Feasting on the Gospels
Matthew, Volume 2

Editorial Board

A Feasting on the Word® Commentary

Feasting on the Gospels

Matthew, Volume 2
Chapters 14–28

CYNTHIA A. JARVIS and E. ELIZABETH JOHNSON

General Editors

WESTMINSTER
JOHN KNOX PRESS
LOUISVILLE · KENTUCKY

© 2013 Westminster John Knox Press

First edition
Published by Westminster John Knox Press
Louisville, Kentucky

13 14 15 16 17 18 19 20 21 22—10 9 8 7 6 5 4 3 2 1

Book design by Drew Stevens
Cover design by Dilu Nicholas

Library of Congress Cataloging-in-Publication Data

Feasting on the Gospels : a feasting on the WordTM commentary / Cynthia A. Jarvis and E. Elizabeth Johnson, general editors. — First edition.
    volumes cm
  Includes index.
  ISBN 978-0-664-23394-5 (v. 2 : pbk.)
  ISBN 978-0-664-23540-6 (v. 1 : pbk.)
  1. Bible. Matthew—Commentaries.   I. Jarvis, Cynthia A., editor of compilation.
  BS2575.52.F37   2013
  226'.2077—dc23

                2013004484

PRINTED IN THE UNITED STATES OF AMERICA

Contents

Publisher's Note

Feasting on the Gospels is a seven-volume series that follows in the proud tradition of *Feasting on the Word: Preaching the Revised Common Lectionary*. Whereas *Feasting on the Word* provided commentary on only the texts in the lectionary, *Feasting on the Gospels* will cover every passage of the four Gospels. *Feasting on the Gospels* retains the popular approach of *Feasting on the Word* by providing four perspectives on each passage—theological, pastoral, exegetical, and homiletical—to stimulate and inspire preaching, teaching, and discipleship.

Westminster John Knox Press is grateful to the members of the large *Feasting* family who have given so much of themselves to bring this new series to life. General editors Cynthia A. Jarvis and E. Elizabeth Johnson stepped from their service on the editorial board of *Feasting on the Word* to the editorship of *Feasting on the Gospels* without missing a beat. Their commitment, energy, and unflagging enthusiasm made this work possible. The project manager, Joan Murchison, and project compiler, Mary Lynn Darden, continued their remarkable

work, bringing thousands of pieces and hundreds of authors together seamlessly.

The editorial board did enormous work under grueling deadlines and did it with excellence and good humor. The hundreds of writers who participated—scholars, preachers, and teachers—gave much of themselves to help create this bountiful feast. David Bartlett and Barbara Brown Taylor took the time and care to help conceive this new project even as they were finishing their excellent work as general editors of *Feasting on the Word*.

Finally, we are again indebted to Columbia Theological Seminary for their partnership. As they did with *Feasting on the Word*, they provided many resources and personnel to help make this series possible. We are grateful in particular to seminary President Stephen Hayner and Dean of Faculty and Executive Vice President Deborah Mullen.

It is with joy that we welcome you to this feast, in hopes that it will nourish you as you proclaim the Word to all of God's people.

Westminster John Knox Press

Series Introduction

At their best, people who write about Scripture are conversation partners. They enter the dialogue between the biblical text and the preacher or teacher or interested Christian and add perspectives gained from experience and disciplined attention. They contribute literary, historical, linguistic, and theological insights gathered over the millennia to the reader's first impressions of what is going on in a text. This conversation is essential if the reading of Scripture is to be fruitful in the church. It keeps reading the Bible from being an exercise in individual projection or uncritical assumption. That said, people who comment on the Bible should never become authorities. While a writer may indeed know more about the text than the reader does, he or she nevertheless writes from a particular perspective shaped by culture, ethnicity, gender, education, and theological tradition. In this regard, the writer of a commentary is no different from the writers and readers of Scripture.

The model for this series on the Gospels is the lectionary-based resource *Feasting on the Word* (Westminster John Knox Press, 2008–2011), now widely used by ministers as they prepare to preach. As central as the task of preaching is to the health of congregations, Scripture is the Word that calls the whole community of faith into being and sends those addressed out as witnesses to the Word in the world. Whether read devotionally by those gathered to pray or critically by others gathered to study, the Bible functions in a myriad of ways to undergird, support, and nurture the Christian life of individuals and communities. Those are the reasons that Westminster John Knox Press has taken the next step in the *Feasting* project to offer *Feasting on the Gospels*, a series in the style of *Feasting on the Word* with two major differences. First, all four Gospels are considered in their entirety, a *lectio continua* of sorts that leaves nothing out. Second, while *Feasting on the Word* is addressed specifically to preachers, *Feasting on the Gospels* is addressed to all who want to deepen their understanding of the Gospels—Bible study leaders and class members, seasoned preachers and seminarians, believers and skeptics.

The advantage of *Feasting on the Gospels* is that the reader encounters multiple perspectives on each text—not only the theological, exegetical, pastoral,

and homiletical emphases that shape the essays, but also the ecumenical, social, ethnic, and cultural perspectives of the authors. Unlike a single-author commentary, which sustains a particular view of a given interpreter throughout, *Feasting on the Gospels* offers readers a broad conversation that engages the text from many angles. In a church as diverse as the twenty-first-century church is, such deliberate engagement with many voices is imperative and, we hope, provocative.

A few observations about the particular challenges posed by the Gospels are in order here. The Gospels were written in a time when fledgling Christian communities—probably in their second generation—were just beginning to negotiate their relationships with Judaism (within which they were conceived and born), a community that was itself in the process of redefinition after the destruction of the Second Temple in 70 CE. Some of that negotiation was marked by great tension and sometimes outright hostility. The temptation for Christian readers to read anti-Semitism into texts that portray intra-Jewish conflict has beset the church almost from its beginnings. Our editors have been particularly mindful of this when dealing with essays on texts where the temptation to speak contemptuously of Jews and Judaism might threaten faithful interpretation.

A second observation involves the New Testament manuscript tradition. In *Feasting on the Gospels* we identify and comment on significant manuscript variants such as Mark 16:9–20 and John 7:53–8:11, something we did not have to contend with in *Feasting on the Word*. We identify those variant readings the way the NRSV does, except that we talk about "other ancient manuscripts" rather than the "other ancient authorities" of the NRSV notes.

The twelve members of our editorial board come from a broad swath of American Christianity: they are members or ministers of Presbyterian, Baptist, United Church of Christ, Roman Catholic, and Disciples of Christ churches. Some of them are academics who serve on the faculties of theological schools; others are clergy serving congregations. All of them are extraordinarily hardworking, thoughtful, and perceptive readers of Scripture, of the church, and of the world. The writers whose work comprises these volumes represent an even wider cross-section of the church, most of them from North America, but a significant number from around the world, particularly the global South.

We could not have undertaken this work without the imagination, advice, and support of David Dobson, Editorial Director at Westminster John Knox Press, and his colleagues Don McKim, Marianne Blickenstaff, Michele Blum, and Julie Tonini. We are deeply grateful to David L. Bartlett and Barbara Brown Taylor, our mentors in the *Feasting on the Word* project, who continued to offer hands-on assistance with *Feasting on the Gospels*. We thank President Stephen A. Hayner and Dean Deborah F. Mullen of Columbia Theological Seminary and the congregation of The Presbyterian Church of Chestnut Hill in Philadelphia, Pennsylvania, who made possible our participation in the project. Joan Murchison, who as Project Manager kept all of us and our thousands of essays in order and enforced deadlines with great good humor, is once again the beloved Hammer. Mary Lynn Darden, our compiler, who corralled not only the essays but also information about their authors and editors, brought all the bits and pieces together into the books you see now.

To the preachers, teachers, Bible study leaders, and church members who will read the Gospels with us, we wish you happy feasting.

Cynthia A. Jarvis
E. Elizabeth Johnson

Feasting on the Gospels
Matthew, Volume 2

Matthew 14:1–12

¹At that time Herod the ruler heard reports about Jesus; ²and he said to his servants, "This is John the Baptist; he has been raised from the dead, and for this reason these powers are at work in him." ³For Herod had arrested John, bound him, and put him in prison on account of Herodias, his brother Philip's wife, ⁴because John had been telling him, "It is not lawful for you to have her." ⁵Though Herod wanted to put him to death, he feared the crowd, because they regarded him as a prophet. ⁶But when Herod's birthday came, the daughter of Herodias danced before the company, and she pleased Herod ⁷so much that he promised on oath to grant her whatever she might ask. ⁸Prompted by her mother, she said, "Give me the head of John the Baptist here on a platter." ⁹The king was grieved, yet out of regard for his oaths and for the guests, he commanded it to be given; ¹⁰he sent and had John beheaded in the prison. ¹¹The head was brought on a platter and given to the girl, who brought it to her mother. ¹²His disciples came and took the body and buried it; then they went and told Jesus.

Theological Perspective

Biblical scholar David Garland observes a fascinating parallel in Matthew's Gospel between Herod and Pilate. Not only is it true that what happens to John the Baptist parallels what happens to Jesus, but it is also true that "Herod's reluctance to execute John (14:9) will be paralleled by Pilate's reluctance to execute Jesus."[1] So one story foreshadows the other not only in the treatment of prophets but also in the deflection of blame: "someone else made me do it." The deflection of blame and its counterpart, the inability to see our complicity in sin, is endemic to the human condition. It is as old as the story of Adam and Eve. When God confronts Adam about his disobedience, Adam deflects the blame to Eve, and Eve, in turn, blames the serpent. So this story of the beheading of John reflects an archetypal pattern that goes to the very heart of sin and our inability to acknowledge our complicity in it.

There is a most curious phrase in the Apostles' Creed: "suffered under Pontius Pilate." Why this mention of the governor of the region where Jesus was crucified? Some claim that it dates the history of the crucifixion, but surely there is more to the mention of Pontius Pilate in the creed that demands our attention, for this phrase is shorthand for the biblical

1. David Garland, *Reading Matthew* (New York: Crossroads, 1993), 154–55.

Pastoral Perspective

There are some arrangements to which the reign of God is not open. Helping Christians see this is a challenge at a time when the value of openness is at an all-time high. A television advertising campaign of the United Methodist Church proclaims churches of "open hearts, open minds." The United Church of Christ proudly announces that "God is still speaking." The Presbyterian Church (U.S.A.) speaks of a "new openness" in its *Book of Order*. The congregation I serve takes pride in being a church that is "nonjudgmental." Certainly these statements offer important correctives as people in the pews examine the checkered history of the church's treatment of anyone labeled different. Many contemporary Christians believe that today's church must demonstrate that the news it proclaims is indeed good, not hateful or harmful to others.

However, no amount of marketing can rescue the church from the gospel's willingness to say no to established power. That willingness means the church must always live ready to pay a price for its faithfulness. The fate of John the Baptist spells this out in graphic terms. Apparently John the Baptist had told Herod flatly, "It is not lawful for you to have [your brother Philip's wife]" (v. 4). Herod was expecting the opposite answer. He was expecting the prophet to bless his choice, perhaps to make it

Exegetical Perspective

The story of the death of John the Baptist is the only episode in the ministry of Jesus in which Jesus does not appear, and the only event in Jesus' ministry that is reported outside the New Testament (Josephus, *Antiquities* 18.116–19). In Matthew it illustrates the proverb that "prophets are not without honor except in their own country" (13:57). It is also a flashback or analepsis, a report of something that has happened earlier in the narrative. Matthew has told the reader that John was arrested (4:12; 11:2) but not that he has been killed. Herod Antipas had scandalously divorced his Nabatean wife and married "Herodias, his brother Philip's wife" (14:3), and Josephus reports that Herod arrested and killed John because he was turning public sentiment against Herod.

The story sounds familiar—and not just because we know it from the Gospels. It is yet another story of the tyrant persecuting the righteous: Pharaoh vs. the Israelites (Exod. 1:15–22; 5:1–23); Joash vs. Zechariah (2 Chr. 24:20–22); Nebuchadnezzar vs. Shadrach, Meshach, and Abednego (Dan. 3:12–30); Darius vs. Daniel (Dan. 6:10–28); Antiochus Epiphanes vs. pious Jews (1 Macc. 1:41–50; 2:15–28), Eleazar (2 Macc. 6:18–31), and the seven brothers (2 Macc. 7); and Herod the Great vs. the innocents in Bethlehem (Matt. 2:16–18). Matthew also

Homiletical Perspective

This is a provocative and energy-charged text. It is filled with guilty consciences, curious alliances, and promises that one wishes had not been made. It also invites reflection about the lengths we might go to in order to retain our security, avoid conflict, and please others. It is rich with the human story and the chaos that ensues when we encounter the Holy.

As the text begins, one can almost imagine Herod pacing the chamber of his palace with dark circles under his eyes from many a sleepless night. He cannot possibly remain seated as one servant after another brings him word of a Galilean teacher who is inspiring the people and drawing energy and attention away from Herod's own government and authority. It is a nightmare he has already lived once before, and the similarities to that debacle are frightening for him. His guilty conscience might be the cause of his assumption that this new teacher, Jesus, is simply a reincarnation of John the Baptist, whom he had beheaded not long before.

The text then recounts for us the awful mess that created this paranoid and fretful reality in which Herod now finds himself. We learn that John the Baptist has spoken out publicly against Herod's marriage to Herodias. She had previously been married to Herod's half brother, and Herod himself had been previously married and chose to be divorced in

Theological Perspective

story of Pilate who washed his hands of any complicity with the crucifixion of Jesus. The creed seems to acknowledge implicitly that blindness to sin is a disease of the human condition.

Just to offer one prominent example, how is it that when we come to the subject of America's primal sin of racism, there is an almost universal tendency among most white people to distance themselves, itemizing, for example, antiracist accomplishments or racially other friendships, but rarely does one hear a confession of how they have been marked and scarred by the sin and how they might be complicit in it.

The biblical story, of course, will not abide any deflection of sin. What is intriguing about the phrase in the Apostles' Creed is that, in spite of Pilate's handwashing, the creed allows the deflection—it acknowledges Pilate's complicity in the suffering of Jesus and so, by implication, calls us to an accounting for our own complicity in the sufferings of others. One of the tragic ironies of Christian history is that the teaching of contempt for Jews was based on the claim that the Jews were Christ-killers—that they crucified God— when, in fact, the creed implies otherwise: that we all had a hand in the crucifixion of God. Moreover, God suffers again every time we fail to acknowledge our complicity with the sins of the world.

A fierce debate has been underway in the Presbyterian Church (U.S.A.) about whether or not to divest financial holdings in Caterpillar, Inc., the heavy-equipment company with headquarters in Peoria, Illinois. Over the last several years, Caterpillar has become a lightning rod because its bulldozers have been used by Israel to construct illegal Israeli settlements, to demolish the homes of alleged Palestinian terrorists and their families, and to construct a separation barrier between Israel and the occupied lands. Human rights organizations have decried these practices. The official response from Caterpillar is, "We can't control how our products are used. We expect them to be used in environmentally responsible ways that are consistent with human rights, but we have no means for enforcement of these expectations."[2] In other words, they deny any responsibility for the how their equipment is used.

The story of Israel's use of Caterpillar equipment is but one example of how easy it is to side with the Palestinians against the Israelis. Before giving into this temptation, it behooves Christians to realize that we are not innocent bystanders in this conflict, nor are we neutral observers of someone else's dispute.

2. Mission Responsibility through Investment of the Presbyterian Church (U.S.A.), General Assembly Mission Council document, August 2011.

Pastoral Perspective

fit into the faith he professed. History is replete with examples of secular power seeking religious sanction or resisting religious censure. The Church of England was born partly because King Henry VIII received a similar no when he sought permission from the pope to annul his marriage to his wife. In more recent years, President George W. Bush all but declared war on Iraq from the very pulpit of the National Cathedral, to the quiet discomfort of many religious leaders who had gathered to stand against using violence as a weapon.

One challenge for today's pastoral leaders is that it is not always clear how to translate what is "not lawful" into contemporary ethical questions. The church's report card is mixed in this area. Hindsight makes it clear, for example, that acknowledging that our planet rotates around the sun is lawful in the reign of God, while slavery is not. The church, or large portions of it, erred on both counts. Still, most church leaders are familiar with the stress created when gospel claims clearly conflict with individual or corporate choices. Pastoral leaders, so often gifted at empathizing with the strain presented by these kinds of choices, must also find ways to make it clear that following Christ comes at a cost.

For most people in the pews, that cost will not compare with John's martyrdom. It could be something more like missing the promotion, losing the account, upsetting the child who wants to skip worship to go to the birthday party. Given the stress I have observed in myself and others over these kinds of decisions, I can imagine that John might have questioned the rigidity of his own convictions. Is it really necessary to give such a strong no in this particular situation? Matthew's Gospel says yes.

Herod's character provides a window into Matthew's view of the dangers of corruption. In the beginning of Matthew's Gospel, Herod is the ruthless leader who orders children put to death to eliminate any possible opposition (2:16–18). One would hardly consider him a man possessing anything resembling a moral compass. Yet here in the middle of Matthew's Gospel, Herod is also portrayed as one who reluctantly orders John's execution because of an oath. An unscrupulous leader would be expected to do whatever serves his best interests, without regard to oaths or other matters of principle. Matthew presents a more complicated individual. This is not an irrational person, but a principled man whose principles have been purposely distorted to malicious ends.

The concern for the church is the possibility that we might slowly but steadily water down the reign of

connects the story with Elijah, Ahab, and Jezebel (1 Kgs. 18–22; 2 Kgs. 9; Matt. 17:10–12).

Only Matthew and Mark report Herodias's role in John's death (cf. Luke 9:7–9). The primary difference between the two is that Mark says that Herodias "had it in for John" while Herod sought to protect John from her. Matthew is less clear. Herod arrested John and wanted to kill him (Matt. 14:3, 5), but was grieved when Herodias manipulated him into killing John (14:9). Matthew typically abbreviates Mark where the two have parallel accounts, but in this case the editing is not consistent, with the result that Mark's plot is both more engaging and more consistent.

Herodias's daughter, presumably Salome, although she is not named in the Gospels, danced for Herod. Mark is unclear about the daughter's identity, but Matthew 14:6, perhaps the earliest interpreter of Mark, reads "the daughter of Herodias." Josephus says that Salome was the daughter of Herodias by Herod Philip (*Antiquities* 18.136). Salome would probably have been twelve to fourteen. We do not know whether the dance was innocent or erotic (as interpreters have often fantasized). Ambrose, for example, condemns the dance: "Is anything so conducive to lust as with unseemly movements to expose in nakedness those parts of the body which either nature has hidden or custom has veiled, to sport with looks, to turn the neck, to loosen the hair?" (*Concerning Virgins* 3.6.27).

The promise to grant whatever she asked recalls King Artaxerxes' repeated promise to Esther (Esth. 5:3, 6–7; 7:2–3). Herod was trapped by his oath in front of his guests (the powerful men of Galilee, Mark 6:21), to whom he had no doubt also made promises.

Although some interpreters have regarded this story as an insertion that interrupts the flow of the Gospel, five observations clarify its place in the Gospel accounts.

1. *John's death foreshadows Jesus' death.* Jesus too will be killed by a tyrant who fears popular opinion (14:9; 27:24) and is manipulated into a killing he did not seek. While Herod's wife prompted her daughter to ask for John's head, Pilate's wife urged him to have nothing to do with Jesus' death (27:19). The report that John's disciples buried his body takes on added significance later, when Jesus' disciples are not present to give him a proper burial.

2. *John's death foreshadows the persecution that Jesus' disciples face.* Matthew develops the pattern that John preached (3:1–12), John was arrested (4:12), and John was put to death (14:1–12). Jesus

order to marry her. John spoke against both actions as a transgression of Jewish law. Furious at having his authority challenged, Herod has wanted to put John to death, but he also has had to contend with the public's high regard for John as a prophet. Herod resolved to put John in prison and bide his time while he pondered his options.

It seems easy perhaps to point an accusing and judgmental finger at Herod. It would be easy to view him as a self-serving monarch, but a pause for reflection and humility might actually land many of us in a place where we resonate with Herod's choice to silence the voice of God's conscience. How often have we encountered God's claim on our lives, or particularly convicting texts such as "Go, sell your possessions, and give the money to the poor" (19:21) or "Do not store up for yourselves treasures on earth" (6:19), and because the claim and the call of those passages make us deeply uncomfortable, we ignore them or imagine they do not apply to us? Living as God's people regularly challenges us to relinquish our desires in favor of following the Holy One, but we are loath to change our path when it costs us something we enjoy.

If we are honest, we can also resonate with Herod's fear of losing power and control as Jesus ascends in popularity. The transformation we make as followers of God is nothing short of dying to self and surrendering to God. Our inner selves fight hard against such changes because we so desperately fear losing control and power, just as Herod fears the ascension of Jesus and John the Baptist before him.

Another character in this drama is Herod's wife. She is not at all pleased with John's disparaging remarks about her choice of husband, either. John is the mirror that shows how she truly appears to the world: as a self-promoting opportunist. She cannot bear that truth and plots with her daughter to silence the man who is calling her to remember God's call to faithfulness. Where Herod seems to want John off the street and away from an admiring audience, Herodias wants him dead.

So Herod's birthday celebration comes with great fanfare and feasting. There are jesters and musicians, and his own stepdaughter wants to honor him and the whole company by performing a dance. It must have been quite a dance, because Herod proceeds to promise her anything she desires in gratitude for her gift. Can you imagine the silence that falls over the room when she tells her stepfather that what she wants is the head of John the Baptist? I am sure Herod thinks she will ask for treasure, perfume, or

Matthew 14:1–12

Theological Perspective

The two-thousand-year history of Christian teaching of contempt for Jews is well documented: the stereotypes, persecutions, pogroms, forced conversions, ghettos, and multiple forms of discrimination. Whether or not Christian teaching of contempt for Judaism led to the Holocaust is a matter of debate; what is without question is that it played an influential role in what became the worst genocide of human history. In light of this, we need to be ever vigilant against anti-Semitic sentiments worldwide and the ever-growing hatred of Israel in the Middle East. This does not mean that we should turn a blind eye toward Israel, nor toward the Palestinian people. We should be both pro-Israeli and pro-Palestinian, but not naively so. The pro-Israeli/pro-Palestinian posture I recommend is grounded in a thoroughgoing acknowledgment of our complicity with the sins of the world.

There is a reason that Christian experience always begins with penance: there is something of Herod and Pilate in all of us. So any serious prophetic impulse arises from a penitential foundation, a base that draws our attention to all the crosses that litter the landscape of our lives, and then draws our vision toward the horizon and the arc of God bringing resurrection and life out of the crucifying patterns of our world. The prophetic impulse does not stem from liberal do-good-ism, because the fact of the matter is that we are not all that good! The prophetic impulse stems from a penitential theology grounded in the sure reality of a merciful God in whom alone is our help, a God who forgives, restores, heals, and empowers us for the prophetic task of healing the world.

It is from this penitent and prophetic standpoint that we can be pro-Israeli and pro-Palestinian, pro-Caterpillar and pro-Peoria, pro-black, pro-white, pro-brown, pro-yellow, pro–Occupy Wall Street and pro–Wall Street, pro-Democrat and pro-Republican, pro-conservative and pro-liberal, pro-gay and pro-straight, pro-human, and always, always pro-creation. We can be pro-reality because the God who made heaven and earth and is revealed in Christ crucified and risen, now rules the world with forgiveness and love.

ROGER J. GENCH

Pastoral Perspective

God through small concessions that, on balance, add up to a betrayal of the faith. This is heavy stuff, but it also means that the daily choices that people make matter. The youth who defends the kid who is bullied, the board member who questions big bonuses going to her company's top management while jobs at the bottom are cut, the parent who raises questions over how the immigrant child is being treated in his child's class: these are matters of faith that matter a great deal. Often we are tempted to believe otherwise. The costs of saying no to an employer, an administrator, a bully, or anyone else who has the power to inflict pain, seem to outweigh anything that could be gained. Indeed, John's head on a platter seems to reinforce this point. Yet it is Herod who lives in fear: first fear of the birth of a king, then fear of John the Baptist, then fear of the crowds, then fear of John the Baptist raised from the dead, with even greater powers to wield.

Herod is wrong on this last point, of course. John is dead. However, the one who now proclaims his message will not only emulate John's costly sacrifice; he will transform it into life that can no longer be silenced by death. This is the good news that a costly faith offers to us: freedom from fearful living. Even with all of his stately power, this is the one thing Herod cannot secure for himself.

During the Arab Spring of 2011, Gene Sharp, whose books on overthrowing dictators have been used by activists around the world, was asked if anything surprised him about the democratic upheavals in the Middle East. Sharp said it was hearing this testimony: "We're not afraid anymore; we've lost our fear." "Once a regime is no longer able to frighten people," he said, "then that regime is in big trouble."[1] The good news for the world is that the regime of death has already been overthrown. We are invited now to live as though we believed this is true.

ANDREW FOSTER CONNORS

---

1. Gene Sharp, interview with Mark Memmott, *Morning Edition*, National Public Radio, February 22, 2011.

Feasting on the Gospels

preached, Jesus was arrested, and Jesus was put to death. So the disciples too will preach (9:37–10:42 [esp. 10:7]; 24:14), be arrested (10:17–23), and be put to death (24:9).

3. *Herod's banquet serves as the antithesis of Jesus' meals.* The banquets of the rich and the powerful were evidence of their wickedness. Origen reported that he found "in no Scripture that a birthday was kept by a righteous man" (Origen on Matt. 10:22), and the Venerable Bede commented: "We hear at the same time of three evil deeds done: the inauspicious celebration of a birthday, the lewd dancing of a girl, and the rash oath of a king" (*Homilies on the Gospels* 2.23). Jesus' ministry, in contrast, is distinguished by his eating with outcasts and feeding multitudes. Jesus ate with "many tax collectors and sinners" (9:10). In contrast to John, Jesus "came eating and drinking" (11:18–19). He fed five thousand (14:13–21), then four thousand (15:32–29).

4. *Serving John's head on a platter anticipates the Last Supper.* At the Last Supper Jesus offers his disciples his body and blood (26:26–29), inviting comparison with Herod's banquet. Jesus offers himself; John is executed because of a rash promise. The head on a platter is a grotesque caricature of the church's sacred observance.

5. *Herod and his "kingdom" serve as the antithesis of Jesus' announcement of the kingdom of God.* Herod was a vassal of Rome, and all the kingdoms of this world are under the authority of Satan (4:8–9). Similarly, two meals are juxtaposed in the Gospel— Herod's feast and Jesus' feeding of the multitude. The true character of both kingdoms is revealed by these meal scenes. The rulers of the Gentiles "are tyrants over them" (20:25). Their festivities are excessive and violent. Herod (or Herodias) exploits the young girl, Herodias manipulates Herod, and Herod takes John's life. Jesus has compassion on the crowd, cures their sick, and then feeds them. One is a kingdom based on privilege and coercive power, the other on compassion and service that ultimately leads to self-sacrifice. The kingdom of God is brought near by the laying down of life: the Son of Man came "to give his life a ransom for many" (20:28). The gospel comes, therefore, with an invitation to a meal.

R. ALAN CULPEPPER

gowns, but to ask for another to be put to death is a dark and bitter request.

Once again poor Herod finds himself torn between his own thoughts and desires and the court of public opinion. He has given his word that she can have anything. He just does not imagine she will ask for this. Matthew tells us he is grieved, but that since so many guests have heard his promise he cannot fail to comply. There is a piercing commentary on oaths and peer pressure here. While Herod is threatened by John's prophetic call against whom he has married, he has not yet acted with finality and violence; but this oath to his stepdaughter places him in an untenable situation. Either he kills John the Baptist, or he is false to his word. Does he value public opinion so much that he is willing to end the life of another? The story tells us he does.

There is a staggering foreshadowing here of Jesus' trial before Pilate. Matthew 27:17–27 tells us that Pilate was hoping to please the crowd as he handed Jesus over to be crucified. This tension between the desire of the crowd and the ones who stand for God is found throughout Scripture. From the early prophets to John and Jesus, the message of salvation and the call to holiness are not often well received. Perhaps it is the knowledge that in following God we will need to leave our places and habits of security in order to enter fully into life with the Divine that keeps us from leaping at God's call when we hear it. So also Pilate's wife is a foil to Herodias; rather than engineering Jesus' death, she speaks up for his innocence (27:19).

At the conclusion of the passage we are left with a gruesome image of John's head on a platter presented by the daughter to her mother. We see in stark relief that pleasing others is costly, and that speaking truth to power may at times have dire consequences.

LIZ BARRINGTON FORNEY

Matthew 14:13–21

¹³Now when Jesus heard this, he withdrew from there in a boat to a deserted place by himself. But when the crowds heard it, they followed him on foot from the towns. ¹⁴When he went ashore, he saw a great crowd; and he had compassion for them and cured their sick. ¹⁵When it was evening, the disciples came to him and said, "This is a deserted place, and the hour is now late; send the crowds away so that they may go into the villages and buy food for themselves." ¹⁶Jesus said to them, "They need not go away; you give them something to eat." ¹⁷They replied, "We have nothing here but five loaves and two fish." ¹⁸And he said, "Bring them here to me." ¹⁹Then he ordered the crowds to sit down on the grass. Taking the five loaves and the two fish, he looked up to heaven, and blessed and broke the loaves, and gave them to the disciples, and the disciples gave them to the crowds. ²⁰And all ate and were filled; and they took up what was left over of the broken pieces, twelve baskets full. ²¹And those who ate were about five thousand men, besides women and children.

Theological Perspective

The Christian life has been described as a movement from the shallow end of the pool to the deep end. Theologian Sarah Coakley suggests three different levels of spiritual practice that enable this movement. The three levels are classic to spiritual theology: the purgative, the illuminative, and the unitive. The purgative is about ethics or establishing the boundaries of the Christian life. The illuminative involves identification with the manner, pattern, or way of Christ. The unitive is transformation by the long, arduous practice of reunion with God and others. All three describe what Protestants have called sanctification, or growth in the Christian life and practice.[1] All three levels can be employed in reading this story of the feeding of the five thousand from Matthew's Gospel.

The *purgative* dimension of this story is the first thing that one confronts. The word "purgative" may sound off-putting, but, in fact, it is a very accurate description of the primal stage of Christian living; it is about differentiating oneself from the brokenness of the world, not for the purpose of isolation, but for ethics or moral reformation. So among the first things we teach children are "do not steal," "do not cheat," and "do not bop your brother or sister on the

1. Sarah Coakley, "Deepening Practices: Perspectives from Ascetical and Mystical Theology" in *Practicing Theology: Beliefs and Practices in Christian Life*, ed. Miroslav Volf and Dorothy Bass (Grand Rapids: Eerdmans, 2001), 78–84.

Pastoral Perspective

Jesus liked to eat. The disciples of John the Baptist noticed enough to question why he did not fast. His enemies noticed enough to ask his disciples why he ate with tax collectors and sinners. They labeled him a glutton and a drunkard. His parables are often about wheat, or fruit trees, or banquets, or vineyards. If he had not traveled by foot so far and so often, it is quite possible that Jesus would have been a little chunkier than he appears in most stained-glass windows.

Eating is rarely listed as a spiritual practice, but it should be. Some of the best stuff in ministry happens over meals. People share shockingly celebratory and devastatingly painful news. Creative ideas are hatched. Relationships are formed and edified. Substantial commitments are made. Every pastor ought to have an expense account to be used to fund the pastoral ministry of feasting. It may be more important than paying the light bill. Mealtime is often where ministry happens.

Jesus knows this well. He says to the disciples, "You give them something to eat" (v. 16). Unfortunately for them, Jesus is referring to a crowd of thousands. The pragmatic disciples recognize that they have been asked to do the impossible, to feed thousands of people with next to nothing.

This seems to be the normal situation in which the church finds itself today. People are hungering

Exegetical Perspective

The feeding of the five thousand declares the fulfillment of Moses and the prophets, the new order of the kingdom, and the good news that under God's rule there is enough for everyone.

The traditional site of the feeding, identified by Helena, Constantine's mother, in the fourth century, is Heptapegon, or Tabgha, the seven springs located south of Capernaum, where pilgrims stopped to eat and rest. A beautiful mosaic of the loaves and fish (mid-fifth-century) still identifies the spot.

Matthew gives particular emphasis to the fulfillment of the Law and the Prophets through fulfillment quotations in the birth accounts and through Jesus' declaration in the Sermon on the Mount (5:17). The miracles that Jesus does are typically wonders like those performed by Moses and Elijah or Elisha. This is certainly the case with the feeding of the five thousand, the only miracle recorded in all four Gospels. Matthew lacks some of the connections drawn by the other evangelists, however. Mark draws a connection to Psalm 23 by saying that Jesus had compassion on the crowd because they were like sheep without a shepherd (cf. also Num. 27:15–17) and by adding that Jesus commanded them to recline on the green grass (Ps. 23:1–2). John connects the feeding with Elisha's feeding of more than one hundred men with twenty loaves of barley

Homiletical Perspective

What Jesus has just heard in this passage is that his good friend and mentor John the Baptist has been beheaded by Herod as a party favor for his daughter. It is no wonder he needs some time alone to pray and, doubtless, grieve. Jesus is not the only one to hear the gruesome news. We are told that the crowds also hear the news of John's demise at Herod's hands. The people are understandably frightened and are seeking Jesus for both comfort and guidance. Thus, while he is out in a boat on the sea, they follow him on foot from the shore.

One can imagine Jesus sensing his own death is nearer now with John's death, and in that anticipation come thoughts about how to prepare for the future of God's ministry among the people. What we encounter in this very familiar passage may be just that: one of the primary messages of what it means to be disciples and to carry Jesus' ministry forward in his absence.

Jesus comes ashore and sees a great crowd. He sees their grief. He sees their fear. He sees their longing for hope and a word of encouragement, and he has compassion on them. He knows what they are feeling, so he reaches out and heals their sick. He spends the day in conversation with them and night begins to fall.

In the next movement of the passage we encounter our own human failings as the disciples try to dodge the responsibilities of ministry. They know

Theological Perspective

head." The reason we teach these things is that the children are going to see plenty of examples of the opposite kind of activity.

This story from Matthew is a textbook case of differentiation or purgation. It begins, "Now when Jesus heard this, he withdrew from there" (v. 13). Heard what? Well, Herod had just thrown a big banquet on the occasion of his birthday, and the daughter of his sister-in-law danced before Herod and so pleased him that he promised her anything in return. She asked for and was granted the beheading of John the Baptist. So upon hearing this, Jesus differentiates himself. Matthew tells us that he retires to a "deserted place," as did the ancient Hebrews in the wilderness, purging themselves for readiness to be the people of God. When the crowds follow him, Jesus embodies the ethics of God; he differentiates himself from Herod by showing compassion for the needs of the crowd. Jesus teaches by example; he reenacts the wilderness wanderings by purging the way of Herod (and Pharaoh) and teaching the way of God.

However, as any teacher of ethics knows, it is one thing to teach morality, and it is quite another thing to acquire moral vision. So we come to the second level of depth, classically called *illumination*. The disciples are in this wilderness; it is growing dark and they are without food. They know the story of their ancestors' wandering in the wilderness without food and of God's provision of manna for them to eat. Like their ancestors, they "murmur." The disciples come to Jesus and say, "This is a deserted place, and the hour is now late; send the crowds away so that they may go into the villages and buy food for themselves" (v. 15). Then Jesus astounds them, saying, "They need not go away, you give them something to eat" (v. 16). The disciples are dumbfounded because they have meager provisions. The disciples may know ethics, but they do not have moral illumination. They must be illumined by the generous heart of Jesus.

The generous heart is the illuminating core of this story; it is the miracle of the story. Some would disagree and identify the miracle of the story as the multiplication of food; but this story is more than a food miracle. Another interpretation of the story suggests that once the sharing of food began, others responded in kind. In this version, the upshot of the story is that we must learn to trust in the resources of our communities. There is a good insight here, but I think the story goes deeper still.

H. Richard Niebuhr taught that in every encounter with another person there is a moment of

Pastoral Perspective

all around us, hungering for a deeper connection with God and each other, hungering for purpose and meaning, hungering for hope in a stagnant economy that was deeply divided long before it was driven into the ditch. Many are hungering quite literally for their next meal. The church has been called to feed all these hungry people with fewer loaves and fishes than we have ever had before.

The disciples are right to notice the limitations. We are not equipped to do what we have been charged to do. We do not have enough. The wise thing would be to send people elsewhere to whoever is serving some helpful fare at the local yoga studio, the coffee shop, the movie theater, or the pub. However, a closer reading of Jesus' words here is helpful: "you give them something to eat." The church is not asked to fulfill every need, is not asked to figure out how a few loaves and fishes are going to feed everyone. Jesus tells the disciples to bring what they have to him and share it. The miracle of the meal with baskets full of leftovers is not the church's miracle; it is God's. The church is as much an observer of that miracle as the people it is called to feed—and perhaps no less amazed.

Preachers know this well. Countless sermons have been offered with weak ingredients and not enough seasoning, stirred together quickly with not enough care in preparation. Yet a week later, someone calls up the preacher and tells her that he has decided to quit his job and work in an orphanage, or become the artist he always knew God wanted him to be—because of some sermon. Amazing transformations happen in a church that has been given very little in the way of substantial sustenance.

The task of disciples today is not necessarily to pretend that we really do have some amazing food to serve a hurting world, but to share what we have been given, trusting that it is enough. Share it freely, wildly, irrationally with others, expecting that God can take our limited, feeble resources and make of them a feast to serve thousands. Perhaps this is where we often get stuck, especially in anxious times. Seeking desperately to name what is wrong with the church and its ministry, we end up creating a fearful environment where people are timid about sharing what they have been given. Their gifts seem too weak, too inadequate to be of any value to a church facing such enormous needs.

This is why we need to eat together more often, why we should examine our schedules and replace committee meetings with more dinners. It is hard to imagine Jesus ever attending a committee meeting.

(2 Kgs. 4:42–44) by adding that the loaves brought to Jesus were barley loaves (John 6:9). The details that Jesus fed the crowd in a wilderness place, that they had bread left over after all had eaten, and that they collected twelve baskets full, invite comparison with Moses' provision of manna in the wilderness (Exod. 16:13–35; Num. 11:1–35). The fact that they had some left (cf. 2 Kgs. 4:43–44) underscores the wondrous bounty of God's provision.

The report that the disciples took up twelve baskets of fragments has evoked various interpretations. The number twelve is often associated with the number of the tribes of Israel, but in this instance it can mean simply that each disciple collected a basket full. The size of the baskets is not specified, but they were probably large baskets used for produce. A basket was standard equipment for the infantry in the Roman army (Josephus, *Jewish War* 3.95), and baskets were so characteristic of Jewish life that Juvenal uses them as a symbol for the Jew in his *Satires* (3.14; 6.542). The count of five thousand men may be related to the Israelite practice of counting men only (Exod. 12:37; Num. 1:2, 20, 22), emphasizing either the exodus or the military overtones of the story. Matthew 14:21 adds "besides women and children."

The strongest resonance is between the feeding of the five thousand and the Last Supper, where "Jesus took a loaf of bread, and after blessing it he broke it, gave it to the disciples, and said, 'Take, eat; this is my body'" (26:26). In contrast to the variations in wording in the rest of the accounts of the feeding, the Synoptic Gospels report the blessing, breaking, giving, and eating of the bread and fish with almost word-for-word agreement. The verbs of the Eucharist echo the feeding: "Taking the five loaves and the two fish, he looked up to heaven, and blessed and broke the loaves, and gave them to the disciples" (v. 19). Luke draws on these same verbs in the account of the meal at Emmaus, where Jesus is recognized "in the breaking of the bread" (Luke 24:30, 35). Taking, blessing, breaking, and giving become the signature by which the risen Lord is recognized, just as it was the pattern of the earthly Jesus' ministry (cf. Matt. 15:36; 1 Cor. 11:23–24).

Through the feeding, the people were connected to a heritage that stretched back to the provision of manna in the wilderness, that would reach its revelatory pinnacle at the Last Supper, that would be celebrated ever after by the church, and that points ahead to the great messianic banquet at the end of time (Isa. 25:6). The feeding of the five thousand is also a lesson for the church. The issue is how we can

the people have expectations and needs. Rather than lean into Christ with faith, they begin to drown in their own fear of insufficiency. They ask Jesus to make an announcement sending the people home. They do not want to deal with the mess and the hunger. It seems overwhelming, and the responsibility seems too great.

Jesus is quick and clear in his response. In one short set of phrases he communicates a vision for community and a trust in the disciples. "They need not go away; you give them something to eat" (v. 16). The first half of the phrase, "They need not go away," is a call to remain together, even when the needs of the group might seem too great. In community we will find what we need; enough to meet our needs and often more. Ephesians 4:12 tells us that each has been given a gift "for building up the body of Christ." Rather than supporting a posture of "every one for herself or himself," Christ invites us to stay with one another and discover another way to collaborate. In remaining together, we may find possibilities none of us could create alone, and surely we will find comfort and companionship in sharing the experience, be it hunger or cold.

The other half of his command, "You give them something to eat," is a profound shift in responsibility. Frequently Jesus himself has done the healing and transforming, but in this moment he calls the disciples to step up and reject the myth of scarcity. Although at first the disciples are still paralyzed by fear and stuck in their limited human imaginations, Jesus is patient with them. They balk and protest about limited resources. There is not nearly enough to go around. There is no way this can work out. They seem to have forgotten the many miracles they have already witnessed.

We know this intersection in our lives so well. We know the familiar feeling of being overwhelmed by what is expected of us. The needs that surround us seem insurmountable. Pick an area of suffering—cancer, global hunger, wars, domestic violence, addiction—and the needs seem beyond our resources to respond. We revert to our own narrow minds, forgetting the expanse and freedom promised by God. So paralyzed by anxiety are we that we forget the thousand other times that God entered in unexpectedly and made a way when there seemed no way. From parting the Red Sea to stilling storms, with manna and miracles abounding, our memories are short when our bellies are empty and night is falling.

Finally Jesus gives them the solution that they need. "Bring them here to me," he says, calling for

Matthew 14:13–21

Theological Perspective

self-transcendence; that is, we move out of our insularity in the encounter so that the other can expand our horizon. He adds that in every encounter, there is a "third" involved, making it a trialogue. The third "does not come to rest until the total community of being is involved."[2] The third, of course, is God, the often forgotten one in every encounter, the one reality with which we have to do in every moment of our lives. Note how the third is critically involved in Matthew's story: "Taking the five loaves and the two fish, [Jesus] looked up to heaven, and blessed and broke the loaves" (v. 19). The blessing is an illuminating acknowledgment of the generous heart of God, an acknowledgment of the transcendent element in every relation, an acknowledgment of the third.

The blessing is also the moment of the final level of depth—the *unitive*. The blessing is an acknowledgment of the deep unitive connection of all beings with one another and with God. The blessing is an acknowledgment of the generosity that connects all beings in God. The blessing is an acknowledgment of the source of all of life, the livingness that we know. As such, the blessing is a means of union with the deep in which we live and move and have our being.

The act of saying a blessing may seem rote, but saying a blessing over and over brings its own blessing. The blessing can move us from the shallow to the deep, from *purging* ourselves of all that is broken in our lives, to the *illumination* of generosity at the heart and core of all that is. The blessing *unites* us with the generous heart of God who does not rest until all are redeemed and blessed. The act of blessing (at a meal, at a celebration, even before a church meeting, or the encounter with another) acknowledges abundance amid seeming scarcity, and inches us ever more fully into the deep.

ROGER J. GENCH

Pastoral Perspective

He preferred banquets and picnics, chats by the watering hole, and conversation over good wine—perhaps because sharing food sets the stage for all kinds of other, deeper sharing that most people yearn for.

I had a professor in seminary who used to shatter the quiet of Communion distribution with words encouraging more healthy appetites. As members of the seminary community, pious and pensive, filed prayerfully forward, carefully tearing off a tiny bit of bread, he would shout, "Go on! Get yourself a big ol' hunk of grace!" Although this disturbed a number of students and professors, a handful of challah filled me much better than the cubed Wonder Bread I dutifully ingested during my youth.

I remember one weekend in college, when a minister invited several church dropouts down to a beach place for a retreat. He had taken an interest in students who had abandoned the church to become "spiritual, but not religious," kids who were rejecting the usual tracks because they wanted to live with the poor, or struggle for change, or organize for justice—kids shaped by the church, but no longer feeling connected to it. I do not remember anything about the weekend except the dinner—good food leading to deep conversation leading to a circle and a loaf of bread, and a jug of wine. Words of Jesus spoken that night certainly did not sound like words of an institution. I just remember thinking, if this is what the church can be—a meal where everybody is filled with good food that leads to deep sharing and a desire to give more—then maybe there is still a place for me. I used to marvel that this minister knew exactly how to reach kids like me. Now I know better. When you have no idea what else to do, plan a meal, invite as many as you can, offer what you have, and prepare to be amazed.

ANDREW FOSTER CONNORS

---

2. H. Richard Niebuhr, *The Responsible Self: An Essay in Christian Moral Philosophy* (New York: Harper & Row, 1963), 87.

Exegetical Perspective

find sustenance "in the wilderness." What do you do when following Jesus has led you to the end of your physical and spiritual resources? What do you do when you do not have what you will need to sustain you on the way home? Translating the situation to the context of the church, where can the church find what it needs to survive in "the wilderness"?

The good news starts with the notice that Jesus had compassion on the people. He saw their need and was moved to respond to it. When we find ourselves in the wilderness, we are not alone. Jesus does for his followers what they cannot do for themselves. What do you do when you find yourself in the wilderness, a long way from home? What do you do when the challenges you face are greater than your resources for meeting them, when what you hold in your hands is so meager and the need is so great?

The first thing Jesus did was to ask the disciples what they had. Often we have more than we realize, if we will only offer it to God. Just five loaves, but when they were offered to God in thanksgiving, they became part of an unlimited treasury of blessing—enough to sustain the people in wilderness, with plenty left over. When we celebrate the Lord's Supper, therefore, we recall this great tradition of blessing, and we testify that even in a few loaves of bread there is more than enough for our needs. They are God's gift, they carry the life of our Savior, and they remind us that God has always provided for the needs of the faithful in times of crisis and distress.[1]

R. ALAN CULPEPPER

Homiletical Perspective

the five loaves and two fish (v. 18). "Bring them here to me," he says, and you can almost hear the disciples breathing a collective sigh of relief and lowering their eyes in embarrassment that they did not think of turning to Jesus for help sooner. "Bring them here to me," he says, and one wonders if he is talking about the people themselves, or the loaves and the fish. The disciples obey, and Jesus invites everyone to be seated for the bounty that is about to be poured out upon the hungry hill.

It really is that simple. Faith tells us that the antidote to the toxic doses of fear and blaring messages of insufficiency is found in taking the meager bits and pieces of what we have and inviting Jesus to bless them and make them more. Over and over again, this invitation and promise are echoed in Scripture: "My grace is sufficient, for my power is made perfect in weakness" (2 Cor. 12:9). Our primary limitation is not a lack of resources but our amnesia, our forgetting to offer up what we have been given to the One whose desire it is to bless us. God in Christ stands ready to heal, redeem, restore, and reconcile; our role is to take responsibility in offering up our part and seeking, with all that we are, to collaborate with God.

In this passage we are shown a new way forward. We learn about our responsibility for one another and about God's trust in us to provide, with God's help, for the needs of the community. We see the miracle that comes when we renounce the message of scarcity and turn to God in faith, offering what we have and allowing God to bless and multiply even the smallest of gifts.

LIZ BARRINGTON FORNEY

1. See R. Alan Culpepper, *Mark* (Macon, GA: Smyth & Helwys, 2007), 280.

Matthew 14:22–36

²²Immediately he made the disciples get into the boat and go on ahead to the other side, while he dismissed the crowds. ²³And after he had dismissed the crowds, he went up the mountain by himself to pray. When evening came, he was there alone, ²⁴but by this time the boat, battered by the waves, was far from the land, for the wind was against them. ²⁵And early in the morning he came walking toward them on the sea. ²⁶But when the disciples saw him walking on the sea, they were terrified, saying, "It is a ghost!" And they cried out in fear. ²⁷But immediately Jesus spoke to them and said, "Take heart, it is I; do not be afraid."

²⁸Peter answered him, "Lord, if it is you, command me to come to you on the water." ²⁹He said, "Come." So Peter got out of the boat, started walking on

Theological Perspective

My childhood faith was framed by kind of naive literalism about stories like Jesus' walking on the water. Jesus became for me something akin to a superhero who could perform wondrous deeds. As I have matured, I have come to appreciate the symbolic power of the biblical stories. For example, the boat and the disciples in the storm-tossed sea were, for Matthew, symbolic of the tormented church wrestling with conflict within and conflict without. To be sure, the church has always had a conflicted existence. Church history is not a story of smooth sailing.

Given this tortured existence, it is not surprising that Matthew characterizes discipleship as a mixture of faith and doubt. Throughout the Gospel, the church is a mixed bag of believing and doubting. Note that Peter himself attempts to emulate Jesus and takes a few significant but faltering steps on water, but then sees the tempest all about him and begins to sink. Thus Jesus says to him, "You of little faith, why did you doubt?" (v. 31). These words are important, because in Matthew when Jesus speaks of "little faith," he conveys both judgment and encouragement. The latter can be seen when Jesus promises, "If you have faith the size of a mustard seed, you can say to this mountain, 'Move from here to there,' and it will move; and nothing will be impossible for you" (17:20). In sum, little faith may be a hindrance

Pastoral Perspective

Advocates for nurturing spiritual practice are quick to point out how often the Gospels report Jesus withdrawing from the demands of daily work to pray. What they do not acknowledge, however, is that these times often correspond to the disciples' getting themselves into trouble. Upon hearing of John's death, Jesus withdraws, only to have the crowds grow into the thousands. The ill-equipped disciples find themselves overwhelmed with sick people and their hungry family members. Jesus sweeps in to the rescue. Later, Jesus sends his top leadership in a boat to the other side of the sea and dismisses the crowds, retreating up the mountain for solitary prayer. Then another crisis erupts, proving again that without Jesus the disciples are a fearful, feckless bunch. The church is not too much different.

In planning a memorial service recently, the family of the deceased indicated their desire not to have Scripture read at the memorial service. A poem about a ship that is no longer seen, but sailing out there somewhere, was chosen by the family as a substitute, along with something else found on the Internet. The widow, realizing the discomfort of her pastor, thought perhaps the concern was over church rules and the need to abide by ecclesiastical order. No, the pastor explained to her, without the good news of the resurrection, the church does not have

the water, and came toward Jesus. [30]But when he noticed the strong wind, he became frightened, and beginning to sink, he cried out, "Lord, save me!" [31]Jesus immediately reached out his hand and caught him, saying to him, "You of little faith, why did you doubt?" [32]When they got into the boat, the wind ceased. [33]And those in the boat worshiped him, saying, "Truly you are the Son of God."

[34]When they had crossed over, they came to land at Gennesaret. [35]After the people of that place recognized him, they sent word throughout the region and brought all who were sick to him, [36]and begged him that they might touch even the fringe of his cloak; and all who touched it were healed.

Exegetical Perspective

Texts have layers, and Matthew's account of the walking on the water is a miracle story that functions as a christological confession that has become two lessons on discipleship. Let us take this one step at a time.

Luke does not report the walking on the water following the feeding of the five thousand, and only Matthew adds the scene of Peter's walking on the water and then doubting. Like most of the miracle stories in the Gospels, this one derives much of its meaning from its resonance with Old Testament passages. Like the feeding of the five thousand, the walking on the water suggests reflection on the exodus. In the flight of the Israelites from Egypt, God parted the waters or drove them back with a strong east wind (Exod. 14:21–29). The Israelites crossed on dry land, but Pharaoh's army perished in the waters. God's sovereignty over the sea at the exodus was connected in Hebrew imagination with God's separation of the land from the sea at creation:

> Was it not you who dried up the sea,
>   the waters of the great deep;
> who made the depths of the sea a way
>   for the redeemed to cross over?
>   (*Isa. 51:10*)

Reflection on God's sovereignty over the creation continues in the Psalms. Between bracketing

Homiletical Perspective

The texts that precede this passage tell us that it has been an exhausting and powerful day for Jesus and the disciples. They have learned that their friend John the Baptist has been beheaded, and they have just witnessed the impossible feeding of more than five thousand people with just a few fish and loaves. It is time for a rest. Jesus sends them across the sea in a boat while he seeks some solitude and time to pray. Time passes. The wind blows the boat, the disciples are far offshore, and night begins to fall. As readers, we are invited into the liminal spaces of night and day, sand and shore, wind and calm. We are in an in-between space, where the human and the holy will meet, to stretch and encounter one another.

Morning dawns and Jesus decides to join the disciples in their boat. Being the Son of God and unimpaired by limitations, he takes a shortcut across the top of the water. Much could be made of this move on Jesus' part. It is a truly significant revelation of power for him to do this. Up until now, his use of holy gifts has primarily been in the service of healing. There is, of course, the wedding at Cana (John 2:1–11), when his mother urges him to change the water to wine, and his response there might inform us of the reason for his decision now to cross the waters in this way. He tells her that his time has not yet come.

Theological Perspective

at times, but a little faith can also enable one to do amazing things, like move mountains and walk on water.

Serene Jones tells a story that illustrates both aspects of faith. She was serving on a long-range planning committee of her church at a critical juncture in the church's life. They had decided to reenergize various ministries of the church, but initial enthusiasm waned when the implementation of the ministries proved difficult. Negativity overtook the leadership of the church. Finally one of the newer members of the church asked, "Is this what it means to be church, believing you should do all these things, and then feeling worn out and guilty because you can't? Is this the Good News we celebrate?"[1] The question was pointed enough that they decided to put their work on hold until they could gain some perspective. It was a teaching moment in which the committee began to talk about classic notions like justification and sanctification.

"Sanctification" is a term John Calvin and others used to describe the gift of grace to be faithful, that is, to perform the faith. The word Serene Jones uses for this form of faith is "adornment," to be clothed in "forms of behaviors, actions, attitudes, and specific practices that conform that person to Christ."[2] Yet sanctification is a form of faithfulness that many Christians emphasize to a fault. Many of us are so concerned about being good Christians that we have lost sight of the fact that we are frail children of dust. Sanctification without justification, the acknowledgment of the free gift of love and mercy, can lead to the belief that practices of faith alone justify us before God and others. We need continually to be reminded that we are saved by grace alone.

"Justification" is the term used to describe what happens when we realize that God loves us and forgives us, despite the fact that we are most unlovable. Yet the unmerited, unconditional nature of the gift of mercy is counterintuitive and countercultural in a world in which everything we do is based on what we have earned. Meritocracy, one of the tyrannies of modernity, leads us to believe that we can save ourselves through our striving, our doing—in our vocations, avocations, education, and relation building. We may be aware of our failures and deceptions about who we are, but nonetheless we strive to earn value and status the old-fashioned way, by "earning"

1. Serene Jones, "Graced Practices: Excellence and Freedom in the Christian Life," in *Practicing Theology: Belief and Practices in the Christian Life*, ed. Miroslav Volf and Dorothy Bass (Grand Rapids: Eerdmans, 2002), 51–53.
2. Ibid., 61.

Pastoral Perspective

much in the way of hope to offer. Without Jesus, we do not have much to offer.

Peter finds the same thing in a more personal and critical way. Alone, walking on the sea, he becomes frightened by the wind. Critics of Peter have long pointed out his lack of faith, which leads to his descent into the sea, but there is an earlier point of criticism. This walking on the water business is Peter's idea: "Lord, if it is you, command me to come to you on the water" (v. 28). It is a foolish idea. You do not step out of a boat in the middle of a storm. You batten down the hatches, put on your life jacket, hunker down in the belly of the boat, and pray that the waves do not get any bigger and the winds do not get any stronger.

This is what most followers of Jesus hope to do in rough times. Perhaps it is what the church hopes to do as the waves of secularism, postmodern uncertainty, and declining membership beat against our aging hull. Meanwhile, the world has hope beaten out of it by economies that cannot recover, violence that never seems to end, and poverty that has become the accepted status quo. The safest way to avoid getting hurt seems to be to stay in the boat. There is no shame in staying in the boat: 92 percent of the disciples do exactly that in this story. Indeed, all Peter seems to receive for his efforts is a rebuke from Jesus: "You of little faith, why did you doubt?" (v. 31).

However, Jesus seems more disappointed than angry with Peter. Jesus is disappointed in Peter because he knows Peter has what it takes to step out of that boat and stay afloat. He knows Peter's history. He knows Peter better than Peter knows himself. Of all people, Peter can walk out on that water with courage. Peter can stand in the middle of the raging sea and walk with Jesus.

The church is built on Peter (16:18). The church should remember that before we huddle down in the boat and pray for safer seas. Peter's church should be willing to take such risks and step out of the boat, step out of the boat and risk preaching news that might disrupt the way we have always done things in the community, in our political life, or in our congregations. The church should be willing to risk our own well-being to try something foolish, borderline crazy in the midst of raging storms. We should be willing to step out of the boat, driven by an impulsive desire to get closer to Jesus, even when he is miles from solid ground.

Peter does not fail because he steps out of the boat. He starts to sink because he notices the wind—the strong wind—and becomes frightened (v. 30).

references to the exodus in Psalm 77:15, 20, the psalmist rhapsodizes,

> When the waters saw you, O God,
> when the waters saw you, they were afraid;
> the very deep trembled.
> . . . .
> Your way was through the sea,
> your path, through the mighty waters;
> yet your footprints were unseen.
> *(Ps. 77:16, 19)*

Walking on the water, following the feeding in the wilderness, Jesus reenacts the exodus. He is the long-expected prophet like Moses (Deut. 18:15, 18) who will deliver God's people. The walking on the water has further significance: it reveals Jesus' divinity. God "alone stretched out the heavens and trampled the waves of the Sea" (Job 9:8). When Jesus walks on the water, therefore, he does what God alone can do, reenacting God's mighty acts at creation and at the exodus. Mark 6:48 underscores this point with an allusion that Matthew omits: Jesus means to "pass by" the disciples, as God passed by Moses (Exod. 33:18–23), Elijah (1 Kgs. 19:11), and Job (Job 9:11).

When the disciples saw Jesus, they cried out, thinking he was a spirit from the deep, but he reassured them, identifying himself, "Take heart, it is I; do not be afraid." The words "it is I," in Greek *egō eimi*, are the divine name revealed to Moses at the burning bush: "I AM" (Exod. 3:14). Jesus' words are also the words God speaks to the people of faith in every crisis:

> But now thus says the LORD,
> he who created you, O Jacob,
> he who formed you, O Israel:
> Do not fear, for I have redeemed you;
> I have called you by name, you are mine.
> When you pass through the waters, I will be with you;
> and through the rivers, they shall not overwhelm
> you.
> . . . .
> For I am the LORD your God,
> the Holy One of Israel, your Savior.
> *(Isa. 43:1–3)*

The first lesson in discipleship, therefore, is that God, our creator and redeemer, the sovereign of the universe, is always present with the community of faith in times of crisis. Surely the One who stretched out the heavens and parted the waters will be present with us in our distress!

Peter asks that, if he really is Jesus, he command Peter to come to him on the water. In the midst of

So perhaps now he feels the disciples are ready to see just how limitless the Son of God really is. It is curious that no one is calling him to come, and no one needs his help in the water as he walks out to meet them. Why does he defy the laws of nature in this way? What does he want the disciples to learn from this encounter?

Halfway between sleep and waking, the disciples are startled to see a figure walking on the water. They cannot make sense of what they are seeing, although it is their friend Jesus, with whom they have traveled and been taught intimately for months now. What prevents them from recognizing Jesus for who he is?

What is it that keeps any of us from seeing God's presence among us? We are told that Jesus seeks us and is present with us, even "to the end of the age" (28:20). However, our anxiety, confusion, and failure to anticipate miracles often have us missing moments of grace that surround us. We expect to meet God in church, or perhaps in the soup kitchen, but do we imagine God's presence could meet us in the laundromat, or carwash, or grocery store? Could God reach out and surprise us in the circus, or on the airplane? Ours is a God who comes at the unexpected hour in unusual, burning-bush ways.

Always patient and compassionate, Jesus hears their cries of fear and alarm. Jesus' arrival is so far from the commonplace and what they expect to see that they immediately fall into superstitious thinking and cry out that a ghost is coming to them. Jesus speaks to comfort and reassure them: "Take heart, it is I; do not be afraid" (v. 27). It seems to be a central aspect of the human experience that our fears and superstitions blind us to the arrival of the holy. In the same way, it seems to be a central and blessed aspect of the character of God that God stands ready with a word of comfort and calm to soothe us: "Take heart, it is I; do not be afraid."

Those words unlock something in Peter. The hot coals of faith are glowing inside him, and he needs just one more good gust of the winds of the Spirit to carry him into action. Peter, like most of us, needs just a bit more reassurance that he is encountering the holy and not playing tricks in his own mind. He speaks out in faith: "Lord, if it is you, command me to come to you on the water." That question echoes the faith of Samuel when he calls out in the night, "Speak, for your servant is listening" (1 Sam. 3:10). Both are articulations of faith needing reassurance, and both are all that God needs to be able to call us to amazing feats of grace.

Jesus responds with one simple word: "Come." Then Peter is off and running. That is all Peter needs

Matthew 14:22–36

Theological Perspective

it. Eventually we must come to terms with the fact that we cannot do so and that God loves us still. This is the judgment side of little faith. The encouragement side of little faith is the assurance that once we begin to ponder the God who loves us still, we are freed for the faithfulness of sanctification.

Once we come to terms with the free love of God, it changes the way we perform the faith, the adornments of the faith that we wear. This realization alters the way we understand and perform ministry, for our ministry embodies an interrelated tension between gift and performance. The phrase Jones uses for this relationship is "adorned in freedom"; that is, faith is both the strenuous work of putting on Christ and the freedom of living out of a love that one does not earn.[3]

Both of these aspects of faith (gift and performance) are reflected in the story of Peter's walking on the water. Let us not forget what happens in the story. Peter does walk on water—albeit only a few tentative steps—and he does it in a storm. Jesus does not chastise him for attempting to perform the faith amid a storm at sea. Why? Because God in Christ does not lead us away from the struggles and the tensions of life, but right into the midst of them, armed with the gift of forgiveness and adorned with the spirit of Christ, who empowers us to follow God's trajectory into the world. Finally, Jesus does not say to Peter, "O you of little faith, why did you think you could walk on water?" but, rather, "O you of little faith, why did you doubt [that you could]?" (v. 31). So it is also for each of us and for our ministry: adorned with the mercy and power of God, we are not to doubt that we can!

ROGER J. GENCH

Pastoral Perspective

Peter's fear gets in the way of his faith. For every disciple who takes her or his call seriously, there is a lot to be afraid of.

What if I take the greatest risk of my faith and God does not meet me? What if the suffering I encounter responding to God's call is larger than the hope my faith is supposed to offer? What if I step out and discover my faith is not strong enough?

The church too faces similar fears. What if our church is not able to respond to the emergent needs of the changing neighborhood or the changing society? What if our newest efforts to revamp worship, or reach out to younger people, or stretch one last time to bring on a pastor do not succeed? What then?

These fears are real, as real as the storm that Peter steps into. Simply focusing on Jesus may not necessarily do anything to calm the storm. No amount of faith may end the difficult times the church is negotiating. No amount of trust may calm the fears of a nation still scared to death by just how vulnerable life is. No amount of prayer is guaranteed to calm the storms that sometimes rage within every life, within every home.

Nevertheless, the words Jesus offers, even before Peter steps out of the boat, could not be more clear: "Take heart, it is I; do not be afraid" (v. 27). Whatever the storm, whatever the uncertainties, whatever the fears, the church that is willing to risk a closer step toward Jesus has nothing to fear. With him, there is courage to engage every change, every uncertainty, every fear. Without him, we do not have much to offer the world. With him, there is little else we need.

ANDREW FOSTER CONNORS

---

3. Ibid., 65–70.

the stormy blast, Peter steps out of the boat and begins to make his way to Jesus, walking on the water. When he becomes concerned about the wind (he is walking on water, why is he worried about wind?), he begins to sink. Sinking into the deep, he cries out to Jesus, "Save me!" This prayer too echoes words of the psalmist:

> Save me, O God,
>   for the waters have come up to my neck.
> I sink in deep mire,
>   where there is no foothold;
> I have come into deep waters,
>   and the flood sweeps over me.
>
>   *(Ps. 69:1–3)*

It is also the cry of the disciples in the earlier sea crossing (8:25). Jesus came to save his people (1:21). He saved others (9:22; 10:22; 16:25; 24:13), but he does not save himself (27:40, 42, 49).

The problem is not the wind or the waves, though: "You of little faith, why did you doubt?" Jesus often chastises disciples for their "little faith" in Matthew (6:30; 8:26; 16:8; 17:20). Here is the second lesson in discipleship: the Lord is always present with us in our times of distress; he bids us come to him, but we must walk by faith with our eyes fixed steadfastly on the Lord. When we fail, as we inevitably do, if we call out to him, he will surely raise us up and draw us to himself. Had Peter not doubted, he would hardly have been human—and certainly not a mentor for those who take one tentative, struggling step at a time. Peter's doubt is less an intellectual uncertainty about what he has seen than it is a hesitation to obey Jesus.

The scene closes with Jesus and Peter getting into the boat and the storm subsiding. The awestruck disciples confess, "Truly, you are the Son of God" (v. 33; cf. Mark 6:51, where they are merely "utterly astounded"). What has revealed Jesus' divine identity to them? Is it the miracle of walking on water, or the fact that he has come to the disciples in their distress, bade Peter come to him, and then lifted him up when he was sinking? Matthew's story invites us to echo Paul's prayer, "Maranatha! Come, Lord Jesus, come!" (1 Cor. 16:22).

R. ALAN CULPEPPER

to get out of the boat so that he can greet his Savior. Just for a moment, just for a tightrope of a second, faith is stronger than doubt. Peter keeps his eyes on Jesus, and everything is possible. Then the world, and wind, and memory, and fear crash in, and Peter begins to sink. "Lord, save me!" he cries (v. 30). As believers we know this moment. It is the moment when we feel as though we have gotten in over our heads, or bitten off more ministry than we can chew. "Lord, save me!" we cry with Peter.

Jesus is so close that he simply reaches out his hand to steady Peter. In the words that Jesus offers Peter we hear both friendly jesting and radical possibility. "You of little faith, why did you doubt?" The subtext is that anything is possible with faith. Walking on water, feeding five thousand, healing the sick—all of it becomes possible if we simply have faith and keep our eyes on Jesus and not the gusting wind and swelling waves that surround us. With a word and a touch Jesus reassures Peter of his presence and the power of God to alter reality.

The passage concludes with Jesus and Peter both in the boat and the other disciples celebrating what they have witnessed. Here in this in-between place, the human and the holy are entwined, and the world is changed by the encounter.

LIZ BARRINGTON FORNEY

Matthew 15:1–11

¹Then Pharisees and scribes came to Jesus from Jerusalem and said, ²"Why do your disciples break the tradition of the elders? For they do not wash their hands before they eat." ³He answered them, "And why do you break the commandment of God for the sake of your tradition? ⁴For God said, 'Honor your father and your mother,' and, 'Whoever speaks evil of father or mother must surely die.' ⁵But you say that whoever tells father or mother, 'Whatever support you might have had from me is given to God,' then that person need not honor the father. ⁶So, for the sake of your tradition, you make void the word of God. ⁷You hypocrites! Isaiah prophesied rightly about you when he said:

⁸ 'This people honors me with their lips,
       but their hearts are far from me;
⁹ in vain do they worship me,
       teaching human precepts as doctrines.'"

¹⁰Then he called the crowd to him and said to them, "Listen and understand: ¹¹it is not what goes into the mouth that defiles a person, but it is what comes out of the mouth that defiles."

Theological Perspective

The theological focus of these eleven verses is essentially ethical, and the central ethical concern is moral hypocrisy. Jesus uses a form of this very word when he bluntly addresses a group of Pharisees and scribes as "You hypocrites!" (v. 7). They have come to complain to him about the fact that his disciples are lax about the tradition of ritual hand washing before meals. This tight focus on a single ethical concern, hypocrisy, is underscored by the several pairs of parallel contrasting terms that appear in the passage: "tradition" / "commandment," "lips" / "hearts," "human precepts" / "doctrines," and "what goes into the mouth" / "what comes out of the mouth."

The theological force of Jesus' retort to the complaint leveled against his disciples is simply to affirm that what a person actually does (or says and truly means) is what makes for righteousness before God and neighbor, rather than even the strictest observation of traditions, practices, and rituals—be they legal (as in vv. 3–5), liturgical (as in vv. 8–9), or dietary (vv. 10–11).

Overall, and in each of these three examples, the criticism Jesus is offering is barbed and discomfiting; indeed it was downright offensive to many of his listeners (see v. 12). This, then, is the central theological affirmation underscored in this awkward encounter between Jesus and his critics: God

Pastoral Perspective

We live by our traditions. They can represent the lived wisdom of prior generations. Traditions structure daily interactions; they guide the important rituals and celebrations that mark life. Traditions express the common values of a community; they give shape and form to deeply held beliefs. Yet traditions can go awry. When traditions become ossified, they rob lives of vitality, integrity, and innovation. When the underlying connection between these traditions and the principles they once embodied is lost, people may find themselves mindlessly following traditions and lose their way on the path God commands. It is all too easy to uphold our traditions at the expense of faithful obedience to God. Religious traditions may even become a cover for not attending to the rigorous demands of the Christian life.

The religious leaders come to Jesus to complain about the disciples' flagrant disregard for their traditions about ritual purity. By not washing their hands before they eat, the disciples are undermining the faith that is embodied in the ritual practices of the community. In answering their question with a question of his own, Jesus exposes their misplaced priorities. Traditions about ritual purity are not as important as the weightier matters of one's obligations to God and to other people that are expressed in the Ten Commandments. Not only do these

Exegetical Perspective

Matthew precedes Jesus' teaching regarding the tradition of the elders and what defiles with stories of the feeding of the five thousand, Jesus' walking on the water, and healing in Gennesaret. In this and the following narratives of the healing of the Canaanite woman's daughter, more cures, and the feeding of the four thousand, the evangelist is largely replicating the Markan context and order of material. The several stories can be heard interacting with Matthew 15:1–11, perhaps particularly in the healing of the child of one who is not of "the house of Israel" and the mother's readiness to eat even the table crumbs. That Matthew had a version of Mark's Gospel before him seems confirmed by their both having the somewhat unusual order "Pharisees and scribes" (Matt. 15:1; Mark 7:5). Mark appears to have done so to refer first to some local Pharisees, while Matthew indicates that both groups came to the Galilean region from Jerusalem.

In verses 3–9, where Jesus is heard responding to the Jewish leaders, the evangelist reorders and adapts the Markan dialogue to make it clearer and more forceful. While it is possible that Mark's explanation of the cleansing of hands and vessels (Mark 7:3–4) was added to this Gospel after it came into Matthew's hands, Matthew finds it superfluous. He then sharpens the contrast between the "tradition"

Homiletical Perspective

This text suggests preaching opportunities on the importance and danger of tradition, the insider-outsider politics of church membership, and the beginning of a discussion of the power of speech. "We have never done it that way before" is often a death knell for, or warning shot aimed at, a new or different idea, practice, or project in the life of the church. It seems that humans, often with no idea of how the practice began, cling tenaciously to what has been, even if contemporarily its practicality has run its course. Church membership rolls and attendance figures rise and fall on the power of tradition in congregations.

Contemporary popular culture is filled with so-called procedural or police dramas from the *Law and Order* and *CSI* franchises to *The Closer* and *Harry's Law*, a plethora of court television shows, and twenty-four-hour food and home design networks. Real and imagined people give advice about how to solve issues, how to make life better, how to save marriages, how to find a guilty party, how to be human, in sixty minutes or less. These icons of culture become the methods for engaging life for millions of people. Lines and processes are quoted more than the biblical text. They become family and friend traditions, like generational support of a favorite college or professional sports team. One may

Matthew 15:1–11

Theological Perspective

demands righteousness of practical action and being, rather that outward forms or practices. As in the more famous parable of the Sheep and the Goats in Matthew 25, Jesus affirms that what finally matters is what we actually do to and for others.

While holding before us the straightforwardness of this affirmation, modern readers are wise to hold three cautionary caveats in mind as they read and interpret the passage. First, we do well to remember that the Pharisees and the scribes were deeply committed, religious people. The Pharisees as a group seem to have been intent on democratizing the Jewish faith centered in the Jerusalem temple, bringing the possibility of purity—in their view, righteousness before God—to those who could not regularly participate in temple practices. The scribes, a distinct but perhaps overlapping professional group, were literate experts on the Mosaic law, trained to interpret and apply the ancient traditions to modern life. It would not be honest to criticize the faith of either group as characteristically hypocritical. More accurately, hypocrisy crept into their ardent religious practice and spiritual zeal just as it can find its way into our practice and our zeal.

Second, Jesus is not condemning tradition or traditionalism as such, but tradition practiced in such a way as to permit hypocritical distance to grow between "lips" and "heart." Ritual can indeed be "dead ritual," but, as many can attest, ritual also can be very much alive, a practiced routine that carves a godly groove into our hearts.

Third, the awkward truth is that some odor of hypocrisy is inevitable for all who feel called to live in righteousness before God and neighbor, simply because none of us can ever become completely the people God would have us be. In point of fact, one might say that the only people who are not in some measure hypocritical are those individuals who either have no standards at all or who have strategically set their standards low enough so that they can always attain them. This note of ethical realism offered, Jesus is obviously criticizing what was a less self-aware and more blatantly cavalier form of moral inconsistency.

A vivid memory serves well to frame Jesus' point. More than two decades ago, I met a man named Fuad Bahnan, an Arab born in Jerusalem, a Christian and a Protestant minister in the Evangelical Synod of Syria and Lebanon. For more than thirty years Mr. Bahnan had served as the pastor of a small congregation in West Beirut, Lebanon, the overwhelmingly Muslim sector of the city. He told me this story

Pastoral Perspective

leaders emphasize the wrong things; they also use their human traditions as a means of not following the law of God. Over time, traditions that were developed to protect, explicate, and apply the law become legal loopholes for rejecting and disobeying the command of God.

In the life of the church, confusing human religious traditions with essential biblical teachings is a constant temptation. It can be as simple as being so caught up in church meetings and programs that there is no time left to love the neighbor in practical and useful ways. There are times people care more about the unspoken rules of the community and how they maintain the church property than they do about the practice of hospitality. Some within congregations can turn a cold shoulder to visitors whose economic, educational, or ethnic backgrounds do not meet their traditions about dress and behavior in worship.

The gospel always takes form in a concrete culture at a particular time and place. The challenge is to discern when the life and teachings of the church are faithful expressions of the gospel and when they compromise the word of God. In the American context, human traditions and laws about slavery, the role of women, sexual orientation, and race have hindered the church from living and proclaiming the liberating power of the gospel.

One of the problems with civil religion is that it clothes the values or concerns of a particular culture or nation in the vestments of religion. The danger is that certain economic theories, immigration policies, military strategies, or partisan politics can be baptized as Christian. Even worship and prayer life can become so compromised by cultural traditions that that they no longer honor God and serve only to glorify vain desires and unholy causes. The result is that religious practices become the servant of misguided ideologies and the church loses its prophetic witness.

The "War Prayer" of Mark Twain, published posthumously, depicts the festive mood and patriotic fervor in a worship service in which the pastor prays for the soldiers of an unnamed country who are going off to war. With grand and glorious rhetoric, the pastor prays for victory and for the total defeat of the enemy. A lone prophetic figure enters the church and speaks to the congregation. He tells them that in praying to crush the enemy they are also praying for the death, destruction, torture, and misery of the people against whom they fight. Is this what they really want?[1] The tradition of a thoughtless civil

---

1. Mark Twain, "The War Prayer," *Harper's Monthly* (November 1916).

Feasting on the Gospels

(*paradosis*) and the "word" (*logos*); some textual traditions have *nomos*, "law," or *entolē*, "commandment," that Matthew reports "God said" (in some versions, "commanded") where Mark has "Moses said."

The net effect of these changes is that Matthew says human tradition toys with God's word, not merely Moses' word. With Mark, Matthew seems to suggest that the example of law avoidance that follows is but a glaring instance of uses of tradition to "break" or "transgress" God's commandment. *Parabainein* is Matthew's word in verse 3, echoing the accusation in verse 2 that the disciples are "breaking" the tradition.

The commandment to honor one's parents is given in positive form (from Exod. 20:12; Deut. 5:16) and then in a negative version with reference to Exodus 21:17 and Leviticus 20:9—the two forms reinforcing the stature of the scriptural commandment. The Pharisees and scribes have "made void" (or "un-ratified" or "a-voided") this commandment and used tradition to allow a person to take what should be devoted to ensure honor and care for parents and to make it into an "offering" or "gift" to God. Matthew does not use Mark's more technical Hebrew *korban* (Mark 7:11) that would need translation. What would have been the motivation for and precise nature of such an "offering" in the first century is not certain. Some commentators suggest from later evidence that a son might have sworn such an oath in anger; in any case, it is clear that the filial duty of the commandment is thus "avoided." Possibly the gift was something like a living gift in modern times, whereby donors may retain benefit from the offerings that then pass to charitable use (in this case, probably for the temple and perhaps its officials) at their deaths.

Jesus is then said to stress the seriousness of such avoidance, since those who allow such are "hypocrites"—a word Matthew uses thirteen times (Mark once; Luke three times) to describe those who "break" God's commandments, which is more the emphasis here than "pretenders," although that nuance would have been present in the common use of the Greek word. Their opposition to the true spirit of obedience to God's commandment is then underscored with the quotation of Isaiah 29:13: "These people . . . honor me with their lips, while their hearts are far from me."

While the general character of such a disputation involving the use of tradition in scriptural interpretation and application sounds apropos for the times,

be penalized and socially ostracized for not joining in support of even a losing season. After all, it is tradition. This text is both a critique and a support of tradition.

Sermonic claims about the value of tradition as the foundation of faith and order in the church are inherent, given a contemporary understanding of Jesus as the fulfillment of, rather than a challenge to, the oral tradition that the Pharisees and scribes were assigned to keep. It is interesting that many preachers forget to step back and view the text in the context of its own culture before they move to its application to the present. Jaroslav Pelikan observed that tradition is the living faith of dead people; traditionalism is the dead faith of living people.[1]

Who are the twenty-first-century Pharisees and scribes who fill pulpits and pews each week? What traditions have we established that impede access to God? Why is the order of worship so important that some faint if a part is skipped or condensed? Why do we do things this way? Why do we dress a certain way, follow a particular style of worship, read a particular text at a certain time of year, recite a prayer repeatedly, celebrate baptism or Communion, pass the peace, or invite persons to become members of the church? How do arguments about things like this relate to everyday existence?

One might explore why humans resist new voices, new practices, or new members who have different ideas or understandings of faith. How much of the Pharisees' and scribes' resistance to Jesus' message stems from fear of loss of power? How much do they represent a rebuke to the challenge of a young teacher who is not as credentialed as they are? The preacher might consider how varied generations understand, value, or reject the traditional values preached each Sunday, while not assuming that young listeners have less knowledge of tradition or have less developed faith than more mature members.

The preacher might investigate how life circumstances were addressed in worship in the biblical text and how they are handled in contemporary times. Are life and worship synonymous, or do we worship only on Sunday? Why is traditional worship often viewed as more correct or closer to the biblical way of worship or holier than so-called contemporary, blended, or emerging worship methods? Procedural and traditional worship and ritual give both law and

---

1. *The Vindication of Tradition: The 1983 Jefferson Lecture in the Humanities* (New Haven: Yale University Press, 1986), 66.

Matthew 15:1–11

Theological Perspective

about an event in his congregation that unfolded in 1983, the year that the Israeli army marched north into Lebanon. No one, he said, knew how far north the Israelis would come; indeed, few thought that they would advance as far north as Beirut. However, members of Mr. Bahnan's church guessed that they would indeed take Beirut and then attempt to starve out any hidden Palestinian fighters. In preparation for the inevitable, the church decided to purchase a large quantity of nonperishable food for the siege they believed would soon be upon them.

It did come, of course. West Beirut was totally cut off; no one could enter or leave; no food was allowed in. The governing board of Pastor Bahnan's church then met to make plans for distribution of the food they had stockpiled. The meeting was long and conflicted. By the end of it, there were two different proposals on the table. The first proposal was that the food be distributed first to members of the congregation, then, as supplies permitted, to other Christians in West Beirut, and lastly, if anything was still left, to Muslim neighbors. The second proposal was very different, the inverse of the first. This motion suggested that the food be first distributed to Muslim neighbors, then to nonmember Christians, and lastly, if there was any left over, to members of the church.

Rev. Bahnan said the meeting lasted six hours. It finally ended when a normally quiet woman, a much-respected elder, stood up and with uncharacteristic volume and impatience shouted to her fellow board members, "You hypocrites! If we do not demonstrate the love of Christ in this place, who will?" The second proposal passed. The food the church had stockpiled was distributed first to Muslims, then to nonmember Christians, and finally to members of the congregation. Fuad Bahnan ended his story with two points. First, he said that there was actually enough food for everybody. Then he added this note: "The Muslims of West Beirut are still talking about it."

MICHAEL L. LINDVALL

Pastoral Perspective

religion that glorifies war and despises the enemy makes void the command of Jesus to love the enemy.

As Jesus said to the scribes and Pharisees, human traditions can become the servants of hypocrisy. Human beings fall into hypocrisy when their moral and spiritual lives do not conform to the truth of the gospel that they affirm with their words. Like actors (*hypocritēs*, the Greek word translated "hypocrite," means "stage actor") we play a part that is not our own authentic life. Without even being aware of what we have done, we may fall into honoring our traditions more than we honor the word of God. We slip into comfortable religious practices that seem to suit our needs, but may be far from what God intends for us. We have trouble stepping outside of ourselves and being self-critical. We rarely examine our beliefs, assumptions, and practices in light of the gospel and from the point of view of others. As Jesus' exchange with the scribes and Pharisees demonstrates, we are not usually the first to see the glaring gap between our words and our actions. We not only play a false part, but we are also no longer able to discern the truth about ourselves. When we lose our moral compass, we may even consciously misuse and abuse our religious traditions for our own selfish purposes.

The gospel convicts us of our hypocrisy. It exposes the way we claim God's forgiveness for ourselves but refuse to forgive others. We talk about justice but enjoy the benefits of unjust relationships. We judge others but make excuses for ourselves. We accept God's good gifts but do not give with glad and generous hearts. The words of Jesus not only convict us of our sin; they also set us free to see ourselves from God's perspective. By his own life, Jesus shows us the way to live with integrity so that our beliefs and actions are congruent. We need one another within the community of faith to hold each other accountable to Jesus Christ. We can help each other examine our traditions, practices, and beliefs in light of the gospel to ensure that our individual lives and our life together honor God and are a faithful witness to Christ.

LEWIS F. GALLOWAY

Feasting on the Gospels

Exegetical Perspective

we know too little about the position of his opponents. The Pharisees gave considerable weight to tradition in application of scriptural laws—more than did some of the Sadducees, who stressed the primacy of the Mosaic Scriptures. More than one rabbi from a later period would have come down on Jesus' side in this dispute, finding that it would be shocking to use tradition to avoid such a significant filial responsibility. Certainly some Jewish leaders in Jesus' time would have agreed with what elsewhere seems to have been part of Jesus' concern: that ways of interpreting and applying scriptural law not be used to avoid the true purpose of the teaching or to make it difficult to live this out in daily life, especially for ordinary people who had neither time nor opportunity to deal with all the details of ritual cleansing and the like.

Hearers of Matthew's Gospel would have been bound to recall Jesus' earlier words regarding the true import of the commandments: "You have heard that it was said . . . but I say to you" (5:21–48), as well as "In everything do to others as you would have them do to you; for this is the law and the prophets" (7:12). Then there was "I desire mercy and not sacrifice" (9:13; 12:7, quoting Hos. 6:6) and the interpretation of the Sabbath law in the stories of the plucking of grain and healing of the man with the withered hand (12:1–8; 9:14).

In verses 10–11 the audience becomes the "crowd" (as in Mark), presumably a reference to "the people of that place" (Gennesaret) in 14:35—a number of whom Jesus had healed, but who now serve as an audience more generically.

Verse 11 connects the passage to verse 2, leading to a question as to whether verses 3–9 may once have been a separate disputation, now placed into the context of verses 2 and 11, continuing on to verses 12–20 (see the exegetical perspective on Matt. 15:12–20). In verse 11 Matthew amends Mark's "nothing outside a person that by going in" and "things that come out" to "into the mouth" and "out of the mouth," clarifying the evangelist's understanding that it is primarily food under discussion as that which goes into a body, but seeming to narrow what comes out to defiling words. Verse 19 views actions as well as words as what defile.

FREDERICK BORSCH

Homiletical Perspective

order to worship. They may also defer the possibility of innovative, inclusive, creative approaches to investigating the mystery of God.

This passage briefly introduces the peril of being so involved in church activities that one neglects family obligations or human relationships. This is a powerful passage for ministers, lay officers, and anyone enmeshed in "doing church" but not honoring the purpose of the commandments to love God, neighbor, and self. This section might be preached on Mother's Day, reminding listeners of the obligation to attend to family with the same passion and zeal with which one serves God. The fragmentation of family is evident in all socioeconomic groups. Seldom do we anticipate a sermon about those who have dedicated themselves to God but ignore or cannot seem to find time to show love to others.

Similarly, the text may work for an ordination service to encourage new ministers to avoid human standards for what constitutes the successful pastor and instead to follow God's instructions to be a holistic pastor. Are we worshiping God, or is the purpose of our service a desire for the people to worship us?

As a former speech language pathologist and current preaching professor, I teach people about the power of spoken words. Reminiscent of the description of the power of the tongue in James 3:1–12, or Eliza Doolittle's lines, "Words! Words! Words! I'm so sick of words!" in Lerner and Loewe's My Fair Lady,[2] or the triumph of fluid speech in the 2010 Academy Award–winning The King's Speech,[3] this passage points to the power of words. Jesus says, "What comes out of the mouth proceeds from the heart. . . . For out of the heart come evil intentions" (15:18).

Consider how words can liberate, destroy, or overwhelm the listener. Clarity of speech is essential in the preaching moment. The caution in this text is that the way in which doctrine is communicated can help or hinder one's faith development. Revisiting the old tradition/new tradition discussion earlier in the passage, the preacher or teacher might invite the church to reflect on language, ways to speak the truth in love, verbal abuse, developing a faith vocabulary, when words are too much, the silent treatment, and salvation speech, as well as "murder, adultery, fornication, theft, false witness, slander" (15:19).

TERESA FRY BROWN

---

2. My Fair Lady, dir. George Cukor (Warner Brothers, 1964; 2009 DVD).
3. The King's Speech, dir. Tom Hooper (The Weinstein Company and Anchor Bay Entertainment, 2010; 2011 DVD).

Matthew 15:12–20

¹²Then the disciples approached and said to him, "Do you know that the Pharisees took offense when they heard what you said?" ¹³He answered, "Every plant that my heavenly Father has not planted will be uprooted. ¹⁴Let them alone; they are blind guides of the blind. And if one blind person guides another, both will fall into a pit." ¹⁵But Peter said to him, "Explain this parable to us." ¹⁶Then he said, "Are you also still without understanding? ¹⁷Do you not see that whatever goes into the mouth enters the stomach, and goes out into the sewer? ¹⁸But what comes out of the mouth proceeds from the heart, and this is what defiles. ¹⁹For out of the heart come evil intentions, murder, adultery, fornication, theft, false witness, slander. ²⁰These are what defile a person, but to eat with unwashed hands does not defile."

Theological Perspective

This passage invites at least two related yet distinct theological considerations. Verses 12 through 14 begin with a report brought to Jesus by his disciples informing him that the Pharisees "took offense" at his teaching (15:1–11). This news is followed by Jesus' response to their negative reaction. A key theological issue raised in this interchange is the nature of the relationship among people who hold sharply different religious views. The second theological consideration suggested is raised by the remaining six verses, in which Jesus clarifies and amplifies to his disciples that same teaching he had offered publicly in verses 1–11, the very teaching that had so offended the Pharisees in the crowd. The theological consideration raised again here is that of faith essentials, specifically in this case what it is that gives people of faith their essential identity—traditional practices or ethical behavior in relationship.

Jesus' response to the indignation of the Pharisees at his teaching about the priority of relational ethics over traditional purity codes offers both blunt and honest critique ("they are blind guides") and counsel to let them be who they are, in peace ("let them alone," v. 14). The tension implied in these words of Jesus is between a critical honesty about those you believe to be theologically wrong on the one hand, and a commitment to peaceful, if awkward,

Pastoral Perspective

The disciples report that the scribes and Pharisees are offended by the harsh words of Jesus. Jesus has declared that God is honored by keeping the commandments and not by upholding religious traditions that interfere with the essential teachings of the law. Jesus responds to the disciples' concerns with a series of parabolic images that leave the disciples puzzled about the meaning of his words. Beneath the controversy and the uncertainty lies the desire to understand what makes a person holy or righteous in the eyes of God. Is it the performance of external rituals or something else? Are the disciples on the right path or not?

Jesus says that true righteousness is not a matter of hand washing or eating ritually approved foods. Using the image of the mouth, Jesus says that what matters is not what goes into the mouth but what comes out of the mouth. True righteousness is a question of the quality of life that flows from the human heart. In these words of Jesus we hear echoes of the teachings in the Sermon on the Mount (chaps. 5–7). In the Sermon on the Mount, Jesus looks behind the act to the disposition of the heart that leads to the act. Behind the sins of adultery and murder lie lust and anger. In contrast, a loving heart will produce fruits of compassion, reconciliation, truth telling, generosity, and even prayer for the enemy. It is an ethic of character.

Feasting on the Gospels

Exegetical Perspective

The larger context of this teaching about things that defile is provided by the framing of the stories of the feedings of five thousand and four thousand before and after it (14:13–21; 15:32–39) that tell of the food that is provided by Jesus. The more immediate context is the dispute with the Pharisees and scribes regarding the oral tradition (15:1–11) and the healing of the Canaanite woman's daughter (vv. 21–28). Verses 12–20 continue the dispute with Jewish leaders and foreshadow events with the Canaanite mother. All can be seen as a kind of test case for stretching Jesus' ministry beyond ritual cleanliness.

As is the case with the preceding eleven verses, Matthew is following Mark but has made a number of significant changes, omissions, and additions. One notes, for instance, how the evangelist brings the concerns and opposition of the Pharisees back into the picture in verse 12, helping further to link the teaching about tradition, the commandments of God (vv. 2–9), and things that defile (vv. 2, 10–20). There is also the possibility, however, that verses 2 and 10–20 could be understood as a separate teaching about what defiles.

In the background one can hear the struggle of the early church over the roles of ritual law and traditions—not least with regard to foods that are clean and unclean. Paul confronts Peter regarding his not

Homiletical Perspective

As the context in Matthew shifts from a public theological confrontation with the Pharisees and scribes to a personal, intimate continuing-education seminar with the disciples, Jesus shows almost parental or seasoned-teacher restraint. I wonder how often he thought, "How many ways do I need to use to teach this group about faith, who I am, and their responsibilities for their own salvation? I know Peter's hand will go up in a minute; he at least asks the questions and wants to know. I am not so sure about some of the others."

The disciples seemingly miss the possibility that Jesus is aware of the level of danger he is provoking by having public arguments and engaging the Pharisees and scribes. In church life the pastor often has insider, confidential knowledge about situations and proceeds in discussion with the other leaders who do not possess it because they have only outsider, public knowledge. A sermon about the trustworthiness of leadership or faith development would be appropriate using this text. Peter's continual questioning of Jesus provides fabric for a word on believers' being able to question God, finding their own voices, growing in surety of faith, reading their contexts, refusing to change, learning new information, or the consequences of speaking one's mind or holding on to one's faith.

Matthew 15:12–20

Theological Perspective

coexistence with them on the other. The unstated implication of such a strategy is that "truth [is] the daughter of time";[1] that is, in the dialectical interaction between differing theological perspectives, the truer one will reveal its truth in time.

This is akin to the intellectually hopeful assumptions behind Gotthold Lessing's famous eighteenth-century poem/novelette *Nathan the Wise*. In Lessing's narrative, a wise and wealthy man named Nathan possesses a ring that for generations in his family has passed from father to son. It is said that the ring offers its wearer wealth, wisdom, and honor, all of which Nathan has known in his life. Lying on his deathbed, Nathan the old man faces a dilemma. He has three sons whom he loves equally. So he calls his jeweler to his bedside, gives him the ring, and asks him to make two perfect copies, exact down to the scratches. The jeweler brings three rings back to Nathan, who mixes them up before privately presenting each to a son, representing it each time as the true ring. Boys being boys, they soon discover the ruse and confront their father, demanding to know which ring is the true ring. Nathan answers that he does not know, but that time will tell.[2]

A second theological consideration, raised in the latter verses of this passage, is much the same as that of the first eleven verses of the chapter. Here, however, Jesus reframes the teaching in an earthy bodily metaphor. The force of the metaphor is to argue against the centrality of the dietary restrictions of purity laws ("whatever goes into the mouth . . . goes out into the sewer," v. 17) and to assert that the evil that "proceeds from the heart" ("evil intentions, murder, adultery, fornication, theft, false witness, slander") is what truly defiles a person (vv. 18–20). However, this is not simply a matter of "meaningless ritual" versus "active faith."

To appreciate the subtleties, one must recall that a core issue in this debate, for both the Pharisees and Jesus, is that of identity. For centuries, the complex system of purity laws had worked effectively to maintain Jewish identity in cultural contexts in which they found themselves a besieged minority pressed to assimilate. A range of distinctive traditions, dietary restrictions among them, had worked to maintain some semblance of Jewish distinctiveness: "purity," if you will. In Jesus' time, Jews were again pressed to accommodate to a pervasive cultural milieu, that of the Greco-Roman world. Among

1. Francis Bacon, *Novum Organum* (1620), paragraph 84.
2. Gotthold Ephraim Lessing, *Nathan der Weise* (1779; repr., Norderstedt: GRIN Verlag, 1998).

Pastoral Perspective

How do we nurture such character in the community of faith? Practicing piety, becoming righteous, and growing in holiness sound to modern ears like words in a foreign language. The old spiritual "Lord, Make Us More Holy" seems to belong to a distant era of church life. Nevertheless, being a Christian is about growing in grace, not staying in place. Sanctifying grace is a gift of God. Jesus says, "Every plant that my heavenly Father has not planted will be uprooted" (v. 13). Every fruitful plant in the church is the planting of God through the Holy Spirit.

The Spirit forms the church and sustains the church. Holiness of life is the work of the Holy Spirit in us. God sets the church apart and equips the church with gifts to nurture faith and to transform lives in the image of Christ. Helping the congregation understand and value the call to a life of holiness is an essential task of leadership in the church. There are so many things that get in the way of this vital work. It is all too easy for church leaders to let this task be eclipsed by the relentless demands of a church calendar crowded with meetings, the minor unexpected crises that seem to consume each day, and the administrative details that drain energy from the church.

Refocusing time, resources, and attention on spiritual growth helps the congregation and its leaders to get their priorities straight. One of the ways individuals and communities grow in faith and in holiness is through spiritual practices. Spiritual practices discipline unruly hearts and awaken lives to the presence of the Holy Spirit. Practices such as worshiping, praying, reading Scripture, singing, caring for the earth, giving generously, living compassionately, serving others, living simply, witnessing, practicing hospitality, and keeping silence all contribute to spiritual growth.

The writings of Craig Dykstra, Dorothy Bass, Henri Nouwen, Richard Foster, and many others provide guidance in spiritual practices. All of these practices offer a way to disconnect the self from cultural norms and social conventions that diminish life and connect the heart and mind to God's presence in the world. When we see God at work in our ordinary daily labors and relationships, then even the mundane tasks that seem so antithetical to the work of the Spirit can become the means of spiritual growth. Spiritual practices lead us into a deeper love for God and love for neighbor.

Growing in holiness is never a solitary journey. Jesus recognizes that his followers need the right kind of guides or mentors if they are to grow in the

Exegetical Perspective

eating with Gentiles (Gal. 2:11–14) and elsewhere offers his own teaching about not judging with regard to food and other matters (Rom. 14:1–12). The whole of 1 Corinthians 8:1–11:1 is concerned with whether or not Christians may rightly attend civic dinner parties, since they are held in pagan temples, or accept dinner invitations from hosts who serve meat that has been purchased in those temples.

Peter himself has a dream vision in which he protests, "I have never eaten anything that is profane or unclean," and hears a voice, "What God has made clean, you must not call profane" (Acts 10:9–16; 11:4–10). Then a Jerusalem council informs the Gentiles that they need not be troubled about many ritual matters, particularly regarding food, although they are instructed to abstain from what has been sacrificed to idols and animals butchered with the blood still in them (Acts 15:1–35). Similarly, John of Patmos rails against "those who say that they are Jews and are not" and are instead "a synagogue of Satan" because they eat food sacrificed to idols (Rev. 2:9; 3:9).

While Luke does not make use of any of Mark 7:1–23, presumably omitting such as no longer relevant for his largely Gentile audience, the evangelist Mark would appear also to regard concern over unclean foods as largely a settled matter: "Thus Jesus declared all foods clean" (Mark 7:19). Matthew, however, does not go this far, and Jesus' teaching about the law and Mosaic tradition in this Gospel seems more complex and nuanced: "Do not think that I have come to abolish the law or the prophets; I have come not to abolish but to fulfill" (5:17). The new teaching Jesus offers does not supersede the law but goes beyond and brings out its true end and purpose: "unless your righteousness exceeds that of the scribes and Pharisees, you will never enter the kingdom of heaven" (5:20), which is then given further explication and meaning in the following antitheses of the Sermon on the Mount. "You have heard that it was said . . . but I say to you" (5:21–48).

A number of interpreters of Matthew's Gospel have concluded that the Gospel was written for an audience that included many Jewish Christians and perhaps had in view potential Jewish converts for whom the role of all ritual laws—including dietary laws—may not have been a settled matter. While Matthew's use of the word "mouth" (*stoma*) in 15:11, 17, 18 may seem to be a play on that which is unclean as food, the list of what defiles in verse 19 clearly involves actions as well as words. Mark's list of thirteen things coming from within and out

Homiletical Perspective

"I once was lost but now am found, was blind but now I see," intones the hymn writer.[1] Spiritual blindness is a reality. There is an African proverb that says, "Blind belief is dangerous." Some believe whatever the preacher says, without any investigation of the source or resource themselves. Even long-standing church members experience sporadic spiritual blindness, astigmatism, or myopic vision. In this text the disciples view the actions of the Pharisees and scribes as problematic, but what if Jesus is describing *their* blindness as well?

The disciples had an up close and personal vantage point from which to view the works of Jesus. They lived with Jesus, walked with Jesus, listened to Jesus, gave up regular lives to follow Jesus. They were taught by Jesus yet had spiritual blind spots. This is evident in Peter's denial of Jesus, those who would later desert Jesus, and the one who would betray him. How many people miss the point of a text, a teaching, a program because of vision problems? As in the first part of this chapter, how many are ritually or textually correct but miss the application of grace that is necessary to live the text?

The preacher must ensure that textual blindness is defined as spiritual and not physical. Every Sunday, listeners are left out of the salvation story due to the preacher's description of a spiritual problem as a physical "because you sinned" issue. The text also points to the critical responsibility of teachers and preachers. "Guides to blind people" are supposed to give them clarity of vision, not further to impair the limited vision they have. The job of the teacher is to assist the student in broader illumination of a passage, practice, or way of life, not to subject their minds into dependency on one who has stopped learning.

An excellent teacher is one who desires to share his or her knowledge and to see the students excel even past where the teacher has developed. The text intimates that the one whose beliefs lead others to fall will also fall. Paraphrasing Carl Jung, one's vision will become clear when we look onto our own hearts. A sermon preparing members for religious education, missionary trips, or evangelism would benefit from use of this text.

Jesus speaks to the disciples in a parable. In my culture, a parable is described as a heavenly message using earthly language. Jesus uses oral tradition, common language that most people understand. Sermons can be so filled with theological, academic, or in-group speech that many listeners miss the

1. John Newton, "Amazing Grace," 1779.

Matthew 15:12–20

Theological Perspective

other goals, the Pharisees were inveterate advocates of maintaining Jewish identity through distinctive practices. The issue was doubtless especially sharp in Galilee, where this interchange takes place, a region where Jews may well have been in the minority. So Jesus' laxity on the matter of hand washing was to the Pharisees a matter not simply of neglecting ritual, but of Jews' not remembering "who they are." Jesus' response is that "who we are" is really defined by the way we live in relationship to others, that which "proceeds from the heart."

This affirmation that how we live with others matters far more than anything else is beautifully unfolded in Ryan White's posthumous autobiography, *Ryan White: My Own Story*. In the book, White, who was dying of AIDS at the age of thirteen, went to church on Easter:

> Normally, at our church, the whole congregation says, "Happy Easter!" to each other this way: our minister steps forward to the front pew, shakes a few … hands and says, "Peace be with you." Then those people turn to their neighbors and shake hands and so on, all the way to the back of the church, where we were sitting. The family in the pew in front of me turned around. I held out my hand to empty air. Other people's hands were moving every which way, all directions away from me. . . .
>
> It wasn't over yet. As Mom, Andrea, and I turned out of the church parking lot, our transmission died in the middle of the lane. . . . Mom tried to flag down some other cars leaving church, but no one would stop. A half hour went by, and then finally a man in a truck pulled away from the auto parts store across the street, nosed up behind us, and pushed our car over to the side or the road. Our rescuer climbed out of his truck and asked Mom, "Need a lift home?" Mom took a deep breath and said, "First I better tell you who we are," and she did. The truck driver shrugged, "Well, it doesn't matter," he said. He drove us home. A couple of months later he stopped by and invited me hang gliding.[3]

The painful point of Ryan's memory echoes that of Jesus: love and mercy take precedence over everything else.

MICHAEL L. LINDVALL

Pastoral Perspective

Christian life. The wrong kind of guidance will only cause one to "fall into a pit" (v. 14). After the resurrection of Jesus, the disciples discovered the Holy Spirit speaking in the church as a guide. They perceived and listened to the Spirit bearing witness through one another. They could learn from each other's successes and failures; they might disagree at times, but they were bound together by the bonds of love.

Christians need one another in the church for mutual encouragement, correction, forbearance, and forgiveness. Small groups within the church that focus on prayer, spiritual fellowship, and mission can be a means of helping one another grow in faithful discipleship. Followers of Jesus also need mentors who can show the way because they have walked in faith through adversity, opportunities, and challenges. As a result, such mentors have a lived wisdom, a mature faith, a compassionate heart, and a spirit open to God.

Being a holy people set apart by God is not an end in itself. Jesus called the disciples to be his witnesses in the world. It matters how followers of Jesus live together, because the Christian community represents an alternative way of being in the world. To be holy does not mean that Christians must withdraw from the world; it means they live in the world by the teachings of Jesus. Such a witness will always be countercultural and offensive.

In the face of the great disparity between rich and poor, the church practices generosity so that the good gifts of God are shared and there is enough for all. With the prevalence of hunger and homelessness even in wealthy countries, the church practices hospitality by feeding the hungry and sheltering the homeless. In a world of violence, the church demonstrates what it means to love the enemy and work for peace among all people. In a deeply polarized society that demonizes those who have different viewpoints, life experiences, and social backgrounds, the church embraces diversity, breaks down barriers that divide people, and builds new community centered in Christ and transformed by this grace.

LEWIS F. GALLOWAY

---

3. Ryan White and Ann Marie Cunningham, *Ryan White: My Own Story* (New York: Signet, 1992), 87.

Exegetical Perspective

of the heart is shortened to seven in Matthew—the last six seeming to be drawn from commandments six through nine of the Decalogue (Exod. 20:13–17). Matthew then brings this teaching to an end by having Jesus refer to Matthew 15:11 and 15:2, linking together the whole of the passage while again opening up the point of view that what does not defile can include a matter such as "unwashed hands."

Jesus' explanation of the saying (v. 11) regarding what does not and what does defile is given (as it is in Mark) to the disciples rather than to the crowd, but Matthew first notes the Pharisees' offense at the saying, followed by Jesus' response, also present elsewhere in the Gospel. The disciples hear of plants that will be uprooted (a familiar biblical theme; in Matthew see particularly the parable of the Weeds among the Wheat in 13:24–30; 36–43), followed by "they are blind guides" (vv. 13–14; also 23:16, 24) and a proverbial saying regarding the blind leading the blind (v. 14) that is also found in Luke 6:39. True sightedness versus blindness on the part of those who consider themselves pious is another familiar biblical theme (see, e.g., Rom. 2:15; John 10:39–41).

It is now Peter (one more indication of his importance in Matthew's Gospel) who, on behalf of the other disciples, asks for an explanation of the "parable," referring back to verse 11. One hears of Jesus' concern with the disciples' lack of understanding (not heard as frequently as in Mark, but still found in Matthew) and Jesus' readiness to offer them his explanation, as is done with several parables in chapter 13. Then and now, hearers of this Gospel are given this new understanding and come to feel themselves part of the circle of informed disciples.

FREDERICK BORSCH

Homiletical Perspective

meaning. Sometimes the sermon language is so common, conversational, or vernacular that the intent is obscured. In the text, Peter just does not get it, for whatever reason, so he asks yet another question. The preacher needs to remember that sometimes, no matter how hard we try, some will not receive the message. The preacher needs multiple levels of language, rephrasing statements in several ways and being multisensory in the presentation, to appeal to every listener. Proverbial language such as "A cutting word is worse than a bowstring; a cut may heal, but the cut of the tongue does not" or "Evil enters like a splinter and spreads like an oak tree" are similar to Jesus' return to the imagery of the power of the tongue or speech in verses 16–20.

The awareness of the injury inflicted by oral tradition, by faith language, and by persons who view themselves as holy is imperative in Jesus' inclusive love ethic. We sin by word and action. Injustice is present in how and what we speak. I would rephrase the old saying: "Sticks and stones do break bones, but words hurt forever." Words are formed in the mind (in biblical language, the "heart"). We say what we think. This text is an object lesson for preachers that our heart language can break listeners' hearts. Refilter the words of a manuscript that may have a homiletically sound form but whose function kills the message and eventually the messenger.

Consider how much violence spews from the pulpit due to word choice. This text is beneficial in preaching topics such as church gossip, "well intentioned advice," political speech and campaign rhetoric, social critiques of "those other people," different faith systems or denominations, and isms or prejudices related to class, race, gender, sexuality, nationality, or economic status. This passage alludes to the weight and repercussions of keeping some of the commandments but ignoring others, of following the worship ritual but texting critiques about church members during worship.

TERESA FRY BROWN

Matthew 15:21–28

²¹Jesus left that place and went away to the district of Tyre and Sidon. ²²Just then a Canaanite woman from that region came out and started shouting, "Have mercy on me, Lord, Son of David; my daughter is tormented by a demon." ²³But he did not answer her at all. And his disciples came and urged him, saying, "Send her away, for she keeps shouting after us." ²⁴He answered, "I was sent only to the lost sheep of the house of Israel." ²⁵But she came and knelt before him, saying, "Lord, help me." ²⁶He answered, "It is not fair to take the children's food and throw it to the dogs." ²⁷She said, "Yes, Lord, yet even the dogs eat the crumbs that fall from their masters' table." ²⁸Then Jesus answered her, "Woman, great is your faith! Let it be done for you as you wish." And her daughter was healed instantly.

Theological Perspective

Two concrete theological issues, both part of a larger and more theoretical issue, arise out of these verses. The first concrete issue is about the scope of Jesus' mission: is it to be to Israel alone or to the larger Gentile world as well? The second concrete issue has to do with the nature of prayer, for prayer is what the plea of the Canaanite woman is. Both of these more specific questions are subsumed under the towering question of the mutability or immutability of God. Does God change God's mind, or is God's will an unchanging constant? In this passage, Jesus—God with us—does indeed seem to change his mind on two matters with one decision. He acquiesces to the eloquent importunity of a courageous mother by changing his mind and healing her daughter. He thereby expands the scope of his ministry to include the larger Gentile world that this woman represents. He does this after having indicated that he had been "sent only to the lost sheep of the house of Israel" (v. 24, also 10:6).

It seems doubtful that either Jesus or Matthew meant to wrestle with the finery of process theology and its speculations about change in God. Rather, Matthew doubtless framed the story he had borrowed from Mark in a way that would help his readers grapple with the tension between those members of his community who understood the gospel of

Pastoral Perspective

The Canaanite woman is an annoyance. Jesus ignores her, and the disciples plead with him to make her go away. Life is often interrupted by people and situations that make inconvenient demands on one's time and get in the way of one's plans. When such interruptions threaten, some people know how to duck the call, take another route home, wait an extra ten minutes, or refer the problem to someone else. If we avoid the unpleasant interruptions in life, are we missing something important that God has for us to learn?

At first glance, this story of the Canaanite woman opens with a disconcerting picture of Jesus. It raises a serious pastoral question: if he does not have time for her, does he have time for *us*? This glimpse into the character of Jesus does not mesh with images of Jesus that many Christians carry in their minds. They see Jesus as the straight shooter who does not play favorites, but embraces all economic groups, social classes, and races. Even though he has the weight of the world on his shoulders, this Jesus has time for everyone. He welcomes sinners into his circle, and outsiders have a place of honor at the table. Even with his eyes set on Jerusalem, he takes time to heal the sick and restore sight to the blind. This is not how the character of Jesus appears as this story opens. The struggle between Jesus and the Canaanite

Exegetical Perspective

The larger context of the story of the Canaanite woman's plea to Jesus and the healing of her daughter is framed by the feedings of the five and four thousand (14:15–21; 15:32–39). Within that frame there is another, narrower context formed by healings done by Jesus near the Sea of Galilee (14:34–36; 15:29–31). Immediately preceding Jesus' dialogue with the woman is the teaching section (15:1–20) dealing with the misuse of tradition versus obedience to the commandment of God and lessons on things that defile a person. All of these passages interact.

Clearly relevant is the setting. The healings done in Galilee would be primarily, if not entirely, among Jewish people, while the encounter with the Canaanite woman is quite deliberately set in the foreign locale of Tyre and Sidon. Matthew has probably added Sidon, which is twenty miles north of Tyre. The two cities are northwest of Galilee on the Mediterranean coast. It may be that Matthew was composed somewhere in the Syrian area and that the evangelist has substituted "Canaanite" for Mark's "a Greek [NRSV "Gentile"], of Syrophoenician origin" (v. 22; Mark 7:26), possibly because the older, somewhat generic term would have been more familiar to Matthew's audience. In any case, this is non-Jewish territory. Jesus' only other encounter with a non-Jew is with the centurion whose servant is paralyzed (8:5–13). What will Jesus do?

Homiletical Perspective

How can Jesus be so insensitive and hateful to this woman? It reminds me of the ways single mothers are sometimes treated today. I thought Jesus was supposed to love everyone. These were questions that relentlessly bombarded my mind when I first preached this text. I was assigned to preach on Mother's Day and encountered this conversation between Jesus and the Canaanite woman. He has left the disciples in the seminary by the side of the road, and the Pharisees and scribes back in the temple, and traveled alone into culturally alien territory. At the time, I was a single, recently divorced black mother raising a daughter, and my heart was pierced by the thought that my sweet, loving Jesus would deny this unnamed woman assistance when her baby was sick. Would he do the same thing to me?

Several sermon possibilities spring from this text, including the depth of mother-child relationships, Jesus' divinity and humanity, cultural and religious prejudice, persistent faith, and the meaning of healing. The text is a difficult dialogue that reflects social stigmatism, racism, and religious discord. What are the cultural barriers evident in the congregation that can be named? What manageable means to remove them can be given? Often sermons urge persons to go save the world, address the "not in our neighborhood" syndrome, or sacrificially volunteer

Matthew 15:21–28

Theological Perspective

Jesus to be the way for Jews to be faithful Jews and those members who believed that the gospel was intended by God for the whole world. That Jesus effectively articulates both perspectives in this passage served to name the tension and to recognize the truth inherent in both viewpoints.

To frame the question as "Does God change God's mind?" is distinctly anthropomorphic. The very question ascribes human characteristics such as "mind" and "change" to God. Of course, all of our imagining of the Divine is necessarily done in the limited terms we understand as humans. What we understand and can speak of is precisely human existence, spoken of in human language. Indeed, in Jesus Christ God has deigned to speak God's truth and nature to us in the very terms we can understand—as a human being who speaks divine truth in human language. The classic Christian affirmation is that Jesus' life and words, his death and resurrection, speak the truth about God perfectly accurately; yet Jesus does not completely or exhaustively speak the entire truth about God, a truth so vast that no human mind could conceive it, so blinding that no mortal eye could bear it.

So a better way to frame the question might be to ask, "How do we imagine God, all the while knowing that God is by definition beyond human imagination?" Some picture God as a passionless, distant, disconnected "entity," perhaps a block of smooth granite in the cold dark of distant space. Others imagine God to be the inevitable, heartless unfolding of natural process, an immovable force, not much different from what some might name "nature." Praying to such a God would be like talking to the wall, of course.

This is not the God of the Bible. God's relationship with Israel is woven into the push and pull of human history. God commands; Israel disobeys; God relents and forgives. Likewise, in the gospel the very presence of Jesus in the world and the nature of Jesus' relationship with the world would have us image God incarnate in the movement and flexing of time, enfleshed in the unfolding, altering nature of human existence as it is: tumultuous, messy, up and down. In this image of the divine nature, God is consummately passionate; that is, God cares and suffers, loves and forgives. Anthropomorphic and naive as the statement is, God would seem to change God's mind. Of course, what does such a statement mean when speaking of a God who exists both inside and outside of time and space? Praying to a God imagined this way is not at all like talking to wall. Rather,

Pastoral Perspective

woman raises and answers questions about Jesus that shape the pastoral care and mission of the church.

Jesus' encounter with the Canaanite woman wakes us up from our biblical slumbers. He tells this woman in desperate need that her need is beyond his concern. She is not one of the family. She kneels at his feet; she pleads with him; she does not take no for an answer. Perhaps her boldness wakes Jesus up to see his mission in the largest possible terms. He is sent not only to the lost sheep of Israel, but to all people—even the ancient enemies of Israel. At the Lord's Table, there is enough food for all. When Jesus feeds the multitudes in the wilderness, there is an abundance left over. Grace abounds for all. In Isaiah, God says it is not enough for the Lord's Servant to restore the lost tribes of Israel. God will give the Servant to be "a light to the nations, that my salvation may reach to the end of the earth" (Isa. 49:6). Through a painful encounter with a Canaanite woman, Jesus grows in his self-understanding and accepts a new vision of his mission.

This encounter with Jesus reminds us that there is no one outside the circle of God's love and compassion. As Jesus walks the roads from Galilee to Jerusalem, people of all descriptions draw near him and follow him. Righteous people criticize him for eating with sinners, lepers, and tax collectors. As his new fellowship spreads into the Roman world, Jews and Gentiles do the unheard-of thing of sitting down together and acting like brothers and sisters. The height, breadth, and depth of God's compassion still trouble some people within the church today. Those who operate out of a mentality of scarcity, fear, or suspicion say that there must be limits. They act as if God's grace is not for everyone. They think that there is not enough to go around.

In our deeply polarized society, people of different political views, economic conditions, ethnic backgrounds. or religious convictions are demonized and dismissed. In such a society, it is easy to decide whom to exclude from the circle of God's love. Yet no one can limit the grace of God. One thing the church has to offer the society is a visible demonstration of how people of different viewpoints, political parties, and backgrounds not only tolerate one another but love and appreciate each other. The doors of the church are wide open to the world. It should always be that way. How else would we have ever come in?

This story helps the Christian community see some of the unwelcome interruptions in busy lives as divine disruptions: God speaks through encounters

Among the things that might be thought to defile a Jewish person in this era could be a close encounter with a foreigner—particularly a foreign woman in a public meeting (see John 4:27 and the disciples' astonishment that Jesus was speaking with a woman who was, in this case, a Samaritan). Jesus has just taught his disciples that only what proceeds from the heart can defile. He does not directly deal with the question of contact with foreigners—much less with extending the ministry of the kingdom of heaven to them. What will Jesus do?

The woman takes the initiative. She "comes out," presumably into the countryside where Jesus is with his disciples, and "starts shouting" (v. 22, the imperfect *ekrazen*: "was crying out," and note also the imperfect *prosekynei*, "was kneeling," in v. 25). In Matthew's version the woman is heard in her own voice, using words also found in Matthean healings of two blind men (9:27; 20:30–31). "Lord" (*kyrios*) can be heard as a title of respect, but it always has greater connotation than that in Matthew's Gospel. "Son of David" is also an important designation for Matthew (beginning at 1:1). The foreign woman shows her fealty and desperate need to honor and yet be heard by Jesus. "My daughter," she pleads, "is tormented by a demon" (v. 22), where Mark notes she "had an unclean spirit" (Mark 7:25). It is typical in the retelling of healing and exorcism narratives that the condition should become more dire, so that the healing miracle will seem grander.

Matthew has Jesus remain silent, heightening the tension and perhaps the sense of question, in his mind and that of hearers, as to what he should do. To the disciples' effort to intervene he responds, "I was sent only to the lost sheep of the house of Israel" (v. 24), similar to what he instructs his missionary disciples in Matthew 10:6: "Go rather to the lost sheep of the house of Israel." It has been suggested that the evangelist is here dealing with the paucity of contacts between Jesus and Gentiles in the tradition and sharing his understanding that Jesus' mission was almost entirely confined to the "house of Israel"—opening up only later to Gentiles. Here then is a breakthrough, proleptic story that acknowledges that the church's ministry does indeed move beyond Israel (cf. 28:19). As in the healing of the centurion's servant, Jesus does not come into direct contact with the one who is healed, perhaps hinting at the distance in time from his earthly ministry until this outreach to non-Jews will take place.

"Send her away," the disciples urge, "for she keeps shouting after us" (v. 23). This perhaps points to a

to work with persons in the Third World (really the Two-Thirds World) but fail to address internal congregational issues. If Jesus could exhibit cultural prejudices, they are also possible within the lives of twenty-first-century believers.

The unnamed Canaanite woman (in Mark she is a Syrophoenician) has deep maternal ties to her child. We are not told how she knew to confront Jesus, but she evidently was well aware of the cultural differences between them. We do not need to know how or what the illness was, just that the mother was desperate for her child's life to be saved. Even speaking to Jesus in public was a violation of the law. Yet she loved her child and needed her child to be healed by any means necessary. Although she has no name, she has a strong voice. The text may be used to describe maternal love, stepping over cultural boundaries, and how a person in the face of insults continues to work for some semblance of equity in society. The mother-child relationship runs deep. One could use the illustration of the number of professional athletes who look into the camera every Sunday and say, "Hi, Mom," or the number of "othermothers" who have not given physical birth to children but daily birth children in classrooms, juvenile shelters, church kitchens, community centers, child-care centers, and corporate boardrooms.

We live in an age where some mothers kill their children, abandon their children, or even prioritize transient satiation from artificial stimulants or loveless relationships over their children. Even in this medically advanced age, there remain millions of women who are unable to give birth to children. This story is a model of how sometimes our intercessors—those who stand in the gap for those who cannot obtain access to assistance—are vitally important to the community. This woman pleads on her daughter's behalf, and we are called similarly to plead on behalf of those whose voices have been silenced.

Jesus is God's Son, and yet he is raised in a culture that had strict rules about contact with other cultures. Jesus has just finished criticizing the Pharisees, scribes, and disciples, but amazingly he demonstrates his own traditional faith roots in this passage. This is a difficult point. The text, however, is clear: Jesus initially denies the woman's request based on religious and cultural differences. His abrupt response to the woman is startling yet expected. He has been raised in a culture of separation by race, gender, class, and ethnicity, just as we have been. He does not refer to this woman as a human being but as a household pet, a dog. How does preachers' language express

Matthew 15:21–28

Theological Perspective

it is like speaking with a parent who loves you more than life itself.

Martin Luther understood this when he said to Philip Melanchthon, "Our Lord God could not but hear me; for I threw my sack before His door, and wearied His ears with all His promises of hearing prayers, which I could repeat out of Holy Writ; so that He could not but hear me, if I were ever to trust in His promises."[1] In the same vein, Rudolf Bultmann wrote, "Prayer is not to bring the petitioner's will into submission to the unchanging will of God, but prayer is to move God to do something which he otherwise would not do."[2] Walter Wink put the same affirmation this way: "When we pray, we are not sending a letter to a celestial White House where it is sorted among piles of others. We are rather engaged in an act of co-creation, in which one little sector of the universe rises up and becomes translucent, incandescent, a vibratory center of power that radiates the power of the universe."[3]

A pastor friend once told me a story about prayer that starkly illuminates the point. An employee of the urban congregation he then served was mugged while walking his dog, stabbed in the heart, and left to die. By the time the man was brought to the hospital, the emergency room staff said that there was only a 2 percent chance that he would survive. Members of the church staff gathered around the dying man's gurney to pray. My friend offered a prayer for peace and acceptance that essentially invited the man's friends to come to peace with God's inscrutable purposes. At this point one of the church's custodians began to pray a different kind of prayer. Clarence got in God's face: "You gotta do something, God! You've done it for me, now you do it again, right here and now, please." The man lived, in fact completely recovered from his wounds.

MICHAEL L. LINDVALL

Pastoral Perspective

with strangers and in situations outside of people's comfort zones. Quite often followers of Jesus have to decide if they are going to let go of their carefully made plans and well-organized schedules in order to respond to the unwelcome demands that arrive without warning. Such moments may become the occasion when God whispers the word a person most needs to hear. It is important for a growing spiritual life to welcome relationships with people outside of the normal circle of family and friends. Disciples of Jesus learn and grow when they brush up against people whose lives, needs, dreams, and struggles are different from their own. The effect of such a relationship is like the effect of sandpaper on a piece of rough wood. It smoothes out the undisciplined edges of life and makes his followers serviceable for some new purpose.

This encounter with Jesus leads the church to reflect on how it carries out Christ's mission. A congregation may have a well-developed mission statement, clearly established goals, and a clear sense of how it will carry out these ministries. As the people go about serving in a particular way or working on a well-established program, God may disrupt their carefully laid plans. Conversations at a soup kitchen may lead a community of faith to become involved in job counseling, mental-health issues, or affordable housing for the homeless. When tutors volunteering in an afterschool program get to know the children and their families, they may come to realize the need for a free preschool for younger children or become advocates for changes in immigration policies.

It is not at all unusual for those who begin doing acts of charity to discover the need for their becoming advocates for justice. Such transformation may happen because someone with different life experiences challenges the assumptions, upsets the agendas, and disrupts the lives of those who come to serve. Compassion grows by sharing life with those who once were strangers; spiritual vision increases by participating in the ever-expanding family of God.

LEWIS F. GALLOWAY

1. William Richard James, *Philip Melanchthon: The Protestant Preceptor of Germany 1497–1560* (New York and London: G. P. Putnam's Sons, 1907), 273.
2. Rudolf Bultmann, *Jesus and the Word*, trans. Louise Pettibone Smith and Erminie Huntress (1926; repr., New York: Charles Scribner's Sons, 1934), 185.
3. Walter Wink, *The Powers That Be: Theology for a New Millennium* (New York: Doubleday, 1999), 186–87.

Exegetical Perspective

later time when disciples too are unsure how far the healing ministry of Jesus should be extended. The woman, however, is persistent—apparently annoyingly so, as far as the disciples are concerned. She kneels before Jesus and repeats her plea in simple words. One is reminded of Jesus' counsel: "Ask, and it will be given to you; search, and you will find; knock, and the door will be opened for you" (7:7). Yet he also says in the same context, "Do not give what is holy to dogs" (7:6). Now he seems to use the word "dogs" crudely when addressing the Canaanite woman: "It is not fair [*kalos*, "good"] to take the food of the children [presumably "of the house of Israel"] and feed it to the dogs" (v. 26). This is the same Jesus who has recently fed five thousand and soon will feed "four thousand men, besides women and children" (15:38).

Attempts have been made to rescue Jesus from the force and tenor of his words. The Greek might be translated "little doggies." He was kidding the woman, at least a bit. He was testing her faith. In any event, she comes right back at him—certainly with spunk, perhaps in an example of what has been termed "peasant good humor."[1]

According to Matthew, it is her "faith" (*pistis*) that makes the difference, while Mark says it is the woman's "word" that changes Jesus' mind (Mark 7:29). Perhaps this suggests that it is the faith of future Gentiles that will make the difference in bringing the healing gospel to them. The faith of the Gentile centurion is also noted (8:10, 13), as it is in several other of Matthew's healing narratives (9:2, 22, 29). Matthew then adds that the healing of the woman's daughter took place "instantly"—apparently to emphasize the miraculous nature of the healing and obviate any suggestion (that hearers might find in Mark's version) that the exorcism/healing took place over time while the woman was away from home.

FREDERICK BORSCH

Homiletical Perspective

cultural difference? How do we preachers refer to persons of different races, ethnicities, abilities, and sexualities in the preached word, due to our social location and our cultural and religious beliefs?

The text is also instructive for the thousands who annually prepare for mission trips. People enter another culture with preconceived notions of saving other people without listening to them or asking what they first need in order to live. Homiletically the proclaimer should examine the differing cultures in the time of Jesus and the differing cultures within the community of the church. It is possible to compose an outreach sermon about being present with persons who have varying beliefs, family structures, occupations, lifestyles, ages, experiences, or even clothing. It might call for the congregation to show grace in difference rather than immediately criticize it.

The serious illness of the child leads to the woman's persistence and insistence with Jesus. She can withstand his insult, if only Jesus will save her child. The text lends itself to a discussion of healing. Jesus employs a variety of methods in the biblical text. Whether touching or being touched, speaking directly and personally with people or across distance, Jesus states that faith is a prerequisite to healing. What happens when one is not healed? Did the person or the family not have enough faith? What is the difference between cure and healing? These questions will arise in the minds of the listener. The preacher should know prior to the sermon what he or she believes about healing.

Finally, these verses would be interesting if preached as a first-person character study, taking the role of either the woman or Jesus. How would you approach Jesus? How would you verbally deflect the insults, all the time knowing that your behavior might determine your child's life or death? What struggles are happening within the mind of Jesus as he navigates his humanity and his divinity? What kind of loving Jesus would deny healing to anyone? Culture notwithstanding, I am glad he did not.

TERESA FRY BROWN

---

1. J. L. McKenzie, "Matthew," in *The Jerome Bible Commentary*, ed. R. E. Brown, J. A. Fitzmeyer, and R. E. Murphy (Englewood Cliffs, NJ: Prentice-Hall, 1968), 90.

²⁹After Jesus had left that place, he passed along the Sea of Galilee, and he went up the mountain, where he sat down. ³⁰Great crowds came to him, bringing with them the lame, the maimed, the blind, the mute, and many others. They put them at his feet, and he cured them, ³¹so that the crowd was amazed when they saw the mute speaking, the maimed whole, the lame walking, and the blind seeing. And they praised the God of Israel.

³²Then Jesus called his disciples to him and said, "I have compassion for the crowd, because they have been with me now for three days and have nothing to eat; and I do not want to send them away hungry, for they might faint on the way." ³³The disciples said to him, "Where are we to get enough bread in the desert to feed so great a crowd?" ³⁴Jesus asked them, "How many loaves have you?" They said, "Seven, and a few small fish." ³⁵Then ordering the crowd to sit down on the ground, ³⁶he took the seven loaves and the fish; and after giving thanks he broke them and gave them to the disciples, and the disciples gave them to the crowds. ³⁷And all of them ate and were filled; and they took up the broken pieces left over, seven baskets full. ³⁸Those who had eaten were four thousand men, besides women and children. ³⁹After sending away the crowds, he got into the boat and went to the region of Magadan.

Theological Perspective

This reading begins with miracles, as Jesus heals the mute, maimed, lame, and blind. Then Matthew continues with a different kind of miracle, feeding a multitude. The feeding narratives are so important they appear six times in the four Gospels. Their significance cannot be fully grasped by those of us who do not experience a lack of security about tomorrow's—or today's—meals. For me, they came to life only in a setting far removed from my everyday existence.

In 1997 I went with members of a Baptist Alliance congregation in Louisiana to visit their sister congregation in Cuba. That congregation sponsors house churches in surrounding villages. One day we traveled out to a house atop a riverbank. Dozens of Christians from all the connected congregations would be baptized in the moving waters by Noé, the senior pastor. After a meal, there would be singing, gift exchanging, and a sermon.

There was great excitement as people gathered. Limited transportation in Cuba means that seeing friends from neighboring communities is an event. Everyone greeted everyone else with a gentle peck on the cheek, the kiss of peace. Then they chattered away, as catching up continued, and continued, and continued.

Finally, Noé announced, "If you don't sit down, you don't eat." Amid laughter, the people sat down

Pastoral Perspective

In 2007, at age fifty-two, Jacob visited his doctor complaining of a dull headache that would not go away. During his preliminary examination, the nurse indicated that his blood pressure was high. Subsequently, Jacob's doctor prescribed a medication and invited him to return in three weeks. During his follow-up visit, Jacob's blood pressure improved. Since he was in relatively good health, the doctor encouraged him to change his lifestyle so that he could wean himself off the blood-pressure medicine. "You should walk briskly for twenty to thirty minutes five times per week," the doctor said, "and once you get into a good routine, add twenty minutes of resistance training twice per week. Reduce your intake of animal fat, drink more water, and incorporate high fiber carbohydrates, like oats, into your daily diet."

After thinking a few minutes, Jacob asked, "Doc, if I do the things you recommend, is it for certain that my blood pressure will return to normal?" The doctor replied, "Well, nothing is for certain, but the likelihood is strong that over time, your blood pressure could normalize without the need for medication."

"Doctor, are you encouraging me to stop eating butter, bacon, fried chicken, and potato chips?" "Yes," the doctor said. "Doc, if I do not make the changes, will my blood pressure stay in the normal range as

Exegetical Perspective

This text combines two miracle stories: one a healing miracle, the other a feeding miracle. The healing miracle (vv. 29–31) is a summative parallel to what is found in Mark 7:31–37. Not only is the Matthean version shorter than its Markan counterpart; it leaves out altogether the exoticness of the Markan rendition. As Daniel Harrington points out, Matthew changes an exotic and dramatic healing story into a generalized healing session.[1] In short, the deaf man of Mark's story falls out of Matthew's altogether.

Matthew is also quiet on two important points. The first is geographical, the second literary. He is unclear in verse 29 as to Jesus' exact location ("along the Sea of Galilee"), whereas in the Markan parallel Jesus is still in non-Jewish territory (i.e., Tyre, Sidon, Decapolis). When Matthew says, "After Jesus had left that place and passed along the Sea of Galilee," it echoes what he says about Jesus in 12:9 ("He left that place and entered their synagogue"), which serves to underscore the itinerant nature of Jesus' ministry. His activity of sitting on the mountain echoes 13:1, but most assuredly it is meant to remind the reader of the Sermon on the Mount (5:1).

Matthew is also unclear about whether Jesus has any physical contact with those he heals, again

1. Daniel Harrington, *The Gospel of Matthew* (Collegeville, MN: Liturgical Press, 1991), 239.

Homiletical Perspective

This healer named Jesus is busy. The crowds of the sick and injured and their friends and loved ones are arrayed before him stretching down the mountain and out toward the sea. He cures those brought before him; the people praise God.

Disability activists today reject the presumptions by many people that being unable to speak or see or walk without assistance are conditions to be fixed, that such challenges are signs of sin or lack of faith, or that cure is the desired end and should alone provoke praise. Here Jesus refuses to imply that illness and disability are punishments for sin or evidence of lack of faith, although he does offer healing when asked for it. People in need sit at his feet and he responds. His are simple, albeit miraculous, responses to simple requests. To provoke praise in our day, perhaps, is to leave old presumptions behind, to listen intently and compassionately to those in need before us, and make similarly direct responses.

At the same time, many of our churches have neglected healing ministries for too long. If Jesus told us to go and preach, to baptize, to break bread and drink a saving cup in his memory, surely he also told us to go and heal (see Matt. 10:1). Such was the source of the people's amazement, of the praise of the God of Israel. Honoring those who want equal

Theological Perspective

Pastoral Perspective

on the ground, arranging themselves more or less in rows, and the steep yard was transformed into a natural amphitheater. Soon people began passing through the crowd with cardboard boxes. A man reached his bare hand into one and gave me an unwrapped sandwich—a square roll with a slab of white cheese in the middle. I found myself thinking that the disciples must have passed through the crowd exactly so, as they distributed the loaves and fishes. My visit to Cuba was life transforming, and that meal ensured that these Gospel narratives would never seem the same to me.

The frequency of these stories increases when we add those about Eucharist: the fourfold action—taking, blessing, breaking, giving—that becomes the heart of the Communion ritual also characterizes the feeding stories. It would have been easily recognized by the early church, where the Gospels were read aloud.

My first pastorate was in a congregation where many elderly members needed to be served the Eucharist at home. Previous pastors who delivered the elements had not used the Great Thanksgiving. I did and discovered the rhythm of those words—"he took the bread, gave thanks for it, broke the bread, and gave it to them"—is still easily recognized, even by those whose hearing has declined. Just as the presence of Christ is key to Eucharist, the presence of Jesus is key to this multiplication of food—but it *is* multiplication, not creation. Loaves and fishes do not appear ex nihilo, out of nothing. People offer up what they have, and seven loaves and a few fish turn out to be plenty for thousands of people. The miracle is that what people have proves sufficient for the day.

The text provides a perfect occasion to talk about hunger, abroad and at home. It should not be an excuse for using a theology of prosperity—if you just trust Jesus, you and yours will never be hungry—but rather an opportunity to work from a theology of sufficiency. We can choose a theology of abundance over against the theology of scarcity, which tends to dominate discussion today and which Thomas Frank calls "rhetoric of crisis" rather than "rhetoric of power."[1]

Leadership expert Janice Virtue says, "You can hear the absolute pragmatism in the disciples' question—where is the food, the money, the resources going to come from? . . . The fear of scarcity, of not having enough, is so ingrained in us that our memory of abundance is slow and vague." She writes,

long as I take the pill every day?" "Based on your response to the medication these last three weeks, I would say so," the doctor replied. "Doc, I think I'll just take the pill."

It would be nice if our problems—health and otherwise—could be remedied with a pill. Or the waving of a wand. Or a broad stroke of the brush. It would be nice if all it took to live a strong Christian life was to show up and let Jesus do the rest.

In this passage from Matthew, Jesus heals a large number of infirm persons over the course of three days. At the end of that time, before sending the people away, Jesus decides to feed them. He gathers bread and fish from the disciples—hardly enough to feed a single family, much less thousands of people—gives thanks, and miraculously feeds everyone present.

At first glance, it appears that Jesus is doing all the work. He receives the people, listens to their stories, fixes their bodies, cures their infirmities, tutors his disciples, and orchestrates a massive picnic. For their part in the story, the people are more like decoration; they are present, but have no voice. The reader of the passage does not hear from them and does not see them do anything to contribute to their own betterment. All they do is show up. Jesus does the rest.

Eduard Lohse describes the character of Jewish life in the days of Jesus:

> The economic circumstances in which the Jews in the homeland lived were generally quite modest. The Jewish population of the country earned their living by farming, handicraft, and small businesses. The peasant population could secure only a modest livelihood through hard labor. Things were not significantly better for the artisans who worked as weavers, fullers, tailors, smiths, scribes, or potters. Many occupations were despised, such as that of the tanner, because he constantly had to make himself unclean, or that of the tax collector, because he was in the service of Gentile masters and dealt fraudulently. There was unemployment, so that anyone who lost his position was necessarily fearful of his future. Poverty and mendicancy were widespread. The roads which traversed the countryside were sometimes made dangerous by robbers who attacked and plundered travelers.[1]

Lohse's depiction provides a snapshot of the very people we read about in Matthew 15: those who "came to [Jesus], bringing with them the lame, the

1. Thomas Edward Frank, *Polity, Practice, and the Mission of the United Methodist Church* (Nashville: Abingdon Press, 2006), 21–24.

1. Eduard Lohse, *The New Testament Environment* (Nashville: Abingdon Press, 1992), 147–48.

unlike Mark. Matthew just says, "And he healed them" (v. 30). Mark never uses the word "heal," although that is clearly what Jesus is doing. Matthew prefers to use the terse aorist indicative active as a replacement for Mark's considerable amount of activity. In many ways, what Jesus is "doing" in Matthew echoes the actions taken by Jesus in chapters 8–9—addressing the enormity of human need.

Matthew ends this healing story with an emphasis quite different from that of his source. In verse 31 the focus is on the "God of Israel," whereas Mark 7:37 focuses on Jesus himself. Scholars will readily admit that the invocation of the God of Israel is odd or awkward. It seems to recall 9:8 ("When the crowds saw it, they were filled with awe, and they glorified God, who had given such authority to human beings"), but this verse is different in that it puts sole focus on God. The possible answer to this oddity of phraseology is that the idea of the God of Israel is a Hebraism meant to point to the place of God in salvation history.

The feeding miracle (vv. 32–39) is the parallel to what is found in Mark 8:1–10. Matthew makes a closer chronological connection between this miracle and the prior one than does Mark. Notice, however, that the time frame—three days—can be found in both. The number three was generally considered to be a divine number. (Four, by contrast, was considered a human number. The sum of the two indicates the joining together of the divine and the human.) Three days, according to some biblical scholars, was a metaphor for the point at which God intervenes. Think, for example, about Jonah's salvation from the great fish and Jesus' resurrection. So it may be that we should think about three days not as a literal passage of time but as a metaphor for the point at which God acts. This may be borne out in verse 32, where Jesus draws attention to the problem, unlike the earlier feeding story where the disciples do so ("Then Jesus called his disciples to him and said, 'I have compassion for the crowd, because they have been with me now for three days and have nothing to eat'").

Matthew also uses the word "crowd" (ochlos) from verse 31 in verse 33 to tie the two miracle stories together in a manner stronger than his source. The loaves and the fish are separated in Mark but put together in Matthew. We are not told the exact number of fish. The Greek diminutive, "little fish" (ichthydion, v. 34), is meant to emphasize the discrepancy between the resources and the amount of food. Also notice that the mention of the fish is suppressed in

dignity, equal access, and an equal voice rather than any predetermined cure of their conditions, can we still find ways to communicate that there is a balm in Gilead, a Great Physician, an abiding Comforter?

The newly cured engage in praise. In fact, they are so caught up in the captivating presence of this healer that they stay for three days, neglecting even their own basic need for food. The healer notes this lack, has compassion, and intervenes. "I do not want to send them away hungry" (v. 32), he says to his inner circle. Is not their response like ours when we face an overwhelming need with scant resources: "Where are we to get enough bread in the desert?" (v. 33). Have they not been paying attention? Would the one who can make a broken body whole with a word, with a touch, be unable to provide simple repast, now that the people's hunger is clearly on his mind? The people's hunger will be addressed.

Besides, there is bread in the desert already. There is only a little for this great crowd, but there is some. "Seven loaves," answer the disciples (v. 34). There are seven loaves indeed. Seven signifies completion, a whole. Seven will be enough. Beyond this, there are a few fish. How can so little provide for so many? Do we not also ask this question every year during budget negotiations, every week when yet another hungry family knocks on the door asking for help, every day when we know that thousands starve while the few grow ill and die of disorders related to habits of gluttony and indulgence?

Jesus takes the loaves and the fish. He gives thanks. He breaks the loaves and divides the fish. He gives bread and fish to the disciples. The disciples share these gifts with the whole crowd. There is enough.

So we find ourselves, suddenly, surprisingly, in a story of Eucharist, Communion, Lord's Supper. Here are the actions on a mountainside: take, give thanks, break, and give. The crowd is so busy praising God for acts of healing that they forget to eat. This is no merely symbolic meal—as if symbols such as bread that multiplies to satisfy a hungry crowd can ever be "mere." Real-world hunger is faced and banished; everyone at this chaotic picnic has food aplenty, so much so that seven baskets (not just seven loaves) remain after all are satisfied. Faced with such abundance, such clear evidence of the divine desire that all who are hungry must be fed, how can our celebrations at Table remain so bland, so removed from actual hunger?

More than thirty years ago, Tissa Balasuriya, a Roman Catholic liberation theologian of Sri Lanka, wrote this:

Matthew 15:29–39

Theological Perspective

"The world approves when the cemetery fund is wisely invested while children in our neighborhood go to school hungry. . . . The gospel, on the other hand, invites us to share our pie, to sit in the company of others and care about their needs, to trust that blessing is more powerful than any market."[2]

In this text, Jesus does not want people fed simply to prevent hunger pangs; rather, he does not want them to faint on the road. They need nourishment for their journeys. Certainly we need spiritual nourishment, since the way of Jesus is not for the faint of heart, but spiritualizing the story to the extent that we neglect its connections to the physically hungry would be a mistake. One good way to begin talking about hunger is to discuss the Heifer Project, which gives milk- or egg-yielding animals to families living in poverty; the families then give the offspring to neighbors. An ecumenical nonprofit group, Bread for the World, teaches how to advocate for the hungry. Oxfam International serves a similar purpose.

Considering what "life abundant" meant to Jesus also requires changing our own expectations about abundance. In Cuba, a host said her shower had sufficient water, but as I told my parishioners later, "In Cuba, 'sufficient' means something else." A roll with cheese for an entire meal at church would not, in our U.S. potluck context, seem like "enough." Nor, I suppose, would some bread and dried fish.

This text opens a space for us to ask, "If the church does not lead society into a rejection of consumerism and a willingness to share, to restructure our lives together with different values, then who will?" The disciples in the story began with what was left among a crowd after three days together. Can the church today offer up what we have left after two thousand years and still find that it is enough to meet the needs of the multitude? We know the earth's resources could be sufficient for humanity. Like the disciples, we are surrounded by the hungry. We do not start with nothing, and we claim the presence of Christ.

ELLEN BLUE

Pastoral Perspective

maimed, the blind, the mute, and many others" (v. 30). These were poor people. They had no clout. Some were unemployed. Some were hungry. Some had been victimized. These disenfranchised persons are the ones who found a way to bring with them the lame, the maimed, the blind, the mute, and many others. This bears repeating. The disenfranchised are not the ones who necessarily sought Jesus' healing for themselves. The disenfranchised in the passage are the ones who brought others to be healed.

When viewed in this light, Matthew 15:29–39 is consistent with Matthew's overarching portrayal of the compassionate Christ. The text recalls the Beatitudes ten chapters earlier:

> "Blessed are the poor in spirit, for theirs is the
>   kingdom of heaven.
> "Blessed are those who mourn, for they will be
>   comforted. . . .
> "Blessed are those who hunger and thirst for
>   righteousness, for they will be filled.
> "Blessed are the merciful, for they will receive mercy.
> "Blessed are the pure in heart, for they will see God."
>   (5:3–4, 6–8)

Do not all of these blessings seem to occur in this account of the curing and feeding of the four thousand?

Further, while it may appear initially that the crowd does not do anything more than show up so that Jesus can heal them, a more in-depth reading reveals that these people made a great personal investment in traveling along the Sea of Galilee up the mountain to be with Jesus. They uprooted their families. They expended personal, emotional, logistical resources to transport those who were immobile. They traveled by foot or beast over rough terrain in an arid climate. Those who traveled longer distances even risked their safety. Certainly these efforts constitute much more than just showing up. They indicate a personal investment.

Perhaps it would be nice if following Jesus were as simple as swallowing a pill. Some persons in today's culture may actually believe it is! However, the biblical record indicates that the Lord loves it when we make a deep, abiding, personal investment in our faith and in others, without concern for personal gain. When we do, the Lord meets us there with abundant displays of mercy, healing, and fulfillment.

PAUL T. ROBERTS SR.

2. Janice Virtue, "Sharing God's Abundance," address to General Commission on Finance and Administration of the United Methodist Church, accessed October 14, 2011, at www.faithandleadership.com/content/sharing-god%E2%80%99s-abundance.

Exegetical Perspective

favor of the bread. This may be meant to point to the Eucharist or Lord's Supper.

We are told in both stories, however, that they have seven loaves of bread. Again, the number may carry more than just quantitative significance. It may be intended to highlight the joining of divine activity to human resources. Notwithstanding, we should avoid the temptation to think that in the face of hunger Jesus regularly miraculously produced food. The feeding on the mountain echoes what we find in Jeremiah 31:10–14 and Ezekiel 34:14, 26–27. For example, in Ezekiel we hear of good pastures that God will provide to feed God's people. In fact, it is Ezekiel 34:26 that evokes the hymn "There Shall Be Showers of Blessing."[2]

Matthew envisions a larger crowd than that found in Mark, where there are "about four thousand people" (Mark 8:9): "Those who had eaten were four thousand men, besides women and children" (v. 38). In addition, we are not able to discern why each evangelist has Jesus depart to a different destination. The location of Mark's "district of Dalmanutha" (Mark 8:10) and Matthew's "region of Magadan" (v. 39) are not known. So it is impossible for us to determine why Matthew would make such an obvious editorial change.

In Matthew 15:29–39 the author develops themes he sounded in 15:1–28 (i.e., the importance of healing and proper nourishment) and prepares the reader for what is found in 16:1–12. The entire section underscores Jesus' vocation as one who has compassion for those in physical and spiritual need. It also shows Jesus exercising his vocation according to the dictates of each situation. Some biblical scholars would also point out that this section points to the concrete presence of Jesus in the life of the church in healing, in table fellowship, and in the sharing of the Lord's Supper.

MICHAEL JOSEPH BROWN

Homiletical Perspective

An agonizing question presents itself to our minds. Why is it that in spite of hundreds of thousands of daily and weekly Masses, the Christians continue as selfish as before? Why have the "Christian" Mass-going peoples been the most cruel colonizers of human history? Why is the gap of income, wealth, knowledge and power growing in the world today—and that in favor of the "Christian" peoples? Why is it that persons and people who proclaim Eucharistic love and sharing deprive the poor people of the world of food, capital, employment and even land? Why do they prefer cigarettes and liquor to food and drink for the one third of humanity that goes hungry to bed each night? Why are cars, cosmetics, pet dogs, horses and bombs preferred to human children? Why mass human sterilization in poor countries and affluence unto disease and pollution of nature among the rich?[1]

Balasuriya's question still haunts. How is it that we can ingest Jesus and yet remain so self-concerned? If we are what we eat and we have been partaking of the Bread of Life every week—or, for many of us, every month—of our lives, why do we still find it so hard to see the hungry crowd, to have compassion and take whatever we have, give thanks for it, break it, and share it until all the world is fed?

We probably would do well to think of how our sharing at table, both the Lord's Table and the tables at which we eat every day, can better reflect the model that Jesus the healer embodies: here is a little one who has been brought to lie at my feet, let me invite him to get up and walk; here is a hungry crowd, let us gather what we have, give thanks to God for it, no matter how meager, and share it with any who are in need. Then we, like him, may get in our boat and simply, so simply, go on.

W. SCOTT HALDEMAN

---

2. Words by Daniel Whittle, 1883.

1. Tissa Balasuriya, *The Eucharist and Human Liberation* (Maryknoll, NY: Orbis Books, 1979), 3.

Matthew 16:1–12

¹The Pharisees and Sadducees came, and to test Jesus they asked him to show them a sign from heaven. ²He answered them, "When it is evening, you say, 'It will be fair weather, for the sky is red.' ³And in the morning, 'It will be stormy today, for the sky is red and threatening.' You know how to interpret the appearance of the sky, but you cannot interpret the signs of the times. ⁴An evil and adulterous generation asks for a sign, but no sign will be given to it except the sign of Jonah." Then he left them and went away.

⁵When the disciples reached the other side, they had forgotten to bring any bread. ⁶Jesus said to them, "Watch out, and beware of the yeast of the Pharisees and Sadducees." ⁷They said to one another, "It is because we have brought no bread." ⁸And becoming aware of it, Jesus said, "You of little faith, why are you talking about having no bread? ⁹Do you still not perceive? Do you not remember the five loaves for the five thousand, and how many baskets you gathered? ¹⁰Or the seven loaves for the four thousand, and how many baskets you gathered? ¹¹How could you fail to perceive that I was not speaking about bread? Beware of the yeast of the Pharisees and Sadducees!" ¹²Then they understood that he had not told them to beware of the yeast of bread, but of the teaching of the Pharisees and Sadducees.

Theological Perspective

The reading begins with a test for Jesus conducted by Pharisees and Sadducees, who ask for a sign from heaven. There is irony in the placement of their request immediately after the record of many healings and the feeding of a multitude. They would not have tried to engage him in this discussion if they had not heard reports about him, and since we have just encountered material on miracles, we suspect they could have discovered his identity if they had genuinely wished to know the truth.

At the same time, most of us should have a secret sympathy for Jesus' questioners. We sometimes find ourselves pleading for a sign from heaven, even while we suspect that an answer regarding what course we should take might be readily apparent if we were able to notice and understand what is right in front of our faces.

Jesus responds to these questioners scornfully, proclaiming that they will receive only the "sign of Jonah" (v. 4). Then he issues a warning to the disciples to beware of the yeast of the Pharisees and Sadducees. Again we sympathize with his hearers, since we would probably have felt the disciples' confusion on receiving this advice. Clueless as ever, the disciples decide Jesus said this because they forgot to bring bread, but Jesus demands to know how it is even possible that they could think he was speaking

Pastoral Perspective

On December 26, 1982, newspapers across the United States published a "Peanuts" comic strip in which America's favorite pooch, Snoopy, and his bird pal, Woodstock, are searching for evidence of Santa Claus and his reindeer. The Charles Schulz cartoon opens with Snoopy coaxing Woodstock from his nest saying, "C'mon, I'll show you." As they walk along snowy paths, Snoopy points to footprints. He says to Woodstock, "You can still see the sleigh tracks in the snow, and the hoof prints from the reindeer. See? Right along here!" Further down the path, Snoopy continues, "Now you can see where the tracks end. This is probably where Santa and the reindeer took off into the air. On Christmas Eve, they had to fly all over the world dropping presents down chimneys for all the kids."[1]

The most pertinent moment in the cartoon occurs when Snoopy exclaims to his friend, "See? Right along here!" The reader wonders, is Snoopy asking whether Woodstock visibly sees the tracks in the snow, or is he prodding Woodstock into a particular interpretation of the facts? After all, Snoopy never once entertains the possibility that the tracks may have come from a source other than Santa Claus.

1. Charles M. Schulz, "Peanuts," United Features Syndicate, December 26, 1982.

Exegetical Perspective

This passage is a triple-tradition pericope (i.e., it is found in all the Synoptic Gospels) and also has a companion passage in the Gospel of John. It is also repeated within the Gospel of Matthew. Each evangelist identifies a different audience for this interrogative. For Matthew it is first the "scribes and Pharisees" (12:38) and here the "Pharisees and Sadducees" (16:1). For Mark it is simply the "Pharisees" (Mark 8:11). Luke and John characterize the questioners as "others" (Luke 11:16) or "they" (John 6:30), unidentified crowds that call for a response from Jesus. In sum, even though this was undoubtedly a pertinent question many believed should have been answered by Jesus and/or his followers, the divergent audiences indicate that it was not a singular group that mounted such an attack.

In opposition to their source, Matthew and Luke prefer the idea of trial or testing (*peirasmos*) to that of argument or disagreement, which is found in Mark. The invocation of the verbal form of trial indicates a more theological interpretation of the event in Matthew. The idea of tempting/testing (*peirazein*), reminiscent of the temptation scene in Matthew 4:1, is still different from its predecessor. Instead of intending to have Jesus succeed in providing the requested sign, it does not appear to be as important to Matthew how Jesus will deal with the challenge of the request.

Homiletical Perspective

 "No sign will be given," says the Teacher (v. 4). No sign will be given to this generation, except the sign that it has already received, the sign of Jonah. What is this sign of Jonah? Is it the storm that arose when he ran in the opposite direction after receiving a divine directive to go to Nineveh and preach and save the city? Is it the fish in whose belly the prophet stewed for three days and nights until he repented and so was released from a watery grave? Is it the response of the Ninevites as they donned sackcloth and ashes and mended their ways? Is it the plant that grew up to give the prophet shade as he grumbled on the top of a sun-baked hill above the city he helped to save? Was it the worm that ate the plant? Was it the divine retort to his lament over the loss of the plant when he should have been rejoicing that so many had been saved?

The question is not only one of interpreting the sign correctly, but also of determining the sign itself. Flooded with data on a daily basis, do we not also face much that is inscrutable—knowing little, not only about how to interpret what confronts us, but even what aspects of our information overload harbor meaning?

Further, what was the test that this cryptic reference supposedly answers? Do the Pharisees and Sadducees consider their question a test because they think Jesus

Matthew 16:1–12

Theological Perspective

about food. It is the things that the Pharisees and Sadducees teach that he is warning them against, he explains.

One of Jesus' "kingdom sayings" refers to a baker-woman (13:33). She would know well that a small amount of yeast affects a much greater volume of foodstuff. The imagery of the woman's hands working the dough, her physical involvement in her task, is a powerful one. As she works, she distributes the yeast among other ingredients so that it can make the whole batch rise. Jesus' comparison of religious teaching to yeast is an apt one, since teaching, especially about theological things, resembles the leavening agent in many ways. The information we receive about the Creator affects our understandings of just about everything else.

Both the Pharisees and Sadducees were quite religious and urged others to attend carefully to proper performance, whether following religious law in every detail or ensuring that rituals were conducted according to certain specifications. The Hebrew prophets, on the other hand, were concerned with calling the people toward what they considered the true nature of their religion—the practices of living justly, welcoming the stranger, and caring for the widow, the orphan, and the poor people of the land.

The suggestion that rule following is a satisfactory substitute for the difficult doing of theology can be insidious, precisely because obedience to rules requires so much less mental and spiritual effort than does acting out justice. It is far easier to follow rules than to make ethical decisions based on Rabbi Hillel's "That which is hateful to you, do not do to your fellow," or on Jesus' "Do unto others what you would have them do unto you," and then to live according to those ethical decisions. It is easier to refrain from doing something forbidden than it is to follow actively the prophet Micah's imperative to do justice, love kindness, and walk humbly with God (Mic. 6:8). The lure of this yeast—of religious fastidiousness unaccompanied by care for the needy—is still abroad and can still distort, or at least change, the shape of our spiritual lives and communities.

Jesus' annoyance with his followers' inability to grasp his meaning is evident. "Do you *still* not perceive?" he demands (v. 9), and all must answer, "Honestly? No." Although his characterization of them as people "of little faith" seems to refer to their forgetting his ability to supply food, it is for us perhaps more useful as a reminder not to despair about the efficacy of our ministries. The yeast of our own teaching will multiply more than we know. For

Pastoral Perspective

It is not at all uncommon for human beings to behave similarly, subjectively. Instead of using the data around us to discover and embrace new truths, we use it to confirm those things we already think and believe. In Matthew 16:1–12, Jesus offers a corrective to this common human behavior.

In verses 1–4, the Pharisees and Sadducees ask Jesus to give them a sign from heaven. By this time in the story, Jesus' interactions with these devout men have become adversarial, so their request for a sign from him seems disingenuous. Based on their beliefs, the Messiah would arrive in a blaze of glory with accompanying political and military might. Jesus, however, has no lofty arrival, no blazes of glory, no political clout, no mighty army. He does not fit their preconceived messianic notions; and they are not interested in discovering other possibilities about the Messiah's identity. As Matthew writes, "They came, and to test Jesus they asked him for a sign from heaven" (v. 1), but it is unlikely the Pharisees and Sadducees are seeking any new truth or discovery. It is more likely they are seeking to confirm their existing belief systems by discrediting him.

In verses 5–12, Jesus' disciples are equally obtuse. Jesus warns them to beware of the yeast of the Pharisees and Sadducees, but they misunderstand and think he is admonishing them because they forgot to bring bread with them. They do not get it! The disciples have heard Jesus' Sermon on the Mount and other public and private teachings. They have seen him perform cleansings and healings of various kinds. They have watched as he cast out demons. They have seen him calm the storm and walk on water. Ostensibly, they have had every opportunity to embrace the new truth of Christ's reality. Yet even they are so rooted in their conventional paradigms that they do not see. Interestingly, the people in the passage who follow Jesus are just as subjective and nearly as intractable as those who do not.

Becoming aware of his disciples' confused conversation, Jesus asks pointedly, "Do you not remember the five loaves for the five thousand, and how many baskets you gathered? Or the seven loaves for the four thousand, and how many baskets you gathered? How could you fail to perceive that I was not speaking about bread?" (vv. 9–11). In questioning them, Christ prods his disciples' consciousness, moving them from their former belief systems into a new way of hearing, observing, and interpreting. Thus the passage concludes, "Then they understood that he had not told them to beware of the yeast of bread, but of the teaching of the Pharisees and Sadducees" (v. 12).

In other words, the "sign from heaven" is interpreted by Matthew as something more meaningful—more in need of direct address—than what is provided in the Markan parallel. This explains why Matthew and Luke provide two additional features missing from Mark: the questioners' lack of ability to interpret the "signs of the times" and the statement that the only sign that will be given is that of "the sign of Jonah" (v. 4; Luke 11:29). Such theological editing, pointing to an apocalyptic context, may demonstrate the complexity of the development of the church in the second and third generations. The figures of speech found in verses 1–4 reflect a Palestinian context, although some biblical scholars still debate if this is unquestionably true. The weather system described is called *sharan* in Hebrew and *hamseen* in Arabic. Thus it may be a conversation that goes back directly to Jesus.

The first demand for a sign occurs in Matthew 12:38–40. Jesus is probably alone when the Pharisees and Sadducees do this in verse 1. We do not hear about disciples again until verse 5. One must admit that this is curious. Are we to understand that Jesus and the disciples travel separately after the feeding of the four thousand and are only now being reunited? The inclusion of the Sadducees makes little intellectual sense. Going back to 3:7, it may be the evangelist's way of demonstrating their shared opposition to Jesus, like their shared opposition to John the Baptist.

To some biblical scholars, the very nature of the question for a sign is misguided, if not malicious. They argue that after the two powerful feeding stories (the feeding of the five thousand in 14:13–21 and the feeding of the four thousand in 15:32–39) any question of Jesus' power is unquestionably malicious. The idea that the sign must be "from heaven" denotes it as a cosmic one, although it is unclear exactly what would count as such a sign (v. 1). The answer—that they will receive only the "sign of Jonah"—appears to point to the process of death and resurrection (v. 4; i.e., Jonah is saved from the belly of the great fish after three days).

The source for verses 5–12, also an apparent triple tradition, is Mark 8:14–21. Luke re-works the passage into one verse (Luke 12:1). Looking at the passages, it is understandable that Matthew omits the distracting loaf of bread found in Mark. Why would the disciples exclaim they have no bread after it is said they have at least one loaf? In fact, there are six editorial changes that occur here: (1) the story does not take place in a boat; (2) the mention of the loaf

cannot give them a sign? Do they assume that he can provide a sign but that whatever sign he gives will reveal that he draws his power to heal and prophesy from some other source than the God of Israel? Do they want to engage in a contest of signs or in a contest of interpretation of signs? We do not know, but we do know their motives are less than pure.

Jesus calls them evil and adulterous (v. 4; cf. 12:39). That seems rather harsh. They are simply doing their job. Honorable teachers and leaders of their day, they have reason to be suspicious of this charismatic wanderer. He draws crowds that might elevate him while diminishing traditional institutions. He provides bread and healing outside of the normal channels. Without proper credentials, he claims authority to reinterpret both the signs of the times and central teachings—even the Law itself.

We struggle too to listen to truth from new corners, to allow new leaders to arise without feeling threatened, to hear criticism of our familiar ways and institutions without defensiveness rising. We too test our critics without pure motives, seeking to humiliate rather than to understand, to marginalize rather than welcome, to vilify rather than embrace. What voices do we resist and why? Where is the new and saving truth that we need to hear but would rather silence?

Jesus does not stick around to continue the fight. He simply speaks his mind and takes off. Perhaps he feels the conversation pointless. Perhaps he finds the opponents unworthy of the debate. Perhaps he thinks it wiser to escape to continue the fight another day. Perhaps he simply has other things to do. We do not know.

We might well consider how we decide when to engage and when to walk away. What conversations do we find worth the effort, and which do we cut off? Whom do we find worthy to debate, and who not? How well do we calculate the risks so as to remain effective in the struggle to speak truth, to communicate mercy, to increase justice?

What we know is that Jesus finds the disciples. Finally they have caught up to him again. What might have been a time for pleasantries, however—or at least constructive strategizing—turns sour. He seems to have trouble letting go of the recent argument. We hear his bitterness: "Beware the yeast of the Pharisees and Sadducees!" (v. 5). They do not have a clue what he is talking about. Why should they? They did not witness the encounter. Like so many of us, they think his anger is all about them. They forgot to bring bread. As is the case with so

Matthew 16:1–12

Theological Perspective

pastors, the warning that inadequate teaching also multiplies is especially important. Many laypeople receive most of their theological instruction within the context of worship, and by no means only during the sermon.

Spiritual teaching is always accomplished through music, prayers, and corporate recitations, both when the pastor has carefully thought through the messages these elements convey and when she or he has not. So-called "problematic" biblical texts that are read aloud but never addressed from the pulpit make their impressions on the hearers, as does the look of physical space used for rituals. Congregants may acquire a picture of a Deity to whom clergy but not laity can come close, who requires certain kinds of clothes for worship, or who does not like laughter or children who make noise. They may fail to recognize that these images bear startlingly little resemblance to the Jesus who insisted that little children be allowed to "bother" him (19:13–15) and who poked fun at people who deemed themselves holy simply because they wore the right things (23:5). These observations are in no way intended to indicate that careful preparation by worship leaders is unimportant. Exactly the contrary is true. Awareness that small things also matter and can have big impacts on worshipers is an appropriate message to take from this text.

Another characteristic of yeast is that it can expire and become useless. Jesus addresses the perishability of another substance when he says, "If salt has lost its taste, how can its saltiness be restored?" (5:13). He tells disciples that they are the salt of the earth, and we like to point out that just a little salt makes a big impact on taste. Yet even salt is not as transformative as yeast. If teaching is like yeast, we should strive not to teach religiosity, but rather to use the yeast of the bakerwoman who is cooking up the kingdom of God.

ELLEN BLUE

Pastoral Perspective

The late Anthony de Mello, a Jesuit priest and renowned spiritualist, said that metaphorically human beings are asleep—all of us. He said it does not matter whether we are Jew or Christian, wealthy or poor, Asian or Latin, white or black. In a compilation of lectures entitled *Awareness*, de Mello opens provocatively. He says, "Spirituality means waking up. Most people, even though they don't know it, are asleep. They're born asleep, they live asleep, they marry in their sleep, they breed children in their sleep, they die in their sleep without ever waking up. They never understand the loveliness and the beauty of this thing that we call human existence."[2] If de Mello is correct, then perhaps our salvation comes not only from Christ's death on a cross, but from Christ's work in awakening us here and now to the eternal truths of God.

Johnson Oatman Jr. expresses a similar thought in his hymn "Higher Ground":

I'm pressing on the upward way,
New heights I'm gaining everyday;
Still praying as I onward bound,
"Lord, plant my feet on higher on ground."
My heart has no desire to stay
Where doubts arise and fears dismay;
Though some may dwell where these abound,
My prayer, my aim is higher ground.

I want to scale the utmost height,
And catch a gleam of glory bright;
But still I'll pray till heaven I've found,
Lord, lead me on to higher ground.
Lord, lift me up, and let me stand,
By faith on Heaven's table land;
A higher plane than I have found,
Lord, plant my feet on higher ground.[3]

Jesus Christ is never content with our status quo, our preconceived notions, our half-truths, our prejudices, our worries and fears, our obstinance, our spiritual slumber. When we are in genuine relationship with him, he quickens us to God's eternal truths and prods our consciousness into a greater awareness.

In the passage, Christ did not throw his hands in the air and walk out on his disciples, despite their continual confusion. Christ's great love for us is apparent in that he stays with us, teaching all along the way, in anticipation of that moment when we finally get it.

PAUL T. ROBERTS SR.

2. Anthony de Mello, *Awareness: The Perils and Opportunities of Reality* (New York: Image, 1990), 5.
3. Johnson Oatman Jr., "Higher Ground" (1898).

is omitted; (3) Herod is replaced with the Sadducees; (4) Matthew makes no mention of hardened hearts, indicating lack of insight; (5) the disciples' answers are omitted; and (6) Jesus changes the meaning of the entire conversation. This makes verses 5–8 sound more consistent than Mark.

Notice that the interaction begins with something of a disconnect. Jesus blurts out what is on his mind. The Matthean evangelist speaks of "the yeast of the Pharisees and Sadducees" (16:6). Mark speaks of "the yeast of the Pharisees and the yeast of Herod" (Mark 8:15), which strikes the reader as odd, since there has been no mention of Herod or the Herodians prior to Jesus' declaration. In addition, the disciples in Mark come across as dim-witted. Matthew instead calls them "you of little faith," a well-known Mattheanism (v. 8; cf. 6:30; 8:26; 14:31; 17:20).

That the evangelist shaped this scene theologically can also be seen in its Lukan counterpart. Luke calls "the yeast of the Pharisees" hypocrisy. This would not work in Matthew's context, since hypocrisy and hypocrites play a distinctive role in his theology. Thus the physical problem of the absence of bread is classified as a misunderstanding and a result of a lack of faith. Mark draws a connection between the absence of bread and the presence of faith. Verses 11–12 make it clear that bread is a metaphor for teaching. In addition, notice that the metaphor of yeast (or leaven) is itself intriguing, since it connotes something that pushes what it inhabits beyond its regular boundaries. In other words, it changes or corrupts that of which it is a part. Jesus' statement here probably points forward to how the Pharisees and Sadducees corrode the positive attitude of the crowd toward Jesus into one that demands his crucifixion (27:22–23, 25).

MICHAEL JOSEPH BROWN

many of our encounters, they are mistaken in thinking it is all about them. He has no need of their bread. Can they remember nothing—not even the obvious signs of who he is? He can produce bread. He just fed four thousand with seven loaves—and they collected seven baskets of leftovers. No, his issue is not with them or with a lack of bread, but with those who ask for signs when signs are all around them and yet they refuse even to see.

How often do we get stuck contemplating our own wisdom, our own efforts, even our own failings and forgetfulness, instead of hearing what another is saying? How often do we convince ourselves that it is all about us rather than stepping back to see what is really going on, so we can act responsibly, differently, effectively?

Signs abound. We notice a few. We miss most of them. Those we notice we interpret. We are fairly good at simple and familiar signs. We can guess what tomorrow's weather may hold by the colors of the evening sky, but the meaning of many signs eludes us. Glaciers recede, yet we deny human involvement in global warming. Towers crumble, yet we persist in seeking global dominance as a nation. With other signs, we too quickly latch on to convenient yet divisive meanings. A tragic and unnecessarily destructive flood is identified as divine judgment upon a great city's cultivation of festivity and freedom.

Perhaps the key is to step back, to remind ourselves it is not all about us, to look again and consider what is a true sign and what is a distraction, and, finally, to listen to the One who provides bread to the hungry for the first clue of what the sign may be all about.

W. SCOTT HALDEMAN

Matthew 16:13–23

¹³Now when Jesus came into the district of Caesarea Philippi, he asked his disciples, "Who do people say that the Son of Man is?" ¹⁴And they said, "Some say John the Baptist, but others Elijah, and still others Jeremiah or one of the prophets." ¹⁵He said to them, "But who do you say that I am?" ¹⁶Simon Peter answered, "You are the Messiah, the Son of the living God." ¹⁷And Jesus answered him, "Blessed are you, Simon son of Jonah! For flesh and blood has not revealed this to you, but my Father in heaven. ¹⁸And I tell you, you are Peter, and on this rock I will build my church, and the gates of Hades will not prevail against it. ¹⁹I will give you the keys of the kingdom of heaven, and whatever you bind on earth will be bound in heaven, and whatever you loose on earth

Theological Perspective

A few New Testament phrases, taken on their own, convey an essential piece of the gospel story. Jesus' question—"But who do you say that I am?" (v. 15)—is one of them. It is completely bound up with the identity of Jesus in terms not only of who he is but also of who he is not. In this material, Matthew is leading up to the transfiguration, which occurs a few verses later. It is a turning point in his Gospel, and this passage's dialogue is crucial in setting the stage for it.

When I was young, if a magazine cover pictured two people together, they had actually been together when the photo was taken. Today, photographs do not always depict what they seem to depict. Tabloids have printed photos of lovers who in fact have never even met. *TV Guide*'s placement of Oprah's head on Ann-Margret's body when they needed a "thin pix" of the talk-show host in 1989 still warrants a prize for creative nonjournalism.

On the other side of the coin, and more relevant for this reading, are people who, before computer-generated imaging, could never be seen together. TV programs never depicted Bruce Wayne and Batman in the same room because Bruce and Batman were really the same person. The same was true for Wonder Woman and Diana Prince. When the Gospels were written, most people gained access to them by hearing them read aloud. They could form mental

Pastoral Perspective

In 1983, Paramount Pictures released a comedy entitled *Trading Places*. The film tells the story of Randolph and Mortimer Duke, owners of a successful commodities brokerage firm who disagree with each other about the factors that influence human identity and achievement. To solve their dilemma, Randolph and Mortimer conspire to reverse the socioeconomic circumstances of two men at different ends of the societal ladder. They identify Louis Winthorpe III, an aristocratic managing partner at their brokerage firm, and Billy Ray Valentine, a street hustler. Winthorpe is framed for petty crimes and subsequently loses his job, assets, and social status. Desperate for his former life, he resorts to hustling to survive. Valentine, on the other hand, is enthroned in a high-powered job and lavish lifestyle. He learns the brokerage business, adapts to his new environment, and adopts the mannerisms of his well-heeled colleagues.[1]

The film humorously revives the decades-old "nature versus nurture" debate and suggests that the formation of human identity is more a product of external conditions such as circumstance, relationships, and community than of internal characteristics like character, personality, and intellect. Might this theory, applied to the life of Jesus, offer us

1. *Trading Places*, dir. John Landis (1983; Paramount, 2002 DVD).

will be loosed in heaven." [20]Then he sternly ordered the disciples not to tell anyone that he was the Messiah.

[21]From that time on, Jesus began to show his disciples that he must go to Jerusalem and undergo great suffering at the hands of the elders and chief priests and scribes, and be killed, and on the third day be raised. [22]And Peter took him aside and began to rebuke him, saying, "God forbid it, Lord! This must never happen to you." [23]But he turned and said to Peter, "Get behind me, Satan! You are a stumbling block to me; for you are setting your mind not on divine things but on human things."

Exegetical Perspective

This passage breaks into two main sections: verses 13–20 and 21–23. This is another triple-tradition passage. The source is Mark 8:27–30, and its parallel is Luke 9:18–21. Matthew agrees with Mark as to the location of the famous confession, while Luke has Jesus praying alone somewhere. The place, Caesarea Philippi, had a non-Jewish association. Emperor Augustus gave the town, originally called Paneas, to Herod the Great in 20 BCE. As a gesture of thanks, Herod built a temple to Augustus there and named it Caesarea. Herod's son Philip, upon the death of the emperor, enlarged the city and added his own name to it in order to distinguish it from Caesarea Maritima, a city on the Mediterranean.

Mark and Luke portray Jesus as speaking in the first person. Matthew has him referring to himself in the third person as the "Son of Man" (v. 13). At this point in the Gospel it has become a Mattheanism, a phrase or word that is used in a technical fashion by the first evangelist. The structure of the language suggests that Jesus is not really interested in the question per se, but uses it as a platform for the confession yet to come.

Jesus is compared to John the Baptist. This recalls Herod Antipas's understanding of Jesus back in 14:2 ("and he said to his servants, 'This is John the Baptist; he has been raised from the dead'"). In this case,

Homiletical Perspective

The question to the disciples remains a question we face every day: who will we say Jesus is? In other words, in our own minds and hearts what do we truly believe he is? Also, what sort of testimony do we offer about him through our words, through our deeds, by our lives? What will our loved ones, our congregations, our neighbors, our communities know about him through us? This may be even more difficult to get right than believing rightly and testifying with integrity.

Peter comes up with the right answer in verse 16, yet finds himself rebuked in verse 23 for completely misunderstanding what that answer might mean. So too we—faithful followers that we are—may know that Jesus is the one who was sent, the one who took flesh, the one who dwelt with us, the one who suffered and died and was buried, the one who rose on the third day. We may declare with pious lips and confident hearts that Jesus is the Messiah, the beloved child of the Most High.

We would be wise, however, to proceed with caution, because there is apparently no guarantee, despite the precision and sincerity of our christological convictions, that we have a clue about what our confession, "Jesus is Lord," actually means.

After all, Peter gets it wrong. Now rebuked in the strongest terms—as Satan, as stumbling block to

Matthew 16:13–23

Theological Perspective

images of the action as they listened. In Matthew's time, a narrative that involved two people standing next to one another would have made it clear to listeners that those individuals were separate people, not just two versions of the same one.

The stage in today's pericope prepares the ground for the transfiguration account by letting us know who it is that Jesus might have been confused with before he appears in chapter 17. When Jesus asks what people say about him, the disciples offer several answers. A resurrected John the Baptist is one, but Matthew has demonstrated that Jesus is not John when they were together at Jesus' baptism. Others suggest Jesus is an important prophet from the past. According to the Hebrew Scriptures, the prophet Elijah never died, having departed for heaven in a chariot. The death of Moses is reported, but no one knows where he is buried; this leaves the door open for something extraordinary to have been in play at the lawgiver's death, as well. Surely enough, we will shortly see Jesus, Elijah, and Moses together.

In these intervening verses, the disciples receive more information about Jesus' identity, as Peter recognizes him as the Anointed One. Jesus declares that Peter knows this because it has been revealed to him, not because Peter's intellect allows him to figure it out (v. 17). Next, Matthew includes a clearly anachronistic saying, as Jesus talks to Peter about "my church" (v. 18). For nearly two thousand years, an incredibly powerful institution has staked its claim to authority on the announcement that the church will be built "on this rock" and on Peter's receiving the "keys to the kingdom."

Although the material about binding and loosing is not completely clear, it is easy to see how it could be applied to shoring up the church's claim that it has authority to forgive. Furthermore, if a member of the clergy can absolve your sin or fail to absolve it or decide necessary conditions for absolution, and can excommunicate you, thus not only isolating you from your earthly companions but also consigning your soul to an eternal hell, then the church's power over your spiritual condition is immense.

When Acts was composed, the writer made the claim that salvation lay only "in the name of Jesus" (e.g., Acts 2:38; 4:18). The next step was the claim that salvation occurs only within the institution of the church. In the West, this trajectory proceeded onward to the pope's pronouncement in 1302 that only those "subject to the Roman pontiff" could hope for happy eternal life. Church folks being what we are, a couple of centuries later new Protestant

Pastoral Perspective

insights about the formation of Jesus' own sense of identity and ministry?

Verses 13–23, commonly (and in some NRSVs) subtitled "Peter's Declaration about Jesus," are largely about identity. The passage is the only account in the New Testament that provides an explanation of the renaming of Simon as Peter. When Jesus asks in verse 15, "Who do you say that I am?" Simon answers, "You are the Messiah, the Son of the living God." Jesus responds, "Blessed are you, Simon son of Jonah! For flesh and blood has not revealed this to you, but my Father in heaven. . . . You are Peter [petros in Greek means "rock"], and on this rock I will build my church, and the gates of Hades will not prevail against it" (vv. 16–18). Jesus' statement is not mere simile. Jesus does not simply tell Peter that he is "like a rock" or has "rocklike" qualities. Instead, he gives Simon a new name ("and I tell you, you are Peter"), informs him of a new role, and empowers him with a new identity. Simon does not assume this identity for himself; it is conferred upon him by Jesus.

Interestingly, Jesus segues into the reshaping of Simon's identity by first inquiring of his disciples about his own identity. In verse 13, he asks, "Who do people say that the Son of Man is?" This is a curious question, since Jesus is aware already of the reports about him. He knows that large crowds follow him. He knows about the Pharisees' public attempts to discredit him. He saw the Spirit of God descending on him like a dove and heard the voice from heaven say publicly, "This is my Son . . . with whom I am well pleased" (3:17). He knows he vexes demoniacs like the two who shout, "What have you to do with us, Son of God?" (8:29).

Perhaps this is the reason Jesus appears unmoved by his disciples' response, "some say John the Baptist, but others Elijah, and still others Jeremiah" (v. 14). So Jesus asks a more probing question: "Who do you say that I am?" Some readers presume that Jesus is testing his disciples' understanding, considering the accolades he heaps on Peter after his "correct" answer. However, there may be other dynamics involved.

The African concept of Ubuntu has its origins in the Bantu languages of southern Africa. While modern culture identifies with Rene Descartes's seventeenth-century postulation, "I think, therefore I am," Ubuntu represents an ancient understanding of ontology, encapsulated by the statement, "I am because we are; and since we are, therefore I am."

In the book *African Proverbs: Wisdom of the Ages*, David Abdulai writes, "In traditional [African] life,

Exegetical Perspective

John the Baptist represents resurrection. Jesus is then connected to Elijah, who was expected to return to earth (see, e.g., Mal. 4:5). This appears to have been a common expectation in the first century, an idea that was connected to John the Baptist earlier in Matthew (3:4). What is singular to Matthew is the inclusion of Jeremiah (v. 14), whose reappearance near the end of time was a much less common tradition. One wonders why the evangelist would draw such an obscure connection. Is Matthew trying to highlight Jeremiah's experience of suffering and rejection, and connecting it with Jesus' experience? This may be the case, but one cannot be absolutely certain. (Luke differs from Matthew by saying that Jesus may be a risen prophet of old.)

Matthew's version of Peter's confession is the best known in the history of Christianity: "You are the Messiah, the Son of the living God" (16:16). The addition of the "Son of the living God" is another Mattheanism. This is also the first and only confession in this Gospel of Jesus as the Messiah/Christ. All other recognitions of who Jesus is are indirect. The concept of the Son of the living God seems to point to an individual—that is, Jesus—who is to be worshiped as one in whom God is immediately encountered. The language here in verse 16 finds its closest parallel in this Gospel in the high priest's words of 26:63. Moreover, to refer to God as "the living God" is to point to God as one who brings all the powers of deity to bear on any situation. In short, in this pithy phrase one finds the proclamation that Jesus is the embodiment of a God who is present and eminently powerful.

Matthew 16:17–19 is probably the best-known block of M material (text that can be found only in the Gospel of Matthew) in the history of biblical scholarship. Its importance to the church and its development is beyond question. However one deciphers the cryptic phrases that make up these three verses, it is almost impossible to understand entirely adequately what the evangelist meant by these verses.

Jesus' response to Peter that his confession is beyond the ability of "flesh and blood" may point to a tradition about divine revelation that circulated in early Christianity rather than to a written source adopted by the evangelist (see, e.g., Gal. 1:16). Contrariwise, the phrase "my church" is unique to Matthew in the Synoptic tradition (v. 18). The "rock" identified in the passage appears to be the Petrine confession. It is upon this revelation that the community will be constructed. Notice that the building activity of Jesus is found again in the testimony of

Homiletical Perspective

Jesus himself—Peter is the one who was lauded for his correct answer just six verses before. As a consequence of his faithful testimony, Peter is named the very foundation of Jesus' church, the rock against which not even the forces of death can prevail. Further, Peter is given keys to free any and all on earth to be heaven-bound and to bind any and all on earth for destruction. If this Peter gets it wrong, who are we blithely to assume that we have it right?

To put it another way, why, like Peter, do we find it so hard to believe that the beloved of God must go to Jerusalem, undergo great suffering, die, and only then be raised by God to new, everlasting, and glorified life? Surely the one known as Son of God will reign without threat, will be honored rather than subjected to suffering, will live and not die, will establish a commonwealth of peace and justice, rather than be executed as a rebel and heretic. However, this is simply not the case. It is also the basis for consistent and destructive false testimony from some of the best-regarded followers of Jesus to this day.

We, of course, live in a postresurrection world. We know what Peter could not accept was true. We know that Jesus went to Jerusalem and confronted both religious and secular authorities with their hubris, exploitive policies, and violence. We know that he was arrested and subjected to both torture and capital punishment. We know he was raised and ascended to the heavenly banquet table and sits at God's right hand and will welcome us to the feast. Still we preach, more often than we ought, that the faithful will not suffer but prosper, will triumph over every adversity, will win rather than lose.

Yes, Jesus won the victory, and death's sting has been swallowed up. Our salvation has been wrought and cannot again be lost. Jesus' work may have been once for all; yet we must avoid Peter's mistake. We must not make what Mary Poppins calls "pie crust promises: easily made, easily broken."[1] We must not say, "God forbid" that the righteous suffer, that saints are killed. Faithful discipleship cannot avoid the walk to Jerusalem and confrontation with the principalities and powers. Jesus leads us in the way we must go, rather than letting us off the hook. That he is Messiah, beloved of God, makes of us members of his body, adopted children of the Most High ourselves—not bystanders in the fulfillment of the promise of his messianic life.

1. Bill Walsh and Don DaGrabi, *Mary Poppins* (Burbank, CA: Walt Disney Studios, 1964).

Theological Perspective

groups began asserting that salvation is only for Christians who are *not* subject to the Roman pontiff. Who knows how many groups have clung to the idea that salvation is limited to members of their particular denominations only?

Images of an authority-laden Peter wearing rich ecclesiastical (and imperial) garments have created an illusion of early Christianity that does not match the Scriptures. There is an old legend about a visit from Dominic (1170–1221) to the pope that alludes to Acts 3:6. The holy father tours Dominic around the Vatican. As they stand in front of Peter's throne, the pope remarks, "No longer can Peter say, 'Silver and gold have I none.'" Dominic replies, "And neither can he say, 'Rise and walk.'"

Jesus' command to Satan (in the guise of Peter) to "get behind me" is usually taken as chastisement for Peter's wrong assessment of what being the Messiah means. The temptation account in chapter 4 also had to do with how Jesus understood himself as Messiah. There he was tempted to take the easy way out—out of hunger, out of risk, out of the slow work of building a community in a world he did not control. Here he seems to view Peter's comment as one more temptation, this one an attempt to persuade him to evade the very hardest and most painful part of his life: his crucifixion.

Given the various churches' consistent claims to exclusive possession of the truth and indeed of salvation itself, it is easy mistakenly to regard the early church as a monolithic institution, perfect in ways that we cannot be today. Yet Jesus surrounded himself with human characters not unlike us, and the New Testament writings actually reveal a group of individuals struggling in serious disagreement about how they should structure themselves as followers of Jesus. Today's reminder that Peter could move at warp speed from a foundation-worthy rock to a stumbling block should be a useful check on our own tendency to believe that we cannot be mistaken about what God is up to in the world.

ELLEN BLUE

Pastoral Perspective

the individual does not and cannot exist alone. He owes his existence to other people, including those of past generations and his contemporaries. He is part of the whole. The community must therefore make, create, or produce the individual; the individual depends on the group."[2] This philosophical understanding exists in one form or another in every traditional ethnic group on the African continent and would have been consistent with the prevailing understanding of identity formation of Jesus' day and locale.

In verses 13–23, might Jesus have been relying on his community of disciples to help "make" him in this way? Might he have been seeking a conferral of his messianic identity from the community that knew him best? Interestingly, of the twenty times in Matthew that the word "Messiah" is used, Jesus never refers to himself as Messiah until after Peter's declaration.

This passage describes a pivotal occasion in the lives of both Jesus and Peter. Each shares his insights with the other, affirms the other's identity, and prepares the other for the ministry that lies ahead. After this mutual conferral takes place, Jesus is transfigured (17:1–7) and enters Jerusalem for the culmination of his earthly ministry (21:1). Peter matures, learns to teach and preach with power (Acts 2), and goes on to become one of the patriarchs of the church. Jesus and Peter help each other assume their rightful identities. This is the principle of Ubuntu: "I am because we are."

This passage stands in stark contrast to Matthew 13:54–58, in which the people of Jesus' hometown ask, "Where did this man get this wisdom and these deeds of power? Is not this the carpenter's son?" Rather than "make" their neighborhood son, their skepticism nearly unmakes him.

Of the innumerable miracles Jesus performed during his earthly ministry, perhaps none was greater than the miracle of inviting twelve poor, pigeonholed, imprudent persons into community and empowering them to live into a new identity. Today, in this age of unprecedented wealth, education, and technology, does not our faith require us to do the same?

PAUL T. ROBERTS SR.

---

2. David Abdulai, *African Proverbs: Wisdom of the Ages* (Denver: Dawn of a New Day Publications, 2000), 7.

Exegetical Perspective

the witnesses in 26:61 ("This fellow said, 'I am able to destroy the temple of God and to build it in three days'"). The triumph over the "gates of Hades" may refer to the incomparable power of the resurrection rather than the activity of the church, whether defensively or aggressively. Alternatively, Peter's reception of the "keys" is a clear consequence of his insight and confession. In this instance, he represents the church, however it may be construed. Moreover, it seems that the "binding and loosing" described in this verse are about the regulation of behavior (cf. 18:18).

The second section of today's lesson is verses 21–23. Again it parallels what can be found in Mark 8:31–33 and Luke 9:22. Although this section closely follows what precedes it, these verses mark a transition from Jesus' ministry toward his suffering and crucifixion. Matthew, unlike Mark and Luke, adds the geographical indicator of Jerusalem. It is not entirely clear why this is the case. Furthermore, Matthew and Luke alter the phraseology of Mark. The verb "be raised" is often designated the divine passive, that is, the activity of God. It also probably reflects the influence of early Christian confession on the evangelist.

Peter's response to Jesus' prediction of his crucifixion ("God forbid it," v. 22) is recorded in Matthew's source, Mark, without giving the reader a statement. Here we find a Septuagintal idiom that means something like "God is/will be kind to you." In other words, it expresses a desire to dismiss an unpleasant idea. It would be similar to someone hearing a dire prediction and saying, "God forbid!" It is not meant to be negative, although Jesus' response makes it so. "Get away from [NRSV "behind"] me, Satan" reminds the reader of 4:11 and the temptation narrative. What Matthew intends is a statement about loyalty and place of investment. Peter, like Satan in Matthew 4, is a tester of loyalties.

MICHAEL JOSEPH BROWN

Homiletical Perspective

This means we do not walk on easy street but must march down the streets of economic exploitation to seek new means of exchange through which all may prosper. We must enter the halls where unjust policies are crafted to voice the concerns of the disinherited. We must visit those in prison while also dismantling the system that locks away so many. We must welcome strangers, even those we consider scandalous and who may make of us a scandal. So we must accept that such confrontations and protests, such opening of doors and hearts and new possibilities, may involve our suffering, our arrest, even our death. Such, it seems, is the way of the one we follow.

Finally, this way of the Messiah seems to imply that we are often wrong about something else. Jesus' final rebuke to Peter is that he has set his mind not on divine things but on human things. We nod approvingly. "We are about spiritual, not earthly things," we say. "That is what Jesus points us toward." In this too we risk further rebuke, if we trust the whole of Jesus' rebuke of Peter. Is it not precisely the avoidance of concrete and material action—with its inevitable concomitant suffering and threat of death—that Peter's mistaken interpretation entails, that demonstrates his human mind-set? Divine things are not ethereal, floating above the mundane, but those things that involve a vision of justice and liberation, compassion and mercy—and the ones who really know who Jesus is are those who, like him, are willing to bear the burden of suffering and death to make that vision real.

The question will not be avoided. Who will we say Jesus is? On our answer, on the answer of those to whom we preach, depends the integrity of our faith and our witness.

W. SCOTT HALDEMAN

Matthew 16:24–28

²⁴Then Jesus told his disciples, "If any want to become my followers, let them deny themselves and take up their cross and follow me. ²⁵For those who want to save their life will lose it, and those who lose their life for my sake will find it. ²⁶For what will it profit them if they gain the whole world but forfeit their life? Or what will they give in return for their life?

²⁷"For the Son of Man is to come with his angels in the glory of his Father, and then he will repay everyone for what has been done. ²⁸Truly I tell you, there are some standing here who will not taste death before they see the Son of Man coming in his kingdom."

Theological Perspective

The theological context for this passage is the liminal, threshold verses that follow Peter's confession at Caesarea Philippi: "From that time on, Jesus began to show his disciples . . ." (16:21). Indeed, Peter's confession serves as the template for this transitional moment in the life of Jesus, that of his disciples, and, by extension, our lives in discipleship. Not only does the journey into Jerusalem represent a shift from the Galilean ministry to the passion; it also reflects a transition in the nature and emphasis of Jesus' teaching and focus. Moreover, we see a developmental shift in the understanding of the disciples' faith, both in terms of what is at stake for them and what may be required of them. Theologically understood, verses 24–28 are not simply a prediction of the future of Jesus' life and ministry. They are at heart an invitation—a "teachable moment" of the most profound kind—to his hearers (and to readers of the Gospel) to discover their true selves, their identities, by choosing to be coparticipants in that future.

It is easy to identify with Peter and the others in these passages. After all, Jesus has not yet helped them understand the theological context for his bleak predictions, or the reasons for them. Peter's response is so human that one wonders at Jesus' stern rebuke. Why not thank Peter, and offer a more measured, reflective corrective? While the disciples

Pastoral Perspective

This passage is perhaps the most unequivocal statement of Christian discipleship anywhere in the New Testament, remarkable for both its brevity and its extremity. Here Jesus teaches that the cost of discipleship is self-denial and the readiness to die for his sake. Although countless preachers across the centuries have attempted to elaborate on what it truly means to take up one's cross, Jesus makes it clear that, whether or not we actually die in the cause, we must be prepared to sacrifice our lives for the gospel. Moreover, he contends that to do less than this is not only a failure of discipleship; it is a failure of life itself.

This is the second time that Jesus has told people that in order to follow him they must take up their crosses. In Matthew 10:36–38, Jesus speaks in absolute terms about how conflicts between the demands of discipleship and those of human relationship, even family life, must be resolved in favor of discipleship: "Whoever loves father or mother more than me is not worthy of me; and whoever loves son or daughter more than me is not worthy of me; and whoever does not take up the cross and follow me is not worthy of me." In this earlier passage, which begins with Jesus telling his followers that he has not come to bring peace, but a sword, the implication is that relationships must be sacrificed if they stand in the way of the gospel. Again, Jesus speaks of this sacrifice in

Exegetical Perspective

Jesus' personal challenge in this crucial passage appears less pointed in the NRSV, due to its use of the plural "If *any* want to become my follower*s*" (v. 24). In an unusual move for ancient teachers, however, Jesus addresses not a group, but each person: "If *anyone* wants to, let that one deny himself [herself]." Jesus is speaking specifically to his disciples, and so the masculine language is appropriate; yet from Jesus' complete teaching we know his instruction is not gender specific. Elsewhere he speaks of those who are his "brother and sister and mother" (12:50). The word used for "deny" (*aparneomai*) is strong: to "repudiate" or to "disown," the word used for Peter's denial of Jesus (26:70)!

English readers may be disoriented by New Testament language, mistakenly equating "soul" with "spirit." "Soul" (Heb. *nephesh*, Greek *psychē*) in the biblical world is the animating principle that God breathed into Adam. In John 20:22 and 1 Corinthians 15:44 we read of the promise that Christians will exchange mere "soul" for the immortal spirit (Heb. *ruach*, Greek *pneuma*). The NRSV rendering "life" gives us a good picture of what Jesus has in mind; some things are even more important than the breath of life. Unless we see the hierarchy implicit in the New Testament view of reality, that the soul is not the highest and greatest gift that we have, we are

Homiletical Perspective

When I entered seminary in 1963, the book at the center of the theological world was *The Cost of Discipleship* by Dietrich Bonhoeffer. Bonhoeffer's life and work come to mind when I consider the exchange between Jesus and Peter about the centrality of the cross in being a disciple. This discussion is also at the heart of what it means to be church and to make disciples who live as witnesses to the gospel. Following Christ requires faithful and courageous living, which is costly.

Much has changed in the last century, but this exchange between Jesus and his disciples in Caesarea Philippi is still central to our understanding of the cost of discipleship and the task of the church. The conversation begins when Jesus asks a question: "What is the word on the street about me?" Peter nails it with his response: "You are the Messiah, the Son of the living God" (16:16). Bingo! Case closed. "On this rock I will build my church" (16:18). Then Jesus tells them the Messiah is headed to Jerusalem and a cross. Peter will have none of that. The rock has become a stumbling block.

This backdrop to our text is important, because Jesus' description of what it means to be a disciple raises the stakes for us. The question of who Jesus is leads inevitably to our own identity and role as disciples. In his description of what it means to follow

Matthew 16:24–28

Theological Perspective

have long since affirmed their belief in Jesus, this shift in the true nature of the mission represents not only a deeper level of understanding of their faith; it also introduces the theological questions of Christology, atonement, and the meaning of suffering. The shift is from being a "hearer" of the word to being a "doer" of it, and this means a shift in traditional wisdom and the introduction of an eschatological theme: "For those who want to save their life will lose it, and those who lose their life for my sake will find it" (v. 25).

As noted, this incarnational expression of Jesus' complete humanity and divinity is hinted at in verse 21, and this represents a shift in both the form and the function of his teaching and ministry. Jesus' convictions, increasingly risky in the political context of the times, require that he make a choice to accept the sacrifice of the cross or seek to escape it. Here we are presented with one of the theological tensions of this passage. In choosing the cross, was Jesus elevating self-denial and suffering for its own sake—intentionally seeking out martyrdom—and in so doing potentially placing all suffering in the context of a punishing, abusive God? Was he, rather, assenting to the cross out of an abiding, deepening, radical love for God and for us?

Too often the pain and humiliation of Jesus on the cross have been used to justify various forms of oppression, such as times when slavery and domestic violence have been cited as examples of one's "cross to bear." Moreover, we are reminded that the phrase "deny yourself" (v. 24) is not meant to suggest forms of asceticism harmful to our mental, physical, or spiritual health. For all who seek discipleship, Jesus' teachings in verses 24–26 call for life-giving affirmation of one's gifts and graces, not ill-conceived and theologically inappropriate self-abandonment.

Each year on August 14 in the Episcopal Church we celebrate the feast day of Jonathan Myrick Daniels. Born in Keene, New Hampshire, in 1939, he was shot and killed by an unemployed highway worker in Haynesville, Alabama, in August 1965. From high school in New Hampshire to his studies at Virginia Military Institute and Harvard, Jonathan Daniels wrestled with the meaning of life and death and vocation. Attracted to medicine and law as well as ministry, he eventually entered Episcopal Divinity School in Cambridge, Massachusetts. In March 1965, the televised appeal of Martin Luther King Jr. to come to Selma, to help secure for all citizens the right to vote, drew Jonathan to a time and place where the nation's racism and the Episcopal

Pastoral Perspective

stark life-or-death terms. He concludes, "Those who find their life will lose it, and those who lose their life for my sake will find it" (10:39).

In fact, in Matthew's Gospel, Jesus begins to prepare his disciples for the high cost of discipleship and its great reward early in his ministry. In 7:13–14, in the Sermon on the Mount, Jesus establishes an absolute, if abstract, choice: "Enter through the narrow gate; for the gate is wide and the road is easy that leads to destruction, and there are many who take it. For the gate is narrow and the road is hard that leads to life, and there are few who find it." Here, if we would say yes to life, we must enter by the narrow gate and go the hard way. Jesus has not yet explained that this "hard way" involves loss, death, even the cross, but he has established that only the narrow gate and the hard way lead to life.

What begins as a counterintuitive choice—that we should take the narrow gate and the difficult path—becomes an absolute reversal by the tenth chapter. If you find your life, you in fact lose it; if you lose your life for Jesus' sake, you will find it. In other words, if we find our ultimate meaning in human relationships with mother, father, daughter, or son, and devote ourselves in an absolute sense to them, then we cannot also devote ourselves to God. We can see, for instance, that a son who is devoted to his father will make the choices his father wants him to make, not the choices that he himself wants to make. It follows the same logic as Jesus' saying that we cannot serve two masters, also in the Sermon on the Mount (6:24).

Like the choice between two divergent paths—in which we may still be able to see the other path for some time after we have made our choice, yet can never be on the other path without returning to the place where the two paths first diverged—it may seem for a time that we do not really have to choose. Yet the way of the cross, which leads to death but ultimately to life, is an absolute choice. In 16:21, then, as Jesus tells his disciples about his own choice—that he will go up to Jerusalem, suffer many things, and be killed—the terms of the reversal are fully revealed. Here Jesus claims in verse 25 that "those who want to save their life will lose it, and those who lose their life for my sake will find it," that those who work to avoid death have nothing, while those who sacrifice for the kingdom of God are immersed in everlasting life.

Jesus speaks all of these words at the end of chapter 16 in response to Peter, who earlier in the chapter both recognizes Jesus as the Christ and also rebukes Jesus for telling his disciples that he must die. Jesus left with an insoluble paradox: how can we not "seek to save our soul," if we understand this as the only place where God meets us?

Jesus does not speak of the wonders of the resurrection, but he does point the disciples to the paradoxical power of the cross. "The one who kills his [or her] soul for my sake will find it" (v. 25b, my trans.). The language is extreme: not simply an involuntary loss of life, but an active putting it to death! One must put to death everything that impedes the new life of God: this is the meaning of "taking up one's cross." In John's Gospel, Jesus bears his own cross. He is the only one who does not cling to his prerogative as God (Phil. 2:5–11), "the representative Die-er of the Universe."[1] In the Synoptic Gospels, however, Simon of Cyrene carries Jesus' cross (27:32): Jesus' followers in their turn "raise up" the cross and follow him. Paradoxically, loss of self involves the finding of one's true self, and everything else besides: "Everyone who has left houses or brothers or sisters or father or mother or children or fields, for my name's sake, will receive a hundredfold, and will inherit eternal life" (19:29). This language concerning human effort is challenging to those concerned about the trap of "works righteousness." Nevertheless, Jesus underscores human participation when he speaks of the time when the "Son of Man" will "recompense to each according to his/her practice" (16:27, my trans.). Somehow the uniqueness of Jesus' action on the cross and our participation work together!

Jesus' scenario of a coming time brings us to the scholarly debate concerning the "Son of Man" (*huios tou anthrōpou,* "Son of a Human Being/Humanity"). Generally, this is a way of speaking about human beings. However, the phrase follows a strange career in ancient Jewish and Christian literature, so that it here means more than simply "someone who is human." We are informed by Daniel 7, where one "like a Son of Man" appears after a series of animal figures who represent godless empires. In contrast, the Son of Man shines with divine light and is human (not bestial), ascends on a cloud to the Almighty, is vindicated by God, and is promised an everlasting cosmic rule of justice (Dan. 7:13). Yet in the interpretation of Daniel's vision, the Son of Man is described in corporate terms: "then . . . the time arrived when the holy ones gained possession of the kingdom" (Dan. 7:22).

him, Jesus directs us toward divine things rather than human things (16:23).

Like Peter, we have trouble putting aside our pursuit of human things. We strive to be independent, self-made, and self-reliant. Getting ahead and getting enough to live comfortably is the goal. Most of us live in a context that rewards these values. When we look for a church, we seek a community that feeds our spiritual needs and the needs of our family. The central figure in this narrative is the self. The smart church will develop a marketing strategy that will reach consumers like us.

This may seem like a stereotype that does not fit or that we may believe is all too accurate. The problem is that there is some of this in all of us. We prefer a faith that encourages rugged individualism rather than an old rugged cross. We want a muscular brand of faith that is committed to being number one and victorious over our foes.

The cross of Jesus Christ stands in stark contrast to this image our culture encourages. The cross was, in the words of the old hymn, "an emblem of suffering and shame." It represented the power of the Roman Empire to demonstrate who was in charge. Maybe the real stumbling block is not Peter's reluctance to accept a suffering Messiah. Maybe the cross is the real problem, as Paul suggests: "a stumbling block to Jews and foolishness to Gentiles" (1 Cor. 1:23).

What was Jesus thinking when he said, "If any want to become my followers, let them deny themselves and take up their cross and follow me" (v. 24)? This still sounds like foolishness. In order to feel better about the embarrassment of a symbol that suggests weakness and failure, in a culture that honors power and success, we dress up the cross and use it as decoration.

To keep us from stumbling, the insight of George MacLeod is helpful:

> I simply argue that the cross must be raised again at the center of the marketplace as well as on the steeple of the church. I am recovering the claim that Christ was not crucified in a cathedral between two candles, but on a cross between two thieves; on the town garbage-heap. . . . Because that is where He died and that is what He died about, that is where the [church] should be and what the [church] should be about.[1]

The church is about making disciples. To be a disciple is to make the way of the cross a way of life

Matthew 16:24–28

Theological Perspective

Church's share in that inheritance were exposed.[1] He was jailed on August 14 for joining a picket line, and then he and his companions were unexpectedly released. Aware that they were in danger, four of them walked to a small store. As sixteen-year-old Ruby Sales reached the top step of the entrance, a man with a gun appeared, cursing her. Jonathan pulled her to one side to shield her from the threats. He was killed by a blast from a 12–gauge shotgun.

Jonathan's papers and letters bear eloquent witness to the gifts he possessed, the flourishing of which led him to participate in the civil rights movement. The cross he chose to bear led to the renewing of his mind and spirit, and a transformation of his understanding of discipleship.

> The doctrines of the creeds, the enacted faith of the sacraments, were the essential preconditions of the experience itself. The faith with which I went to Selma has not changed: it has grown. . . . I began to know in my bones and sinews that I had been truly baptized into the Lord's death and resurrection . . . . with them, the black men and white men, with all life, in Him whose Name is above all the names that the races and nations shout, we are unspeakably one.[2]

These verses in Matthew, with their concomitant theological tensions and ambiguities, call us to follow Jesus in both the risk of suffering and the blessing of redemption and resurrection.

To deny ourselves is to lose ourselves in the service of compassion and life in the body of Christ. The way of the cross is unpredictable and sometimes frightening. Peter and the disciples came to know this in ways that they had not planned for and could not have predicted. In naming aloud for the first time what it meant to live into and participate in the body of Christ, Peter and the others show us what it means to live into the mystery of the incarnation, in discipleship.

J. WILLIAM HARKINS III

Pastoral Perspective

blesses Peter as the rock upon which he will build his church but then, six verses later, calls Peter Satan, because Peter has set his mind "not on divine things, but on human things" (v. 23). Together Peter and Jesus articulate our challenge as human beings: to lay aside our personal claim to what is precious to us in this life, and to choose the risk and reality of pain and loss for the sake of Christ's love for the world.

The stark reality of taking up one's cross becomes hopeful in the light of the reversal in verse 25; "those who lose their life for [Jesus'] sake will find it." The two questions posed by Jesus in verse 26 answer themselves: "For what will it profit them if they gain the whole world but forfeit their life? Or what will they give in return for their life?" As we sing in the African American spiritual: "I heard my mother say, Give me Jesus. Give me Jesus. You may have all this world. Give me Jesus."[1] The passage concludes with the promise that everyone will be repaid for what they have done.

SUSAN B. W. JOHNSON

---

1. *Lesser Feasts and Fasts 2000* (New York: Church Publishing Inc., 2001), 330.
2. Ibid., 331.

1. "Give Me Jesus," traditional, in *African American Heritage Hymnal* (Chicago: GIA Publications, 2001), #561.

Exegetical Perspective

Throughout the New Testament, "Son of Man" is a phrase used only by Jesus, except in Stephen's vision prior to his martyrdom (Acts 7:56) and in Revelation 1:13; 14:14. A curious feature of Jesus' teaching about the Son of Man is that he is involved with suffering—something not clearly apparent in Daniel. It would seem that Jesus joins together the picture of the vindicated and victorious Son of Man with that of the Suffering Servant figure—both corporate figures in their original contexts (Dan. 7; Isa. 53)—in order to show that victory is to come by the cross and to indicate solidarity with his people.

Certain scholars, taking their cue from nineteenth-century scholar William Wrede, believe that Jesus made no such claims, but that the identification of Jesus as Servant, Messiah, and Son of Man was a creation of the early church. Theories like this require reading between the lines of the Gospels, where the clearest and most obvious reading suggests otherwise. Here Jesus speaks about carrying the cross and the recompense given by the Son of Man in one breath, just as elsewhere he commends self-denial done for his sake by others. Here the Son of Man comes in the glory of the Father; earlier Jesus shockingly declares, "All things have been handed over to me by my Father" (11:27).

Is Jesus then mistaken that some would not die before they saw the "Son of Man coming in his kingdom"? A long train of scholars going back to Albert Schweitzer has thought so, and seen the failure of the kingdom to "come" as a sign of Jesus' flawed greatness. Does Matthew here intend for us to picture a return of Jesus, or is this about Jesus' imminent vindication?[2] A prophetic "failure" does not seem to have disturbed our evangelist. The structure of Matthew's Gospel would indicate that the fulfillment is found, at least partially, in the subsequent episode, where Jesus is transfigured and ratified by the divine voice.

EDITH M. HUMPHREY

Homiletical Perspective

that we follow because it reveals what we believe about God and ourselves. The suffering and death of Jesus on the cross demonstrate the depth of God's love and compassion. This is the way God exercises power to save and redeem. Therefore, in the cross we discover that the way to self-fulfillment is the way of self-denial.

John Calvin said this is central to the Christian life. "We are not our own; therefore, as far as possible, let us forget ourselves and the things that are ours. On the other hand, we are God's; let us, therefore, live and die to him (Rom. 14:8)."[2] When I was a student at Yale Divinity School, William Sloane Coffin visited with students and remarked that self-interest is not wrong. The question is, what kind of self are you interested in being? For both Calvin and Coffin, the call to discipleship is the call away from a self-centered life to a Christ-centered life.

Following Christ is not denying the value and worth of the self as a child of God. Rather, it is an affirmation that our true worth is found in giving ourselves on behalf of others. A deep sense of satisfaction is found in standing with and for those who have no voice, caring for neglected children, building homes for those with none, lifting your voice and moving your feet in support of those in need.

The community that participates in formation of disciples who give their lives away for the sake of the gospel will also walk the way of the cross. Whatever the church does in worship, education, and mission should be a witness to the cross. In losing our lives for the sake of the gospel we gain them. Try it!

JOSEPH S. HARVARD III

---

2. On this, see N. T. Wright, *Jesus and the Victory of God* (Minneapolis: Fortress Press, 1996), 340–64, 512–17.

2. John Calvin, *Institutes of the Christian Religion*, trans. Henry Beveridge (Peabody, MA: Hendrickson, 2008), 449.

Matthew 17:1–13

¹Six days later, Jesus took with him Peter and James and his brother John and led them up a high mountain, by themselves. ²And he was transfigured before them, and his face shone like the sun, and his clothes became dazzling white. ³Suddenly there appeared to them Moses and Elijah, talking with him. ⁴Then Peter said to Jesus, "Lord, it is good for us to be here; if you wish, I will make three dwellings here, one for you, one for Moses, and one for Elijah." ⁵While he was still speaking, suddenly a bright cloud overshadowed them, and from the cloud a voice said, "This is my Son, the Beloved; with him I am well pleased; listen to him!" ⁶When the disciples heard this, they fell to the ground and were overcome by fear. ⁷But Jesus came and touched them, saying, "Get

Theological Perspective

This text represents another of the remarkable transitional passages in Matthew, connecting as it does Peter's confession of his faith in Jesus as the Messiah, the Son of God (16:16), and the subsequent journey on the long road to Jerusalem. The transfiguration story immediately follows Jesus' first prediction of the passion (16:21–23). Now, in the presence of three of his disciples (Peter, James, and John), as well as Moses and Elijah, there is confirmation of both Peter's conviction about Jesus (16:16) and Israel's conviction about God. Here Jesus appears in a form that both confirms Peter's earlier confession and anticipates the glory of the postresurrection paschal mystery.

One identifies with Peter's desire to remain on the mountaintop and in so doing to preserve the mystery and power of the experience. It is tempting to compare this with the other two christophanies in Matthew, in both of which the living and glorified Christ appears to the disciples (14:25; 28:17–18). One is particularly aware of the contexts of fear, doubt, awe, and wonder in each of these passages. One is a postresurrection appearance on a mountain in Galilee, and the other on the Sea of Galilee during a storm. Both evoke hints of the theophanies in Exodus. Indeed, in some ways the basic template from the Moses story is recapitulated here, replete with six

Pastoral Perspective

The transfiguration of Jesus is one of the most consoling and encouraging Gospel narratives about Jesus and his disciples. The story speaks to us without mediation and suggests many applications to our lives. So many themes present themselves in thirteen verses: retreat, the vantage point of the mountaintop, revelation, spiritual legacy, indwelling, fear of failure, fear of success, the return to reality, the messianic secret, the power of sacrifice, the impotence of death. It is a narrative revealing of Jesus' ministry, his sacrificial death, and his resurrection; it is also a narrative revealing of the disciples' (and our) limits and possibilities in the light of these.

Six days can seem like an eternity. The transfiguration took place six days after Jesus had confided in his disciples that all of his captivating teaching and all of his energizing and hope-filled healing would lead to his suffering at the hands of authorities, to his execution, and finally to his rising from the dead. It is six days after Peter had pulled his teacher aside and rebuked him, in response to what Jesus had said; six days since Jesus had, in turn, rebuked Peter in the strongest terms and then turned to the rest of the disciples to tell them that if they wanted to follow him, they had to deny themselves and take up their cross. He told them that in attempting to save their

up and do not be afraid." ⁸And when they looked up, they saw no one except Jesus himself alone.

⁹As they were coming down the mountain, Jesus ordered them, "Tell no one about the vision until after the Son of Man has been raised from the dead." ¹⁰And the disciples asked him, "Why, then, do the scribes say that Elijah must come first?" ¹¹He replied, "Elijah is indeed coming and will restore all things; ¹²but I tell you that Elijah has already come, and they did not recognize him, but they did to him whatever they pleased. So also the Son of Man is about to suffer at their hands." ¹³Then the disciples understood that he was speaking to them about John the Baptist.

Exegetical Perspective

Matthew shares the transfiguration with Mark and Luke. He places his account in a structurally significant place, following Peter's identification of Jesus as Messiah, and prior to Jesus' return to Judea and Jerusalem, where he will face the cross. The transfiguration is a key element in the disciples' learning process, since they must be willing, like their Lord, to take up the cross (16:24). It is also a key element in the revelation of Jesus' full identity: he is not only the Messiah, but also the One who "must go to Jerusalem and undergo great suffering . . . and be killed, and on the third day be raised" (16:21). Indeed, to "see the Son of Man coming in his kingdom" (16:28) is to embrace this Jesus who will suffer and die; this is the deepest manifestation of divine glory.

Immediately after Jesus' teaching in the previous chapter concerning his passion, three disciples are taken up the mountain, where they see the glorified Lord. Peter, James, and John, the three closest disciples to Jesus, are given this privilege, but they will pass on what they have seen at the appropriate time—"after the Son of Man has been raised from the dead" (v. 9). It is not that these apostles are privy to secrets about Jesus denied to others. Rather, they are learning as apprentices what it means to acknowledge Jesus as Lord, and they themselves will

Homiletical Perspective

Barbara Brown Taylor advises against talking about the transfiguration of Jesus. She reminds us that neither Jesus nor the three disciples who were with him talked about it.[1] I have found it helpful to follow her advice. Jesus told the disciples to tell no one until after the resurrection.

Have you ever tried to keep a secret about something out of the ordinary that happened? It is not easy, but the disciples may have pulled it off. Eventually the story got out, however, and we have it before us. What Taylor suggests is not to attempt to give some reasonable explanation of what happened on that mountain. Strange things happen on mountains in Scripture. When the Bible says someone is going up a mountain, an epiphany is about to happen.

We all need mountaintop experiences. These are sacred moments when God's presence comes near to assure us or to challenge us. Peter, James, and John were assured that in leaving everything to follow this Jesus they were on the right track. There had been moments of doubt. What about all the push-back from the religious authorities? What about all this talk of a cross? The cross was the empire's last resort

---

1. Barbara Brown Taylor, *Home by Another Way* (Cambridge, MA: Cowley, 1999), 57.

Matthew 17:1–13

Theological Perspective

days, three companions, and God speaking to those gathered from a cloud.

In this passage, as at Jesus' baptism in 3:17, a voice from heaven says, "This is my Son, the Beloved; with him I am well pleased." This repeats a common thread in the use of the term "beloved" and adds the command to pay attention: "Listen to him!" One suspects this is directed to Peter, who is still struggling to manage the events as they unfold around him, to bring order to the mystery and chaos of the moment. The vision is to be kept secret until after the resurrection, but the appearance of Elijah already prompts a discussion in which Jesus explains that the ministry of John the Baptist has fulfilled the ancient prophecy (Mal. 4:5). This the disciples seem to understand. With this the mountaintop experience comes to an end, and it is time to return to the everydayness of life and to a journey that may lead into unknown territory.

What might it mean to "practice transfiguration," theologically understood, once one has descended the mountain? Keeping with two of the identified themes of this passage—light and listening—how might this inform our practices of paying attention to the light of the transfiguration in the everyday moments of our lives, not just those occasional mountaintop experiences? Perhaps paradoxically, this may mean being mindful of the mystery and awe of the uniqueness of Christ portrayed in this passage, while recognizing that in some way we too are to be bearers of that light. A theology of the incarnation might hold in tension both the Word become flesh, well acquainted with the human condition of suffering, and Christ as intercessor and redeemer who suffers with us.

Moreover, the journey down from the mountaintop and the return to level "valley" ground is an appropriate opportunity for further theological reflection on this tension. The valley is where Jesus continued his ministry. This might be informed by thoughtful inquiry, for example, on the nature of the Eucharist and of the beloved community as the body of Christ. How do we embody our mountaintop experiences, including our journey into Christ in the Eucharist, once we have returned to the valley of day-to-day life to "Go in peace, to love and serve the Lord"? How do our disciplines and practices inform both our mountaintop experiences and life upon our return to level ground?

Some time ago I journeyed with my two sons to the northern Cascades for a mountaineering trip, the ultimate goal of which was to summit Mount Baker.

Pastoral Perspective

life they would lose it, but that to lose their life for the gospel would be to find life itself.

The message was simultaneously clear and opaque; they understood what he was saying about himself, and they were devastated by what it meant for him and for them. Six days later, when Jesus took Peter, James, and John up a mountainside, one can only imagine that it relieved for them a terrible tension inside. It must also have engendered another tension as well. Having the confidence of a mentor is both powerful and fearful.

He called them away to a mountaintop, not only a place set apart (as the wilderness was), but also a place of perspective, wonder, and possibility. From there they could see the whole world as they knew it. In some ways we might say they were primed for revelation, yet Jesus had once been delivered to a very similar vantage point by Satan and asked about the view (4:8). Once on the mountaintop, Jesus was visibly transfigured. It was as though all of the confusion six days before had been swept away; Jesus *was* the Christ, just as Peter had said. In this way the transfiguration was the kind of confirming revelation that corroborated for them what they had felt and known. We too have that amazing sense from time to time in our lives, when our vision is confirmed by something outside of ourselves, when—even if only for a moment—we see things so clearly it is as though they gleam.

Moses and Elijah were a very special part of that corroborating vision. They represented the legacy of the prophets and spiritual leaders of the Hebrew people, those most favored by God. In the Hebrew Scripture, it is Moses and Elijah who are taken up at their end. Moses was taken by God and buried where his people knew not; Elijah was taken up from the banks of the Jordan in a chariot of fire. If Jesus were not to live forever—and Jesus himself had just told his disciples that he would not—then Moses and Elijah were indeed the people one would want to see at his side. Theirs was a spiritual legacy of vision and power and even eternal life with God.

So who could blame Peter for wanting to stop there? "It is good for us to be here; if you wish, I will make three dwellings here, one for you, one for Moses, and one for Elijah" (v. 4). In some ways this attempt at indwelling is the most natural human response we can imagine. Let us stay here together in this hallowed place. Let us never come off this mountain, now that we have seen all we ever need to see.

There is nothing quite like revelation for its excitement, its privilege, its security, and its

be called to follow the path of humility as martyrs in an echo of what they have learned.

Both Matthew and Mark detail this momentous event as occurring "six days later" than Peter's confession, perhaps recalling God's creating power (according to Ambrose[1]), but more probably to recall the feast of Booths (or Tabernacles), a celebration kept for seven days, with a moment of complete rest on the eighth and final day (see Lev. 23:39). This feast was a perpetual reminder to the Jewish people of an earlier era, when God led them through the wilderness, keeping them safe and guiding them to the promised land by means of his shining glory (Exod. 24:16; 33:22; 40:35; 40:38).

Peter himself makes the connection as he responds to what the three have seen and requests to erect "booths" or "tabernacles" as a memorial. We are meant, then, to understand the experience of Peter, James, and John on the mountain as a ramped-up version of the wonders that Moses and the Hebrews beheld in the wilderness, when they lived in tents and encountered the glory of the Lord, both on the mountain and in the tabernacle that traveled with them. In the Gospel, the divine glory is also among the disciples, but in the person of Jesus, not just in a fiery cloud or majestic voice.

Jesus appears before their eyes with Moses, who spoke directly with God "mouth to mouth" (Num. 12:8; my trans.) and himself shone with a borrowed glory, and with Elijah, who was visited by God's still, small voice (1 Kgs. 19:12) and who saw the fire upon his offering (1 Kgs. 18:38). Moses and Elijah are also symbolic of the Law and the Prophets, whom Jesus fulfills (5:17), since the divine voice prompts "Listen to him!" (v. 5). Some have noted that Moses died, while Elijah did not, and so they may be seen as representing the "living and the dead," all under the care of the Lord. It is Jesus, not these two, who takes center stage. He shines, and the three apostles are directed to heed him; he touches them, comforting and interpreting to them what they have seen.

In the book of Daniel, those who are wise will, we are told, "shine like the stars" (Dan. 12:3); here, Jesus outranks all the wise, shining like the sun, the major luminary of the sky. His luminosity is so strong that it affects not only his face but his clothing, and indeed casts its light upon the disciples. Because of them, they will eventually become like their master,

to keep order and maintain power. Somehow such things seemed out of place for a conquering king who would establish God's rule.

"Sometimes I feel discouraged and think my work's in vain," says the old spiritual.[2] There are moments when the question arises, what was I thinking when I agreed to sign on to work for justice and reconciliation? It simply will not work in a divided and hostile world like ours. Then, in some remarkable way, forgiveness is offered, a corner turned, or a roadblock removed, and God's peaceable kingdom comes near. There is no logical explanation for the way God's power works.

Bruce Rigdon, pastor and church historian, has been leading travel seminars to Russia and the Middle East for many years. In orientations for the trip, he often reads the story of the transfiguration. He re-creates an experience he had as a graduate student at Yale studying with Roland Bainton. While doing research, he came across a manuscript written by a monk in the sixth century, who suggested that there is a miracle in the transfiguration story we have often ignored. The disciples had their eyes opened, and they saw a new reality. It was revealed to them that the way of Jesus was God's way in the world. The one whom they had been following had the power to transform them into agents of God's love and justice and to heal a broken world. Wow! "They . . . were overcome by fear" (v. 6).

Fear raises its head one more time. Jesus understands that we are fearful creatures. Over and over again, Jesus tells us not to be afraid, not to let our hearts be troubled. Some of our fears grow out of the precarious nature of life. We do not know what is coming toward us tomorrow. It may be a storm, a frightening person, or a scary medical diagnosis. Fear can dominate our lives. Fear can stop us in our tracks and envelop us. Such fear is addressed with the promise that nothing can separate us from God's steadfast love.

I think there is a different kind of fear that overcame the disciples at the transfiguration. The disciples had their eyes opened to the new reality God is bringing about in Christ, and they were afraid. Encounters with the presence and purpose of God can be frightening. Things may not be running smoothly when we are at the controls; but if God is really running things, then we are not! You never know what to expect. We can never be sure what God may be up to and what God might call us to do.

---

1. Ambrose, *Exposition of the Gospel of Luke 7:6–7*, quoted in Arthur A. Just Jr., ed., *Ancient Christian Commentary on Scripture: New Testament III: Luke* (Downers Grove, IL: InterVarsity Press, 2003), 159.

2. "There Is a Balm in Gilead," traditional.

Matthew 17:1–13

Theological Perspective

So I thought. After several days of preparation, we departed our base camp at 2:00 a.m. for the summit attempt. The night was clear and cold, and our team, roped together, ascended steadily. Each deliberate step brought us closer to the hoped-for sunrise on the summit of this jewel of the Cascades. Soon, however, lightning appeared off to the west as a line of powerful, predawn thunderstorms announced a fast-moving cold front. In consultation with our wise guide, we made the group decision to return to camp, with the wind, rain, and lightning close behind. I wanted the mountaintop, and I got a storm. I was disappointed and, worse, felt the disappointment of my sons.

Later our older son, the most experienced mountaineer among us, said something I will never forget: "Dad, you never climb into a storm. That's Mountaineering 101. We did the right thing." What I remember most about the trip now, back in life in the valley, is not the fact that we did not summit, but that we were together and that our disciplines and practices led us to remember what was most valuable and important. Like Peter perhaps, who wanted to remain on the mountaintop, I had to reconcile my return to level ground with a deeper awareness of the nature of the journey, a journey perhaps more ambiguous and risky.

Indeed, Jesus' rebuke of Peter in Matthew 16 finds here its penultimate meaning. They would descend the mountain, but—and this is where our Mount Baker narrative and the transfiguration narrative part company—they would climb into a storm of life-changing proportions in Jerusalem. Perhaps with Peter we are tempted to say, "Let's stay on this mountain, and build huts here," when practicing transfiguration on level ground may mean transformation and change beyond anything we have imagined. The transfiguration is in part a living into a sense of wonder about the mystery of such transformations.

J. WILLIAM HARKINS III

Pastoral Perspective

tranquility. All is right with the world at such a moment. Who would go back down? A bright cloud and a startling voice interrupted him. "This is my Son, the Beloved," the voice says. Then, as if in rebuke of Peter yet again for not hearing: "Listen to him!" (v. 5).

The disciples were overcome by fear, but was it fear of failure, fear of success, or perhaps fear of God? They would prefer to stay on the mountain, but they were left with Jesus alone, whose touch and voice told them not to fear. They came down the mountain and returned to reality. Jesus told them not to speak of what they had seen until he had risen from the dead. Again they were confused. According to tradition, Elijah comes first, then the messiah. This was not as strong a response as Peter's first reaction to suffering and death, but they would have liked to hold on to Jesus, even as they returned to the world.

Like our response to hearing the terminal diagnosis of a friend, they work to deny it. We work to prove that it is not true. Jesus, however, tells them that Elijah has come already (in John the Baptist). The transfiguration they must hold inside because they cannot yet see beyond the suffering he will endure, although we, as the later readers of a completed Gospel, do. Only when they see the fruit of Jesus' suffering, that he has risen from the dead, will they be able to proclaim this vision they have seen.

SUSAN B. W. JOHNSON

as he himself promised: "the righteous will shine like the sun in the kingdom of their Father" (13:43).

Matthew tells his story in a striking fashion that reminds us of great revelatory events and visions of the past. His narrative is twice pierced by the expostulation "Behold!" or "Lo!" (vv. 3, 5), a directive word that reminds us of other visions, such as the nativity appearance of the angelic choir (Luke 2:13). This repeated word is obscured in the NRSV, which translates it as "suddenly." Indeed, the episode displays the rhythm of an apocalyptic vision such as that found in Daniel 10:4–11. Like Daniel, the apostles see a wondrous sight, one whose face "shines like the sun" (v. 2). This glowing One is greater than the mere angel observed by Daniel, whose face was "like lightning" (Dan. 10:6).

After beholding this wonder, the three hear a divine *bath qôl* (a rabbinic term that means literally, "the daughter of a voice," the echo of God's own word on earth). At this, they fall on their faces in awe and like Daniel are touched and are raised up, for God has something for them to do. Finally, on the way down the mountain, Jesus says that the apostles have seen "a vision" (v. 9), which they are not to recount for the time being.

Then he assumes the role of interpreter, a figure frequently found in visionary literature. He explains the meaning of what has been revealed, so that the Gospel can comment: "then the disciples understood" (v. 13). Part of the instruction means understanding that the martyred John the Baptist has played the role of Elijah, preparing God's people for their visitation. His death, however, points beyond itself to what Jesus himself will do. It is not merely Jesus' interpretation on the spot, but his entire direction of life—down to the cross, and up beyond that ordeal to the resurrection and ascension—that provides the full interpretation of the vision. The disciples must continue on the road with Jesus for full understanding and in order to be incorporated into the life of this unique Son of God.

EDITH M. HUMPHREY

Martin Luther King Jr. must have been afraid many times in the struggle to bring an end to racial injustice. Attack dogs, fire hoses, thrown rocks, and angry crowds were dangerous and frightening. One moment late at night, when King was sitting alone at the kitchen table, he heard what he called an "inner voice" telling him to do what he thought was right. From that point on, he knew that the hand of the Lord was upon him, and it gave him the courage to face what was ahead. God was moving through him to set his people free.[3]

God gives us mountaintop experiences that are transformative. They change the way we see the world and ourselves. Business as usual is no longer possible after you have seen the vision of God's good future revealed to us in Jesus Christ. Such experiences give us confidence in the presence and power of God's steadfast love that endures forever, and they sustain us through trials and tribulations.

Between the baptism of Jesus and his journey to the cross, Jesus and three of his disciples had an epiphany, and the lives of those disciples were never the same. The transfiguration signaled that a new day was on the way in Jesus and that God was moving us toward the beloved community Martin Luther King Jr. preached about and died for. The message was clear. God is about the business of bringing hope and healing to a broken world. When your eyes are opened to God's good future, then you cannot go back. However, you can go back down the path to be a healing presence to those who are hurting, to work for justice and peace, and to offer hope. People are hungry to experience this good news. We may not be able to explain the transfiguration story, but we can tell about the power and purpose of God in Jesus Christ to make all things new.

JOSEPH S. HARVARD III

---

3. Taylor Branch, *Parting the Waters: America in the King Years, 1954–63* (New York: Simon & Schuster, 1988), 162.

Matthew 17:14–21

14When they came to the crowd, a man came to him, knelt before him, 15and said, "Lord, have mercy on my son, for he is an epileptic and he suffers terribly; he often falls into the fire and often into the water. 16And I brought him to your disciples, but they could not cure him." 17Jesus answered, "You faithless and perverse generation, how much longer must I be with you? How much longer must I put up with you? Bring him here to me." 18And Jesus rebuked the demon, and it came out of him, and the boy was cured instantly. 19Then the disciples came to Jesus privately and said, "Why could we not cast it out?" 20He said to them, "Because of your little faith. For truly I tell you, if you have faith the size of a mustard seed, you will say to this mountain, 'Move from here to there,' and it will move; and nothing will be impossible for you." [21But this kind does not come out except by prayer and fasting.]

Theological Perspective

This passage follows the wonder and mystery of the transfiguration. Thus it represents a return to the challenges awaiting Jesus and the disciples in the valley after they have been on the mountain. The confrontation with the reality of suffering in the form of an epileptic boy (Mark 9:14–27; Luke 9:37–42) reinforces the subtext of the preceding passage: that the glory of the transfiguration will not be without suffering. Matthew's account of the encounter with the boy implies that he suffers some form of demonic possession. As is the case in earlier miracle narratives (see 8:1–9:8) the theological issue at stake is Jesus' authority, particularly in light of the recent mountaintop revelation.

What are we to make in our postmodern age of what looks to us like Matthew's equation of epilepsy with demonic possession, and its healing with exorcism? Those of us who engage in pastoral counseling and other forms of clinical work may view this ostensibly immediate healing by exorcism with both skepticism and curiosity. Perhaps the narrative is instructive, however, with regard to the central theological issue in this passage. In approaching Jesus on behalf of his son, who does not speak—or at least from whom we do not hear—the man tells Jesus that the disciples have been unable to heal his son. Those named the "unbelieving and perverse generation"

Pastoral Perspective

As Jesus comes down the mountain with Peter, James, and John following his transfiguration, there is no doubt of his immediate depth of compassion for the father and son he meets at the bottom. A man emerges from the crowd that waits for Jesus, and as he kneels at Jesus' feet he begs Jesus to have mercy on his son. He describes his heartbreaking story, that of a parent whose child's illness makes it impossible for him to protect his son. The dual images of a child who might at one moment burn to death or at another moment drown are powerful reminders of the very real desperation people feel when someone they love is seriously ill. It is terrifying and tragic when we are not able to protect or care for the people we love, and there is perhaps no greater feeling of helplessness than when we cannot take care of a vulnerable child.

As is so often also the case among those who suffer, the father's helplessness and his son's suffering are further compounded by their frustration when people who they have been told can help are no help at all. The man explains that he brought his son to the disciples, but they could not cure him. As urgent and impassioned as Jesus' concern for the boy is, his impatience and even anger with the disciples over this failure is palpable.

One might be tempted to describe this passage of Scripture as a particularly low point in Jesus'

Exegetical Perspective

This vignette brings to an abrupt end the disciples' mountaintop experience. On their return from the transfiguration, everyday life awaits them. Although the story does not emphasize sin, only lack of faith, the pattern reminds us of Moses' return from Sinai, and the failure of the Hebrews to keep faith with the Lord. Matthew does not emphasize this link with the exodus as strongly as Mark does, for he does not begin with a scene of chaos (Mark 9:14–16). Rather, Matthew calls the reader to identify with the suffering father who cries out, with words that will become a part of Christian worship in perpetuity, *Kyrie eleison*, "Lord, have mercy!" (v. 15). The plight of the boy and his illness are underscored.

Considering the dramatic emphasis placed upon Jesus in the previous episode, the transfiguration, we are not surprised—as the father and the disciples seem to be—at the disciples' failure to cure. In the flow of Matthew's story, however, their failure must be read as a serious setback, since in 10:1 the Twelve are sent out to proclaim, heal, and exorcise, and presumably they meet with success on their mission. It would seem that Matthew intends to show us that those following Jesus must be brought to a deeper level.

We are perhaps astonished that Jesus does not take the disciples' inability in stride. After all, they are not the Messiah, and he is! Jesus' response,

Homiletical Perspective

It is easy to understand why Peter wants permanent residence on the mountain of transfiguration (17:4). When he and James and John come down from the mountain, the "glow" wears off in the face of a desperate father with a sick son. The disciples on the mountaintop have experienced the power of God. Now they are faced with human pain and suffering.

The church is in a similar situation. I am alarmed by the number of children in our culture who suffer from all kinds of diseases, mental and physical. Youth leaders who lead retreats tell me that keeping up with young people's medicine is a huge task. It is a helpless feeling to seek to minister to families dealing with chronic mental illness. The father of this boy is honest in describing the condition of his son, and he is hopeful that Jesus can provide some help. After trying for assistance from the disciples, to no avail, he turns to Jesus.

"Why could we not cast it out?" ask the disciples (v. 19). Have you not experienced the frustration reflected in the disciples' question? The challenges before us seem much greater than our ability to respond. Jesus is exasperated with the disciples and has some tough words for them. Jesus' outburst against them brings back memories of the responses to the faithlessness of our ancestors in the Old Testament by Moses ("[You] perverse and crooked

Theological Perspective

with whom Jesus is angry and exasperated are principally the disciples.

One empathizes with the plight of the father, who has clearly been on a long and difficult journey because of his son's illness. One feels for all parents whose children suffer chronic and debilitating illnesses. Were the son to speak, one imagines that his narrative, of suffering and the chaos of the seizures that indiscriminately cause him to fall into fire and water alike, would show him to be exhausted and in despair. Thus this encounter is in radical contrast to the mountaintop glory of the transfiguration and thus places the lack of faith (v. 20, "little faith") of the disciples in stark contrast with what they have only recently observed.

This echoes the shift, first observed in 16:21 ("From that time on, Jesus began to show his disciples . . ."), from the Galilean ministry to Jerusalem and all that awaits them there. This transition has implications for the ministries of both the *being* and the *doing* of the disciples. In this encounter with the epileptic boy, they struggle to demonstrate an understanding that the nature of their faith—and the concomitant actions it might inspire—has changed. Contextually, then, one understands Jesus' anger and frustration, clearly evident in this passage, as he sees both the urgency of what lies ahead, and what is at stake in the faith it will require.

Regardless of how one understands the connection between illness, possession, and healing, it is clear that participation in any form of healing requires some measure of authority and faithfulness. It also requires relationships of trust. Jesus earlier gave the disciples authority to cast out demons (10:1). Yet, at least in this case, their faith proves insufficient to exercise that authority. Comparisons with the Markan account of this story are fascinating for the absence in Matthew of the reference to prayer: "This kind can come out only through prayer" (Mark 9:29). One asks questions about the theological nature of authority and the relationship between authority, faith, and healing, particularly in the context of the transitions from the Galilean ministry to the Jerusalem road—shifts, that is to say, in both the form and function of the ministries of Jesus and the disciples.

The liminal, threshold nature of these passages may also require a change in how the disciples in particular understand their relationship to God. Again, in Mark 6:7 (parallel to Matt. 10:1), there is reference to the temptation to believe that the gift they have received is theirs to control and dispense as they wish. This may have suggested faith in their

Pastoral Perspective

teaching ministry. His disciples, whom he has commissioned in 10:1, and to whom he has given "authority over unclean spirits, to cast them out, and to cure every disease and every sickness," have accomplished very little with their newfound authority. In seven chapters, they are recorded as failing to feed crowds of five thousand and again of four thousand, failing to walk on water, and failing to understand anything more in Jesus' parables than the crowds around him have. They have eaten with him, traveled with him, spoken with him privately. Yet, when it comes to bringing the kingdom of God into this world, proclaiming the good news to the poor and oppressed, the sick and those imprisoned, the disciples are still neophytes and bystanders. Even their devotion to him as disciples seems to have emptied them rather than filled them with power.

The narrative of the child with epilepsy picks up after a sequence of hemming and hawing on the part of the disciples. At one moment Peter declares that Jesus is the Christ, the Son of the living God, and Jesus blesses him as the foundation of his church; in the next moment Peter pulls Jesus aside and reprimands him for speaking of his impending suffering and death (16:13–23). In an earlier passage, Jesus has attempted to explain that in his death, death itself will lose its power (16:21), but the disciples cannot seem to hear or comprehend this. Sternly Jesus warns them that in order to follow him, they too must deny themselves and take up their cross. Jesus' transfiguration (17:1–12) fills Peter, James, and John with awe, yet they fail to understand that the work of the kingdom awaits them at the base of the mountain. Peter wishes to remain on the mountaintop indefinitely (17:4).

The background to the story of the boy with epilepsy is that Jesus' disciples are content to be passive, if worshipful, disciples. Jesus has given them authority to cast out spirits and heal diseases, but they have not accepted it. As followers, they are eager yet timid, devoted yet retiring, willing yet unprepared. They are, as Jesus bluntly tells them, faithless and perverse. He is angry; there is no other way to read his words. Every bit as much as the boy's illness moves him to pity, the endless equivocation of his disciples exasperates him. It is one of the moments when, in the midst of his divinity, Jesus' utter humanity comes into full view. This is the second of the three times he speaks to his disciples in explicit terms about his approaching death and its meaning. "How much longer must I be with you? How much longer must I put up with you?" (v. 17) can be read

Exegetical Perspective

from the human perspective, seems severe. Why should the apprentices be able to do all that their master does? On the other hand, Jesus' disapproval is perhaps not directed only at them, but also at an implicit criticism from the suffering father: *your* disciples could not do anything. Coming directly after conversation with the glory-tinged Elijah and Moses, perhaps this confrontation is a real disappointment to Jesus, just as Moses' discovery of idolatry was a blow to him (Exod. 32:19–20).

The Lord's response is mysterious, but indicates that he sees more here than we do as casual readers. In any case, it is a strong reminder of the high expectations that the Lord has for us: God is not content to leave us in our childish complaining or our ineffective lives, any more than Jesus leaves this boy in his dangerous condition. Indeed, there is more than one patient here: not only the boy, but also his father, and the disciples of "little faith" (see 6:30; 8:26; 14:31; 16:8)—not to mention present-day readers! Jesus, embedded as he is in a ministry among those who are truly needy, demonstrates his fatigue and sacrifice—along with a suggestion that this is not his natural home—with the words, "How much longer must I be with you?" (v. 17). His statement is at once both fully human and intriguingly other: human in the fatigue and outburst, divine in the longing for the divine dwelling place!

Despite the disappointment, Jesus acts: "Bring him here to me" (v. 17). He casts out the demon, and the child is instantly cured. In a usual report of a miracle, the healing would immediately be followed by the wondering admiration of the crowd. However, the Gospel writer is using this miracle to teach something else. He follows instead with the wonder of the disciples that they had not been able to heal. Why? Jesus' answer comes to us as something of a shock, if we hear it with new ears and not simply as a saying that we have heard many times before. We are assured that faith—even just a very little faith—moves mountains. We must think carefully here. Frequently English-speaking Christians imagine that "faith" is a quality, a personality or character trait like blue eyes or a sense of humor. Faith is seen as a kind of substitute for "confidence," with that word defined in the manner of Maria's song in *The Sound of Music*: "I have confidence *in confidence ALONE!*"[1]

Biblical faith is something different: it is an action of belief directed toward God, a confidence that God

Homiletical Perspective

generation" [Deut. 32:5]) and by the Lord ("How long shall this wicked congregation complain against me? I have heard the complaints of the Israelites, which they complain against me" [Num. 14:27]).

Often, when I feel overwhelmed by a situation that has no obvious solution and seems way beyond me, I will recognize that the only hope is divine intervention. It is time to turn to God in prayer. The church has recognized this and offers this suggestion on an occasion like what the disciples face:

> Mighty God,
> in Jesus Christ you deal with spirits that darken our
>   minds and set us against ourselves.
> Give peace to those who are torn by conflict, cast
>   down, or lost in worlds of illusion.
> By your power, drive from our minds demons that
>   shake confidence and wreck love.
> Tame unruly forces within us, and bring us to your
>   truth,
> so that we may accept ourselves as your beloved
>   children in Jesus Christ.
> Amen.[1]

I find this prayer helpful because it acknowledges our dependence on the power of God. Jesus diagnoses the problem of the disciples as "little faith," a common malady that often afflicts the disciples in Matthew (6:30; 8:26; 14:31; 16:8). Thomas Long suggests that in Matthew "little faith" is not agnosticism or unbelief but "*distracted* faith . . . because it has drifted away from its anchorage . . . [and the disciples] lose their confidence in God's care."[2]

The prayer refocuses our attention on the God we have encountered in Jesus, who offers hope and healing. Often we ask someone in a crisis, "What can we do to help?" The response, "Please pray for me," may not sound like much help. Having prayed and been prayed for in time of need, I know that it is one way to deal with the problem of "little faith." Prayer reminds us that we are not left to our own resources.

Prayer may seem like a little thing in the face of the enormous obstacles to healing and wholeness. Jesus contrasts little faith with faith the size of a mustard seed (v. 20). A mustard seed is small, but it can yield a large shrub. In a similar manner, "mustard-seed faith" believes in the power of God to bring to fruition the future God has promised in Jesus Christ.

How often have we allowed "little faith" to paralyze us? The odds seem so great in a world with so

---

1. Richard Rodgers and Oscar Hammerstein, *The Sound of Music* (New York: R&H, 1959).

1. *Book of Common Worship* (Louisville, KY: Westminster/John Knox Press, 1993), 991.
2. Thomas G. Long, *Matthew* (Louisville, KY: Westminster/John Knox Press, 1997), 181.

Matthew 17:14–21

Theological Perspective

gifts, graces, and power—trust in their own power rather than in God.

Thus, in light of 16:24–28, with its profound shift in understandings of "bearing one's cross," and "denying oneself," and of 17:1–13, with the deepening understanding of their ministries seen in the light of the transfiguration, the disciples are living into the invitation to live out in profoundly deeper ways the meaning of their mission and their relationship with God. In saying, "If you have faith as small as a mustard seed" (v. 20b), Jesus is teaching them that availability to relationship in the moment—and faithfulness here, now, with God—is more important than the size of the gesture or their perceptions of their own power and authority. Denying themselves and taking up the cross will profoundly change their theological understandings of authority, power, and, yes, faithfulness, in ways much needed on the road to Jerusalem.

In a sense, these related passages in 16:24–17:21, a theological tone poem in three parts, are *harrowing* transitions. Theologically understood, this is not limited to the culturally familiar and pejorative understanding of the word "to harrow," meaning "to vex, torment, or cause mental distress."[1] When I was growing up, my paternal grandfather owned a hardware store in an agricultural community. One of the farm implements he sold was a disk harrow, designed to turn over and break up the soil in late winter and early spring, in the service of "harrowing" the soil. One could see farmers harrowing their fields, folding the detritus of last year's crop into the soil in preparation for planting, new growth, and eventual harvest. In this sense, then, "harrowing" can be a life-giving term. Indeed, the root of the word "harrow" is *harwe*, from which we also get our word "harvest." The road to Jerusalem will be *harrowing* for Jesus and his disciples in both senses of the term, and the life-giving harvest for all promised in the transfiguration will require mustard-seed faith—seeds planted in soil harrowed by faith, and a hoped-for harvest nurtured and sustained by that same faith.

J. WILLIAM HARKINS III

Pastoral Perspective

in human terms as an angry plea that they realize how short the time is, although it may also be read as public impatience, even condemnation.

This is a story that, from a pastoral perspective, is difficult to talk about. Anger, even righteous anger, is hard to hear and hard to swallow, and most seekers and believers would find it offensive to think of Jesus calling them faithless and perverse. Yet American culture is replete with calls to action in the midst of endless equivocation, and within every church there are responses to the gospel that are simultaneously eager and timid, devoted and retiring, willing and unprepared.

Finally, it is more than a postscript that this passage is actually about faith. When the disciples, obviously perplexed, come to Jesus privately and ask why they could not heal the boy, Jesus tells them that it is "because of [their] little faith" (v. 20). He challenges them that even the smallest glimmer of faith, faith like a mustard seed, would do plenty. They do not trust in God's power to heal; is this because they trust only in themselves? Since they are filled with their own sense of weakness already, is there any room for trust in God?

Nevertheless, Jesus ends on a very positive note: "If you have faith the size of a mustard seed, you will say to this mountain, 'Move from here to there,' and it will move; and nothing will be impossible for you." The eschatological moment is continuously breaking forth. Jesus not only heals a child no one could heal, but he tells his disciples that with faith in God the impossible will be possible. The kingdom of God is at hand.

SUSAN B. W. JOHNSON

---

1. *Webster's New World College Dictionary*, 4th ed. (New York: Macmillan, 1999), 650.

Feasting on the Gospels

Exegetical Perspective

is the Lord of the living and the dead and that the Holy One hears our prayers, cares, and acts. Abraham was commended for faith because he believed that God could raise the dead (Heb. 11:19) or open the womb of Sarah (Rom. 4:18). Similarly, Jesus responds to this man, one of a faithless and crooked generation, because he has properly directed his faith, tiny though it is.

Jesus encourages us to practice our confidence in God, and so our faith is bound, like a seed, to grow. "Nothing will be impossible" is not an absolute statement, but Jesus' response to the disciples' confession that they were unable to heal: when trusting in the God of compassion, Christians will no longer ask, "Why did we not have power?" (*ti . . . ouk ēdynēthēmen*, v. 19), for nothing will be beyond God's power in them (*ouden adynatēsei hymin*, v. 20).

Our understanding about faith is to be galvanized by such astounding statements as that which Jesus makes here. Our growth in faith requires that we not think about it in childish terms, however, as though it is the business of Christians to force God's hand. Careful study of the quality of faith as expressed by those who die for the Lord is key here. Especially important is to trace the steps of Jesus, who himself, we are told, "grew in wisdom and in stature" (Luke 2:52) and had to "learn obedience" (Heb. 5:8). Faith is not magic; it is mature participation in the work of God.

Verse 21 of this section, whether it is original or an additional explanation of Jesus' words,[2] is an important part of the Christian tradition: true faith will exhibit itself in prayer, in waiting upon the Lord to show mercy. True faith also is exercised, shaped, and chastened by fasting, for through this action we are reminded of our dependence upon God for all things that are good, and we learn (as did Jesus in Gethsemane) to bring our wills into harmony with the will of the Father.

EDITH M. HUMPHREY

Homiletical Perspective

much pain and suffering. We can easily become distracted with programs that entertain and with concern about the growth in numbers. Instead, the church is called to do the things we can do, like praying with and for those who are diseased in body and mind, being a presence with them and an advocate for them. We do all this with confidence in God's power to work through us.

A number of years ago my "little faith" encountered "mustard-seed faith." During the time when apartheid had a stranglehold on South Africa, Bishop Desmond Tutu was touring the United States to raise support for the struggle. We invited him to Durham to speak at a community gathering in Duke Chapel. I was amazed that he was so small in size and so huge in spirit. On that evening, he announced to us that the oppressive system of apartheid would not survive. I thought to myself, "What is he thinking?" His confidence was based on a letter from an elderly woman who wrote to him that she was on her knees every morning, praying for deliverance from apartheid. Tutu had the audacity to suggest that despite its tremendous power, apartheid did not have a chance against this woman's prayer to God, who can be trusted. That is mustard-seed faith. Reflecting on this incident over the years has convicted me of my "little faith." I needed the vaccination of mustard-seed faith that I received from Stanley Saunders:

> Too often we live as if we are moonstruck, casting ourselves from fire to water. Like the disciples, we may sometimes fail to exorcise the demons, but, like them, we ought to keep trying, for resurrection faith knows no wall that God's power cannot overwhelm. Even a little faith, even the tiniest shred of faith, even faith that sometimes fails, is sufficient for God to use.[3]

JOSEPH S. HARVARD III

---

2. This verse about prayer and fasting is not found in the earliest manuscripts that we possess.

3. Stanley P. Saunders, *Preaching the Gospel of Matthew: Proclaiming God's Presence* (Louisville, KY: Westminster John Knox Press, 2010), 173.

Matthew 17:22–23

22As they were gathering in Galilee, Jesus said to them, "The Son of Man is going to be betrayed into human hands, 23and they will kill him, and on the third day he will be raised." And they were greatly distressed.

Theological Perspective

Jesus startled the disciples with a blunt warning of his coming fate. Calvin suggests that Jesus had been doing this for some time and that the disciples should not have been surprised.[1] Perhaps they were not surprised, but had managed to ignore the warnings that Jesus had given them. As Calvin points out, followers of Jesus are frequently unwilling to follow where the Lord leads. This insight orients us to the other points that the pericope suggests: the reception of the gospel, the reactions of the disciples and by extension other believers, and the way believers conceive of Jesus.

For several thinkers in the Christian tradition, it has been a crucial matter to notice that the human reaction to the gospel is distress. Perhaps more even-handedly, we might say that when the gospel message comes plainly and clearly, one of two opposing reactions must occur. Søren Kierkegaard wrote that when humans are confronted with the gospel, the genuine response must be either faith or offense.[2] He meant that if one truly understood Jesus existentially (contemporaneously), one would either be angered or moved to faith.

1. John Calvin, *A Harmony of the Gospels Matthew, Mark and Luke*, trans. T. H. L. Parker (Grand Rapids: Eerdmans, 1972), 2.211.
2. Søren Kierkegaard, *Practice in Christianity*, ed. and trans. Howard V. Hong and Edna H. Hong (Princeton, NJ: Princeton University Press, 1991), 81–121.

Pastoral Perspective

Of course the disciples are "greatly distressed" (v. 23). Who would not be, after hearing a dear friend announce his coming death? It is the kind of moment that becomes a turning point: one minute, the disciples are watching Jesus cure a young boy (vv. 14–20); the next, they are learning that he is going to die (vv. 22–23). Of course they are upset. Anyone who has been with someone they love when they deliver that kind of news knows that words cannot describe the shock, grief, sadness, or anger we feel when we learn that someone we love is going to die. One minute, life is humming along, and the next, everything is different. Life completely changes when you get that kind of news about someone you love.

It is not as if the disciples do not already know about Jesus' future. He has revealed his coming death to them already, before the transfiguration. In his initial sharing, the disciples react with shock and defiant anger, as Peter rebukes Jesus for demonstrating such notions about his death: "God forbid it, Lord! This must never happen to you" (16:21–23).

In this text, Jesus again shares the news with the disciples that he is going to die. He waits until he is alone with them to deliver the news about his death ("As they were gathering in Galilee," v. 22). Jesus tells them plainly, succinctly, and clearly. Previously, Jesus has *shown* the disciples about his coming death. This

Exegetical Perspective

This is Jesus' second passion prediction. The first followed Peter's confession at Caesarea Philippi (16:21). Matthew depended on Mark for the location and timing of the prediction, but he introduced some significant variations. He shortened Mark's introduction to Jesus' words and presented the disciples as saddened rather than baffled.

Whereas Mark 9:30 depicted Jesus and the disciples "passing through Galilee" on their way to the Passover in Jerusalem, Matthew envisioned them "gathering in Galilee" (v. 22). He knew that Caesarea Philippi was not in Galilee, so he had Jesus and his company return there. He may already have had in mind Jesus' departure from Galilee (19:1) for the last time, to go to Jerusalem. Galilee was important to Matthew as the locus of Jesus' ministry (4:12), as the place where he had called disciples (4:18), and as the site where he launched the church (28:16). Matthew knew that Jesus chose Capernaum on the Sea of Galilee for the fulcrum of his mission (4:13). Consequently, 17:22, 24 underscored the connection of Jesus with Galilee.

Matthew did not share Mark's concern to preserve the "messianic secret." Where Mark presented Jesus conducting a seminar with this inner circle of disciples, perhaps to caution them against betraying the secret, Matthew reduced the introduction to the

Homiletical Perspective

This brief passage is prophetic in nature. It is the second of three prophetic passages about Jesus' death and resurrection in Matthew's Gospel (the first is found in 16:21–23; the third at 20:17–19). Jesus is foretelling the pattern of his life's conclusion, and it is devastating. It is noteworthy that Jesus reiterates in detail the future set of actions against him. Indeed, reluctant and disbelieving followers would have a difficult time accepting the fact that their leader's life will take this horrific course.

Warnings of negative circumstances to come are difficult to accept. Many have had the experience of bad news repeated to them when a tragedy occurs; we are often incapable of taking in such information on first hearing. Jesus' words are repugnant to us. Who wants to hear such words of impending disaster and death? We sometimes meet bad news with refrains such as "No, that's impossible!" or "You're kidding!"

Jesus' announcement is shared in Galilee, his home environment. He describes himself indirectly as the "Son of Man." The phrase is sometimes used to describe "the future figure of glory and authority."[1] Jesus then details future events with three verbs: he will be betrayed, killed, and raised.

1. R. T. France, *The Gospel of Matthew* (Grand Rapids: Eerdmans, 2007), 664.

Theological Perspective

Instead of expressing either true faith or genuine offense, far too many followers of the Lord are blissful in their triumphal imaginings of the world that is to come because of the goodness of Christ. It is far more pleasant to imagine a transformed world that has arrived in an earthly paradise wherein Christ is Lord of all than it is to concentrate upon the process by which Jesus will startle the world out of its inertia and sinfulness. Do we imagine that following Christ will represent no disruption of our old lives? Why does Paul call baptism a baptism into Christ's death (Rom. 6:3)?

The truth is that the gospel arouses the hatred of the world. The gospel message arouses a number of indignant offenses in the spirit of the world. Kierkegaard called these offenses those of loftiness, of lowliness, and of the established religious order.[3] The world hates Christ for claiming to be God—he offends through his loftiness. The world rejects Christ for claiming to be human—he insults through his lowliness. Finally, even without the special claims of divinity and humanity about Jesus, he upsets the established religious, political, and social orders. We see all three possibilities in the disciples' distress.

Jesus called himself the Son of Man. This had been a term of apocalyptic significance since the composition of Daniel. The Son of Man was a messianic figure, well understood by first-century Jews. The disciples had little difficulty in grasping that Jesus was not simply claiming humanity for himself when he implicitly took on this title. However, the all-too-human tendency is to bring the divine into the mundane realm, to make it common and acceptable. The disciples—and by extension all believers—want to settle into a life and habit of regularity. We want a tamed Christ who will not startle us. We desire a predictability to life that stems from our own autonomy. The Son of Man offers none of this.

The disciples are troubled by Jesus' lowliness. Why should he accept betrayal? Why is Jesus apparently unwilling to announce this disastrous future so as to escape it? The human tendency, and an excellent plot device, is to uncover treachery so as to prepare for it. That is the opposite of Jesus' plan. This is more than distressing; it is devastating. How can we accept a God who knowingly accepts tragedy? What does Jesus' acceptance of his own fate portend for God's care of those calamities that will befall us?

Finally, the disciples and later believers are agitated by Jesus' clear opposition to the established

3. Ibid., 85–121.

Pastoral Perspective

is the first time Jesus *tells* them that he is going to die. This time, when Jesus tells them plainly what will happen, they are not angry, but rather "greatly distressed" (v. 23). As is often the case when preparing for a loved one's death, anger turns to deep sadness.

Jesus reveals three important details about his death in this foretelling of his crucifixion. First, he tells the disciples that he is going to be "betrayed into human hands." It is difficult to know how the disciples heard this first part of Jesus' news, but Jesus' choice of words foretells a political deception that results in falling into the power of human hands. After traveling with Jesus, hearing him teach, and watching him perform miracles, the disciples know well Jesus' power and his ability to inspire awe and wonder. How then do the disciples hear this part of the news: that this man, this Son of Man, will fall prey to human powers? Does it make them question Jesus' identity?

The second part of Jesus' revelation to the disciples is that the human hands into which he will be betrayed will kill him. This is an intense announcement; not only will Jesus die, but he will die at the hands of some who want him dead. Again, the political nature of Jesus' foretelling is hard to miss. Someone will deceive him, and the deception will result in murder. Of course the disciples are "greatly distressed." Questions must have raced through their minds: Who will betray him? Who will kill him? When will this happen? Where will we be when this happens? Can we do anything to prevent it? The disciples probably feel shocked and afraid. Jesus has just told them about something that will change their lives forever.

The last part of Jesus' revelation to the disciples is the most important: "and on the third day he will be raised" (v. 23). Of course he also foretells the resurrection, God's awesome power over death. However, the disciples are not yet ready to hear the good news on the other side of the crucifixion. They are standing in the moment when bad news is dropped like an anvil, hitting hard on the lives they have built following Jesus. They are not yet ready to hear the good news. When you find out that someone you love is going to die, it is hard to hear anything else after that. The disciples will hear it again, and of course eventually will live through it. For now, though, they need time to stand in the sadness that takes over when you get the kind of news no one wants to hear about someone they love.

The Rev. William Sloane Coffin, pastor of the Riverside Church in New York City from 1977 to 1987, lost his son Alex in a car accident at age twenty-four.

simplest form possible: "Jesus said to them" (v. 22). Since he depended so heavily on Mark, you may wonder why he did not share Mark's notable concern to keep the secret. The most obvious answer has to do with timing. Mark wrote *before* the destruction of the temple, Matthew *after* it. By this time, thanks to the Hellenists and Paul, the nascent church had established a pretty clear identity independent of Jerusalem. Matthew's Gospel, in fact, may have supplied a manual for missionaries[1] based in Syria, and its author took a keen interest in the transition of the movement beyond Judaism.[2]

Matthew also tinkered with the prediction of Jesus' betrayal, death, and resurrection. Circulation of different oral versions near the end of the first century could account for some variations. Both Matthew and Luke, for instance, inserted the auxiliary Greek verb *mellei*, "is about to." How much that would have altered Mark's present passive infinitive is open to question: Matthew's "The Son of Man is about to be betrayed" (v. 22, my trans.; NRSV "is going to be") versus Mark's "The Son of Man is to be [or is being] betrayed" (Mark 9:31). At least it indicates the *imminence* of Jesus' betrayal and death, not its *necessity* (which would require Greek *dei*).

Paradidōmi, "to hand over," is often used in its literal sense. The word clearly has christological connotations. In its literal sense it could refer either to an informal or to a formal process by which Jesus ended up in the hands of religious and Roman authorities. As they approached Jerusalem, Jesus told the disciples that "the Son of Man will be *handed over* to the chief priests and scribes. . . . then they *will hand him over* to the Gentiles" (20:18, 19). As Passover approached, Jesus alerted his companions to the fact that "the Son of Man will be *handed over* to be crucified" (26:2). Following Jesus' arrest, the authorities "*handed him over*" to Pilate (27:2). After releasing Barabbas, Pilate "*handed [Jesus] over* to be crucified" (27:26).

Matthew used *paradidōmi* in the sense of "to betray" when referring to Judas. Judas Iscariot was "the one who betrayed him" (10:4). He asked the chief priests what they would give him "if I *betray* him to you" (26:15). From then on Judas looked for an opportunity to *betray* Jesus (26:16). As Judas approached to deliver the telltale kiss, Jesus said, "See, my *betrayer* is at hand" (26:46).

First, little in human experience can compare to the bitter emotions elicited by betrayal. Who has not felt betrayed by one's choices or the decisions of others? Jesus is not describing, however, the many betrayals that make up life in general. The kind of betrayal he refers to will result in his death, caused specifically by betrayal "into human hands" (v. 22).

Listeners will experience a liturgical echo on hearing the verb "betrayed." Paul uses the word in his mention of the church's words of institution for the Lord's Supper in 1 Corinthians 11:23–26. It is profoundly ironic that the act of betrayal is perpetually remembered as the backdrop for the church's sharing of the Lord's meal. We remember with thanksgiving and humility that we share in Jesus' invitation to break bread with him—despite the betrayals of ourselves, others, and God on a regular basis.

The second verb Jesus uses, "kill," is unambiguous. Jesus is telling the disciples bluntly that he will be murdered. The act of murder is nothing new to the human condition. Cain's killing of his brother Abel is ready witness to that fact. More than ever, today the acts and effects of murder are continually available for scrutiny through a multitude of televised crime programs as well as the news. Children go missing, serial killers roam anonymously, and victims of crime suffer. We are reminded of the ultimate steps human beings take against one another in the willful destruction of life, even to destroying the Lord of life.

Finally, the third verb, "raised," comes couched within an astonishing statement: "and on the third day he will be raised." When the disciples hear Jesus' words, is it possible they actually *hear* the third and final part of his statement? No one comes back from the dead! Is Jesus engaging in wishful thinking? Is he merely fantasizing that his death is not the end? Jesus' concluding sentence is an assertion of new life. As with the other two verbs, Jesus indicates here that he is the passive recipient of others' actions toward him. He does not say he will raise himself but rather "he will be raised." Jesus' final verb places the action of resurrection within the will of God. At the end of Jesus' prediction is the expression of an ultimate act of faith: Jesus is stating that death does not have the last word in God's view! Indeed, we acknowledge this sequence of events in our recitation of the creeds.

The response of the disciples concludes this brief passage. They are described as "greatly distressed" (v. 23). Who would not be? Jesus has told them that they have signed on for a seemingly failed mission. Their leader will be betrayed and killed. As to being

1. See Krister Stendahl, *The School of St. Matthew and Its Use of the Old Testament* (Uppsala: C. W. K. Gleerup, 1954).
2. Joachim Jeremias, *Jesus' Promise to the Nations*, trans. S. H. Hooke (London: SCM, 1958).

Matthew 17:22–23

Theological Perspective

orders, especially the established religious order. Humans crave the predictability of establishment; very few true anarchists exist. Jesus blithely accepts that his end has already been signaled by the existing powers. Further, he foretells that after three days, he will be raised. What might be the consequence of such an action? While we wish to domesticate that message into a sense of the certainty of a heavenly reward for Jesus' followers, he predicts no such thing. Why might it not as easily be judgment of those who have failed to protect their Lord?

The opposition to the gospel stuns the disciples, and even today dumbfounds followers. Believers wish to imagine a world of triumph. We want to move from the joy of conversion directly into the magnificence of an earthly and heavenly kingdom where all obstacles have bowed before the glory of the Lord. Martin Luther rightly denied this in his concentration on a *theologia crucis* (theology of the cross). The actual task of Jesus was to come in humility and weakness. Only the *theologia gloriae* (theology of glory) denies this. Of course, the theology of glory is our preferred metaphor. We wish to see our Lord in glory, and then to share in that glory.

No gospel message has proven harder to resist than the prosperity gospel. It reflects our sense of shared success, and our desire for Jesus to crown our own good sense in choosing his kingdom. The prophet is unwelcome in his or her own land (13:57). Perhaps this statement becomes true in our day because true prophets who bring the message of change and are conformed to Christ are always unwelcome. In this pericope, we find Jesus' stark answer. The Lord is in control of the present and future, and the task of the disciple is to follow willingly. Nothing more is promised than that, and only faith can grasp that stark reality.

R. WARD HOLDER

Pastoral Perspective

Reflecting on his experience of grief in a 2004 interview with Bill Moyers, Coffin said, "Chirping optimism is terrible. . . . And [people] think that emotional mediocrity is the good life. No. We should be able to plumb the depths of sadness and rise to the heights of joy, even ecstasy, though at my age, it's not too easy."[1] Coffin knew what it meant to experience shock, anger, and sadness in suffering the loss of his son, whom he loved deeply. Coffin also knew that he needed to be able to dwell in the sadness as long as necessary in order to heal.

The disciples' emotional reaction to learning of Jesus' coming death offers the opportunity to name and embrace a very human reaction to loss. In this telling of Jesus' coming death, the disciples miss the good news of the resurrection. In those moments when the news of a loved one's death is new, when you are standing in shock and sadness, it is understandable that you cannot see beyond the tremendous loss. Jesus tells the disciples of his coming death one more time, but it is not clear whether the disciples in Matthew's Gospel ever fully embrace the good news of Jesus' resurrection.

At the end of the book, there is a hint that at least some of the disciples may have accepted the reality of the resurrection, for when the risen Jesus appeared to them, "they worshiped him; but some doubted" (28:17). Standing on this side of the resurrection, it can be difficult to let ourselves feel the disciples' distress upon hearing Jesus tell of his coming death. In this text, where the disciples are not yet able to hear the good news of the resurrection, they offer us permission to embrace whatever emotions we experience in the face of loss.

KATE FOSTER CONNORS

1. Bill Moyers, *NOW*, PBS, March 5, 2004, http://www.pbs.org/moyers/faithandreason/print/coffin_print.html; accessed November 9, 2011.

The passion prediction contrasts "Son of Man" and "human hands." What a paradox! The Son of Man is the one who assures true justice, rewarding each person according to that person's deeds (16:27). He is a life giver. "Human hands," Jewish opponents and Roman authorities (20:18–19), are those who take his life unjustly. Later Matthew could say as an equivalent phrase, "The Son of Man is betrayed into the hands of sinners" (26:45).

Matthew differed quite strikingly from Mark on resurrection. According to Mark, "*three days after being killed*, he will rise again" (Mark 9:31; also 8:31; 10:34). Matthew (16:21; 17:23; 20:19) and Luke (Luke 9:22; 18:33) spoke of resurrection "*on the third day*." The variation may not have seismic importance, but the Matthean and Lukan phrasing agrees with the earliest formula, that of Paul (1 Cor. 15:4). We probably should assume that Mark derived his phrasing from another oral source, which Matthew and Luke felt obliged to correct. Jesus died and was buried on Friday. The women who very early on Sunday, the first day of the week and the third day after his death, went to tend the body did not find him in the tomb.

Matthew pictured a different response to the passion prediction than Mark. After the first prediction he followed Mark in reporting Peter's rebuke of Jesus for suggesting such an outcome and Jesus' remonstrance of Peter for tempting him to forsake his calling (16:22–23; Mark 8:32–33). Luke, on the other hand, bypassed that narrative entirely. After this second prediction, Matthew and Luke switched strategies. Luke elaborated two reactions of the disciples that Mark reported: their incomprehension and their fear to ask Jesus to explain. Matthew envisioned a quite different reaction: grief.

This divergence seems significant. What lay behind it? Did Matthew think that Mark made the disciples, with whose company he may once have consorted, look too much like dummies and fraidycats? Even though this was the second time Jesus had predicted his death and resurrection, Mark says, "They did not understand what he was saying and were afraid to ask him" (Mark 9:32). Matthew restored a little dignity to the disciples. "And they were greatly distressed" (v. 23). Grief was much more acceptable than stupidity and cowardice.

E. GLENN HINSON

raised? Could the disciples move past the first two verbs in order to reach the third and hear the good news in that? It would seem not.

Jesus' predictions of the events surrounding his death meet contemporary listeners in a postresurrection frame of mind and life. We know the end of the story—but do we? The passage must give us pause if we take Jesus' words seriously in view of daily events unfolding domestically and globally. There is always much to be "greatly distressed" about in terms of both personal and worldly responses to Jesus. Even today there are those who are being betrayed and killed for his sake. Various Web sites detail the contemporary martyrdom of Christians globally. Jesus' words are not merely about events in the past, but repeat themselves daily in the present lives of true disciples who are willing to live out the pattern of his sacrificial life.

Jesus' words offer a portrait of the true pattern of all faithful Christian communities. The description of the disciples' reaction as those "greatly distressed" is a reminder that their Lord's earthly life ended in tragedy—in human terms. His leadership is founded on his body sacrificed for the world. Jesus' words are a reality check. Will we associate with him in the midst of injustice, tragedy, and violence? Will we stand with him in both his death and his resurrected life?

The film *Romero*[2] is a narrative about the archbishop of El Salvador, Oscar Romero, who was assassinated on March 24, 1980. It concludes with a striking scene. As the assassin prepares to pull the trigger from the shadows at the back of the church, at the altar Romero lifts the Communion chalice upwards—and is murdered. Jesus' words are forthright, stressful, and real. Can we stand with him?

SUSAN K. HEDAHL

---

2. *Romero*, dir. John Duigan (Paulist Pictures, 1989).

Matthew 17:24–27

²⁴When they reached Capernaum, the collectors of the temple tax came to Peter and said, "Does your teacher not pay the temple tax?" ²⁵He said, "Yes, he does." And when he came home, Jesus spoke of it first, asking, "What do you think, Simon? From whom do kings of the earth take toll or tribute? From their children or from others?" ²⁶When Peter said, "From others," Jesus said to him, "Then the children are free. ²⁷However, so that we do not give offense to them, go to the sea and cast a hook; take the first fish that comes up; and when you open its mouth, you will find a coin; take that and give it to them for you and me."

Theological Perspective

The history of the interpretation of this passage reflects both the concerns of the interpreting communities and the state of the historical understanding that was current when thinkers grappled with its meaning. For instance, when examining the hermeneutical stances of interpreting communities, for those interpreters who wished to make a claim about Petrine authority, the linking of Peter with Jesus could not have been a clearer statement that Peter enjoyed at least a mantle of reflected authority. Not surprisingly, very few Protestant reformers accepted this linkage. In the same way, the question of when Rome began to collect the temple tax made an impact on the interpretation. Calvin's interpretation depends upon Matthew's being a faithful historian of the facts of Jesus' life; later scholarship has demonstrated that it was the Roman emperor Vespasian who demanded the temple tax be collected from the Jews for Rome, and this happened in 70 CE.[1] Certainly Rome collected the temple tax during the time when Matthew was written, but just as certainly, not when Jesus was alive.

The text begins with a conundrum: the realm has taken to itself the rightful gain that was demanded for the maintenance of divine worship. Should Jesus pay?

1. John Calvin, *A Harmony of the Gospels Matthew, Mark and Luke*, trans. T. H. L. Parker (Grand Rapids: Eerdmans, 1972), 2:236.

Pastoral Perspective

In one way, this is the perfect stewardship text. It is easy to read Jesus' instructions to Peter to go catch a fish, take the coin out of its mouth, and give it to the temple as the perfect command to churchgoers everywhere: "Go, take the gifts that God has given to you, and share what you have with the church." It would be a no-brainer to use this text in a stewardship sermon: "Here it is. Jesus said it himself: we should give back to God (through the church) a portion of what God gives us." Although Jesus argues for freedom from the *obligation* to give to the temple ("then the children are free," v. 26), still he advocates giving, reframing it as a choice, not as a matter of following someone else's rules. In the end, Jesus tells Peter to support the temple with the resources God provides (the coin in the fish's mouth, which only God could have provided). A perfect message for stewardship season.

As is usually the case, there is more to the text than what is obvious on a first read. When the collectors of the temple tax come to Peter and ask him whether or not Jesus pays his portion of the tax, their question is about more than money. More than whether or not he has made a contribution, they want to know if Jesus is playing by the rules. In Jesus' time, Jewish men were required to pay a tax to the temple. So the collectors of the temple tax want to

Exegetical Perspective

Matthew alone reported this curious incident concerning the temple tax. In line with his use of Mark he connected it with Jesus' and the disciples' entrance into Capernaum. Capernaum would fit, of course, because the Jewish authorities collected the temple tax there as the residence of both Jesus and Peter. Why did Matthew interrupt the Markan narrative to insert the story? What point did he want to make? Where did the story come from?

Regarding the last query, we probably could assume that it circulated orally, perhaps cited in sermons. There is much material peculiar to Matthew, especially parables, for example, the Unmerciful Servant (18:23–35), the Laborers in the Vineyard (20:1–15), the Two Sons (21:28–32), the Ten Virgins (25:1–13), and the Last Judgment (25:31–46). Whether Matthew intended it or not, this story portrays Jesus as a law-abiding Jew who supported the temple—not, as later charged (26:61; 27:40), a renegade who wanted to destroy the temple.

To explain why Matthew preserved the story, we must look more closely at the temple tax. The tax consisted of a half-shekel or double-drachma for support of the temple. Each free adult Israelite—excluding women, children, and slaves—paid it annually to defray expenses of the temple cult. It was a relatively late assessment and originally not a

Homiletical Perspective

Sermon preparation on this passage is best approached by reviewing the list of its many unresolved questions as a means of finding a sermon focus. This passage comes in the well-known form of a conversation between Jesus and a disciple. It centers on a painful human fact: taxes. The events in this passage play out at two levels, the explicitly financial and the spiritual. At its most obvious, this incident revolves around an issue familiar to all listeners and shows that not even Jesus was tax exempt! What makes this particular tax notable is that it was not levied from outside the Jewish community but from within it. It was the annual tax all adult Jewish males were to pay for the upkeep of the sanctuary in Jerusalem. So any quibbles Jesus might have about this tax are not at the political level of Roman assessments, but go to the heart of support for the temple system and the question of who pays for it.

There are several interpretations that can be derived from this dialogue. First, this is the tax required of all adult males for the upkeep of the temple in Jerusalem, which was collected at the local level, in this case at Capernaum. This dialogue may also be a subtle sign of Jesus' discomfort with the way the financial matters of temple affairs were handled, a matter of passive political resistance on his part. It is also possible that Jesus was using language

Matthew 17:24–27

Theological Perspective

If he does, is he accepting the authority of the realm to order godly worship? If he does not, is Jesus subversive to the realm, and a bad Jew, unwilling to pay his fair share for the preservation and continuation of traditional religion? Certainly that question comes before Christians of every age. What does Caesar have to do with Christ? Jesus' question to Peter forces the logic of the rhetoric into these questions: the issue is not the ability to pay, but the rights and habits of kings and their subjects. Jesus established that the tax fell on the "others." Thus, the children of the king were free. In parallel fashion, the true children of the true king are free. Jesus then arranged to avoid offense, but only to maintain peace, not to set a precedent for the children of the king.

This text deftly opens the questions of loyalty and fidelity to the Lord, as opposed to an earthly sovereign. From the days of Caesar to the present, earthly kingdoms—whether empire or kingdom or Reich or democratic republic—have sought to claim that which truly belongs to the Lord. The Barmen Declaration, written in 1934 in the context of Nazi Germany, argued that loyalty to anyone or anything over loyalty to God was a form of idolatry. It stated, "We reject the false doctrine, as though the State, over and beyond its special commission, should and could become the single and totalitarian order of human life, thus fulfilling the Church's vocation as well" (see footnote 2).

Alas, earthly kings and kingdoms, princes and principalities, have ever eyed the possibility of an allegiance that demands the highest commitment as a worthy goal. Unfortunately, too frequently Christians have fallen prey to this temptation themselves. Reinhold Niebuhr pointed out that, especially in times of war, a dangerous simplicity was introduced into modern life, one where a human's responsibilities were so simplified as to resolve the necessary paradoxical tensions of living with both a state and a God. As subjects of both worldly and heavenly kingdoms, Christians have a special balancing act to perform. This has been noted across the Christian era; Augustine spoke of the difference between the earthly city and the city of God, and Martin Luther noted that believers have a paradoxical tension between their responsibilities in the two kingdoms.[2]

Pastoral Perspective

know if Jesus participates in the custom; they are wondering, "Is he one of us?"

That is a question people get asked all the time. When the Democratic Party or the Republican Party or the Green Party calls asking for financial support, are they not asking, "Are you one of us?" When your alma mater calls to solicit your support for the annual fund, are they not asking, "Are you one of us?" When we stand and sing the national anthem, are we not singing to proclaim that we belong to our country? When we pass legislation regulating immigration, are we not making decisions about who gets to be one of us? The question is aimed at finding out what Jesus' priorities are. When the collectors of the temple tax ask Peter whether Jesus pays his tax, they are asking about Jesus' loyalty.

Today loyalty is a dying phenomenon. People are not loyal to their workplace; loyalty would be naive in a world where companies no longer provide job security to their employees. People are not loyal to brand names; in a time of economic difficulty, they tend to purchase whatever is most cost efficient. People are not loyal to denominations; most mainline denominations are in decline. People today are not even necessarily loyal to their spouses; almost half of marriages now end in divorce.

As personal loyalty declines, organizations that in the past benefited from loyal patrons seem to be working harder to capture the allegiance of anyone who will take notice. Schools, companies, organizations, and churches all compete for our attention. One market research firm estimates that "a person living in a city thirty years ago saw up to 2,000 ad messages a day, compared with up to 5,000 today."[1] Maybe the barrage of messages aimed at influencing where we spend our money or our time has turned people off enough that they have given up on the idea of loyalty.

The only place today where loyalty seems commonplace is when someone is talking about their favorite sports team, their hometown, or their pet. In the workplace, with political parties, and with organizations and companies that ask for our money, there is distrust. How can we be sure you will not betray us by laying us off from our job, by taking our contribution for your political campaign only to commit the next political scandal, by convincing us to spend money on your product only to have it break soon after we buy it? People have to make

2. The Theological Declaration of Barmen Declaration, in *The Constitution of the Presbyterian Church: Part I, The Book of Confessions* (Louisville, KY: The Office of the General Assembly, 2004), 8.23, 250; Reinhold Niebuhr, *Leaves from the Notebook of a Tamed Cynic* (1929; repr., Louisville, KY: Westminster John Knox, 1990), 19–22; Augustine, *The City of God*, trans. Marcus Dods (New York: Random House, 1950); Martin Luther, "Temporal Authority: To What Extent It Should Be Obeyed," in *Luther's Works* (Philadelphia: Fortress Press, 1962), 45:81–129.

1. Louise Story, "Anywhere the Eye Can See, It's Likely to See an Ad," *New York Times*, January 15, 2007; retrieved from http://www.nytimes.com, April 21, 2012.

Feasting on the Gospels

regular tax. When it became obligatory is uncertain, but there are good reasons to believe it dated from the time of Alexandra Salome[1] (78–69 BCE). The Essenes did not collect or pay the tax. The destruction of the temple in 70 CE, of course, ended it as a requirement. The Romans replaced it with the *fiscus Iudaicus*, which was not optional. Contrary to the conjecture of some scholars, the emperor Nerva (98–107) did not abolish the tax. Composing his Gospel after the destruction of the temple, Matthew would not have included the story to encourage Christians to pay the temple tax, but he may have inserted it to encourage them to pay the obligatory *fiscus Iudaicus*. Nonpayment could get them into serious trouble with Roman officials.

The story features two scenes: between tax collectors and Peter (vv. 24–25a) and between Jesus and Peter in the house (vv. 25b–27). Had Peter not already given the tax collectors a positive answer, the pericope could have ended at verse 26, which seems to suggest that Jesus had a negative attitude toward the tax. So the fish story served to make the pericope a unit. Nevertheless, reliance on this kind of ATM to pay taxes makes us wonder whether Jesus and the disciples had such limited funds that he needed a small miracle to show his respect for the temple. The tax collectors sounded skeptical as they approached Peter to ask about Jesus' taxpaying habit. "Does your teacher not pay the temple tax?" They doubtless had solicited people who refused to pay, especially if it remained unsettled whether they had to pay. In Galilee they probably encountered many of that stripe. With a mixed population, less religious and more remote from Jerusalem, Galilee did not provide the best conditions for collecting the tax.

Presuming on his intimate connection with his teacher, Peter answered with a simple and straightforward yes. As he entered the house, however, Jesus, presumably by foreknowledge rather than supersonic hearing, picked up the tax issue with a tangential question, an approach frequently witnessed in his debates, for example, about tribute to Caesar (Matt. 22:15–22; Mark 12:13–17; Luke 20:20–26): "From whom do the kings of the earth take toll or tribute? From their children or from others [strangers]?"[2]

both ironically and humorously when he invited Peter, in the words of a well-known legend, to seek his funds in a fish.

Local tax collectors visit Peter, meeting him outside his home in Capernaum. It is apparent there are hidden motives in this visit. It is not Peter they have come seeking, but rather the perceived head of the group he affiliates with: Jesus. They wish to know if Jesus has paid the tax, to which Peter answers simply, "Yes."

The second layer of this episode unfolds as Jesus, who has obviously overheard the exchange outside, questions Peter. Jesus asks a familiar question: who should pay taxes? His analogy suggests that the sons of kings do not pay their fathers' taxes; only the citizens and strangers do. When Peter agrees with Jesus that the sons do not pay, Jesus responds that "the sons are free."

What is not obvious to anyone except Jesus is that *he* is a true son of God's house and therefore free from worldly obligations. Jesus knows, however, that expressing such a self-understanding will be greeted with derision. It will be viewed as an arrogant and blasphemous excuse for not paying the required tax. Using the tax question to argue for his divine identity will be the wrong issue for the wrong time and circumstances. Jesus thus wisely instructs Peter to pay the tax. What is unusual is the *way* he tells Peter to pay the tax; Peter should do what he always does: Peter should go fishing.

The end of this conversation does not offer evidence that any such miracle of finding money actually occurs. Peter is not described as either doing what Jesus tells him or returning to the disciples with the money. In fact, one scholar notes the folktale history behind Jesus' command to find the needed tax in the belly of a fish: "the most famous [story] is the recovery of Polycrates' ring (Herodotus 3.41–42), but there are similar Jewish stories. . . . Such a background in popular folktales makes it questionable whether Jesus would have issued such instructions in all seriousness."[1] Jesus was perhaps indulging in humor in the fanciful, semidesperate way many people do when it comes to paying taxes: Let us see what is buried in the backyard! Maybe I will win the lottery!

Jesus' direction to Peter, however, is prefaced by something that is very serious, and focused on Jesus' priority of maintaining the mission to proclaim God's good news. Jesus understands that enabling mission to move forward is more important than picking peripheral battles, which might jeopardize what he

1. Alexandra Salome was the wife of the Hasmonean kings Aristobulus I and Alexander Jannaeus and the mother of the high priest John Hyrcanus II and Aristobulus II, a pretender to the throne. On Alexander Jannaeus's death in 78 BCE, she took control of Jerusalem, crowned herself queen, and appointed her son John Hyrcanus high priest.

2. The word *allotriōn* can also be translated "strangers." The nuance of the question seems to favor a contrast between children of the rulers and persons not related to them.

1. D. T. France, *The Gospel of Matthew* (Grand Rapids: Eerdmans, 2007), 671.

Matthew 17:24–27

Theological Perspective

Kingdoms and nations have desired that first allegiance for themselves, whether in fusing the role of the Holy Roman Empire and the church, or in declaring that America is a nation under God to differentiate between it and the godless communists.

Jesus' comment clarifies the relationship for believers. First, believers must note that he does not attempt some form of religious commonwealth that denies the state. To avoid offense, he pays the tax. At the same time, he assures his disciple that the children are free. Christian freedom is briefly suggested here. This is not the whole of the doctrine of Christian freedom, which Martin Luther would so thoroughly portray in his treatise of that name, a doctrine that illustrates how Christ's grace received through faith frees the Christian from the impossible task of earning salvation. There is a corollary: the state or realm has no claim upon the believer's allegiance to God.

Thus, when kingdoms or nations claim to take up the mantle of the work of God, they not only fall short of the glory of the kingdom of God; they also act in an idolatrous manner. The state can never be the true and holy commonwealth. The Christian must therefore live as a resident alien, a person whose true citizenship is held by another lord. Bernard of Clairvaux called this earthly life that of the person who lived in the region of dissimilitude, a place where we do not truly fit.[3] The Christian can pay the tax but can never allow the power of the state to blind him or her to the true allegiance and worship owed to the true sovereign, Christ the Lord.

R. WARD HOLDER

Pastoral Perspective

careful choices about where to place their loyalty. Read in this light, Jesus' answer to the temple-tax collectors is particularly poignant.

The collectors of the temple tax want to know about Jesus' loyalty: "Does your teacher not pay the temple tax?" (v. 24). In talking with Peter about their question, Jesus shifts the conversation from a question of who is in and who is out to a matter of spiritual loyalty. Jesus implies that his loyalty is to God, not necessarily to the temple institution. For those who have decided that the church is not for them, that they are "spiritual but not religious," this text seems to provide justification. That is a real challenge for the contemporary church, as it declines in numbers and relevance and worries about its future.

Even so, Jesus offers a clear reminder that loyalty is not about blind devotion or playing by the rules. It is about making choices, choices about what is most important, about where to put your trust, your time, your resources, your energy, your imagination, your whole self. There are a lot of organizations, a lot of product lines, a lot of sports teams, that work hard to gain the allegiance of as many people as possible, that work hard to win the time and the resources of as many people as they can. However, as Jesus reminds Peter, "the children are free" (v. 26) from the "kings of the earth" (v. 25).

This is good news that the church is called to proclaim. Perhaps the church can grasp that news and make it the next big marketing campaign: You are free to live for God. So thank goodness that loyalty to employers is down. Thank goodness that loyalty to brand names is declining. Because there is only one place for loyalty, and that is with God.

KATE FOSTER CONNORS

---

3. Martin Luther, "The Freedom of a Christian," in *Martin Luther: Selections from His Writings*, ed. John Dillenberger (New York: Anchor, 1962), 42–85. Bernard of Clairvaux, *On the Song of Songs*, trans. Kilian Walsh (Kalamazoo: Cistercian Publications, 1971), 178–79.

Feasting on the Gospels

(v. 25). Although familiar with his teacher's dialectic, Peter must have wondered, "What has that got to do with the temple tax?" Still, he replied. "From others [strangers]" (v. 26). Rulers did not tax their children; they taxed persons outside their own households.

To this, Jesus responded, "Then the children are free" (v. 26). "Children" could be construed in different ways. Does Jesus mean Jesus himself as the one who knows God intimately? He certainly had a strong filial consciousness (Matt. 11:25–27; Luke 10:21–22) that let him correct Moses (Matt. 19:7–8). Does he mean Israelites as God's elect not bound by human legislation? As "children," Jesus and Peter did not have a binding obligation to pay. They would pay, however, to avoid a ruckus. According to Matthew's understanding, Jesus knew already at this point some criticisms hurled in his direction for sitting loose in relation to Judaism's two most basic institutions, the law and the temple. In the Sermon on the Mount, Matthew had Jesus give assurance about the law (5:17–20): he came "not to abolish but to fulfill." Here he had Jesus prescribe something like an acted parable offering assurance about the temple.

The directive is terse and to the point: "Go to the sea and cast a hook; take the first fish that comes up; and when you open its mouth, you will find a coin [*statēr*]. Take that and give it to them for you and me" (v. 27). Nothing miraculous in that, although the operation might seem like a little miracle! In Matthew's view Jesus would possess more-than-human ESP so as to know what Peter had said to the tax collectors and that his directive would supply him and Peter with the money they needed to pay the tax. As astonishing as it seems to us, numerous ancient legends told of finding a jewel or coin in a fish's mouth. In this case the Greek *statēr* provided exactly the double-drachma the temple tax called for. To Christians of Matthew's day, the story said, "Pay the *fiscus Iudaicus*. It is not a big deal!"

E. GLENN HINSON

and his disciples are doing. This is reflected in his words to Peter in verse 27: "However, so that we do not give offense to them . . ." Jesus is willing to pay the tax. How that happens is not answered in this passage, although the tax itself was not a minor amount.

Today more than ever, there are many public debates over taxes of all kinds. Taxes are natural territory in one sense for all of humanity. Taxes pay the bills of a society or a group. While many churches and denominations assess members to support mission work today, those assessments are not necessarily measures of any given mission's importance. Taxes can never be levied in any real or justifiable sense on the gift of the gospel. Jesus is attempting to demonstrate that paying the temple tax cannot reflect the larger spiritual reality to which Jesus is pointing. This reality is that God's gifts are free of conditions.

This passage raises two related issues: paying taxes and doing God's mission. Are the taxes just? Who is levying them and for what reasons? What would happen to the rest of life if one did not pay the required taxes? Are any daily demands impinging inappropriately on mission? Something is quietly and subtly emerging in this passage. Behind Jesus' words and ideas is a growing challenge to the old structures of worship that his gospel is addressing. When Jesus talks about the tax with Peter, he is stating a paradox. Taxes should be paid for the temple's upkeep for the time being, but Jesus is also hinting at a new reality to come, one that will be tax free and reembodied in the person of the risen Lord Jesus Christ! Not only is the temple system itself on the brink of destruction and replacement, but the replacement will come through the life, ministry, death, and resurrection of Jesus himself. He will be the new temple. Ultimate and unconditional freedom is found in Jesus himself, free of charge.

SUSAN K. HEDAHL

Matthew 18:1–11

¹At that time the disciples came to Jesus and asked, "Who is the greatest in the kingdom of heaven?" ²He called a child, whom he put among them, ³and said, "Truly I tell you, unless you change and become like children, you will never enter the kingdom of heaven. ⁴Whoever becomes humble like this child is the greatest in the kingdom of heaven. ⁵Whoever welcomes one such child in my name welcomes me.

⁶"If any of you put a stumbling block before one of these little ones who believe in me, it would be better for you if a great millstone were fastened around your neck and you were drowned in the depth of the sea. ⁷Woe to the world because of stumbling blocks! Occasions for stumbling are bound to come, but woe to the one by whom the stumbling block comes!

⁸"If your hand or your foot causes you to stumble, cut it off and throw it away; it is better for you to enter life maimed or lame than to have two hands or two feet and to be thrown into the eternal fire. ⁹And if your eye causes you to stumble, tear it out and throw it away; it is better for you to enter life with one eye than to have two eyes and to be thrown into the hell of fire.

¹⁰"Take care that you do not despise one of these little ones; for, I tell, you, in heaven their angels continually see the face of my Father in heaven." [¹¹For the Son of Man came to save the lost.]

Theological Perspective

This passage begins with the disciples questioning Jesus about the ranks of those in the kingdom of heaven. Perhaps it is simply impossible for humans to avoid the will to power that is inherent in the question. Certainly that was the point Reinhold Niebuhr was trying to convey with his idea of sin as a will to power and the anxiety that accompanied that sin. While Valerie Saiving's cautions about overgeneralizing from the experience of men without the leavening experience of women are crucial to finding a better discussion of the human predicament, her work is not without problems of its own. First, Saiving suggested that there was a social norming that perhaps was stronger in her construction than it was in reality. Second, it can be argued that Saiving's ideal of the feminine sin that was not a will to power but self-abnegation represents a competition for the most virtuous sin.[1] While that may seem absurd, can it be any more absurd than the disciples coming to their Lord and servant and asserting their priority in the kingdom of heaven?

In the sixteenth century John Calvin wrote about the human desire to outstrip the other and noted how this tendency knew no bounds. He examined

1. Reinhold Niebuhr, *The Nature and Destiny of Man: A Christian Interpretation* (Louisville, KY: Westminster John Knox Press, 1996); Valerie Saiving, "The Human Situation: A Feminine View," *Journal of Religion* 40 (1960): 100–112.

Pastoral Perspective

There are times when we need to be confronted head-on in order to grow, times when we cannot see clearly, when we are stuck seeing things one way, when our world needs to expand so we are able to see things from other vantage points. In those times, we can be grateful for the teachers in our lives who notice that we need to grow and who push us to see things in a new way.

It must have been the disciples' question that gave them away: "Who is the greatest in the kingdom of heaven?" (v. 1). The question betrays a desire for Jesus to confirm that they are important. It is a question many parents have heard as their children, fueled by healthy rivalry with siblings, grapple with their place in the family and their significance to their parents: "Whom do you love the most?" As would most parents, Jesus sees through their insecurity. Jesus could have just talked to the disciples about children. He could have told them a story about children. Instead, "he called a child, whom he put among them" (v. 2).

Just as he has called each of his disciples, Jesus calls a child, and puts the child among them. In Jesus' time, children had very low social status; so to put a child in the midst of any group of adults would be uncomfortable for the adults. The text does not tell us anything about the child—how old,

Exegetical Perspective

Matthew 18:1–11 belongs to the community discourse of 18:1–35. Jesus addressed the message to the disciples or to Peter as representative of the disciples. Scholars have described the theme as church order, rules for God's household, or kinship in the church.

Verses 1–5 establish the fundamental principle of unself-conscious humility. "At that time" connects this unit with the preceding one. As in 13:36 and 24:3, the disciples came to Jesus and posed a question that became the point of departure for the longer discourse. Matthew omitted the dispute among the disciples in Mark and had them frame a larger question about basic principles: "Who is the greatest in the kingdom of heaven?"

As so often, Jesus did the unexpected. He used a child as a parable (vv. 2–3). He demanded a fundamental change in his disciples—that they become like little children. The Greek word *paidion* that Matthew used in this account is a diminutive of *pais*. *Pais* means "child," but it was used frequently to mean "servant." Jesus was himself the *pais theou*, "servant of God" (12:18, citing Isa. 42:1). Unless they changed and became like little children, they could not expect to enter the kingdom.

Through the centuries interpreters have debated what childlikeness means. Both Mark and Luke left

Homiletical Perspective

This passage is sure to provoke anxiety and attention in many listeners. It refers to three very significant and potentially painful issues: the care and status of children, the reality of hell, and the treatment people afford one another in the church. Jesus' words tie all three matters together, yielding several implications for Christian discipleship. In his responses, the church is warned against living in his community without regard for others. The mood of this passage is sharp, even severe. Jesus does not mince words about consequences for inappropriate ethical behavior.

In preparing this passage, preachers need to observe the following. First, the reference to children in this passage is divided into two sections: verses 1–5 and verses 6–10 (many manuscripts omit v. 11). In the first section, Jesus is responding to a question from a disciple about what constitutes "greatness." Jesus uses his own visual aid to help the disciples understand his answer. He calls a child over and tells them: this is who is "great." Here Jesus' reference to children is literal and explicit.

In verses 6–10, however, "child" and "little ones" shift to *all people* who have come to believe in Jesus, particularly those—like children—who are vulnerable, innocent, and easily manipulated. Believers who disdain such as these are sinning against them and against God, whose kingdom is reflective of

Matthew 18:1–11

Theological Perspective

the phenomenon in terms of scrupulous asceticism and noted that, even in this case, self-denial for the Lord or religion can be a slippery slope. Commenting upon this tendency, Calvin wrote that one might begin with teetotaling, the avoidance of wine. Eventually humans would push this scruple to the point that one "will not dare touch water if sweeter and cleaner than other water."[2] People seem unable to stop comparing themselves to each other, to find that advantage, even if in a distant future.

To stop this tendency, Jesus placed a child before the disciples as the true example of humility. Children cannot plan far enough ahead to use humility for grandiose ends. Children accept the grace that is given them and the gifts that Jesus offers. There is an old saying that claims the one-eyed man is king in the land of the blind. The proverb attempts to illustrate that different realms value different gifts. Jesus claimed that the highest value in the kingdom of heaven is that of simplicity and acceptance of the divine gifts. He then identified himself with these, much as he did in the parable of the Great Judgment (25:31–46).

The passage then seems to change from the consideration of who would be greatest in the kingdom of heaven toward a discussion of those things that the disciples and other believers should avoid so as to reach heaven. However, the passage makes more sense if all of verses 6–9 is understood as Jesus giving further explanation about treatment of those who are childlike in their simplicity and humility. These little ones must be protected more than one's own freedom, as Paul states in 1 Corinthians 8:13.

Verses 6–9 concern the obstacles disciples put in front of childlike believers. The history of Christianity is replete with such obstacles, whether human institutions that religious authorities have required of believers, as if they were revealed articles of faith necessary for salvation, or discussions of erudite theology that led away from the simplicity of the gospel. (My personal favorite was the discussion in the fourteenth century about whether God could have made it the case that believers would merit salvation for hating God. At least one theologian believed that God could have done that.) Even in the biblical period, Paul had to fight the Galatians for their desire to keep the works of the law as a way of ensuring their holiness, instructing them that Christian freedom rested on Christ rather than observance of any law, even holy laws.

2. John Calvin, *Institutes of the Christian Religion*, ed. John T. McNeill, trans. Ford Lewis Battles, LCC (Philadelphia: Westminster Press, 1960), 3.19.7.

Pastoral Perspective

whether he or she stands still and quiet, or whether the child has a conversation with the disciples. In a way, it does not matter what happens between the child and the disciples. What matters is what Jesus *does* to make his point. He puts a small, dependent child in the middle of grown-up, self-important disciples. Jesus puts a child, who is considered lowly, in the midst of adults, who consider themselves more important. When it is embodied, an idea is hard to ignore.

Jesus knows the disciples well by this point, and he probably knows they need to be confronted with something that will be hard for them to discount, something that will be concrete, right in front of them, that will help them see in a new way. It will be difficult to ignore a child, especially if that child is young and squirmy and needy and right in their midst. There are times when God knows we need to be confronted in order to grow, times when God puts people right in our midst who make us uncomfortable, who challenge us to offer the kind of welcome that Jesus was teaching his disciples about.

A church I know was focusing on learning how to be a more inclusive community. As part of this effort, the congregation planned an adult education class about how to welcome people with disabilities. Over the course of the class, church members talked about physical barriers at the church that hindered the access of people with disabilities, and particularly wrestled with the fact that the nineteenth-century building had no elevator, which meant that some of the third-floor youth Sunday school classrooms were inaccessible. A month later, a teenager in a wheelchair visited the church and was interested in getting involved with the youth program. The idea of being a welcoming church, so easy to discuss in an adult class, had suddenly become a real challenge about how to be inclusive. Soon after, the congregation—forced to engage quickly with what it means to welcome someone with a disability—moved the high school Sunday school room to an accessible space and made adjustments to the youth programs to make them more inclusive.

When the congregation was merely *talking about* welcoming people with disabilities, the idea of welcome could remain an abstract idea, something the church was open to, but an idea that might become a reality sometime in the future. When *a real person* showed up, though, when Jesus called the boy in the wheelchair and put him in their midst, the idea of welcome had to become the reality of welcome. It was not easy for this congregation to welcome

that query unanswered, but Matthew did not leave in doubt his interpretation. "Whoever becomes humble like this little child is the greatest in the kingdom of heaven" (v. 4). In his woes against the Pharisees, Matthew had Jesus reinforce the perception, with emphasis on the other model of humility, the servant: "The greatest among you will be your servant [*diakonos*]. All who exalt themselves will be humbled, and all who humble themselves will be exalted" (23:11–12).

Verse 5 is loosely related to what goes before it, an aside: "Whoever welcomes one such child in my name welcomes me." Accepting the humble establishes Christian identity. In verses 6–9 Jesus issued a warning against the snares or stumbling blocks (*skandala*) that might trip up the humble. The verb *skandalizō*, "cause to stumble," connected the four sayings. Matthew used it elsewhere in connection with rejection of Jesus (11:6; 13:57; 15:12; 26:31, 33) and apostasy (13:21; 24:10). In this passage Jesus spoke of leading into apostasy Christians, as "those who believe in me" would imply. In Matthew, apostasy entails not only embracing false doctrine but also doing deeds not corresponding to the will of God (7:21–23). Seducing people to sin has such drastic consequences that the seducer should be drowned in the depth of the seas with a giant millstone tied around his or her neck. Both Jews and Greeks used this method of punishing terrible crimes, but they considered it especially barbaric.

Jesus referred here to the upper millstone (*mylos onikos*), usually made of basalt, turned by an ass (*onikos*). It had the shape of a double funnel and served as the hopper into which the miller poured grain. The lower funnel rested on a cone-shaped stone. When the upper stone turned, it ground the grain. Matthew found the phrase "one of these little ones" in Mark 9:42. He used the term a number of times (10:42; 18:6, 10, 14; 25:40, 45). It was not a fixed designation for Christians, and it is difficult to say if "these little ones" were a particular group in the church or all members. The contrasting of "little ones" with prophets and the righteous in 10:42 suggests that they were ordinary Christians not included in those special groups. Readers of Matthew's Gospel would probably associate them with the humble of 18:3–4. Ulrich Luz concludes, "The expression is thus a programmatic shorthand for what Christians are and should be." They may have no significance in the world's eyes, but they are of great importance in God's. All Christians, therefore, would fit the category of "little ones" insofar as "they

such people. Jesus employs hyperbolic language to describe the fate of those who sin against the "little ones." He uses a second image from his day—a millstone—to make his point. Examples of millstones may still be seen in Israel and Palestine today and in other agrarian cultures. The millstone, often pulled by a donkey or ox, is enormous. A stone a hundredth of its size would be sufficient to drown anyone.

Jesus' description of such a punishment for those who mislead others underscores how seriously he views sins against the fragile of this world. In verse 7a Jesus makes clear that indeed bad things do happen to good people (however innocent) in the world. In verse 7b, though, he sharply admonishes those followers who knowingly act as causes of sin for others. While the former is always a possibility, there is no excuse for believers acting negatively.

"Who is great in the kingdom of heaven?" is further pursued in terms of how seriously people are willing to deal with their sin. The innocent are part of the kingdom, but what of those who sin against them? Verses 8–9 show Jesus introducing a third image—that of "eternal fire" and "the hell of fire"—to emphasize steps believers must take to avoid sin. Here Jesus again uses hyperbolic language to show that changing lifestyles and actions might involve acting radically to ensure avoidance of sin.

It is important for the preacher to remark on the fact that the words "stumbling" and "stumbling block" are used *six times* in verses 6–9. Indeed, Jesus is aware of the inevitability of sin, but simultaneously he urges his followers knowingly to seek means to avoid it and warns of the consequences for those who do not. Jesus is not, however, simply telling the disciples to avoid sin. He is calling them to a greater goal so that they can "enter life" (vv. 8, 9). What is at stake relates back to the original question posed by the disciples in verses 1–5: who has entrance into the kingdom of heaven?

This section concludes with yet another admonishment tied to a third image. Jesus warns listeners not to disdain the "little ones," because they are represented in heaven by "their angels." Lest the mention of angels devolve into something inane, such as discussion of so-called guardian angels, it is important for the proclaimer to point out that Jesus means God's vulnerable ones *already* have their portion in heaven in some fashion. They are represented by one of the powers attendant on God, namely, angels.

The demands of this text are obvious and strenuous, and Jesus' words raise several familiar issues. He is clear that believers are responsible for one

Matthew 18:1–11

Theological Perspective

Of course, believers have not only sought to bind the consciences and lives of the simple, but have also sought to bind themselves. This effort always demonstrates some effort to find the human key to heaven. Humans never tire of attempting to find what level of asceticism, spiritual exercise, self-denial, or even self-punishment would attract the Lord's favor. Such was even the basis of Western monasticism, *The Rule of St. Benedict*, which proclaimed that following the rule was the path to heaven.[3]

The point is not to argue that efforts to lead the holy life that the Scriptures require are wrongheaded (see Rom. 12:2). However, the all-too-human tendency is to take the effort to live within the boundaries that the Lord sets for believers as helps to avoid occasions for sin, and to mistake such rules for the basis of the Christian life and the path to salvation. Jesus recognized that tendency in his disciples, and placed before them the simplicity and authenticity of children—children who would simply accept the love and care that was offered.

The passage ends with the concern to protect the childlike innocence of these and to avoid leading them astray. This theme of concern both to avoid the straining after preferment and to avoid leading the truly humble astray comes again to clarify the structure of the argument. While the Son of Man has come to save the lost, clearly some are becoming lost through the example of the leaders, whether in the leaders' desire to grasp the honors in the kingdom, or their teaching to those who are truly coming to the Lord as children. Jesus' point, that the child's humility is the greatest gift, represents his own remedy to the human tendency to grasp after tawdry gain.

R. WARD HOLDER

Pastoral Perspective

someone who had a significant disability, someone whose mind was sharp but whose body required substantial assistance to move around, to go to the bathroom, to eat meals. Being a welcoming community of faith has required a lot of energy, creativity, flexibility, and commitment in that church. It has forced the congregation to see their facility and their programs through a completely different lens, one that now includes what it is like to live with a disability.

It also has brought in the extraordinary gifts of intellect and humor, of courage and determination, that the young man has contributed to the life of the youth group and the congregation. It has not been easy, but there have been many blessings, and the congregation has expanded its understanding of what it means to be the community of those who follow Jesus. Now the congregation can see that it needed to grow in its understanding of what it means to be inclusive. The congregation can see that it needed to be confronted with a concrete challenge to the idea of welcome it had discussed in the adult class.

Jesus tells the disciples, "Whoever welcomes one such child in my name welcomes me." Whoever welcomes the most unlikely person welcomes Jesus. To be the church, to call ourselves followers of Jesus, means welcoming the people Jesus called into the places where he ate and worshiped and lived. Jesus always put himself with the people the world most wanted to leave behind. It sounds as though that is what he wants his disciples to do too. Those who want to follow Jesus can be on the lookout for those whom Jesus has called into their midst, always looking for ways to offer welcome. For whoever welcomes the one Jesus calls and puts right in front of us, the one who makes us uncomfortable, the one who is despised, the one who is difficult to include, welcomes Jesus.

KATE FOSTER CONNORS

3. *Rule of St. Benedict in English*, ed. Timothy Fry, OSB (Collegeville, MN: Liturgical Press, 1982), 17.

Exegetical Perspective

affirm their insignificance and practice it as humility and love."[1]

In using the term "little ones" three times in the discourse (vv. 6, 10, 14), Jesus called on his disciples to think small. They should want *not* to be great (20:25–26), rabbis, fathers, or masters (23:8–10). They should be like children. Because the little ones are great in God's eyes, causing them to fall is an awful sin.

To whom was verse 6 addressed then? The words were likely a comfort to readers who thought of themselves as "little ones." Those who lead them astray will come to a horrible end. Verse 7 would seem to confirm this. In Matthew, *skandala* always refers to persons. These should be expected, because evil will prevail in the last days before the Son of Man comes; but woe to the seducers!

According to Matthew, Jesus knew no distinctions regarding sins and left no middle ground. He featured an ethical severity based on the unconditional will of God, as expressed in the antitheses of the Sermon on the Mount. Matthew wanted to shake up Christians by confronting them with the severity of the last days.

In verses 8–9 Matthew followed Mark in issuing a warning to members of the church likely to be seduced. Although repeating the warning of 5:29–30 about severing a hand and plucking out an eye, he applied it differently. Where 5:29–30 warned about sexual seduction, 18:8–9 challenged "little ones" to avoid all contact with people who want to destroy their faith. Whereas 5:29–30 paralleled rabbinic warnings, this text came closer to Hellenistic exhortations that compare radical separation, from bad friends or from evil in general, to physicians who may have to amputate parts of the body.

It is not easy to fit this section into the rest of chapter 18. How does it relate to the lowliness of verses 3–4 or to what follows? It does not comport well with the image of seeking lost sheep (18:12–14) or forgiving seventy-seven times (18:21–22). Verse 10 may serve, therefore, as a sort of transition statement, one more shot across the bow on behalf of "little ones." The best manuscripts of Matthew 18 do not include verse 11, "for the Son of Man came to save the lost."

E. GLENN HINSON

Homiletical Perspective

another. They are to employ ethical means in their dealings with one other and to offer special care for those who are vulnerable, because it is God's will that they do so. Matthew's text is directed to a growing church struggling with the typical competitive issues of who is in or out: who is great? Although not directly stated here, what is implicit in this passage is the issue of leadership, not simply participation. The disciples' question about the ordering of individuals is not without merit. Jesus has already predicted he will be removed from their presence through death. Without the physical presence and leadership of Jesus, who leads? It is a normal question in all worship communities.

Jesus indicates he is aware of how easy it is for those in positions of leadership to use their power to create injustice in a community by manipulating and deceiving others. The "little ones" need not be mentally or physically challenged in any way (although such do exist in most communities). They may simply be those who are knowingly locked out of resources, knowledge, and power by those who seek earthly power for themselves alone in the church.

Taking radical means to curb and avoid sin in a believing community that cares about the "little ones" also raises another potential direction for proclaiming this text. How seriously do today's Christians take church discipline in situations in which people are hurting one another? Most congregations have some form of ecclesial process that attempts to curb sin and resolve conflicts. The directives in verses 8–9 show that, indeed, radical steps might have to be taken to restore a community to peace and protect the vulnerable. Jesus does not shy away from bluntly telling believers that true faith commitment also means radical choices to maintain both individual and corporate life in Christian assemblies as a true foretaste of God's kingdom of heaven.

SUSAN K. HEDAHL

---

1. Ulrich Luz, *Matthew 8–20: A Commentary* (Minneapolis: Fortress Press, 2001), 434.

Matthew 18:12–22

12"What do you think? If a shepherd has a hundred sheep, and one of them has gone astray, does he not leave the ninety-nine on the mountains and go in search of the one that went astray? 13And if he finds it, truly I tell you, he rejoices over it more than over the ninety-nine that never went astray. 14So it is not the will of your Father in heaven that one of these little ones should be lost.

15"If another member of the church sins against you, go and point out the fault when the two of you are alone. If the member listens to you, you have regained that one. 16But if you are not listened to, take one or two others along with you, so that every word may be confirmed by the evidence of two or three witnesses. 17If the member refuses to listen to them, tell it to the church; and if the offender refuses to listen even to the church, let such a one be to you as a Gentile and a tax collector. 18Truly I tell you, whatever you bind on earth will be bound in heaven, and whatever you loose on earth will be loosed in heaven. 19Again, truly I tell you, if two of you agree on earth about anything you ask, it will be done for you by my Father in heaven. 20For where two or three are gathered in my name, I am there among them."

21Then Peter came and said to him, "Lord, if another member of the church sins against me, how often should I forgive? As many as seven times?" 22Jesus said to him, "Not seven times, but, I tell you, seventy-seven times."

Theological Perspective

Behavior Becoming God's Kin. The mission of Jesus, carried on by his disciples after his death on the cross, was to establish the kingdom of God. Jesus' kingdom is in stark contrast to Rome's. While the Roman Empire depended on military might to control and dominate, Jesus' kingdom centers on love and justice, having as its goal to become the family of God. To live according to Jesus' message in the face of the strict controls the Romans had over the Jewish population was demanding. Verses 12–22 exhort the community to care for each other, no matter what.

The Good Shepherd parable employs the metaphor of sheep and shepherd used throughout the history of Israel; its use could well indicate that Jesus' followers thought of themselves, as did all Jewish people, as the people of God. The disciples of Jesus, just like the sheep, could go astray; it would be surprising if they did not. What is surprising is the willingness of the shepherd, not only to put himself at risk, but also to risk ninety-nine sheep to save one. Verse 14 summarizes the teaching of this pericope: not a single person should be lost; no one is expendable; each one is worthy of being pursued to the point of risking everything. The rejoicing when the lost sheep is found emphasizes this point—even if, in a way, it minimizes the faithfulness of the ninety-nine.

Pastoral Perspective

The Galilean ministry is finished, and Jesus is at home. In the next chapter, Jesus begins the trip to Jerusalem and the cross. In the important time between the public ministry and the journey to Golgotha, Matthew records Jesus' teaching about how the church ought to behave. At first glance, it might seem a bit trivial. In just a few chapters our hearts will start racing, as the story of the crucifixion begins to unfold, but for now, Jesus is at home sounding like Dear Abby. Jesus talks about how to care for even one church member, what to do if conflict arises, and the lengths to which forgiveness should be extended.

In the first section of this teaching, Jesus underscores an important Matthean theme and speaks of the pastoral call to attend to "the least of these" (25:40). In Matthew, Jesus has come as the fulfillment of the prophetic hope. In his Galilean ministry he has been teaching about the big theme of the kingdom of heaven, and the coming passion narrative will conclude: "All authority in heaven and on earth has been given to me. Go therefore and make disciples of all nations" (28:18–19a). Yet within the enormous scope of his teaching and ministry, there are always individual people with names and faces. The one who leaves the ninety-nine, the two who are fussing at church, the church member who "sins

Exegetical Perspective

How wonderful is it that Jesus begins, not by laying down the law or dictating divine truths, but by asking, "What do you think?" Those who first heard Jesus were not accustomed to being asked for their thoughts—they were poor nobodies who scraped by—and Jesus honors them by asking, "What do you think?" Not only does he honor them; he invites them in as participants in the holy reflection on the ways of God in the world. Jesus never lays down seven or a dozen nonnegotiable rules for living; he tells a story, opens a window, and asks what his listeners think.

His arresting image is that of a shepherd, someone whom people of status would have looked down on. However, the Israelites had always been poor and relied on sheep for survival, and they were not inclined to despise lowly status. An average, respectable flock would be about a hundred, but this shepherd is not concerned to keep the size respectable. He is attached to all the sheep, and his listeners would have known what it felt like to be just one more, disposable, forgettable. The picture Jesus paints of the shepherd who cannot bear to lose even one would have surprised, comforted, and emboldened each in the crowd.

Interestingly, Matthew and Luke use Jesus' story of the one lost sheep for different purposes, which is

Homiletical Perspective

Rejoicing over the One (vv. 12–14). In the context of celebration, the opening verses of this text break open God's amazing grace. In a pastoral context, they offer the preacher a gentle way to lead those who feel as though their actions, or the vicissitudes of life, have led them astray from the fold of God. When the context calls for challenge, the passage asks members of a congregation to decide where they are in relationship to the Good Shepherd.

Many congregants may find initial fascination with the image of being the one lost sheep sought after by the Lord. Yet the text makes demands upon us as Christians by forcing us out of this comfort zone. Is it not also possible that we have become the ninety-nine left behind? Perhaps, as Christ's gathered body here on earth, we should stop waiting for our shepherd to find us, and instead join him in his search for "these little ones" (v. 14).

Some congregants may find themselves resistant to the notion that so many are left behind for the sake of finding just one. There is also the challenge of understanding why the shepherd rejoices more over the one "than over the ninety-nine that never went astray" (v. 13).

Giving sound historical background to this difficult text may contribute to a sermon wherein a congregation can hear the passage challenge them to

Matthew 18:12–22

Theological Perspective

By referring to the community of Jesus' followers as the "little ones," verse 14 indicates that Matthew's community was in danger. Why? Although they continued to be observant Jews, its members had a different religious practice and a different way of life, which certainly meant that they left much to be desired as Roman subjects. Jesus counterposed the will of God to the will of the emperor, and it was the will of God that was to rule the life of the community. It is this different way of life that makes present and operative God's will that all are to be saved. This verse is a commandment from God to the community: the community must be like the shepherd who risks it all to save each and every one. God's will is to be done by the disciples "on earth as it is in heaven" (6:10). This parable of the Good Shepherd, then, more than anything else, admonishes the community how to behave toward each other.

The second part of this reading addresses what Jesus' followers ought to do when one of the members sins, causing division and hurting the community. The community, not being perfect, grapples with what to do when one of its members goes astray, keeping in mind obviously what Jesus had taught and how he had conducted himself. Being the family of God, the kin-dom of God, the community understands sin as the breaking of the relationship between brothers and sisters (v. 15).[1]

When this happens, the community must attempt reconciliation, no matter what the cost. Those offended are to act like the good shepherd, who goes after the lost sheep. If the offending person "listens"—that is, if the person understands how she has broken the family ties and is willing to change her behavior—reconciliation is possible. More than one attempt needs to be made to bring about reconciliation. Perhaps if several members of the community talk to the offender, she might reconsider her behavior and the divisions caused in the community will be healed. What if all attempts fail?

The community is never to give up; it must always continue to seek reconciliation. If the community's attitude is reconciliation, then it is not the community that is responsible for the offender's being excluded. If he is not willing to change, the offender excludes himself. The call to treat him as a Gentile or a tax collector is not a call to exclude him permanently; after all, Jesus ate with Gentiles and tax

---

1. For a full explanation of the followers of Jesus as the family of God, the "kin-dom" of God, see Ada María Isasi-Díaz, "Kin-dom of God—A *Mujerista* Proposal," in Benjamin Valentin, ed., *In Our Own Voices: Latino Renditions of Theology* (Maryknoll, NY: Orbis Books, 2010), 171–90.

Pastoral Perspective

against me"—all are at the center of Jesus' personal ministry.

I was once part of a group that went to spend the day with the pastor of a large and vibrant Presbyterian church in our city. One of the guests asked the pastor, "What is the secret to growing a big church?" The pastor answered, "If you want to get big, you must learn to think small." He went on to say that the leadership of his church was continually asking questions like, "What is the full experience of a single mother with a ten-year-old and a toddler who arrives at our church on Sunday morning? Does she know where to park? Is there help for her when it is raining? Does she know where she is supposed to go and how to get her children to the right places?" He explained to us that his leadership had adopted a disciplined approach of thinking small.

This might have been mostly about church growth; however, it may be that he was cultivating an important gospel theme. The story of the shepherd with a hundred sheep calls every church to think smaller. How do we assure that we do not get so caught up in the big ideas of our church and community that we fail to meet the ministry needs of the one? How do we adopt a pastoral sensitivity that personalizes the gospel for individual persons?

"If another member of the church sins against you, go and point out the fault when the two of you are alone" (v. 15a). Can you just imagine what your church would look like if every member took this vow? What if conflict were contained to the smallest possible circle with a hope for resolution and treated as an opportunity to build up rather than tear down?

At lunch with several work colleagues, I said a careless word about another minister. After returning from lunch, one of my lunch mates came to my office and confronted me. His coming to see me, one on one, was an act of Christian maturity. He risked my response because he cared enough about me to push me toward more careful speech. His response to me could not have been easy for him. He used conflict as a way to build me up, not tear me down. If he had gone to someone else's office that afternoon and talked about me and taken the easy course, his actions would have diminished me in the same way that my carelessness diminished our mutual friend. His mature response modeled the principle of this passage. By speaking truth, containing the conflict, and loving me enough to confront me, he strengthened the body of Christ rather than eroding it.

While Jesus' teaching about conflict may seem, at first blush, a small matter in the larger themes of

a problem only if you take a narrow, cynical view of Jesus' teachings. Surely he told a story expecting it to be heard in unique ways. In Luke 15:3–7, the lost sheep is the sinner needing salvation, but in Matthew 18:12–14, the lost is the one from within the church who has strayed from the body.

In whatever context Jesus' parable of the Diligent Shepherd occurs, it is all about grace. The *Gospel of Thomas* reiterates the same story but adds that the lost one is "the largest." As Joachim Jeremias clarifies, "it was not the high value of the animal that caused the shepherd to set out on his search, but simply the fact that it belonged to him, and without his help it could not find its way back to the flock."[1] The lost sheep may have been scrawny or—if we think about life within the congregation—one that was especially annoying or difficult. Yet we are to seek the one who is estranged and tirelessly to pursue reconciliation.

How far-fetched Jesus' process may seem to us! Typically, if someone offends us, we boil with rage, we talk to somebody else or quit the church. Jesus lays out a path toward healing, not just an Oh-it-doesn't–matter kind of patching things up, but a candid confrontation in which two people deal with what has split them apart. The Essenes utilized a similar process: private reproof, then a small group, then the whole community.

Bringing wrongdoers to repentance is fraught with peril. Concern for and exposure of someone's sin might be nothing more than a pious veneer masking anger, vested interests, or petty agendas. No wonder Christians have not done this sort of thing for a long time: the potential for abuse, shame, and harm is great. Craig Keener says, "Professing Christians never repudiated by the church have perpetrated many evils throughout history, bringing shame to the body of Christ."[2] However, such occurrences are overshadowed by the nasty habit, which the church has justified by this very text, of abusing, belittling, and even killing their fellow faithful.

Jesus' process is not designed to get rid of anybody. Jesus is not establishing principles of inquisition but instilling a mood of serious commitment to keep strong arms around every member of the community. The church has always had its lapsed members; Augustine tried to settle the controversy once and for all by debunking the Donatists, who saw no path back for those whose faith had failed. Like Alcoholics Anonymous, we are to combine firmness

protect the helpless, encourage the offended to seek pastoral help, and urge offenders to seek reconciliation. Even so, it should be emphasized that such challenge ought not be approached in a flat-footed way that makes mission and evangelism into a salvo to the guilty middle-class soul. Who are the little ones that we are willing and ready to recognize as such? Who are the little ones that we would rather ignore, allowing them to wander off while we look the other way?

Pointing Out the Fault (vv. 15–20). This passage is unique to Matthew, presenting procedural material as part of the extended teaching of the Messiah. Its detailed description of how members of the church should confront offending members may not only be difficult to hear; it can also be misused when it is put into practice.

Healthy communities have boundaries that, when respected, ensure that all parties feel welcome and safe. Refusing to set solid and proper boundaries in the name of "the gospel of being nice" allows bullies to stay in control and vulnerable people to be hurt. At the same time, some congregants may be too eager to put this passage to "good use" by turning it against someone whom they have been waiting to confront. While it may prove difficult or pastorally inappropriate to make a direct analogy between this passage and a concrete situation in the congregation, it may still be possible for the preacher to focus the sermon on the helpful and unhelpful ways that church people set boundaries and deal with conflict.

It is more likely, however, that many in the congregation will find the notion of rebuking or shunning another human to be a dangerous or at least an uncomfortable suggestion. In this case it may be important to emphasize the importance of setting boundaries for safety. While we are committed to welcoming all people, this commitment does not include neglecting those who may be harmed if we allow unacceptable behavior. There may also be individual Christians in the congregation who believe that they are called to martyrdom in this life, but this does not obligate the rest of us to accept that call on their behalf.

This passage has traditionally been associated with the church's discipline of excommunication, or what many Protestant traditions called the ban. With regard to enforcing the ban, it is important to provide some historical context for how first-century Galileans and Judeans viewed tax collectors and Gentiles before making too swift an analogy with a

---

1. Joachim Jeremias, *The Parables of Jesus* (New York: Scribners, 1972), 134.
2. Craig S. Keener, *Matthew* (Downers Grove, IL: InterVarsity Press, 1997), 289.

Matthew 18:12–22

Theological Perspective

collectors and sinners. So considering the offender to be like one of them is not a call so shun him, but a call to reach out to him. The community must continue in its efforts to make reconciliation a reality.

The third part of this reading makes clear that "the missioning, reconciling, and praying community of disciples committed to Jesus is the place of Jesus' presence, represented by and encountered in these acts."[2] It is a bold claim, since insistence on effecting reconciliation mirrors God's way of acting. God ratifies the decisions of the community. Verses 18–20 make clear that the community, as a community, is responsible for deciding what is the right conduct of the members of the kin-dom of God: "whatever you bind on earth will be bound in heaven, and whatever you loose on earth will be loosed in heaven" (v. 18). God sanctions the decision made by the whole family through which God is present in the world (vv. 19–20). It is daring to assert that God, in the person of Jesus, is in the midst of this community, one that is inclusive and forgiving, rather than one that controls and executes its offenders.

This pericope ends by once more emphasizing how to deal with a community member who has committed an offense. This ending verse does not focus on the offender but on the behavior of the offended community. The community is called to be always the good shepherd.

"Be perfect, . . . as your heavenly Father is perfect" (5:48) forthrightly proclaims that the community has to model its behavior on God's behavior. The attitudes and behaviors that Jesus expects of his disciples, therefore, are modeled on who God is and how God behaves. The God of Jesus and his disciples is a forgiving God, a reconciling God, and a God that will do all that is possible to save each and every one.

ADA MARÍA ISASI-DÍAZ

Pastoral Perspective

Matthew, there have been few things as damaging to the Christian witness or as destructive to Christ's church as escalated conflict. Again, how would your church look different if every member took a vow to live by the principle of Matthew 18:15?

There seems to be a progression in the intimacy and difficulty of the three sections of verses 12–22. The first call is to care for the lost sheep, the furthest from our experience and arguably the easiest of the three ways the church needs to act. If we fail at this, people who live on the edge of life are hurt the most. Next, Jesus introduces the difficult principle of contained conflict that calls on mature Christians to disagree in ways that build up rather than tear down. If we fail at this, it is the witness of the church that is hurt the most. The final appeal of Jesus is the most personal and the most difficult. We are to forgive, "Not seven times, but, I tell you, seventy-seven times" (v. 22). If we fail at this hardest command, it is our most intimate relationships and ourselves that are hurt the most.

We could make the case that the church of Jesus Christ has suffered from not thinking big enough and bold enough. We could also make the case, however, that Jesus is calling us in this chapter of Matthew's Gospel to think smaller. If we continue to give pastoral attention to the small matters of church life, then the weeds of discord will not strangle the growth of God's kingdom (see 13:7). We have a pastoral challenge to think small enough to chase down the lost sheep, small enough to confront each other in private so that conflict does not become toxic and damage the larger congregation, and small enough to extend and accept forgiveness for personal transgressions.

DOCK HOLLINGSWORTH

---

2. Warren Carter, *Matthew and the Margins: A Socio-Political and Religious Reading* (London: T. & T. Clark, 2004), 369.

Exegetical Perspective

and grace. With Jesus' process, if excommunication happens, it is the one outside who insists on being outside.

How odd then that Jesus says, "Let such a one be to you as a Gentile and a tax collector" (v. 17). Does he mean the way they were accustomed to treating Gentiles and tax collectors, with contempt? No, for Jesus had a great love for tax collectors and Gentiles!

The stakes are eternal when we deal with the lost member. Whatever is "bound" or "loosed" on earth will be "bound" or "loosed" in heaven. Our own ultimate forgiveness is tied up with whether or not we forgive others. Matthew also seems to imply that God delegates the judgment process to us down here. When Jesus says that if two agree, it is God's will, and that when two or three gather, God is there, Jesus is not fixing the threshold for a quorum or declaring that God answers prayer. Rather, God seems to trust the wisdom of the people who are striving faithfully to discern what should be done for the life of the church. Therefore that wisdom can be trusted by members of the church.

What a responsibility! Moreover, the promise is that leaders of the church can count on God's guidance. The method, after all, is not majority rule. Those who enter into the bonds of the family of God expect nothing less than holiness, humble prayerfulness, patient kindness, and grace. Forgiveness, not expulsion or punishment, is the way of the followers of Christ.

Are there limits to forgiveness? Jesus surprisingly supplies a number after which we need no longer forgive. Start counting, each time you forgive, and when you get to seventy-seven (as the NRSV translates it; the RSV renders it as seventy *times* seven, which is also possible), you need not forgive any longer. The huge number had to elicit a chuckle or two, and we laugh at ourselves as much as anyone, realizing that there simply is no end to forgiving. We can be thankful that God has forgiven us. How many times? Seventy-seven? Seventy times seven? Seventy-seven times four hundred ninety?

JAMES C. HOWELL

Homiletical Perspective

contemporary Christian congregation. The point of Matthew's teaching on the subject is not to encourage those in power to look down on those who are out of power. On the contrary, the point is to see "Gentiles and tax collectors" as outsiders who might yet be welcomed into the church as disciples.

The preacher might link this passage about the offending member back to the Sermon on the Mount in general (chaps. 5–7) and in particular to the passage concerning the offering of gifts (5:23–26). In the case of offering one's gifts upon the altar, the question to ask is not "Who has offended me?" but "Whom have I offended?" That places a different spin on the passage under examination here. When members voluntarily submit to examination, that makes the passage less about confrontation and more about discipleship. Perhaps this passage is not so much a call to conflict management as it is a call to discipleship.

As we become aware of ourselves as individuals, we can gain the strength to be aware of ourselves as a community. As a community, how have we offended in the past, and how are we offending now? In what way does our complacency or comfort keep us from seeing our faults? On the other hand, in what ways might we be part of a community that has been offended? Is it time to take this to the offending party? How do we do so out of mutual love rather than retaliation?

Discerning whether or not one has been harmed, and then determining how and whether to set an appropriate boundary, is not something either an offended party or an offender can do alone. Discernment of an issue requires a broader community, so that no one is either inappropriately shamed or inappropriately excused. The church needs its members and its pastors in order for all of its members to live into their ministries of reconciliation in their reconciling Lord.

NATHAN JENNINGS

Matthew 18:23–35

²³"For this reason the kingdom of heaven may be compared to a king who wished to settle accounts with his slaves. ²⁴When he began the reckoning, one who owed him ten thousand talents was brought to him; ²⁵and, as he could not pay, his lord ordered him to be sold, together with his wife and children and all his possessions, and payment to be made. ²⁶So the slave fell on his knees before him, saying, 'Have patience with me, and I will pay you everything.' ²⁷And out of pity for him, the lord of that slave released him and forgave him the debt. ²⁸But that same slave, as he went out, came upon one of his fellow slaves who owed him a hundred denarii; and seizing him by the throat, he said, 'Pay what you owe.' ²⁹Then his fellow slave fell down and pleaded with him, 'Have patience with me, and I will pay you.' ³⁰But he refused; then he went and threw him into prison until he would pay the debt. ³¹When his fellow slaves saw what had happened, they were greatly distressed, and they went and reported to their lord all that had taken place. ³²Then his lord summoned him and said to him, 'You wicked slave! I forgave you all that debt because you pleaded with me. ³³Should you not have had mercy on your fellow slave, as I had mercy on you?' ³⁴And in anger his lord handed him over to be tortured until he would pay his entire debt. ³⁵So my heavenly Father will also do to every one of you, if you do not forgive your brother or sister from your heart."

Theological Perspective

This pericope is instruction about behavior expected of Jesus' followers. It makes clear how they must not behave. They must not hold a grudge; they must not seek revenge; they must not require compensation or redress. The proper behavior is to seek out the offender and bring him or her back into the fold. The behavior of the community must reflect what happens in heaven (Matt. 6:10). Jesus' followers are to be followers of Jesus, not admirers of Jesus. Admirers praise and proclaim the wonders of those who hold their attention and imagination, but followers concentrate on taking to heart and imitating the behavior of Jesus, continuing his mission to make the kin-dom of God a reality.[1]

Followers of Jesus organize their values according to the principles presented in the Gospels: justice and peace (*shalom*), that is, fullness of life. Jesus' disciples are to judge what is good and right (grace) and what is evil and wrong (sin) according to the teachings of Jesus exemplified in his life. Reconciliation was fundamental to the message and mission of Jesus; Matthew 18 focuses precisely on bringing back into the family of God those who have gone astray.

1. For an explanation of the followers of Jesus as the "kin-dom" of God, see Ada María Isasi-Díaz, "Kin-dom of God: A *Mujerista* Proposal," in Benjamin Valentin, ed., *In Our Own Voices: Latino Renditions of Theology* (Maryknoll, NY: Orbis Books, 2010), 171–90.

Pastoral Perspective

It is a funny parable. The characters and amounts of money are so absurd. A servant owes a king ten thousand talents (a talent is equal to about fifteen years' pay for a laborer). It is all so laughable until the end of the parable, where it moves a great distance from silly and ends with jail and a flurry of words like "distressed," "wicked," and "anger." We laugh our way into the parable until the story catches us in our betrayal.

The pastoral implications for this parable are both systemic and personal. The pastor can read this as an indictment of corporate greed and systems that continue to forgive major societal excess and exploitation while condemning small offenders. It can also be read as a devotional reading that leads the individual believer toward deeper gratitude for the size of God's grace and the pettiness of our response.

The bizarre debt amounts in this parable cause our imaginations to move quickly to governmental and corporate excess. Besides, who else has fifteen years' salary 10,000 times over? Once, when I was teaching this parable to a Wednesday night Bible study group at church, I asked the group to explore practical and contemporary implications of the parable. One of the men said, "I think I'm going to send a copy of this parable to GMAC. When the government gave GMAC sixteen billion dollars to bail them

Exegetical Perspective

It is astonishing to realize how much of Jesus' teaching has to do with debt. Obviously, in Roman Palestine, debt was a very real, agonizing, often brutal reality. Forms were not mailed from the Roman Revenue Service, but strong men who could break your knees showed up and demanded payment. The unfairness of it all, the desperate craving for mercy, proved to be Jesus' best window into the hearts of his listeners when he was trying to talk about divine and human forgiveness.

In verses 23–35, Jesus compares the kingdom to the most absurd debt collection scenario imaginable. A certain king (we see again how Jesus made up stories to depict the heart of God) decided it was time to settle accounts, and one man owed him 10,000 talents. There is simply no way to translate this into modern dollars, as it is an absurd, laughable amount. The talent (and we should remember this when we read the story in 25:14–30 of those who used or hid their talents) was the largest denomination of money in the ancient world. We can reckon 10,000 talents as roughly 100 million days' wages for the average worker. One hundred million days? Josephus reports that the total tax for all Judeans combined in a year was only 600 talents.[1] This lone individual,

1. *Antiquities* 17.11.4, cited in Donald Wagner, *Matthew 14–28* (Nashville: Word, 1995), 538.

Homiletical Perspective

Much of the material in Matthew 18 appears also in the other Synoptic Gospels, but Matthew's arrangement of it is unique, and this parable occurs nowhere else. It is a rich text to preach, because the parable demands forgiveness of others and of ourselves. Jesus teaches the practice of forgiveness as our acceptance of God's forgiveness.

The sheer amount of debt the slave owes is surprising. Another surprise that can often be overlooked is the way the king forgives the slave's debt so easily. This surprising ease of forgiveness is often overlooked because, of course, rhetorically the point is to concentrate on the way in which the slave will go on to interact with his fellow slave after receiving this miraculous debt relief. Nevertheless, it might serve the homily well to point out the amazing ease with which the king grants forgiveness.

Congregants less familiar with the parable may be shocked by the slave's lack of forgiveness toward his fellow slave. It may also be very difficult for some of them to hear the king renege on his forgiveness of the slave when he learns of the slave's own lack of forgiveness. This parable does not mesh well with a gospel of a "nice" God. Some may hear the ending as merciless. Furthermore, and a bit more concretely, many contemporary Westerners experience debt not merely as a political problem but as a lived, personal

Matthew 18:23–35

Theological Perspective

It is important to notice that the focus is not just on forgiveness as a private matter, but on reconciliation—bringing back into the fold those who have strayed. Each and every member of the kin-dom of God has to be a good shepherd, willing to take risks to find and return to the family those who have become strangers.

The parable of the Unmerciful Servant makes this point about reconciliation from a different perspective than that found earlier in Matthew 6:12. The focus here is on what will happen to those who do not show mercy, who do not forgive, who are not agents of reconciliation. This pericope does not contradict what has been said, but it does have a different emphasis. It is impossible to reconcile the behavior of the master in this parable with what Jesus has said in the immediately preceding verses concerning forgiving seventy-seven times (18:22). This parable does not exhort repeated forgiveness. "Not only does the king not forgive repeatedly; he takes back the forgiveness already offered when the servant fails to forgive just one."[2]

The emphasis is not on the attitude and behavior of the master but on the actions of the servant and on the consequences of such actions. The parable makes clear that the servant is held responsible for what he does and for the consequences of his actions. The master's understanding of human weakness and his being merciful do not trump personal responsibility. The servant is held responsible for what he does, because the mercy of his master does not supplant or in any way diminish the responsibility of the servant for his behavior. Were the servant to choose to follow the master's lead and be understanding and merciful with others, he would be rewarded. However, since he chooses not to imitate the master's way of acting, he has no one to blame but himself for what befalls him. He brings upon himself a terrible punishment; it is done to him as he has done to others, as the Lord's Prayer indicates: "forgive us our debts, as we also have forgiven our debtors" (6:12).

In this parable, the master should not be in any way demonized. The punishment the servant receives is not because the master is evil or intransigent or because he wants to get even. Getting even is not the point of this parable; if it were, it would indeed contradict Matthew's immediately preceding

Pastoral Perspective

out, it seems like the least they could do was forgive the $11,000 I still owe on my Buick." We laughed, of course, but it was a painful sort of laughter.

The parable has hints of the biblical year of jubilee, when all debts are forgiven and all prisoners are set free (Lev. 25:8–12; Isa. 61:1–11). We know that it is not likely that our banks will forgive our debts or our prisons will open their gates. This parable might speak an important word, however, to two systems that are crippling our society. The race and class discrepancies in indebtedness and in the prison population raise serious pastoral concerns. This may invite the pastor to consider how the church can respond to the debt and incarceration crises in our culture.

One of the parable's absurdities is that the servant who did not forgive his fellow servant who owed him a hundred denarii (about a hundred days' wages) had him thrown into prison until he could pay the debt. Of course people in prison do not have a way to earn the wages needed to pay off indebtedness. The forgiven servant will never get satisfaction for the debt, and the imprisoned servant will remain in prison, unable to produce wages. United States governmental data in 2010 estimates that it takes about $25,500 a year to house, feed, protect, guard, and provide medical attention for each federal inmate and $26,000 for each state prisoner. If nonviolent offenders were released on parole, it would cost $2,800 per year, and $1,300 if they were on probation.[1] In both cases, they could work and pay into the tax system. If in prison, they cannot pay their debts. Instead, and ironically, the taxes now paid by the people they owe are what sustain them. At the end of the parable, the king has the servant with outrageous debt thrown into prison too. Of course now he too has no way to earn. One way to deal pastorally with this parable is to look for absurdities in our own system and to raise awareness about systemic justice issues.

One way to avoid the sting of this parable is to deflect the attention to the superrich and powerful and to rail against systemic injustice, and never let the story shine its light on us. While this parable may have systemic implications, it also has a personal and devotional dimension that intends to catch us in our own pettiness. It is too easy to forget that the king is the one who did the gracious thing. In this parable, the most powerful person was also

---

2. Warren Carter, *Matthew and the Margins: A Socio-Political and Religious Reading* (London: T. & T. Clark, 2004), 370.

1. John Schmitt, Kris Warner, and Sarika Gupta, "The High Budgetary Cost of Incarceration" (Washington, DC: Center for Economic and Policy Research, 2010), 11.

as Jesus tells the story, owes the king more money than was actually in circulation in Judea at the time! How could one get in such a hole? Why does the king allow so much debt to accumulate before this reckoning?

Why does Jesus use such hilarious, impossibly extravagant hyperbole? Partly he wants to undercut, in advance, any counterarguments—like, if someone owed four talents and it was forgiven, then what about someone who owed six? No one could ever, ever owe 10,000 talents. Jesus also wants to astonish his listeners with the immense largesse in the heart of God. How much can be forgiven? Not manageable, believable amounts of sin, but any, all, no matter how high the mountain, no matter how awful the infractions.

Some writers have suggested that Jesus taught effectively because he used down-to-earth, practical, understandable metaphors from life on the farm, among animals, within families; but in most of Jesus' stories there is something that would make first-century listeners roar with laughter or raise their eyebrows because of the crazy hyperbole. The king, once the man quite obviously cannot pay, is offered an initial plan for redress that is just as ludicrous as the debt itself: sell the debtor into slavery to repay the 10,000 talents! The most expensive slave on record from Roman times would have gone for just a single talent, while the average slave's price would have been a mere fraction of that.[2] The debt would still be astronomical. So why not just go ahead and cancel the debt?

Where Jesus transports his audience next is, if anything, even more outlandish than the notion of a single man accumulating more debt than the entire nation had in its pockets. The forgiven slave is himself owed a microscopically small sum, and yet he shows no mercy after being forgiven a zillion times the amount himself! The crowd would chuckle, to be sure, and then perhaps realize that Jesus was underlining what God might expect of us. How much do I owe God? I owe God plenty, an incalculably large amount, for the grief I have laid on the heart of God, by my sin, by simply ignoring God, by my failure to do and be what God wants me to be. I also owe God that much and even more for all the benefits, for God's immense goodness in huge and quite small ways, every day throughout my life and the life of the world.

How is such a debt to be repaid? It cannot be; we only fling ourselves on the mercy of God, and when

problem. Many in the congregation may be in debt, even severe debt. In order to guide the congregation beyond an initial resistance to the text, place the passage in its broader historical, Matthean, canonical, and worship contexts.

In its historical context, this passage witnesses to Jesus' messianic proclamation of the jubilee age. When sins are forgiven and debts released, it is hard to enjoy the kingdom of heaven while still holding on to the obligations of others, real or imagined. For a community grounded in forgiveness, witnessing to the jubilee proclaimed in Jesus challenges the powers and principalities of this age, which often justify their regimes with a promise of this-worldly "justice."

It may be hard for some to hear the demand to forgive in this passage, especially if they misunderstand forgiveness to mean accepting unacceptable behavior. Verses 21–22 provide a context for the teaching, setting up the parable that follows as a narrative answer to Peter's questions. One thrust for the preacher could be to remind listeners that even those who seek genuine reconciliation should expect to deal with human beings who will continue to suffer from the same bad habits that led them to poor behavior in the first place. This passage invites reflection on a realistic anthropology that includes the persistence of sin. In that context, the passage demands that we be more forgiving of others, and of ourselves as well.

The preacher could bring in the Lord's Prayer (6:9–13). In our most common and familiar prayer as Christians, we pray what this parable is demanding of us. The Lord's Prayer links forgiveness of others with God's forgiveness of us: "forgive us our debts, as we also have forgiven our debtors." Another way to provide context for this pericope and aid the congregation in hearing the gospel in it would be to bring the wider canon into dialogue with this passage. The preacher could connect the message of forgiveness in this parable with Paul's "ministry of reconciliation" in 2 Corinthians 5:16–21. Jesus' own ministry, especially as unfolded in the paschal mystery, involves the members of his body in reconciliation.

In a worship context where there will be a formal or corporate confession of sin, the preacher might relate the parable to confession and absolution (or the declaration of forgiveness) in Christ. Our ritual reception of Christ's forgiveness becomes real for us only when we forgive others, which links the parable to the Sermon on the Mount (Matt. 5–7, esp. 5:23–26). It is our responsibility as Christians not

2. Joachim Jeremias, *The Parables of Jesus* (New York: Scribners, 1972), 211.

Matthew 18:23–35

Theological Perspective

insistence on the obligation to forgive again and again and again. Verse 35, however, does introduce a reversal from what Jesus' teachings about God have led one to expect: God will indeed act the way this master has acted with the servant, if Jesus' disciples do not forgive one another. God's mercy does not erase personal responsibility for one's actions.

Verse 35 summarizes the chapter's intention to teach the disciples that they are God's family and must behave accordingly, seeking to be reconciled. Reconciliation is not a formality but must be from the heart, which is "the core of a person, the center of a person's willing, thinking, knowing, deciding, and doing self."[3] This is especially true within a family, which is the way the followers of Jesus are presented here: "if your brother or sister sins . . ." (v. 15). It is not the master of the parable who is the one in charge but "my heavenly Father." The head of this family is a loving parent who holds the kin of God accountable for their actions. Since God is the patriarch of this family, God's behavior of mercy and forgiveness is paradigmatic. God's mercy and forgiveness are even more than paradigmatic; they are a transforming power, what in religious language is called God's grace (v. 19).

The parable teaches that God's grace is not a magician's trick; grace will not operate if it is not embraced wholeheartedly. A direct connection exists between God's preoccupation with saving each and every one (18:10–14) and the behavior that is demanded of the family of God. The behavior in the kin-dom of God must make obvious who God is and what God is like.

ADA MARÍA ISASI-DÍAZ

Pastoral Perspective

the most forgiving and the most gracious. The judgment was pronounced on the servant who remained ungracious.

The second pastoral consideration is the very personal challenge that asks us all to consider the size of our gratitude in response to the blessings given to us. Economics aside, each of us has been the recipient of God's constant favor and forgiveness. Each of us has known God's steadfast love in the face of our regular betrayal. Not one of us hopes we are judged on the ledger of our own goodness in response to God's abundant gifts. As a matter of personal devotion, this parable asks us to consider the liberality of our own forgiveness and generosity in light of God's favor to us. While we all have power structures to whom we are accountable, we also have people who depend on us or owe us. How we exert our power over the less powerful is a serious matter of Christian maturity.

If we read this parable against the backdrop of the pericope before it, we might be led to consider how our response to being forgiven has made us more forgiving. "Seventy times seven" is certainly the forgiveness we have received from God. Like the debt numbers in this parable, we have been recipients of grace in amounts that we can hardly count. If we do not forgive the minor transgressions of our human experience in light of the outrageous abundance of the way we have been forgiven, we are at risk of being convicted alongside the servant. We are being called to a liberal forgiveness.

DOCK HOLLINGSWORTH

3. Ibid., 375.

it comes, we humbly give thanks and praise and unstinting service. We also look at any forgiveness required of us, from anyone who has hurt or caused our little worlds to shiver, and we forgive. Jesus' classic, simple prayer teaches us the daunting petition: "Forgive us our debts, as we also have forgiven our debtors" (6:12). We ask God to forgive us with the measure with which we have forgiven others. The man in Jesus' parable cannot pray this prayer for a single moment. Can we?

W. D. Davies and Dale Allison doubt that the amount of the debt in the story is original. Since it is such a preposterous amount, they speculate that the amount of the debt, when Jesus first told the tale, was perhaps 10,000 denarii (not talents, but still a gargantuan sum, decades of wages). In their minds, it might have been Matthew himself who expanded things and substituted talents for denarii.[3] Perhaps, although the theological edge goes to whoever thought of substituting talents for denarii, and we ascribe the daring theological brilliance to Jesus, not his biographer. Either way, massive, unpayable debt is remitted, but then the one who is so stunningly and undeservedly off the hook cannot find a way to relieve the tiny bit owed him. Such is human nature, but Jesus would have it otherwise.

Failure to forgive is not just bad form or something God frowns upon. Failure to forgive is failure to be like God; failure to forgive digs out a massive gulf between us and God. If we take Jesus seriously, the parable is not merely saying that God wishes we would be a little better. In this parable, the king sends the unforgiving debtor for torture. Jews did not practice torture, but the Romans did. Jews listening must have been flabbergasted that Jesus would suggest such a thing, but his searing demand for forgiveness, his tender invitation to forgiveness, was so very serious that he pressed the limits to underline the awful consequences of the unwillingness to forgive.

JAMES C. HOWELL

just to forgive those we believe have harmed us, but also to seek forgiveness from those we believe that we have harmed.

In order to preach the passage with image and story beyond strict analogies, it may prove helpful to take the time to rehearse the story again, in your sermon or homily, very carefully. There is a lot going on in this short parable that might be lost when it is read aloud only once. Draw out the irony of the parable. Use the tension inherent in the parable itself to strengthen the rhetoric of your own homily. Draw out the shock felt by the fellow slave when he is not forgiven.

Help the congregation to experience the passage by imagining a similar situation in contexts more familiar to them. When have we needed forgiveness? When have we been refused forgiveness? Whom are we begrudging it even now? Are we in debt? What would it feel like to be freed from the burden of so great a debt? Forgiveness is at the heart of Jesus' gospel. Guide the congregation to its challenge and its gift.

A sermon on this pericope could take a narrative form, making use of a local-contextual retelling. It could take the form of a classic expository sermon, giving solid exegetical and historical background to the existential demand at its conclusion. It could also focus more on Jesus' own preaching, asking what problem his teaching addresses. How does our congregation share this problem? How is Jesus addressing our problem through this text today?

The text demands that we forgive others and that we forgive ourselves. It demands not simply that Jesus' disciples be forgiving people, but that they constitute a community of forgiveness. The deeper demand of the text is to forgive others *as our acceptance* of God's forgiveness. It is not so much that God's forgiveness is contingent upon our forgiving others as that our forgiveness of others *performs our acceptance* of God's forgiveness. Without that performance, how can we enjoy the gift we have been given? Enjoying a gift as truly *gift* means sharing that gift with others.

NATHAN JENNINGS

3. W. D. Davies and Dale C. Allison, *A Critical and Exegetical Commentary on the Gospel according to St. Matthew 8-18* (Edinburgh: T. & T. Clark, 1991), 2:197–98.

Matthew 19:1–12

[1]When Jesus had finished saying these things, he left Galilee and went to the region of Judea beyond the Jordan. [2]Large crowds followed him, and he cured them there.

[3]Some Pharisees came to him, and to test him they asked, "Is it lawful for a man to divorce his wife for any cause?" [4]He answered, "Have you not read that the one who made them at the beginning 'made them male and female,' [5]and said, 'For this reason a man shall leave his father and mother and be joined to his wife, and the two shall become one flesh'? [6]So they are no longer two, but one flesh. Therefore what God has joined together, let no one separate." [7]They said to him, "Why then did Moses command us to give a certificate of dismissal

Theological Perspective

We should not gloss over the second verse of this passage, where Matthew points out that Jesus continued with his ministry of healing, even when the focus of the story that follows is teaching. Jesus' preoccupation with the bodily or material well-being of people does not take second place to his teaching about the kin-dom of God.[1] The importance Jesus gave to healing makes clear that the human person cannot be split into body and something else. The teaching of the Bible leaves no doubt that at the core of what the church is and does must be the physical well-being of the community.

This pericope presents a discussion Jesus has with the Pharisees that shows them, the religious elite of Jesus' world, questioning Jesus' authority and resisting his ministry. Jesus uses the incident to instruct his followers about the values, attitudes, and behaviors that are expected of them as members of the kin-dom, or family, of God.

This text leaves no doubt that the Pharisees are testing Jesus, trying to catch him with a trick question. It should also leave no doubt that Jesus uses the question posed by the Pharisees to resist the

1. For a full explanation of the use of "kin-dom" instead of "kingdom," see Ada María Isasi-Díaz, "Kin-dom of God: A *Mujerista* Proposal," in Benjamin Valentin, ed., *In Our Own Voices: Latino Renditions of Theology* (Maryknoll, NY: Orbis Books, 2010), 171–90.

Pastoral Perspective

The ministry in Galilee is finished. Jesus is on his way to Judea and is stopped by the Pharisees to be tested about the issue of divorce. Where were they when Jesus was teaching the disciples and the crowd (5:31–32)? Jesus has already weighed in on his thoughts about divorce, but the Pharisees are not satisfied. While it is clear that most Pharisees of Jesus' day were sincere searchers after truth, the Scripture is direct in saying that this small group came to test Jesus, not to learn from him. They are trying to trick Jesus about loopholes in the law or about making deals with God. While Jesus sets a high standard and takes a hard line on divorce, those testing him are looking for ways to circumvent the high demands.

Our current church situation demands that we deal with at least three pastoral issues in this teaching. First, how do we take the countercultural, high demand of Jesus' teaching seriously without becoming irrelevant literalists with regard to divorce? Second, we must shape our own pastoral response to a church that includes many divorced persons who want to be full citizens within their faith community. Finally, we should explore whether this might be a continuation of Jesus' teaching with regard to the care and protection of the powerless.

There is a tension in this story. Jesus has posted God's ideal starkly, "Therefore what God has joined

and to divorce her?" [8]He said to them, "It was because you were so hard-hearted that Moses allowed you to divorce your wives, but from the beginning it was not so. [9]And I say to you, whoever divorces his wife, except for unchastity, and marries another commits adultery."

[10]His disciples said to him, "If such is the case of a man with his wife, it is better not to marry." [11]But he said to them, "Not everyone can accept this teaching, but only those to whom it is given. [12]For there are eunuchs who have been so from birth, and there are eunuchs who have been made eunuchs by others, and there are eunuchs who have made themselves eunuchs for the sake of the kingdom of heaven. Let anyone accept this who can."

Exegetical Perspective

In our day, a delicate artfulness is required for us to say anything theological about divorce. This was no less so in Jesus' day. Jesus does not seem worried that his listeners will be annoyed with the strength of his position; and he is still full of love and hopefulness, which they must have sensed.

Before we consider Jesus' position, we need to attend to the vast differences between marriage in the first century and marriage in our own day. While we have romantic notions of weddings and anniversaries, visions of fulfillment and inner angst, in antiquity people married quite young (by the middle teenage years) and out of necessity. There was virtually no privacy, as people lived with extended family and within a couple of feet of their neighbors; there were no careers or date nights. Husband and wife labored hard all day long just to survive, fell asleep exhausted at day's end, and got up the next morning to toil for a little bread and meager shelter. So divorce was not the end game, after twists and turns in the relationship and months of counseling; divorce was not the result of one partner's search for greater happiness. Divorce was generally the result of bad moral behavior. Women often were the losers, as it was generally the husband who had the right to initiate divorce. Women were victims—and in the face of belittlement and abuse had not one legal leg to stand on.

Homiletical Perspective

Looking at the brokenness of culture and family with a pastoral eye and tone may be the preacher's best approach to this text. Many families in the contemporary Western world have been broken or affected by divorce. Passages concerning divorce may be hard for some in a congregation to hear. This text requires gentle handling by the preacher. There is nevertheless no need to deny or smooth over the difficult demands of Jesus' gospel represented within a pericope such as this one. In fact, exactly because so many have been adversely affected by divorce, it does little good to dismiss or condone divorce. People know it to be an evil, either because of guilt or shame or because of a broken family of origin. Instead of quoting statistics (congregants are not numbers in a chart) or decrying a corrupt culture, this passage may demand a word of comfort to those hurt by divorce. The preacher of this text need not condone divorce in choosing to comfort those adversely affected by it.

Although this seemingly strict teaching concerning divorce appears in the other Synoptic Gospels, only in Matthew do we receive a record of the disciples' reaction. The disciples show surprise at the difficulty of this teaching in their own day: a difficulty many in our congregation may feel—for different reasons of course—in our day. In their historical

Matthew 19:1–12

Theological Perspective

patriarchal view of marriage common in the Greco-Roman world. Matthew 19 continues the teaching that has been going on in previous chapters about how the community ought to behave, concentrating here on how it should organize itself as a household and how its members are to deal with one another.

The household in antiquity was considered, as it is today, the basic unit of the city or kingdom. It revolved around three relationships—husband-wife, father-children, master-slave—and the task of the father/husband/master as head of the household was to earn wealth and increase honor for the whole family. The household was hierarchical; the male held all the power and ruled over the rest. The point of the teaching of Jesus here is precisely to subvert this hierarchical order and to set up an egalitarian one. The husband is not to rule over the wife but, rather, is to become "one flesh" with her, creating a mutual relationship.

This teaching about loving egalitarian relationships is one of the main markers of the kin-dom of God. The other one, which is interrelated with love, is justice. The early Christians were known precisely by the love they had for one another: "See how they love one another," is the well-known phrase reported by Tertullian as a way of identifying Jesus' followers.[2] The household of Jesus' followers was run differently from the norm. Jesus' disciples indeed lived "a marginal existence, as societal participants yet as outsiders, over against dominant societal values."[3]

In Acts 4:32–35 the way a household in the family of God functioned is laid out very specifically. They obviously had a process for discussing important matters, for they not only loved each other but also were of one mind (4:32). This love for one another meant that there were no needy persons among them (4:34–35). Given the clarity of this teaching in Scripture, church preaching must give much more consideration than it does to the fact that all private property carries a social mortgage, that is, that no one has the right to buy whatever he or she can afford or wants without taking into consideration the needs of others. The needs of others trump private property.

Throughout the Gospels, Jesus is seen as setting up a different type of family from the normative one of his time. The fact is that the poor did not have the means to maintain the type of family society prescribed. It is not far-fetched, then, given Jesus' option

Pastoral Perspective

together, let no one separate" (v. 6). God's chosen one, Moses, however, has offered a compromise. In fact, the law of Moses is more liberal than this new teaching from Jesus. In the Old Testament divorce is permissible for "indecencies" (Deut. 24:1), which is certainly broader than Jesus' more specific "unchastity."[1] Any number of specific behaviors could qualify as indecencies, and many in the Christian church have practically adopted the looser Old Testament rendering. For example, spousal abuse is certainly a break in covenant and a clear and serious "indecency." Only a few extremists would encourage a person to stay in a physically abusive relationship because divorce is a sin. This rendering, however, is in keeping with the Old Testament teaching but not with this passage in Matthew. What are we to do?

Jesus is making high demands in the face of opposition that is looking for loopholes. Jesus makes the same hard statement about divorce in the Sermon on the Mount (5:31–32). As in other parts of that teaching, Jesus is raising the bar. Jesus says, "You have heard it said . . ." and then reinterprets the Old Testament teaching to a higher standard. In each case, the higher standard is impossible. Anger is judged as murder. Lust is judged as adultery. It may be that Jesus keeps elevating the standard of God's expectation in response to the Pharisees' (and our) tendency to look for ways not to take it seriously enough.

While few of us would argue for the strictest rendering of this high standard about divorce, we must also take seriously that the highest standard is God's ideal. Even if we adhere to the looser Old Testament standards, it is countercultural to treat marriage as a high and holy covenant that is broken only in the most extreme circumstances. In his 2008 study, George Barna noted "that Americans have grown comfortable with divorce as a natural part of life." One of his researchers went on to conclude, "There no longer seems to be much of a stigma attached to divorce; it is now seen as an unavoidable rite of passage. Interviews with young adults suggest that they want their initial marriage to last, but are not particularly optimistic about that possibility."[2] Pastoral fidelity to the teaching of Jesus demands that we continue to hold the marriage covenant in high regard, even if the larger culture is going in the other direction.

Our churches, however, are still filled with believers who are divorced. A second pastoral issue is

---

2. Cited in Warren Carter, *Matthew and the Margins: A Socio-Political and Religious Reading* (London: T. & T. Clark, 2004), 377.
3. Ibid., 378.

1. Joe M. Sprinkle, "Old Testament Perspectives on Divorce and Remarriage," *Journal of the Evangelical Theological Society* 40 (1997): 549–50.
2. "New Marriage and Divorce Statistics Released," Barna Group, http://www.barna.org/barna-update/article/15-familykids/42-new-marriage-and-divorce-statistics-released?q=divorce; accessed November 30, 2011.

Exegetical Perspective

Mark 10 is our earliest Gospel account of Jesus' teaching on divorce; to which Matthew makes two fascinating edits. Whereas in Mark Jesus taught the crowds, in Matthew Jesus healed them. The church could use some healing words about marriage. Matthew's Jesus also asks if they have read the Scriptures—and in this story, everything hinges on how the Scriptures are read.

The Pharisees test him, in effect asking him to give his interpretation of Moses' strictures on divorce in Deuteronomy 24:1, a hotly debated text. As Craig Keener points out, the school of Shammai interpreted Deuteronomy to mean that unfaithfulness was sufficient cause for a man to divorce his wife; but the school of Hillel was more liberal, allowing a man to divorce for any cause, including burning his toast.[1]

Jesus would have echoed Malachi 2:16: "I hate divorce, says the LORD." We hate it too, but did Jesus hate it so much as to forbid it entirely? He sounds rigorous, but he probably has in mind a crucial distinction between the perfect will of God—what God deeply prefers, not taking into account human fallibility and rebellion—and what God concedes to us, given our hardheartedness and the fallen world in which we find ourselves.

Jesus seems uninterested in the question of rights: does a man have the right to divorce? Jesus clings to a holy vision that ignores loopholes and seeks God's perfect will—and believes it can happen. His basis is the quotation from Genesis about two becoming one flesh. In our society, two become one flesh long before the marriage vows are made. However, for Jesus the "one flesh" is not merely sexual union. It is the children, shared labor, bearing illness and hunger, lives joined not merely in spirit but in the harsh and delightful realities of the body.

We also might speculate that, in saying when divorce is reluctantly *permitted*, Jesus is out of sync with much teaching of his own day, which insisted that Jewish husbands were actually *required* to divorce their wives in cases of adultery. If divorce is permitted, then the healing of the marriage, even after sexual immorality, is conceivable.

Being unmarried in the community of Jesus' followers is also conceivable, and perhaps even admirable. The mystifying comments about eunuchs may make more sense when we see that the rabbis of the day taught there were two sorts of eunuchs: the "eunuch of man" was a male who had been castrated or had by illness or accident lost his procreative

1. Craig S. Keener, *Matthew* (Downers Grove, IL: InterVarsity Press, 1997), 295.

Homiletical Perspective

context, the disciples question whether marriage is worth the risk, given their expectation of a coming this-worldly kingdom of God. Many in congregations today might ask if it is worth marrying, but for different reasons indeed. After romanticism and the sexual revolution in Western countries, many might even question whether such a fuss need be made about marriage at all. Perhaps marriage as a contract is an old institution best placed firmly in the past.

There may be, however, a handful of folks in a congregation who would love to brandish a large moral rhetoric, employing this passage to decry what they perceive to be the degeneration of current culture. If congregations and preachers have worries about divorce rates and broken families, a challenge sermon could ask the question: how can the church be a community that mitigates or witnesses against the cultural, societal, and economic conditions that lead to divorce in the first place?

Another interesting or unexpected twist in the text comes from Jesus' response to the disciples' reaction. Not many contemporary congregations are going to have a notion of what a eunuch is, much less any experience with one. If the preacher wishes to take this up, some historical and especially cultural background is going to be necessary. In urban Western culture after birth control and the sexual revolution, it is difficult to recognize that marriage, fertility, and family went together in ancient cultures and still do in many non-Western cultures today. The preacher may need to explain the making of eunuchs for the "safety" of the ancient Near East court and especially its harems and concubines. Remind the congregation of Jesus' use of hyperbole, for example, cutting out eyes and cutting off limbs in Matthew 18:8–9.

Depending upon your community's tradition, this passage may be an opportunity to explore the church's ongoing tradition of ascetic practice in general and celibacy in particular. If so, before using such a text as a call to members of the congregation, be sure to describe what this text meant historically in terms of the ancient prophetic call, and compare and contrast that with its development within the tradition.

Within the text itself, we see that Matthew places this interaction with the Pharisees immediately after his long discourse on the nature of forgiveness and church life. What follows is Jesus' command not to stop the little children from coming to him. Within its immediate context, the Pharisees are trying to show Jesus' teachings in general to be contradictory or inconsistent with Torah. His clear teaching

Matthew 19:1–12

Theological Perspective

for the poor, that he worked to set up a different type of family—the kin-dom of God—based not on power and wealth but on love and justice. The Gospels give ample evidence of Jesus' struggle against the world order established by the Roman Empire, with its own Jewish strand upheld by the priestly class and Herod Antipas.

Therefore, it seems logical to conclude that for Jesus the kin-dom of God was not modeled on the Roman household imposed on the Jewish people. It is Jesus' relationship with God that grounds how he conceives his relationship with the disciples and among them. To constitute his disciples as kin, with God as "Father," can be read as a way for Jesus to counter the Roman Empire's societal organization, which had the emperor as father. This subversive way overturned the submission of women, children, and slaves, indeed making it possible for his followers to be a discipleship of equals.

Verse 12 introduces "eunuchs for the kingdom of God." Eunuchs were considered total outsiders to society, with no place in the households. They had different roles from males and females. Even if some eunuchs had a specialized role in society and attained certain levels of prestige and power, they remained marginalized members of society. This seems to be the point that Jesus is making: both eunuchs and Jesus' followers live a marginalized existence, participating in society but without being intrinsic parts of it. Establishing a parallel between eunuchs and his disciples leaves no doubt as to how strong are the demands that Jesus places on his disciples. The necessary sacrifices are not only personally demanding; they also alienate one from society. Jesus unequivocally affirms that no one is to be excluded from the kin-dom of God, whether eunuchs or disciples who do not marry or divorce and not remarry. Inclusion is the telltale sign of the family of God.

ADA MARÍA ISASI-DÍAZ

Pastoral Perspective

how these people will be treated. Many churches have treated divorce as a never-expiring blemish that keeps divorced believers from serving in some church capacities. As this teaching on divorce immediately follows Jesus' admonition to forgive "seventy-seven times" (18:22), it is unlikely that treating divorced Christians as anything less than full citizens of the church was ever the intent of Jesus' teaching. Divorce should not be seen as an absolute impediment to church leadership. If anything, Jesus is radically welcoming in the way he treats the marginalized and scandalized.

Speaking of the way Jesus treats those on the margins, this strong word about divorce may also have been a way that Jesus sought to protect those with less cultural power. Since many women were not financially self-sufficient, divorce could leave a woman abandoned with no good way to care for herself. This teaching from Jesus was directed toward the men who gathered around him: "And I say to you, whoever divorces his *wife*" (italics mine). It may be that some men in that culture were searching for the loopholes in the law so they could pursue new interests. A divorce in that day would not result in the wife's getting the house and the Buick while the husband keeps the dog and the Town Car. The wife could be relegated to the margins. The teaching of Jesus here carries overtones of the consistent theme of his care for the powerless.

Jesus' teaching on divorce sets the very highest standards of God's hope for us. The pastor must stay in the tension of trying to proclaim and live into the seriousness with which God takes covenant relationships, while also modeling God's expansive grace and forgiveness. We are called to serious fidelity to God's ideal and to be forgiving, loving, and protecting of those who find themselves needing to live with Moses' compromise.

DOCK HOLLINGSWORTH

potential; the "eunuch of the sun" was one born impotent.[2] In this text we see yet a third type of eunuch: a man who has not married, not because he cannot marry, but because he chooses not to; his God-given vocation seems best discharged outside the bounds of marriage.

While many of the church fathers used this text to denigrate marriage, Matthew 19 takes a high view of marriage and also of those who choose not to marry for the sake of the kingdom of God. Jesus was unmarried, as were Francis of Assisi, Mother Teresa, and a holy host of saints. Many Christian heroes of history were barely married, and perhaps should have remained single, given their dogged devotion to ministry and seeming inability to honor domestic life. Paul too was single, and we sense in 1 Corinthians 7:25–35 and 9:5 that he believed marriage could be an obstacle to service to Christ.

Jesus speaks optimistically about the vocation of the eunuch for the kingdom. Could it be critics poked fun at him, unmarried as he was, for being a eunuch? Might Matthew's first readers have heard of the dramatic conversion of the Ethiopian eunuch (Acts 8:26–40)?

What is the overlap between the challenges of discipleship for the married and for the single? Both are challenged to learn holiness of body. Perhaps marriage is peculiarly daunting when it comes to holiness and forgiveness; it is interesting that right after Jesus speaks at length about forgiveness (chap. 18) he turns to the subject of marriage and divorce. Eugene Rogers writes that marriage "ought to be understood as an ascetic practice—so much so that marriage and monasticism are but two forms of the same discipline, in which human beings are formed by the perceptions of others to whom they are so committed that they cannot easily escape. Marriage like monasticism exposes the worst in human beings, so that it can be healed."[3]

JAMES C. HOWELL

favoring the "little ones" (18:10), both literal (children) and figural (the marginalized, therefore, including divorced women) seems to deny divorce; but Torah allows a certificate for divorce. The Pharisees of this story seem to imply that such legislation means that divorce is an acceptable choice for men. Jesus retorts that legislation for properly, legally, and justly dealing with an already bad situation is not the same thing as condoning the bad situation itself. "From the beginning" (v. 8) it was not so, and ought not therefore be considered a paradigm for marital relationships.

This text continues Jesus' care to honor the "little ones." In Jesus' day his little ones included women who were economically devastated by divorce. In many contemporary congregations, his little ones also include men, women, and their children, either still young or now fully grown, who have suffered from the emotional pain caused by divorce.

Verse 6 contains a line now made famous by many Western wedding ceremonies: "Therefore, what God has joined together, let no one separate." It seems a bit ironic that a line so often used in wedding ceremonies comes from a text that would almost never be read at a wedding. Drawing that out may be helpful for the preacher. Focusing on this verse, the preacher could take a theological turn and focus, as did Paul in Ephesians 5, on the marital relationship between Christ and the church. That may work for some congregations, or as a portion of the homily or even an interpretive lens for the passage as a whole. However, such a theological turn would probably be a difficult stretch for many congregations and without careful handling could do violence to the text.

This pericope resists any straightforward analogy between Jesus' teaching, in its historical and textual context, and our contemporary congregations and their members. Giving some sound historical background to this passage should aid in meeting the pastoral needs and avoiding pitfalls. Discuss the nature and abuse of divorce in the ancient world. Show how Jesus' teaching is a radical challenge for social justice and the respect of women and children in his day and ours.

NATHAN JENNINGS

2. W. D. Davies and Dale C. Allison, *The Gospel according to St. Matthew* (Edinburgh: T. & T. Clark, 1997), 3:22.
3. Eugene Rogers, *After the Spirit* (Grand Rapids: Eerdmans, 2005), 188.

Matthew 19:13–15

¹³Then little children were being brought to him in order that he might lay his hands on them and pray. The disciples spoke sternly to those who brought them; ¹⁴but Jesus said, "Let the little children come to me, and do not stop them; for it is to such as these that the kingdom of heaven belongs." ¹⁵And he laid his hands on them and went on his way.

Theological Perspective

Although this story is brief in all the Synoptics, Matthew's telling is different from that of Mark and Luke in several particulars (cf. Mark 10:13–16 and Luke 18:15–17). Matthew states that the people wanted Jesus to pray for the children, rather than merely to touch them. More notably, Matthew does not say Jesus is indignant with his disciples, and Matthew does not place here the strong warning that if one does not receive the kingdom as a little child, one will not enter it (he moves that saying to another context, 18:1–4). This scene in Matthew is simpler, gentler. Jesus loves the little children, which, as hymns and nursery art show us, is very good news.

The story is simple, but weighty.

One can stretch it toward contemporary ethical debates about when after conception someone is actually a child welcomed by Jesus, to whom the kingdom of heaven belongs and who therefore is not to be treated lightly and fatally. One must admit, though, that this is to stretch the passage. Jesus was dealing with children who had actually been born. These children's parents, whether they personally welcomed their births or not, did in fact bring them to Jesus for prayer.

It is the disciples who were the problem. The disciples spoke sternly to those who brought children, keeping them away from Jesus. It is today's

Pastoral Perspective

The image of Jesus welcoming the children is one of the most beloved in Christendom. It is pastoral. It affirms our belief in family. It reminds us of the innocence of childhood. These three verses have been the subject of many paintings since the story was first told in the Gospels. One painter has Jesus sitting on a rock with the children gathered around. Another has Jesus sitting on the steps of a great temple with the mothers and their children, but no disciples. Yet another has both. More modern paintings illustrate Jesus holding hands with children from around the world.

The popularity of Jesus' blessing the children is an enduring image. It goes perfectly with a song many learned in church:

Jesus loves me! This I know,
For the Bible tells me so.
Little ones to him belong;
They are weak but he is strong.[1]

What many may not know about this hymn is that the words were originally part of a novel, written as a poem offered to comfort a dying child. The words of the song capture the message of Matthew's

1. Susan Bogert Warner and Anna Bartlett Warner, *Say and Seal* (New York: J. B. Lippincott, 1860).

Exegetical Perspective

This is a story of Jesus blessing little children while on the way to Jerusalem. It follows Jesus' debate with the Pharisees on divorce and marriage (19:1–12) and precedes his conversation with a rich young man about eternal life and discipleship (19:16–30), in the same sequence found in Mark 10. These three pericopes may not be sufficient to constitute a Christian household code, but the dialogues reveal some of Jesus' important teachings about the relationships between husband and wife, adults and children, and Jesus and his disciples.

This story has a few details significantly different from its parallel in Mark 10:13–16. Jesus does not rebuke the disciples and does not turn indignant, nor does he hold the children in his arms. He does not say that one may not enter the kingdom of God without receiving it like a little child (Mark 10:15) either—perhaps because that saying has just been cited in the previous chapter (Matt. 18:3). Noteworthy is that the little children are brought to Jesus, not simply for him to touch them, but for him to lay hands on them and to pray for them. The narrative is thus framed by the idea of the laying-on of hands, with its focus on the little children. The little children should be allowed to come to Jesus to receive his blessing, for the kingdom of heaven belongs to them.

Homiletical Perspective

Matthew 19:13–15, short as it is, is nevertheless important. Each of the Synoptics includes the little story, and each one is different. Matthew begins with Jesus' wanting to lay hands on the children and pray. It ends with Jesus' laying hands on the children and going on his way. The middle involves the clash between the disciples, who want to shoo the children away, and Jesus, who wants the children to come to him. There are then three concerns in the text: Who are the children? How are we to "lay hands" on them? Can we understand reciprocity between younger children and older children, that is, adults?

Who are children? We assume that a child is someone between birth and puberty. However, we do not know for sure that all cultures and faiths assume that. For example, when I arrived in Niger, in 1965 as a Peace Corps volunteer with some thirty others, we were instructed by Boubou Hama, the president of the National Assembly of Niger, about our work in his country. His first words were "Mes enfants" (my children), and throughout his talk he called us, people in our twenties and thirties, "my children."

There are biblical examples of the same thing. Paul says, "in Christ Jesus you are all children of God through faith" (Gal. 3:26; cf. Rom. 8:14–17; Phil. 2:15), and he repeatedly addresses his readers as his beloved children (1 Cor. 4:14; cf. 4:17; 1 Thess.

Theological Perspective

communities of disciples, today's congregations of Christians, who need to hear and heed what Matthew presents as Jesus' gentle correction, as they deal with actual children. Adults gather to be in Christ's presence at worship, speaking their prayers and singing their praises, hearing his Word and receiving his grace. It is precisely here that many churches make children unwelcome—even baptized children who are members of the church.

Christians across traditions differ strongly about whether, or when, baptized children can come to the Lord's Table, where his presence is celebrated most profoundly. Apart from formal barriers, congregations have other ways of "speaking sternly" to those who bring children near. People turn and glare at a crying baby or a wriggly toddler, or urge parents repeatedly to make use of the nursery. Even if children are officially welcome, adults rarely plan the various parts of worship services with an eye to whether or not children can understand and participate at their own level.

Welcoming children is a theological matter in this text—it is a particular and necessary expression of the call to love our little neighbors as we love our big selves. Jesus said that actual children were welcome in his presence. He said that the kingdom of God belongs to them. We are therefore forbidden to hinder them from coming to him in the places and times that we ourselves seek to be with him.

Historically this text has been used in discussion of a much more typical doctrinal issue. The question is whether Jesus' welcome of the little children should be taken to imply that the church should go so far as to baptize them. By the Reformation era, baptism of infants had long been the norm. Then the sixteenth-century Anabaptists noted that there is no explicit command to baptize infants, nor any clear biblical example of doing so. Therefore, they concluded, baptism is not for children but instead is only for those who have come to a mature commitment of faith. On the other hand, John Calvin (1509–1564), leading theologian of the Reformed tradition, used this passage prominently in his arsenal of arguments for infant baptism. If it was not, strictly speaking, commanded by Scripture, surely it was an expression of what this passage and others, properly interpreted, taught the church to practice.

In his commentary on this passage, Calvin noted that when Jesus welcomed, prayed for, and embraced the children, his actions embodied the very things baptism communicated sacramentally. Calvin was out on a limb when he said confidently that Jesus'

Pastoral Perspective

story. True, children are physically weak and vulnerable, and Jesus, an adult man, is strong. He will keep little ones safe. They have a place to belong if the world does not seem to care. We teach this song over and over because it is reassuring to hear.

Another illustration comes to mind. In the chancel area, parents hold their infant child dressed in a white baptismal gown; their young daughter stands nearby. The minister begins, "Forbid them not, for it is to such as these that the kingdom of heaven belongs." As she reads the baptismal vows to the parents, their young daughter reaches up, puts her hand in the baptismal font, and touches her forehead with water. She has, for all intents and purposes, just reaffirmed her baptism. She knows Jesus' inclusion and, without reading more into the action, reminds those watching that it is just that simple. No ceremony. Jesus loves me!

What does not appear in the sweet and gentle interpretations of this passage is a depiction of how Jesus' welcome of children is a radical action in his first-century Greco-Roman world. For the mothers to come forward with their children is a courageous act of faith. They are transgressing societal norms. Jesus could have rejected them, as he initially did the Canaanite woman in 15:23–24. Instead, by welcoming them, Jesus shows they are equally valuable to God. His actions are a cultural reversal of the expected. Suddenly the kingdom of heaven gets bigger: children, even children, are welcome. Throughout Matthew's Gospel, we see Jesus crossing social, political, and religious boundaries to associate with people whom others consider inappropriate, immoral, or contemptible but who are invited to become the growing reign of God.

One chapter earlier the disciples ask, "Who is the greatest in the kingdom of heaven?" Jesus says, "Whoever welcomes one such child in my name welcomes me" (18:1–5). Have they forgotten already? They were just told the importance of children in the kingdom, and now they are trying to push them away. The disciples represent those who think they know what is best. They know what God wants. They are the gatekeepers, the ones who say you are welcome or you are not. We know people like this; we know churches and denominations like this.

The disciples see the children as a waste of time. They have bigger fish to fry. They have an agenda for Jesus: he is their king-to-be. Stopping along the way does not fit their idea of achieving royalty. Whether the disciples get the message is not clear, but it is the same one they encounter all along the journey with

Exegetical Perspective

The little children (*paidia*) are probably under the age of seven. Perhaps because they are not yet productive members of the family, little children are often invisible or ignored by the adults, as attested by the disciples' attempt to block them off. God loves them all the same, and Jesus is never too busy to see them. In fact, Jesus' strong advocacy for them is rarely heard among other religious leaders. To uphold the value of little children, Jesus announces that the kingdom of heaven belongs to them.

When Jesus cleanses the temple in Jerusalem, it is the children who praise him, shouting, "Hosanna to the Son of David"; to defend them against the angry chief priests, Jesus cites Psalm 8:2: "Out of the mouths of infants and nursing babies you have prepared praise for yourself" (21:15–16). Following his discourse on community life in the previous chapter, this story also shows how Jesus practices what he preaches in 18:1–5, where he commands his disciples to welcome children in his name. In Christ, all are welcome—rich and poor, men and women, grown-ups and little children.

Laying-on of hands is a ritual practice in biblical tradition. Aaron lays hands on the head of the bull to sanctify it as an acceptable sacrifice to the Lord (Exod. 29:10). Moses lays hands on Joshua to consecrate him as new leader of Israel (Deut. 34:9). Jacob lays hands on Joseph's two children, Ephraim and Manasseh, to bless them and wish them well (Gen. 48:14–18). In New Testament times, the apostles also lay hands on seven people to ordain them as deacons for the church in Jerusalem (Acts 6:6). Ananias lays hands on Saul in Damascus so that his eyesight may be restored and he may receive the Holy Spirit (Acts 9:17). The prophets and teachers of the church in Antioch lay hands on Barnabas and Paul to commission them as missionaries (Acts 13:3).

Laying-on of hands is thus a ritualistic gesture of seeking and receiving God's approval, benediction, and commission. It is performed by an authoritative mediator such as Moses or Peter, priests or parents, to secure God's blessings on others. The fact that people wish for Jesus to lay hands on their children and pray for them indicates that they believe Jesus is a reputable servant of God whose intercession will be effective. Jesus' action shows that he is glad to grant the parents' good wishes for their children.

Jesus explains why he accepts the little children by saying that "it is to such as these that the kingdom of heaven belongs" (v. 14). The phrase "such as these" suggests that the kingdom of heaven belongs not only to little children but also to people like them.

Homiletical Perspective

2:7, 11), as does the Elder (1 John 2:1, 12, 14, 18, 28; 3:1–2, 7, 10, 18; 4:4; 5:2). These words from 1 John and Paul's letters are clearly aimed at more than chronologically young children. Biblical scholar Judith Gundry-Volf also affirms that "the Gospels teach more than how to make an adult world kinder and juster for children. [They] teach the reign of God *as a children's world*, where children are the measure, where the small are great and the great must become small."[1] Preachers must preach to *all* children.

The children's sermon is offered in many churches. Some children's sermons are quite good, although many set children up to be laughed at by adults and so unintentionally humiliate them. This essay engages some approaches to preach from this little text to the whole congregation, rather than simply preach a sermon to children. The sermon should be useful in some way for children, youth, adults, and seniors. Such a sermon should generate memories, good or bad, and encourage people, young or old, to move toward love, hope, and reciprocity.

The second concern in the text involves the phrase "He laid his hands on them." Some two thousand years ago, the disciples of Jesus wanted the children to go away. Jesus wanted the children to come to him instead, so he could touch them and pray. In our time we do not want the children to go away from Jesus. It is quite possible, though, there is someone in the congregation who wants to touch children in an inappropriate way.

Almost every day one finds in the newspaper stories about the activity of such people. It means that seeing or receiving loving hugs from good, loving people makes some people nervous. I know a pastor who wants to hug everybody on Sunday, and some of his parishioners are visibly nervous about that. A woman once gave me her card that said: "You receive one free hug." I also had a student who came up to me at the beginning of the semester and said softly, "I want you to know that I do not like to be touched." People are different, and touch can be ambiguous.

We have to admit the dark side of our culture around us and the fact that many people do not know how to respond to it. They are deeply confused and hurt when charges of pedophilia are sustained against a clergyperson. I believe that pastors and priests should preach on this text to say that Jesus laid his hands upon us and prayed for us, a kind of baptism and loving touch. Those six words, "he

---

1. Judith Gundry-Volf, "Jesus and Children: 'To Such as These Belongs the Reign of God,'" *Theology Today* 56, no.4 (January 2000): 480.

Theological Perspective

prayer over the children was that they would be counted among God's children, but he was firmly on the ground when he said that Jesus' actions indicate that he saw the children as part of his flock. This is the message of the gospel. The children belong to Jesus, not because of their own faith or discipleship, but because of Jesus' love. Jesus' acceptance of them indicates free forgiveness, gracious adoption, regeneration, the hope of salvation. "And if they were partakers of the spiritual gifts which baptism figures, it is absurd that they should be deprived of the outward sign."[1]

It is unlikely that Calvin's argument changed the minds of many in his day who were convinced that baptism is for believers only. It is even less likely that his views will change people's views today. The idea that baptism must follow faith as a testimony of the believer's discipleship was radical in sixteenth-century Europe, but it has become the norm in North American Protestantism—even for many in denominations that practice infant baptism. It is not unusual in Presbyterian or Methodist congregations for parents to refrain from presenting their children for baptism and to wait until those children make their own professions of faith and ask to be baptized. This contrasts sharply with Calvin's understanding that baptism is primarily a promise of grace that God makes to us.

Quite apart from the question of infant baptism, Calvin's exposition points us to the theological riches of the passage. Jesus wanted these little ones to come near him, without expecting any kind of righteous action on their part—a fact thrown into sharp relief by the man in the very next passage who asks what good deed he needs to do to gain eternal life. Jesus' invitation, his embrace, his prayer, all graciously claim the children as his own. From this we know that he welcomes us too. It is the same message that Karl Barth saw as central to his understanding of the faith, summarized in the children's hymn: "Jesus loves me—this I know, for the Bible tells me so."[2]

GARY NEAL HANSEN

Pastoral Perspective

Jesus: all are welcome. Songwriter Marty Haugen wrote a hymn with the same message, "All Are Welcome." Those words are the refrain, with the stanzas about building a house, like the kingdom of God, where "all can safely live and hearts learn to forgive."[2]

It is a fair question, then, to ask ourselves whom we see as a waste of our time. Our awareness of the desperate need of children around the world, even in our own neighborhoods, can be overwhelming. Let us be courageous, like the mothers who dared to bring their children to Jesus. Let us dare to cross the social norms as Jesus did, to stop, listen, and bless those who cross our path. Let us leave our comfort zone and step into the hospitals, prisons, homeless shelters, and soup kitchens, caring about and welcoming all.

The familiarity and popularity of these verses in paintings, songs, and moments of grace cannot keep them domesticated. Their power can and must go beyond the four walls of the church. It is a message ready to go viral on YouTube. Imagine a video with a hip-hop artist singing "Jesus Love Me" or "All Are Welcome" verses in a new tune with segments such as these:

an Iraqi child survivor of a bombing with limbs lost entering a VA hospital
a starving child from Congo eating a meal at a soup kitchen
a teenage meth addict from Middle America checking into rehab
an infant in Africa with AIDS being held and rocked
a high school student reading a letter to the Gay Student Alliance from a juvenile incarcerated for killing a gay classmate
an orphan from the streets of Haiti finding shelter and adult protection
a young girl with anorexia finding a support group

Were this to go viral, all would see, sing, and act for the love of God.

OLIVE ELAINE HINNANT

---

1. John Calvin, *A Harmony of the Gospels Matthew, Mark and Luke*, trans. T. H. L. Parker, in *Calvin's New Testament Commentaries*, ed. David W. Torrance and Thomas F. Torrance (Grand Rapids: Eerdmans, 1972), 2:251.
2. Cited in Hugh T. Kerr, *The Simple Gospel* (Louisville, KY: Westminster/John Knox Press, 1991), 4.

2. Marty Haugen, "All Are Welcome" (Chicago: GIA Publications, 1994); http://www.mljmusic.com/Portals/0/Lyrics/All%20Are%20Welcome.pdf; accessed March 6, 2012.

Exegetical Perspective

Little children can be a model for adults. What then are the traits of the little children worthy of the kingdom of heaven? The childlike qualities may refer to the character of the children, such as innocence, trust, joy, and eagerness to learn. They may also refer to their low social status, such as vulnerability, dependence, powerlessness, and exploitability. In Matthew, the references to both character and social status may be found. In 18:4, for instance, Jesus says to the disciples: "Whoever becomes humble like this child is the greatest in the kingdom of heaven." Humility is a character trait of little children featured as a virtue for the kingdom of heaven. This echoes the first beatitude in the Sermon on the Mount, "Blessed are the poor in spirit, for theirs is the kingdom of heaven" (5:3).

Jesus also warns the disciples not to scandalize "one of these little ones who believe in me" (18:6), and says in the parable of the Sheep and Goats that the righteous people will be rewarded because of their acts of kindness to "one of the least of these who are members of my family" who are hungry, thirsty, estranged, naked, sick, or imprisoned (25:40). The "least of these" are followers of Jesus who, like little children, are suffering at the bottom of the social pyramid. The little ones and the least of these are not the little children, but they are the people such as them to whom the kingdom of heaven belongs. Jesus' action shows that God has a preferential love for the little children, the humble, and the poor, because God is merciful.

In the historical debates between Reformers and Anabaptists, this story has sometimes been cited to support the practice of infant baptism. One needs to be cautious, however, because the blessing of little children is not infant baptism. The main point of this story is Jesus' love for little children, whose character is overlooked and whose dignity ignored. Adults can learn from them, and should bring them to Jesus to be blessed.

JOHN YIEH

Homiletical Perspective

laid his hands on them," may have encouraged the later church's baptizing of children.[2] Beyond that, the pastor or priest can say in a sermon that touch can be good, bad, or confusing,[3] and we need to be sensitive to that. Almost every denomination has an educational program to prevent child sexual abuse that would be helpful. The preacher's sermon might become an occasion to introduce a program of such training.

The last concern in the text suggests a reciprocity between little children and grown-up children. We often think that we adults do everything for little children, make all the decisions. That is not the whole truth. Children do a plethora of things for us. A pastor once told me that he sat in his rocking chair, puzzling over whether or not to take a new call. He was afraid that his little son had so many friends where they lived that he would be lost in the new place. He then felt his son come up and touch him on the shoulder. He said, "Daddy, I think we should go to the new place. It would be a lot of fun, and I would make a lot of friends. Let's do it." This decision was made not by him alone but also with his son. The love between them was huge, and both of them were children, in the sense that the Bible speaks of all of us as children of God. We teach our children, but our children also teach us. We learn together that Jesus loves us.

JOSEPH R. JETER

---

2. See W. D. Davies and Dale Allison, *Matthew: A Shorter Commentary* (London: T. & T. Clark, 2004), 319.
3. This phrase derives from the FaithTrust Institute founded by the Rev. Marie M. Fortune (http://www.cpsdv.org/).

¹⁶Then someone came to him and said, "Teacher, what good deed must I do to have eternal life?" ¹⁷And he said to him, "Why do you ask me about what is good? There is only one who is good. If you wish to enter into life, keep the commandments." ¹⁸He said to him, "Which ones?" And Jesus said, "You shall not murder; You shall not commit adultery; You shall not steal; You shall not bear false witness; ¹⁹Honor your father and mother; also, You shall love your neighbor as yourself." ²⁰The young man said to him, "I have kept all these; what do I still lack?" ²¹Jesus said to him, "If you wish to be perfect, go, sell your possessions, and give the money to the poor, and you will have treasure in heaven; then come, follow me." ²²When the young man heard this word, he went away grieving, for he had many possessions.

²³Then Jesus said to his disciples, "Truly I tell you, it will be hard for a rich person to enter the kingdom of heaven. ²⁴Again I tell you, it is easier for a camel

Theological Perspective

In Matthew the story of the rich young man functions as something of a commentary on the previous scene. The two passages are paired in all the Synoptics, but they contrast most strongly here (cf. Mark 10:17–31; Luke 18:18–30). After Jesus generously welcomes little children who have done nothing to earn his love, this fellow rushes up to ask how he can get eternal life. Rather than calling Jesus "good" as in Mark and Luke, in Matthew he asks what "good deed" he must do; rather than wanting to "inherit" eternal life, here he simply wants to "have" it.

Eventually Jesus answers on just these terms: if he wants to get life for his good deeds, the man should do what God has defined as good. Jesus recites most of the second table of the Decalogue, plus the summary command to love neighbor as self (see also 22:39). The man brashly claims to have kept them all. Then comes the theological crux of the scene: Jesus tells him that if he really wants to be "perfect," he should sell his many possessions and give the money to the poor. Then he should come back and follow Jesus.

Jesus' offer of a way to be "perfect," found only in Matthew, has had particular theological resonance historically. For many centuries this verse has been taken to mark two different standards of discipleship. Ordinary Christians are called to virtue, but not to

Pastoral Perspective

At first glance it seems this text is better suited for the wealthiest 1 percent in the United States. We might secretly be glad to hear that for the rich it will be impossible to enter the reign of God. For the 99 percent who hear this story, it stirs up a response not unlike the disciples': what about us? We go to church, serve on committees, feed the poor, give our time and talent, and we want our fair share. We may not be as perfect or as rich as this man claims to be, but we deserve too. Something seems unfair here. Not only has the rich young man managed to get wealthy. He has managed to do so while keeping all of the commandments and at a young age.

The rich man in Matthew's story is part of the 1 percent crowd. Having become successful in the eyes of others, he asks, "Teacher, what good deed must I do to have eternal life?" (v. 16). The rabbi replies, "There is only one who is good [and that is God]. If you wish to enter into life, keep the commandments." It is curious that Jesus does not reply with the same words "eternal life" but with "life." Is Jesus shifting to a "here and now" focus? The rich young ruler is thinking ahead; Jesus is thinking about today.

The man's response to keeping the commandments is almost humorous: "Which ones?" As if there are some commandments that can be left out or some that do not really matter. Interestingly

to go through the eye of a needle than for someone who is rich to enter the kingdom of God." [25]When the disciples heard this, they were greatly astounded and said, "Then who can be saved?" [26]But Jesus looked at them and said, "For mortals it is impossible, but for God all things are possible."

[27]Then Peter said in reply, "Look, we have left everything and followed you. What then will we have?" [28]Jesus said to them, "Truly I tell you, at the renewal of all things, when the Son of Man is seated on the throne of his glory, you who have followed me will also sit on twelve thrones, judging the twelve tribes of Israel. [29]And everyone who has left houses or brothers or sisters or father or mother or children or fields, for my name's sake, will receive a hundredfold, and will inherit eternal life. [30]But many who are first will be last, and the last will be first."

Exegetical Perspective

As part of Jesus' teaching on discipleship on the way to Jerusalem, this pericope begins with Jesus' dialogue with a young man about eternal life (vv. 16–22), continues with a lament over the challenge to rich people (vv. 23–26), and finishes with a response to Peter about the rewards of discipleship (vv. 27–30). Eternal life and following Jesus are key themes, while wealth is the major concern. The final warning, "But many who are first will be last, and the last will be first," is a bridge to the parable of the Laborers in the Vineyard, which ends with the same saying (20:16).

Several differences from its parallel (Mark 10:17–31) are noteworthy. In Mark a man addresses Jesus as "good teacher," but in Matthew it is a young man who asks about the "good deed" (v. 16). Matthew adds the idea of becoming perfect (v. 21) and the promise of twelve thrones (v. 28). All three changes reflect Matthew's special concepts and concerns.

The young man asks Jesus three questions: how to receive eternal life, which commandments to keep, and what more he should do. First, by changing "good teacher" to "good deed," Matthew shifts Mark's christological question to a soteriological issue and focuses the conversation on the commandments. Jesus' answers to the first two questions make it explicit that, since God is good, God's

Homiletical Perspective

To preach from Matthew 19:16–30 is not easy for preachers, and there is good reason. Many pastors may read the text and fear that the wealthy folk in the congregation who provide the funds that keep the church rolling may be peeved when they are told to "sell your possessions, and give the money to the poor" (v. 21). They may even take themselves and their funds away from the church.

There are also several approaches used by preachers to deal with an uncomfortable text. The first one is to laugh off what we ought to take seriously. You may have heard that lightsome song called "Prayin' for the Camel":

> Come on, camel, squeeze on through;
> Come on camel, this rich man's prayin' for you![1]

Audiences laugh when they hear this song, but they may also wonder. We, like the disciples, wonder if anyone can be saved. Jesus mercifully reminds them that "for mortals it is impossible, but for God all things are possible" (v. 26).

Next is the Francis of Assisi approach. Francis was a wealthy young man, but changed his life and became God's pauper and the founder of a Christian

1. "Prayin' for the Camel," by Lindy Hearn and Lynn Adler (Spring Hollow Records, February 3, 2005).

Theological Perspective

perfection. Others, though, the "religious" (priests, monks, and nuns), are called to follow the "counsels of perfection." These include the poverty Jesus teaches here, as well as chastity and obedience. Protestants tend to dislike this idea of a two-tiered standard, and many traditions strongly object to any sense that perfection is possible in this life. Pelagius, a British monk in Augustine's day, claimed that perfection was possible and therefore required of Christians. He was judged a heretic. Yet here is the possibility of perfection, from the very mouth of Jesus.

Confusion about perfection comes from a misunderstanding of the text. The word *teleios*, typically translated as "perfect" here, does not indicate the kind of perfection measured in unswerving obedience to the law. That is what the rich man already claimed. The word instead has to do with being aimed at the proper end or goal. That is, Jesus is aiming the man at the real target of life, calling him to the "perfection" of being complete and mature. Real maturity for this particular man would start with using his resources for God's purposes in practical love. Jesus seems to be pressing him on the honesty of his claim to have obeyed all God's laws. For this rich man to love his actual poor neighbors as he loves himself is quite a test, and the man walks away, knowing he has failed it. Even if he had passed that test, he would not have reached the goal. Jesus' call to perfection concludes with the gospel's model of the human goal: he calls the man to come and follow him. This is the target to which all our lives are to be aimed.

The rest of the passage plays out the paradoxical implications of Jesus' interaction with the man in a conversation with the disciples. First, Jesus portrays the difficulty of a rich person's coming to salvation. It is as difficult as threading a needle with a camel. He seems to be saying that no rich person can possibly be saved.

The disciples are of two minds about this, perhaps depending on whether they focus on what they have or on what they have left behind. As a group the disciples ask, "Then who can be saved?" If the standard is so strict, the aim so high, perhaps no one at all may enter the kingdom. Perhaps they see themselves as rich, because they walk with Jesus and receive all they need. Maybe they know that, although poor, they are mighty attached to what they have.

Jesus flatly denies that salvation is impossible, but only by shifting their understanding of the source of salvation. That is, the rich young man came asking what *he* could do to get eternal life. This is the futile way. No human being can do what needs to be done

Pastoral Perspective

enough, Jesus confirms this by naming commandments five through nine, which are the social commandments, the ones about how we treat each other. Then Jesus adds the commandment "You shall love your neighbor as yourself." These commandments also have to do with the here and now, not with eternal life. The rich young man, confident that he has kept all of these, presses Jesus further: "What do I still lack?" (v. 20). For some reason, he wants more: a piece of paper confirming his ticket to heaven, a price tag on eternal life, a promise of security in the afterlife, because it is the only thing he finds lacking in his life on earth, or simply because he is used to always getting more. He wants full disclosure, so Jesus gives it to him. "Go, sell your possessions, and give the money to the poor, and you will have treasure in heaven; then come, follow me" (v. 21).

The text says he goes away grieving. It has always been assumed that he will not sell his possessions. However, imagine for a moment, if the rich young man went off grieving because he knew the impact this would have on his family. Maybe he went to talk with them about this decision or to talk with his hedge-fund manager. Surely this is a decision to consider and not take lightly. Maybe he left to pray about it. To sell all his possessions is to move from Wall Street to roaming the city streets. This is generally true for any of us.

Depending on our social locations and life experiences, our reactions will no doubt vary upon hearing this text. There may be feelings of guilt because we too have no intention of selling our possessions, or annoyance that the rich young man thinks more of material things than following Jesus, or regret because we have not kept the commandments anyway.

Going beyond our personal responses, though, consider that this text is also read in countries that see the United States as the 1 percent in the world. The people in these countries are the 99 percent asking, like the disciples, what about us? We need water, food, housing, and a healthy economy too. Perhaps this text is good news or great news to 99 percent of the world, because Jesus says it is hard for a rich person to enter the kingdom of heaven, and they know they are not rich. Then there is greater news. For the rich to enter the kingdom or have eternal life, they must give up what they have, so that others may have. They must love their neighbor. They must face their dependence on God alone.

The disciples are stunned by this news. Initially they feel left out, now they are wondering, "Then

commandments are the good deeds that are key to eternal life: a life blessed by God now and in the future. Second, Matthew adds loving neighbors (Lev. 19:18) to the list of examples, because it is a great commandment (22:36–39) and a reminder of loving enemies (5:43–44). Jesus' endorsement of the law echoes what he declares earlier: "For truly I tell you, until heaven and earth pass away, not one letter, not one stroke of a letter, will pass from the law until all is accomplished" (5:18). The law remains binding for the Christian church in Matthew.

To the third question, Jesus answers, "If you wish to be perfect [*teleios*], go, sell your possessions, and give the money to the poor, and you will have treasure in heaven; then come, follow me" (v. 21). Perfection is a higher step. To receive eternal life, it suffices to keep God's commandments as prescribed in the law and prophets. To be perfect, however, this young man is advised to do three extra things. His relations to his possessions, to the poor, and to Jesus determine his way of life and its consequences. The idea of perfection has appeared in the Sermon on the Mount as the goal of Jesus' radical discipleship: "Be perfect, as your heavenly Father is perfect" (5:48). What is "perfection"? First of all, it is modeled on God the heavenly Father. In Greek philosophy it means true knowledge and true virtue. In Jewish tradition it means "completeness" (*tamim*), so Ulrich Luz, a Swiss professor of New Testament, defines it as "undivided obedience to God."[1] Luz has also proposed that it has three connotations in Matthew: unlimited love (loving enemies, 5:43–48), complete obedience (exceeding righteousness, 5:20), and following Jesus (total commitment, 19:21).[2]

One major debate in the history of interpretation is whether the call to perfection is issued to the young man only or to all the baptized. Catholic tradition regards it as an "evangelical counsel" for religious elites. Protestant tradition often sees it as a challenge for all Christians to detach themselves from money. Given Jesus' commission to make disciples of all nations by baptizing all believers and teaching them to obey all of Jesus' commandments (28:19–20), the invitation to become perfect seems intended for all followers. The three radical demands—giving up possessions, helping the poor, and following Jesus—are the costs of discipleship.

Seeing the young man walk away in grief, Jesus laments that it is harder for a rich person to enter the

order. He has been venerated by millions. Even today people love his poverty, like that of Buddha, Gandhi, the desert fathers and mothers, and so forth. Francis sought perfection but felt that he had never reached it and scolded himself. Nikos Kazantzakis's brilliant novel about Francis demonstrates this in a call and response between Francis and his disciple Brother Leo. Francis says to Leo, "Say 'Woe is you Francis! You committed so many sins that you won't be saved, but shall go to the very bottom of hell!' Say that!" Leo says, "Joy to you, Brother Francis. You committed so many good deeds in your life that you shall go and sit at the very summit of Paradise!"[2] The condemnation and encouragement go back and forth in the book. The point is that we need to love and care for those who try their best to help others but feel that they have failed.

Another approach might be called the Leo Tolstoy or Stephen King approach. Tolstoy's short story "How Much Land Does a Man Need?" tells of a man named Pahon who wants more land. The Bashkir people have much land, and their chief tells Pahon that for one thousand rubles he can buy all the land he can circle from dawn to sunset. Pahon runs and sees more and more nice land he wants and keeps running around more. He sees that the sun is going down and he runs as fast as he can to get back to the starting place. He makes it. The land is his—but he drops dead and is buried in his land, a six-foot grave.

Author Stephen King has been called the scariest man in America—and one of the richest. On June 19, 1999, he was walking alongside a road when he was struck by a van, hurling him into a ditch, close to death. He was hospitalized for weeks, and years later he remains in pain. He walked slowly to the lectern to speak at a Vassar College commencement on May 20, 2001, and said:

> A couple of years ago I found out what "you can't take it with you" means. I found out while I was lying in the ditch at the side of a country road, covered with mud and blood. . . . I had a Master-Card in my wallet, but when you're lying in a ditch with broken glass in your hair, no one accepts MasterCard.
>
> In the months that followed, I got a painful but extremely valuable look at life. We come in naked and broke. Warren Buffett? Going to go out broke. Bill Gates? Going to go out broke. Tom Hanks?

1. Ulrich Luz, *Matthew 8–20: A Commentary* (Minneapolis: Fortress Press, 2001), 513.
2. Ibid., 513–14.

2. Nikos Kazantzakis, *Saint Francis*, trans. P. A. Bien (New York: Touchstone, 1962), 256. The story in the next paragraph is from Leo Tolstoy, "How Much Land Does a Man Need?" in *The Kreutzer Sonata and Other Short Stories* (Mineola, NY: Dover Thrift Editions, 1993), 1–15.

Matthew 19:16–30

Theological Perspective

to enter the kingdom of God. For God, however, all things are possible. God can bring anyone God wants into the kingdom. The direction is reversed, and salvation becomes possible. This is where it is helpful to see the story of the rich young man in contrast to the story of the blessing of the children. Jesus' loving welcome of the children came not because they did something to get it—they came at their parents' behest, and the obstacles were overcome because Jesus intervened. Salvation of the rich or the poor will look like that, rather than like the rich young man's striving.

Peter, on the other hand, seems more conscious of having done just what Jesus asks the rich young man to do: he has left all and followed Jesus. "What then will we have?" he asks (v. 27). Jesus' answer acknowledges the truth of Peter's perspective. His followers, who have indeed left all, will sit in high places in the kingdom, on thrones of judgment over God's people. Jesus broadens the promise beyond the Twelve, saying that anyone who has given up anything for his name's sake will receive a hundred times as much. In addition to that abundance, they will inherit eternal life. The choice of terms again emphasizes salvation as gracious gift. Matthew's rich young man wants to "have" eternal life, to possess it by his own actions. Jesus says his followers will "inherit" eternal life, receiving it as part of the family.

Jesus' answer to Peter does not quite fully affirm Peter's own claim to a reward for his sacrifice. Jesus indicates that at a human level these things remain shrouded in mystery: many who appear to be first will in the end be last, and vice versa. The Twelve will see this clearly when one of their own betrays their Lord; and Peter himself will learn to his own sorrow how fragile his own claim of devotion is.

GARY NEAL HANSEN

Pastoral Perspective

who can be saved?" "None of us," is basically Jesus' response. Even more dismayed, Peter wants to know what they will have for leaving everything and following Jesus. It is not unlike what the rich young man is seeking—or what we are seeking. We want to be told everything is going to turn out all right, that we will be taken care of, no matter what we do. When we worry about the future, we lose sight of today; when we think we have done good and kept all the commandments, it is still not about our playing God.

Usually people do not recognize they are not God until they have lost everything. One particular group learns this lesson the hard way. People in Alcoholics Anonymous hit bottom when they lose their families or work or home or possessions or all of these. At that point they realize they are not in charge, if they ever have been, and that they need each other to survive. One of the sayings in the 12-step program is this: Alcoholics Anonymous works for those who believe in God. AA works for those who do not believe in God. AA does not work for those who are God. We cannot be God. We learn that by living one day at a time.

Jesus is very clear about what to do with our possessions. If our possessions rule us, then that is where our treasure is. Eternal life is not something we can buy or do or possess. It is something that God does daily; it is what God gives.

OLIVE ELAINE HINNANT

Exegetical Perspective

kingdom of heaven than for a camel to go through the eye of a needle (v. 24), which is a hyperbole. Since the pursuit of possessions often takes priority over one's concern for the poor and mutes Jesus' call for discipleship, can anyone be saved? Recognizing the seductive power of wealth, Jesus concedes that it is impossible for mortals to resist wealth. However, he adds, "but for God all things are possible" (v. 26). If we trust God the Father, who loves us more than the birds in the sky and the lilies in the field (6:26–30), we will not be worried about our own needs and will be freed to give possessions away to help the less fortunate.

Trusting God is therefore the cure for fear and the remedy for greed. On verse 25, Clement of Alexandria, in a sermon entitled "Who is the rich man that shall be saved?" argued that one can be rich externally and spiritually.[3] Possessions are neither good nor bad. It is the spiritually rich—"the poor in spirit" who use money to help the poor—who will be saved. The point is to worship God, not mammon.

Since the disciples have given up everything to follow Jesus, what are their rewards? To answer Peter's question, Jesus promises three stunning rewards: the privilege to cojudge the twelve tribes of Israel; houses, families, and fields a hundredfold; and eternal life (vv. 28–29). The rewards will come at the "renewal of all things," which may mean the resurrection of the dead, the restoration of Israel, or the re-creation of the world. To cojudge Israel with the Son of Man is an incredible honor for any human. The hundredfold is the utmost number in biblical symbolism. Both promises are eschatological prizes that await the disciples.

Since every believer is encouraged to become a disciple in Matthew, the promises are offered to everyone. These rewards provide incentive and hope for Jesus' followers to strive for the kingdom of heaven and its righteousness in an entangling and hostile world. They also assure them of God's justice. Finally, the warning that "many who are first will be last" encourages disciples not to become complacent on their faith journey.

JOHN YIEH

Homiletical Perspective

Going out broke. Steve King? Broke. Not a crying dime.

Should you give away what you have? Of course you should. I want you to consider making your lives one long gift to others, and why not?[3]

No words in King's speech are a better statement than, "I want you to consider making your lives one long gift to others." So said Jesus. So lived Jesus.

A fourth approach can be found in an early nineteenth-century painting by Heinrich Hofmann, *Christ and the Rich Young Ruler*, which hangs in the Riverside Church in New York City. In the painting are four persons: an older man, probably ill; a young woman, perhaps his daughter, on whom he is leaning; a young man, dressed in finery; and in the center, Jesus. The faces of the characters are unusual. The woman has worry on her face; the young man's countenance is a disappointed expression. Jesus is the center of the painting; his expression, perhaps to our surprise, is plain and modest. His hands sweep from himself toward the poor, sick, and worried, a response the young man is not expecting. Many struggle these days to try to help others, but are afraid that Jesus will sweep his hands toward the ones we do not have in mind.

A song, a novel, a story, a speech, a painting: each suggests that our culture seeks ways to understand a text that is not easy. A sermon may begin with the difficulties found in the community, the experiences of people as they struggle. We tell their stories and ours. Then the truth: in King's words, "we're going out broke"; in Jesus' words, "you will have treasure in heaven" (v. 21). We are called to make our lives one long gift to others.

JOSEPH R. JETER

---

3. Clement of Alexandria, "Who is the rich man that shall be saved?" in *The Ante-Nicene Fathers* (Grand Rapids: Eerdmans, 1983), 2:589–604.

3. Stephen King's speech is found at http://www.beliefnet.com/Love-Family/Charity-Service/2001/06/Scaring-You-To-Action.aspx?p=1; accessed February 17, 2012.

Matthew 20:1–16

¹"For the kingdom of heaven is like a landowner who went out early in the morning to hire laborers for his vineyard. ²After agreeing with the laborers for the usual daily wage, he sent them into his vineyard. ³When he went out about nine o'clock, he saw others standing idle in the marketplace; ⁴and he said to them, 'You also go into the vineyard, and I will pay you whatever is right.' So they went. ⁵When he went out again about noon and about three o'clock, he did the same. ⁶And about five o'clock he went out and found others standing around; and he said to them, 'Why are you standing here idle all day?' ⁷They said to him, 'Because no one has hired us.' He said to them, 'You also go into the vineyard.' ⁸When evening came, the owner of the vineyard said to his manager, 'Call the laborers and give them their pay, beginning with the last and then

Theological Perspective

Only Matthew includes this parable in his Gospel. What goes before it and what comes after it follow the pattern found in Mark and Luke. The parable comes on the heels of Jesus' saying, "But many who are first will be last, and the last will be first" (19:30), and concludes with its repetition, albeit in reversed order, "So the last will be first, and the first will be last" (20:16). Not only does this bracketing serve to maintain the flow Matthew shares with Mark and Luke, but it marks the parable as a kind of commentary on the saying.

This bracketing is not mere elaboration, however. In the context of the parable, the terms "last" and "first" are temporal, not hierarchical. Jesus' saying is given expanded meaning: it is not only about who ranks higher or lower; it is also about who comes earlier or later, who follows longer or more briefly. If the saying in 19:30 is cautionary against the backdrop of Jesus' remarkable promise that "you who have followed me will also sit on twelve thrones, judging the twelve tribes of Israel" (19:28), the added parable reaches back to the danger lurking in the question of Peter that occasioned the promise, "Look, we have left everything and followed you. What then will we have?" (19:27). The parable's laborers who were first in the field and longest at work "thought they would receive more" (v. 10).

Pastoral Perspective

In Matthew 20:1–16 Jesus shares the story of the landowner and the hired workers. Five groups of laborers come to the vineyard at different hours of the day. When they gather to be paid, all receive the same wage, regardless of the time they clocked in to begin their efforts. The parable's placement is immediately after the provocative statement of 19:30 that "many who are first will be last, and the last will be first," a saying that reappears as a concluding and framing declaration for the parable in verse 16. On initial reading, it seems that the purpose of the story is to offer a vivid illustration for this proclaimed truth of the coming kingdom—but there are also hints that open the possibility of additional interpretations.

As a parable the passage shares classic elements with others found elsewhere in the Gospels. It is constructed with everyday imagery and populated with recognizable characters. It lays out a common-sense progression of expectations and then brings a kingdom twist to its ending, leaving the listener with a sense of violated logic and disorientation. At its conclusion all of us, as readers and listeners, and as hired hands for the work of the vineyard, are standing before the bemused eyes of the landowner, who is trying so hard to teach us something vital about our living.

going to the first.' ⁹When those hired about five o'clock came, each of them received the usual daily wage. ¹⁰Now when the first came, they thought they would receive more; but each of them also received the usual daily wage. ¹¹And when they received it, they grumbled against the landowner, ¹²saying, 'These last worked only one hour, and you have made them equal to us who have borne the burden of the day and the scorching heat.' ¹³But he replied to one of them, 'Friend, I am doing you no wrong; did you not agree with me for the usual daily wage? ¹⁴Take what belongs to you and go; I choose to give to this last the same as I give to you. ¹⁵Am I not allowed to do what I choose with what belongs to me? Or are you envious because I am generous?' ¹⁶So the last will be first, and the first will be last."

Exegetical Perspective

The parable of the Laborers in the Vineyard is a startling biblical text that stirs the emotions of the interpreter. For many, it is a moving depiction of God's grace toward humanity. For others, however, it is an incomprehensible parable that eschews fair play.

The details of the parable are clear. First, as in most parables, its main topic is the kingdom of God (v. 1a). Second, the parable compares the kingdom of God to a man who owns a vineyard (v. 1b). Third, the landowner goes "out" to hire day laborers to work in his fields. The first group is hired, as customary, at dawn (v. 1). However, the landowner also hires groups of day laborers at nine in the morning (vv. 3–4), at noon, at three in the afternoon (v. 5), and at five in the evening (vv. 6–7). Fourth, the day laborers receive their pay at the end of the day, which usually means sundown (v. 8). Fifth, a discrepancy or dispute ensues when all the workers—including the group hired at five in the afternoon—receive the same pay for their work (vv. 9–10). Sixth, the disgruntled workers voice their grievance to the landowner (vv. 11–12). Seventh, the landowner defends his actions (vv. 13–15). Finally, the parable ends with a saying about the great reversal that the gospel brings (v. 16).

The main topic of this parable, which appears only in Matthew, is God's outrageous generosity.

Homiletical Perspective

"Are you envious because I am generous?" asks the owner of the vineyard (v. 15). You bet we are! If we are not envious, we are not hearing the parable. The parable rubs us the wrong way. Its visions of fairness and equality chafe. We cringe at what it seems to say about God. We shrink before what it seems to say about us! The parable of the Workers in the Vineyard catches us quickly into the narrative, because we carry around notions of what is fair and what is not, and this story offends most of them.

We may be entrepreneurial enough to agree the owner of the vineyard can run his business any way he pleases, but we cannot rest comfortably with his payroll policies. We want to agree, yes, everyone needs a job, needs a fair day's wage to keep food on the table; but if the master is determined to be generous, why not pay those fellows who worked all day a bonus? That also would be fair. The way generosity gets passed around in this tale abrades our sense of justice.

So we take our places with those who were hired first, paid last, and who now complain. We join the chorus of grumbling at the back of the line. It is not fair, they say—we say—as we take our place at the end of the line. Indeed, the parable presses that the sermon be written from the back of the line.

We have a good view from here. We see everything that is happening. We see the others being

Matthew 20:1–16

Theological Perspective

It is tempting to read this parable, as many commentators do, in terms of grace and works, as though it points to what Paul summarizes in Ephesians 2:8–9: "For by grace you have been saved through faith, and this is not your own doing; it is the gift of God—not the result of works, so that no one may boast." After all, is not the parable about laborers and their work in the landowner's vineyard? Does its climax not revolve around the generosity of the landowner? A close reading of this parable, however, cautions us to look elsewhere for its theological trajectory.

Nowhere here is there a hint that work is depreciated, and its value is certainly not overrun by the landowner's (God's) generosity. If anything, being idle is what is questionable (vv. 3 and 6). Moreover, the word "grace" does not appear in Matthew's Gospel. A grace-versus-works dichotomy is not characteristic of his theological perspective; therefore, such a theological framework should not be imposed on this parable. While the grace of God—in Paul's terms and our understanding—is certainly generous, the parable's mention of the landowner's (God's) generosity is not sufficient to draw us into a grace-and-works framework and should be allowed to stand on its own.

What the parable asserts is this: "The kingdom of heaven is like a landowner"—who, we discover as the parable unfolds, is therefore also an employer and labor manager. As in most of Jesus' parables, the manner of divine governance in heaven is revealed by some likeness to things we know or can imagine in everyday life. Sometimes, what a parable is showing is something that bears likeness to the way divine governance ("the kingdom of heaven") plays out—its dynamic, its effects, its ultimate ends (see, e.g., the parables in Matt. 13). This parable is even more pointed, drawing out the likeness between a particular character (the landowner) and the God whose reign is being revealed. It does not portray a likeness between the realm of heaven and the landowner's estate, but accents how similar to the God who reigns in heaven is the behavior of this particular landowner—precisely in the shocking way he manages workers, time, and wages. The grumblings against the one are the grumblings brought against the other (vv. 11–12).

The point of the parable lies in the interplay between "whatever is right" (the landowner's promise, vv. 4–5) and "I am generous" (the landowner's self-identification, v. 15). It comes to its critical moment in the complaint of those hired first, "you have made them equal to us" (v. 12), and

Pastoral Perspective

The feeling this brings is reminiscent of the one generated in Luke's Gospel as we stand in the field with the elder brother of the returned prodigal son (Luke 15:11–32). There are the sounds of a party in progress. "My brother is receiving a celebration? What is going on here? This is certainly not fair." This violates what is supposed to happen. Likewise, Matthew's parable of the Workers in the Vineyard has built to a crest and creates a sense of anticipation. Our minds are being teased toward the possibility of a new awareness; the air carries forward the tantalizing scent of a fragrance of grace that is perplexing.

Within the rhythm and energy of Matthew's parable, the landowner is the still point, just as the father of the returned prodigal is the anchored still point within Luke's telling. The landowner of this parable demonstrates by his actions that the grace of God for those of the kingdom is radical, shaking the foundations of expected economics and everyday ethics. Because each worker has come to the vineyard by his own choice after accepting the owner's invitation, there is no question of social justice to be debated. No rights are being violated. The landowner is not being deceitful or duplicitous. He remains calm before the grumbling of the gathered workers as they speak of the burdens of the day and the scorching heat. When he refers to a representative of this group as "friend" (v. 13), it is not in a sarcastic or sardonic voice. This is the tone of someone earnestly wanting to make an important point and to redirect the question in order to focus on the true cause of the disgruntlement.

A key to one understanding of the passage is suggested by the owner's discernment of the source of his workers' grumbling. He ponders aloud the cause of their discontent and wonders if its source lies more within themselves than within his own decisions and actions. There is an invitation for deeper reflection here. From a psychological vantage point, we might consider this to be the recognition of the operation of unconscious projection on the part of the workers, as they cast their own anxieties and assumptions onto the behavior of their employer. The landowner is simply asking them to realize and claim their part in the interaction.

Yet there seems to be something more, especially as we remember that Jesus is offering this parable as a template of the kingdom and that the story is set within a vineyard, bringing to mind John's Gospel and the metaphor of vines and branches (John 15:5). What does it mean to be truly connected to the spirit

Exegetical Perspective

Furthermore, some interpreters see this parable as a statement about the establishment of an alternative egalitarian society.

My ethnicity heavily influences my interpretation of the parable. As a Latino, I have seen how day laborers stand in corners from the early hours of the morning, waiting for someone to hire them. I know that workers who are standing at the corner of the park, the market, or the hardware store in the early afternoon have probably been up since four or five in the morning. I also know that those who are not hired will probably have nothing to eat that night.

Joachim Jeremias in his seminal book on the parables of Jesus misunderstands the situation. The mid-twentieth-century German scholar states that the workers hired last are a clear example of "Oriental indolence."[1] Jeremias evidently thinks that they were not hired early in the day because they were at home resting or sleeping. The contemporary interpreter and the parish preacher must reject such an interpretation of the text.

The parable of the Laborers in the Vineyard continues the topics addressed in the previous chapter. The first topic is God's love for those who are vulnerable in society. The parable illustrates God's love for the poor, as Matthew 19:1–12 illustrates God's love for divorced women and 19:13–15 illustrates God's love for children. The second topic is the correct attitude toward wealth. The parable contrasts the generosity of the landowner with the greed of the rich young man who rejects Jesus' call to discipleship in 19:16–29.

Verse 1 presents the landowner as a man who rules his fields as God rules the divine kingdom. The landowner is wealthy, and the day laborers are poor. The "usual daily wage" (NRSV) is a denarius (v. 2). However, we must note that the wage is established after a mutual agreement between the landowner and the workers (v. 2), thus invalidating any claims of injustice.

The text does not explain why the landowner continues to hire workers during the day (vv. 3–4). At no point does the story suggest that the day laborers hired early in the morning cannot handle the job. By the same token, the landowner does not agree on a wage for the workers hired late in the day; he just promises to pay "whatever is right" (v. 4). Nothing is promised to the last group hired by the landowner, who simply tells them to "go into the vineyard" (v. 7). This group works only about an hour, given that the usual workday ended at six in the evening.

1. Joachim Jeremias, *The Parables of Jesus* (London: SCM Press, 1954), 26.

Homiletical Perspective

paid. We see the owner's generosity to those others whom we consider undeserving. If we watch and wait long enough, perhaps we can see something else too. Perhaps we will even see ourselves in a new way.

Watching and waiting at the back of the line, we begin to see that our issue is greater than just a question of hours worked and equal pay. We see that it is not just equality, not just fairness, but something else we want: if the owner is going to play favorites, we want to be the favored ones. If the owner is going to be ridiculously generous, we should like some of that generosity. "Are you envious because I am generous?" asks the owner of the vineyard. You bet we are! At the back of the line the preacher can scarcely avoid the theological protest: "Why is God not that good to *me*?" "Why does God not love *me* that much?"

Questions raised by this parable are dramatized in Peter Shaffer's play *Amadeus,* which asks what it means to be "beloved of God." The question emerges in a dramatic confrontation between Antonio Salieri, an eighteenth-century court composer in Hapsburg Vienna, and his nemesis, Wolfgang Amadeus Mozart.

As Salieri tells us—at great length—he was a virtuous man, a hard-working man. From his youth Salieri wanted only to write music. As a teenager Salieri had slipped into church and made a bargain with God: he would write God glorious music, and God would grant him fame and fortune in return. As we meet Salieri in the play, it seems clear his bargain has been accepted. A successful and admired composer, all Vienna sings Salieri's praises—and to his own tunes.

Enter Wolfgang Amadeus Mozart, who as a child prodigy wrote his first symphony at five. Mozart, as portrayed in the play *Amadeus,* is vulgar, a notorious womanizer, tactless, conceited, irreligious, disrespectful, and *enormously talented.*

Salieri has worked hard to write beautiful music, but Mozart does not work hard. Music flows from him effortlessly, as if by grace, as if Mozart were a musical instrument and God the musician. Salieri recognizes Mozart's genius. Salieri knows the music proceeds directly from God, that Mozart is indeed *Amadeus,* literally, "the beloved of God." Salieri has received all the acclaim and reward he bargained for, but Mozart has talents beyond imagining, beyond negotiation.

"Are you envious because I am generous?" the owner of the vineyard asks. You bet we are. We begrudge generosity that goes to others and does not come our way. We stand at the back of the line, stewing in bitterness.

Matthew 20:1–16

Theological Perspective

the response of the landowner, "I am doing you no wrong" (v. 13). The matter turns on two things: the first hired "thought they would [and should!] receive more" at the end of the day (v. 10); and the landowner declares, "I choose to give to this last the same as I give to you" (v. 14).

It feels to us readers, as it did to the laborers in the parable and undoubtedly to those who heard Jesus tell it, that generosity seems arbitrary when not calculated fairly. Likewise, if we get any sense of the perspective of one whose intention it is to be generous, strict fairness seems inimical to generosity. The parable wants us to enter this tension and sit for a while with the recognition that with God the contradictions so apparent to us are not at work. We are encountering here a different calculus, one in which being entirely fair (think God's covenant faithfulness) and lavishly generous (think God's mercy to the Gentiles) flow together in an unbroken whole (cf. Rom. 15:1–13). It is like God to act in this way. God refuses to play fairness and generosity off against each other.

The concluding question from the landowner (and from God?!) invites us to reconsider the calculus that has been more natural to us and to welcome God's alternative calculus. It puts our own responses into a new perspective: "Am I not allowed to do what I choose with what belongs to me? Or are you envious because I am generous?" (v. 15). Faith has to do with what, in our minds, we do or do not "allow" to God. Faith is the willingness to trust when God must remind us, "For my thoughts are not your thoughts, nor are your ways my ways, says the Lord" (Isa. 55:8). Faithfulness has to do with refusing envy and welcoming God's lavish expressions of generosity on those who came in later than we did, have not followed as long and hard as we have, were not the pioneers and builders that we have been. To welcome God's generosity lavished on others is to welcome the formation of the same generous spirit in ourselves.

GEORGE R. HUNSBERGER

Pastoral Perspective

of the kingdom? Is it about living in a distracted state of anticipating potential rewards? Is it about living fully in the moments that you have, regardless of when you enter into a kingdom connection? We will see this message yet again in verses 17–28.

Southern writer Flannery O'Connor's short story "Revelation" draws its inspiration directly from this parable. Her story centers on the character of Ruby Turpin, a pious and patronizing lady of self-proclaimed virtue who has a violent encounter with a young woman named Mary Grace in a doctor's office waiting room. Mrs. Turpin is confronted with her Christian smugness and condescending manner of seeing the world and those around her. The story's end finds her hosing down the pigs on the farm she works with her husband. She is gazing into the twilight sky and seeing a vision of a long line of persons dancing into heaven, the column being led by members of her society that she has always considered to be the least deserving. It is a moment pregnant with the question of whether, like the prodigal son or like the workers before the landowner, she will come to herself and realize the meaning of grace.[1]

We are left disquieted by the action of radical grace in the kingdom and the adjustments required of those who would receive it. From O'Connor's collected letters we find her wonderful comment, "All human nature vigorously resists grace because grace changes us and the change is painful."[2]

The landowner is confronting the workers with their own limited understandings. He is inviting them to consider a kingdom awareness that is centered on the state of their own souls, to live "mindfully" in this moment, the parable teasing the hearer's or reader's mind into something subversive of the everyday with regard to what it means to live fully. We end the parable waiting for their decision.

SKIP JOHNSON

1. Flannery O'Connor, "Revelation," in Flannery O'Connor, *The Complete Stories* (1965; repr., New York: Farrar, Straus & Giroux, 1981), 488–509.
2. Sally Fitzgerald, ed., *The Habit of Being: Letters of Flannery O'Connor* (New York: Farrar, Straus & Giroux, 1979), 307.

Feasting on the Gospels

Exegetical Perspective

The last workers to be hired are paid first (v. 8), a detail that anticipates the great reversal affirmed in verse 16. When the workers hired early in the day see that the ones hired later receive a denarius for their toil (v. 9), they expect a higher reward for themselves. However, they receive only the amount agreed upon in verse 2 (v. 10), which triggers bitter complaints against the landowner (vv. 11–12). The verb translated "grumble" (NSRV) is common in the New Testament, where it usually refers to gossiping by Jesus' adversaries or to conflicts at local churches (see Luke 5:30; John 6:41, 43; 1 Cor. 10:10). In most cases, the disgruntled people complain about God's merciful acts toward those who have nothing.

The landowner's rebuttal is a beautiful example of grace (vv. 13–15). First, he defends his actions, indicating that he has paid the amount previously agreed upon (v. 13). There is no foul. Second, the landowner states that he "chooses" to give a full day's pay to the laborers hired late in the day (v. 14). Third, he asserts his right to use his own money as he pleases. He also confronts the disgruntled workers, asking if the real motive of their complaint is envy, not justice (v. 15).

The parable ends with a logion or saying that summarizes the gospel of the kingdom: "So the last will be first, and the first will be last" (v. 16, cf. Mark 10:31; Luke 13:30). Disciples who accept the message of the gospel must undertake the values of the kingdom of God, which tend to contradict the values of the dominant society. In this case, the core values presented by the parable are generosity, mercy, and love.[2]

PABLO A. JIMÉNEZ

Homiletical Perspective

There is an alternative view, however, a good view from this position. Note that Jesus could have told this parable differently—with those hired first paid first, avoiding conflict later. But Jesus did not tell his parable that way, because for those hired first who wait at the back of the line, there is something *more to see.*

The phrase translated, "Are you envious because I am generous?" is literally rendered, as it is in the King James Version, "Is your eye evil?" The problem is not with the owner's generosity but with our eyesight—our angle of vision—and there is another way of looking at things that the sermon can expose.

If we wait and watch long enough, we come to see that the only way we come to know the goodness of God, the only way we can see the goodness of God, is as it is given to others. We can see the goodness of God more clearly in the lives of others, quite simply because they are other than us. The back of the line offers perspective.

We are too close to ourselves, too wrapped in our own skins, too bundled in our own terrible needs, to see truly what God gives us. What God, in goodness and generosity, gives us we are likely to assume is our due, something we have earned, a goodness we have fabricated for ourselves. We see other people more clearly than we see ourselves. Thus when we see God's goodness to others—to people we love, to friends, to colleagues, but most especially to those people we do not think deserve such generosity—then we can see the goodness of God for the wondrous miracle that it is. If we can look at this world through the parable of the Workers in the Vineyard, we will discover the vast truth of the master's generosity: all of us are beloved of God. The first and the last, Salieri and Mozart, those at the front and those at the back of the line.

PATRICK J. WILLSON

2. Pablo A. Jiménez, "The Laborers of the Vineyard (Matthew 20.1–16): A Hispanic Homiletical Reading," *Journal for Preachers* 21, no.1 (Advent 1997): 35–40.

17While Jesus was going up to Jerusalem, he took the twelve disciples aside by themselves, and said to them on the way, 18"See, we are going up to Jerusalem, and the Son of Man will be handed over to the chief priests and scribes, and they will condemn him to death; 19then they will hand him over to the Gentiles to be mocked and flogged and crucified; and on the third day he will be raised."

20Then the mother of the sons of Zebedee came to him with her sons, and kneeling before him, she asked a favor of him. 21And he said to her, "What do you want?" She said to him, "Declare that these two sons of mine will sit, one at your right hand and one at your left, in your kingdom." 22But Jesus answered,

Theological Perspective

At first glance, it would seem that we have here three separate conversations only minimally related to each other.

First, now for a third time (as Matthew, Mark, and Luke all report it), Jesus anticipates his suffering and death at the hands of religious leaders who will condemn him and Roman officials who will mock, flog, and execute him (by crucifixion, only Matthew adds). Two things are different this time: "the Gentiles" are implicated in the deed, and now it is not a vague or distant prophecy. It is about to happen: "See, we are going up to Jerusalem" (v. 18).

Second, the mother of the sons of Zebedee (James and John) approaches Jesus asking a favor. Perhaps she and her sons (Mark and Luke do not mention the mother) remain fixated on Jesus' recent statement that "at the renewal of all things, when the Son of Man is seated on the throne of his glory, you who have followed me will also sit on twelve thrones" (19:28). The request is that the two may sit in the preferred seats (thrones?), a request Jesus says is not his to grant but is his Father's to determine.

Third, when the anger of the other ten arises against these two, Jesus sits them all down for a lesson in the alternative way ruling is to be conducted by them—not like the Gentiles—and the way

Pastoral Perspective

While the setting of Matthew 20:17–28 shifts away from the narrative preceding it, the intent of the passage continues to be parabolic. It focuses on the challenge of understanding what it means to accept an invitation to the radical meaning of the kingdom.

Jesus and his disciples are traveling toward Jerusalem. During the journey, we are told that Jesus takes the Twelve off to the side to provide them with particular details of what is about to take place. He provides a direct and unambiguous statement about what is waiting for him at the end of their journey. His statement is marked by the explicit naming of the circumstances that will surround his own death. The clarity of his speaking makes what follows appear all the more questionable and strange: the juxtaposed exchange with two of his disciples and their mother.

As in the chapter's earlier parable with its disgruntled workers standing before the landowner in the vineyard (20:1–16), one stands on the outskirts of this passage shaking one's head over misunderstanding and misconstrued meanings. The request by the mother of James and John for her sons to be granted positions of power and prestige in the coming kingdom bears more resemblance to a borrowed sketch from the British comedy group Monty Python

"You do not know what you are asking. Are you able to drink the cup that I am about to drink?" They said to him, "We are able." ²³He said to them, "You will indeed drink my cup, but to sit at my right hand and at my left, this is not mine to grant, but it is for those for whom it has been prepared by my Father."

²⁴When the ten heard it, they were angry with the two brothers. ²⁵But Jesus called them to him and said, "You know that the rulers of the Gentiles lord it over them, and their great ones are tyrants over them. ²⁶It will not be so among you; but whoever wishes to be great among you must be your servant, ²⁷and whoever wishes to be first among you must be your slave; ²⁸just as the Son of Man came not to be served but to serve, and to give his life a ransom for many."

Exegetical Perspective

This text contains two related stories. The first is the third announcement of Jesus' death and resurrection (vv. 17–19). The second is the request of the mother of James and John, who desires places of privilege for her children in the kingdom of God (vv. 20–28).

Both stories come from Mark (Mark 10:32–34, 35–45), where they are located in a section that highlights the disciples' inability to comprehend fully Jesus' message. In Mark, that section, from chapter 8 to chapter 10, is framed by two miracle stories in which Jesus heals blind men: one who is not named at Bethsaida (8:22–26) and Bartimaeus at Jericho (10:46–52). Matthew's versions of these stories closely follow Mark's account, although Matthew does not stress the subject of incomprehension as strongly as Mark does.

The third announcement of Jesus' death and resurrection presupposes the first two (16:21–23; 17:22–23). The number three, like other numbers in the Bible, has symbolic value. It appears in the phrase "on the third day," as in Matthew 20:19. However, the number is also used in 26:34, in reference to Peter's denial of Jesus. Solemn oaths are also repeated three times (see John 21:15–19). In general, the number three refers to that which is divine.

The announcement takes place on the way to Jerusalem (20:17). Given that the Holy City is in a valley

Homiletical Perspective

If we leap into an ongoing conversation, we may misunderstand the thrust of the discussion; we may say things that sound unfortunate and inappropriate as we respond in ways that belong to some other conversation. That is the problem with the request made here by "the mother of the sons of Zebedee." It is also the dilemma the preacher faces in reading this pericope. The boundaries of any selected text are always somewhat arbitrary, and that is so with verses 17–28 as a discrete and preachable unit. Matthew began a series of conversations in 19:27 with Peter asking, "What then will we have?" The topic of conversation appears to be, what can disciples of Jesus expect to receive? The prior parable of the Workers in the Vineyard, with its controversial parceling out of payments, is one piece of that conversation.

Now the mother of the sons of Zebedee hears Jesus announce that "the Son of Man is seated on the throne of his glory" and that "you who have followed me will also sit on twelve thrones" (19:28). She was not privy, however, to a later side conversation when Jesus "took the twelve disciples aside by themselves" and explained how "the Son of Man will be handed over . . . to death" (20:18). The mother of the sons of Zebedee has heard about the triumphant victory of the Son of Man "at the renewal of all things" (19:28),

Matthew 20:17–28

Theological Perspective

greatness is to be sought (by being a servant) and position gained (by being a slave).

On closer observation, it becomes evident that there is something like a deep ocean or river flowing beneath these three episodes, binding them together and bearing them along. Jesus and the disciples are on their way to the cross, and it is being made ever clearer that to follow Jesus is to follow in the way of the cross. Markers in the narrative make this apparent: Jesus will be handed over, condemned, mocked, flogged, and crucified. To the request of the mother, Jesus says (to her and the sons), "Are you able to drink the cup that I am about to drink?" (v. 22).

Jesus contrasts the way of the disciples with the way the rulers of the Gentiles "lord it over them" and the way their great ones are "tyrants over them" (all of which will be so vividly displayed soon in Jesus' crucifixion). "It will not be so among you" (v. 26). Instead, what will be so among them is likeness to the Son of Man, who "came not to be served but to serve, and to give his life a ransom for many" (v. 28).

Jesus' impending death—his crucifixion, the cup he is about to drink, the life he is giving as a ransom—is the deep undercurrent that determines everything, in these episodes and for the whole company of Jesus' followers, then and now. The spirituality of the apostle Paul, the insight of the sixteenth-century Protestant reformer Martin Luther, and the writings of a contemporary gathering community of theologians (Douglas John Hall, Gerhard Forde, Jürgen Moltmann, and Alan E. Lewis, to mention a few) lead us to attend to this undercurrent: what Luther called a theology of the cross, which stands over against a theology of glory that has allured so many in the church's history.

More pointedly, Luther drew the contrast as one between being *theologians of the cross* and *theologians of glory*—see, for example, the *Heidelberg Disputation*. For Luther and present-day theologians who appropriate his distinctions, to be a theologian of the cross means much more than having a theory or theology about the cross and its meaning. It means, rather, in Forde's words, having "a particular perception of the world and our destiny, what Luther came to call looking at all things through suffering and the cross. It has to do with . . . the way the cross is put to use in our lives."[1] As Hall puts it, "the theology of the cross is . . . a spirit and a method that one

1. Gerhard Forde, "On Being a Theologian of the Cross," *Christian Century*, October 22, 1997, 949.

Pastoral Perspective

than to an appropriate and true interaction between Jesus and his most intimate associates.

The conversational exchange we witness is taking place on two different language levels. Jesus is simply not being heard, or at least his words are not being attended to with the necessary eagerness and depth of comprehension. His listeners overlook, misinterpret, or disregard the weight of what they are being told, distractedly looking instead to personal reward and position. When the circle of conversation widens to include the other ten disciples—we are not told whether their mothers are also present to lobby on their behalf!—we find indignation reflected among the entire group, perhaps because the idea of approaching Jesus with a special appeal for such privilege did not happen to occur to them first.

A key phrase in the passage is found in Jesus' initial reply to the request for a specific reward (v. 22). One can imagine him speaking with a tone of frustration mixed with sadness in his reply to James, John, and their mother: "You do not know what you are asking." He goes on to question their ability to drink the cup that he is about to drink. They answer unreservedly with a speedy, "We are able" (v. 22). One can imagine Jesus' eyebrow arching quizzically upward. It seems apparent that something has been lost in translation. Did you hear anything that I said?

The full-day workers in the vineyard parable of 20:1–16 were unable to acknowledge the distortion they had brought on themselves by their envy of the wages received by the laborers who came last. Now the focus shifts to the twelve disciples, Jesus' closest followers. This is his circle of intimates, yet they demonstrate a self-centered naiveté, missing the point in self-aggrandizing delusion as to what a connection with Jesus is really all about. They are looking for benefits. Jesus reminds them it is about something altogether different.

For me as a reader, it is reminiscent of the easy affirmations and vows sometimes made in the most significant of life decisions, which are confirmed, pledged, and sworn without any reflective comprehension as to the import and consequences of their meaning. Be they couples entering into a covenant of marriage, parents accepting responsibility for a child at baptism, or men and women responding to words of ordination or consecration into Christian service, there is always much that is not fully understood and yet is readily agreed to, for reasons more selfish than selfless.

Ironically, the expressed displeasure of the other ten disciples to the request of their two colleagues

surrounded by mountains, people usually "go up to Jerusalem" (v. 17). This expression has cultic implications, evoking the Psalms of Ascent (Pss. 120–134) sung by pilgrims on their way to the temple.

Jesus offers a succinct summary of the events that will soon take place, telling the disciples that the "Son of Man will be handed over to the chief priests and scribes, and they will be condemn him to death" (v. 18). The new element here is his condemnation, a detail not mentioned in the earlier announcements.

In a veiled reference to Judea's colonial status, Jesus asserts that he will be "handed over to the Gentiles" (v. 19). This implies that Jewish religious leaders collaborated with the colonial government in order to kill Jesus. Why? Because Romans, like most colonial powers, reserved to themselves the right to apply the death penalty. Jesus will endure mocking, flagellation, and crucifixion. Flogging was a form of torture, performed with a short whip called "flagellum," multiple strands of leather with sharp pieces of metal or bone at the tips. Crucifixion was also a form of torture, used mainly against rebels accused of sedition. Inefficient as a form of capital punishment, death on a cross was meant as a deterrent to would-be enemies of the state. These insights may help the interpreter to construct a postcolonial reading of the text.

The "good news" is that Jesus will conquer death, rising up "on the third day" (v. 19). Nonetheless, the brief reference to the resurrection suggests that the main intention of the text is to prepare the reader for Jesus' arrest, trial, and gruesome death.

The second story is the odd request by the mother of James and John (vv. 20–28). In Mark's version, the sons of Zebedee ask for themselves. Probably this story echoes the many times where people ask for Jesus' patronage in the kingdom of heaven. This would explain the awkward literary structure of the text.

The first part of the text (vv. 20–23) affirms that only God decides the positions of honor in the kingdom, hinting that martyrdom may determine how God grants such positions. The second part (vv. 24–28) addresses the issue of who is the greatest in the kingdom, stressing that in the Christian community greatness is achieved through service and mutual love.

The mother of James and John, the sons of Zebedee, kneels before Jesus (v. 20) and asks him to grant positions of honor to her children (v. 21). Jesus asks the brothers if they are capable of drinking the same cup he is about to drink (v. 22). "Drinking a cup" is a metaphor for enduring suffering and punishment

but she has not heard that the Son of Man "will be handed over," die, and be raised. She is only about to discover the wholly unanticipated truth that "the Son of Man came not to be served but to serve." In this respect she models those who first listened to Matthew's Gospel, alongside those who gather around it now in the twenty-first century.

Far from providing preachers an occasion for joking asides about Jewish mothers or parents who are excessively ambitious for their children, her request offers a promising homiletical platform from which to engage the text. Adopting a posture that may be recommended for preaching, she kneels before Jesus and does not speak until spoken to. Jesus recognizes a supplicant's pose and asks her, "What do you want?" Then and only then does she make requests on behalf of her children. She knows enough of the Son of Man to want to respond to him, but she does not know enough of the character of the Son of Man to respond fittingly. Surely we can sympathize.

The request the mother of the sons of Zebedee makes is derived from the repertoire of social aspirations provided by a culture that understood reality as a hierarchy of honor and power. At the bottom were slaves and servants; at the top were thrones and those who sat upon them. She hears Jesus' words about "Son of Man . . . seated on the throne of his glory" with other thrones descending from his, and she hopes that her sons, who are, after all, Jesus' disciples, might find a place within such a glorious vision.

Does that really seem so odd, so out of place? Do parents—except in BBC television classics like *Upstairs, Downstairs* and *Downton Abbey*—hope their children will be servants? Have parents anytime or anywhere longed for their children to become slaves? Nevertheless, that is precisely what Jesus proposes to those who follow him. Authentic greatness in that kingdom of the Son of Man authorizes a reevaluation of the lives we imagine for ourselves. Previously servants and slaves were what we wanted to *have*; now servants and slaves are what we strive to *be*.

This vision of verses 26–28 has always worked better as a stimulus to critical thinking than as an institutional framework for the church. Within only a few years the apostle Paul would dramatically upgrade the status of "slave of Christ" as a formal self-designation (Rom. 1:1), and before the New Testament was completed, "servant," *diakonos*, would apparently be the title of an office in the first-century church (Rom. 16:1; 1 Tim. 4:6). Institutionalize those titles though we may, the names still offer sharp

Matthew 20:17–28

Theological Perspective

brings to all one's reflections on all the various areas and facets of Christian faith and life."[2]

In this portion of Matthew 20, Jesus presses the disciples to recognize in the cross upon which he will shortly hang the inconceivable logic that "the surrender of power is *the* form, and the *only* form, that God's power takes" and is God's means for "bringing history powerfully to its fulfillment." Lewis calls this living "between the cross and resurrection" as an Easter Saturday community whose mode of life is that of "confessing and obeying Christ's cruciform, grave-shaped lordship over all."[3]

Following in the way of Jesus' self-relinquishing, God-entrusting love cuts a path at odds with the self-reliant and self-serving optimism that presents itself in some way or another in virtually every age and place—nowhere more strongly perhaps than in contemporary North America. The self-confidence that takes delight in determining the fate of others (read "lords it over them") and the easy equation of greatness with tyranny—whether social, economic, political, or psychological—are habits of "the Gentiles" to which disciples are not naturally immune (as the request of Zebedee's family and the offense taken by the other ten disciples illustrate). Again and again, and particularly when it comes to this most crucial of issues, the nature and form of leadership and authority, Jesus' words come echoing in reminder: "It will not be so among you; but whoever wishes to be great among you must be your servant, and whoever wishes to be first among you must be your slave" (vv. 26–27).

GEORGE R. HUNSBERGER

Pastoral Perspective

suggests that their understanding of what it means to drink of the cup is equally lacking. What is intriguing is the overarching allusion to an ongoing pastoral theme of Matthew regarding those who are able to properly hear and see the good news. In 13:16 we read, "Blessed are your eyes, for they see, and your ears, for they hear." The persons who are able to accomplish this are not necessarily the ones that you would expect. This idea will be further developed in the final passage of Matthew 20, when Jesus provides sight to two blind men on the roadside outside of Jericho (vv. 29–34).

The entire chapter is fraught with themes of reversal, along with questions of who is capable of attending to what is truly significant in the kingdom. It concludes with an implied question as to who the blind really are and redirects our attention from the front of the line to its end point, surprising us about who is found where, and reminding us of the radical nature of the kingdom and of God's gift of grace.

Jesus' response to the perceived dullness of wits and perception among his disciples shows a triumph of compassion over anger. In verses 25–28 he is gentle in his explanation of what his statements portend, modeling before his followers a way of rebuke that is in stark contrast to the exercise of authority by the Gentiles. He is modeling what they are to learn and to practice. The "first to be last" kingdom truth is reiterated twice (19:30; 20:16), as Jesus asks his listeners to seek to be servants and slaves to others, surrendering the self and its ego needs. Perhaps there is recognition here that the development of reflective wisdom, of kingdom awareness, is stirred by behavior as well as by insight. Live out the actions of the servant, Jesus seems to say, and you will find your way to understanding. Watch my example in the days ahead, and follow my lead into the grace of the kingdom.

SKIP JOHNSON

---

2. Douglas John Hall, "The Theology of the Cross: A Usable Past," *Seminary Ridge Review* 8, no. 2 (2006): 7.
3. Alan E. Lewis, *Between Cross and Resurrection: A Theology of Holy Saturday* (Grand Rapids: Eerdmans, 2001), 303.

(see, e.g., 26:39, 42). Therefore, Jesus asks them if they are willing to endure martyrdom for their faith.

The brothers answer that they are able to endure suffering (v. 22), revealing in the process that their mother has voiced their question. Jesus affirms that they will indeed be martyrs (v. 23), but that granting positions of honor in the kingdom of God is a prerogative of God the Father. According to Acts 12:2, James died as a martyr under the government of Herod Agrippa I, who ruled Judea from 37 to 44 CE. In early Christian tradition, the story of John the apostle has been conflated with that of John of Patmos, who endured persecution and incarceration for his faith. Contemporary scholars tend to believe that they are two different persons.

The other disciples react angrily to the brothers' petition (v. 24) with indignation (ēganaktēsan). The reader wonders if the real motive of their anger is envy, not holy zeal. In any case, Jesus uses the occasion as a teaching moment (v. 25), proceeding to discuss the criteria for determining who is "the greatest" one in the kingdom of God. Jesus contrasts true and false greatness, affirming that nonbelievers (called "Gentiles") wield power in tyrannical ways (v. 25) and instructing the church to exercise power in a different way (v. 26). Greatness in the Christian community must be determined by service to the other (v. 27), particularly to those whom Jesus served ("the least of these," 25:40, 45).

The text ends by presenting Jesus as the model of discipleship, leadership, and service: "the Son of Man came . . . to serve, and to give his life a ransom for many" (v. 28). Therefore, disciples who want to achieve greatness must emulate Jesus' life of self-sacrificial service.

PABLO A. JIMÉNEZ

critique of the church and those who serve within it: "Whoever wishes to be great among you must be your servant, and whoever wishes to be first among you must be your slave" (vv. 26–27).

The request the mother of the sons of Zebedee makes is not so much inappropriate as it is untimely. She does not know what time it is and what the present moment requires. At the end, "at the renewal of all things" (19:28), there will indeed be thrones of glory, and glory aplenty to be passed around, as common and sweet as cotton candy at the state fair. Now, however, they are "going up to Jerusalem . . . and the Son of Man will be handed over" to the bitterness of suffering and death (20:17, 18); and now in this present moment we are invited to comprehend that "the Son of Man came not to be served but to serve" (v. 28).

Along that trajectory of service traced by the Son of Man's service, sacrifice, suffering, death—and eventual resurrection and enthronement—we who follow will discover whatever honor and greatness we may be given. Like the mother of the sons of Zebedee, we entered this conversation wondering what we shall receive; in the end we discover it is about the servant work of the Son of Man. Like the consumers that we always are, we thought we were talking about what would be given *to* us; instead the conversation is about what the servant Christ gives *for* us.

His service is a gift, and coming to terms with Jesus' words is also a gift. The words dazzle us and baffle us, just as they have dislocated the expectations of disciples for centuries. If we can hear them at all, we receive them, not as an achievement of our understanding, but a gift given with the same generosity as the landowner in the vineyard parable that preceded this text. May it be a gift that we ask for, as in the story immediately following, as two blind men pray to Jesus, "Lord, let our eyes be opened" (20:33). Let us see the servant way you are going, so that we may follow.

PATRICK J. WILLSON

Matthew 20:29–34

²⁹As they were leaving Jericho, a large crowd followed him. ³⁰There were two blind men sitting by the roadside. When they heard that Jesus was passing by, they shouted, "Lord, have mercy on us, Son of David!" ³¹The crowd sternly ordered them to be quiet; but they shouted even more loudly, "Have mercy on us, Lord, Son of David!" ³²Jesus stood still and called them, saying, "What do you want me to do for you?" ³³They said to him, "Lord, let our eyes be opened." ³⁴Moved with compassion, Jesus touched their eyes. Immediately they regained their sight and followed him.

Theological Perspective

Here we move to the final chapter of Jesus' life and ministry. Doing the work of God in word and deed, Jesus and those following him encounter opposition and rejection in the Galilee region. After Peter's confession at Caesarea Philippi, Jesus tells the disciples of his impending death and turns toward Jerusalem.[1]

Jesus walks the road from Jericho to Jerusalem, a journey he believes he will take for the last time. He has told those closest to him that he will be handed over to the chief priests and then to the Romans, who will flog, mock, and execute him (20:17–19). A large and excited crowd, convinced that he is the promised Messiah, follows him. Then from the side of the road comes an anguished cry from two blind men, "Lord, have mercy on us, Son of David" (v. 30). Members of the crowd, eager to accompany Jesus on his triumphal entry into Jerusalem, tell them to shut up and stop bothering the new king, who they believe has more important things to do than help them. The blind men, however, will not be quiet and shout even louder, "Have mercy on us, Lord, Son of David." Jesus stops in his tracks, turns toward them, and asks, "What do you want me to do for you?" They answer, "Lord, let our eyes be opened." Moved with

1. Donald Senior, *Matthew* (Nashville: Abingdon Press, 1998), 227–28.

Pastoral Perspective

It is a road oft traveled, particularly by clergy in small, older-skewing congregations. A beloved member's gradual decline with age suddenly shifts into a landslide. Perhaps it is cancer or congestive heart failure. Regardless, it is the brief, often physically painful completion of the earthly journey. In many ways, each round of "death watch" in a congregation is strikingly similar. Still, in almost every instance, there are those moments that stand out—that make the final days of this beloved child of God different from the final days of those before her who have taken a similar path. Each of us clings to life, or lets go of life, in ways that reflect and define how we have lived. One is resigned, one is defiant, one is at peace, one is in denial.

With that in mind, these six verses that transition out of Jesus' pre-Jerusalem ministry show him undertaking that journey. Just ten verses ago, Jesus announced his call to go to Jerusalem, knowing that he would be crucified there (20:17–19). The question of how he will face his fate is largely addressed by this brief healing story. Jesus' steadfast identity in the face of death raises questions for the church's faithfulness in every age, but particularly in our era.

First, *Jesus will not allow his impending death to change who he is.* Here, two blind men encounter

Exegetical Perspective

All three Synoptic Gospels include at least one miracle of Jesus restoring the sight of someone who is blind, and the Gospel of John includes the story of Jesus granting sight to someone blind from birth. In two of these stories from Matthew, two blind people are healed rather than one (see also 9:27–31). There is no clear reason why Matthew doubles the number of those healed; perhaps he wants to make Jesus' miracles more remarkable, or maybe he is just dramatizing the plural form that is in Jesus' words in 11:5 ("The blind receive their sight"). More important than the number of those healed for the proclamation of this text are the contrasts Matthew highlights within it. In these contrasts we see clearly that Jesus is who Matthew called him at the start of this Gospel: "Christ" and "son of David" (1:1).

The reading begins and ends with references to following Jesus. At its beginning, a great crowd follows Jesus as he leaves Jericho. As the story ends, the two who were formerly blind now also follow Jesus on the way to Jerusalem. In between, Matthew contrasts the crowd and the blind ones: the great crowd is following, while the two who are blind are lying alongside the road. These two are on the margin of the action swirling around Jesus, and they are stuck there. Something that will come to look like a royal

Homiletical Perspective

In Matthew, Jesus' healing ministry is an essential element of his mission to proclaim the good news of the kingdom of heaven. Matthew consistently portrays Jesus as a powerful and compassionate healer who is concerned for people marginalized in Jewish society and identifies the healer as the Messiah, the "Son of David." This text is one of the stories of Jesus' healing miracles.

For preachers, miracle stories of healing in Scripture are a challenge, since miracles are normally understood as irrational or supernatural events. On the one hand, contemporary Christians no longer live in a premodern world, and many want to disregard such unscientific stories in the Bible or "demythologize" them as "husks" of the Christian gospel. On the other hand, many still want to believe biblical stories of healing as facts and anticipate that miracles like those in the Bible happen in their own lives as supplements to the achievement of modern science. How, then, can the preacher or teacher deal with this text? Should it be taught as an assurance of belief in the miracle of healing? Should it be deleted from the list of sermon texts? If neither is the case, how can contemporary listeners find relevance in the story?

One of the homiletical ideas to preach a theologically meaningful and contextually relevant sermon

Theological Perspective

compassion, Jesus touches them and restores their sight. They follow him (vv. 31–34).

In asking for sight, did they know they would see not only people, trees, and sunsets, but also the effects of Rome's imperial rule on their people and their homeland? Did they know that they would see the divisions that that rule caused among their brothers and sisters—prophetic Pharisees over against accommodating Sadducees and high priests; violent Zealots and sicarii against sectarian Essenes; large landowners against displaced itinerants?[2] Did they know that following Jesus meant standing with him against that rule and the disorder it causes in God's creation? Did they know that Jesus was to be flogged, mocked, and executed when they got to Jerusalem? When they got up to follow Jesus, did they know that they would be following him on "the way of the cross"? Does anyone?

The young Dutch Reformed pastor Beyers Naudé probably did not. The youngest member ever admitted to the Afrikaner Broederbond—South Africa's most powerful political group—Naudé became acting moderator of the Transvsaal Synod of the Dutch Reformed Church (1961), which endorsed the government policy of apartheid. Many believed he would be the future premier of the country. Sitting on his own road to Jerusalem, however, Naudé's eyes were opened as he taught and mentored seminary students doing field work in the racially segregated homelands of South Africa. He dismissed as exaggerated their reports about the conditions blacks endured—until he accepted his students' invitation to see for himself. He began to visit the homelands—something he and many like him had never done. Those who lived there were out of sight and out of mind. Among other things, he saw the unsanitary conditions and the overcrowded quarters, and he witnessed a massacre of people demonstrating against the pass laws.

What Naudé saw changed him forever. He withdrew from the racist Broederbond and called upon the Reformed Church to repudiate its support of the government's policy of apartheid. The church refused. One Sunday morning in September 1963, after preaching a sermon entitled "Obey God, Rather than Man," Naudé descended the pulpit of the prestigious Aasvoelkop Church in suburban

2. See Howard Thurman, *Jesus and the Disinherited* (1949; repr., Boston: Beacon Press, 1996), 23–27. For an interesting description of the tension between village landowners and those who had lost their land through debt and foreclosure, see John Dominic Crossan, "Jesus and the Kingdom: Itinerants and Householders in Earliest Christianity," in Marcus Borg, ed., *Jesus at 2000* (Boulder, CO: Westview Press, 1991), 21–53.

Pastoral Perspective

him and call out to him, "Have mercy, Son of David," the exact words two other blind men used in seeking his aid much earlier in his public ministry (9:27). Who is this Jesus? He is Son of David, Matthew's shorthand for Messiah. He is merciful, one whose steadfast love for those he encounters is not passive or internalized, but on display in acts of compassion and restoration.

For Christians today, it can hardly be doubted that the mainline church of the mid-twentieth century is in decline, if membership lists (and median ages) are taken as an indicator of life and liveliness. If that is true, if the historic Protestant churches in North America are approaching their demise in the coming generations, will this change the church's identity in meaningful ways? Will the church surrender its compassion, its mercy, its core identity, in order to survive?

Second, *Jesus continues to find his identity on the margins.* Here Jesus is on the precipice of confrontation with the powers and principalities, particularly the religious leaders and educated people, who would be expected to know about and recognize the Son of David. Very shortly we will learn that those powers will not recognize him. Indeed, they will be irritated, belligerent, and murderous—clearly demonstrating they do not "know" him at all.

In our post-Christendom world, as the Western church ends its seventeen centuries at the center of power and is returned to the margins by the shifting center of an increasingly secularized and globalized culture, will it reclaim its first-century roots at the margins? Will it adapt its expectations and structures to engage the world, not from a position of power and influence, but with prophetic and healing ministries? Like Jesus, can the church move from setting the agenda to asking what is required or needed of us, and then responding as opportunities present themselves? Further, will the church still be able to recognize the Jesus it encounters on the margins?

It is ironic that the (physically) blind men recognize Jesus even though they cannot see him. Perhaps it is their open acknowledgment of their need and powerlessness that grants them faithful vision. Perhaps it is their very powerlessness, which removes the blinders of self-delusion as to their own personal power and autonomy, that gives them the ability to "see" true power, true strength, true compassion in the Jesus who is passing by. Can the church as willingly claim its newfound second-class status as an invitation to greater dependence on the steadfast mercy of a loving God?

procession into the holy city is passing them by. Even so, the blind ones are aware of the crowd, and when they hear that Jesus is going by, they cry out, "Lord, have mercy on us, Son of David" (v. 30). The crowd rebukes the two, telling them to be silent, with the result that they cry out all the more.

Like "Christ," the title "Son of David" calls to mind the restoration of Israel's fortunes and that time when God will rescue God's people from subjection to pagan rule. David's reign was recalled as a high point in Israel's history. A ruler like David would surely be good news. Yet scholars have puzzled over why the title is on the lips of people who seek healing. David did not heal anyone. How did the title come to be part of requests for healing? One of the most plausible answers connects the title to Ezekiel 34, where God announces that, in the absence of good shepherds among the trusted leaders of Israel, God will shepherd the people: "I myself will be the shepherd of my sheep, and I will make them lie down, says the Lord GOD. I will seek the lost, and I will bring back the strayed, and I will bind up the injured" (Ezek. 34:15–16a). As shepherd, David would have ministered to the injured of the flock; such healing is part of the work that Ezekiel says God will take up. This is the work, then, that Matthew shows Jesus doing. Jesus the healer is also Son of David.[1]

The blind ones by the road cry out for mercy to "Lord, Son of David." Jesus stops and calls to them. This pause in the action gives the reader time to consider how the story arc might be drawn differently. Jesus might pass by these two on the outskirts of town, distracted by his own thoughts about Jerusalem. He might be swept along in the excitement of the crowd, or "protected" by the crowd's attempts to silence the needy at its edge. These things do not happen. Instead, Jesus engages the two who are calling to him.

Jesus asks, "What do you want me to do for you?" (v. 32). When the two ask for their sight, Jesus is moved with compassion and touches their eyes, and they can see again. Up to this point in Matthew, we have heard of Jesus' compassion three times; in each case Jesus' concern is with the needs of the crowd following him. He has compassion when he looks out on the crowd and sees them as "sheep without a shepherd" (9:36), when he heals the sick among the crowd (14:14), and when he provides food for

is to read the text attentively and imaginatively from the perspective of Matthew's theology, the theology of the kingdom of heaven. At first glance, this passage seems to be just one of many healing stories of Jesus. In fact, the story is similar both in structure and vocabulary to the healing of two other blind men in Matthew 9:27–31. The text is, however, distinctive from the other healing story in at least two aspects.

One is that, in the narrative plot of the Gospel, the text is placed between the passage of Jesus' foretelling of his death and resurrection in Jerusalem to his disciples (20:17–19) and the passage of his messianic procession into the city of Jerusalem (21:1–11). In this plotted schema, the text functions as the climax of Jesus' ministry for the kingdom of heaven before he is going to be proclaimed as the Messiah to the public in Jerusalem.

The other distinctive aspect of the story is that this text emphasizes Jesus' compassion as the key factor that makes the miracle of healing happen. In 9:27–31, the two blind men's faith contributes to the healing miracle. This story, however, witnesses that Jesus' compassion for the two blind men made the miraculous healing happen (v. 34, "Moved with compassion, Jesus touched their eyes") and that they were transformed from disabled and marginalized persons to active participants in Jesus' ministry of proclaiming the kingdom of heaven.

For Matthew, God consistently exercises sovereign power on behalf of the marginalized in society, and God's saving intervention in their lives is the sign of the kingdom of heaven, a sign of future hope promised in Jesus' crucifixion and resurrection. The healing story in the text exemplifies this sign. Through this miracle, the crowd who have been following Jesus witness again a strange new world in which no one is excluded. Indeed, where compassion is, the kingdom of heaven is present, in which "the birds of the air come and make nests in its branches" (13:32).

The reading of the text from the perspective of the kingdom of heaven suggests at least three important homiletical insights. First of all, the text should not be demythologized but should function as a paradigm through which the preacher or teacher and listeners can think theologically about the meaning of the miracle on a deeper level and reflect on our contemporary experiences of miracles. What kind of miracles have we experienced in our personal and communal lives? What kind of transforming events have we witnessed?

---

1. For more on the connection between this title in Matthew and Ezekiel 34, see Wayne S. Baxter, "Healing and the 'Son of David': Matthew's Warrant," *Novum Testamentum* 48, no. 1 (2006): 36–50.

Matthew 20:29–34

Theological Perspective

Johannesburg, took off his clerical robe, and renounced his ordination in the Dutch Reformed Church. He became active in the movement to end South Africa's institutionalized racism, eventually succeeding Desmond Tutu as the general secretary of the South African Council of Churches.

The regime placed him under house arrest for seven years. Despite restrictions on visitors and travel, Naudé led the Christian Institute, whose theological perspective challenged racial segregation and discrimination. When apartheid ended, Naudé was the sole Afrikaner (white) among the principal negotiators for the African National Congress that established the interim government and constitution for the new South Africa. Nelson Mandela said that Naudé's "remarkable witness continued to be a great source of inspiration" and "living proof that *baaskap* [air of racial supremacy] is not an essential characteristic of the Afrikaner people."[3]

There is a difference between the two men in our Gospel story and Beyers Naudé: they knew they were blind, while he did not—at first. However, once Naudé's students offered to show him what he had not seen, he had to decide: Would he look, or would he not? Did he want to be healed, or did he not? He probably did not know at the time he accepted his students' invitation to see that it would set him on a life course in which so much would be taken from him, and so much hatred directed at him. Neither did he likely know the ways in which his life would be immeasurably enriched by the new relationships there, because of his choice to see and act.

This passage invites us to consider hard questions too. In what regard might we be blind? Whom and what do we not see? Who and what are not in our field of vision? Do we want to see, if seeing entails taking responsibility for doing something about what we see? What if doing something brings with it a high cost and an uncertain reward? With the blind men on the road to Jerusalem, we are invited to ask whether we will have the courage to shout and ask to see the truth.

STEPHEN BOYD

Pastoral Perspective

Third, *Jesus is undergoing a "coming out" of sorts.* Eleven chapters ago, when he healed those first two blind men, he instructed them (without success) to tell no one what he had done. Here, on the brink of the moments that will define him as Christ, his secrecy is gone. Jesus is not uncertain about who he is or cautious about anyone's finding out.

In a contemporary culture where declarations of faith are too often equated with a flat-earth, science-denying, willful ignorance, can the mainline reclaim the foolishness of faith in a resurrected Lord—not in opposition to intellectual and philosophic vigor, but as the motivation for a defiant hope and uncynical compassion that is more concerned with mercy than doctrine?

Finally, *Jesus makes it clear that he will not bow to the will or expectations of the masses.* Before, Jesus silenced those he healed. Now, the crowd seeks to silence those who would be healed. They have bigger fish to fry than tending to two marginalized beggars. They have a revolution to undertake, but Jesus will not let the crowd's agenda become his agenda—with, at least for a time, fatal results.

Remarkably, the two men who are healed in this passage do not return to their families and communities to report all that happened to them (as the men did in chapter 9); instead, they join Jesus and the crowds that journey with him to Jerusalem. Their example of faithfulness is not to become Jesus, but to follow him.

This passage invites us to follow Christ's example of steadfastness to his true identity, even in the face of death. Even more, perhaps the ultimate invitation in the text is to stop assuming that the church is the soon-to-be-martyred Jesus and, instead, to claim our own blindness. Then, as we prepare to answer the question of what we want Jesus to do for us, and awaken to the healing we have been given, may we respond by following, trusting the new vision we have been given, even if the road ahead is leading us to unfamiliar territory.

MICHAEL D. KIRBY

---

3. Charles Villa-Vicencio and Carl Niehaus, eds., *Many Cultures, One Nation: Festschrift for Beyers Naudé* (Cape Town: Human & Rousseau, 1995), 6.

Exegetical Perspective

thousands (15:32). The difference this time is that it is not the needs of the crowd that move Jesus to compassionate action, but the needs of two individuals whom the crowd around him has tried to hush.

This text is about physical healing, yet the response of the formerly blind ones—they see and follow Jesus—is itself a vivid contrast to the response in this Gospel of Israel's leaders, who, like the would-be leaders in Ezekiel's time, cannot see the way of God or participate in God's will and reign. In the story of the man born blind (John 9), John draws a sharp contrast between the formerly blind man, who comes to see and confess Jesus to be the Christ, and the Pharisees, whose willful refusal to recognize Jesus as sent from God plunges them into ever deeper darkness. Something like that contrast is present also in Matthew's Gospel. Only in Matthew does Jesus call the scribes and Pharisees "blind guides" (15:14; 23:16; 23:24) and "blind fools" (23:17).

Preachers will want to use care in the way they appropriate this metaphor of blindness: hymns, texts, and sermons that speak of our "blindness to God's will" and so on can be experienced as thoroughly insensitive to the real lives of those who are, in fact, blind, and who are also faithful followers of Jesus Christ. The sermon can avoid such insensitivity by simply drawing hearers' attention to these two by the side of the road and to the way Jesus responds to them—and they to him—even as he and a great crowd travel on to Jerusalem. Both when these two are blind and when they are seeing, they recognize Jesus as Son of David and their healer. As we share in their story, we are able to see him this way as well.

MARY HINKLE SHORE

Homiletical Perspective

The second homiletical insight comes from reading the text with imagination. For example, imagine that we are on the biblical scene and hear the cries of the two blind men as Jesus does. Do we have a feeling of empathy? Do we feel compassion for them? Are we willing to touch their eyes with love? Like Jesus, we hear the cries of the people on the margins of our own church, society, and world. Do we respond to their voices with compassion and grace? Honestly, for many of us who were born and raised in an individualistic culture, listening with compassion to the desperate cries of the marginalized is a difficult, humbling, lifelong process of learning, for our individualistic culture has hardened our hearts and has taught us to cover our ears and close our hearts to the cries of others. Where there is no compassion, no miracle happens. Yet, in the direction of becoming a more compassionate community, we experience that every increase in our capacity for empathy with those who are marginalized by their physical and other disabilities makes it possible for God to intervene. God exercises sovereign power to make the miracle of healing happen in our personal and communal lives.

The last homiletical insight is that the text is ultimately an invitation to the community of solidarity. Rather than simply describing the miracle story as a personal experience of God's miraculous power, Matthew intends through the story to invite his readers to the formation of a new community that represents the kingdom of heaven here and now. In this community, members empathize with the weakness and pain of others and share in their suffering, as Jesus did. Where solidarity is built among the members, the miracle of healing happens unexpectedly through God's intervention beyond human reason, as it did in the story. Such a community is a sign of the kingdom of heaven that Matthew describes in his Gospel.

EUNJOO MARY KIM

Matthew 21:1–11

¹When they had come near Jerusalem and had reached Bethphage, at the Mount of Olives, Jesus sent two disciples, ²saying to them, "Go into the village ahead of you, and immediately you will find a donkey tied, and a colt with her; untie them and bring them to me. ³If anyone says anything to you, just say this, 'The Lord needs them.' And he will send them immediately. ⁴This took place to fulfill what had been spoken through the prophet, saying,
5 "Tell the daughter of Zion,
   Look, your king is coming to you,
      humble, and mounted on a donkey,
         and on a colt, the foal of a donkey."

Theological Perspective

According to Matthew, Jesus knows that by entering Jerusalem he begins the final chapter of his life. It will end here, not with fanfare and enthronement, but with torture and disgrace. Those who have accompanied him and those who welcome him cry out for the healer-king, the Son of David, to save them, the city, and the nation; they chant praise to the messianic deliverer. For now, they believe in him, they are with him. Later in the week they will not be.

He was, after all, a strange king. A millennium before, believing the confederacy of tribes and judges to be insufficient to protect them from their enemies, the people of Israel had pleaded with Samuel—a prophet and judge—to appoint a king to rule over them. With the permission of the Lord, Samuel did so, but he conveyed the Lord's warning that the king would take their sons to be his horsemen, to make implements of war, to plow his ground, and to reap his harvest. Their daughters the king would take to be his perfumers, to be his cooks, and to be his bakers. Their fields, vineyards, and olive orchards the king would take and give to his courtiers. He would tax their harvests and produce, take the best of their cattle and donkeys, and everyone eventually would become his slaves. "You want a king? You will have one, but do not come crying to me when you do not

Pastoral Perspective

Poor Jerusalem. For centuries, its residents have been represented as the most fickle among ancient municipalities. In popular interpretation they are the definition of populism at its most dangerous: moving from enthusiastic revolutionary fervor to condemnatory, bloodthirsty revenge in five short days; displaying an almost schizophrenic relationship with Jesus, loving then violent, manically adoring then angrily rejecting. A closer examination of the text reveals that, at least for Matthew's Gospel, we hasty interpreters have engaged in a massive case of mistaken identity.

In this Palm Sunday text, there are two groups responding to Jesus' entry into Jerusalem: "the crowd" and "the city." Who are the adoring crowds? By all appearances, they are not residents of the city, but Jesus' "posse," his own band of followers—those same folks who have been on the road with him all the way back to Galilee, together with those they have picked up along the way. Jesus is not hailed as the Messiah by strangers who have heard of his revolutionary reputation, but only by the crowd of his own followers. The residents of the city are referred to but once in Matthew's version of Jesus' triumphal entry, at the end (v. 10). Their initial response is not to step into the parade and follow Jesus. Rather, it is to stare and ask, "What the heck is going on here?" They are in turmoil, wondering.

⁶The disciples went and did as Jesus had directed them; ⁷they brought the donkey and the colt, and put their cloaks on them, and he sat on them. ⁸A very large crowd spread their cloaks on the road, and others cut branches from the trees and spread them on the road. ⁹The crowds that went ahead of him and that followed were shouting,

"Hosanna to the Son of David!
Blessed is the one who comes in the name of the Lord!
Hosanna in the highest heaven!"

¹⁰When he entered Jerusalem, the whole city was in turmoil, asking, "Who is this?" ¹¹The crowds were saying, "This is the prophet Jesus from Nazareth in Galilee."

Exegetical Perspective

In *Matthew as Story*, Jack Dean Kingsbury notes that this Gospel can be divided into a beginning, middle, and end, which are bounded by the phrase, "From that time, Jesus began . . ."[1] In 4:17, Matthew writes, "From that time Jesus began to proclaim, 'Repent, for the kingdom of heaven has come near.'" Then, in 16:21, Greek words identical to those in 4:17 begin the verse: "From that time on, Jesus began to show his disciples that he must go to Jerusalem and undergo great suffering." Between these two verses, most of Jesus' ministry in Galilee unfolds. After 16:21, the end begins, as the Gospel's focus begins to shift to Judea and ultimately to Jerusalem. Three times between 16:21 and 20:20, Jesus tells the disciples that he is going to Jerusalem and there will suffer, die, and be raised.

Now, in chapter 21, he enters the Holy City. The text relates an event that today we might call performance art. Jesus enacts a prophetic word that looks toward the arrival of one who will rule God's people in a time of peace.

Without giving any more reason than "The Lord has need of them," Jesus directs two disciples to fetch two animals for him. The disciples find the animals as Jesus has predicted, and they bring the two to

1. Jack Dean Kingsbury, *Matthew as Story*, 2nd ed. (Philadelphia: Fortress Press, 1988), 40.

Homiletical Perspective

The event of Jesus' procession into the city of Jerusalem is narrated in all four Gospels, and preachers are challenged to deepen their understanding of who Jesus is in relation to the four different descriptions. While the four Gospels include common elements in describing this event, some unique features are found in the Matthean text. One of them is that the text describes Jesus' entry into Jerusalem as a big event of the whole city that resulted in a great commotion among the people. Significantly, Matthew ends the story with the question of the people in the city about the identity of Jesus, "Who is this?" (v. 10), and with the answer of the crowds to the question, "This is the prophet Jesus from Nazareth in Galilee" (v. 11).

In the previous passage (20:29–34), Matthew identified Jesus as the Messiah by describing him as a compassionate healer, through whom God intervened in the suffering and pain of human lives. In this following text (21:1–11), Matthew continues to identify Jesus as the Messiah, but with a different image: Jesus is the one who fulfills the prophetic oracles about the eschatological figure of the humble and gentle king, foretold by prophets in Jewish history (Isa. 62:11; Zech. 9:9). Among all the characters in the narrative, including disciples and religious leaders, it is the crowds who have followed Jesus to

Matthew 21:1–11

Theological Perspective

like what he does. I will not listen," says Samuel; "and neither will the Lord" (1 Sam. 8:4–18).

By the time of Jesus, this warning aptly describes the life of the people of Israel under Roman rule, overseen by the emperor's client, King Herod, and his sons. Many in Judea, Galilee, and the Transjordan did cry. True to his word, the Lord did not answer them, in Samuel's day or that of Jesus (1 Sam. 8:18).

Jesus is deeply committed to bringing about what Matthew calls "the kingdom of heaven"—the rule of the Lord "on earth as it is in heaven" (6:10). He is not, however, the kind of king described by Samuel. Much to the disappointment of many praising him as he enters Jerusalem that day, he will not become that kind of king in order to throw Caesar out of Judea or Herod Antipas out of Galilee.

We should not be surprised that Jesus' understanding of kingship is vastly different from the people's. Early in Matthew's account, Jesus rejects that kind of kingship and way of ruling. When the devil offers Jesus "all the kingdoms of the world and their splendor," in exchange for his loyalty, Jesus responds, "Away with you, Satan! For it is written, 'Worship the Lord your God, and serve only him'" (4:8–10). No, that kind of kingship and glory serve Satan's purposes, not God's.

Now, in the days before entering Jerusalem, Jesus once again repudiates the coercive, exploitive character of the kingship Samuel described and that the people of Israel experienced. This time the encounter is with the mother of James and John, who asks Jesus to allow her sons to have places of power and honor when he comes into his kingdom. After explaining, again, that anyone following him will drink the cup of suffering, Jesus responds, "You know that the rulers of the Gentiles lord it over them, and their great ones are tyrants over them. It will not be so among you; but whoever wishes to be great among you must be your servant, . . . just as the Son of Man came not to be served but to serve, and to give his life a ransom for many" (20:25–28).

The one who enters Jerusalem on a donkey does so as one who serves the purposes of God and God's kingdom of justice and healing. That one willingly and nonviolently accepts the judgment and violence of those who demand to be served for their own purposes.

If that is the kind of king Jesus is, then what kind of God does he serve? What kind of God allows those who serve God's purposes to be humiliated, beaten, tortured, and savagely killed? Dietrich Bonhoeffer, the German pastor and theologian, reflected

Pastoral Perspective

We cannot be certain, then, from which of these two groups will emerge the third throng: those who will shout, "Let him be crucified" (27:22), a few days hence. Scripture tells us many of the faithful will flee and abandon Jesus. We do not know whether the lion's share of those who will be manipulated into seeking Jesus' death are from among Jesus' followers or from among the befuddled and wondering denizens of the city. Regardless, history supports the idea that bewildered people and political leaders with an ax to grind are a potentially deadly combination.

Likewise, much has been speculated about people who want a warrior Messiah being further inspired to revolutionary expectations by this triumphal entry. Yet that interpretation does not seem to do justice to Matthew, for whom this entry into the city is all about fulfilling prophecy (vv. 4–5). The specific prophecy quoted, from Zechariah 9, continues:

> He will cut off the chariot from Ephraim
>   and the war-horse from Jerusalem;
> and the battle bow shall be cut off,
>   and he shall command peace to the nations;
> his dominion shall be from sea to sea,
>   and from the River to the ends of the earth.
>   *(Zech. 9:10)*

This is hardly the description of a coming warrior king. Thus it appears that the reference to triumph and victory is not the result of war, but the result of its elimination (Zech. 9:9). This king who will "cut off" chariots, war-horses, and battle bows from Jerusalem commands only peace (Zech. 9:10). Those who are paying attention to the prophecy would not be thinking violent revolution at all—just the opposite, in fact. Further, if the crowd who acclaims Jesus Messiah is the crowd who has journeyed with him, then they well know that he is no warrior, that he is instead a teacher and a healer, a miracle-making philosopher/rabbi whose only firepower is his compelling presence and word.

Sometimes it appears as though we in the church expect the world outside of the sanctuary to behave like the Palm Sunday Jerusalem that we have misread into the text: instantly, if fickly, enthusiastic, capable of seeing the parade of the pious (the church), and miraculously seeing the positive need for and the desire to be a part of the inbreaking kingdom of God. We are puzzled when they respond as the actual Jerusalem of the text—with skepticism and confusion about the church, its motives, and even the Christ we purport to proclaim.

him. All three Synoptic Gospels include a scene of the disciples borrowing a ride into Jerusalem for Jesus. The fact that the disciples find things as Jesus describes them demonstrates his prescience, as well as the care with which he prepares to enter the city.

Matthew cites Zechariah 9:9 as that portion of the prophet's words that Jesus brings to life as he rides into Jerusalem. There Zechariah paints the picture of God as a ruler returning to Zion, triumphant and humble at the same time. In two lines structured according to the parallelism present in much of Hebrew poetry, Zechariah names two animals, and in Matthew's literal reenactment the disciples collect two animals and Jesus "sits on them" (v. 7). It is unfortunate that the plural language in Matthew creates a picture that resembles a circus trick more than a royal procession. In Mark and Luke, Jesus directs the disciples to bring him just one animal on which he rides. More important than the number of animals is the point, as W. D. Davies and Dale C. Allison note, that "Jesus, unlike the normal pilgrim, does not approach the city on foot. Instead he rides. This reflects his extraordinary status: the king sits."[2]

The disciples offer their cloaks to Jesus as saddle blankets. Crowds surround him, and those in front spread garments and branches in his path. It is a kind of "rolling out the red carpet" at the arrival of a celebrity. In the context of Israel's history, the action recalls the response of King Ahab's officers upon hearing that a prophet of the Lord had secretly anointed Jehu king, at a time when everyone thought Ahab still reigned: "Then hurriedly they all took their cloaks and spread them for [Jehu] on the bare steps; and they blew the trumpet, and proclaimed, 'Jehu is king'" (2 Kgs. 9:13).

Like the officers who were ready to change allegiance from Ahab to Jehu, the crowd around Jesus hails the one in their midst in the way crowds would hail a new king. For their shouts of praise, the crowds borrow a line from Psalm 118, "Blessed is the one who comes in the name of the Lord!" (v. 9; Ps. 118:26).

All the activity causes a stir among the inhabitants of Jerusalem. At the start of Matthew's Gospel, when visitors from the East come, trying to find the one born king of the Jews, we hear that Herod is troubled, and the whole city of Jerusalem with him (2:2–3). Now, the whole city is shaken again as the adult Jesus enters in royal procession. The word used in chapter 21 to describe the state of the whole city (*seiō*) is the same word used for the shaking of

the city who proclaim this identity of Jesus to the public.

The crowds, a mixed group of multitudes, may have followed Jesus for many different reasons. Obviously, the two blind men who were healed in the previous passage and others who were set free from their incurable diseases by Jesus would be in the crowds. Others may be the witnesses to Jesus' miraculous feeding of thousands of people. Others may be the learners who were enlightened by Jesus' teaching of the kingdom of heaven through parables. By the lips of these diverse people, Matthew announces Jesus' identity to the capital city of the nation.

Who is Jesus? This is a question that has been asked by a number of characters in the Matthean text since the infancy narratives and has found its ultimate answer in the confession of 16:16 within the circle of Jesus' disciples. Now Matthew puts this question to the people in Jerusalem and has the crowds answer the question, rather than the disciples, who have been privileged to learn in advance about the messianic secret of Jesus' death and resurrection.

Is Jesus a prophet? In other words, is the crowds' answer right? Commentaries differ on the matter. Some say that the answer is wrong, since Jesus is not the prophet but the Messiah, the Suffering Servant; some say that the answer is partially correct, since the prophet is an important title for Jesus in light of his ministry; and some say that the answer is right, because the title prophet is interchangeable with the title Messiah for the Jewish people. Matthew probably regards the title prophet as the most comprehensive title to the attributes of Jesus as the Messiah.

More precisely, what Matthew means by the title "prophet" in his Jewish context of his particular historical time is not limited to one who addresses the oracle of God to people. Rather, the title prophet implies broader roles, such as a charismatic miracle worker like Elijah (Mal. 4:5), a lawgiver with kingly leadership like Moses (Deut. 18:15–18), and a visionary like Daniel and other prophets (Dan. 7:1–8:26, etc.). It is also notable that many prophets in Scripture were described as "suffering servants" of God who had to go through enormous physical and psychological pain for the sake of God's saving plan for the people (1 Kgs. 19:1–21; Jer. 11:18–23). With these multiple implications of the title prophet, Matthew has the crowds tell the world, "This is the prophet Jesus from Nazareth in Galilee" (v. 11).

The emphasis on "Nazareth in Galilee" reminds the reader of the nature of Jesus' messiahship. The

2. W. D. Davies and Dale C. Allison, *Matthew: A Shorter Commentary* (London and New York: T. & T. Clark, 2004), 346.

Matthew 21:1–11

Theological Perspective

from his prison cell on this God who seemed to allow many innocents to suffer at the hands of the Nazis, as well as those like him who believed they served God in trying to stop them. Of that God, Bonhoeffer declares: "The God who is with us, is the God who forsakes us; we must live as if God is not a given. Before God and with God we live without God; God lets himself be pushed out of the world on to the cross; He is weak and powerless in the world, and that is precisely the way, the only way, in which he is with us and helps us."[1]

God does not swoop in and save Jesus from the machinations, manipulations, and schemes of Pilate, Herod, or the kind of people who praised him as he entered Jerusalem and yet turned on him within a week. The human heart is not won by coercion and violence, but by a willing offer that must be willingly received. Once that offer is received, the recipient acts in the world on behalf of God's order. That, according to Bonhoeffer, is how God is experienced—in the strengths, gifts, and actions of those who respond.

Jesus makes clear that his loving Parent repudiates the exploitation of the people by those who would be king, but he does so without violence—without a club, chariots, horsemen, and swords. Jesus accepts the consequences of standing resolutely for God's order and justice. For those who would be great, this is the way—the way of service to God's order. They too must take up the cross (16:24). They too must participate, in Bonhoeffer's words, "in the sufferings of God in the secular life."[2]

STEPHEN BOYD

Pastoral Perspective

Perhaps the modern call of the triumphal entry is for us to ask ourselves pastorally if we have forgotten the confusion the parade inspires. Like the highly organized, well-meaning mother in *Miracle on 34th Street*, has the church gotten so caught up in the details of the parade as to lose sight of whose arrival it heralds and how earth shattering he is?[1] Convinced of the inherent attraction of the message, is it possible that we have become too concerned with organizing the triumphal pageantry?

The steed of divine strength we have clothed in symbols of earthly power and might. The humble donkey we have virtually disguised in doctrines and grandiose displays of piety. Both of these bearers of our hope we have harnessed in stifling and burdensome ecclesial equipage. We have set entrance exams for the branch bearers and organized the cloak layers to a fare-thee-well. The city looks on in confusion, too often turning away from the spectacle before they encounter the One who is heralded. In large part due to what they see in the parade, many are as disinclined to encounter one they interpret as our spiritual Santa Claus as the jaded parade watcher is to stick around for the jolly man at the end of the Macy's Thanksgiving Day parade.

Ideally, a fresh approach to this text will give us—both "the crowd" and "the city"—the benefit of the doubt. On that Sunday centuries ago, those who proclaimed Jesus' presence moved from flinging down their coats to fleeing when the confusion of the onlookers turned to fear and anger. We face a time when, with plenty of justification, many look to the church of Jesus Christ with fear and anger. Faith history provides two options—leave the palms behind and join those cheering for the demise of the church, or run away and hide. Surely there is a third option: turning outward to the befuddled, even angry, city and saying in every word and deed, "This parade is not about us but about this One we have come to know . . . this One who has changed our lives along the way . . . this prophet, Jesus of Nazareth."

MICHAEL D. KIRBY

1. Dietrich Bonhoeffer, *Letters and Papers from Prison* (1953; repr., New York: Macmillan, 1972), 360.
2. Ibid., 361.

1. *Miracle on 34th Street*, dir. George Seaton (Twentieth Century-Fox, 1947).

Exegetical Perspective

the earth when Jesus breathes his last (27:51), and for the quaking of the guards at the tomb when they behold an angel of the Lord (28:4). The word names the action of an earthquake. The details of the story—the donkey and colt, the cloaks, the crowds, the shouts of "Hosanna!"—signal that something astonishing, hopeful, and frightening is happening. Tectonic plates are shifting.

Unique to Matthew's account is the puzzlement of the bystanders in Jerusalem, prompting an explanation from the crowds praising Jesus: he is a prophet. While it is high praise to be hailed a prophet, it is also an ominous label. In the chapters to come, as Jesus is teaching in the temple, he will lament over the city, saying, "Jerusalem, Jerusalem, the city that kills the prophets and stones those who are sent to it!" (23:37a). After Jesus is condemned to death, those with the high priest spit on Jesus, strike him, and then mock him with the demand, "Prophesy to us, you Messiah! Who is it that struck you?" (26:68).

The pronouncement of Jesus as a prophet is just one of many ways that this reading is a turning point from the journey toward Jerusalem to the events that will occur within the city itself. In their commentary on Matthew, Davies and Allison note seventeen elements of this text that reappear in the Gospel's remaining chapters: the setting of the Mount of Olives; citations of Zechariah; crowds again shouting, "Hosanna!" to Jesus, and so on.[3] The entry into Jerusalem functions as an overture to the last act of the Gospel, sounding themes of Jesus' meekness and his royal identity, presaging the earth-shattering conflict and redemption that is about to unfold.

MARY HINKLE SHORE

Homiletical Perspective

Messiah does not come from the famous capital city of the nation or from an affluent upper-middle-class residential area. Instead, he is from Nazareth, an isolated small village of the poor, located in Galilee, a region of political and social unrest with racially and culturally mixed people. Jesus' messianic ministry to proclaim the good news of the kingdom of heaven began from "Galilee of the Gentiles," a place of darkness and death for both the land and its people (4:16). Matthew's modified citation of Zechariah in 21:5, which leaves out the words "triumphant and victorious," underscores the fulfillment of the prophecy about the gentle and humble Messiah in Jesus of Nazareth in Galilee.

Our pluralistic and interreligious culture challenges Christian churches to rethink what Jesus means for them. Like the people in the city of Jerusalem, many people ask, "Who is this?" Under the clerical hierarchy, it seems that such a question should be answered by ordained pastors and professionally trained preachers. In the text, however, Matthew puts the answer to the question on the lips of the crowds, the multitude of followers, rather than on the lips of the disciples. With the disciples, the crowds followed Jesus to Jerusalem, where he was to suffer and be sentenced to death.

Like the crowds in the text, people today follow Jesus for many reasons. Some have witnessed God's miraculous power in their lives; some have found the truthful way for the journey of their lives through Jesus' teaching. If they are asked, "Who is Jesus?" their answers vary, based on their different experiences of Christ Jesus. It is important to note that in the text Matthew summarizes the crowds' diverse answers in one sentence: "This is the prophet Jesus from Nazareth in Galilee." This answer is the theological and biblical criterion for us to discern who Jesus is for us.

Thus, the text suggests that sermon preparation should begin with listening with discernment to the congregants' witness to Jesus Christ. Just as Matthew's crowds proclaim who Jesus is in their particular Jewish context, church members may surprise the preacher with their particular personal and communal experiences of Jesus in their lives. Who is Jesus? It is supposed to be answered in collaboration between the congregation and the preacher.

EUNJOO MARY KIM

---

3. Ibid., 348.

Matthew 21:12–13

¹²Then Jesus entered the temple and drove out all who were selling and buying in the temple, and he overturned the tables of the money changers and the seats of those who sold doves. ¹³ He said to them, "It is written,
'My house shall be called a house of prayer';
        but you are making it a den of robbers."

Theological Perspective

Having entered Jerusalem, in Matthew's account Jesus goes directly to the temple. Disturbed, Jesus drives out all who buy and sell there. Echoing Jeremiah's criticism of the First Temple and Isaiah's word of promise for this, the Second Temple, Jesus declares, "'My house shall be called a house of prayer'; but you are making it a den of robbers" (v. 13).

Jesus' words recall Jeremiah's: when Assyria occupied the northern kingdom of Israel and Babylon threatened the southern kingdom of Judah, Jeremiah received a word to stand in the gate of the Lord's house and proclaim, "If you truly amend your ways and your doings, if you truly act justly one with another, if you do not oppress the alien, the orphan, and the widow, or shed innocent blood in this place, and if you do not go after other gods to your own hurt, then I will dwell with you in this place" (Jer. 7:5–7).

Rather than heed his warning, the temple became a "den of robbers," and eventually the Babylonians destroyed it in 586 BCE.

Later, Isaiah prophesied Israel's return from exile and a rebuilding of the temple that would be called "a house of prayer for all people." To those returning from exile Isaiah conveys this message from the Lord: "Maintain justice, and do what is right, for soon my salvation will come, and my deliverance be revealed" (Isa. 56:1). Rather than let the eunuch

Pastoral Perspective

The Girl Scouts who meet on Tuesdays want to set up a cookie table this Sunday; the youth group wants to hire that hot Christian singer/songwriter to perform a concert in the sanctuary and sell tickets to raise money for next summer's mission trip; the mission committee needs the fellowship hall for two weeks in December for its annual fair-trade Christmas market; and the stewardship committee wants to include an insert in the bulletin and take a minute (or five) during announcements to explain the new direct-deposit program for pledged giving. It is enough to make any disciple wonder, "Which table would Jesus overturn first?"

The sordid topic of coin. Whatever our preferences may be, the reality is that ministry in the contemporary world must live and breathe in a world where virtually every decision has a measurable financial or opportunity cost in real dollars—despite a hermeneutic that is focused on the eternal, the holy, and the faithful. What crosses the line into twenty-first-century money changing? How do we pastorally address these realities for Christians in the world today?

In the fall of 2011, in hundreds of cities in dozens of countries, protesters took to the streets in what came to be known as the "Occupy" movement. Efforts to delineate clearly the specific goals of the

Exegetical Perspective

Israel's prophets often combined speech and actions to proclaim the word of the Lord. Jeremiah ruins a perfectly good loincloth, breaks a pot, and walks around wearing a yoke, all to make God's word vivid to the people. At God's command, Hosea marries a prostitute, turning his family into a metaphor for God's relationship to Israel. Isaiah walks naked and barefoot for years on end, enacting the indignity to be visited upon Ethiopia and Egypt (Jer. 13:1–9; 19:1–13; 27:1–7; Hos. 1:2; Isa. 20:2–3).

In the tradition of these prophets, Jesus combines speech and action to proclaim God's word. E. P. Sanders understands Jesus' outburst in the temple as the second of three symbolic actions that Jesus performs during the last week of his life. Like the first action, riding into Jerusalem on a donkey, and the third, sharing a meal with the disciples in anticipation of sharing wine anew with them "in my Father's kingdom" (26:29), the ruckus in the temple is a prophetic word-and-deed that signals the intervention of God to bring about a new age. These three actions, Sanders notes, "all point to the coming kingdom and Jesus' own role. He will feast with his disciples, there will be a new or improved Temple, and he will be 'king.'"[1]

---

1. E. P. Sanders, *The Historical Figure of Jesus* (London: Penguin, 1993), 264.

Homiletical Perspective

The text is well known as the "the cleansing of the temple," in which Jesus drives out the buyers and sellers from the temple precincts. Jesus is portrayed as a prophet outraged at the failure of the Jewish religious leadership, because they practice injustices in the temple rather than being responsible leaders of Israel. Unlike Luke (but with similarities to John), Matthew describes Jesus' action of cleansing the temple concretely by adding that Jesus "overturned the tables of the money changers and the seats of those who sold doves" (v. 12; cf. Luke 19:45; Mark 11:15; see also John 2:13–14). This gives an impression that Jesus in the Matthean text is more concerned about the commercialization of the business in the temple and judges that as soon as he arrives in Jerusalem. Indeed, this text seems to demonstrate immediately the crowd's announcement of Jesus as the prophet in the previous verse (21:11).

Not surprisingly, many sermons based on this text focus on Jesus' action as the prophetic judgment on the commercialized temple and call for the church to repent of its corresponding sins and to restore its ministry. For the Jewish people, however, the temple had been the place for offering many kinds of offerings and sacrifices under the direction of the priests, and the practice of selling animals and exchanging money in the temple area had been customary for

Matthew 21:12–13

Theological Perspective

believe himself simply a "dry tree" or the foreigner fear separation from the Lord's people (Isa. 56:3), the Lord assures them that if someone—no matter who that person might be—keeps the covenant, "I will bring them to my holy mountain, and make them joyful in my house of prayer" (Isa. 56:4, 7).

The ancient prophets remind the people that the temple is to be a place where justice is honored. It is a place where the virtues of reverence for the Lord, respect for elders, truthfulness, generosity, hospitality, compassion, and courage, which are required to keep the covenant, are fostered and transmitted to new generations. It is a place where everyone—Jew or Gentile, man or woman, slave or free, blind or sighted, lepers or nonlepers, foreigner or native—who is willing to participate in that covenant and learn and practice those virtues is welcome. It is a place of hope, encouragement, flourishing, and joy for "all people." The inference is that when the temple is not such a place, the Lord no longer dwells there, and it might as well be destroyed. Jesus in today's passage from Matthew declares that the temple is no longer such a place.

Mexican theologian Carlos Bravo, SJ, comments on Jesus' outburst from the perspective of one whose people were targeted by European colonial powers for economic exploitation, cultural genocide, torture, and death. The ostensible purpose and justification for the colonization was to bring civilization, principally understood as the sharing (or, frankly, imposition) of the gospel of Jesus Christ and the attendant oppression that the colonizers brought with it. Why does Jesus denounce the temple and the religious establishment? Bravo believes he does so because "the travesty the religious leaders make of God and his project is the principal obstacle to the people's hope."[1] God's kingdom, or reign, belongs not to the important, to the rich, or to the powerful, but to the poor in spirit, to those who mourn, to the meek, to those who hunger for justice, to the merciful, to the pure in heart, to the peacemakers, and to those who are persecuted for the sake of justice (5:1–12).

As Jesus enters Jerusalem and heads for the temple, this moment is not, says Bravo, "the moment to flee or resist violence." Instead, it is the moment "to renounce [the temple], so that [Jesus'] death will openly show the murderous nature of that power which is so seductive, especially when it is exercised in God's name, but which continues to cause the

1. Carlos Bravo, "Jesus of Nazareth, Christ the Liberator," in Jon Sobrino, SJ, and Ignacio Ellacuría, SJ, eds., *Systematic Theology: Perspectives from Liberation Theology* (London: SCM, 1996), 117.

Pastoral Perspective

movement proved difficult, but the almost universal adoption of the slogan "We are the 99 percent!"—an apparent allusion to the enormous concentration of global wealth in the top 1 percent of the population—made it clear that economic disparity and its resulting injustices were at the heart of the protests. Ironically, tradition has long called Jesus' violent temple reaction to economic actors (the buyers, sellers, money changers, and sacrificial-dove merchants) an "occupation." Just as many pundits expressed frustration at a lack of clear goals in the Occupy movement, discerning a clear understanding of the specific goals of "Occupy the temple" is equally frustrating, particularly for church leaders seeking to navigate the perilous dance of church and commerce.

In these two short verses, Jesus upsets more than just a cashbox and a few cages of doves; he violently condemns long-standing practices that are part of the apparently legitimate business of the temple. Further, he exorcises practices that are both practical and arguably mandated by the Law of Moses. Sacrificing doves is a mandated faithful practice on many occasions, including the birth of a child (Lev. 1:14–17; 5:7; 12:8; 15:14; Luke 2:24). Further, the people who have traveled from all over for Passover cannot use their Roman currency to pay their alms at the temple. They *need* the dove sellers in order to fulfill their sacred obligations and to worship decently and in order. They *need* the ecclesial ATM of the money changers to give all these visitors a chance to help the temple stewardship committee offset the costs of hosting the festival (and presumably to ensure that there are enough turkeys and cans of green beans to fill the food baskets for the needy).

Here comes Jesus, spouting Scripture about "a house of prayer" (Isa. 56:7) and a "den of robbers" (Jer. 7:11) and creating chaos. What does he think? That "prayer" is going to feed the people who show up hungry? That the pilgrims are going to bring their doves with them from throughout the Diaspora? Just what is Jesus thinking and, more importantly, what is he trying to teach the disciples (including those a couple of millennia later who are struggling with whether to hold a churchwide rummage sale to buy new paraments for the sanctuary)?

The traditional view of Jesus' intent is found adjacent to the Jeremiah quotation—where the prophet stands at the gates of an earlier iteration of this same temple (Jer. 7:2) and announces its future destruction if the people persist in oppressive or exploitive practices within the presumed legitimacy

Exegetical Perspective

Sanders's discussion points to one of the abiding questions associated with this text and its parallels in the other Gospels. Does Jesus mean by his action to call for reform of corrupt practices associated with the temple, or to signal the temple's imminent destruction? In support of a "reform" reading is the fact that in the Gospel of John, Jesus objects to the making of the temple into a marketplace (John 2:16), and in all three Synoptic Gospels, Jesus alludes to Jeremiah 7:11 about the temple's having been turned into a "den of robbers." From these texts, one might conclude that Jesus is objecting not to the changing of money to pay the temple tax or the selling of sacrificial animals per se, but to the "highway robbery" being visited upon pilgrims for whom the changing of money elsewhere and the hauling of animals from home were not feasible. Moreover, neither Jesus nor his disciples refuse to worship in the temple or pay the temple tax. Luke reports that after the resurrection Jesus' disciples "were continually in the temple blessing God" (Luke 24:53). Jesus and his followers do not abandon the institution, like, for example, those in the pious Jewish community of Qumran.

On the other hand, seeing Jesus interested only in reform of the present temple does not explain the witness of the Gospels that he spoke of its destruction. The testimony against Jesus at his trial before the high priest is, "This fellow said, 'I am able to destroy the temple of God and to build it in three days'" (26:61; cf. Mark 14:58), and Jesus says to the disciples as they marvel at the temple's construction, "Not one stone will be left here upon another" (24:2; cf. Mark 13:2; Luke 21:6). In these verses, Jesus looks toward something catastrophic: not mere reform—better exchange rates or fairer prices on pigeons—but something altogether new. While it is true that Jesus and his disciples worship in the present temple, that worship does not itself preclude their expectation that God will soon do something so different as to be discontinuous with the current temple and its practices.

A study of these verses would do well not to dismiss too quickly the prospect that Jesus could honor the dominant religious institution—calling its sanctuary the dwelling place of God (23:21)—and at the same time criticize it vehemently (21:12–13) and look toward its destruction (24:2). The temple is God's dwelling place, but it does not contain God, and it is not God's only way of being among God's people.

This is a hard word. The exiles had struggled to rebuild the temple, and their offspring continued to

Homiletical Perspective

the convenience of worshipers (Num. 3:47). Definitely, Jesus' action against this business as usual must have shocked the people around him. They might have been stunned by his disrupting action, although Matthew does not mention this in the text.

Does Jesus then overreact to the business in the temple area? In other words, why does Matthew describe Jesus as the prophet doing such a nonsensical action? Matthew does not explain why Jesus speaks so harshly about the temple. Rather, he answers this question through Jesus' words quoted from the prophets Isaiah and Jeremiah: "It is written, 'My house shall be called a house of prayer'; but you are making it a den of robbers" (v. 13). Perhaps it is not necessary for Matthew to explain further, for his original readers already know what is going on with the business in the temple that makes it deserve to be called "a den of robbers" (Jer. 7:11) by Jesus.

Rather, it seems urgent for Matthew to remind his readers that, since the kingdom of heaven has come near (3:2; 4:17; 10:7), now is the time to stop what has been conventionally practiced in the temple and to fulfill what the prophet Isaiah had foretold: "My house shall be called a house of prayer." Isaiah called the sacred space where people offered burnt offerings and sacrifices to God's altar the house of prayer and prophesied that God's house "shall be called a house of prayer for all peoples" (Isa. 56:7).

The people in the temple must have been preoccupied with external things—numerous ordinances and regulations concerning burnt offerings and other sacrifices commanded in the Law—but they had forgotten the intrinsic things, that the sacred space should be the place of prayer and that such ritual activities should be the vessels of prayers in the house of God. Jesus' actions and words tear down the old order in the temple and establish something new, a new order of the kingdom of heaven in the sacred space.

Just as the temple was called the sacred space for the Jewish people in Jesus' time, so is the church building called the sacred space for Christians. What, then, is the church supposed to be, from the perspective of the kingdom of heaven? Like the temple, the church is the place where a number of activities are going on: fellowship and other social gatherings, evangelism and outreach projects, Bible study and educational programs, cultural and artistic performances, and even commercialized businesses for the convenience of the members, in addition to worship. Like the temple, many churches seem to have forgotten that the intrinsic thing is to be

Matthew 21:12–13

Theological Perspective

death of every prophet, because it continues to cause the death of God's children."[2]

What is one to say, what is one to do, when the very "houses of prayer" that are to be centers of justice, courage, and hospitality betray their calling? The German Lutheran theologian Dietrich Bonhoeffer faced this question during the rule of the Nazis, who transported to concentration camps, executed, and cremated millions of Jews, gay people, gypsies, communists, and political dissenters. In his *Letters and Papers from Prison*, Bonhoeffer suggested why more German Christians did not speak up or act to stop the deportations:

> Our church, which has been fighting in these years only for its self-preservation, as though that were an end in itself, is not capable of taking the word of reconciliation and redemption to mankind and the world. Our words then are bound to lose their force and cease, and our being Christians today will be limited to two things: Prayer and righteous action.[3]

For Bonhoeffer, too many in the German churches had lifted neither their voices nor their hands to stop the shedding of innocent blood. Too many had not understood that everyone—Jew, gypsy, gay, communist, and the physically or mentally challenged—was included in God's promise to draw all nations to the holy mountain to "make them joyful" (Isa. 56:7). The church had therefore forfeited its right to speak the word of healing and reconciliation until it learned once again, in Isaiah's words, to "maintain justice, and do what is right" (Isa. 56:1).

Jesus asked then and asks us now: Are our churches houses of prayer for all people? Are our churches sources of succor for widows, for orphans, and for foreigners? Agreeing with Jeremiah's critique of the First Temple, and Isaiah's word of promise for the Second Temple, Jesus challenges us to discern the extent to which we too are guilty of his judgment: "'My house shall be called a house of prayer'; but you are making it a den of robbers.'"

STEPHEN BOYD

Pastoral Perspective

of YHWH's temple (Jer. 7:6–10). Jesus appears to be condemning the money changers because they are exploiting others. However, Matthew (or Jesus) refuses to make it easy. Other than the quotation from Jeremiah, he provides no actual evidence of exploitation. "Business as usual" is enough to incite Jesus' violent outburst. What Jesus *sees* appears to be enough. Why?

Jesus does not appear to be simply condemning traditional sacrificial practices. If that were the case, his quotation from Isaiah (concerning welcoming the stranger into the temple) would prove problematic, as it contains specific positive references to "offerings and sacrifices" in the "house of prayer" (Isa. 56:6a–7). Apparently that house (at least for now) should still include burnt offerings.

Rather, the problem may actually be the "selling and the buying" (v. 12). After all, it does not have to take place here. Try as anyone might, there is no way to prevent buying and selling in a community from having a stratifying affect upon those gathered there. Some can buy, some cannot. Some can afford more, some cannot. Does any of this have anything to do with their righteousness, the true value of the people involved?

Perhaps the pertinent questions are these: What are we buying and selling in the church today? What is it that, try as we might, cannot help but make some people "less than" if it is on public display? Do we offer systems that stratify or exclude, that mimic an exploitive consumerist culture or that do not make the stranger "joyful in my house of prayer"? It is messy and it is uncomfortable to think that anything we do in a desire to meet needs or expectations could inspire Jesus' ire.

Perhaps that is the point. In one of his last public acts, Jesus "turns the tables" on even well-intentioned religious systems that make purely worldly distinctions among God's people. Perhaps sometimes the church's pastoral starting point should be, like that of the Occupy movement, "I am not certain what the right way to do this is, but this is not it."

MICHAEL D. KIRBY

---

2. Ibid.
3. Dietrich Bonhoeffer, *Letters and Papers from Prison* (1954; repr., New York: Touchstone, 1971), 172.

sacrifice to support it (see the widow in Mark 12:41–44 and Luke 21:1–4). Clearly the authorities whose livelihoods were connected to the temple had a stake in its continued operation, but so would the pilgrims streaming into it for the Passover festival. To get a feel for how radically uncomfortable Jesus' words and actions with respect to the temple would have been in his time and place, postmodern Christians need only imagine the response to any similar words and actions with respect to the Scriptures, or the Christian church, or a beloved denomination or congregation, or some other dominant religious institution. How would someone be received who honored such as these, and also vehemently criticized them, and even looked toward their destruction?

In these verses, of course, Jesus does not say anything about the destruction of the temple, and his actions, disruptive as they are, stop short of bringing down its buildings and walls. Yet he does act in such a way as to describe an alternative to business as usual.

First, Jesus borrows from Isaiah to define the temple as "a house of prayer" (Isa. 56:7). In Matthew, the prayer at the center of the Sermon on the Mount asks that God's will be done and God's kingdom come "on earth as it is in heaven" (6:10). In the garden of Gethsemane, Jesus prays, "Your will be done" (26:42). As the temple, or any other place of God's abiding, becomes a house of prayer, it will be a place where God's people ask God to accomplish God's purposes among them.

Second, Jesus introduces an alternative to usual temple activities by healing the blind and lame who come to him in the temple (21:14). It was healing like this that Jesus cited as information with which to answer John's question, "Are you the one who is to come, or are we to wait for another?" (11:2–6). Here again, the healings Jesus performs, like the manner of his entry into Jerusalem and the event of his disruption of the usual temple practice, are signs of the coming kingdom of God.

MARY HINKLE SHORE

the sacred place. We can be thankful that the text reminds us of the identity of the church in the reign of God: it is supposed to be the house of God, the house of prayer.

How many church leaders and members are aware that the church is the place of prayer? Most churches are overwhelmed by numerous activities that are supposed to be done by other social sectors and institutions and misplace worship's priority in the list. Other Christians and their churches seem not to feel the necessity of prayer, do not give credit to the power of prayer, and disregard the practice of prayer. For them, the church is no longer the house of God but the house of people who have common interests in their social and personal lives. The absence of attention to the presence of God in the church makes the church no longer a sacred space where people renew their intimate and abiding relationship with God through prayer.

This reality challenges the preacher to ponder what prayer means for people in our modernized society and high-tech culture of communication. Prayer and associated practices have been widely shared aspects of human life. Today, however, prayer tends to be less and less interesting to people. Many of them say that they gain inspiration through Facebook or by clicking on other Web sites of virtual communities, rather than through praying to God. Again, it is a challenging task for the preacher to reconfigure the significance of prayer from the perspective of the kingdom of heaven.

In Scripture, prayer is normally defined as a way of communicating with God, and the temple and the church are the places where this union between God and believers is enacted. In a variety of practices of prayer, ranging from conversational prayers in private and in small groups to formal prayers recited in liturgical settings, the believers renew the covenant with God and respond to God's sovereign activity by living a life according to God's will. Especially for Matthew, the kingdom of heaven is part of a continuing activity of prayer for repentance and forgiveness.

EUNJOO MARY KIM

Matthew 21:14–17

¹⁴The blind and the lame came to him in the temple, and he cured them. ¹⁵But when the chief priests and the scribes saw the amazing things that he did, and heard the children crying out in the temple, "Hosanna to the Son of David," they became angry ¹⁶and said to him, "Do you hear what these are saying?" Jesus said to them, "Yes; have you never read,
'Out of the mouths of infants and nursing babies
    you have prepared praise for yourself'?"
¹⁷He left them, went out of the city to Bethany, and spent the night there.

Theological Perspective

To understand this text, begin with a quick look back at its context. In the immediately preceding verses, Jesus has forcefully condemned and physically disrupted the normal preparations for worship in the temple. Overturning furniture, he drove out the people who were doing the standard things to help prepare for worship in that setting: changing imperial money into temple money, selling birds for the prescribed religious offerings (v. 12). Quoting Scripture and adding his own commentary, Jesus drew a contrast between the temple's God-given identity and its actual functioning: God intends for the temple to be a "house of prayer," but in actual practice it is a "den of robbers" (v. 13). The temple, which is supposed to be a place where good happens, has been made into a place that harbors injustice. Jesus' disruption of temple practice—and his sharp condemnation of what the temple has become—endear him neither to the chief priests, who preside over the temple, nor to the scribes, the theologically learned Scripture scholars who assist them.

In verses 14–17, Jesus offers the positive alternative. If the people running the businesses that make possible the temple sacrifices are thieves, by contrast Jesus demonstrates what should happen in God's house of prayer. Jesus offers healing welcome to those who cannot see and cannot walk on their

Pastoral Perspective

After acts of healing, recovery from pain, and relief of suffering, it is sadly often the case that some people only complain. In this passage, instead of celebrating the curing of the lame and the blind, the religious leaders of the day did not, indeed would not, rejoice. Envy and jealousy can blind us to the amazing things that are possible through God's good grace. The desire to be the ones in charge of other people's religious and spiritual experiences can make it difficult for us even to see the hand of God in other peoples' lives.

Everyone saw the "amazing things that he [Jesus] did" (v. 15); that was not what the contention was about. What raised the ire of the chief priests and scribes more was what the ordinary people shouted out in the temple: "Hosanna to the Son of David!" How dare they interpret what they all saw? What did they know of the law and the prophets? How could they attribute to Jesus titles and accolades to which only they (the chief priests and scribes) felt entitled? How could they imply that this untutored carpenter's son could be praised in titles reserved for the Messiah? Moreover, how could Jesus receive these words and not rebuke the crowd or restrain them from using such loaded language?

Acts of kindness and deeds that promote healing and well-being for the many often disturb the

Exegetical Perspective

Matthew 21:14–17 is the end of a larger and very dramatic passage, 21:1–17, that includes Matthew's version of the triumphal entry and the cleansing of the temple. As such, this short paragraph rarely gets a careful reading for its own sake from the pulpit or in Christian education classes. To be sure, we need to recognize it as the denouement of the high tensions accompanying Jesus' entry into Jerusalem and his provocative actions in the temple. Even so, this small story is worth its own regard. It has its own conflicts and serves a subdued but nevertheless important function both within the unit and in the Gospel more broadly, serving as a turning point toward Jesus' passion.

The beginning of this passage is a stark contrast to what has gone before. The temple clash was high energy: Jesus physically drove out livestock and people. He threw tables and chairs around. He tendered charges against the temple practitioners in tones that still ring through the centuries. Now, as this text begins, there is the simple statement that blind people and lame people were coming to him in the temple, and he healed them. The subtext is the normalcy of Jesus' ministry. Nothing is more usual than people in need coming to Jesus and his attention to their needs. Here in the temple—after the pageantry of the triumphal entry and the turmoil

Homiletical Perspective

It is getting hot indeed in the kitchen of the temple. Jesus engenders fierce loyalty and unabashed praise from crowds and children, but provokes ever more entrenched opposition from leaders. Each scene in Jerusalem takes Jesus closer to the cross, pressing toward Matthew's vision of the joyful life of discipleship as contrasted with the grim, empty lives of the political and religious leaders. Jesus follows his prophetic upending of the money changers' tables with unrestrained acts of mercy and healing. His power to heal and his judgment of corruption set him on a direct collision course with the chief priests and scribes. They are bent on preserving the status quo and the perks that accompany it. As we consider our own congregational context, we might ask how this cast of characters would look in our town and temple.

Who are the blind and the lame in our midst? They are those who for various reasons rank as second-class citizens, tolerated but not entirely welcomed. Texts such as Leviticus 21:18 prohibited priests with physical deformities from offering sacrifices. Religious leaders in the time of Christ allowed them in the outer courtyard, but not enthusiastically. Their presence detracted from the scenery, the carefully designed sets they had erected to preserve the illusion that all was flourishing in the temple pageantry. Like many a corporate leader of recent

Matthew 21:14–17

Theological Perspective

own and who for those reasons are not supposed to approach the altar. In God's house of prayer, Jesus instructs the chief priests and scribes to hear the voices of children praising God by speaking the truth. Jesus' image of a house of prayer—with inclusion of the outcast, and healing, and children's cries of praise—upsets the chief priests and the scribes.

Tension between Jesus and various groups of institutional religious leaders characterizes not only this text, but also every other section of chapter 21 in Matthew's Gospel. Both the chapter as a whole and these specific verses teach us to be suspicious of institutional religious leaders.

Suspicion of the "chief priests," "scribes," "Pharisees," "Sadducees," and "teachers of the law" comes easily to many Christians. Time and again in the Gospel, one or another of these groups of religious leaders is at odds with Jesus, trying to make his life difficult, even seeking to have him killed. The specific pairing "chief priests and scribes" is especially ominous in Matthew. (E.g., it is precisely these groups that the child-murdering King Herod consults in response to the visit from the magi in Matt. 2:4.) Shortly before our passage, in 20:18, Jesus tells his disciples that "the Human One will be handed over to the chief priests and scribes, and they will condemn him to death" (my trans.).

Such negative references become more troubling if we let them hit closer to home. Although terms like "chief priests" and "scribes" may strike many Christians as foreign, belonging to a distant time and religious situation, in Jesus' own life he was not struggling with exotic groups. He was struggling with the familiar religious leaders, the recognized, institutionalized, and respected leaders of his faith community.

One thing to learn from Jesus is suspicion of institutional religious leaders. There is no reason to assume that institutional religious leaders today would escape Jesus' critique. This suspicion extends to the author of this little section of theological commentary—an ordained pastor and a seminary professor. An author with such an institutional pedigree is liable to oppose Jesus and to seek to squelch the truth that is spoken by and about him. Let the reader beware!

One important strand of twentieth-century Protestant theology is a critique of religion in the name of the gospel. The Swiss Reformed theologian Karl Barth said that the gospel subverts every religion—the Christian religion as much as any other—because religion is the human project of "getting right with

Pastoral Perspective

few. The privileged and the powerful often become disturbed when things are done that raise the level of participation of the many. The control of resources has often lain in the hands of designated people. This is true of both material and interpretive assets. The control of physical or material resources lies with the social organizations that have been established for specific purposes. Interpretive capital in this case was deemed to lie with the chief priests and scribes. They were those who had the learning and authority to explain religious themes and interpret God's activity.

Jesus' actions disrupted the established lines of control in both physical and interpretive terms. He not only cured the sick; he also pointed them in the true direction of the Divine. The people recognized in Jesus not merely a magician or physician able to cure their diseases, but also the Messiah ("Son of David") able to save their souls, now ("Hosanna!"). Amazingly, these ordinary suffering people were granted this deep insight, whereas the chief priests and scribes did not get it. Blinded by their own privilege and unconcerned with the responsibility to do all they could to relieve the suffering of the poor, these religious leaders were envious and angry when one appeared who was deeply committed to the well-being of the poor, and did all in his power to relieve their suffering.

For us, this is a crucial reminder that religious authorities and communities need constantly to check our place and perspective when it comes to the suffering of the poor. Are we on the side of the privileged or the needy? Do we use our power and resources to relieve suffering and increase the access of the many, or to shore up the privilege of the few?

God's acts of care are directed at all people. They aim at granting all of us greater access to the divine abundance; they demonstrate that all are loved by God and have a place in God's reign and realm. We are called to participate in delivering healing and well-being to ever-increasing circles of people in our communities, neighborhoods, and indeed the whole world. We must realize, however, that pastoral acts such as these often imply turning the tables on those who have held exclusive rights to power, access, and privilege in our world.

Churches, congregations, organizations, and individuals who engage in relief work often find themselves embroiled in political battles. As we strategize to deliver relief to the most needy, we must reckon on upsetting, albeit unwittingly, some people's applecarts. Relief agencies must not be naive. Doing good for ordinary suffering people never goes without

of his parabolic restoration of God's purpose for the temple—the life and times in the ministry of Jesus return to normal. People come; he heals.

What is, of course, not usual is that Jesus is healing them in the temple. It is not that the blind and lame were not welcome there. As Ulrich Luz notes, there were no rabbinic prohibitions preventing them from entering the temple.[1] However, the healing ministry that Jesus has begun in Galilee is now taking place at the very center of Jewish thought and life. Not only has he arrived at the heart of Jewish faith; he has claimed it for his own. His unusual and upside-down procession into the city has been unopposed. His emphatic rejection of the commercialism and avarice of the temple practices has been unopposed. Now he resumes his healing ministry in this time and place with a quiet but real authority. Jesus is here showing a composure that in its own way makes a point.

Later, in verse 23, the religious leaders will directly challenge this authority, but at this moment of healing and normalcy, they challenge Jesus only indirectly. These leaders, the text tells us, are upset about the wonderful acts of healing he is doing, but they focus their complaint on the cries in the temple of the children, who are still calling out, "Hosanna to the Son of David!" "Do you hear what they are saying?" the leaders ask Jesus, as if he will surely join them in their condemnation of the children. It may be that carrying the procession into the temple is unseemly in itself, but it is more likely that the designation of Jesus as the Son of David is upsetting. It is a title that not only puts Jesus in the line of the most elevated ancestor, but makes certain claims about his own kingly power and authority. It may not be a blasphemous claim, but it is certainly an arrogant one. The very way Jesus processed into Jerusalem renders kingly expectations ironic and lends an anti-royal flavor to any Davidic claims, but this eludes the opponents at this point.

Jesus, as the evangelist portrays him, responds to this indirect challenge with a quotation from Psalm 8. In reminding his opponents of Psalm 8, he is using their complaint about the children as a point of entry into conversation with them. At the same time, he is speaking to the heart of their challenge, their discomfort with his care for the vulnerable. In throwing out the ones who were using the temple for their own aggrandizement, he made space literally

decades, the rulers were blind to their own institution's bankruptcy and impending collapse. It is the sightless ones who see clearly, who know enough to come to Jesus and ask for what they most need. The text invites comparison with Acts 3:1–10, where leaders of the early church lived into the healing power of the resurrected Christ, causing amazement from crowds and opposition from those in power. In our preaching, we will want to call our congregations to ministries of hospitality and healing for those who seem to disturb the smooth running of our show.

From the beginning of Matthew's Gospel, genuine worship and jealous anger are juxtaposed. The wise men, having nothing to lose, freely offer their worship and allow themselves to be "overwhelmed with joy" (2:10), while Herod, at the center of power, seethes with fury and fear and so murders innocent children. This scene foreshadows the clashes that come to a head as Jesus enters Jerusalem. Those who see most clearly are on the borders of society, and like the children in our text, they are free to respond with joyful worship. Who are the children in our midst, as we at the center of the church belabor debates over worship styles and structure? The pure in heart more readily see God, Jesus proclaimed, but angry, resentful people have trouble bringing gifts to God's altar.

Not all anger is out of place; some of it makes way for a purified and more inclusive worship. In the verses preceding our text, Jesus exercises holy anger on behalf of those who have been kept from full participation in communal life. Jesus does not lash out at random. He targets his anger with laserlike precision at those who would enforce barriers to worship. Seats and tables are cleared and then reset for the banquet he longs to host. Like gleeful victors in a mad-scramble round of musical chairs, the blind and lame rush to take those seats, and Jesus gladly serves them. Children, never ones to miss much, proclaim his true identity in the temple. These children freely offer their praise to the Davidic king, just as the wise men were bowled over with joy and humbly knelt before Jesus.

The children's cries provoke indignant protests from the temple leaders who, like Herod, see only threats to their status and privilege. They ask Jesus if he hears the children—an irony in Matthew, since Jesus has been calling people to purified hearing throughout the Gospel (7:14; 13:14–16). They imply that he should share their outrage at this obvious blasphemy, and suppress the children's unruly chants. Jesus parries with the strange strategy of God

---

1. Ulrich Luz, *Matthew 21–28*, Hermeneia: A Critical and Historical Commentary on the Bible (Minneapolis: Augsburg Fortress, 2008), 13.

Matthew 21:14–17

Theological Perspective

God," while the gospel announces that that entire project is unnecessary: God is with us and for us in saving love by divine initiative, regardless of our own actions.[1] Writing from a Nazi prison cell, the German Lutheran theologian Dietrich Bonhoeffer struggled to articulate a "nonreligious" interpretation of the gospel. Bonhoeffer was afraid that religion relegates God to one dimension of our lives, while the gospel insists that God is with us and for us in the fullness of our creaturely existence. Religion, for Bonhoeffer, might help us become saints, but the gospel seems more interested in helping us to become genuine human beings.[2]

As an institution, the church is always at odds with itself.[3] The fundamental purpose of any institution, as an institution, is to survive. We found and cultivate institutions in order to continue some worthwhile function into the future, beyond the current energies and even beyond the lifetimes of those who establish the institution. It is the job of institutions to perpetuate themselves.

The church has a good reason for institutionalization, if ever there was one. The church exists as an institution in order to ensure that the gospel keeps being communicated in word and in deed into the future, even beyond the lives of any current members of the church. Here is the rub: an essential part of the gospel message is the recognition that you live only by ceasing to cling to your life, by ceasing to make self-preservation a top priority. This gospel conviction stands at odds with the fundamental commitment to self-preservation inherent in every institution. The church is in the odd position of existing as an institution to preserve and perpetuate a message that undercuts the very dynamic of institutionalization, a message that tells us that we are free from the need to be obsessed with self-preservation.

JOHN F. HOFFMEYER

Pastoral Perspective

some political name-calling and even opposition from persons in powerful positions. It is important that those who would follow Jesus in relieving the suffering of the poor be aware that they will face misunderstanding, persecution, and at times outright opposition.

Far from becoming disturbed or distracted by the obvious anger of the elders, Jesus not only continues to care, but also offers scriptural support for the activities of the people. Their praise is sanctioned by the Word of God. What they do and say has scriptural backing. They may be "infants and nursing babies" (v. 16), but they are a part of God's humanity. God has ordained that they too have a voice. They have a place in praising God. The praise of God will forever rise from the earth—no matter what.

Moreover, Jesus does not abandon the people he has healed to the anger of the religious leaders. He stands with them and by them, assuring them of a place in God's grace and affirming them as people in the heart of God's love. It is not sufficient to cure the sick; we must also support and encourage them. It is not enough to perform acts of kindness. We must also provide religious, material, and emotional support for them in their newfound freedom. We are summoned not only to act on behalf of the needy, the poor, and the suffering. We can and must assist them to speak with their own voices. Advocacy is a crucial part of care. The witness of a caring community encourages and ennobles the "least of these" to find their identity as people of God. It affirms their ability to discern the presence of God in the world and establishes their right to praise God at all times in the manner of their choosing.

At the end of this passage, Jesus leaves for Bethany to take some rest and care for himself. He does so only after he is assured that the people he has ministered to are safe and secure, out of harm's way.

EMMANUEL Y. LARTEY

1. Karl Barth, *Church Dogmatics*, I/2 (Edinburgh: T. & T. Clark, 1956), §17.
2. Dietrich Bonhoeffer, *Letters and Papers from Prison*, ed. Christian Gremmels et al., trans. Isabel Best et al., in *Works* (Minneapolis: Fortress Press, 2009), 8:361–504.
3. This paragraph and the next follow Robert W. Jenson, *Story and Promise: A Brief Theology of the Gospel about Jesus* (Philadelphia: Fortress Press, 1973), 86, 188–89.

and metaphorically for blind people, lame people, and children.

That Matthew's Jesus has Psalm 8 in his heart and mind at this juncture is important to note. This hymn of praise to God, for creating human beings, caring for them, and valuing them, is the spirit in which Jesus is approaching Jerusalem. It is the spirit in which he enters, cleans, and claims the temple. It is the spirit in which he opens space there for people to come for healing, for children to claim him freely as their Son of David, their hope. It is the spirit in which he confronts those who would deny such healing and hope.

In this short text, which completes Jesus' entrance into Jerusalem, Psalm 8 also underlies the irony and sorrow with which Matthew paints this beginning of the passion narrative. Consciously or not, those who sing "Hosanna" recognize Jesus rightly as one to whom Psalm 8 also belongs: with all humanity, created in the image of God; with all humanity, graced with God's care. Yet Jesus, God's dearest one, is about to be treated in ways that do not accord with his humanity, let alone his status as Son of David. However we understand Jesus' self-awareness, he undoubtedly intuits that he is about to be treated as one who is less than human. He knows and sees that the scribes and priests are not caring for the blind, the lame, and the children in the ways that God cares for them.

The priests and the scribes are not living up to their calling as religious leaders. Psalm 8, as Jesus speaks to them, should recall for them the way of righteousness regarding all humankind—and especially the most vulnerable. It should, but it does not.

MARY H. SCHERTZ

outlined in the Psalms, which portray God receiving praise from a host of unlikely sources.

As we prepare to preach this text, Matthew's Gospel invites us as leaders to explore the places of fear in our own hearts. Our hands may be gripping tightly to the levers of control in our congregations and governing bodies. Clenched hands have trouble turning upward in worship. Throats too spent from appeasing every faction rarely have the gusto left to cry, "Hosanna!" like innocent children. Ears all too finely attuned to the complaints of influential members about the length of the pastoral prayer may miss the boisterous praise emerging from unlikely corners of our sanctuaries.

In 2007, virtuoso violinist Joshua Bell donned jeans and a baseball cap to play in the L'Enfant Plaza subway station in Washington, DC. It was only children who strained to stop and hear him. They were pulled on by parents frantic to get them squared away in daycare, so they could get on with their days. Other commuters barely glanced his way as they dashed to their trains.[1] Is our church at risk of missing the best part?

It would do our sermon-bearing souls good to reflect upon our own flares of anger within the halls of ministry, and upon the subtle yet troubling displays of indignation and impatience we observe in our congregations. The same events that trigger worship from the children trigger anger from those who fear the crashing down of their cherished order, an order in which their exalted place seems set in granite. Turning and praising would involve too much loss. The ruts in our familiar roads of church life are too deep. The proverbial children among us simply hop out of the car and make a mad dash to the magnetic source of their joy, but the drivers, their hands clenching the wheel, may miss the magic altogether.

LISA WASHINGTON LAMB

---

1. Gene Weingarten, "Pearls before Breakfast," *The Washington Post,* April 7, 2007 (http://www.washingtonpost.com/wp-dyn/content/article/2007/04/04/AR2007040401721.html); and the YouTube of Bell's performance at http://www.youtube.com/watch?v=hnOPu0_YWhw; accessed August 11, 2012.

Matthew 21:18–22

¹⁸In the morning, when he returned to the city, he was hungry. ¹⁹And seeing a fig tree by the side of the road, he went to it and found nothing at all on it but leaves. Then he said to it, "May no fruit ever come from you again!" And the fig tree withered at once. ²⁰When the disciples saw it, they were amazed, saying, "How did the fig tree wither at once?" ²¹Jesus answered them, "Truly I tell you, if you have faith and do not doubt, not only will you do what has been done to the fig tree, but even if you say to this mountain, 'Be lifted up and thrown into the sea,' it will be done. ²²Whatever you ask for in prayer with faith, you will receive."

Theological Perspective

This is probably not the favorite passage of many tree lovers! At one level it seems like the story of a snippy miracle worker who gets in a bad mood and takes it out on an innocent tree. In the middle of chapter 21, however, which is filled with tension and confrontation between Jesus and various groups of religious leaders, the story of the fig tree and Jesus' subsequent words about faith are an important part of what Matthew has to say about Jesus' confrontation with religious leaders.

A hungry Jesus comes upon the tree and finds no fruit, only leaves on its branches, so he condemns it to fruitlessness forever. The word "fruits" (*karpoi*) comes up three times in chapter 21, appearing twice (translated "produce" in the NRSV) in the closing parable of the Vineyard and the Tenants. When the time for the ripe fruit of the vines is at hand, the owner of the vineyard sends servants to take the fruit from the vinedressers. The vinedressers abuse the servants, even killing some, so that no fruit makes it back to the owner of the vineyard. After recounting more bad behavior by the vinedressers, Jesus asks his hearers what the owner will end up doing with the vinedressers. They reply that the owner will give the vineyard to others who will give him the vineyard's fruit. In the commentary after the conclusion of the parable, Jesus says to the chief priests and other

Pastoral Perspective

Jesus has begun his final journey in his life on earth. The cross already seems to loom large on the horizon in Matthew's account in the passage for today. On his way back to the city, where he has utilized his divine power in curing the blind and the lame, he is hungry. He comes across a fig tree—a tree that in its time would have yielded abundant fruit. Although the tree is in full leaf, there is no fruit. Herein lies the challenge for all: churches, congregations, and individuals who are signs of God's reign in the world. The prophet Isaiah uses a similar metaphor when he takes up the song concerning God's unfruitful vineyard (Isa. 5:1–6). God has done all that a diligent vine keeper could be expected to do for his plant, yet when God "expected it to yield grapes, . . . it yielded wild grapes" (Isa. 5:2). In frustration, disappointment, and, no doubt, anger, God says, "I will remove its hedge . . . break down its wall . . . make it a waste . . . command the clouds that they rain no rain upon it" (vv. 5–6). Verse 7 states the reason for this harsh action:

> For the vineyard of the LORD of hosts
>   is the house of Israel,
> and the people of Judah
>   are his pleasant planting;
> he expected justice,
>   but saw bloodshed;

Exegetical Perspective

Ulrich Luz describes the parable of the Fig Tree as a "somewhat unhappy text."[1] The tone, beginning with verse 19, seems in bleak and abrupt contrast to the last passage, where Jesus was healing blind and lame persons and defending the children in the temple. After the scene in the temple, Jesus goes to Bethany to stay the night. We often associate Bethany with Jesus' friends, but in Matthew's Gospel, this is the first mention of the town. We see it again later in 26:6 at the home of Simon the leper, where an unnamed woman anoints Jesus. Here the hospitality that Jesus receives leaves some of his needs unmet. As he returns that morning to Jerusalem, and to the temple that he has newly reclaimed for the purposes of God, he may be well rested, but he has not been well fed. He is hungry.

Walking down the road, Jesus sees a single fig tree and goes to it hoping for fruit, only to find none. Jesus speaks to the fig tree with what sounds like a curse: "May no fruit ever come from you again!" (v. 19). The tree dries up immediately. Both these words and this action seem out of character for Jesus. We think of the temptations in the wilderness, where Jesus, hungry after forty days without

Homiletical Perspective

This text is notoriously difficult to preach and yet rich with homiletical promise. If Eugene Lowry is right, that "trouble in, around, with and about the text is often the occasion for a fresh hearing,"[1] we are in good shape with this passage. While embracing difficulty is a worthy and indeed essential first task for preachers, our listeners are right to expect some resolution, some tying off of all the threads we let roam free, as we explore the more problematic texts of Scripture.

Hearers may protest that Jesus appears to be capricious and even cruel. Others might conjecture that his nerves have worn thin after one too many altercations with religious leaders; the strain is getting to him. Context will clarify but not entirely smooth out the ragged edges of Jesus' actions here. Jesus' miraculous power delights us when it is used to heal and feed; when used to judge and end life, even the life of a tree, it is less appealing and more troubling. The story shows Jesus' affinity with the prophets of Scripture, who at times turned to absurdity to convey tough truths to the recalcitrant people of God. From shattering pots to letting loincloths go to mildew, the prophets made dramatic use of

1. Ulrich Luz, *Matthew 21–28*, Hermeneia: A Critical and Historical Commentary on the Bible (Minneapolis: Fortress Press, 2008), 24.

1. Eugene Lowry, *How to Preach a Parable* (Nashville: Abingdon Press, 1989), 33.

Theological Perspective

leaders (variously labeled "elders of the people" in v. 23 and "Pharisees" in v. 45) that the dominion of God will be taken from them and given to others who will produce its fruits (v. 41).

Thus the fruitlessness to which Jesus consigns the fig tree symbolizes the fruitlessness of the religious leaders. This connection finds reinforcement in Jesus' words to his disciples: when the disciples are amazed at the fig tree's drying up, Jesus tells them that with faith, not only could they do the same thing, but also they could tell "this mountain" to be cast into the sea and it would happen. Although this text is the basis for the notion that faith can "move mountains," Jesus does not seem to be referring to a general miraculous power to displace huge objects. He says specifically "this mountain." Since this passage follows directly upon Jesus' provocative disruption of temple business and occurs while Jesus is on his way to the temple the next morning, it seems that the particular mountain to which Jesus is referring is the hill on which the temple is built. The present temple establishment may loom as impressive as a mountain, but it is full of thievery and injustice. To establish the alternative, a house of prayer, does not require an equally huge, an equally "mountainous" institution, but simply faith. Faith can remove the present distortion of right worship of God and replace it with the prayer that welcomes the blind, the lame, and noisy children in the sacred space before God.

In verse 22, Jesus directly connects prayer and faith. The promise that the disciples will receive whatever they ask, provided that they pray in faith, can be troubling. Can this mean that disciples can pray for anything they want, and it will be granted, or that the content of the prayer does not matter? This is not what Jesus is saying. Faith is not sincere conviction irrespective of content. Jesus does not tell his disciples that if they pray with faith for the glorification and perpetuation of the current temple establishment, the "den of robbers," they will receive what they ask for. Jesus does not say that with faith his disciples could lift up "this mountain" and then drop it down again, crushing the outcast and vulnerable underneath it. Faithful prayer is in accordance with Jesus' vision of the temple as a house of prayer rather than a den of robbers. Indeed, faithful prayer relies upon Jesus' vision, in which those who might otherwise be outcast are also welcomed to bring their prayer and praise.

As much as these verses stand in continuity with the preceding scene of Jesus' disrupting the temple routine, in the hope that the temple could be a house

Pastoral Perspective

righteousness,
> but heard a cry!

Where is the fruit? Where is the evidence of the nurture and care of God for God's people? Where is the expected outcome of all that God has invested in God's people? The response of Jesus to the unproductive tree unfolds along similar lines. It bespeaks divine disappointment and frustration at human unproductivity in spite of divine investment. What can be more disappointing than to see advertisements that portray certain products in the most glowing terms, only to find that what is promised is very far from what is delivered? The mission of the church is not only to be an advertisement for the gospel, but actually to bear fruit delivering what is promised. Promissory notes are only as good as what is actually available in the bank account of the one who promises

The productivity of the tree—and the people of God—is only a secondary point. What this incident primarily points to is the power of Jesus' faith. His word has all the backing and power of God, because it is a word uttered in faith and complete dependence upon God. One thing is clear: this man Jesus has great authority at his disposal. He knows how to unleash phenomenal power through simple trust. Not only is he able to cure the sick; he also has authority over the elements of creation. The divine creator is mightily present through this man. Such is his love, commitment, and obedience to the divine will that he does not call upon this incredible power to save himself from the cross in days to come. Rather, he elects to suffer in order to secure the redemption of the world in accordance with the divine plan. In this way he demonstrates that power is to be used to fulfill the will of God—not merely the whims and caprices of humanity.

This is the mark of the truly powerful person: one who makes choices that are in line with the divine will, and therefore always for the benefit and well-being of humanity. The cursing of the fig tree is to act as a challenge for the people of faith: Be fruitful or be cut off. Produce evidence of the faith, or else you will prove useless. It is also a challenge to trust in the power of fulfilling the will of God. John's Gospel puts the same challenge in these words: "Those who abide in me and I in them bear much fruit, because apart from me you can do nothing. . . . If you abide in me, and my words abide in you, ask for whatever you wish, and it will be done for you" (John 15:5, 7). The power available to Jesus is present

food, tells the tempter that human beings do not live by bread alone (4:4). We think of the feedings of the multitudes, where Jesus takes compassion on the crowds who have followed him out of town and parlays a little fish and several loaves of bread into abundance (14:14–21; 15:33–39). What is Jesus—who seems to understand food as God's providence—doing, cursing a fig tree just because it does not meet his own immediate needs for refreshment? When did Jesus' own needs somehow become the standard by which trees live or die? These words and this action seem radically opposed to the kind of person that he is, and the ethos around human needs that he has shown in his ministry of teaching, preaching, and healing.

Our astonishment about these developments is but an echo of the disciples' astonishment. They are surprised that the fig tree withers at once; surely they are also taken aback on several other levels as well. Jesus answers only their presenting marvel—and turns it into a lesson about faith. In fact, he gives them an example of faith that outshines even the shrunken fig tree in preposterous incredulity. "Take a mountain and cast it into the ocean," he tells them; "if your faith is sufficient and you do not doubt. Moreover, if you trust, you can ask anything in prayer and receive."

So, yes, this small passage is knotty on a couple of counts. Its historical basis as well as its theological direction and import may be questioned. What actually happened to the fig tree that morning we will never know for sure. We may understand it as miracle or metaphor for religious practices that are more form than function. We would be hard pressed, however, to imagine that Matthew, or Jesus for that matter, ever intended the lesson about moving mountains to be taken literally. We have in this Gospel—and in this Jesus—any number of illustrations, parables, and teachings of one or another sort that are more provocative, and perhaps even more playful, than anything else. This is the Gospel—and this is the Jesus—who talks about logs in eyes (7:3–4), cutting off hands that offend (5:30), and hanging millstones around necks (18:6). In these days when millstones are rare in our experience, we likely miss the humor of the idea of hanging a millstone around anyone's neck. We might hang someone from a millstone, but the opposite, the way Jesus said it, is unlikely, to say the least.

To be sure, it is a rough humor, a kind of humor that would hardly fly in our own atmosphere of sensitized and politicized language. Let us recognize,

whatever was at hand to make their points with vivid impact.

In Mark, the fig tree incident more explicitly frames the cleansing of the temple (Mark 11:12–25) and happens over two days; here it follows the temple scene and happens in an instant. In both, the connection is clear: the tree vividly symbolizes the failure of the people to bear the good fruit that God desires. Matthew's description of its having "nothing at all on it" echoes the lament of God in Jeremiah: "When I wanted to gather them, . . . there are no . . . figs on the fig tree; . . . what I gave them has passed away from them" (Jer. 8:13; cf. Hos. 9:10, Joel 1:7). Although it was not the season for fully formed figs, small knobs, forerunners of figs called *taqsh* in Arabic, would be forming in fruitful fig trees. These were sometimes eaten by the poor. The tree evidently showed no evidence of becoming fruitful, although it was lush with leaves.

The poet Denise Levertov gives the fig tree a voice in her poem "What the Fig Tree Said." The tree is bemused by the shocked reaction of the disciples, and asserts,

> But I, I knew that,
> helplessly barren though I was,
> my day had come. I served
> Christ the Poet,
> who spoke in images; I was at hand,
> a metaphor for their failure to bring forth
> what is within them (as figs
> were *not* within me).[2]

Levertov's creative imagining of this scene reflects a theme of Psalm 119:91, "For all things are your servants." In her understanding, the tree was a willing, even glad servant of the purposes of Christ, grateful for the chance to emblazon his message. Jesus sought to embed a truth deep into the hearts of his disciples. He wanted them to bear fruit that would last, to avoid the traps of empty religion that he saw all around him in Jerusalem. He also wanted them to know the power of faith-filled prayer.

The religious leaders, in their sneering contempt for Jesus, miss the childlike stance Jesus invites his disciples to adopt when they pray. He calls them to a level of boldness in prayer that may disturb our sensibilities nearly as much as the cursing of the tree. What can this promise of Jesus mean, when we see unanswered prayers all around us? How can we

2. Denise Levertov, "What the Fig Tree Said," in *Evening Train* (New York: New Directions, 1992), 111.

Matthew 21:18–22

Theological Perspective

of prayer, there is an important tension between the two texts. It is the tension between two different responses to a corrupt and fruitless institution. One response is to cleanse and heal the corruption. That is the approach that Jesus takes in seeking to reclaim the temple as a house of prayer. Another response is to think that the corrupt institution must be not just cleansed, but uprooted and cast out. This is the approach suggested by Jesus' image of faith uprooting "this mountain" and casting it into the sea. We too are called to work against corruption and fruitlessness in the church. Some of us may be more inclined to the former, more reforming approach. Others may be inclined to the second, more revolutionary approach. We may feel the tug of both approaches in tension within us. Jesus apparently did. There is no general theological principle that one approach is the correct one and the other is misguided.

In the meantime, it is a good practice for churches to continue to pray for their leaders. Leaders are exposed to temptations and pressures; they need prayerful support to be faithful in the midst of those temptations and pressures. The leaders whose call is to serve the God to whom Jesus prays as "Abba" are prone to work at cross-purposes to Jesus, but knowing this does not mean that the Christian community should scorn its leaders. The constant emphasis of Matthew 21 on the tension between Jesus and religious leaders is no reason to cease praying for our current religious leaders. Jesus tells his followers in Matthew 5:44 to love even their enemies and to pray even for those who persecute them. This is good news for all the religious leaders reading this theological perspective—and for the religious leader who is its author.

JOHN F. HOFFMEYER

Pastoral Perspective

to believing disciples who remain in vital communion with him.

Here then is the message of the fig tree to believing disciples: In Christ you have a choice about what power you will have, and how you will use the power you have. Faith in and communion with Christ offer disciples access to incredible resources. How can we access this power? What will we choose to use the power of Christ for? Jesus uses the power available to him in two ways, namely, to heal and defend the sick (21:14–17), and to warn and teach his people about faithfulness and fruitfulness (21:18–22).

Jesus, supreme example, type, and pattern of our lives as Christians, charts the course for the life of believing Christians. The witness of the church lies in believing Christians who embody and live the life of Christ in today's circumstances. We may or may not be called to "curse fig trees," but we are all called to access, through faith in Christ, the power of God to seek the well-being of people around us. Caring entails seeking the welfare of those who are entrusted to us. Care includes warning and teaching in the manner of Christ. Caring sometimes requires that we confront behaviors that may be self-defeating and self-destructive on the part of those entrusted to us. The disciples were amazed at how rapidly the fig tree withered following the words of Jesus. This graphic lesson would no doubt stay with them for a long while. Caregivers have at times to seek memorable ways of implanting lessons in the lives of the people they care for—acts and words that will motivate change in their behavior in ways that may ultimately work in them for good. The withering fig tree may well have been just the lesson the disciples needed to motivate them to be fruit-bearing followers of Christ. What lessons might we learn from this for today? How might we impress upon our fellows the need to be faithful and fruitful today?

EMMANUEL Y. LARTEY

therefore, that our reluctance to attribute any roughness to Jesus may be more our cultural problem than his or Matthew's. A young and quite loving father I know once told his three-year-old twins that if they did not return to their seats at the dinner table until they were excused, he would cut off their legs. The twins, of course, collapsed in giggles along with their preposterous father—and sat down. Humor, especially exaggeration, is all in a relational context.

Still, even if Jesus was going for a quick grin from his hungry disciples that morning as they headed into Jerusalem, he was making a point—and quite a serious point at that. It is a point that leaves us, as it left Jesus' disciples, in a familiar quandary: the promise and the problem of sincere prayer.

There are the poignant cases, the cases that try all our faith, the prayers of those who in all sincerity and all good faith pray for deliverance from their own looming, terrifying mountains: painful illnesses that diminish us, debilitating poverty, wars out of anyone's control, ravishing disasters of many sorts. There are also the imaginative and creative cases that try our faith in different ways: the prayers of those who also in sincerity and good faith pray for the fulfillment of dreams, visions, new possibilities for great human good.

Lest we forget, however, none of the prayers that have reverberated around that immovable mountain down through the centuries are all that different from the prayers of the disciples that morning. Let us not ignore the narrative context in which these teachings on prayer are set. This is chapter 21 of Matthew's Gospel. Tensions are mounting, controversies abounding. Both disaster and dream are in sharp focus. The question, for Jesus' disciples and for us, is, whom do you trust? The call Jesus issues that morning is not for naive faith, but for seasoned faith in the one, the only one, who is not afraid to curse fig trees and indeed can move mountains.

MARY H. SCHERTZ

preach such a preposterous promise to stage-four cancer patients and foreclosed-upon homeowners frantic to find work? Jesus makes expansive promises to his disciples, to infuse them with a radical boldness as they enter into leadership in his new community. They will not see every prayer answered, but they will see astonishing miracles happen as they ask for them with faith, as the book of Acts chronicles. In our preaching, we need to be responsible in what we promise our listeners, but we must not shrink from calling them to bold faith and to persistent, importunate prayer.

As we preach this text, we will want first to consider where our own lives are dense with the foliage of busyness and external piety, yet devoid of the fruit of authentic discipleship. In Matthew, Jesus relentlessly calls his listeners to act upon the words they hear (7:24; 12:33; 13:23), insisting that acts of righteousness and mercy toward the stranger are among the telltale marks of a disciple. Shortly after the scene with the fig tree, he describes a process in which the kingdom will be given to people whose lives "produce the fruits of the kingdom," after being taken from those whose lives fail to reflect the radical priorities of God (21:43).

As we consider the social locations of our listeners, we will consider where they (and we) may be overly impressed by systems or symbols of power, wealth, and significance, which tower like mountains in our lives, threatening to overshadow our faithful journeys. Some of the mountains in our lives may have expanded as we have granted them prominence—for example, the esteem of our supervisors or the approval of our peers. We pile up fears of their disapproval to the size of massive crags as well. True words, spoken in faith, go a long way toward leveling those exalted peaks.

However we wrestle with this text, we preachers must ultimately turn from our congregations to face Jesus and point to him. This is the same Jesus who welcomed children and fed crowds. Here his anger sobers and disturbs us, but the time has come for a potent act of judgment on hypocrisy. Troubled though we may be, we will ideally come, as we prepare to preach, to a place of embracing the *chutzpah* of Jesus in this narrative.

LISA WASHINGTON LAMB

Matthew 21:23–27

²³When he entered the temple, the chief priests and the elders of the people came to him as he was teaching, and said, "By what authority are you doing these things, and who gave you this authority?" ²⁴Jesus said to them, "I will also ask you one question; if you tell me the answer, then I will also tell you by what authority I do these things. ²⁵Did the baptism of John come from heaven, or was it of human origin?" And they argued with one another, "If we say, 'From heaven,' he will say to us, 'Why then did you not believe him?' ²⁶But if we say, 'Of human origin,' we are afraid of the crowd; for all regard John as a prophet." ²⁷So they answered Jesus, "We do not know." And he said to them, "Neither will I tell you by what authority I am doing these things."

Theological Perspective

In this verbal skirmish with Jesus, the chief priests and elders of the people do not say what they really think because they are afraid of the crowd (v. 26). At the end of chapter 21, fear of the crowds will restrain the chief priests and the Pharisees in their desire to seize Jesus. Institutional leaders may seem to have a lot of power on their side, yet they are surprisingly susceptible to fear. In addition to these explicit references to fearing the crowds, verses 15–16 recount that the chief priests and scribes are even upset at the children in the temple for repeating what the crowd has been shouting in the streets. How secure can heads of the religious institution be about their power, if even children unnerve them?

One of the repeated messages of the Gospel according to Matthew (and Mark and Luke, as well) is not to be afraid. Jesus speaks this encouragement on three different occasions (14:27; 17:7; 28:10). It is reinforced by other messengers from God (e.g., the angel's word to the women at the tomb on Easter morning in 28:5). The fact that this is a repeated message from God attests to its importance. Underlying the encouragement not to be afraid are two truths: one about human beings and one about God. The anthropological truth is that fear is a big problem for us humans—whether or not we are religious leaders. The theological truth is that God is loving

Pastoral Perspective

Issues of power and authority are often the hidden causes for conflicts in communities and between people. French philosopher Michel Foucault argued that power is basically a kind of relation between people. Leadership turns on how we use, abuse, or respond to issues of power and authority. In Foucault's terms, then, leadership has to do with how we manage relations between ourselves and others.[1]

When people in power fear that their position is under threat, or when they perceive potential challenges to their privileges or influence over others, they react sometimes with violence. The regimes in the Middle East and North Africa that have seen challenges to their privilege and power from ordinary unarmed citizens in some cases have resorted to the use of force and violence to try to protect their positions. Another response to threats to one's power is to manipulate the people concerned through their access to information or to force them into situations where they will be required to make choices that could lead to their own downfall or destruction. Violence and manipulation of people and information were resorted to unsuccessfully by unpopular regimes in different countries during the so-called Arab spring of 2011.

---

1. Michel Foucault, *Power*, ed. James D. Faubion, trans. Tobert Hurley et al. (New York: The New Press, 1994), 234.

Exegetical Perspective

In Matthew 21:23–27, the central issue of authority, simmering in the background of the previous episodes in this chapter, emerges into the foreground. Still hungry after the fig tree fails him, Jesus is teaching in the temple that he has purged of commercialism and claimed as a place of healing just the day before. What he has not gotten rid of in that decisive action are the critics. It is a slightly different group of opponents that he meets on this day. Previously, his challengers were the chief priests and the scribes. Today the chief priests are back, but they are joined by the elders rather than the scholars. The new group means that he has arrayed against him not only the religious leaders but also the influential families, the Jewish aristocracy.

The chief priests and elders ask him forthrightly about his authority. Since Jesus is neither a chief priest nor a scribe nor an elder, they want to know his authority for doing these things. The issue of authority is not new at this point of this Gospel; it has been there from the beginning of Jesus' ministry. The teaching on the mountain in Matthew 5–7 concludes with Matthew's comment that Jesus taught with authority and, interestingly, *not* as one of the people's scribes (7:29). In Capernaum, the centurion with the sick servant recognizes that he and Jesus are both men of authority (8:5–13). In the story of

Homiletical Perspective

Throughout Matthew, Jesus has preached crisp, clean words with a level of authority that has refreshed the crowds and disturbed those in power. Nevertheless, for all his bold proclamation, he has chosen to withdraw from conflict several times in Matthew (12:14–15; 14:13; 15:21). Now, by entering Jerusalem, he has waded deep into the stream of his opponents' power and confronts their objections head-on. Like Aragorn, the rightful king of Middle Earth in J. R. R. Tolkien's *Lord of the Rings*, he faces resistance to his claims to rule, from those whose preconceptions do not allow them to recognize his legitimacy and power. Here chief priests and elders react to his teaching in the temple, both to his confrontational choice to teach there and to the affrontive content of his message. They do not ask with receptive openness, but hoping to garner evidence against him. In keeping with the format of rabbinical dispute, he parries their question with a question in return.

His query seems simple enough, but it stymies them. It entraps them or, better said, exposes the trapped, narrow space they occupy as they live in fear of the crowds. (This they share with Herod, 14:5.) Like elected officials, ever checking their approval ratings, the religious leaders huddle to calculate their options and downsides, and find that they are unable to answer at all. They are undone.

Matthew 21:23–27

Theological Perspective

and faithful. From this theological truth comes a second truth about human beings, more fundamental than the first: because of God's faithfulness to us, we do not need to be afraid.

The insecurity of the chief priests and elders is likely behind their questions to Jesus about his own authority: Does Jesus' authority call theirs into question? Is it possible for them to have the authority that they would like to claim, if Jesus also has authority?

In the view of Matthew's Gospel, Jesus' authority is not something that he possesses simply in his own right; it is given to him (28:18). Jesus, in turn, does not simply hold the authority for himself; he gives it to his disciples (10:1). The crowds react to Jesus' authority in two ways. First, they say that it makes his teaching different from that of the scribes, the theologically learned Scripture scholars. Second, the crowds praise God because Jesus uses his authority to forgive sins. Significantly, they praise God not for Jesus' authority as an individual alone, but for the authority given by God "to human beings" to forgive sins—precisely as they have just seen this authority embodied by Jesus (9:6–8).

The authority Jesus possesses and displays has its source in God, the sole giver of authority. Interestingly, nowhere does Matthew refer to any religious or governmental institution—or to any leader in those institutions—as possessing authority. The only connection between institutional religious leaders and authority is a negative one, when the crowds contrast the authority of Jesus' teaching with the lack of such authority in the teaching of the learned Scripture scholars. Matthew goes out of his way to deny authority to the "authorities." Particularly in 21:23–27, when the chief priests and elders ask Jesus defensively about his authority and refuse themselves to answer his question honestly because of their fear of the crowds, Matthew urges us to be suspicious of religious "authorities." The only legitimate authority that they could have would be shared with and derived from Jesus, since "all authority" is given to Jesus (28:18).

Jesus' authority, as Matthew 21 emphasizes over and over, challenges and subverts the institutional religious leadership of his day. Christians may sometimes harbor the unexamined assumption that our religious leadership should fare better, since Christian leadership supposedly recognizes the true identity of Jesus, unlike the Jewish leaders of Jesus' day. However, Jesus' critique of his own religious leaders has nothing to do with their not being Christian. (Although the Christian church is

Pastoral Perspective

Jesus' return to the temple sets a similar scene. There are those who perceive in his presence and gracious actions a threat to their positions. The chief priests, scribes, and elders choose the path of manipulation, querying Jesus about his power and authority, to try to achieve the end of discrediting Jesus in the eyes of his followers and showing him to be out of line with the correct teaching of the faith. Their motivation is far from hidden. They blatantly seek to trap Jesus with a very loaded, highly manipulative question, just as they have done before. Any answer he would give could signal trouble for him, either from the people who followed him or else from themselves. In making a response to their question, Jesus has a choice: to be rejected by the people, to be condemned by the religious leaders, or to be untrue to what he knows of God.

Trick questions demand trick answers. That is exactly the response of Jesus. He poses the same question to them, requiring them to give a judgment about John called the Baptist. The discussion among his protagonists reveals the thinking that lies behind their question to him and shows the dilemma with which they try to destroy him.

Fear, especially of people who are influenced by and have influence on leaders, is closely related to the issues of power. The chief priests and elders of the people confess that they "are afraid of the crowd" (v. 26). Political leaders and religious leaders, because they deal with, have influence over, and are influenced by people, are also frequently very sensitive to the views of the people they are called to serve and lead. Herein lies the challenge of pastoral power. In all matters of leadership, fear can warp and distort the judgment of those called to lead. Truth calls for fearlessness and courage. Leaders especially need to be motivated by truth, rather than the opinions or pressures of "the crowd." We are called to witness to the truth, not to be swayed by fear of the people we seek to influence.

The Akan people of West Africa have an ancient saying: "Power is like an egg. When held too tightly it may break, or it falls and breaks when held loosely." This saying is symbolized in a golden sculpture of a chief sitting in state holding an egg, which was an emblem of office for Akan traditional rulers. Akan leaders were by this emblem constantly reminded of the sensitive nature of their office and the care that the responsibilities of leadership required of them. Religious and communal leaders do well to bear in mind how delicate issues of power and authority are. Wisdom is needed to

Exegetical Perspective

the healing of the paralytic in 9:2–8, Jesus claims his authority in the face of challenges from the scribes. Finally, in 10:1, he bestows like authority on his disciples. At that point the question seems to have been put to rest for the time being.

Here, however, in this interlude after he comes into Jerusalem, Jesus' authority faces new questions as the priests and elders close in around him and challenge his legitimacy for "doing these things" (v. 23). These things are most immediately his chasing the bankers and vendors from the temple, as well as his teaching and healing there. As radical and unorthodox as Jesus has been all along, he has upped the ante by continuing his ministry of word and action in the temple itself. Note that no one has attempted to deny him his place in the temple—although surely these questions from the legitimate authorities are preliminary to making an effort to oust him. Note also that the chief priests and elders are not denying that he has authority. Instead, the questions are what kind of authority and, more importantly, who gave him authority.

Jesus does not answer their questions about his authority directly. Rather, he asks them a question in return, rendering his answer to their question dependent on their answer. This style of argument, typical of a controversy story, involves him asking his opponents whether the authority of John's baptism was divine or human. As Ulrich Luz notes, from the perspective both of Matthew as the narrator and of the reader for whom Matthew is writing, Jesus and John the Baptist share one mission, the proclamation of the kingdom of the heavens.[1] What is true of John is also true of Jesus, and what is true of Jesus is also true of John: the one who sent them is the same; they proclaim the same message and ultimately will share the same fate.

Jesus seems to be counting on John's popularity with the people. As the priests and elders talk over their answer among themselves, they realize that they are caught. They are afraid. If they say the answer that the people want them to say—that John's authority came from God—then Jesus will ask them why they did not believe John. If they say that John's authority was merely human, then they will face the wrath of the people who believe that John was a prophet of God.

The crucial contrast between Jesus and his interlocutors in this episode is between fear and fearlessness. The high priests and the elders are operating

1. Ulrich Luz, *Matthew 21–28*, Hermeneia: A Critical and Historical Commentary on the Bible (Minneapolis: Fortress Press, 2008), 29.

Homiletical Perspective

This passage begins a series of encounters in which Jesus refutes faulty logic to silence his detractors; far from convincing them, the conflicts leave them only more entrenched in their opposition to him.

Jesus' move to shift the discussion to the source of John's baptism is brilliant. He refuses to be drawn into their web and deftly weaves one of his own, beckoning them to enter. John's baptismal ministry insistently pointed away from himself and toward the greater power and authority of Christ; his message was preached to prepare the way for Christ to install God's kingdom. Acceptance of John's message would thus require an open receptivity to Christ's authority. If John's baptism was undergirded by God's endorsement, then it was indeed ushering in a new order, brought fully in the ministry of Christ.

John's baptism and proclamation was also an explicit challenge to the Pharisees and Sadducees. When they came for baptism, John called them to repentance for their failure to bear the fruit that should flow from transformed lives. We do not learn their response to John's public challenge of them in Matthew 3, but it cannot have been one of eager receptivity. While it is intriguing and initially promising that they venture forth to be baptized, after that foray they apparently retrench, dispassionately watching the action unfold and plotting their next moves. As it becomes clear that honest engagement with Jesus will involve letting go of the systems that have served them so well, their ears and minds close, but they lack the courage to oppose him outright. Their fingers are in the wind to test public opinion, and they are loath to speak against the beloved John. In an act of cowardice they punt and feign ignorance.

As we preach this text, we will want to call our congregations to consider how our fears of disapproval and cravings for approval actually limit our own ability to perceive and respond to Jesus Christ. By clever questioning, Jesus has succeeded in revealing his listeners' lack of commitment to truth. To hearers such as these, he declines to disclose the full truth about his identity and authority. Of course, he does in fact answer them, in parabolic form, for John's heaven-endorsed message endorsed him. They have shown themselves to have the hardened hearts Isaiah lamented (Isa. 6; Matt. 13:14–15), so they will get only parables, without explanation or understanding. Understanding is reserved for those who intend to respond to his words with obedience. Unhappy with this treatment, the elders and chief priests move swiftly toward condemning Jesus to death.

Matthew 21:23–27

Theological Perspective

chronically tempted to forget it, Jesus himself was not a Christian.)

Jesus' authority has its particular character—coming from beyond him, not confined to him as an individual—because of the triune identity of God. The source of Jesus' authority lies beyond him; it is a divine gift to him. At the same time, he has the full exercise of divine authority: what has been given to him is "all authority in heaven and on earth" (28:18). Still, Jesus' authority is not something limited to his own individual person. Wherever his followers go in space and time, Jesus—through the power that other parts of the New Testament identify as the Holy Spirit—accompanies them with his authority (28:19–20). This is the promise already anticipated when Jesus, during his lifetime, gives the twelve core disciples "authority over unclean spirits, to cast them out, and to cure every disease and every sickness" (10:1). This is the promise anticipated when the crowds marvel that God has given to human beings the power to forgive sins (9:6–8).

The doctrine of the Trinity concerns the source and scope of the divine power present in and as Jesus Christ. This is a power that does not conform to many of our usual assumptions about power. This divine power, the power of God's own life, often looks more like powerlessness to us. It is often at odds with what we think would be the most effective way to get something done. That is why this divine power is so frequently at odds with the ways in which we organize and implement our religious institutions. That is also why there is so much tension between Jesus and the religious leaders of his day, and why Jesus poses such sharp challenges to institutional Christian religious leadership today.

JOHN F. HOFFMEYER

Pastoral Perspective

make decisions and choices where power is at stake. Courage is needed, in order not to succumb to the manipulations of others in power and the fear of the power of the many. In all cases, there is the need for integrity when faced with threats and wisdom when challenged.

Leaders and communities of faith need to be nurtured to be respectful of the ultimate source of power, namely, God. They need also to understand that issues of power and the use of power are always fraught with danger. Power itself is not an evil. We all have and need some power to live our lives. There is no human alive today with absolutely no power. The question has more to do with whether we can recognize our power and utilize it for the benefit of others. This is the call to all who would exercise influence over others. Fear of people will distort any leadership. While sensitivity to the needs and concerns of people is necessary and crucial for influence, fear will always paralyze and damage the best intentions.

Care for communities entails recognizing need, being respectful of the power of the people, having the integrity to see truthfully and the courage to act thoughtfully. Jesus meets the challenges of the chief priests with divine wisdom and the calm courage of one who knows what is at stake. He understands the manipulative games they are playing, and he responds wisely, turning the spotlight back on his questioners and in a sense requiring them to look first at themselves. When they do, they are confounded and unable to answer Jesus' question truthfully in public. Those called to lead always have to take an "inward look." Before we ask anyone to do anything, we must ascertain our own preparedness to respond to the same question, lest we ask someone to do what we are not prepared to do for others.

EMMANUEL Y. LARTEY

Exegetical Perspective

out of fear. Their answer to Jesus is that they do not know, but that answer reveals both their lack of belief in John's message of repentance and the fear that is holding them hostage. They fear the crowd, and their fear governs their answer to Jesus. Jesus in turn answers them: since they did not tell him whether John was from God or from humans, neither will he tell them by what authority he is doing these things.

The story does not quite end here, even though this is the point at which the commentary divides the readings. What follow are two of the most pointed and critical parables Jesus tells in all of Matthew's Gospel. The parable of the Two Sons (21:28–32) and the parable of the Tenants and the Vineyard (21:33–43) follow this contentious dialogue with the chief priests and elders. Looking at those texts is not the task of this essay, but notice verses 45 and 46. There the chief priests are joined by the Pharisees, and together they take umbrage at Jesus' parables because they perceive that they are the brunt of the stories. They take action, or try to take action, by trying to arrest Jesus. However, their fear of the people who think Jesus, like John, is a prophet stops them. Once again, the opponents show themselves to be people of fear.

In Matthew's Gospel, the heart of discipleship is releasing fear, becoming free to take up the cross of following Jesus wherever compassion compels. Nowhere is that more evident than in the mounting tensions of the controversy stories in this interlude between Jesus' entry into Jerusalem and the beginning of the passion narrative. In contrast to the religious leaders, Jesus' actions—claiming the temple as the house of God, teaching and healing with the authority that comes from God—demonstrate that freedom from fear, that freedom to take up the cross.

MARY H. SCHERTZ

Homiletical Perspective

As we preach it, this text offers us an opportunity to dig into the themes of hearing and obeying that pervade the Gospel of Matthew. The Gospel opens with a series of announcements and a wide range of responses, from fearful rejection to joyful embrace. The mark of true, faithful disciples is their capacity to receive words and let those words effect real change within them. In discussing the nature of parables, Jesus notes that the disciples have been blessed with the capacity to hear and respond in fruitful ways (13:10–17). Those who have placed themselves outside of a dynamic relationship with Christ can neither formulate a true question nor come near to receive a true word. They are capable only of antagonistic questions that elicit enigmatic answers.

Finally, here, as elsewhere in the Gospel, Jesus welcomes sincere questions and spirited dialogue. However, his answers always call for change. Jesus' reply to the rulers houses just such a call, given how central the theme of repentance was to John's baptismal message. Jesus' very next parable praises a son who initially walks away from his father but then has a striking change of heart. When we approach God we always run the risk that a disruptive call to repentance will emerge. Jesus Christ may stop us in our tracks and set us on a whole new road. It did not happen in this story, but it could happen to us; the text invites us to be more open than Jesus' opponents were.

A commitment to a stance of receptivity will alter the shape of our questing and the tone of our questioning. True worship is a disturbing adventure; the looming possibility that we will hear an invitation to change is part of the reason we do it so little. As we preach this text, we will want to consider what it means to engage God with our own questions in a lively, honest, and yet humbly receptive manner. Our sermon then can call people to risky engagement with God.

LISA WASHINGTON LAMB

Matthew 21:28–32

28"What do you think? A man had two sons; he went to the first and said, 'Son, go and work in the vineyard today.' 29He answered, 'I will not'; but later he changed his mind and went. 30The father went to the second and said the same; and he answered, 'I go, sir'; but he did not go. 31Which of the two did the will of his father?" They said, "The first." Jesus said to them, "Truly I tell you, the tax collectors and the prostitutes are going into the kingdom of God ahead of you. 32For John came to you in the way of righteousness and you did not believe him, but the tax collectors and the prostitutes believed him; and even after you saw it, you did not change your minds and believe him."

Theological Perspective

"What do you think?" Jesus poses this question, first to Simon concerning the temple tax (17:25), and next to the disciples about a shepherd who leaves the ninety-nine in search of the one (18:12). Now the question is put to the chief priests and elders in an escalating exchange that will culminate in Jesus' arrest, trial, and crucifixion. Save for the textual discrepancies that reverse the order of the sons and so the sense (or nonsense) of the authorities' response, most commentaries presume the question to be rhetorical: the son who first refuses his father's command and later goes to work in the vineyard is the son who does his father's will, actions trumping words. Even the judgment of the religious experts appears to be swift, pronounced without hesitation, and in direct contrast to the consternation provoked by Jesus' previous question (21:26–27). What matters in Jewish theology and tradition is obedience; what is essential, if one is to be judged righteous, is doing the truth.

What if the unresolved textual confusion signals a reversal of cultural norms, norms presumed by the parable but missed by readers at a remove of two millennia? Only after years of living in the Middle East did Roland Muller, a lifelong missionary, begin to notice that he was living in a culture oriented not toward guilt and innocence but shame and honor.

Pastoral Perspective

The parables of Jesus have teeth. At times, they bite. This may be the first challenge in sharing with a congregation the three consecutive parables beginning in Matthew 21. Congregants worn by the responsibilities of life bring with them a hunger for the Jesus who warmly gathers his flock. However, this is a Jesus caught in the middle of a matrix of religious, economic, and political powers that has raised his hackles; and he will not be cowed. How will you describe the tensions—both for Jesus and for Matthew—and make this conflict resonate in the life of a listener who may wonder why Jesus uses harsh words?

The parable about the two sons is the first confrontational story Jesus tells to "the chief priests and elders" in the area of the temple, after they question his authority to teach there (21:23–27). In the parable, Jesus asserts the priority of righteous deeds over righteous words as the foundation for authority in the life of faith. It is not what you say, but what you do, that matters to God. The story he tells appears clear: the first son verbally defies his Father's order to work, but later changes his mind and goes to the vineyard to complete the assignment; the second son says he will go, but he never does. Which one, Jesus asks, does the will of the father? It is the one who gets the work done, despite his initial refusal.

Feasting on the Gospels

Exegetical Perspective

In order to find nourishment from the three parables in Matthew 21:28–32, 33–45; and 22:1–14, for one's own community and for others, it is necessary to name and confront aspects of these texts that have done damage in the history of interpretation. In much of Christian history, rather than provoking Christian readers to self-examination and repentance, these texts of judgment have been the basis of self-justification and projection of Jesus' condemnation onto Jewish "others." The themes of disobedience, replacement, and punishment in these vineyard and wedding parables have underwritten Christian supersessionism. In addition, when the parables are read as allegories, the violence of the king's response to dissatisfaction with his sons or tenants portrays God as a vengeful tyrant. Finally, if not named and explored, the patriarchal setting of the parables—male owner and male sons, weddings without mothers or brides, and prostitutes and tax collectors as gendered stereotypes of sinners—will severely limit the power of the parables to speak to all readers. There are many ways to hinder readers from hearing good news in this Scripture.

In the plot of Matthew, this parable and the two that follow it take place in the setting of the temple in Jerusalem, in the context of Jesus' confrontation with and condemnation of the Jewish leaders, the

Homiletical Perspective

When Jesus rides into Jerusalem, it is a ride into the heart of high-stakes conflict. The crowds' acclaim has enraged the Jewish religious leadership ("chief priests and scribes," 21:15). When Jesus appears at the temple the next day, they are waiting for him: "By what authority are you doing these things, and who gave you this authority?" (21:23).

Jesus' counters with a question on a related subject: by what authority, he asks the investigative committee, did John baptize? The experts confer in a corner. Deliberations include a fair amount of beard pulling. They cannot say John's baptism was merely human unless they are prepared for a riot and possibly being mauled. The crowds will not stand for it. On the other hand, to admit John's ministry was divinely ordained is unthinkable. They collect themselves and return to Jesus: "We do not know." Since they provide no direct answer to Jesus' question, Jesus provides no direct answer to theirs (v. 27), but responds indirectly in three parables. Before us is the first of these.

"What do you think?" (v. 28) invites rabbinic deliberation and debate. The parable of a Vineyard Owner and His Two Children is unique to Matthew. (The Greek refers to the two offspring as *tekna/ teknon*, "children/child," not "sons/son.") The first child, summoned by the father to go labor in the

Matthew 21:28–32

Theological Perspective

"Everywhere I moved in the Middle Eastern culture," he recalls, "there were things that pointed to honor or shame. What chair I chose to sit in, who entered the door first . . . the very way I walked and held myself, all communicated to others around me 'my place' in the world."[1]

Consider the stories having to do with shame and honor that preface this parable in Matthew's Gospel. The day before, Jesus has entered Jerusalem "humble, and mounted on a donkey" (21:5); overturned the tables of money changers in the temple (21:12); and healed the unclean in holy space (21:14). Each act challenges assigned places; each episode shames those who presently occupy places of honor. After this parable, if we continue to read with the lens of honor and shame in place, we encounter in the next parable (21:33–41) another son, whom the landowner sends to the vineyard with the expectation that he will be "respected," that he will be honored. Then there are the invitees who dishonor the king by refusing his invitation to the wedding banquet (22:1–10) and a single guest whose dishonoring garb leaves the same king speechless, even as the king's extreme reaction leaves twenty-first-century readers dumbfounded (22:11–14). Elsewhere, there is Jesus' advice to take the lowest seat when invited to a banquet where one is due the seat of honor (Luke 14:10) or his judgment of those who appear to be righteous on the outside while they are full of hypocrisy on the inside (Matt. 23:28) or his warning that "nothing is covered up that will not be uncovered, and nothing is secret that will not become known" (Luke 12:2). With each parable and every encounter between Jesus and the various representatives of religion, the conventional places of honor are reversed, as the one shamed in the eyes of the world continues to obey his Father's will all the way to Golgotha.

Now what do you think of these two sons, if the paradigm through which you do your thinking is ordered not by right and wrong or guilt and innocence, but rather by honor and shame? The first refuses but later goes to work. The second answers his father, "I go, *sir*," but stays put—emphasizing his acute awareness of his place by the use of words that show honor. In a culture of honor and shame, the son who obeys his father to his face is the righteous son, the son who has kept his place, the son who has maintained the relationship, the son who has not shamed the father.

1. Roland Muller, "Honor and Shame in a Middle Eastern Setting," http://nabataea.net/h&s.html; accessed August 11, 2012.

Pastoral Perspective

This is not a simple story about good guys finishing first. Jesus is not lifting up the person who always does the right thing. In effect, both sons have done wrong, one in word and his sibling in deed; all have sinned and fallen short. In a world in which there is enough moral failing to go around, are there any who can be called righteous? Surely it is those who have done their best to follow the rules.

Jesus, however, says it is the tax collectors and the prostitutes who are cleared to go into the kingdom of God ahead of the chief priests and elders, because they "believed" John's message of baptism and repentance. The tax collectors and prostitutes have clearly and consciously violated the ethical teachings of the Torah; but they, according to Jesus, are the ones chosen for the kingdom over those who have fastidiously obeyed and kept the law of God. What expresses the will of God, according to the story, is not your history of righteous deeds but, rather, your embrace of repentance and your need for mercy. We mistake our own arrogance for faith. Like the first son, the prostitute, and the tax collector, those who turn away from God may learn humility in the process. What matters for the kingdom life is your recognition of your own frailty and acting upon your own need for personal change.

This is a shocking—even unjust—idea. It is hard to be good and to follow the rules; it takes self-discipline, restraint, and courage. Can it be that the behaviors and values that feel like honest expressions of faithfulness to God in our inherited tradition might be demeaned, and God would grant favor to those who simply confess their own brokenness?

No church can *exist* in which every person consistently breaks the rules and comes back saying, "I am sorry," expecting to be fully restored. It would be mayhem and moral chaos. However, this story is not a book of church order. It simply says that no *church* can exist if people who consistently break the rules and come back saying, "I am sorry," are *not* fully restored to membership. For the new church, obediently following the rules requires forgiveness.

Matthew characterizes the Jewish authorities as those who have said they will obey the Father's will, but who fail to respond to the repentance and forgiveness that God issues through John and now through Jesus. God wants the kingdom to include those who have been excluded; those who resist, risk being excluded themselves. The substance of the critique transcends the particulars of the setting and reaches our age—and our communities—as well.

Feasting on the Gospels

"chief priests and elders." This parable is linked to the preceding controversy about Jesus' authority by the reference to the controversy over John's authority; it is linked to the following parable by the setting of the vineyard. The question that introduces the parable, "What do you think?" is designed to provoke response from the listeners.

The simple setup, "a man had two sons," evokes the stories of two sons in the narratives in Genesis 25:21–23 (cf. Rom. 9:12–13) and influences the form of the expanded parable of the Father and Two Sons in Luke 15:11–32. On one level the setting of the story is a literal plot of land, set in a culture and time in which a father would normally expect his sons to work. On another level, the vineyard evokes the image for Israel expressed in the prophets (Isa. 5:1–7). The symbolic setting creates the expectation that this parable will speak of God and God's people.

The man tells the first son to go work in the vineyard today. The son verbally refuses, then later changes his mind and goes. The second son agrees, but does not go. A further question asks a conclusion of the listener: "Which of the two did the will of his father?" (v. 31). Again, here the phrase "will of the father" suggests that the parable has a symbolic dimension alluding to the "Father in heaven," used frequently in the Gospel of Matthew. The scribes and elders give the obvious answer, "The first" (v. 31).

Jesus' interpretive conclusion, addressed to the leaders, states that "the tax collectors and the prostitutes are going into the kingdom of God ahead of you" (v. 31). Jesus' explanation draws out parallels to the parable that do not match perfectly. The two despised groups, tax collectors and prostitutes, are equivalent to the first son who said no and then obeyed. Those to whom Jesus addresses the parable correspond to the second son, who agreed in word but refused to go, as Jesus explains, because they did not believe John and then did not change their minds. The parable itself, verses 28–30, contrasts verbal agreement and practical disobedience with verbal refusal and practical acquiescence.

However, the conclusion goes a different direction, emphasizing the fact that John came in the way of righteousness and they did not believe him, nor did they change their mind; but the tax collectors and prostitutes did believe. The contrast in Jesus' interpretive conclusion is between the powerful leaders, who do not believe John and Jesus, and the unrighteous sinners, who do follow John and Jesus. Matthew's adaptation of this parable is shaped by the conflict of Matthew's community with competing

vineyard, flat out refuses, but eventually *does* go, for reasons unexplained. By contrast, the second child says yes—but never follows through.

Jesus' listeners are on thoroughly familiar ground with this story's features. First, its vineyard symbolism resonates with Isaiah's song of the vineyard (Isa. 5:1–7), an impassioned divine lament over Israel. The vineyard of God's own planting yields "wild grapes." In anguish, God cries, "What more was there to do for my vineyard that I have not done in it?" (Isa. 5:4a). Second, the motif of laborers of different sorts, diligent or lazy, dutiful or distracted, appears in ancient moral tales.

Thus it is to experienced interpreters of such catechetical tales that Jesus turns when he asks his opponents, "Which of the two did the will of his father?" (v. 31). Eager for vindication, they answer quickly, "The first." Jesus' next move is devastating: "The tax collectors and prostitutes are going into the kingdom ahead of you!" (v. 31). This is the linchpin that clicks everything into place. Suddenly we know who is who, who are the inert yes-men and who the transformed sinners. As befuddled as the temple leadership may be about the authority of John, Jesus makes *his* position perfectly clear: John's was the voice of the prophetic tradition raised again after long silence; woe to those who ignored his summons. While notorious sinners, discerning that voice as God's own, plunged into the river of repentance, those who should have been the first to get it instead watched and analyzed.

An important caution is in order as preachers consider how to interpret this parable and the two that follow. It is not the Jewish people as a whole that Jesus is confronting for unresponsiveness to the present work of God. Jesus is engaged in intramural, thoroughly in-house Jewish debate: how rightly to interpret, in terms of their shared tradition, the authority of John's ministry and of Jesus' own. Jesus' interpretation of his own parable makes this plain.

Before turning to possible preaching approaches, some false avenues can be eliminated. Consistent with the prior caution, it is indefensible to paint a derogatory caricature of the Jewish religious leadership and congratulate Christian disciples that, thank God, we are smarter than they were. Nor will it be enough to tell a congregation what the parable was intended to do—back there, back then. Such sermons leave a congregation better informed but underfed. Preachers will also need to resist any temptation to moralize about the "all talk, no

Matthew 21:28–32

Theological Perspective

Then comes the surprising turn in the parable. Jesus does *not* ask, "Which of the sons showed honor to the father?" but, "Which of the two did the will of the father?" His question shifts the paradigm from shame and honor to obedience. "The first!" can be the only correct answer to his question, an answer that ironically shames the assembled authorities. Just in case this point is missed by the audience in the temple and by the audience reading the text, Jesus spells out the metaphor: the place of honor on the way into the kingdom of God will be given to those who presently occupy places of shame but who do God's will, while the religiously righteous will bring up the rear.

Looking back on this parable from the vantage point of Gethsemane, we also might wonder if even Jesus takes the answer to his parable for granted. For Jesus, the question of obedience to God's will cannot be an idle question, especially at this point in Matthew's Gospel. In the garden, he will twice ask to be excused from the obedience he knows to be his Father's will. His beseeching is met with silence; wordlessly he obeys, going forth to meet his betrayer. Borrowing the words of the preacher in Hebrews, he obeys God's will, disregarding the shame of the cross (Heb. 12:2); borrowing the words of Paul, he who has humbled himself now becomes obedient to the point of death (Phil. 2:8). In his birth and in his death, he assumes the shame of creatures who have lost their place, and their way, in the garden of their disobedience.

One last detail in this text catches the attention of any who are still trying to decide what to think. Unlike his pronouncing the harsh judgment in the parables ahead, for slaves who dishonor the son and for guests who refuse the king's invitation and for one who fails to dress for the occasion, Jesus says to these opponents, "The tax collectors and the prostitutes are going into the kingdom of God *ahead of you*" (v. 31). The implied soteriology is that a child is a child eternally, even a Christian child with an unchanged mind.

CYNTHIA A. JARVIS

Pastoral Perspective

As individuals in a congregation sit and listen to this story, they will recognize their own failings in both the first son and the second. The line that Matthew draws between the Jewish leaders and the followers of Jesus gets redrawn down the middle of every listening heart.

We are sympathetic to the first son. In moments of honesty and transparency, each person can acknowledge that we have not said yes to the "way of righteousness." We have made bad choices and hurt people through those choices. We reject parts of Christian discipleship because we find them too hard, too inconvenient. Still, like the first son, we have also had hidden moments of profound desire for our own transformation. We want to please God—and that longing counts for something—even as we botch the particulars of the Christian life. We are relieved and delighted to be included in communion with Jesus as a first son.

Nevertheless the gospel message—and the functional tension in the Christian life between grace and judgment—never lets us rest easy. God's call to repentance and renewal never stops naming our enduring hypocrisy. We have been included in God's kingdom in spite of our sin; but we persist in judging the sin of others.

Jesus' critique of religious hypocrisy is not limited to individuals; his anger falls on every church family. A searching and fearless moral inventory of the lives of our churches will reveal more of a second-son culture than we regularly admit in our leadership-team meetings. We are a group of people who profess one thing and do another. Too much of our church work is institutional maintenance; we serve our own needs first and serve others with the leftovers. The urgent, edgy grace of the Jesus community fades into a warm place to belong. A warm gathering of second sons is not an unpleasant place to be. It is just not the kingdom of God.

DAVID LEWICKI

Jewish groups who do not share their belief that Jesus is the fulfillment of Torah.

A contemporary reader of this parable recognizes the cultural setting in which male sons could be expected to work the land of their male father. Male characters in the parables reflect the understanding of men as religious agents who may represent and include female actors as well, but they are not named explicitly in the text. Here female "prostitutes" are a notable explicit mention of female believers and followers of John. Both tax collectors and prostitutes engage in professions that the establishment deems dishonorable—they are illegitimate workers, as opposed to the legitimate workers who are portrayed as the father's sons. While the sons can agree to work, refuse, or change their minds, it is unlikely prostitutes have a choice. Poverty and desperation likely made this work not a lifestyle option, but a necessity. Tax collectors play a role in an exploitive system for their own advantage, but do not have control over the system itself. In the Gospel of Matthew, "tax collectors and sinners" are those with whom Jesus dines (9:10–11). He is called a "friend of tax collectors and sinners" (11:19) and criticized by the Pharisees for his association with them.

One subversive strategy for reading this parable is to read it not from the point of view of the chief priests and scribes, or even from the perspective of the Jesus believers who were Matthew's audience at the end of the first century, but instead from the position of the prostitute or tax collector who saw and identified the righteousness of John and followed him as a popular prophet and preacher. They feasted with Jesus, their friend, and when he was maligned for these meals, stood with him. Matthew portrays John and Jesus as allies, both children of Wisdom (11:19).

The reference to *pornai* (prostitutes) in this text makes it clear that the motley group dining with Jesus is indeed a group of women and men. That Jesus announces that these enter the kingdom ahead of the chief priests and scribes expresses how shocking is the movement of John and of Jesus.

CYNTHIA BRIGGS KITTREDGE

action" child as a prod toward congregational follow-through on annual pledges to the budget.

The parable instead begs us to invite listeners to imagine the vineyards to which they are sent. We can think in terms of the spiritual nurture of our children, the spiritual and material needs of our neighbors, or the vineyard that is the church's immediate neighborhood. Making the vineyard concrete and local is true to the text itself and keeps us from trading in grand abstractions that typically generate minimal imagination, energy, or motivation.

Little is gained by skewering a congregation with a choice between the two children ("So, which one are *you*? Are you the one who says yes, but then . . . ?"). Congregations know how to attend tactfully to the bulletin announcements at such points. The preacher is better served simply to tell the truth: that, as individuals or congregations, we have been and will be *both* children. Our "no" is not necessarily a rebellious sneer. It may be the offhand, even apologetic excuse of the busy and preoccupied. Then one gracious day we discover that what we have mistaken for a yen for success or affection, knowledge or adventure, is in fact a hunger for the vineyards of God, and nothing will do but to give ourselves over to those vast fields, sowing God's mercy, justice, and compassion.

We are the other child too: all "yes" and "send me," our zeal fueled by the exciting new preacher, the edgy new book, the (very exclusive?) prayer group. Months later, the embers have cooled. Then, parked in our traditional pew out of sheer habit, we may find ourselves recalled by a phrase of Scripture or sermon, hymn or prayer that cuts to our souls.

Whether resistant or eager, devoted or distracted, we can take heart: both children are the father's. Both are summoned, both are sent. The fact is, we do not really know how it ends for either of them. Jesus does not say. Now it is our story. It is open ended.

SALLY A. BROWN

³³"Listen to another parable. There was a landowner who planted a vineyard, put a fence around it, dug a wine press in it, and built a watchtower. Then he leased it to tenants and went to another country. ³⁴When the harvest time had come, he sent his slaves to the tenants to collect his produce. ³⁵But the tenants seized his slaves and beat one, killed another, and stoned another. ³⁶Again he sent other slaves, more than the first; and they treated them in the same way. ³⁷Finally he sent his son to them, saying, 'They will respect my son.' ³⁸But when the tenants saw the son, they said to themselves, 'This is the heir; come, let us kill him and get his inheritance.' ³⁹So they seized him, threw him out of the vineyard, and killed him. ⁴⁰Now when the owner of the vineyard comes, what will he do to those tenants?" ⁴¹They said to him, "He will put those wretches to a miserable death, and lease the vineyard to other tenants who will give him the produce at the harvest time."

Theological Perspective

Standing in the temple, the place of God's dwelling on earth (the house already destroyed, the Presence departed, by the time Matthew writes his Gospel), Jesus tells a story to those who have been set apart to keep God's household in order in the meantime. We know two things about Jesus' listeners: they do not believe Jesus has divine authorization to speak to them (v. 23), and their minds have remained unchanged in response to another messenger claiming God's imprimatur, John (21:32). Continuing to spar with these same religious authorities, who have walked into Jesus' verbal trap but a moment ago (21:31), he tries again. "Listen to another parable" (v. 33).

This parable is drawn from one first told by the prophet Isaiah (Isa. 5:1–7). Both are juridical parables. In a juridical parable, the story is designed to be plausible and the characters morally reprehensible; the characters are humanly recognizable, yet kept at a remove from the identity of the audience, lest their judgment of the characters' actions be tainted by self-interest. Once judgment is pronounced, often accompanied by self-righteous indignation, the jig is up. The storyteller lifts a mirror to the listeners' lives and says, in so many words, "You are the man!" Juridical parables tend to have one of two effects on those who hear them: either they convict (2 Sam. 12:7) or they inflame (Matt. 21:45–46).

Pastoral Perspective

Despite its ubiquity in the Gospels and the likelihood that some proximate version of the story is traceable to Jesus, the parable of the Wicked Tenants makes very few lists of most beloved parables. The parable has parallels in Mark and Luke, and in the *Gospel of Thomas*, but Matthew alone sandwiches it between two other parables that escalate Jesus' conflict with the temple leadership to a boiling point. In Matthew's Gospel, the story is an allegory—an extended metaphor in which the characters' identities are concealed so as to reveal deeper truths—about the salvation of Israel redirected through Jesus. Tenants charged with the task of keeping a vineyard while the owner is away mistreat and kill a succession of persons—first slaves and finally the vineyard owner's son—who are sent by the owner to collect the produce. The tenants face dire consequences for their actions.

The cultural limitations of the allegory employed by Matthew here (and in the succeeding banquet parable) mean that few modern listeners connect sympathetically to a symbolic world that assigns divine sanction to the rejection of Jesus as the Messiah—and to subsequent punishment that comes to the Jewish leaders and people. Moderns who are sensitive to living in a multifaith (and in particular a Jewish Christian) culture will feel anger at hearing this story from the mouth of Jesus and will perceive

⁴²Jesus said to them, "Have you never read in the scriptures:
'The stone that the builder rejected
   has become the cornerstone;
this was the Lord's doing,
   and it is amazing in our eyes'?
⁴³Therefore I tell you, the kingdom of God will be taken away from you and given to a people that produces the fruits of the kingdom. ⁴⁴The one who falls on this stone will be broken to pieces; and it will crush anyone on whom it falls."

⁴⁵When the chief priests and the Pharisees heard his parables, they realized that he was speaking about them. ⁴⁶They wanted to arrest him, but they feared the crowds, because they regarded him as a prophet.

Exegetical Perspective

The parable of the Wicked Tenants, their mistreatment of the emissaries of the owner of the vineyard, and their punishment as a result raises difficult problems of interpretation as sacred Scripture in contemporary life. The landowner's replacement of the tenants with "a people that produces the fruits of the kingdom" (v. 43) has been read to justify the replacement of the people of Israel by the Christian church. In the parable's portrait of the slaves' being seized, beaten, stoned, mistreated, thrown out, and killed, readers have seen a reflection of the Jewish religious establishment's mistreating Jesus and persecuting his followers. Even when historical criticism contextualizes this parable as a product of Matthew's community's view of their rivals, the rabbis in the late first century, the construction of the unjust persecution of the innocent continues to have interpretive power. Identifying the polemical focus of the parable as the Jewish leaders and not the Jewish people does not adequately mitigate the strong anti-Jewish thrust. The obvious allegorical dimensions of the parable—God as the landowner, the vineyard as Israel, the tenants as the leaders, the owner's son as Jesus—lead to the potential conclusion that it is God who "will put those wretches to a miserable death and lease the vineyard to other tenants" (v. 41). The impact of the cornerstone on those on the outside will be to break

Homiletical Perspective

The parable of the Murderous Tenants is the second of three parables that Jesus tells in the presence of Jewish leaders in his final week in Jerusalem. Vineyard symbolism carries over from the previous parable in the same setting (21:28–32).

Tenants are entrusted with a vineyard, but they beat, stone, and ultimately kill the owner's emissaries who come to collect their master's rightful share of the yield. When, as a last resort, the owner sends his son, the tenants have no regard for him. Instead, they plot the killing that will pave the way for their seizure of the property. (Legally, if the legal heir to a property had died and left the property unclaimed, the land could be claimed by others.[1])

Treating his opponents as equals in rabbinic deliberation and experts in jurisprudence, Jesus invites them to provide a fitting ending to the story. Their verdict? Those "wretches" should suffer "a miserable death" and be replaced by others more worthy (v. 41). Jesus immediately pins the parable to the present situation. *They* are the resistant tenants, and more fitting keepers of the vineyard *will* replace them. Before they can recover, Jesus picks up the judgment theme, splicing texts familiar to

---

1. Rudolf Schnackenburg, *The Gospel of Matthew* (Grand Rapids: Eerdmans, 2002), 211.

Matthew 21:33–46

Theological Perspective

Taking Jesus' own interpretation of the parable as our guide, we begin at the end of the pericope. Note that he uses Scripture to interpret Scripture, beyond borrowing the parable from Isaiah for the scaffolding of his story. The interpretive lens he gives us is Psalm 118:22–23, a psalm whose substance invites us to consider religion's rejection of revelation. The immediate context is the rejection of Jesus by those authorized to oversee the temple in Jerusalem; yet, if we are to refuse the anti-Semitic and supersessionist uses made of this parable historically,[1] we would do well to let Jesus' parable have its way with us as present-day caretakers of the church's faith and theological tradition.

In the first place, as our minds are made up about the grasp we have on the truth as zealous guardians of the church's doctrines, the parable enrages us. We come to this parable knowing we know God through Jesus Christ. We have honed our christological formulas over the centuries; we have anticipated what God will say to us on the basis of what God has already said to us; no less than those who have gone before us, we have mistaken certainty for faith in the living God. Such was the case with the temple authorities in Jesus' time, and with the church authorities in Luther's time; such is the case with the religious guardians of received theological wisdom in our own time.

Karl Barth rings the changes on the rejection of revelation by Christianity when he writes, "What we have here [in the Christian religion], in its own way—a different way from that of other religions, but no less seriously—is unbelief, i.e., opposition to the divine revelation, and therefore active idolatry and self-righteousness. . . . It is in place of and in opposition to the self-manifestation and self-offering of God."[2] As the gospel is said to be the possession of the church and under the church's idolatrous control, religion inevitably becomes what people are led to believe in instead of God. In the end, we kill the living Son, so that we may get his inheritance, may possess what can be received only as a gracious gift.

The parable also convicts us. Religious institutions function in most societies to conserve the beliefs, morals, and reigning social order. Priests of that order are reluctant to change their minds

Pastoral Perspective

here Christian roots of anti-Semitism. Their response is warranted.

Pastorally, it is essential to note Matthew's edgy relationship with Judaism. In his world (approximately 85 CE), there were rancorous feelings on both sides in the wake of the church's still-recent separation from the synagogue, and both groups were in critical periods of identity formation. Matthew's community struggled with the representatives of emergent rabbinic Judaism, with each side claiming to represent authentic Torah interpretation. For Matthew, the knife edge of division is Jesus himself, who Matthew believes fulfills and interprets the law. This belief is evident in the allegory. Matthew warns that those who reject Jesus face being "crushed" and "broken," yet in his desire to distinguish the church from the synagogue, he avoids assigning any culpability to the Romans for the "rejection" of Jesus.

One fruitful way of reading this passage in community is to read toward—rather than away from—our discomfort with it. Identity formation, like that in which Matthew was engaged, is a long process of telling and retelling a people's story. It includes shaping a coherent history, choosing sacred texts, establishing rituals for communal meaning making, and clarifying the ethical actions that set the community apart from other groups. Matthew is fervently engaged in this process, using this story to remap the arc of ancient and recent historical events. He makes frequent use in his Gospel of familiar sacred texts of Hebrew Scripture to paint a new reality for his nascent community. As is often the case when communities are in formation, Matthew identifies enemies. Common enemies unite communities. Whether wittingly or unwittingly, Matthew gave the church stories of rhetorical violence—stories that modern readers know have contributed to horrific physical and spiritual violence inflicted by Christians against Jews.

What does a community do with founding stories that not only have lost their initial function but continue to cause harm to the community's life in the present day? A long sideways glance at the founding and development of the United States can be instructive. In this nation, the impetus toward establishing a unique people with a divinely sanctioned destiny had consequences: extermination of native peoples and religious persecution, to name just two. It can be pastorally instructive to explore the tensions and conflicts of community formation in the particular history of the area where your congregation is located.

A common contemporary cultural response to Scriptures with inflammatory characteristics is to

---

1. See Marcus Bockmuehl's chapter "God's Life as a Jew," in *Seeking the Identity of Jesus,* ed. Beverly Gaventa and Richard Hays (Grand Rapids: Eerdmans, 2008), 74. Bockmuehl argues that this parable is "deeply antisupersessionist in relation to Israel. The whole object of the action of the Father and the Son is the protection and prospering of the vineyard of Israel in the purpose for which it was made."
2. Karl Barth, *Church Dogmatics,* I/2 (London: T. & T. Clark, 2004), 327.

and to crush. These very difficulties press us toward a fresh reading of the text.

The parable is the second in a sequence that continues to portray controversy with the chief priests and Pharisees. Matthew has revised the parallel version in Mark 12:1–12, simplifying the sequence of return visits by the slaves and their fates, adding phrases that indicate an eschatological dimension: "season for fruit" and "finally." The detail that the son is thrown out of the vineyard may be connected with the tradition in Hebrews 13:12 that Jesus was killed "outside the camp." The pattern of the parable resembles that of a synagogue sermon that begins and ends with a quotation of Scripture. The opening evokes the love song of the vineyard in Isaiah 5:1–7, which describes the planting of the vineyard: "Let me sing for my beloved my love-song concerning his vineyard: My beloved had a vineyard on a very fertile hill." As in Isaiah, the vineyard in the parable in Matthew is an image for Israel. Thus the vineyard is both a literal vineyard, managed according to the customs of Palestinian agriculture, and a literary vineyard, sharing the symbolic weight of prophetic description and denunciation.

The parable concludes with Jesus' quoting Scripture: "The stone that the builders rejected has become the chief cornerstone. This is the LORD's doing; it is amazing in our eyes" (Ps. 118:22–23), drawing a pointed conclusion, predicting that the kingdom of God "will be taken away from you" (Matt. 21:43) and amplifying the impact of the stone on those who fall on it. The expanded allegorical parable in which violent rejection of the son leads to punishment by God represents Jewish thinking about how to understand political disaster, the destruction of Jerusalem. Other first-century examples of this reflection are in *4 Ezra* and *2 Baruch*. The parable shows Matthew's community interpreting defeat in the war with Rome as God's punishment for rejection of Jesus. Understanding the apocalyptic theological scheme that Matthew shares with *4 Ezra* and *2 Baruch* can help to put into historical context this parable and the one that follows.

Meaningful engagement with this parable in the present requires the reader to ask questions of the text in order to bring this historically specific parable/allegory into the present without replicating its violent supersessionist rhetoric and effect. For example, we might ask, "Do we Christian readers share the parable's understanding of God's punishment in the time of the wars with Rome or in political conflicts today?" Contemporary interfaith theological

his listeners. The rejected stone that has become the cornerstone (Ps. 118:22) aligns with Isaiah's chosen stone on which some stumble (Isa. 8:14–15; 28:16). His listeners see themselves in the mosaic Jesus has assembled, marked for the very judgment they themselves have just rendered.

The path to preaching this text is thorny. One challenge is that Matthew's portrayal of Pharisees, chief priests, and teachers of the Law is unrelentingly negative. As Graham N. Stanton points out, in Matthew there is no gracious Pharisee who invites Jesus to dinner, no mention of the fact that the centurion whose child is healed was a friend of the Jews or built a synagogue, no scribe commended for his faith.[2] Sadly, this pejorative characterization of the Jewish religious elite has fueled sermons that claim Israel *as a whole* has been rejected by God; this parable in particular has been cited as evidence that the Christian church supplants Israel as God's chosen. Nevertheless this very problem can provide a prompt for preaching. This parable may provide an ideal opportunity to confront the fact that, all too often, Christians have read not only Jesus' parables, but the New Testament as a whole, with an anti-Jewish slant. While Matthew draws the division within the Jewish house in starkest terms in his Gospel, he does not envision (much less celebrate) its utter collapse. Debates about appropriate interpretation of Jesus' identity and ministry in light of Jewish Scripture continued in Matthew's communities, but they remained thoroughly in-house Jewish struggles. Moreover, a Christian canonical reading of the Gospels supports God's relentless dedication to Israel (consider Rom. 9). This text provides a chance to preach thoughtfully on the relationship between Christianity and Judaism.

A second potential problem is the violence we find here and in other Matthean parables. Matthew reworks parables found in other Gospels, intensifying the conflict and sometimes adding scenes of violent judgment. Where Mark says that the vineyard owner will "destroy" the rebellious tenants (Mark 12:9), Matthew reads: "He will put those tenants *to a miserable death*" (v. 41). Similarly, Matthew's version of the wedding banquet story that follows this parable includes scenes of violence altogether absent from Luke.

Here again, precisely what is problematic in this text lends itself to an illuminating sermon. New

2. Graham N. Stanton, "The Communities of Matthew," *Interpretation* 46, no. 4 (1992): 382–83.

Matthew 21:33–46

Theological Perspective

when confronted with a contrary witness to the truth—with a living word that invariably surprises them if it turns out, through the working of God's Spirit, to be God's word. This is especially so when that witness and that word threaten their authority. Looking back, we remember with shame the church's response to prophetic voices concerning racial injustice and the role of women. Presently, we stone those whose words challenge the reigning economic order or definition of the family.

Seen in its best light, ministers and theologians are humbled by the enormous responsibility placed on them to safeguard the gospel from apostasy and unrighteousness or impurity; seen in its worst light, we are blind to the light of God's glory shining from unauthorized sources, especially when that light illumines our own error, our misunderstanding of Scripture, our rejection of those always unlikely (unclean? immoral? secular?) witnesses used of God to bring us to faith. Only when we look back from the distance of time is any of this marvelous in our eyes.

Finally, if we do not realize that Jesus is speaking about us, we miss the truth of the matter: that the one telling the parable is himself a living parable. When the living Son of God shows up in the vineyard that we have been set apart to tend, threatening the inheritance of sedimented religious beliefs and practices, we will know we are having to do with the living God because, as Robert Jenson puts it, "the minimum difference between a live man and a dead one is that [a live man] can surprise us: a dead man is dead in that he cannot."[3] The one we have made into a dead doctrine is alive. He is the mirror held up to our lives as leaders of God's people, that we may behold even ourselves redeemed in him. If we are convicted or enraged, we have heard the word of the Lord.

CYNTHIA A. JARVIS

Pastoral Perspective

claim that if one is found faulty, then the whole of Scripture is suspect. Faith communities have an obligation to face our own challenging sacred texts and criticize them and redirect their trajectory of interpretation.

Successful reform movements will often use the best parts of the community's identifying story to reshape its worst parts. The rhetoric of Frederick Douglass and Martin Luther King called on America to become *more itself* in order to reform the nation's racial immorality. In the same vein, it can be helpful for Christians to read Matthew against Matthew. Matthew is, after all, a proponent of loving and serving one's enemies (e.g., 5:44) in such a way that the category of "enemy" itself collapses; he is a teacher of the hermeneutic of mercy and a fierce and determined advocate of forgiveness. Perhaps the best solution for Matthew's anti-Jewish allegories is more Matthew.

Another way of letting Matthew reform Matthew is by transplanting his agrarian allegory into our contemporary setting, thereby shifting the object of its harsh judgment from the Jewish leaders to our own leaders and ourselves. The vineyard could be our patch of earth—or Earth itself—and the tenants those of us entrusted to be stewards of its fruitfulness for all people. Have we been left in charge only to allow the fruits to be hoarded by some, while others literally starve within its walls? Have we spoiled the soil by dumping the toxic byproducts of our industrialized culture back into the fields? Are we silencing the voices calling us to account for our stewardship? Have we taken seriously the inevitable judgment that is coming?

It may be, however, that the allegory itself needs to yield to a new story that nurtures the community's sense of its kingdom identity. Experiment with writing your own allegory. If challenged to reimagine this parable in a contemporary setting, many moderns would find the fault lying not in the tenants, but in the irresponsibility of an absentee landlord—a form of ownership that is synonymous today (as it was then) with exploitation. Movements abound in the world to localize and personalize our economic life so that the economic expressions of our community's life are fully consistent with our vision of a God whose ultimate destiny is to dwell—making God's very home—among mortals.

DAVID LEWICKI

3. Robert Jenson, *Story and Promise* (Mifflintown, PA: Sigler, 1989), 43.

Exegetical Perspective

discussion understands that the heirs of the Pharisees and rabbis and the Christian church can live in respectful relationship and collaborate with God's purposes. As we reconstruct a background for this text that understands Matthew's group in fierce rivalry with the Pharisees, about who are the rightful interpreters of Torah, we might better understand the rhetorical function of the language of replacement in the first century, but reject that language in the present.

We would try instead to reconstruct and analyze the power dynamics of the community of Matthew in relation to its rival Jewish groups and within the Roman Empire. At the time of the writing of Matthew's Gospel, both the community of Jesus believers and the Pharisees were marginal groups with little military or political power in the Roman Empire. However, when Christian readers of this text did become politically dominant, such language of violent seizure and replacement could serve to justify violence.

The parable employs and does not question the economic system of tenant farming, slavery, and the use of violence as punishment and revenge, and it uses that model as an allegory for God and the people. Contemporary readers are challenged to make the difficult move of bringing this parable into dialogue with current economic systems and with contemporary political constructions of persecutors and victims. Readers might imagine the current market economy as a contemporary parallel of the system of tenant farming in the Roman Empire. When the rhetoric of enmity in Matthew is understood to have the purpose of forming community—to cause its hearers to identify with Jesus and his values and oppose the values of their enemies—faithful readers can reflect on how effective this strategy is and what its limitations are.

As they engage the text, readers may recognize that the images of violence in this parable are in tension with Jesus' instruction in Matthew 5:44–45a: "But I say to you, Love your enemies and pray for those who persecute you, so that you may be children of your Father in heaven." By asking questions of the text that go beyond the constructions of Judaism, gender, and society within the biblical text, interpreters of Matthew's Gospel can bring the Scripture into fruitful conversation with the realities of our own historical and social context.

CYNTHIA BRIGGS KITTREDGE

Homiletical Perspective

Testament scholar Barbara Reid notes that the violent imagery in Matthew trades on "stock" paradigms of Jewish apocalyptic and therefore suggests eschatological, divine judgment—not a model for Christian ethics.[3] Matthew, writing from and for Christian communities that have been mistreated by the socially, religiously, and economically powerful, reassures them of ultimate divine justice. Contemporary congregations also include sufferers yearning for justice. The message that God is not unmoved by abuse and will pursue justice is good news. God's determination to deal with those who abuse power can reinforce a congregation's own efforts to identify and challenge oppressive systems, as well as care for those who are victims of such abuse.

Another approach is to focus on the way this parable takes the measure of our own vineyard keeping. A preacher might let the vineyard image function almost literally. We tenants on God's earth are realizing that at least *some* changes in soil, water, and weather are traceable to the impact of (profitable) human technologies. While we may not have stoned or beaten the messengers who question our profit-driven priorities, we have not necessarily been kind or even respectful to them, either. Those of us who recognize the earth as God's own are answerable to more than future generations for the fruits of our labors, whether those fruits look like food enough for all or, tragically, poisoned water for millions.

Other congregations may simply need eyes to see that, wherever they worship and witness, it *is* God's vineyard. Sometimes congregations and their leadership need to remember this, lest they lament that the soil is too hard, the climate too inhospitable, to expect any fruit. One congregation is posted on the corner of Third and Broad in a diverse city crackling with volatility as well as promise, another nestles amid gated enclaves of wealth and influence, while still another prays its way through flood and drought in the heartland. In God's eyes, each occupies fertile ground worthy of faithful labor.

Finally, the preacher might focus on the strange behavior of the vineyard owner. Who would keep sending servant after servant, when one after the other they come back bruised and broken, or not at all? *Who?* Only someone with unquenchable hope and almost unthinkable mercy. Surely judgment will come one day; but mercy hopes beyond hope for change.

SALLY A. BROWN

3. Barbara Reid, "Violent Endings in Matthew's Parables and Christian Nonviolence," *Catholic Biblical Quarterly* 22, no. 2 (2004): 251, 253.

Matthew 22:1–14

[1]Once more Jesus spoke to them in parables, saying: [2]"The kingdom of heaven may be compared to a king who gave a wedding banquet for his son. [3]He sent his slaves to call those who had been invited to the wedding banquet, but they would not come. [4]Again he sent other slaves, saying, 'Tell those who have been invited: Look, I have prepared my dinner, my oxen and my fat calves have been slaughtered, and everything is ready; come to the wedding banquet.' [5]But they made light of it and went away, one to his farm, another to his business, [6]while the rest seized his slaves, mistreated them, and killed them. [7]The king was enraged. He sent his troops, destroyed those murderers, and burned their city. [8]Then he said to his slaves, 'The wedding is ready, but those invited were not worthy. [9]Go therefore into the main streets, and invite everyone you find to the wedding banquet.' [10]Those slaves went out into the streets and gathered all whom they found, both good and bad; so the wedding hall was filled with guests.

[11]"But when the king came in to see the guests, he noticed a man there who was not wearing a wedding robe, [12]and he said to him, 'Friend, how did you get in here without a wedding robe?' And he was speechless. [13]Then the king said to the attendants, 'Bind him hand and foot, and throw him into the outer darkness, where there will be weeping and gnashing of teeth.' [14]For many are called, but few are chosen."

Theological Perspective

In the 1541 French edition of his *Institutes of the Christian Religion,* John Calvin locates the discussion of Jesus' parable of the Wedding Feast in a chapter on God's predestination and providence. Leading up to his exposition, Calvin addresses the question of the confidence believers may have in their election, a confidence represented by the "P" in the five Calvinist doctrines known as TULIP. The doctrine of the perseverance of the saints was meant to effect, in the life of the elect, an assurance about salvation that freed believers to lead a life of gratitude and service, "because we have once been made [Christ's] own."[1]

What then is to be made of Jesus' ominous warning at the conclusion of the parable of the Wedding Feast concerning the many that are called but the few who are chosen (v. 14)? In a word, says Calvin to the elect, nothing! He explains to his flock, in this touchingly pastoral edition of the *Institutes,* that there are two kinds of calling: a universal calling in which all are invited to Christ, and a special calling made to the faithful few through the work of the Holy Spirit. Calvin imagines Jesus looking upon the general public, much as Calvin did fifteen hundred years later, and telling this parable in order to shine

1. John Calvin, *Institutes of the Christian Religion, 1541 French Edition,* trans. Elsie Ann McKee (Grand Rapids: Eerdmans, 2009), 435–36.

Pastoral Perspective

This is the last of three parables by which Jesus engages the temple authorities. They have confronted him about his authority (21:23–27), and he responds with a series of stories that eviscerate them rhetorically. Matthew proves to be an equally rigorous judge of the faithfulness and integrity of members of his own emerging Christian community. This story holds the prospect of fierce and final judgment *for all* in tension with the possibility of an outlandishly inclusive grace *for all.*

Matthew's story is an allegorized rendering of the "banquet invitation" God extends to Israel. Prophets were sent, and they were rejected; Jesus was sent, and he was killed. In Matthew's telling, the sacking of Jerusalem by the Romans in 70 CE is repayment for the ungrateful response of the people that dishonors the Lord's generous invitation.

As with the previous allegory (21:33–46), if congregants are savvy to the story's identification of the king with God, the invitees as Israel, and the rejected servants as the prophets (including Jesus), they will be uncomfortable with the parable's first section. There may be an identification in our frantic culture with citizens who were "too busy" to respond to the invitation to the banquet, but few will be content to see Jews—even Jewish leaders—in the historically tendentious role as killers of the messenger.

Feasting on the Gospels

Exegetical Perspective

The third parable in this sequence in Matthew about membership in the kingdom of heaven (21:28–22:14) employs the biblical motif of the wedding feast: the feast used in the prophets to speak of the messianic age (Isa. 25:6–8); the wedding used elsewhere in the New Testament to refer to the time of fulfillment (John 2:1–12). Both Luke 14:16–24 and *Gospel of Thomas* 64 have stories that are parallel to this parable. This Matthean version is expanded with detail that lends itself to allegorical interpretation. The scenario of invitation, refusal, and the inclusion of surprising guests has conventionally been understood to describe salvation history from a Christian perspective.

In this series of parables, the protagonists are first a father (21:28–32), then a landowner (21:33–45), and in this parable a king who hosts a wedding banquet for his son. Consistent with the patriarchal perspective, mother and bride are unnamed and of no consequence for the purpose of the parable, whose action focuses on the contrast between those invited and those who attend. Slaves are intermediaries who execute the will of the king and are sent twice to call those who are invited.

As the three invitations are described, each refusal escalates the rejection: from simple refusal, to disrespect and return to farm and business, and

Homiletical Perspective

If we were confronted with this version of the parable of the Wedding Banquet, absent any indication of its source, we could probably guess that it is Matthew's version. Both Matthew and Luke include a parable where originally invited wedding guests dismiss the invitation and are replaced by others (Luke 20:9–19), but Matthew ups the ante in several ways. First, in Matthew this is the wedding of the king's son, which assigns it particular social and political importance. While in Luke the first-invited offer excuses, in Matthew they simply (unthinkably) refuse. This amounts to treason; little wonder the king burns their city. Finally, Matthew adds a scene absent from Luke: a guest who did not bother to dress for the occasion is discovered in the hall. As if it is a deliberate insult, not an oversight, he is not ushered out, but thrown out—"into outer darkness," no less, "where there will be weeping and gnashing of teeth" (v. 13).

Matthew's version, as we have come to expect, is glossed with a strong theme of judgment. The consequences of ignoring the host's invitation are pointedly violent. As we approach this Matthean telling of the story, it is important to remember that setting and audience make a difference to interpretation. Matthew has set this parable amid intense debate between Jesus and the Jewish religious elite over

Theological Perspective

the light of the gospel's judgment on the many who refuse the gospel. Therefore the names on the original guest list (v. 3), as well as a nameless multitude eventually brought in from the streets to fill the hall, both good and bad (v. 10), are those who have received a general call. (Never mind that elsewhere Calvin understands the original guest list to stand for God's election of Israel.) In other words, they are not necessarily the elect; in fact, they likely are not the elect.

What interests Calvin the most is the ill-clad guest. Ignoring the violence visited on the slaves by those first called (v. 6) and the king's rage against the murderers of his servants (v. 7), Calvin's pastoral instincts instead zero in on the one who has been justified but remains unsanctified. You could say that this is the man in Calvin's flock who confesses Christ, is baptized, and then lives his life as it suits him. This is the Christian who is present for the festivals at Christmas and Easter but thinks nothing of the cost of discipleship. Like Calvin, if we bracket the question of the original identity of the characters in the parable, and ask how the parable is a living word to those within earshot of the gospel today, we need look no further than the membership rolls of the church to wonder about the disparate responses of the baptized to the gospel.

Once they were born anew into a living hope; once their names were placed on the invitation list by the grace showered on them in baptism. Now every invitation to a foretaste of the banquet falls on deaf ears and busy lives. Even a second invitation, issued after some thought has been given to "marketing the menu," elicits hostility. According to Calvin, at the end of the day of the Lord, these are those whose hearts have never been rooted in the teaching of the Spirit. As for the few who have been made Christ's own, "it is not from this calling that we teach the faithful to estimate their election."[2] No doubt this reading of the parable holds in solution the judgment Matthew originally meant to visit upon believers whose prior election was presumed.

Karl Barth offers a very different understanding of the theological import of this parable. His exposition is placed in a lengthy discussion of the command of God that follows from the divine election of grace. Although Barth does not say this, one could surmise from his tendency to skate on the thin ice of universalism that, because the wedding feast is being thrown for the son, in Christ we are already included

Pastoral Perspective

Moreover, most will be outraged at the image of God as a vengeful king. Even if you explain the strange incongruities of the story and plead, "It's just an allegory," it does not feel right. The story through verse 8, passed through the filter of the church's history of anti-Semitism, tastes bitter.

In verse 9 the tenor of the story tips from judgment to grace. The king sends the servants into the streets to invite *everyone*. In the most true-to-life line in the passage, the servants gather into the banquet hall (in the allegory, now the church) "both good and bad" (v. 10). This is consistent with Matthew's unromanticized portrayal of the church as consisting of both "wheat" and "weeds" (13:37–43). For all kinds of reasons, the menagerie of those invited came.

Is that not the church you know? If there are 100 people in worship, there are 150 reasons for being there. They come to honor the Lord . . . or to obey their parents . . . because of unshakable guilt left over from childhood . . . to meet a future lover . . . to keep the peace in a marriage . . . to grieve. Their mind lights up over questions of spirit. It is the only place they receive a warm embrace. It is the only place they can be quiet without also being alone. We are good *and* bad, each of us, in some measure. The patterns of our church life largely protect us from knowledge of one another's sins, but they are no less offensive for remaining anonymous. The same is true for one another's virtues. We rarely get to see them on full display, but we fill the church with uncommon goodness every time we gather.

In a world in which people are dividing themselves into smaller and more homogeneous groups, the random variety of every church gathering is a persistent image of the grace of the kingdom of God. Churches can be ugly places when seen up close—callous, cruel, and small-minded, just like the people brought in off the street. Churches can also be beautiful places when seen up close—generous, loving, and just in ways that the world never is, just like the people God brings in off the street. The church's diversity mirrors our own soul—as the poet Walt Whitman said, "We are large, we contain multitudes."[1] God invites us—all of us—to the feast.

One wonders what the king thinks of this banquet. The one he ends up with is different from the one he planned. The king has been dishonored, and all he has managed to pull off is a banquet feast of the marginally honorable. The long-awaited

2. Ibid., 437.

1. Walt Whitman, "Song of Myself," in *The Portable Walt Whitman*, ed. Mark Van Doren (New York: Penguin, 1973), 96.

finally to the seizure, mistreatment, and murder of the king's slaves. The king's first overture is simply refused. In the second, the king speaks an invitation that elaborates on the preparation of the food. These words echo those of the female figure of Wisdom in Proverbs 9:1–6, who invites the simple, "Come, eat of my bread and drink of the wine I have mixed. Lay aside immaturity, and live, and walk in the way of insight." She, like the king in the parable, has slaughtered her animals and made ready her feast. The king is portrayed as impatient and unforgiving to those who refuse his invitation. The third violent response, unrealistic as a response to a wedding invitation, fits the pattern of betrayal and murder expressed in the previous parable of the Vineyard Owner and the Slaves. In his enraged response the king "sent his troops, destroyed those murderers, and burned their city." These military details lead commentators to conclude that Matthew's retelling of this parable has been influenced by the community's experience of the sack of Jerusalem in 70 CE.

The king's next step is equally implausible: he pronounces that those invited to the feast were not worthy, so he instructs his slaves to call people in from the streets. This again reminds the reader of Proverbs: calling in the streets and public places is also a feature of Wisdom in Proverbs 9:3. In Matthew's parable, the slaves do not discriminate between worthy and unworthy, but include both good and bad and fill the hall. The morally mixed character of the church is the focus of the parable of the Weeds and the Wheat in 13:24–30. Its force is that the act of dividing up and judging is to be postponed and left for God.

Intriguingly, rather than concluding with the image of morally mixed inclusion, the story resumes with an additional episode of judgment, disappointment, and punishment. The king notices a man without a wedding robe and asks how he was able to enter. Again the response is illogical; the king's reaction does not make sense, since no dress requirements were specified in the previous passage about the invitation. Nevertheless, the king commands the guest to be tied up hand and foot and thrown into the outer darkness, where in Matthew's characteristic expression "there will be weeping and gnashing of teeth" (v. 13). In the final pronouncement, "many are called, but few are chosen," the "many" may refer to those who attend the banquet, and the "few" to those who are prepared with the proper garments.

The logical gaps in the episodes and the lack of fit between the saying and the scene may be explained

the nature and source of his authority. In contrast, Matthew's other wedding parable—the story of the prudent and the careless bridesmaids (25:1–13)—is addressed to disciples (see 23:1 and 26:1, bracketing the Mount of Olives discourse to disciples). Here the audience is made up of those "in the know," keepers of the tradition with political clout and the power to mete out judgment. They are by no means novices in the will and ways of God. While the later parable is designed to equip the faithful for coming days, the present parable is Jesus' final thrust to the Jewish leadership directly—one last effort to penetrate their resistance to God's overtures.

Before considering preaching routes, two cautions: First, Matthew is interested in an intramural debate between Jesus (and later, his followers) and other interpreters of Jewish biblical tradition—specifically, a debate about the possibility and nature of God's saving intervention in the life of the nation through Jesus. Matthew does not pit an entity called the "Christian church" against the Jewish faith as a whole. This rules out from the start identifying the first-invited with Jews, the second-invited with Gentiles. Such interpretation distorts and limits the range of the parable.

Second, the violent endings of Matthew's parables function as symbols of ultimate divine justice, not as models for Christian behavior toward anyone the community deems unworthy. To say "there will be weeping and gnashing of teeth" (v. 13) is not necessarily to say that God has designed these horrors. Perhaps there are horrors we bring upon ourselves, the inevitable fruit of rushing headlong through lives so self-absorbed that the whispers or even shouts of God's messengers cannot reach us until it is too late.

We can imagine several directions for preaching. It can be worthwhile to take on the violent features of the parable, taking into account their eschatological import and the rhetorical intent of the parable, as noted above. This would likely involve a side-by-side reading of Matthew's version of the parable and Luke's (Luke 14:15–24). The invitation is unique and urgent, but ultimate justice is in God's hands, not ours.

Another sermon would concentrate on the invitation itself. First, it is an exceptional invitation; this is an invitation to the wedding of the king's son. Second, if we believe that the Spirit of God who spoke by the prophets still speaks, then the prophetic word still comes—and it demands utmost attention! God has not gone silent. It is possible to be intensely religious, as were the religious leaders of Jesus' Jewish community, and yet turn a deaf ear to the Spirit

Matthew 22:1–14

Theological Perspective

at the table prepared for us by his sacrifice. We simply continue to live as though this were not the case. We put off his call, make light of it, work the fields, go about our business, and even mistreat those who persist in reminding us that all is ready. Our resistance notwithstanding, the one who is telling the parable continues to call all who are within earshot: calling us out of the un-freedom, represented by every other claim on our lives, to the freedom of the one claim that gives us permission to be the persons we are, to be those who were made to be with God.

What does Barth make of the one who ends up bound and thrown into the outer darkness? In a reading very different from Calvin's, Barth sees him as the one who is there by compulsion, because it is his solemn and sober obligation to obey God's call rather than his joy and delight to be a guest at the wedding banquet of the son. "In the last resort, it all boils down to the fact that the invitation is to a feast, and that he who does not obey and come accordingly, and therefore festively, declines and spurns the invitation no less than those who are unwilling to obey and appear at all."[3]

Whether we follow Barth's or Calvin's reading, one thing is clear. If the Lord's Day and the Lord's Table are a foretaste of the eschatological banquet, then this parable invites us to consider the eternally fraught drama played out temporally among those who find themselves, by God's invitation, at table together even now. From a remove, we listen, as present-day religious leaders and congregants whose backdrop includes congregations no less conflicted than Matthew's and religious institutions barely less in ruins than the Jerusalem temple was post-70 CE. Entering into the parable's world, we listen, as servants sent to issue the king's invitation, servants who are, in the same breath, potential guests invited to enter into the joy of God's presence that is our salvation.

CYNTHIA A. JARVIS

Pastoral Perspective

messianic banquet looks like life on the streets, not a dinner party of elites.

Matthew says that the king enters the banquet hall to survey the guests. He has been generous to the last detail, even providing appropriate attire to those he gathered in haste. However, there is one person not wearing a wedding robe. "Friend," the king says, "how did you get in here without [the right clothes]?" (v. 12).

The man stands in the banquet hall of the king, feasting at a grand table—but he shows no evidence that he understands where he is. Brought in off the street, he shows no gratitude. The king responds with a brusque judgment we have seen already: "bind him . . . and throw him into the outer darkness, where there will be weeping and gnashing of teeth" (v. 13; see 8:12; 13:42, 50).

In the parable of the Two Sons (21:28–32), the ethical imperative is to embrace repentance and change. Here is the same imperative, evocatively portrayed as a wedding garment—a symbol for the Christian life. The image of clothing is employed at other places in the New Testament (see Col. 3:12; Eph. 4:24; Gal. 3:27), where the metaphor refers to outward evidence of the inward transformation that occurs when a person is joined to Christ through baptism.

For Matthew, ethics are paramount. If a person receives unmerited grace and does not respond with humility, compassion, kindness, and gratitude, that person is judged just as those who begged off the initial invitation. In truth, it may be that an ungrateful life is its own judgment—an "outer darkness" that is desperately lonely and devoid of joy.

It is striking too that the man cast out of the banquet is not just underdressed, but speechless. Not every church community practices testimony— sharing in a warm and genuine and personable way the good news about our own salvation. Still, for those who dwell in the warmth and security and abundance of the banquet hall, it is not unreasonable to expect that someday you will find yourself face to face with the host of the party. When that day comes, you will do well to be prepared with a word of personal thanks.

DAVID LEWICKI

---

3. Karl Barth, *Church Dogmatics*, II/2 (Edinburgh: T. & T. Clark, 1957), 588.

as a result of the parable's development from its origins in Jesus' ministry to its elaboration to interpret relationships of the community with others in the time of Matthew. For example, in the course of the composition of the Gospel, the parable in verses 11–14 may have been a separate parable about being prepared, similar to the wedding parable about the ten bridesmaids in 25:1–13.

Comparing this parable with its parallels in Luke and the *Gospel of Thomas* shows the distinctive emphasis of Matthew. While it shares the structure of invitation, refusal, and corralling people from the street, *Gospel of Thomas* 64 does not include the allegorical details of Matthew. In Luke 14:16–24 the giver of the dinner is not specifically a king. When the invited guests refuse on various grounds, the owner instructs the slave to gather the poor, the crippled, the blind, and the lame. When there is still room, others are invited also to fill the house. The saying that concludes the parable in Luke, "none of those who were invited will taste my dinner" emphasizes those who are excluded rather than the surprising inclusion. Matthew's parable is more violent and polemical than the parallels. The addition of the episode of the missing wedding garment and ensuing punishment places the emphasis strongly on exclusion and rejection.

The parable of the Wedding Feast raises sharply the difficulties for contemporary interpretation presented by the previous two parables. The parable's portrait of the king's son's wedding, the hostile rejection of the invitation, and the violent punishment of the unprepared guest reflects the violence of the parable's imperial context. To engage this text as Scripture, readers might reflect on how the trauma of war with Rome and painful competition between heirs of the Pharisees and those of the Jesus movement have shaped this parable and its history of interpretation. Those who seek nourishment from these parables may expand beyond the image of God as father, slave owner, and king that operates within the parables. The figure of Wisdom that lies behind the words of invitation to the wedding feast and that has influenced the portrait of Jesus as one of Wisdom's children in 11:19 may provide an alternative image to that of the revenging and violent king.

CYNTHIA BRIGGS KITTREDGE

in our time. While there is much focus on individual vocation, preachers need at times to address the question of vocation to the congregation as a whole. Might the call to worship itself be framed as an urgent invitation? What if we came together asking, "What is the Spirit saying to the churches today? How is God's future already taking hold of our present? What is our part to play?"

The most evocative option might be to wrestle with the question of worthiness and unworthiness that seems to be at work here. All seems well until we stumble upon the underdressed, second-invitation guest. (Incidentally, scholars are virtually unanimous that no custom of wedding hosts handing out wedding outfits to invited guests can be established with any certainty; so, appealing as that easy out may be, it is not plausible.) For all the breadth of the invitation, Matthew's story sounds as if, in the end, one has to earn the right to be there.

On closer reading, a single line undermines that idea. Notice that when the slaves go out for the second set of guests, they gather up "all whom they found, the good and the bad." Not only the "nice" people are invited; so are the despicable. Matthew's parable of the Dragnet comes to mind (13:47–50). Everyone is worthy of an invitation. The invitation is scandalously broad. In fact, there are only two ways to end up on the outside of this party: either you disregarded the invitation completely; or you imagined an invitation this broad could not be worth much, so you stumbled in still dressed for the gym, in case the party was a bore.

The message of Matthew is that God's intervention in Jesus is at once broadly inclusive and utterly decisive. The wedding invitation has gone out. The question is not whether you can manage to fit this party into your schedule. This is the invitation that changes your schedule—and your life. This is an invitation to give oneself up to God's future in Jesus Christ, which rushes toward us with unstoppable power, overtaking our present with a costly summons.

SALLY A. BROWN

Matthew 22:15–22

¹⁵Then the Pharisees went and plotted to entrap him in what he said. ¹⁶So they sent their disciples to him, along with the Herodians, saying, "Teacher, we know that you are sincere, and teach the way of God in accordance with truth, and show deference to no one; for you do not regard people with partiality. ¹⁷Tell us, then, what you think. Is it lawful to pay taxes to the emperor, or not?" ¹⁸But Jesus, aware of their malice, said, "Why are you putting me to the test, you hypocrites? ¹⁹Show me the coin used for the tax." And they brought him a denarius. ²⁰Then he said to them, "Whose head is this, and whose title?" ²¹They answered, "The emperor's." Then he said to them, "Give therefore to the emperor the things that are the emperor's, and to God the things that are God's." ²²When they heard this, they were amazed; and they left him and went away.

Theological Perspective

The overarching question that will arise out of these three passages (22:15–40) is the overarching question of the entire book of Matthew: Who is this Jesus, the son of David? In one sense, Matthew answers the question in the first chapter with Jesus' lineage, but that is merely the genealogical account of Jesus as son of David. The rest of the book can be seen as a fuller explication of what it means to be the "son of David."

These texts are framed by two key events. The first is Jesus' entry into Jerusalem, the seat of power both politically and religiously (21:1–11). Here Matthew provides a hint of what the Matthean king looks like. This king is not what many were anticipating. He is not the warrior king who liberates Israel from their oppressors by force; rather, he is the dying king who sacrifices himself freely. His triumph is manifested in surrender, his victory in defeat.

The second event that frames these pericopes is Jesus' cleansing of the temple (21:12–17), where Jesus denounces the religious leaders. The thrust of that narrative is not that Jesus is rejecting Israel or its religion, but rather that judgment begins in God's house, that the Lord corrects whom he loves. Jesus is not rejecting the nation of Israel, or even Judaism; rather, he is reaffirming his commitment to the covenant. That Jesus first cleanses the temple reaffirms

Pastoral Perspective

This is the first of three debates between Jesus and various religious leaders. These debates, colored by later conflicts, paint a picture of Jesus as a threat to the religious and political powers that be. Jesus' interlocutors in this first episode are the Pharisees and the Herodians. We know little about the Herodians, except that they were supporters of Herod Antipas. That is enough to tell us that this conspiracy against Jesus is made up of strange bedfellows indeed. We might expect the Pharisees, fastidious observers of the Law, and the Herodians, collaborators with Rome, to be at each other's throats, but in this text they are united in their opposition to Jesus.

They have decided to use taxes to trap Jesus. After an opening bit of flattery we get right to the heart of the matter: the poll tax. This was a Roman tax administered by Jewish authorities. Like many taxes, it was especially burdensome for poor people. So is it lawful to pay the tax or not? As far as trap questions go, this is a good one. If Jesus says yes, he risks alienating both the Pharisees, who consider entanglement with Rome unrighteous, and the poor people who are oppressed by the tax. If Jesus says no, he risks sedition, and you can be sure the Herodians are prepared to report any whiff of that to Rome. Collaboration or treason: these are the horns of the

Exegetical Perspective

Matthew borrows this series of confrontations from the Gospel of Mark. In Mark the chief priests, the scribes, and the elders send the Pharisees to trap Jesus. In Matthew, whose community is in conflict with the Pharisees, the Pharisees are the instigators and the Herodians join them as loyalists to the empire. This confrontation with the Pharisees allows Matthew the opportunity to express his community's struggle with their contemporary rivals in the synagogue. As always, we are reminded that this conflict is not *against* the Jews but *among* the Jews.

Although we are told the Pharisees come "to entrap him" (v. 15), it is superfluous information. All the way back in 12:14 they have already decided "to destroy him." Compliments or not, the question subsequently posed is a minefield with a purpose: "Is it lawful to pay taxes to the emperor, or not?" (v. 17). Although there is a strong tradition of theological debate and scuffle in the temple, the question posed to Jesus is far from abstract. In 6 CE the Roman head tax was instituted when Judea became part of a larger Roman province. The annual tax of a denarius was roughly the amount a laborer would make in a day. The coin to pay the fee was imprinted with this inscription: "Tiberius Caesar, august son of the divine Augustus and high priest." Many faithful Jews, instructed to eschew all idolatry, were incensed by

Homiletical Perspective

In 1789, Benjamin Franklin wrote a friend, "In this world nothing can be said to be certain except death and taxes."[1] Given that Franklin shared his sentiments six years *after* the end of the Revolutionary War, perhaps he was more certain than ever of the inevitability of taxation, whether with or without representation. While some preachers may wonder whether Jesus uttered today's pronouncement about taxes with a similar world-weariness, I suspect there was more at play. Detecting just what Jesus meant by his ambiguous statement, however, let alone how to apply it to our situation, is no easy task.

First, some background. It is not simply taxes in general that are up for debate here. Jews in first-century Palestine paid numerous taxes: temple taxes, land taxes, and customs taxes, just to name three. The tax in question was a particular—and particularly onerous—one. It was the imperial tax paid as tribute to Rome to support the Roman occupation of Israel. That is right: first-century Jews were required to pay their oppressors a denarius a year to support their own oppression.

Not that everyone saw it this way. Those put in power by the Romans, represented in this passage by

1. Letter to Jean-Baptiste Leroy (November 13, 1789), available at http://archive.org/stream/writingsofbenjam10franuoft/writingsofbenjam10franuoft_djvu.txt (accessed May 25, 2013).

Matthew 22:15–22

Theological Perspective

God's faithfulness to love Israel, despite Israel's unfaithfulness to God.

The Pharisees were good at their job. They were trained in both rhetoric and the Scriptures and were skilled in argumentation. In this text they pose a question, seeking to "entrap him" (v. 15). Jesus is faced with two choices: he can agree to the tax, casting his lot with the Herodians, in which case he is a traitor to the nationalistic movement; or he can rebuke the tax, in which case he is an insubordinate rebel against the state. Both put Jesus in serious jeopardy; either he betrays his people, or he declares war on Rome.

Rather than get stuck on one of these two options, Jesus poses a counterquestion, "Whose head is this?" (v. 20). In pointing out the likeness of the emperor on the coin, Jesus calls to mind the prohibition on constructing idols and graven images (Exod. 20:4). What faithful Jew would have any likeness of Moses or Abraham? Nevertheless they failed to see the problem with possessing as many likenesses of a pagan ruler as possible.

In demonstrating what should be a problem for observant Jews, Jesus poses his response in terms of ownership. This coin belongs to the emperor; his likeness declares his kingdom. This kingdom is marked by wealth, military strength, and brutality, and all the political power rests with the emperor. He is the personification of all the wealth and strength of Rome, and the tax belongs to him. By contrast, what can we say "belongs" to God? With a tax we know exactly how much is due, and the remainder is ours. What can we expect to hold back from God? What is "ours" in contrast to God's? As the psalmist states: "The earth is the LORD's and all that is in it" (Ps. 24:1). What in creation does not have the imprint of God? Did God not make humans in God's image (Gen. 1:26)?

Jesus rebukes the Pharisees, calling them "hypocrites," first for their uncritical loyalty to the crown, but also for their underlying belief that they can treat God like a great tax collector who can be appeased with a minimal "tax." They are hypocrites because they honor the pagan emperor and are happy subjects of his kingdom, yet they hope to hold back from the Lord of the covenant and neglect their true citizenship in God's kingdom.

It is important to note that Jesus is not establishing dual kingdoms. He is not declaring that the state is autonomous in its sphere, while the reign of God is confined to its corner. In pointing out their misguided loyalty, Jesus is declaring the preeminence

Pastoral Perspective

dilemma, and the Pharisees and the Herodians hope to stick Jesus with one or the other.

Jesus begins his thread-the-needle answer with this: "Give to the emperor the things that are the emperor's" (v. 21). Given our political climate, in which the legitimacy of government itself is sometimes called into question, it is important to note that Jesus does affirm some duty to the emperor. The parameters of this duty are not clearly defined, however. The emperor is due what belongs to him. Implicit in this claim is the counterclaim (made explicit in just a moment) that not everything belongs to the emperor (regardless of what the emperor may believe). We are to give the emperor his due—but no more. We are not to give to the emperor things that do not belong to him. Again, in our context, where national loyalty and Christian faith too often merge into one another, this is an important suggestion of limits: give to the emperor what belongs to the emperor, but no more.

The implicit becomes explicit as Jesus' answer continues: "[Give] to God the things that are God's" (v. 21). Now our duty to the emperor is resituated within a broader, indeed universal, context: our duty to God. This broader duty to God may not exactly annul the duty to the emperor, but it does massively reconfigure it. We are to give the emperor his due, but only insofar as this is consistent with—indeed an expression of—our more expansive duty to God.

Many commentators have seen a connection between the image on the coin, indicating the coin belongs to the emperor, and the theological claim of *imago Dei*, indicating that human beings, created in the divine image, belong to God. This can be a helpful insight, but we must be careful not to allow it to become a dualism, as if coins and money were always only matters for the emperor, and human beings were always only matters for God. This reading would be inconsistent with the rest of the Gospel according to Matthew. The point is not that some things belong to the emperor and other things belong to God. Every Jew standing there would have known Psalm 24: "The earth is the LORD's and all that is in it; the world, and those who live in it" (Ps. 24:1). *Everything* belongs to God, not just human persons created in the divine image, but also coins and emperors and Pharisees and Herodians and fish and water and bread and wine. Everything belongs to God; thus we owe everything to God. That means whatever we give to the emperor can and must be an expression of our deeper allegiance to God.

their forced participation in such activity. There was an immediate revolt, and a larger and disastrous revolt by the Zealots from 66 to 70 CE.

"Is it lawful?" An answer in the affirmative puts Jesus in the pocket of the Romans and therefore dismissed by many faithful Jews. An answer in the negative makes him a common revolutionary to be arrested by the empire. The ones asking the question do not say under whose law the act should be judged, Rome's or YHWH's. Jesus is aware of their motivation. In Mark, Jesus recognizes their hypocrisy, but Matthew demonstrates his particular disdain for the Pharisees by noting their "malice" (*ponēria*, v. 18), which includes a connotation of evil.[1] He requests to see the coin used for such payment. Note that Jesus does not possess one on his person, but those questioning him do. He is not a part of the system in question, while they clearly are. He gets them to name the authority of the system in verse 21, when he asks whose "head" and "title" are on the coin: "The emperor's." Jesus' response confounds their efforts to label him so easily: "Give therefore to the emperor the things that are the emperor's, and to God the things that are God's" (v. 21). It is a fine political move on his part, but is that all it is? Matthew's Jesus would never miss an opportunity to teach us the ways of higher righteousness, so this is obviously not a moment of mere political sleight of hand.

For many years this text was interpreted as an acknowledgment of the separation of church and state. It has been argued that Jesus is providing a framework by which we seek to delineate under whose power different parts of our lives lie. This could not be further from the truth. In 6:24, Jesus clearly states, "No one can serve two masters." If one cannot serve two masters, surely Jesus is not now discussing how to divide one's loyalties.

Matthew's Jesus is always raising the ethical bar for us all, and this text is no different. There is no opportunity given to compartmentalize our loyalties. Jesus is calling us to offer our entire lives to the Divine. Perhaps more accurately, Jesus is calling us to recognize to whom we already belong. When he announces to his opponents that they are to "give therefore to the emperor the things that are the emperor's, and to God the things that are God's," the conversation is deeper than the coins in our pockets. It is we who are God's, each and every one created in the image of God. Human systems throughout

the Herodians, advocated supporting Roman "governance" of Israel. Nationalists opposed to Rome, perhaps comprising much of the crowd, found the tax galling, as it was a constant reminder of their humiliation. The religiously devout, represented by the disciples of the Pharisees, had to pay the tax with a coin engraved with a picture of Tiberius Caesar and a proclamation of his divinity, forcing them to break the first two commandments.

All this made the topic of the imperial tax tremendously divisive and one's opinion on it immediately revealing. Herein lies the cunning demonstrated by two normally fractious parties, united only by their shared opposition to this young rabbi who the day before had entered Jerusalem to great acclaim and had been stirring things up at the temple ever since. With their question about the imperial tax, Jesus' foes thought they had him trapped, as he would either disappoint the people by advocating for the tax or put himself in jeopardy with Roman officials by arguing against it.

Jesus not only evades their snare but entangles them in their own devices. "Whose face is on the coin?" he asks. Perhaps overeager to advance their plot, Jesus' opponents forget that by procuring a coin they betray their own complicity in the Roman system. For those not paying attention, Jesus makes explicit their self-indictment by asking whose image and proclamation adorn the coin. "The emperor's," they answer (v. 21), assuring those in attendance that they know full well the face and blasphemous confession of divinity they carry.

All this sharpens the bite of Jesus' response: "Give therefore to the emperor the things that are the emperor's, and to God the things that are God's" (v. 21). Suddenly the tables are turned, as all in attendance confess that everything belongs to the Holy One of Israel, the one who made humanity in the "image" of God (Gen. 1:27). With just a few words, Jesus reveals the truth about his would-be accusers and simultaneously calls them to a higher fidelity than they had imagined.

Might he also be doing that to us? So many sermons on this passage seem to turn on political and ideological concerns. Conservatives argue that Jesus directly affirms traditional divisions between church and state, while liberals insist that Jesus stands against complicity with oppressive forces. No matter how we try to press Jesus' statement into service for our political convictions, it defies definitive interpretation.

Perhaps that is by design. While our relationship to government authority (including the matter of

---

1. Donald Senior, *Matthew* (Nashville: Abingdon Press, 1998), 248.

Theological Perspective

and priority of God's kingdom. God's kingdom is the original will and plan of God for humanity and creation. It is not the case that we need to carve space for God's kingdom out of the secular empire. There is no rival kingdom, no divided loyalty for Jesus' followers. The problem is not how to partition the power in proper proportion; the problem for the believer is how to justify allegiance to the emperor while remaining faithful to God. No one can have two masters (6:24).

It is likewise noteworthy that in Matthew's account Jesus does not appear to distinguish between the tax associated with the coin and the political power the likeness represents. There is an inherent connection between the economic structure and the political power of the kingdom. Jesus rules out the facile bifurcation between wealth and political allegiance. He sees that with the emperor's coin comes loyalty to the emperor. He calls out the hypocrisy that thinks that faithfulness to God can coexist peacefully with faithfulness to empire, with allegiance to mammon. They are hypocrites because they fail to see the problem with being rich in the emperor's money while claiming fidelity to the one who himself became poor. Jesus himself makes this point: "It will be hard for a rich person to enter the kingdom of heaven. . . . It is easier for a camel to go through the eye of a needle than for someone who is rich to enter the kingdom of God" (19:23–24). It is difficult for a person whose life is marked by self-aggrandizement and self-service to enter a kingdom marked by sacrifice and self-giving.

Do riches and political allegiance necessarily mean you are living outside of God's kingdom? Perhaps not, or perhaps it does. Jesus never states that the rich and politically invested are *necessarily* outside of God's kingdom, but riches clearly present a marked risk. Jesus repeatedly warns against the perils of riches and divided loyalties. We would do well to heed these warnings and understand riches and political allegiances not as a blessing, but as a dangerous threat to our well-being in the kingdom of God.

KEITH ERRICKSON

Pastoral Perspective

Of course this does not offer us much in the way of concrete guidance. What do we do when conflict arises between loyalty to God and loyalty to the emperor? What do we do when it becomes seemingly impossible to give the emperor his due as an expression of our duty to God? As in much of Jesus' teaching, he is not giving us concrete rules to live by, but a vision that reconfigures our loyalties. Ultimately it is up to us to sort out what this means in the quotidian decisions of life. No doubt we have more concrete hints, for example, in the Beatitudes (5:1–12) and in the parable of the Last Judgment (25:31–46). Perhaps Jesus' teaching here could be summarized as, give the emperor his due but love God and neighbor. However, that still provides little guidance when the loyalties diverge.

It may be enough simply to recognize that this can be a question. Given the perennial temptation to collapse loyalty to emperor and loyalty to God, state and church, into one, or the equally perennial temptation to separate them into distinct spheres, as if one had nothing to do with the other, it may be enough to recognize that Jesus is rejecting both approaches. Thus he leaves us with a difficult task, the task of sorting out our loyalties, of discerning how to make our duty to the emperor an expression of our duty to God. There are no answers in the back of the book.

Of course it is easy to be confused about our loyalties, given the way the emperor rules our lives in so many subtle and not so subtle ways. Just four chapters later in Matthew's Gospel we see the ultimate expression of imperial might as Jesus is crucified for blasphemy and sedition. However, this is not the end of the story. The emperor may seem to rule the world and our hearts, but Easter promises that God, not the emperor, gets the last word.

RICHARD A. FLOYD

history have sought to claim ownership over people and their ultimate allegiance. This text radically challenges all those claims of ownership. The totality of who we are belongs to God, and any human institution or doctrine that says otherwise is false.

This does not literally preclude the payment of the tax, though. In 17:24–27 Peter and Jesus discuss the payment of the temple tax. Jesus states that the "children are free" from the tax, yet sends Peter out to find a coin to pay it. Matthew's Jesus is not demanding payment or nonpayment of the tax. Jesus is calling us to do all things with an understanding of who is truly sovereign.

When Jesus' opponents compliment him at the start of this interaction, they say to him, "Teacher, we know that you are sincere, and teach the way of God in accordance with truth, and show deference to no one; for you do not regard people with partiality" (v. 16). A closer translation of the final phrase, "for you do not regard people with partiality," could be "you do not look to the faces of humans." In fact, Jesus does "look to the face of humans," and he looks upon the imprint of Caesar's face on that coin, and in both of them he sees the image of God reflected in creation. What he does *not* see is anyone or anything worthy of our ultimate allegiance.

In 5:18, Matthew's Jesus tells us "not one letter, not one stroke of a letter, will pass from the law until all is accomplished." Matthew's original audience would immediately be reminded of the injunction "You shall have no other gods before me" from the Ten Commandments (Exod. 20:3). They would hear Jesus' words and know that none of their ultimate allegiance belonged to Caesar or any other human system.

In an age when we are skeptical of offering ultimate allegiance to anyone or anything, we are not as likely to worship our human institutions. However, this text reminds us that there is indeed someone worthy of our worship, the God to whom we belong in all times and all places.

DOUGLAS T. KING

taxes) differs considerably from that of first-century Jews, there is at least one way in which we are similar: there is no way to flee participation in, and perhaps even complicity with, the "powers that be." This is neither to assume that such participation is always bad—read Romans 13—nor to affirm that it is always good or inevitable. There are times Christians cooperate with civil authority and times we resist, and telling the difference often takes more than a modicum of wisdom.

Whatever alliances we may make with the powers of this world—or with those who oppose them—these alliances are always temporary, dictated perhaps by the demands of the circumstances, but ultimately directed by our relationship with the One who created us and whose image we bear. This means that following Jesus' counsel is always a matter of discernment, prayer, and confession, as we will frequently fail and always struggle to discern what God-fearing participation with government requires.

It would have been nice, of course, if Jesus had given clearer instructions; but perhaps the ambiguity of his words mirrors the ambiguity of our lives and invites a sermon that advocates not simply reflection but action that is simultaneously judicious and penitential. That is, we may be sent into the world to engage in a series of "faithful compromises" as we try to discern what is Caesar's and what is God's, only to be drawn back weekly to the fellowship of forgiven sinners to hear again that we are made in God's image, beloved of our Creator, and sent to care for this world God loves so much.

Nor is everything ambiguous in this passage. Keep in mind that this exchange is but one of numerous tension-filled episodes that take place during the week we name Holy. The standoff begins with Jesus driving the money changers from the temple (21:12–17), intensifies with his debates with and denunciations of the Pharisees (chaps. 22–23), and climaxes with his adversaries plotting his death (26:1–5). However, the story does not end here. Three days after Jesus' opponents are once again sure they have dealt with this young rebel, his followers are declaring his resurrection. The empty tomb stands as witness that there is something beyond even death and taxes that is certain in this world: God's absolution given in response to ambiguity, God's mercy and grace offered to those in need, and God's new life granted to all who are dying.

DAVID J. LOSE

Matthew 22:23–33

²³The same day some Sadducees came to him, saying there is no resurrection; and they asked him a question, saying, ²⁴"Teacher, Moses said, 'If a man dies childless, his brother shall marry the widow, and raise up children for his brother.' ²⁵Now there were seven brothers among us; the first married, and died childless, leaving the widow to his brother. ²⁶The second did the same, so also the third, down to the seventh. ²⁷Last of all, the woman herself died. ²⁸In the resurrection, then, whose wife of the seven will she be? For all of them had married her."

²⁹Jesus answered them, "You are wrong, because you know neither the scriptures nor the power of God. ³⁰For in the resurrection they neither marry nor are given in marriage, but are like angels in heaven. ³¹And as for the resurrection of the dead, have you not read what was said to you by God, ³²'I am the God of Abraham, the God of Isaac, and the God of Jacob'? He is God not of the dead, but of the living." ³³And when the crowd heard it, they were astounded at his teaching.

Theological Perspective

In this pericope Jesus engages a new segment of religious leaders. The Sadducees are a religious sect who closely follow the Torah but reject the rest of the Hebrew Bible. They, like the Pharisees, are well trained in biblical tradition and rhetoric, and they too seek to entrap Jesus.

Their riddle is theological in its nature, but their aim is the same as that of the Pharisees in the preceding story (22:15–21). The Sadducees begin their questioning with the title "Teacher," a title of honor that places Jesus in a position of authority and appears to position them as his students. Yet from the outset it is clear that their goal is to trick Jesus, to demonstrate his limitations as a biblical scholar, and to discredit him as a teacher. How much can a carpenter's son from Nazareth really know?

The Sadducees cite Deuteronomy in their attempt to pull Jesus into a hopeless debate over the nature of the resurrection. They intend to drag him into a debate about the resurrection of the dead played by their rules. They present an absurd scenario and invite Jesus to defend belief in the resurrection, to *prove* to them the resurrection.

The resurrection of the dead is a key doctrine that is essential to Jesus' life, work, and teachings (17:22–23), but that is not the discussion Jesus undertakes. The Sadducees need to understand something much

Pastoral Perspective

It is a bizarre question the Sadducees asked Jesus that day. Following the practice of levirate marriage (Deut. 25:5–6), a woman is passed along from one doomed husband to another. So, ask the Sadducees, if "husband and wife" means "husband and wife" now and forevermore, whose wife will this woman be in the resurrection? We might rightly recoil at the gender politics implied in this scenario, but that is not what the Sadducees are concerned about. They want to know how this woman and her seven husbands will be sorted out in the world to come.

Before we expend too much energy trying to answer this casuistic riddle, we should recognize that—at least as Matthew tells the tale—the Sadducees are not interested in a real answer, because they have not asked a real question. They do not want to know about the resurrection; they do not even believe in the resurrection. This is a trap, an attempt to expose Jesus, to make him look foolish.

The Sadducees are not the first people in Matthew's Gospel to do this, to ask Jesus a trick question in the hopes of exposing him as a fraud. The Pharisees also try to ensnare Jesus with questions that are not really questions. They believe in strict adherence to God's law, and they seek to ambush Jesus with the finer points of that law. The Pharisees think faithfulness means holiness, and they try to set themselves

Exegetical Perspective

The theatrically charged debate in the temple between Jesus and his opponents continues with the arrival of the Sadducees. The Sadducees were traditionalists who based their beliefs solely on the Pentateuch, as opposed to the Pharisees, who drew upon the entirety of what would become Hebrew Scripture. In Jesus' time the Sadducees had great influence through their cultic role in the temple. They were not a factor in Matthew's community, because they had been decimated by the revolt in 66–70 CE and the destruction of the temple. Thus they appear much less frequently in Matthew's Gospel than the Pharisees, who were a powerful presence in the time of Matthew as well as that of Jesus. In this section of confrontations in the temple, Jesus squares off against the gamut of temple authorities: the Pharisees, the Sadducees, and the scribes. Matthew loves to challenge the scribes and Pharisees, but this question about resurrection can come only from the mouths of the Sadducees, who argue against it because it is not addressed in the Pentateuch. As in the preceding text, Jesus' opponents come to him with a question designed to leave him with no good response.

The Sadducees' question about seven grooms for a single bride presents a metaphysical puzzle for those who claim the reality of the resurrection. The story, although an unlikely scenario, has its roots

Homiletical Perspective

On some level, preaching is always about carefully and creatively crossing the channel between the historical "then" of a biblical passage and the homiletical "now" of what it may mean for us today. Rarely, however, will the differences between these two elements be as acute as they are with this passage.

Let us start with the "then." The question posed to Jesus about the resurrection of the dead will make little sense to our contemporary hearers, as it hinges on two arcane pieces of information few of them possess. First, the Sadducees: this group of religious leaders had primary authority over the temple; recognized only the Pentateuch, the original five books of Moses, as fully authoritative; and did not believe in the resurrection of the dead (since the Pentateuch does not explicitly refer to resurrection). Although normally rivals of the Pharisees, the Sadducees put their typical biases aside to join forces against Jesus, likely because Jesus only a day earlier had attacked the sacrificial practices of the temple.

Second, levirate marriage: the law the Sadducees refer to, found in Deuteronomy 25:5–10, describes what is called levirate marriage (from the Latin *levir*, "brother-in-law") that sought to ensure the preservation of the family name by stipulating that a man should marry the childless widow of his brother.

Theological Perspective

more basic: the Scriptures and the power of God. In ignoring their trap and instead teaching them about the Scriptures and the power of God, Jesus is ironically fulfilling their feigned praise and demonstrating the authority he has as the son of David. Jesus first juxtaposes his authority to theirs and begins to demonstrate what the term "son of David" means. It is not a title merely of genealogy or bloodline; it entails an authority foreign to the Sadducees. He will address this point more fully later (vv. 41–46), but it is clear that Jesus possesses authority unlike that of anyone else.

From his position of authority Jesus addresses the Sadducees' initial problem: they do not understand Scripture. They interpret Scripture through the lens of their preconceived notions of possibility. Rather than allowing Scripture to inform them of what is possible, they rule out the possibility of the resurrection from the outset. They invite Jesus to construct a logical argument that will "prove" the resurrection. Jesus bypasses their preconceived notions of possibility and instead asserts the reality of the resurrection at the outset. Rather than argue for the resurrection, he begins his teaching with the fact of the resurrection. Instead of starting with an abstract notion of what is possible, and weaving a logical defense of the possibility of the resurrection, he authoritatively declares it: "In the resurrection . . ."

For Jesus there is no need to argue about the possibility of the resurrection; it is possible because it is real. For God, reality precedes and informs possibility. God does not operate within the bounds of possibility. God declares reality in God's own creative will and power. What we understand as possible is not based upon our limited experiences or our even more limited logic; rather, what is possible is understood by what God declares as real. God did not first inquire about the logical possibility of the Creator becoming a creature, of the Lord of heaven dying a criminal's death. God willed the incarnation, and as a result it became possible. God's reality precedes possibility.

The Sadducees err in their understanding of Scripture because they rule out that which appears impossible from the outset, and they fail to allow God's creative power to inform them of what is possible. The resurrection is unlike any reality they can fathom. It does not correspond to our understanding of marriage in a one-to-one fashion. Rather, the resurrection is a reality that God's revelation makes clear to us. By faith we understand the resurrection, not by preconceived conceptions of what is possible.

Pastoral Perspective

apart from sinful people and a sinful world. Jesus says they have misunderstood what faithfulness is about. Jesus says faithfulness means compassion, and so he invites them to embrace the very people they want to exclude. They never can see eye to eye on this, so the Pharisees view Jesus as a threat and try to undermine him at every turn.

The Sadducees are a different story. They are the elites, the well educated and well heeled. They take their religion seriously, of course, but have little patience for the superstitions of the masses, including the belief in the resurrection of the dead. So when they meet Jesus and ask their question about the resurrection, it is not because they want an answer. It is a way for them to show their cleverness, to enhance their credibility, to expose Jesus as a fool and a fraud.

Jesus ultimately rebuffs the Sadducees, just as he rebuffed the Pharisees, and for the same reason: they lack imagination. Jesus' claim that we will be "like angels in heaven" (v. 30) serves to swat away the common assumption that marriage endures in the resurrection. It also seems to throw up an impenetrable barrier. To say that we will be "like angels in heaven" is to say we do not know what we will be like, and so there is no point speculating. Jesus' response to the Sadducees' phony question is, in effect, to say that they cannot even imagine resurrected life. It is too capacious, and their imaginations are too cramped.

The Sadducees cannot imagine resurrected life because they are too busy clinging to the status quo (which has served their interests rather well), too busy looking after themselves and protecting their corner of the market. Notice how Jesus answers their question: God is "God not of the dead, but of the living" (v. 32). The Sadducees cannot imagine a *living* God and do not want to. They much prefer a dead God, a God who sits still and stays put, a God who never threatens their security, never threatens to overturn their little worlds.

Here is where this story may challenge us as well. Surely there are times when we seek a dead God, a God who will not interfere with our grand conquests in life, a God whose only job is to secure a place for us beyond this life and then get out of the way. Jesus challenges our cramped imaginations. We too are tempted to recoil from a living God.

We also are tempted to imagine resurrected life in self-serving ways. The Sadducees assume Jesus shares the common belief that resurrected life stands in great continuity with this life. In this passage Jesus

in the book of Tobit, where Sarah does indeed out-live seven husbands. Levirate marriage (from *levir*, "brother-in-law") was a critical obligation handed down by Moses in Deuteronomy 25:5. Moses was credited by the tradition as author of the Pentateuch, and thus the ultimate human authority for the Sad-ducees. To preserve the family line into the future, it was expected that a man would marry his brother's widow and have children with her. It was a human construct to ensure a form of immortality through one's descendants. In effect the Sadducees are asking which of the brothers would have a claim of owner-ship over the woman and, through her children, immortality.

None of the possible answers looks very good for Jesus. Speaking out against the tradition of levirate marriage puts him in opposition to Moses. Choosing one of the husbands denies the sanctity of the other marriages. Not having an answer suggests that the resurrection is absurd—or that Jesus is not so wise a teacher as some claim. The Sadducees have crafted their question well and very likely believe they leave Jesus with no appropriate response.

Jesus sees beyond the limited choices provided. His response begins with the ultimate insult from the Gospel of Matthew, "You are wrong, because you know neither the scriptures nor the power of God" (v. 29). For Matthew's Jesus, who is consumed with the fulfillment of the law (see 5:17–20), these are explosive words thrown at the ones who believe they are most staunchly defending the tradition. He then informs them that their very categories are of no importance in what will come: "For in the resurrec-tion they neither marry nor are given in marriage" (v. 30). Marriage, understood as a patriarchal institu-tion of ownership of one by another, will no longer be a reality. The resurrection will not merely create some new and improved version of how we live in this world.

At this point Jesus has angered the Sadducees but has yet to say anything to change their minds. There is no explicit reference to the resurrection in the Pentateuch. The first clear-cut discussion of the resurrection does not occur until the book of Dan-iel (12:2), which was the last book of the Hebrew Bible to be written and was not even recognized by the Sadducees as Holy Scripture. Now Jesus quotes directly from the Pentateuch: "I am the God of Abra-ham, the God of Isaac, and the God of Jacob" (Exod. 3:6). At first it is not clear what God's announce-ment to Moses has to do with the question of the resurrection.

What might be easier for our hearers to appre-ciate is that the Sadducees' question is entirely hypothetical, meant to take an ancient practice to the extreme in order to show that the whole idea of resurrection is foolish, thus undermining Jesus' authority, as well as embarrassing their "frenemies" the Pharisees, who also believe in the resurrection. We have heard these kinds of questions before, and perhaps on our worst days even asked them.

Having put this passage briefly into context, however, we can turn profitably to the "now" of the text, only by admitting honestly that few if any of our hearers care about old Jewish religious rivalries or archaic marriage practices. Rather, when they hear the term "resurrection," they will think almost immediately of loved ones they have lost. What reg-isters for most hearers is that in this story someone seems to be questioning Jesus about the resurrection and—now that you come to it—that they have a lot of questions too. The preacher therefore has good reason to depart from strict attention to the histori-cal or literary details of the text to consider three significant questions that may be sparked by hearing it read aloud. (In trying to address this theme, how-ever, be prepared to admit that we are speaking of things with which none of us has direct experience, so a certain degree of modesty is appropriate!)

The first question that strikes many people when discussing resurrection is, perhaps not surpris-ingly, "What will resurrection life be like?" We are naturally curious about what comes next, both for our loved ones and for ourselves. Admittedly, the passage in front of us gives few details. It does, however, insist that resurrection life is qualitatively different from life as we know it. This is, in fact, the heart of the mistake Jesus points out the Sadducees are making. Their whole question is premised on the assumption that eternal life is just "more of the same"; hence, the absurdity of the situation they describe. Resurrection, Jesus insists, is different. The things by which we track our journey though this mortal life—marriage, childbirth, graduations, retire-ments, and the rest—do not characterize our eternal lives, because resurrection life is not merely an extension of this life. It is something wholly different.

The second question prompted by this passage may therefore be, "Is Jesus saying we will not know our spouses and family members?" This is an under-standable next step, given Jesus' words about not marrying and our previous emphasis on the qualita-tive difference of resurrection life. Let us be clear, though, Jesus is not answering this question. He does

Matthew 22:23–33

Theological Perspective

The rules of the afterlife are not bound by our logic or limited by our creative imaginations. God's self-revelation is both trustworthy and reliable. We need no other normative starting point for our theological thinking. God's self-revelation in Christ is both the origin and governing epistemological basis of all our knowledge of God and reality. By faith we understand.

It is noteworthy that Jesus does not give us details regarding what "like the angels" (v. 30) entails. While some might get caught up searching for the meaning of "like the angels," Jesus opts not to address it, reinforcing his point that God's self-revelation is trustworthy and sufficient. Our theological inquiries must remain disciplined and guided by the reality God has revealed and not delve into speculations that produce neither love nor faithfulness; God's grace is sufficient.

The Sadducees' second error is similar to the first: they fail to understand God's power. As with their first error, the Sadducees start their understanding of God's power with an abstract notion of possibility. It is absurd to believe that a person who died can be resurrected, so it is likewise absurd that a woman can have seven husbands simultaneously. Their understanding of God's power is so limited that they fail to see that the Lord is the God of the living, not the dead. The power of God is not limited by death; rather, death is limited by the power of God. The resurrection of the dead is God's affirmation of life, the demonstration of God's power over death.

The Sadducees fail to understand God's power because they begin their understanding of God and Scripture with their preconceived notions of power and possibility. Jesus reframes their entrapping question, asserts his authority as the son of David, and addresses the Sadducees' fundamental failure to approach God and Scripture in a receptive posture marked by faith, gratitude, and humility.

Far too often in our churches today our understanding of God and Scripture is based upon our preconceived notions. We filter what we believe about God, salvation, and humanity through the lens of what we "know" to be true apart from God's self-revelation in Christ. Let us learn the lesson of the Sadducees and understand, first, that we know neither the Scriptures nor the power of God.

KEITH ERRICKSON

Pastoral Perspective

not only dismisses their question; he also confronts our own commonly held beliefs about resurrected life. There is never a short supply of books purporting to reveal all the mysteries of what lies beyond this life. We are sorely tempted to imagine the resurrection as nothing but the eternal perpetuation of our personal projects of self-actualization and self-fulfillment. When Jesus says we will be "like angels in heaven," he short-circuits our self-involving resurrection fantasies. He turns the question and our attention back to God—not the dead God who attends to our needs and baptizes our causes, but the living God.

It is striking that in this text where Jesus speaks most directly to what happens when we die—and we must admit that this has become the sum total of the Christian gospel for many—he deflates our curiosity, our self-serving need to be assured things will turn out as we wish, and points us toward God and life. Many are tempted to make heaven the whole point of the Christian gospel, but here Jesus closes the door to such self-serving speculation. He reminds us that God is a God of *life*, and so we are called to turn our attention to life and to the beautiful and fragile creation that sustains it. It is not our calling to sort out the eternal destiny of any creature or to figure how things can and must be in the world to come. Our calling instead is to fix our minds and hearts on the living God, and that means fixing our minds and hearts on our own living, and on the living of others, and on the whole creation that sustains that living. Here in this seemingly heavenly minded text, Jesus invites us to do earthly good.

RICHARD A. FLOYD

Exegetical Perspective

Then Jesus draws the Sadducees' attention to the verb tense God uses. God is speaking in the present tense about Moses' ancestors, Abraham, Isaac, and Jacob: "He is God not of the dead, but of the living" (v. 32). If the divine is speaking in the present tense of his relationship with these ancestors who have died, they must be alive once more in some way for the relationship to continue to exist. Jesus does not specify the nature of how they are alive, and that is frankly inconsequential to us. Our categories and understandings will not circumscribe God's transforming power. Jesus has quoted from the call narrative of Moses, the one who has provided the entire tradition the Saducees revere, to demonstrate a scriptural basis for the resurrection. The use of this very significant text of God's defining Godself before Moses as evidence of the resurrection is a very potent argument in this debate.

In the previous confrontation (22:15–22), we are told that Jesus' opponents were "amazed." In this confrontation we are told that the entire crowd is "astounded." The Sadducees may have called Jesus "teacher" with a suggestion of irony, but his authority as a teacher is confirmed by the people's response of astonishment.

It is particularly interesting that in Matthew, a Gospel so committed to fulfilling the law (as seen in 5:17–20), we get this story of Jesus contradicting the Sadducees who challenge him with the minutiae of the law. As valuable a gift as the law may be, it is never a tool that binds God's hands from acting in transformative ways beyond what we can yet imagine. The Sadducees, who do not believe in the resurrection, can only imagine the resurrection life as an eternal, static continuation of our present existence. Jesus' image of the resurrection is a far larger and more reality-altering idea. In the previous passage debating the ultimate power of the Roman emperor (22:15–22), Jesus' opponents raise a question that explores the potential limitations of God's sovereignty. In this passage, the opponents raise a question that explores the potential limitations of God's power. Jesus brings the strong word that both God's sovereignty and God's power are without limits and beyond the control of any system or religious authority.

DOUGLAS T. KING

Homiletical Perspective

not say we will not know those who have been dear to us, only that resurrection life will not be marked by the same features as this one. Indeed, given his next statement about Abraham, Isaac, and Jacob (chosen judiciously from the Pentateuch, take note), it seems that the relationships defining our current life may persist, certainly with God, and likely with each other.

The third, and perhaps broadest, question may run something like, "Is resurrection the same as immortality?" Actually, few of our hearers may articulate this question explicitly, but you can nevertheless count on the fact that many of them regularly confuse these two things. Whereas immortality of the soul assumes that some spiritual element of a person persists beyond the physical death of the body, resurrection promises that the whole person will in some way be united with God (see 1 Cor. 15, esp. vv. 35–49).

While affirming the importance of this distinction—and, indeed, our larger discussion about resurrection—the point of the sermon should not be to scold our hearers for an inadequate piety or offer remedial instruction about life after death. Rather, our homiletical aim is to offer a deeper sense of the comfort and promise of the gospel. After an adult forum on resurrection some years ago, a parishioner came to me very upset. Her husband had died the previous year, and her belief in the immortality of the soul had brought her comfort. As gently as I could, I said that I did not want to take that comfort away, but rather to make it stronger, more complete. "What I want and hope for you," I said, "is more than the wispy essence of your husband. I want the whole person for you, the whole person created, loved, and now redeemed by God in and through Christ." That seemed to help her reckon with her grief, not by denying it, but by promising that there would be an end to it, indeed, an end to all our grief, tears, limitations, and suffering, as the God of Abraham, Isaac, and Jacob, the One who raised Christ from death, promises to do the same also for us. For God is the God not of the dead, but of the living, both then and now!

DAVID J. LOSE

Matthew 22:34–40

³⁴When the Pharisees heard that he had silenced the Sadducees, they gathered together, ³⁵and one of them, a lawyer, asked him a question to test him. ³⁶"Teacher, which commandment in the law is the greatest?" ³⁷He said to him, "'You shall love the Lord your God with all your heart, and with all your soul, and with all your mind.' ³⁸This is the greatest and first commandment. ³⁹And a second is like it: 'You shall love your neighbor as yourself.' ⁴⁰On these two commandments hang all the law and the prophets."

Theological Perspective

This passage presents the third in a series of confrontations between Jesus and his challengers. Here the Pharisees notice the Sadducees' failure to entrap Jesus, and they regroup. Rather than trying to ensnare him with a no-win question, they now approach Jesus with an open-ended theological question: "Which commandment in the law is the greatest?" (v. 36).

While this may appear to be innocent, Matthew tells us that the Pharisees intend to "test him." They are attempting to trick him into a misstep by encouraging him to engage in an unwise topic; once again, how much can a carpenter's son really know?

The question immediately poses a theological problem for Jesus. How can one law be greater than another? There was a tradition of bifurcating the laws of the Hebrew Bible into "greater" and "lesser" commands. This had the unintended effect of ranking some commandments as important and others as unimportant. Is there a hierarchy of laws in the Torah? Do some laws mean more to God than others? Can we not simply disregard the insignificant and follow only the significant laws? Further, if some laws are irrelevant, is the law of the Lord no longer "perfect" (Ps. 19:7)? Their question attempts to goad Jesus into devaluing the law and discrediting himself as a teacher. Yet Jesus did not come to abolish the law, but to fulfill it (5:17–20).

Pastoral Perspective

Recently I had a conversation with a friend with whom I had not spoken in years. This friend is bright and compassionate; I find her politics generally agreeable. Yet in the course of our conversation I discovered that I have a habit that she does not have. On most topics, regardless of where we started, I found myself habitually reflecting on it using the categories of God and neighbor and self, as if I could not truly understand it apart from this triadic way of thinking. My friend does not have this habit. She could begin and end a topic with reflection on the self, without moving on to God or neighbor. This was not because she is particularly self-regarding; she was simply reflecting the expressive individualism of our culture. My friend has almost no formation in the church, whereas (for better or worse) I have been deeply formed by the church. It occurred to me that this habit, this reflexive consideration of God and neighbor and self, is a learned response, learned through the stories and practices of ecclesial existence. The conversation left me wondering: where else in our culture is this habit being cultivated, and how do we endure as a species without it?

Our text from Matthew invites us into this triadic habit of thought and practice. In Matthew's version of the story, the lawyer's question is asked with bad intentions. It is but one more example of

Exegetical Perspective

The third in this series of temple showdowns between Jesus and his opponents brings the Pharisees back to question Jesus once more. Matthew continues the pattern of these interactions he inherited from Mark, but with a different tone. Matthew's context of a community of Jews in conflict with a local synagogue is on full display. This Gospel writer often uses the Greek term for the way in which the Pharisees gather together (*synēchthēsan*, v. 34) in the sense of plotting against Jesus (2:4; 22:41; 26:3; 27:17; 28:12).[1] What is a neutral encounter in Mark is used by Matthew as a hostile and adversarial encounter. The anonymous scribe who questions Jesus in Mark becomes a lawyer (*nomikos*, v. 35) in Matthew. It is the only time Matthew uses the term. Some have suggested that the questioner is a professional theologian. Whoever he is, it is clear that he is chosen carefully for the task at hand, "to test him." The verb "test" (*peirazō*, v. 35) is used in Matthew only in reference to the devil and the Pharisees (4:1, 3; 16:1; 19:3; 22:18).

As in the two preceding encounters, the questioner addresses Jesus with the respectful title of "Teacher," but clearly this is spoken with great irony. The question follows the pattern of the previous two encounters in its challenging nature: "Which

1. Donald Senior, *Matthew* (Nashville: Abingdon Press, 1998), 252.

Homiletical Perspective

Do you ever think about what is at the center of your life? How you answer may change. At one age it may be work, at another family, at another friends. Wherever you are, it is a question both interesting and important to ask. Hence a sermon on this passage might provide the opportunity to invite others to ask it as well: What is my center? What am I making a priority? What am I willing to save or sacrifice for? What is most important to me?

Sometimes it can be a little hard to tell what is at our center. We may say it is our children, but discover too late that, from all the missed suppers and trips away from home, they could not tell. We may say it is our faith, but wonder if anyone from the outside notices anything that is different about us because we are Christian.

One way to tell what is at our center is to pay attention to the rules we make for ourselves. These may be formal rules, but often they are more informal things we do not name but regularly follow. For example: "Put 10 percent of your paycheck into savings." "Always be home in time to read to the kids." Paying attention to the rules we make is revealing, because by and large the rules we live by orient us to our center, to what is most important, to what we want to make sure we attend to.

Matthew 22:34–40

Theological Perspective

As in the previous two exchanges, Jesus transposes their question into the discussion he desires. He uses this open-ended question, not just to teach about the law, but also to reveal who God is and who the son of David is.

In his response, Jesus speaks from a posture of authority unfamiliar to the Pharisees. He does not cite rabbinic tradition or even the patriarchs; he boldly quotes from the Shema (Deut. 6:5), the most prominent prayer in Hebrew tradition. The Shema can well be called the cornerstone of Jewish faith and practice; its importance for Judaism cannot be overstated. While often used as a prayer, fundamentally the Shema is a statement of who God is: "the Lord our God is One." Monotheism was and is the defining characteristic of Judaism. It distinguishes the Abrahamic faith from all others. The Shema reinforces this basic truth about God and in turn commands Israel to love the Lord with all their heart, soul, and mind. This command and this truth about God are intricately linked. Because the Lord your God is One, you shall love the Lord with the entirety of your being. The Lord is distinct from all the pagan deities in unique Oneness, and as a result you may love the Lord without reservation.

Jesus' response was likely respected by the elders and scholars in attendance. Then he quickly surpassed their expectations by including a lesser-known command from Leviticus 19:18: "You shall love your neighbor as yourself." This inclusion was marked by the important phrase "a second is like it." This phrase was radical to Jesus' audience, yet we often overlook its significance. To put this command on equal footing as the Shema was surprising, particularly to the Pharisees.

Jesus does just that: he equates the command to love your neighbor as yourself with the holistic love commands of the Shema. The result is not simply a command to act; it amounts to a statement about God. The God of the Shema is One and unique and elected the nation of Israel to be God's one, chosen people. God's oneness and uniqueness correspond to the uniqueness of the covenant.

Jesus' addition of the neighbor-love command in the discussion of the greatest command—even calling it "like the first"—reinforces the image of God who loves the "neighbor" as much as the nation of Israel. Given Jesus' broad interpretation of "neighbor," this implies that God reaches out to the nations and establishes a covenant with "all flesh" (Gen. 9:17). Here we see a reinforcement of the picture of God sending his messengers out into the main

Pastoral Perspective

the religious leadership trying to test Jesus. However, in Mark and Luke the question appears to be a sincere effort to sort through the hundreds of commandments, the tangles of shalts and shalt-nots, to find the essence of the law, the heart of the matter. Kierkegaard said purity of heart is to will one thing.[1] So what is the one thing? What is the greatest commandment?

Of course Jesus answers with two things: "You shall love the Lord your God with all your heart, and with all your soul, and with all your mind." "You shall love your neighbor as yourself" (vv. 37, 39). When Jesus says the second is "like" (*homoia*) the first, he is suggesting that these two things are not really two at all. There is an intimate connection between the two, a unity, as if they were two sides of the same coin. There is no love of God without love of neighbor (see, e.g., 1 John 4:20), and love of neighbor *is* love of God, whether we know it or not (which seems to be the whole point of Matt. 25:31–46). Also implicit here is the recognition that love of neighbor is inextricably tied to a properly ordered self-love. One cannot give oneself away in love to God and neighbor if a healthy self has never been formed in the first place.

So Jesus answers the question about the greatest commandment with two things (love God and love your neighbor as yourself) that are also three things (love of God, love of neighbor, and love of self) that may also be considered one thing (God-neighbor-self love). This is the triadic habit of thought and practice to which Jesus calls us. It is a calling to reflect on every issue, every decision, every action, in this triadic way, to ask in all things: how are we loving God and neighbor and self in this?

This is the question that should attend all our discernments as individuals and as congregations. Whether in how we allocate resources or choose to support this or that mission project, or what constitutes creative and faithful worship, or what the proper relationship is between church and state, or any of the countless other issues we must sort through in the daily journey of faith: we must discern how we might love God and neighbor and self in all we say and do.

Too often and too easily this triadic habit breaks down. Our culture entices us to begin and end with a kind of expressive individualism: What are my needs, my rights, my desires? What will bring me

---

1. Søren Kierkegaard, *Purity of Heart Is to Will One Thing*, trans. Douglas V. Steere (1846; repr., New York: Harper, 1956).

Exegetical Perspective

commandment in the law is the greatest?" (v. 36). It was conventional wisdom that there were 613 commandments in the Scriptures (*Makkot* 23b), and it was believed that all should be upheld with the same rigor. It was not unusual for rabbis to offer summations of the law, but naming a single commandment as the greatest was filled with potential pitfalls. Any commandment chosen leaves one open to criticism in debate for neglecting others.

Jesus responds by reciting a section of the Shema, the primary confession of the Israelites. For some reason Matthew edits out of Mark's version the opening of the Shema (Deut. 6:4), the proclamation of God as one. It is a rather strange edit for a Gospel that is so quick to quote Hebrew Scripture. Perhaps Matthew wants to bring an immediacy to the command. Eugene Boring notes that Matthew chooses to adhere more closely to the Septuagint reading of this text by eliminating the fourth "with" clause of "strength."[2] While Mark refers to "the second commandment," Matthew appears to bind the two commandments as equal partners: "This is the greatest and first commandment. And a second is like it: 'You shall love your neighbor as yourself'" (vv. 38–39). This would suggest that Matthew wants to ensure that the second commandment is not considered as lesser than the first in any way but that they are equally important. You cannot love "God with all your heart, and with all your soul, and with all your mind" without also loving your neighbor.

When Jesus speaks of loving one's neighbor, he is quoting from Leviticus 19:18. This understanding of loving one's neighbor is not some vague concept of goodwill. This section of Leviticus is explicit in its understanding of what this looks like. Warren Carter writes:

> The command presents not just an exhortation to occasional loving acts but a societal vision. Leviticus 19 requires just human relations, including respect for parents (Lev. 19:3), provision of food for the poor and alien (19:9–10), no stealing, lying, false dealing or swearing falsely by God's name (19:11–12), no defrauding or reviling of the deaf and blind (19:13–14), no biased judgments or slander (19:15–16), no hatred or vengeance (19:17–18).[3]

Matthew's Jewish audience would have knowledge of this section of Leviticus and would understand

2. M. Eugene Boring, "Matthew," in Leander E. Keck, ed., *The New Interpreter's Bible* (Nashville: Abingdon Press, 1995), 8:424.

3. Warren Carter, *Matthew and the Margins: A Socio-Political and Religious Reading* (Maryknoll, NY: Orbis Books, 2000), 445.

Homiletical Perspective

The same was true in Jesus' day. So perhaps it is not surprising that one of the Pharisees asks Jesus about which rule, or commandment, is most important. We do not know exactly why he asks. Matthew says he is testing Jesus, so maybe, like some of his colleagues earlier, this Pharisee is trying to trap Jesus, to trip him up with a particularly difficult question. Maybe, having devoted his life to studying God's law, he is a little overwhelmed with it all. After all, tradition says there are 613 commandments in the Old Testament,[1] and maybe he is tired of juggling them all and wants to know which he should focus on. So maybe he tests Jesus hoping that Jesus will pass his test and, in turn, help him be more faithful. Maybe, just maybe, he wants to know more about Jesus, about what matters most to him, and he figures the best way is to ask him what commandment is the most important. What, that is, stands at the center of the kingdom Jesus preaches?

Interestingly, Jesus does not give him a single commandment but names two, both from the heart of the Jewish tradition. "Love the Lord your God with all your heart, and with all your soul, and with all your mind," Jesus says first, naming what many considered the central commandment. Then he adds a second. Actually, he says this second one is just like the first, in fact even defines the first: "Love your neighbor as yourself." Love your neighbor, that is, in the same way you hope to be loved. Take care of your neighbor as you want to be cared for. Then he goes even further, saying that everything—all the law and everything the prophets said—is summed up in these two commandments.

So, after all his preaching and teaching, after all his travels and miracles, here, just days before his crucifixion, our Lord names his center—the center of his ministry, the center of his mission, the center of the kingdom he has been sent to proclaim and build—and it is love. Love of neighbor, care and concern for each other.

By naming his center, Jesus reveals something not only about himself, but also about God. That can be easy to miss, because so many of us learned somewhere along the way that while Jesus may have been a pretty nice guy, his Father was another matter altogether. Many of us, that is, learned that while Jesus talked about love, God was primarily interested in righteousness; that God, in this sense, was very much like a judge, waiting to catch us in any and all

1. JewishEncyclopedia.com, "Commandments, The 613," the Kopelman Foundation, http://www.jewishencyclopedia.com/articles/4566–commandments-the-613; accessed May 12, 2012.

Matthew 22:34–40

Theological Perspective

streets, gathering all they find "so the wedding hall was filled with guests" (22:9–10). We see in graphic detail that God does not want any to perish (2 Pet. 3:9) and seeks all those who are lost (Luke 19:10). This is an image of the self-giving God who chooses self-abasement and dies a criminal's death in order to restore a relationship with all of humanity. Here we see that God truly loves the creation as much as "himself." This love is revealed perfectly in the son of David, who in his very life reveals the self-giving love of God for all peoples and nations.

Because this second command is like the first, Jesus can hold that on these two commands hang "all the law and the prophets" (v. 40). Every revelation of God's character contained in the law and the prophets rests on the revelation of God as the loving God who includes all the nations in God's covenant.

To many of the Pharisees, this image of God is at once unsettling and a stumbling block. If the God of Israel loves all nations as much as Israel, then everything about their identity is threatened. If God esteems all people groups as God's chosen, and requires a corresponding love by the chosen people, are the Pharisees now supposed to love others as much as themselves? Are they called to love the unclean and rejected as much as this Jesus loves them? This "son of David" is now calling into question the foundation of their religious identity and practice.

This in turn leads them to question just who this man is. He too is Jewish, indeed a teacher of Judaism. Has this teacher the authority to challenge their understanding of both God and the covenant? This radical carpenter's son is threatening to upend all of the Pharisees' work and identity. This image of the Lord in covenant with all flesh was not new to Judaism (see, for instance, Isa. 55:5; 66:18), but in Matthew's Gospel, it presents a firm challenge to the practice and power of the Pharisees. The authority and radicalness of his message leave the Pharisees with one overarching question: Just who exactly is this man?

KEITH ERRICKSON

Pastoral Perspective

self-actualization and contentment? This kind of solipsistic thinking contributes to the disintegration of our society (whither the common good in a world of expressive individualism?) and the impoverishment of our planet (the concupiscent desire to seek self-satisfaction through consumption is the root of many of our ecological problems).

Congregations are not immune to the acids of this expressive individualism. Many congregations are tempted to turn from self to God without consideration of the neighbor. Thus we begin with my needs as a sinner and end with God's salvation in Christ, cleanly circumventing the hurting neighbor (which must be understood to include the whole of suffering creation). Other congregations are tempted to turn from self to neighbor without consideration of God. Thus their ethical passion easily dissipates into self-righteousness or despair.

The church is called to cultivate the habit of triadic reflection and practice, to recognize that no discernment process is complete until love of God and neighbor and self has been expressed. This triadic practice, this love of God-neighbor-self, is not some innate human capacity. It is not a natural state for the human animal. The habit must be formed in a grace-filled community of faith where it is proclaimed and sung and embodied over and over and over again.

My mind returns to my childhood friend: bright and compassionate, politically engaged, yet caught in a web of expressive individualism, a web she (and we) can hardly escape from, because it is simply the milieu of our lives. Thus all the more critical is the mission of the church. We must hear the stories, stories that render another way of being in the world, a way free of solipsistic delusion and despair, a way that opens out to the neighbor and ultimately to the God who is the source and end of all things. Jesus offers us the one thing that empowers our freedom: a triadic habit of God-neighbor-self love. Our lives and the life of the world depend upon our picking up the habit.

RICHARD A. FLOYD

the full implications of loving one's neighbor. It is important to note that the "neighbor" referred to in Leviticus is one's fellow Israelite. Matthew's Jesus, though, has already radically reshaped the definition of "neighbor": "You have heard that it was said, 'You shall love your neighbor and hate your enemy.' But I say to you, Love your enemies and pray for those who persecute you" (5:43–44). Love for one's neighbor is both very specific in the ways in which we should treat each other and universal in who is included in receipt of such treatment.

Jesus concludes his response by confirming the importance of the commandments he has chosen: "On these two commandments hang all the law and the prophets" (v. 40). It was commonly understood that the phrase "the law and the prophets" referred to the totality of the Hebrew Scriptures. The two commandments he has named are the lens through which we view the purpose behind all scriptural injunctions.

At this point in the original account from Mark, the scribe responds by praising Jesus' answer and by echoing it back to him for further evidence of approval. In Matthew there is no praise or approval from the temple authorities. The tension between Jesus and the temple authorities, especially the Pharisees, will not be broken so easily. This text once again allows Matthew the opportunity to affirm that Jesus came to fulfill the law. A question that opened the door to choosing one law over another, and thus potentially denigrating the law, has been answered in a way that is foundational to the purpose of the entire law.

Instead of choosing a single rule to follow, Jesus chooses the motivation behind all of the rules given to us by God: love. Matthew's Gospel is often thought of as a class in Christian ethics, challenging us to live lives of higher righteousness by following Jesus' example of fulfilling the law. This text gives us the most succinct and perhaps the most challenging charge about how we accomplish this task, which is beyond our ability to accomplish on our own.

DOUGLAS T. KING

of our moral misdeeds. So any talk of the law may make us nervous, anxious, even a bit afraid.

Here Jesus points to the true character of all God's laws: to help us love and take care of each other and in this way to love God. Take the Ten Commandments, for instance; while the first few are about our need to trust and honor God, the rest are about caring for each other. Further, these laws—that we should not murder, lie, steal, covet, and the rest—are not all that remarkable when you think about it. They are the essential building blocks of any healthy community. What is remarkable is that the Israelites confessed that *God* gave us these laws, that God cares deeply about how we treat each other.

God's law, finally and forever, is the law of love. It is that simple . . . and that difficult, because loving others means putting them first. It means sacrificing. It means being vulnerable to the needs of those around us. All of this can be scary, which is why Jesus does not just come teaching and preaching God's law; he also embodies it. Just a few days after this encounter, Jesus will gather with his disciples, take some bread and wine, and invite them by eating and drinking to share his very life. After that meal, he will go out from that place of safety to embrace his destiny, going to the cross not to *make* God loving but to show us how much God loves us already, because ultimately the only way we can love each other is first to recognize just how much God loves us. This is why perhaps the most faithful sermon on the law will ultimately point us to Jesus, where we discover that we—*all* of us—are at the center of God's love and attention, grace, and mercy, now and forever.

DAVID J. LOSE

Matthew 22:41–46

⁴¹Now while the Pharisees were gathered together, Jesus asked them this question: ⁴²"What do you think of the Messiah? Whose son is he?" They said to him, "The son of David." ⁴³He said to them, "How is it then that David by the Spirit calls him Lord, saying,
⁴⁴ 'The Lord said to my Lord,
  "Sit at my right hand,
    until I put your enemies under your feet"'?
⁴⁵If David thus calls him Lord, how can he be his son?" ⁴⁶No one was able to give him an answer, nor from that day did anyone dare to ask him any more questions.

Theological Perspective

In this final encounter with the Pharisees—the fourth of four questions—Jesus becomes the questioner, and he does so in a way that brings the religious leaders finally to silence. For both Jesus and the author of Matthew, however, more is at stake in this encounter than the establishment of Jesus' teaching credentials. Jesus and Matthew are turning the ears of their hearers away from the penultimate question of the nature of the Law to the ultimate question of the hope of the gospel.

At the most basic level, this encounter establishes Jesus' religious authority. Jesus begins the week entering Jerusalem with the crowds hailing him as "the Son of David," as "the one who comes in the name of the Lord," and as "the prophet from Nazareth in Galilee" (21:9–11). Once inside the city, he enters the temple, drives out the merchants, overturns the tables of the money changers, and loudly accuses those he encounters there with turning God's house of prayer into a den of thieves (21:12–13). When the blind and lame come to him, he heals them (21:14).

Witnessing this amazing series of actions by the "prophet from Nazareth," the chief priests and the scribes—the ultimate authorities in charge of order—become angry and challenge him, for he is acting like a king and a prophet: "Do you hear what these

Pastoral Perspective

"By what authority do you do these things?" This was a common question directed at Jesus by the religious leadership of his day. In chapter 21 the chief priests and the elders of the people posed this question following Jesus' triumphal entry into Jerusalem on a donkey, his confrontation with money changers in the temple, and his healing of the blind and lame. This continues as the Pharisees and Sadducees ask Jesus question after question in chapter 22, in their attempts to expose him as a false prophet. The Pharisees in particular, according to Matthew, were descended from the "proper" line, had an esteemed educational pedigree, and were exacting in their adherence to Torah.

Jesus, in contrast, was a nobody from Nazareth who hung out with the "wrong" people, told subversive stories, and persistently challenged the religious establishment and the social status quo in his interpretation of the law. According to the Pharisees earlier in Matthew, Jesus even transgressed the law by healing on the Sabbath and presumptuously took on the authority of God to forgive sins. These tensions are coming to a head in this passage, and Jesus, recognizing the game that is being played by the Pharisees, uncharacteristically turns the question about authority back on them.

While the Pharisees are gathered together, Jesus asks them this leading question: "What do

Exegetical Perspective

The Big Question. Who is this Jesus? The Gospel narratives are consumed with the question of Jesus' identity. Perhaps the entire mission of any first-century Gospel story is to present an answer to this perennial first-century question (see John 20:30). While this question is important to the early church, as expressed by the authors of the Gospel narratives, this may not have been the query of Jesus, who constantly avoided titles and preferred this simple response, "Just call me the son of humanity." For first-century followers, however, the response was varied: Jesus was the Elijah who had mysteriously returned; a master teacher schooled in rabbinic knowledge; a resurrected John the Baptist; or a blazing prophet destined to name and tame social ills (Matt. 16:13–14). To the readers of Matthew's Gospel, however, Jesus clearly must be the Son of David. Matthew's genealogical prologue states the fact: "The book of the genealogy of Jesus Christ, the son of David, the son of Abraham" (1:1). However, that report of Jesus' family tree, despite its almost catechetical nature, does not fully answer the question in Matthew's Gospel. The unanswered question still murmurs under the breath of Matthew's narrative (13:13–20). In Matthew 12:1–8 Jesus plucks grain on the Sabbath and breaks the law like David (1 Sam. 21:1–6). In 12:23 the crowds who see Jesus

Homiletical Perspective

The Pharisees have already decided to kill Jesus (12:14). Yet in this series of controversies (21:23–22:40) the battle lines are drawn. The Pharisees will take counsel, plot, and lay plans to kill Jesus. Jesus will be clever in his answers, as he is asked about taxes, the resurrection, and the greatest commandment. He will stump and amaze the crowd, or decide not to answer at all.

We feel the tension; we have felt it since Jesus entered Jerusalem, a city in turmoil about who Jesus is. Jesus has a temple tantrum, throwing out the money changers who make God's house of prayer a den of robbers instead. The gathered children sing Jesus' praises and anger the chief priests and scribes. Tension mounts, and we know that violence will ensue. Jesus has fielded a question from the Sadducees and answered in such a way that they are silenced: "You are wrong, because you know neither the scriptures nor the power of God" (22:29).

Fighting words, to my ears.

Core to the tension, perhaps, is the central teaching of Jesus itself. Both to his followers (7:12) and to his opponents (22:34–40), love is the commandment on which hang all of the law and the prophets. Love, not power; love, not heritage; love, not law.

Now it is time for Jesus to ask a question. Once again Matthew replaces Mark's general audience with

Matthew 22:41–46

Theological Perspective

[people] are saying?" (21:15b–16a). Jesus rebuffs them.

When Jesus enters the temple again the next day and begins teaching, the religious authorities challenge his authority: "By what authority are you doing these things, and who gave you this authority?" (21:23). Jesus refuses to answer (21:27).

When Jesus proceeds to teach the crowds, telling three parables of recipients rejecting prophets sent by God, sons sent by fathers, and invitations sent by kings (21:28–22:14), those in charge of the religious and political life of Jerusalem—the Sadducees, the Pharisees, and the Herodians (22:15–16, 23, 34–36)—mean to weaken his appeal to the crowd by asking him questions that he cannot answer or that will force an answer that will fracture his audience or get him arrested. They ask him the politically dangerous question of whether it is lawful to pay taxes to Caesar (22:17), the spiritually contentious question about belief in the resurrection of the dead (22:23–28), and the debatable question about which commandment is supreme (22:36). In each case, Jesus' answer only amazes the crowds more fully (22:22, 33).

The fourth question changes the pattern (22:41–46). Jesus this time asks the Pharisees a question: How can the expected Messiah be a descendant of David, yet during David's lifetime, David called the Messiah his "Lord"? It is a time-sequence conundrum that the Pharisees are unable to answer. They become the ones discredited in front of the crowds, and Jesus, revealing his superior knowledge of the Scriptures, silences their queries.

Matthew thus establishes Jesus' credentials as the divinely authorized teacher (see also 5:2–7:29; 28:16–20), before Jesus is questioned by religious and political authorities at his trials later in the week, trials at which he primarily remains silent (26:63a; 27:11–14).

There is a deeper layer of meaning, however, to Jesus' concluding encounter with the religious authorities. The time-sequence conundrum of David's relationship to his descendants and to the one he calls "my Lord" is solved only if his Lord is the Messiah, and this Messiah somehow transcends time and is owed loyalty by David. The Pharisees cannot figure this out, but the Christians in Matthew's community, who know the resurrected Jesus as Lord, do see this solution. So Matthew implies that Jesus is the long-awaited Jewish Messiah, the son of David (v. 42).

The religious authorities, though, do not recognize him, and in a few days even the crowd will no longer

Pastoral Perspective

you think of the Messiah? Whose son is he?" They answer, "The son of David." During this time, there were not only a number of would-be Messiahs, but many people claiming to be descended from David. How many people do we have today claiming to be descended from Thomas Jefferson and other American founding fathers? How many in my Reformed tradition—both liberals and conservatives—claim to be the true theological descendants of John Calvin? People and institutions stake a claim to descent from heroic figures such as David as a shortcut to establishing their own credibility. Jesus knew that the Pharisees counted on this all-too-easy route to authority, an authority based on some assumption of royal lineage. This form of arbitrary supremacy endures, unfortunately, to this day.

Jesus then responds to the Pharisees, "How is it then that David by the Spirit calls him Lord, saying, 'The Lord said to my Lord, "Sit at my right hand, until I put your enemies under your feet"'? If David thus calls him Lord, how can he be his son?" (vv. 43–45). It is almost unheard of in an ancient Near Eastern context for a sovereign like David to call one who comes after him "Lord," thereby granting the descendant even greater authority than the patriarch. By conventional logic, this threatens the stability of the whole patriarchal system, which depends on the head to retain permanent authority, which then gives security, identity, and stability to those who follow in the line. This is why the Pharisees are stunned and unable to give an answer to Jesus, who is arguing that David, in his enigmatic statement in Psalm 110:1, is daring to expect that someone even greater than he will emerge in his wake, to whom he will gladly submit. The Pharisees, recognizing that this could undermine the whole basis of their authority, grow silent and cease from asking Jesus any more questions. He has just one-upped them in their game.

The questions that emerge after this exchange, which the text does not directly answer, are: Who is the one of whom David speaks, the one who will surpass David? How will the people know when this person is in their midst? Again, the question of authority has not been answered, but those around can infer from some of Jesus' other exchanges what he is suggesting. When he makes a distinction between false prophets and true disciples earlier in Matthew, for example, he states plainly, "You will know them by their fruits" (7:15–20). Shortly after in the text, when John's disciples approach Jesus to ask, "Are you the one who is to come, or are we to wait for another?" Jesus responds, "Go and tell

heal the blind and the demoniac are unsure and ask, "Can this be the Son of David?" When Jesus teaches in the synagogue, the listeners question, "Is not this the carpenter's son?" (13:55).

Now, in the theological workshop of the religious leaders of the first century, the voice of Jesus asks: "What do you think of the Christ [the Messiah]? Whose son is he?" (v. 42ab). The educated, experienced religious leaders, the Pharisees, deeply schooled in Hebrew Scriptures and sincerely committed to the patriarchal faith of their ancestors, respond by saying the very obvious: "The son of David" (v. 42c). The Messiah, God's long-awaited anointed one, will come in the flesh, in the form of David's son. To any faithful religious person of the day, this was clear—the Messiah will be the son of David. David, the great historical figure who had united the Israelite nation, who began the Israelite story of spiritual and economic prosperity with political unification and spiritual structures in the holy city of Jerusalem, was the honored and elevated one. David's son, the messianic role as expressed in patriarchal succession, would assume that wonderful legacy, of course! The long-awaited "anointed one" appearing in the first century would obviously be the son of David. It was the way that history had planned it to be, so the religious leaders determined.

The Tradition Is Challenged. Is it really that way? Even though this traditional line of thought—that the Messiah was the son of David—was a highly respected and accepted understanding (Isa. 11:1, 10; Jer. 23:5), did this concept find unanimous agreement? In the mind of Jesus, as reflected in verses 43–45, there is grave doubt. A high level of argumentative debate reveals the weakness of this tradition that identifies the Messiah as the son of David. Pause for just a moment; check out the logic here in verses 43–45. If the son of David is the Messiah, then how is it that David, the king of Israel, calls the Messiah Lord? This response uses a familiar citation from Psalm 110:1 (LXX Ps. 109): "The LORD says to my lord, 'Sit at my right hand until I make your enemies your footstool.'" In this quotation, David calls the Messiah Lord. Thus, how can the Messiah be David's son? If the Messiah is David's Lord, then the Messiah must be greater and better than the son of David, just as he is greater than Jonah, Solomon, and the temple (12:6, 41). The voice of Jesus, who questions religious orthodoxy of the day, as well as the author of the genealogical prologue of Matthew's Gospel, deconstructs the hard-core

the Pharisees. Jesus poses a question that is not easily answered, not without faith. With Psalm 110 as the backdrop, Jesus asks a question that confounds their ears: "What do you think of the Messiah? Whose son is he?" "The son of David," they say (v. 42). Right answer—but Jesus is not finished. "How is it then, if David calls him Lord, how can he be David's son?" There is no answer forthcoming, and there are no more questions either.

I confess, I do not really enjoy the way the Pharisees are characterized, that they are set in opposition to Jesus. I do not really feel comfortable with the bickering, the feeling that Matthew does not like the Jewish authorities, and we are not supposed to like them either. Post-Holocaust, in relationship to all of the ways we work for Jewish, Muslim, and Christian cooperation, I do not like the sense that this text might lead to anti-Semitism.

I might, because I am uncomfortable, try to move to my head, get stuck in the work of exegesis when preaching this text. I want to dig around in these questions, perhaps to engage head rather than heart for the answer. How *is* Jesus both son of David and Lord of David? I could spend hours in the psalm, digging around in there, avoiding the belly feeling of tension.

In the end, though, it is our hearts that bring us to know what Jesus knows. He is the humble king who has arrived in the city of David. He is son of David, and he is Son of God. He has come to help us to understand the core of what God expects of us: to love God with our whole selves and to love God with all we have. In light of his simplicity and the simplicity of his message, the quibbling of the synagogue leaders then and congregational leaders now fades away. In light of the simple message to love, in the silence that follows the arguing, what we have left is a Son who is faithful, a Messiah who calls us to love, and a life that eventually will lead to death—and then life again.

We may want to avoid the feeling of tension, of combativeness, and the clash between the sweet Jesus in our hearts and this one who is a formidable opponent. The primary function of these passages is to cast Jesus as the winner; he defeats his opponents in four contests. Jesus is victorious; they are silenced. Before Jesus turns to address the crowds around him, before he turns his face to the cross, he is victor. Opponents are silenced. They can only stand in wonder and amazement. There is nothing else left for them to say.

What of those early followers? How did they experience Jesus, Mary and Joseph's boy, when they

Matthew 22:41–46

Theological Perspective

recognize him as the longed-for "son of David." This is because although he is a king, indeed the *Lord* (v. 44; cf. Ps. 110; 1 Cor. 15:20–26, Eph. 1:20–23; Heb. 1:3, 13; 10:12–13), and although he defeats evil and reestablishes God's good created order, his means of victory are unexpected. He is not a militaristic savior who conquers by violence, like Herod killing the innocents (2:1–18). He is the all-powerful one who saves in a nonviolent way. He saves by healing and feeding (15:29–39). The Pharisees and Saducees seek a sign (16:1–12). Jesus gives an unexpected demonstration of power: he continuously offers the unconditional, nonviolent love and grace of God.

In a threefold combination of symbols, Matthew paints a scandalous portrait of the one who has now arrived in power: he is the *son of David*, but he is not like the militarily savvy warrior-king; he is also the expected *Son of Man*; and, shockingly, he is both of these figures *as one who suffers* (16:21–28). He loves the enemy, intercedes for his persecutors, forgives (see 5:38–48; 18:21–22). Such a combination neither the religious leaders nor the crowds could imagine (11:6; 13:20–21, 57; 15:12; 16:21–23; 26:31).[1]

However, not only are the leaders and crowds of Jesus' day, as well as the later Jewish onlookers challenging Matthew's own community, thinking wrongly about the meaning of the messianic "son of David"; they are thinking too small (see 12:6, 41–42). For the good news is not merely that a son of David, a "King of the Jews" (27:37), will come to restore the house of Israel (1:1). For Matthew, the one who comes is also, and more fundamentally, a *son of Abraham* (1:1), the fulfillment of the hope for Jew and Gentile of a restored humanity and of social reconciliation (see Gen. 12:1–3).

Finally, for Matthew, the deepest truth of all is that this particular son of David can conquer evil and death on God's behalf, and can fulfill God's promises to Abraham, because he is not just another talented human king. He is, most fundamentally, the *son of God* (see 3:17; 11:25–30; 16:16; 17:5; 24:36; 28:19; also 1:23). He comes to heal all things.

That is why his presence is good news.

GREGORY ANDERSON LOVE

Pastoral Perspective

John what you hear and see: the blind receive their sight, the lame walk, the lepers are cleansed, the deaf hear, the dead are raised, and the poor have good news brought to them" (11:3–5). For Jesus, the test of legitimacy is the fruit of one's faith; therefore, the true Son of David is the one who embodies the faith of David, not simply his genealogy.

The faith of David was an unself-conscious faith immersed in awareness of God and desire to follow God's ways. David was a sinner, to be sure, but according to tradition, he acknowledged himself as such. His predecessor Saul never recovered from an episode early in his reign in which he made multiple excuses when confronted with his sin, and sought above all to save face. By contrast, when David sinned boldly, he repented boldly (Ps. 51). In addition, if he felt like dancing before the Lord in joy and exuberance, he went ahead and did it, unaffected by what people around him thought (2 Sam. 6:14). This is why Jesus, not the Pharisees, is the legitimate heir to David's legacy. Jesus sets aside the accoutrements of the Davidic tradition and lives into the heart of it. Jesus is not self-conscious or insecure, but enters into the joy of life by being attentive to those around him and by trusting his heavenly Father for daily bread.

This means that Jesus often acts out of line with what is deemed appropriate by the religious leaders of his time, who cling to their professional and genealogical claims to the authority of David. Jesus embodies and indeed surpasses the spirit of David; people around him affirm this, and his fruits bear witness to it. Like David, Jesus wishes that those who follow him would also surpass his own works when he says, "The one who believes in me will also do the works that I do and, in fact, will do greater works than these" (John 14:12). May we all strive to live fully into the faith that Jesus embodied, and live simply in God's secure embrace.

JIN S. KIM

---

1. Concerning christological titles, Matthew uses the term "Messiah" 17 times; "king" 8 times; "Lord" 34 times; "the coming one" 7 times; "Son of David" 10 times; "Son of Man" 30 times; and "Son of God" 9 times.

theological assumptions of a Davidic Messiah with this quotation. The argument is troubling. For in this passage, the voice of Jesus in verses 41–44 seems to contradict the opening statement of Matthew's narrative, as well as the traditional religious thought: "The book of the genealogy of Jesus Christ, the son of David" (1:1).

The Logic of the Argument Is Honored. That the Messiah would be the son of David is affirmed in ancient Hebrew texts, even in the narrative of Matthew's Gospel. That the Messiah would be the son of David, however, is also refuted in Matthew's Gospel. Will the real Messiah please stand up? How can one story both affirm and refute that the Messiah is the son of David? Matthew's Gospel says both statements are true, using powerful Hebrew argumentation. The entire Synoptic tradition also follows the powerful logic, providing broad support for this understanding in the theology of the early church. The argument to undermine the traditional Davidic messianic thought using David's speech in Psalm 110 begins with Mark's Gospel (12:35–37), borrowed by Matthew and also used by Luke (20:41–44).

The scene and the audience change with each Gospel, but the basis of the argument remains. In Mark, Jesus argues against the traditional thinking in the temple; in Matthew, Jesus uses the argument in debate with the Pharisees. In Luke, Jesus uses this argument with the Sadducees. Yes, the Messiah is the son of David. No, the Messiah is not the son of David, but greater than Jonah, David, Solomon, the temple—even greater than the entire religious tradition. The argument, haggadic in nature, a kind of argumentation found in the Mishnah, can hold opposing positions in such a careful balance that truth can be mediated even in the midst of the opposing realities. Matthew's Gospel uses this method to witness to the revelation of God's presence in the world. The nature or style of debate is lodged deeply within the Hebrew tradition. This passage attempts to solve the apparently conflicting scriptural propositions. This is Scripture correcting Scripture, and they both are right!

LINDA MCKINNISH BRIDGES

heard him arguing with their leaders? Did they feel that slightly queasy feeling we get when we watch a fight on the street, or hear tense talk in the political arena or from the talking heads on the news, or read fighting words in the blogosphere? How did they feel when telling the story? Rehearsing the events? Was this the Messiah of expectations? Were they surprised, as we are, that there is toughness here?

This is not a soft, gentle, weak lamb led off to slaughter. This is a warrior, not unlike David, who has in his quiver not arrows but wisdom and the power of the Word. This is Word made flesh, unafraid to duke it out with the powers and principalities. Can our Christ be Christ like this? Do you feel the tension in the belly? We know how the story ends, and yet we can feel the curtain going up on the drama. He could have been quieter, more cooperative. He could have been more conciliatory, more accommodating. This son of David whom David calls Lord is Lord of words, anointed to speak truth to power, to tell it like it is.

Preachers, we might need to be prepared to disabuse our people of the nice Jesus in their minds; this one has words to say about injustice. This Messiah speaks of love and is unafraid to call a spade a spade. He is smart, biblical, up on current issues, and quick to shut up the foolish. If preaching to other preachers, I would want to say that prophetic preaching is required of us. To my laypeople, I would want to say there is something about the Word that defeats the status quo. I would want to talk about how our words can be used to turn the world toward justice.

Choose your words to speak truth to power, and to re-present Christ to a hurting world that needs a savior.

JACQUELINE J. LEWIS

Matthew 23:1–12

¹Then Jesus said to the crowds and to his disciples, ²"The scribes and the Pharisees sit on Moses' seat; ³therefore, do whatever they teach you and follow it; but do not do as they do, for they do not practice what they teach. ⁴They tie up heavy burdens, hard to bear, and lay them on the shoulders of others; but they themselves are unwilling to lift a finger to move them. ⁵They do all their deeds to be seen by others; for they make their phylacteries broad and their fringes long. ⁶They love to have the place of honor at banquets and the best seats in the synagogues, ⁷and to be greeted with respect in the marketplaces, and to have people call them rabbi. ⁸But you are not to be called rabbi, for you have one teacher, and you are all students. ⁹And call no one your father on earth, for you have one Father—the one in heaven. ¹⁰Nor are you to be called instructors, for you have one instructor, the Messiah. ¹¹The greatest among you will be your servant. ¹²All who exalt themselves will be humbled, and all who humble themselves will be exalted."

Theological Perspective

This text begins a judgment discourse that is multi-layered. Within the text, Jesus' audience includes his disciples and potential followers among the crowd. The author of Matthew shapes the text to speak broadly to the Christians in his community in the latter part of the first century CE and to the leaders of that community. While the text seems burdened with overly harsh polemics, in fact what is at issue for all audiences is the very heart of the gospel.

Jesus begins by affirming the religious authority of the scribes and Pharisees. They "sit on Moses' seat" (v. 2). As Moses was given a chair from which to express and explain the meaning of God's law, so Jesus acknowledges that the scribes and Pharisees now occupy that teaching office, and thus they are to be listened to. Further, these teachers discern the way toward life on the same basis as did Jesus and Matthew's Christian community: the exposition of the Torah (see 5:17–48).

After insisting on respect for these teachers of the law, Jesus gives a harsh criticism: they do not practice what they teach, so do not follow them as models (v. 3). A person's conduct must cohere with her or his proclaimed values and loyalties (7:21–23; 21:28–32). Since the scribes and Pharisees of Jesus' day and the Pharisees of Matthew's time equally insisted on the importance of such coherence of

Pastoral Perspective

In the previous passage Jesus questions conventional understandings of David's authority, and in so doing begins to move the basis of true religious authority from professional and genealogical claims to the fruit of one's life. Here, as Jesus addresses the curious crowds and disciples who have gathered around him, he sharpens his critique of the religious establishment of the day by talking about the teaching office of Moses. He begins with an affirmation of the authority of Moses by recognizing the legitimacy of the scribes and Pharisees to "sit on Moses' seat" (v. 2).

To the modern ear, this may sound like some reference to an endowed chair of a professorship. Jesus legitimates Moses' permanently endowed chair—his teaching authority—that the scribes and Pharisees occupy. Immediately after he affirms their right to teach, however, he upends the whole patriarchal system, striking at the heart of the false notions of authority that are oppressing the people. Jesus senses that the religious leaders exploit this system in order to prop up their credibility and esteem. By exposing this before the crowds of followers, he increases the pressure for a new form of religious leadership to emerge.

In contrast to the Sadducees, Jesus here affirms the right of the scribes and Pharisees to teach the law. What he challenges is the rigid adherence to

Exegetical Perspective

Continuing to Put the Religious Tradition in Its
Place. If the messianic expectations regarding the
son of David tradition were successfully decon-
structed in the previous passage (22:41–46), then
this section continues the challenge. Direct shaming and coarse speech, rather than sophistry and
logic, are used in this section. The audience shifts
from Pharisees in the previous section to a more
intimate group of disciples and followers. Matthew's
Jesus works hard to put the religious leaders and
their orthodoxy in their rightful place—far below
where they want to be! The current religious tradition wants full authority; they want to be seated on
Moses' seat (vv. 2–3). This was a literal stone seat
placed in front of the synagogue, intended as a place
of authority for the teacher or scribe, honoring the
religious legacy of Moses.

Jesus' admonition is clear to those who might follow them: honor the position they hold, but do not
follow their actions. These religious leaders place
the yoke of the law on others but not on themselves
(v. 4). Furthermore, they wear religious symbols in a
very ostentatious manner (v. 5a), intending to draw
attention to their elevated piety. With traditional
practice, phylacteries, small cases of parchment or
leather containing a piece of vellum inscribed with
texts from the Law, such as Deuteronomy 6:4–9 and

Homiletical Perspective

It has been a busy Tuesday. Jesus is still in the temple
precincts, now talking to his followers and to the
crowds. By the time Matthew is writing this, there
are tensions between the synagogue and the new
church, between Jews who follow Christ and Jews
who do not. The temptation to anti-Semitism may
be real, but should be resisted; that is not Matthew's
message. Most modern exegetes recognize that this
address really does belong to Matthew, who puts
words into Jesus' mouth about the ethics that belong
to his new faith community.

"Moses' seat" represents the Jewish leadership,
tradition, law. Matthew uses Jesus' teaching as a rhetorical device to find common ground here. There
is validity to the Pharisees' teachings, so heed them.
The Torah is relevant to our life, so read it. However,
do not do what these leaders do, because there is a
disconnect between what they teach and how they
behave. This criticism applies to both Jewish leaders and early Christian leaders; both have lessons to
learn about a life of faith.

The teachings lend themselves to a list.

First: *Make your walk and your talk the same.* In
other places in the Gospel (see also 6:1–18; 7:21–23;
21:28–32) Matthew contrasts mere talking with
doing. Christians in the early church and those of us
in the church now are invited here to examine the

Theological Perspective

speech and action, the warning may be aimed most fully at Matthew's own Christian community.

As Jesus' criticisms go further, however, it becomes clear that the more significant moral incoherence involves a split within one's inner life itself. While claiming to honor God, certain persons are really seeking the admiration of others by claiming marks of high social status. The scribes and Pharisees pray three times a day, and wear the required small leather boxes containing portions of the Torah and the blue-and-white tassels on the four corners of their prayer shawls. While both were meant to remind the praying person of God's law, they were being worn in such a manner as to draw public attention to superior piety (v. 5). Similarly, they sought seats of honor at banquets and the seats occupied by teachers and respected leaders in the synagogue, facing the congregation (v. 6). They want to be called "rabbi," a term of respect in Jesus' day, and a term restricted to official teachers of formative Judaism in Matthew's day (v. 7). In contrast, both Jesus and Matthew want a person's religious actions to be aimed at gaining the approval of God alone (see 6:1–18).

Again, even the Pharisees, both in Jesus' day and in Matthew's, would have cared about internal integrity. However, Jesus disagrees with the scribes and Pharisees—and Matthew with the Pharisaic leaders who are guiding the main competition to Matthew's Christian communities—not on the importance of the Torah, or of personal integrity, but on the meaning of the Torah. What are the signs that mark a person as a citizen of God's inbreaking kingdom? What is the basis of unity in the new community? What is the meaning of purity for these community members?

The Pharisees of Matthew's day were not hypocrites interested in external signs in contrast to the interior life. Rather, after Jerusalem's destruction and the scattering of the Jewish community after 70 CE, the emerging rabbinic leadership emphasized external signs of piety as distinctive markers of God's people within a pluralistic society. They were concerned about the loss of identity. The problem is that such external signs—phylacteries and fringes, honorific seats and titles—identify an in-group by identifying those excluded. They also create hierarchies of worth: some persons are more important than others. In contrast, Jesus advocates identity markers in which all can be included and have equal worth. The citizens of God's kingdom are to be identified by their love, mercy, forgiveness, and mutual service.

Pastoral Perspective

Torah that disguises their disregard of the hardships of regular people. Their teaching may not have been technically outside the bounds of the law, but they failed to understand the law's purpose, and therefore lived falsely. In particular, "they tie up heavy burdens, hard to bear, and lay them on the shoulders of others; but they themselves are unwilling to lift a finger to move them" (v. 4). Jesus calls others to take up their cross and follow him to the point of suffering, humiliation, rejection, and death, so he is certainly not against placing heavy burdens upon the people! However, the temptation for teachers of the law and the sacred texts in that day was to lay the burdens of God on the people, then leave it to them to do the heavy lifting on their own. How many pastors in our day preach a powerful word on Sunday, only to retreat into their office for the rest of the week? How often do we avoid the mess of intimacy and the cost of solidarity with congregation members, while preoccupied with the pursuit of personal knowledge and righteousness?

The approach of the scribes and Pharisees in this text is the exact opposite of Jesus. They seek to be seen by others, making their phylacteries broad and their fringes (or their academic gowns and ministerial robes) long, relishing the place of honor at banquets and the best seats in the synagogues (or churches and assemblies), looking to be greeted with respect in the marketplaces (or by potential donors) and to have people call them rabbi (or Reverend and Doctor).

In contrast, Jesus, instead of lifting himself up and setting himself apart, gets dirty with the people, taking on their sin and shame so that he might lead them out of it. The burdens of God are not designed to elevate the few who have the time to follow them in an exacting manner—as in the 613 commandments in the Old Testament or more contemporary forms of Christian moralism. God's intention is to liberate all people from self-obsession to an attentiveness to the other. This is why Jesus can claim that "my yoke is easy, and my burden is light" (11:30), even as he calls people to follow him to the cross.

Jesus then strikes at the heart of what is oppressing the people by returning to a familiar theme, the smashing of patriarchy. The religious professionals of the day borrowed their authority from Abraham, David, and Moses, just as pastors today borrow from Luther, Calvin, Barth, Martin Luther King Jr., their seminary, or the denomination that ordains them. Jesus relativizes all of this: "You are not to be called rabbi, for you have one teacher, and you are all

Exodus 13:2–10, were tied to forehead and left arm of the faithful Hebrew in accordance with Exodus 13:9, 16.

Jesus' admonition does not negate these symbols, but rather calls for smaller bands and shorter fringes, less showy and ostentatious display of religious piety. In similar manner, fringes, tassels worn on the corners of outer garments in accordance with Numbers 15:38 and Deuteronomy 22:12, were important symbols identifying the faithful in the religious tradition. In fact, Jesus wears fringes (9:20; 14:36), but they become a symbol for the healing of others, rather than a display of individual religious piety. In addition, places of honor at banquets and seats of power in the synagogue become abused by the religious leader who seeks attention and self-aggrandizement (v. 6). Grand entrances by religious leaders in the marketplaces, where the common people call these leaders by honorific titles such as rabbi, are denounced.

Originally the term "rabbi" was used like the term "sir" or "master." Later the term would be used for teachers in the religious tradition. At this moment, however, in first-century religious life, this term is not common and is elevated to honorific status, reserved only for Jesus, according to Matthew's Gospel. In similar manner, the term "father" is to be reserved for God. Religious leaders who demand that followers call them rabbi, master, or father are drawing attention to themselves, not to the faith that they serve.

The Featured Proverb. The language of this section is both culturally conventional and unconventional. Jesus' manner of speaking is filled with shame. Shaming the listener to corrective action was a typical response by a person in the Mediterranean cultural web of honor and shame. Honor and shame are two pivotal cultural attributes of the first-century world. Honor was not only the product of one's birth—where one was born and to whom—but also given by social recognition. Marcus Borg writes, "Much behavior was therefore dictated by the desire to acquire, preserve, or display honor to avoid its opposite, shame. Honor and shame are still major motivators of behavior in much of the Middle East as well as elsewhere."[1] The irony of this section, however, is that in trying to achieve honor, the religious leaders are fully shamed.

Perhaps the greatest shame is paying too much attention to the exterior life and forgetting the

connection between word and deed. The preacher might use a story that affirms that connection, rather than illustrations of the negative. A timeless story about a woman from Minneapolis named Mary Johnson who forgave the man who killed her son illustrates radical forgiveness.[1] Certainly she grieved the senseless murder of her twenty-year-old son Laramuin, who was shot to death by Oshea Israel, then a sixteen-year-old, after an argument at a party in 1993. Oshea went to prison, and Mary, a devout Christian, began thinking of ways to forgive him. She began to visit him in prison and, when he was released, arranged for him to live next door to her. She says, "Yes, he murdered my son, but the forgiveness is for me." We can help our congregants to feel their way into this kind of forgiveness and faithfulness with stories that illustrate the best of humankind. There are many living testimonies of people who love in a manner that reflects God's love.

Second: *The burden of the law is crippling God's people; the lighter burden is love directed toward others.* This yoke Jesus promises is light (11:28–30). The religious leaders were encouraging all of the people to live the priestly codes. The law of love is simpler and easier, because it is outer directed. A text like Isaiah 58 can support the preacher's point here about the kind of fasting that God desires. Works of justice—feeding the poor, clothing those who are naked, visiting those who are sick—are the kind of lighter yoke to which Jesus refers. Again, a story that illustrates the kindness of a familiar saint might help: the woman who knits prayer shawls for the poor, the family who pays the mortgage for another family suffering in this economy. It could be compelling to seal this message with a memorable and heartwarming story of the law of love in action.

Third: *The Pharisees acted pious for the wrong reasons, to make an impression on others.* After the destruction of the temple in 70 CE, Jewish leaders sought to emphasize external expressions of piety, to distinguish Judaism from its neighbors. The early church was tempted to conform to these practices. Here they and we are challenged to make piety an internal affair and, most importantly, not to impose our pious expectations on others. Imagine the importance of this teaching when we are reaching out to the unchurched teen who finds his way to our youth group, or to the millennial who already believes that churches are hypocritical and

---

1. Marcus Borg, *Jesus: Uncovering the Life, Teachings, and Relevance of a Religious Revolutionary* (New York: Harper Collins, 2006), 212.

1. "Woman shows incredible mercy as her son's killer moves in next door," June 8, 2011, http://www.dailymail.co.uk/news/article-2000704/Woman-shows-incredible-mercy-sons-killer-moves-door.html; accessed February 11, 2012.

Matthew 23:1–12

Theological Perspective

In a fallen world, social unity is gained through coercive power and hierarchical relations. In contrast, Jesus forms a community in which unity is gained not through relations of super- and subordination, but through relations of equality, mutuality, and reciprocity. This radical leveling of worth for the members of God's kingdom is gained by Jesus' insistence that there is only one "great one" (rabbi), the Messiah, and only one "Father," God (23:8–11; see also 12:46–50).

Paul creates an identical leveling of worth and form of unity based upon mutual service by saying there is only one body, one Spirit, one (eschatological) hope, "one Lord, one faith, one baptism, one God and Father of all, who is above all and through all and in all" (Eph. 4:4–6). By focusing on traits that can be shared by all—believers are filled with the same God, and go toward the same new creation— a radical commonality of worth forms the basis of communal unity: "There is no longer Jew or Greek, there is no longer slave or free, there is no longer male and female; for all of you are one in Christ Jesus" (Gal. 3:28).

Finally, both Jesus and the scribes and Pharisees (and Matthew and the emerging Pharisaic Judaism) are concerned about purity. However, they interpret purity differently, and this marks the greatest point of divergence. The Pharisees encouraged the people as a whole to live out their vocation as a priestly nation (see Exod. 19:6). With his Sermon on the Mount, Jesus implies a similar goal (5:17–20, 48). After the destruction of the temple in 70 CE, the Pharisees applied the priestly purity laws to all Jews as the markers of identity. Jesus viewed the purity laws as difficult to perform (v. 4) and, more importantly, misdirected (15:1–20). For Jesus, the key traits of purity are love, mercy, and a desire to serve and lift up others, in particular those of lower social status (vv. 11–12). These purity traits are more difficult to fulfill, yet also easier, for Jesus gives the love that is to be shared (11:28–30). On the basis of these traits, one will be evaluated at the last judgment.

The scribes and Pharisees, concerned with upholding the purity laws that function to reinforce social hierarchies, while refusing to "lift a finger" to aid those upon whom they place the burdens, are warned (v. 4).

GREGORY ANDERSON LOVE

Pastoral Perspective

students. And call no one your father on earth, for you have one Father—the one in heaven. Nor are you to be called instructors, for you have one instructor, the Messiah" (vv. 8–10). Jesus rejects an easy funding of religious authority through a quasi-patriarchal line that is then used both to control and to create a safe distance from the people, eventually creating unnecessary divisions. There is one patriarch, the heavenly Father, and there is one instructor, the Messiah, and all who follow are sisters and brothers.

Jesus smashes patriarchy in order to reconfigure it. When his mothers and brothers wanted to speak to him elsewhere, he pointed to his disciples and responded, "Here are my mother and my brothers! For whoever does the will of my Father in heaven is my brother and sister and mother" (12:49–50). From this point on, patriarchy does not run through the line biologically or through endowed chairs or through pedigree or through some cultural heritage; this new patriarchy, new family, and new authority are based completely on those who do the will of God, which is a turning from the self toward the neighbor.

Thus "the greatest among you will be your servant. All who exalt themselves will be humbled, and all who humble themselves will be exalted" (vv. 11–12). Jesus is creating a new community out of all the old tribes of this world, including those religious tribes that burden and divide the people, by calling them out of old patriarchal structures into the people of God, where burdens are shared. This starts with courageous leaders who dare to humble themselves and serve among the people, that all might learn to help each other bear the yoke of Christ—a yoke that leads to freedom.

JIN S. KIM

central core of values and attitudes of service. The denouement of this passage describes the interior life of the religious leader in proverbial form: "The one who is greatest will be the servant, and the one who is exalted will be humble, and whoever is humble will be exalted" (vv. 11–12, my trans.). Religious symbols, such as ancient stone monuments in the yard of the synagogue, special clothing, honorific titles, and special seats of honor at banquets, do not make a religious leader.

Although these religious symbols can hold meaning for the tradition, these symbols can be misused and abused. For leaders, humble service is most required. Popular wisdom, as featured in this proverb, says that self-promotion leads to demotion. Those who demote themselves will be promoted. This is a striking contrast to the religious leaders who flaunt their title and position with special names, seats, and garments.

The Gospel Narratives and the Religious Tradition. The words of Jesus in Matthew are intended to shame the one who is so very concerned with honor: They "love the place of honor at feasts and the best seats in the synagogues, and salutations in the marketplaces" (23:6–7, my trans.). These words found in the Gospel narratives, several in almost verbatim form, shape the Synoptic worldview by permeating the entire Gospel tradition, perhaps revealing their popularity among first-century Christians, as well as a strong authentic core belonging to the words of Jesus in the early tradition.

In Mark's Gospel Jesus admonishes, "Beware of the scribes, who like to go about in long robes, and have salutations in the marketplaces and the best seats in the synagogues and the places of honor at feasts" (Mark 12:38–39, my trans.). Luke's Gospel repeats the same admonition, almost verbatim (Luke 20:46). John 13:1–20 uses the story of the washing of feet to give an illustration of Matthew's proverb in verses 11–12. The entire Gospel tradition echoes these important words, directing them in culturally powerful ways to the religious leaders of the day by saying in a multitude of forms that "those who lead will serve."

LINDA MCKINNISH BRIDGES

judgmental. An illustration of the kindness of an ordinary person in the community might be used to illustrate this point.

Fourth: *Matthew's framing of Jesus' speech addresses the leadership of the early church.* For him, no one should be called rabbi ("my teacher") except for Jesus. The new church is a family of equals, of brothers and sisters, with one Father or Holy Parent. There are implications here for the priesthood of all believers. How do we engage our laypeople in partnerships of ministry?

Rather than taking a high tone here, the preacher may want to own that all human beings like to matter, to be important, to be honored. We all want to be known and loved; this is what it means to be human. Hearers might better find their way in without our judgment. How important is it for all of us to feel as if we matter and are appreciated! We want promotions, raises, bonuses, good grades. We are they—the finger points back to us, because we are all human. We can find our way to an ethical universe in which all people are valued, all are cherished.

On the way to the cross, on the way to a hill called Golgotha, Jesus is teaching those who would hear him about new rules. Perhaps the lines between "us" and "them" feel drawn too sharply for our contemporary interreligious contexts, but the invitation is there to seek lighter burdens for all of God's people. A life of faithfulness, we are reminded in this pericope, is about outer-directed love to neighbor and to God, and to love of self. This is the lighter burden. A life of faithfulness means recognizing in the family of God the giftedness of all—older people, children, the differently abled, those traditionally marginalized due to race or ethnicity, gender, sexual orientation, or class. We are invited to put ourselves last, to find ways to affirm and cherish others. These are ethical teachings for the church then and for the church now.

JACQUELINE J. LEWIS

¹³"But woe to you, scribes and Pharisees, hypocrites! For you lock people out of the kingdom of heaven. For you do not go in yourselves, and when others are going in, you stop them. [¹⁴Woe to you, scribes and Pharisees, hypocrites! For you devour widows' houses and for the sake of appearance you make long prayers; therefore you will receive the greater condemnation.] ¹⁵Woe to you, scribes and Pharisees, hypocrites! For you cross sea and land to make a single convert, and you make the new convert twice as much a child of hell as yourselves.

¹⁶"Woe to you, blind guides, who say, 'Whoever swears by the sanctuary is bound by nothing, but whoever swears by the gold of the sanctuary is bound by the oath.' ¹⁷You blind fools! For which is greater, the gold or the sanctuary that has made the gold sacred? ¹⁸And you say, 'Whoever swears by the altar is bound by nothing, but whoever swears by the gift that is on the altar is bound by the oath.' ¹⁹How blind you are! For which is greater, the gift or the altar that makes the gift sacred? ²⁰So whoever swears by the altar, swears by it and by everything on it; ²¹and whoever swears by the sanctuary, swears by it and by the one who dwells in it; ²²and whoever swears by heaven, swears by the throne of God and by the one who is seated upon it.

Theological Perspective

This collection of seven woes is painful to read. It displays a Jesus who uses shockingly polemical language, and who by doing so portrays God as a demanding judge. Further, given the deadly history of Christian anti-Semitism, the harsh attacks on the religious leaders, of Jesus' day as well as of the late first century CE, seem dangerous and incendiary. However, as with the previous section, in which Matthew's Jesus warns his hearers not to follow the behavior of the scribes and Pharisees (23:1–12), this judgment text reflects conflicts in interpretation of the Jewish law central to Jesus' teaching, and thus to the ethical import of the gospel.

The woe form is taken from the prophets of the Hebrew Scriptures (e.g., Isa. 45:9–10; Jer. 13:27; 48:46; Ezek. 16:23). It reflects the dismay of the prophet or of God at the wretchedness that has come upon a rebellious people, and it also reflects God's condemnation of the evil human acts that cause the wretchedness. The woe form is probably one form of Jesus' own prophetic pronouncements. Further, Jesus did have conflicts with the Jewish leaders (as seen in the earlier Q source behind Matthew and Luke 11:39–52). Matthew adapts this material primarily to address the opponents of his Christian community, which faced opposition from the leaders of the Pharisaic Judaism emerging after 70 CE. For the

Pastoral Perspective

Religious leadership is dangerous. This is clear in the passages leading up to this text, where Jesus issues stinging rebukes to the primary leadership of his day, the Pharisees and Sadducees. No wonder James warns his readers: "Not many of you should become teachers, my brothers and sisters, for you know that we who teach will be judged with greater strictness" (Jas. 3:1). Nowhere in the Bible is this clearer than in the seven woes that Jesus pronounces upon the scribes and Pharisees. Jesus rarely has a harsh word for tax collectors, prostitutes, criminals, or even the Roman soldiers who kill him, but he has a litany of curses lined up for the religious authorities of his day. While Jesus has compassion on the people, he has little patience for the powerful who profane God by pursuing their own self-righteousness at the expense of the people they claim to serve.

The problem with religious leadership is presented plainly in Jesus' first two woes to the scribes and Pharisees (vv. 13–15), in which he confronts the danger of blocking others from the kingdom of heaven, or even making them children of hell! How often does it happen in our own church contexts, for example, where someone starts to confront the depth of his or her own lack of faith, begins asking difficult questions and making risky confessions, and then ends up unsettling the typically formulaic faith

²³"Woe to you, scribes and Pharisees, hypocrites! For you tithe mint, dill, and cummin, and have neglected the weightier matters of the law: justice and mercy and faith. It is these you ought to have practiced without neglecting the others. ²⁴You blind guides! You strain out a gnat but swallow a camel!

²⁵"Woe to you, scribes and Pharisees, hypocrites! For you clean the outside of the cup and of the plate, but inside they are full of greed and self-indulgence. ²⁶You blind Pharisee! First clean the inside of the cup, so that the outside also may become clean.

²⁷"Woe to you, scribes and Pharisees, hypocrites! For you are like white-washed tombs, which on the outside look beautiful, but inside they are full of the bones of the dead and of all kinds of filth. ²⁸So you also on the outside look righteous to others, but inside you are full of hypocrisy and lawlessness.

²⁹"Woe to you, scribes and Pharisees, hypocrites! For you build the tombs of the prophets and decorate the graves of the righteous, ³⁰and you say, 'If we had lived in the days of our ancestors, we would not have taken part with them in shedding the blood of the prophets.' ³¹Thus you testify against yourselves that you are descendants of those who murdered the prophets. ³²Fill up, then, the measure of your ancestors. ³³You snakes, you brood of vipers! How can you escape being sentenced to hell?"

Exegetical Perspective

This section contains statements that appear to be some of the harshest words found in the New Testament. Matthew's Jesus leaves no stone unturned in his condemnation of the religious leaders of the day. Positive attributes belonging to this group of deeply devout Jews are difficult to find in the Gospel narratives, especially in this section. Perhaps related to the group of brave, pious Jews called the Hasidim, who stood against Antiochus IV Epiphanes in the Maccabean Revolt (1–2 Maccabees), the Pharisees work to preserve the Jewish tradition from Roman political, social, and religious influence. They also protect the Jewish tradition from the more liberal first-century reform movements, such as the Jesus movement—the Hebrew followers of Jesus, who refuse to follow the religious codes of purity and separation.

An honest appraisal of the Pharisees is necessary. Acknowledging that this passage reflects an inner struggle between two factions that are working within the Jewish tradition is important. Positive traits of the Pharisees exist, even though it is difficult to see them through the harsh polemic of Matthew's Gospel. Without these conservative leaders, the Pharisees, the Jewish tradition would not have been preserved. With these leaders, however, religious vitality appears to be lacking.

Homiletical Perspective

Whenever I am presented with a picture of Jesus as beyond humanity, I must admit that this text is one that comes to mind. It is really clear that Jesus is not above cursing a blue streak, when he calls the scribes and Pharisees hypocrites, snakes, and a brood of vipers. In true prophetic tradition, Jesus who is Son of David and Lord of David, Jesus who is Messiah, has a rant, not for the Pharisees per se, but for those who actually opposed the Matthean Christians, the opponents of Matthew's own time, represented by the scribes and the Pharisees. The charge of hypocrisy was about being inconsistent in one's faith and actions, about putting too much emphasis on looking faithful rather than being faithful.

What was at stake in the historical context was that some teachers discouraged their students from becoming Christian in the first place. Matthew's scribes, trained for the kingdom, were at odds with the scribes who did not believe in Jesus. What was also at stake was an emerging identity: who was the new community and who was it becoming?

We have to admit that the church too often acts as gatekeeper, shaping its identity with strong assertions of who is in and who is out. So we might ask our congregations: Are we gatekeepers? Do we see ourselves as the ones called to keep out of God's kingdom those who are "unworthy"? How do we feel about those

Theological Perspective

Pastoral Perspective

author of Matthew, his Christian community and the Pharisaic Judaism represent not differing doorways into the same realm of peace created by God, but alternate kingdoms. The Christian community is of God, while that of the Pharisees of his day leads to nothing but destruction (see 23:36–38). The stakes here are very high.

The overarching problem with the scribes and Pharisees, according to Matthew, is that they are idolatrous, yet blind to their own idolatry. They are called "hypocrites," not because they are insincere, but for the same reason that they are warned in 23:1–12: their actions fail to reflect their faith (the same behavior for which Paul rebukes Peter at Antioch [Gal. 2:11–14]). Further, even their faith is divided, for they place value on how they appear to others rather than on pleasing God.

These spiritual divisions in their hearts render the scribes and Pharisees inadequate to guide others toward the inbreaking reign of God. They "lock people out of the kingdom of heaven" (v. 13) because they do not see the presence of God's kingdom entering the world, nor the presence of God's Messiah who inaugurates it. When Jesus heals a demoniac who is blind and mute, the Pharisees attribute the work to "Beelzebul, the ruler of the demons," rather than to the Spirit of God and to God's Messiah, "the Son of David" (12:22–37). They call God's work of restoration evil, and this is an unforgivable sin (12:32). Failing to perceive and respond to God's Spirit, they also act to block others from responding (12:23–24; 23:13).

Further, they convert Gentiles to their own wrongheaded understanding of the kingdom of God, and these converts further block people from responding to the work of the Messiah and the Spirit (v. 15). It is doubtful that a large-scale Pharisaic mission to the Gentiles existed, but Christian missionaries from Matthew's community may have faced opposition from the Pharisees and from Gentile converts to Judaism, who opposed the Christians' lax attitude to the Torah. These woe sayings have behind them the pain of religious conflict.

The scribes and Pharisees are "blind guides" (vv. 16, 24) because they misunderstand how to fulfill the law of God. They focus on exterior or minor obligations in the law, while neglecting to fulfill the personally all-encompassing and central ethical obligations to God and neighbor: justice, mercy, and faithfulness (v. 23; cf. Mic. 6:8; Matt. 9:13; 12:7). Matthew's Jesus does care about the commandments, up to "the least" of them (5:17–20). Nevertheless

of the religious leadership? When someone is on the verge of the kingdom of heaven in this way, is not the temptation to block his or her path because it threatens to expose the shallow, professional faith of the leaders?

In Jesus' time, there was the same missionary zeal to create new converts in faraway places that we have today (v. 15). This can also be dangerous. In a religious system that is exacting in its expectations and laws for behavior, imposing these foreign burdens on a new convert, without the willingness to walk step by step with them through daily discipleship, sets them up for unnecessary failure, making them twice as much a "child of hell" as those who perpetuate the system.

In the next two woes (vv. 16–24), Jesus confronts the foolishness of some of the customs of the scribes and Pharisees, which he claims miss the point of God's law. First, they were swearing by the gold of the sanctuary in order to make their oaths, as if swearing by the sanctuary was trivial by comparison. Jesus puts the horse before the cart with this simple logic: It is the sanctuary that makes the gold within sacred, and the altar that makes the gift holy. In the same way, God must be the central reference point for all honest human interaction, not some external object, which apart from a holy God is merely an objet d'art. Jesus taught elsewhere, "Let your word be 'Yes, Yes' or 'No, No'; anything more than this comes from the evil one" (5:37). A myriad of oaths cannot overcome people's inability to trust their neighbor.

Second, the leaders were faithful in tithing, but they had become so insistent on minutiae—tithing mint, dill, and cummin—that they neglected the greater call to justice, mercy, and faith. Thus they "strain out a gnat but swallow a camel" (v. 24). To prioritize a natural fruit of righteousness, such as tithing, over righteousness itself is to risk fetishizing religious practice. Jesus is calling them to make the main thing the main thing again.

In Jesus' fifth and sixth woes against the scribes and Pharisees (vv. 25–28), he highlights their hypocrisy and self-deception. As religious leaders they are hypocrites because they maintain appearances by keeping clean the outside of the cup or whitewashing the tomb, while their insides are filled with "greed and self-indulgence," death, and "all kinds of filth." This can easily become the danger of formal ministerial training today, a training that all too often equips ministers to hide sin and struggle, to whitewash brokenness and fear behind the façade of "professionalism" and "boundaries."

In typical Hebraic style, Jesus condemns the Pharisees with a series of woes similar to the list found in Isaiah 5:8–23. This material belongs to a tradition developed even earlier than the Gospels (called Q), discovered by parallel material in Matthew and Luke. In this section we are also reading texts formed by Matthew's community alone. This material belongs to the period in the early stages of the Jesus movement (perhaps 40–50 CE), even though Matthew's Gospel may not have been written until later in the first century.

On Hindering Others (v. 13). Jesus, in Matthew's Gospel, accuses the Pharisees of keeping others, including themselves, from entering the kingdom of heaven, the place of God's presence. Rather than introducing God's reign to earth, these religious leaders are accused of keeping people from entering God's blessed kingdom. This denunciation has no other Gospel parallel; this particular concern perhaps belongs specifically to the Matthean community.

For a Proselyte (v. 15). Note that verse 14—"Woe to you, scribes and Pharisees, hypocrites! For you devour widows' houses and for the sake of appearance you make long prayers; therefore you will receive the greater condemnation"—is omitted in most texts. This verse appears in other Greek manuscripts but is absent in the earliest and best authorities. In verse 15 Jesus admonishes the Pharisees for their zealous behavior, crossing the "sea and land to make a single convert." However, in creating a new convert, they have created a "child of hell."

Swear by the Temple (vv. 16–22). The logic of the rule of the Pharisees is challenged here. The tradition affirmed that when a person swore by the temple, by the altar, or by heaven, the oath was not obligatory. However, if a person swore by the gold in the temple or by a gift at the altar, the oath was obligatory. Jesus' words affirm that it is the temple that makes the gold holy and the altar that makes the gift holy. In other words, all vows are sacred—wherever and whenever they are made. This admonition, similar in pattern to verse 14, is unique to Matthew. All other denunciations in this section have parallels in Luke (Q) or the *Gospel of Thomas.*

Mint, Dill, and Cummin (vv. 17–24). The Pharisees are such close observers of the tithing law that even the herbs and spices from the garden are tithed. The irony of such attention to detail is that the weightier

who do not share our theological framework? How do we feel about those who belong to a different racial/ethnic group? How do we feel about those who are gay, lesbian, bisexual, or transgender? Is my congregation a highway unto our God, or do we feel somehow responsible to restrict access to God's reign? It will be the honest preacher who can confess that much of church life is about who is in and who is out. Woe to those of us who feel called to sit at the gate and restrict access to God's amazing grace.

The second woe (v. 15) continues to address what it means to be missional. What is required of people before they belong to God? Must they convert to our way of thinking? A preacher might encourage her congregation to see themselves in the ancient church with some holy imagination: "This would never happen here in our congregation, but can you believe that in Matthew's church they could not imagine that God could welcome the new converts unless they became Jewish first? Can you imagine that they thought God's *hesed* (covenant faithfulness) was too small, too limited, God's love too puny to receive the people just as they were?" Humor is good sugar for the bitter medicine of the gospel in times like these.

Woe to those of us who split hairs, who major in minors, who sweat the small stuff. Justice, mercy, and faithfulness trump straining gnats out of drinks. Sometimes denominational meetings can encourage thinking about gnats. The minutiae of congregational life that lead to conflicts among God's people (I think we should sing only these kinds of hymns, serve only this for brunch, relate only to these kinds of people, serve Communion only with white gloves, use only this order of worship) are gnats. How we love to major in the minors, how we love to spend our spiritual capital on the small stuff, and to feel safe and secure behind the barriers of legalism we set up for ourselves. Let's laugh at that!

Woe to those of us who focus on the outer rather than the inner. Purity of thought, purity of heart, is as essential as the outward appearance of righteousness. What if our people thought of ritual cleanness as both an internal and external project? In many congregations, as soon as worship is over, there is grousing on the way to the fellowship hall or to the parking lot. An invitation to laugh at how much dissonance there is between the inner work and the outer work at the congregation on the other side of town, in the city in which you grew up, or back there in the first century, might get your congregation ready to confess this issue in the here and now in your context. A wonderful companion text is Psalm

Theological Perspective

the weightier ethical obligations are to guide one's response to the minor ones in a given situation.

That Jesus thinks the scribes and Pharisees miss the forest for the trees is clear from woes three and four (vv. 16–24). The leaders focus on hairsplitting distinctions between invalid and valid oaths, which Jesus believes distract people from the heart of what is at stake in social commitments: one's honesty and truthfulness before God and neighbor (see 5:33–37; Jas. 5:12). The leaders go beyond the law's tithing requirement, setting aside even mere garden spices, while neglecting the heart of the moral law: God's call for just, compassionate, and faithful relations with neighbors (v. 23). They focus on gnats and miss the camels (v. 24).

This focus on the form of the law while missing its substance is also seen in the leaders' misunderstanding of the purity demanded by God (woes five and six, vv. 25–28). They focus on the fine points of the external purity of dishes, or keeping ritual purity on the way to the Passover festival, while forgetting to ask the deeper question of whether one is acting morally or immorally throughout one's life.

The climax of this condemnation—that those who think they are being lawful are actually lawless and godless—comes in the seventh woe. The leaders think they are honoring the martyred prophets. In fact, when God's prophets appear, ushering in God's reign—John the Baptist, Jesus, the Christian missionaries of Matthew's community—the Pharisees resist and kill them (vv. 29–36; see 5:11–12; Heb. 11:32–38). Despite their attempts at ritual purity, the leaders' hearts reflect the homicidal tendencies of the human race.

Jesus' pronouncement of woes forces his hearers, the disciples and potential disciples in the crowd, to make a choice. Which guides will they follow? To which kingdom will they give their allegiance (cf. chaps. 24–25)?

In a few days, the crowds will give their answer. They will violently reject Jesus as guide, as well as the kingdom that he claims to inaugurate (see 26:55; 27:25). Already in proclaiming these woes, Jesus knows what is coming.

GREGORY ANDERSON LOVE

Pastoral Perspective

In the seventh woe (vv. 29–36) Jesus uses the braggadocio of the scribes and Pharisees against them by accusing them of inescapable culpability and thus complicity in the martyrdom of the ancient prophets. The key word for Jesus was "our," as in "our ancestors" (v. 30). Jesus may very well have been charging them with idolatry, as he seems to refer to the Second Commandment: "You shall not bow down to [idols] . . . for I the LORD your God am a jealous God, punishing children for the iniquity of parents, to the third and the fourth generation of those who reject me" (Exod. 20:5). The idolatry at hand is the self-serving exaltation of the prophets by the scribes and Pharisees. Their paean to the faithful heroes of old is a cover for their own vanity.

In America, for example, people are fond of saying "*our* founding fathers" when discussing the admirable parts of history, but quickly exempt themselves from the genocide of Native Americans and the chattel slavery of African Americans. Brutality and inhumanity are also at the heart of our country's founding and history. Real leaders, according to Jesus, take collective responsibility for the good and the bad.

Jesus' rebukes sound harsh to modern sensibilities, but that is because there is so much at stake in religious leadership. When leaders block the people's way to genuine faith with unconfessed hypocrisy, they become "snakes" and a "brood of vipers," devouring the people for their own gain. This hard word can also be a liberating one in twenty-first-century America. As institutions continue to lose their standing and appeal, especially religious institutions, and as contemporary church leadership entails fewer and fewer concrete benefits, the time is ripe for the kind of courageous leadership that will take collective responsibility for the past, and move beyond a preoccupation with the instruments of religion to a cruciform discipleship.

JIN S. KIM

concerns of the first-century world, such as justice and faithfulness, are ignored. The Pharisees tithe the smallest items but neglect justice and mercy (see Luke 11:42), thus straining out gnats and swallowing camels (Matt. 23:24).

Cleaning the Outside and Inside of Cups (vv. 25–26). Luke attaches this saying to a story about Jesus and a Pharisee sharing a meal (Luke 11:39–41). When Jesus fails to wash his hands before dinner and the Pharisee is astonished, Jesus retorts that it is not enough to wash the outside of the cup, for the inside is also dirty. Hands are of lesser concern when the heart is dirty, Jesus implies.

Whitewashed Tombs (vv. 27–28). Not lacking for graphic imagery, this denunciation is the most vivid of all. The interior of the tombs is filled with dead, decaying flesh and bones. From a Jewish perspective this is a very unclean place and is to be avoided at all costs (Num. 19:16). The irony of this scene is that on the inside of the tomb one finds the epitome of decay, yet on the outside the tomb appears bright and beautiful, featuring freshly painted walls carefully hiding the death and decay on the inside. The decay is not hidden in the Pharisees. This severe criticism underscores the hypocrisy of the religious leaders. This passage has a parallel text in Luke 11:44.

Prophets' Tombs (vv. 29–32). Important people were honored even in death. The building of majestic tombs and monuments provided yet another way to show religious arrogance. Jesus calls the religious leaders to be honest when they quickly declare that they would not have been the ones to kill the prophets, if they had been alive at the same time, as they honor their dead ancestors in the graveyard. Thus Jesus declares that these first-century religious leaders are guilty of killing the ancient Hebrew prophets by their association with the ancient ancestors and their ostentatious funerary monuments.

Brood of Vipers (v. 33). Reaching back into the negative images of the garden of Eden, where the serpent is deceitful and cunning (Gen. 3:1–4), Matthew's Jesus declares that the Pharisees are a bunch of snakes—a brood of vipers (cf. Matt. 3:7; 12:34). They are going to hell.

LINDA MCKINNISH BRIDGES

139, in which the psalmist knows that God already knows all that is going on inside. When we acknowledge that there is nowhere to hide, we are free to present ourselves to God, just exactly as we are, and to be cleansed and made whole. God wants our outer self and our inner being; God wants to claim all of us, our total being. The issue here is integrity between what is in our hearts and how we behave.

This concern is echoed in the woe about whitewashed tombs (v. 27). To encounter a tomb by accident was to risk incurring uncleanness. A tomb that was whitewashed made itself plain, so it could be avoided. Once again, Matthew points out the danger of inconsistency between exterior and interior. The issue for the modern hearer might be about holiness and wholeness, and a ritual in worship might support the sermon, something about clean hands and heart, perhaps a renewal of baptism with the sprinkling of water.

Where is the good news in a text like this? Jesus knows our humanity and tendency toward failings, and still we are loved. God knows the humankind God created, and still we are loved. These texts make us laugh with a nervous kind of laughter, if we are honest. The concepts feel archaic; the metaphors do not really work for us. Yet we feel the judgment and know that it is true for us: we are imperfect, we will take shortcuts to look as if we have it together, and we cannot fool God.

If we say we have no sin, we lie, and the truth is not in us. If we confess our sin—our failings, our brokenness, our desire to cheat and whitewash what is dead within us—God is swift and just to forgive us and to cleanse us (1 John 1:8–9). That is the good news.

JACQUELINE J. LEWIS

Matthew 23:34–39

³⁴"Therefore I send you prophets, sages, and scribes, some of whom you will kill and crucify, and some you will flog in your synagogues and pursue from town to town, ³⁵so that upon you may come all the righteous blood shed on earth, from the blood of righteous Abel to the blood of Zechariah son of Barachiah, whom you murdered between the sanctuary and the altar. ³⁶Truly I tell you, all this will come upon this generation.

³⁷"Jerusalem, Jerusalem, the city that kills the prophets and stones those who are sent to it! How often have I desired to gather your children together as a hen gathers her brood under her wings, and you were not willing! ³⁸See, your house is left to you, desolate. ³⁹For I tell you, you will not see me again until you say, 'Blessed is the one who comes in the name of the Lord.'"

Theological Perspective

These passages conclude the seven woes that indict the Pharisees as hypocrites. Whereas in other places Jesus warns against being taken in by false prophets, here the people are chastised, not only for *not* recognizing true prophets, but indeed for killing them. This is offered as a description of future action with the prophetic words that "all this will come upon this generation" (v. 36). Indeed, Jesus himself will be one of those whom the people "will kill and crucify" (v. 34). His death will continue the long line of "righteous blood shed on earth," stretching as far back as Abel (v. 35). Jesus the prophet speaks on behalf of God, and the tone shifts from one of condemnation and indictment to lament.

In the lament, Jerusalem is singled out as "the city that kills the prophets" (v. 37). Luke extends this claim with bitter irony, adding that "it is impossible for a prophet to be killed outside of Jerusalem" (Luke 13:33). For Matthew, these lines function within the Gospel as Jesus' recognition that he will be killed. They also serve to explain to Matthew's community of Jewish Christians why the temple was destroyed (in 70 CE), an event mentioned in the opening lines of chapter 24; the destruction of the temple is a form of divine judgment and is also connected to the unfolding of the end of time. As one who continues in the line of prophets, Jesus also will not be

Pastoral Perspective

Cheery primary colors illustrate the delightful children's book that begins, "God is like a Mother Hen . . . who protects her little chicks."[1] A smiling mama hen stretches her loving wings in a wide embrace beneath a bright buttercup sun. Around her pointy chicken feet, a brood of baby chicks scuttles here and there as they nibble on lush and tasty green grass. Hearing Jesus say, "How often have I desired to gather your children together as a hen gathers her brood under her wings" (v. 37), a listener might be drawn to picture in one's mind's eye an image that is meant primarily to comfort children. For readers of Matthew's Gospel, however, the image of Jesus as a mother hen was not a bedtime story intended to rock children gently to sleep; it was an image intended to buoy the faith of adults struggling and gasping to stay afloat amid the swirling waters of persecution.

The image of Jesus as a hen who gathers a brood of chicks under her wings appears in a lament that falls from his lips like tears, as he moves closer and closer to a death-dealing Jerusalem. For those who read these words in the first century, surely the image of a mother hen—who would draw her chicks

1. Carolyn Stahl Bohler, *God Is Like a Mother Hen and Much, Much More* (Louisville, KY: Presbyterian Publishing Corporation, 1996), no page numbers.

Exegetical Perspective

This pericope begins with *dia touto* ("on account of this"), a concluding sentiment that suggests the entire pericope is best understood in relationship to what precedes it, the discourse that began at least at the beginning of chapter 23. Verse 34 parallels Luke 11:49 and foreshadows Jesus' death, particularly as it refers to the killing and crucifixion and flogging of unnamed "prophets, sages, and scribes." The figures mentioned here serve to unite Jesus to the Hebrew prophetic and wisdom traditions, as well as link him to the "scribes" (*grammateus)*, with whom he is frequently in conflict. Jesus' hostility toward the scribes is clear throughout 23:13–29, as he denounces both "scribes and Pharisees" in a series of "woes."

The discussion of "righteous blood" in verse 35 foreshadows Jesus' own death as an innocent sacrifice. The reference to Abel calls to mind the story from Genesis 4, one that is both familiar in our context and known to the original hearers of this Gospel. The story of Zechariah's death is less familiar to us, although likely familiar to the original audience. The reference to Zechariah comes likely from 2 Chronicles 24:17–22, where the story of Zechariah ben Jehoiada is recounted. This prophet, slain by supporters of King Joash, is more consistent with the details of this narrative than is the account of Zechariah ben Barachiah, the prophet who lends his

Homiletical Perspective

Preachers know the importance of the audience. The crowds and the disciples are the actual hearers of these words that come at the tail end of woes specifically directed to the scribes and Pharisees. The crowds will not appear again in Matthew's Gospel until the arrest of Jesus. While the crowds are not the intended addressees of Jesus' accusations, they are most certainly aware of the seriousness of Jesus' words. One wonders if the crowds and the disciples looked at each other and said, "Why is Jesus telling us this? He should save this speech for when the scribes and Pharisees show up." We might compare the scene to overhearing a monologue meant for someone else, but that somehow speaks to you as well. That the hearers of these words of woe are eavesdroppers, not the proposed recipients, suggests that the warnings and indictments could just as easily be directed to us. Before we point the finger at the scribes and Pharisees, for all of their waywardness and wrongdoings, Jesus asks us to examine our own penchants for hypocrisy, exclusion, and self-righteousness.

This then is the narrative context for what appears to be a self-fulfilling prophecy for Jesus. The verse immediately preceding this last section of Matthew 23 reads, "You snakes, you brood of vipers! How can you escape being sentenced to hell?" (v. 33). Jesus

Theological Perspective

accepted and will face death. When these sentences are read in conjunction with what follows, they offer warning to Matthew's struggling community, which is still awaiting the second coming, and some of whose members will be tortured and put to death (24:9).

These lines at the end of chapter 23 do not have the apocalyptic certainty that is found in chapter 24. Whereas chapter 24 describes in greater detail the time of great suffering, when "the sun will be darkened, and the moon will not give its light" (24:29), chapter 23 can be read as God's lament over the people's rejection, expressed through their murderousness and their unwillingness to accept God's love. Extending the covenant to the new community, God offers protection and love "as a hen gathers her brood under her wings" (v. 37), and yet the people continue (and will continue) to turn away. The tone is one of lamentation, God's grieving the painful irony that God's people (now in its broadened sense) are incorrigible, but are not irredeemable. We are those people.

As New Testament scholar Donald Senior has suggested, Matthew emphasizes the "legacy of rejection."[1] We reject and often kill our prophets; we always have. Is it a rejection of the uncomfortable truths that they present? Is it to avoid the harsh light of scrutiny? Is it because we cannot stand or fathom the consequences of their claims? What would we have to give up, what habits and actions would need to cease, in order to heed their call? Does the rejection stem from stubbornness, from pride, or from something even deeper?

These passages tell us something about God as well, something equally paradoxical and confounding. Matthew's God is the God of wrath and judgment, the one who will destroy the temple, leaving the house desolate (v. 38). That same God is also the one who, in love and protection, will gather the people "as a hen gathers her brood under her wings" (v. 37). As Dale Allison has put it, the seeming contradiction in Matthew "between the God of love and the God of wrath goes back to the beginning, to Jesus himself, and beyond him to the Jewish theology in which he was raised, . . . There is, from the Gospel's point of view, no theological contradiction in its portrait of God."[2] It is we moderns who struggle with understanding how God can be both; this difficulty does not belong to Matthew.

1. Donald Senior, *Matthew* (Nashville: Abingdon Press, 1998), 263.
2. Dale Allison, "Deconstructing Matthew," in *Studies in Matthew* (Grand Rapids: Baker Academic, 2005), 249.

Pastoral Perspective

close beneath protective wings, even though it might mean her own death to save them from a hen-house-raiding fox—could not be separated from the image of the cross.

There is an honesty in Matthew's Gospel that refuses to take refuge in pious platitudes, but is willing to face the brutalities of life as first-century Christians faced it—and as twenty-first-century Christians face it too—with courageous resolve. In the image of a mother hen, as in the image of the cross, we see the love of the One who weeps and cries out from the pain of betrayal, abandonment, loneliness, physical and emotional suffering, and, finally, death. In this image, we come to know that whatever terrifying things we may encounter in this life (and, yes, we will face them—disappointment, rejection, loss, death), God spreads divine wings over our pain and weeps with us and for us toward the day of salvation, when the whole world exclaims in joy, "Blessed is the one who comes in the name of the Lord."

How may this image of a mother-hen Christ who lays down her life for her chicks work toward the salvation of those who suffer?

A woman who remembers a time in her life when violence in her marriage was an everyday occurrence tells of not being able to drive or handle money. She was not allowed to do the family shopping. She was not permitted to speak to, or even look at, the neighbors. Her husband had arranged for their home phone to be an extension of his office phone, so that she was unable to make a single phone call without the fear that he was listening. He censored her mail and would not leave her alone, even with his own relatives.

Then, one day she was at home in prayer. She was meditating upon an image of Jesus hanging on the cross. Suddenly the cross seemed to move. Instead of being in front of her, it shifted to her side, as if Jesus were hanging on the cross beside her as she too was being crucified. She knew somehow that she was not alone. When she hurt, God hurt. When she was hit, God was hit. When she was bruised, God was bruised. When she could not bear the pain anymore, God bore the pain for her.

This God was not exactly the God for whom she had hoped. She had prayed for a knight-in-shining-armor God who would gallop in on a charging steed, waving a holy wand, sweeping her away from the torture of her violent marriage. The God she found, however, was a God who spread divine wings over her pain and wept with her and for her. It was this image, the image of a crucified God, the image of a

name to the minor prophetic book, whose death is not described in the Hebrew Bible. The connection of Zechariah's death with the temple brings to mind the notion of the cultus and worship practices of the larger Jewish community, and associates a system of sacrificial atonement with Jesus' own death.

In this passage we find the image of a God who is constantly supplying access to God's will, but an obdurate people not only reject the word from God, but also kill the messengers who bring it. This calls to mind other narratives, like the parable of the Vineyard Keepers in Matthew 21:33–41, which tells of people who kill those sent to retrieve part of the produce for the owner and then kill even the owner's son, often interpreted by Christians as Jesus himself. This passage can be dangerous if not carefully considered, since Jesus here blames his own Jewish contemporaries for the brutality against the faithful servants of YHWH. When we recognize that this is one Jew speaking to others of the same faith, then we hear the invective as less about condemnation of one ethnic group, and more about condemnation of all who reject God's words. As Gentile Christians, we should be cautious that we do not interpret this passage as an invective against Jews.

Jesus' condemnation of "this generation" (*genean tautēn)* for the deaths of the prophets in verse 36 echoes from Matthew's time, when the temple has fallen and the people of Jerusalem have fallen as well. There is an even greater danger lurking in this verse, based upon which word we choose to use to translate this term. If *genean* is understood to be "race" or ethnic "kind," then this passage can well serve as a basis for anti-Semitic thought, conveying a sense of responsibility to the "entire people" for the deaths of the prophets (and remember, this statement is also a foreshadowing of Jesus' own fate, so their responsibility for Jesus' death is also implied). If the word is instead taken as "generation," the term, while still somewhat troubling, seems to resonate with the temporal assumption of the larger pericope of punishment for those whom Jesus is addressing: the particular group of "scribes and Pharisees" (v. 29) who are "children of the prophet killers" (v. 31, my trans.). Further, the general Jewish Christian context of Matthew makes the former reading of *genean* as "ethnic kind" problematic, and makes a temporal "generation" more likely. It resonates with the apocalyptic feel of this verse, which portrays the judgment of God soon coming upon them. It still does not alleviate fully the hazard inherent in the text, however, nor should this aspect of the passage

then talks about sending prophets, sages, and scribes who will be killed and crucified, flogged in the synagogues, and pursued from town to town. Sounds an awful lot like what will happen to someone we know. It is here that we need to remember the other half of the audience for this discourse, the disciples. The very near future for Jesus will also be a probability for the truly righteous. Jesus' fate could quite likely be theirs. Persecution is the reality for the righteous.

So this passage is a very direct lesson as to what righteousness needs to look like, not only for the sake of the self, but for the sake of the church. This is a critical theme for Matthew and comes at an important place in the story. These are Jesus' last public words in Jerusalem and in the temple before his arrest. As a result, one of the most significant aspects of this passage is how we as a community define and adjudicate righteousness. In communities of faith, when are the times when we quite easily determine and detect false practices in others, especially on the outside of our walls, and yet are unable and unwilling to acknowledge our own halfhearted and self-regarding attempts at righteousness?

Moreover, the location of righteousness is called into question: not only whom we expect to display it, but also where we expect to find it. The people and places that represent righteousness are not who and what we think. Jerusalem should be the center of righteousness and religiosity, yet in the next chapter Jerusalem's destruction will be foretold. The scribes and the Pharisees should be the practitioners of righteousness, yet their actions reveal that righteousness does not reside in their hearts. This passage also suggests that whom you listen to can very well determine your own behavior. The words you take in may just manifest themselves in correlate actions on the outside.

Given this theological context, the lament for Jerusalem is all the more poignant. The likely historical context of the Gospel, after the destruction of the temple, situates the lament of Matthew's community in a time of looking back, trying to make sense of what has happened. The touching and gentle image of a hen gathering her brood under her wings is in striking contrast to the behavior of the Pharisees and scribes, and gives us a portrait of what righteousness should look like and feel like. Righteousness is the tenderness of a mother's embrace, the warmth of a mother's protective arms, the feeling of being safe and loved.

It imagines that righteousness is not simply an autonomous act of religiosity but is also given and

Matthew 23:34–39

Theological Perspective

There has been some debate about how to interpret the enigmatic conclusion of chapter 23: "you will not see me again until you say, 'Blessed is the one who comes in the name of the Lord'" (v. 39). Many hear in these words a continuation of the spirit of indictment found in the seven woes. To read in these lines, however, only indictment and threat is to miss the joy-filled promise of Psalm 118: 26 that Matthew cites here: "Blessed is the one who comes in the name of the LORD." Graham Stanton offers the helpful suggestion that these passages be read as an example of Sin-Exile-Return, a pattern from the Hebrew Bible taken up by Matthew as part of the Christian-Jewish polemic and apologetic of this Gospel.

First, there is the denunciation of sin, followed by a declaration of punishment (often exile and the destruction of the temple). This is then followed by the promise of return. The offering of the promise of salvation in verse 39 may seem odd as the conclusion to an extended statement of judgment. However, as Stanton shows us, "the juxtaposition of judgment and salvation . . . is a thoroughly biblical and well-established Jewish pattern: it goes back ultimately to Deuteronomy, where blessing sometimes follows curse."[3] Matthew's community understood itself as still within the fold of Judaism; the anti-Pharisee polemic stems from a struggle *within* the tradition, as the new community of Jewish Christians wrestled with rabbinic Judaism after the destruction of the temple.

The promise of salvation comes right on the heels of stern judgment: these words foretell a future that will include enormous suffering but will end with the beginnings of the new age and a new kingdom. Rather than a crescendo of anger, the seven woes conclude on a note of sadness. These passages should not be read with a finger pointing at the scribes and the Pharisees. *We* are the ones who live out the "legacy of rejection," who kill the messengers sent by God. We are the ones who are desolate, yet always still redeemable.

HANNAH SCHELL

Pastoral Perspective

mother-hen Christ who loved her with a wondrous love that willingly joined her in her pain, that led her to begin the hard work of freeing herself from violence and entering into a resurrected life of hope and possibility.

What would the church formed in the image of a mother-hen Christ look like?

Perhaps it would look like the Bag Ladies at Lakewood Presbyterian Church in Jacksonville, Florida, who gather one Saturday each month to sew bags and stuff them with supplies—a miniflashlight on a rope, a handmade pillow, a towel, a washcloth, a toothbrush, a coloring book, and a snack—for the children who come with their mothers to Hubbard House, Jacksonville's shelter for domestic violence survivors. The ministry was begun by Pat Bloebaum, whose commitment grew out of the tears that she shed when she learned of her daughter's experience. When her daughter arrived at Hubbard House with two young sons, it was necessary for them to use T-shirts to dry off after showering, because there were no clean towels left, and her four-year-old grandson was so scared that he kept a dim toy lantern on all night.

Pat's inspiration came when she thought about how many women experience what her daughter experienced but do not have family and friends to help them. She enlisted fellow church members in her efforts, and the ministry grew. Pat's two grandsons, who once stayed at Hubbard House, have joined the effort as well, collecting snacks for other Hubbard House children in a program they call Grocery Bags for Kids.[2]

"How often have I desired to gather your children together as a hen gathers her brood under her wings?" (v. 37). On the cross, Jesus did precisely this, and he invites his body, the church, to do the same.

ELIZABETH MCGREGOR SIMMONS

---

3. Graham N. Stanton, *A Gospel for a New People: Studies in Matthew* (Louisville, KY: Westminster/John Knox Press, 1991), 250.

2. Bridget Murphy, "10 Who Make a Difference: Making a Difference for Domestic Abuse Victims," *Florida Times-Union*, January 10, 2010.

escape the preacher's or teacher's notice. In our day, a sermon that reflects on the dangers of anti-Semitic readings might prove to be a timely reminder of the pre-Holocaust Christian interpretive traditions that led to the horrors of retribution against the Jews.

Verse 37 may well be an allusion to scriptural tradition (Ps. 57:1; 61:4). This verse could be dependent upon 2 Esdras 1:30: "I gathered you as a hen gathers her chicks under her wings. But now, what shall I do to you? I will cast you out from my presence." This passage from 2 Esdras reflects the notion of God's desire to gather together the scattered exiles; but because of their recalcitrance, God determines in the end to send them back into the Diaspora. The interpreter should not miss the wonderful feminine metaphor for Christ as a female bird exerting her protective and nurturing duties for her vulnerable and often wandering brood. Unlike the Esdras version, where God rejects the people, here it is the people's rejection of Jesus that leads to their demise.

The desolation mentioned in verse 38 foreshadows the impending destruction of Jerusalem and may well reflect the language of the Old Testament prophets, like Jeremiah, who declares, "But if you will not heed these words, I swear by myself, says the LORD, that this house shall become a desolation" (Jer. 22:5). This pericope ends in verse 39 with a direct quotation of Psalm 118:26, which both affirms the divine mission of the prophetic ambassador of the Lord (and thus Jesus) and links this instruction to that found in the Psalter: "Blessed is the one who comes in the name of the LORD. We bless you from the house of the LORD."

RODNEY S. SADLER JR.

received. In the end, this is what the scribes and the Pharisees had forgotten. Righteousness is not just about the self, but must be given away. Your acts of righteousness have an impact on others, and therefore those others need to be in view. In the end, the scribes and the Pharisees had abandoned that which is intrinsic to righteousness, especially when it comes to God. God cannot *not* direct God's acts of righteousness toward that which or whom God loves. If righteousness reveals the very nature of God, then it must reflect the character of God, and the character of God is inherently relational. God's righteousness is who God is, but it is simultaneously who God is for us.

A deeper question in all of this, particularly for the disciples at this point, is this: in whom or what can you trust? If the founts of righteousness are no longer the expected and well established, where will we find them? The answer to this question points to two unsettling yet surprising possibilities. The proximity of Jesus' arrest, trial, crucifixion, and resurrection indicates that the entire passion narrative reveals God's view of and acts toward righteousness. So the event of Jesus' passion is where we will find righteousness, and where the nature of righteousness will be fully revealed.

The second possible source of righteousness resides in the disciples themselves. "Who, me? I am a conduit of righteousness? How can this be?" Jesus is counting on the disciples to act out his righteousness in the world when he is no longer present. The Great Commission will send them into all nations with the power of the Father, Son, and Holy Spirit, to baptize, to teach, and to keep all that has been commanded them. In other words, Jesus is counting on the disciples to act out his righteousness in the world when he is no longer present. Yet Jesus promises to be with his disciples always (28:20), and this promise and presence assure them that the righteousness of God goes with them.

KAROLINE M. LEWIS

Matthew 24:1–8

¹As Jesus came out of the temple and was going away, his disciples came to point out to him the buildings of the temple. ²Then he asked them, "You see all these, do you not? Truly I tell you, not one stone will be left here upon another; all will be thrown down."

³When he was sitting on the Mount of Olives, the disciples came to him privately, saying, "Tell us, when will this be, and what will be the sign of your coming and of the end of the age?" ⁴Jesus answered them, "Beware that no one leads you astray. ⁵For many will come in my name, saying, 'I am the Messiah!' and they will lead many astray. ⁶And you will hear of wars and rumors of wars; see that you are not alarmed; for this must take place, but the end is not yet. ⁷For nation will rise against nation, and kingdom against kingdom, and there will be famines and earthquakes in various places: ⁸all this is but the beginning of the birth pangs."

Theological Perspective

Matthew 24 shifts the location of the action from the temple to the Mount of Olives. This shift is significant and accords with the shift in the discourse, from condemnation and lament to apocalyptic prophecy. The temple, once the *axis mundi* (sacred center) for the people's relationship to their God, has become inhabited, and therefore tainted, by hypocrites. The Mount of Olives, associated with words of final judgment (see Zech. 14:4, "his feet shall stand on the Mount of Olives, which lies before Jerusalem on the east") serves as the appropriate site for Jesus' words describing "the end of the age" (Matthew's preferred phrase, one that is unique to the first Gospel).[1]

There is also a shift in the audience for Jesus' words. He has gone from speaking to "the crowds and his disciples" (23:1) to now speaking directly to his disciples, responding to their questions about the end times: When? How? What will be the signs? Their questions are our questions, and indeed Jesus' discourse as it unfolds seems to be addressed to an even broader audience than just the disciples.

Predictions and descriptions of the end times are serious business. We want to believe that history, and our small, brief role in it, is going someplace, that it

Pastoral Perspective

Jesus and the disciples leave the temple, whose stately splendor embodies enduring religious tradition, and they travel to the Mount of Olives. Sitting on this symbolic promontory jutting forth from the familiar old order into a fearsome future, Jesus speaks to his disciples: "See that you are not alarmed."

Thomas G. Long writes, "The rock-solid temple with all its trusted and established structures was behind them; the cross with all its fearful uncertainties and demanding sacrifices was ahead of them."[1] Like Jesus and the disciples, like Matthew and his first-century audience, Christ followers in every time and place live between the established structures of the past and the uncertainty of the future. How then are present-day disciples to stave off a sense of anxiety and alarm as they live life while perched on the promontory of the present? Jesus does not provide an explicit checklist for such living. Implicit in his words, however, is the counsel that disciples are to be patient and prayerful as they watch and wait, all the while keeping their hearts open to signs of God's coming.

Presbyterian pastor Carol Clark had gone to the hospital to visit someone, and it started out badly. She had a hard time finding a parking place. She got

---

1. Jack Dean Kingsbury, *Matthew: Structure, Christology, Kingdom* (Minneapolis: Fortress Press, 1989), 28.

1. Thomas G. Long, *Matthew* (Louisville, KY: Westminster John Knox Press, 1997), 266.

Feasting on the Gospels

Exegetical Perspective

This passage begins curiously. Why in verse 1 would the disciples point out the temple buildings if Jesus were just inside of them (21:12–17)? Were they not all in the temple with him? The Markan version (Mark 13:1–4) seems to clarify what the disciples were doing in the Matthean account; there, a single disciple focuses on the distinctiveness of the stones and buildings of the temple complex, thus providing the context for Jesus' subsequent invective against the central focus of Jewish worship.

Jesus' prediction in verse 2 are intended to shock his hearers and are tied to the fact that the temple is not just a celebrated religious relic; it is also the seat of the domination system that plays a large part in the oppression of the people. Although we might like to think of Jesus' words as a subsequent reflection from later Christian community who saw the temple in ruins, their rhetorical power in the moment that he spoke them should not be ignored. In Jesus' day they would have been a powerful pronouncement of the end of the temple, a product of the oppressive Herodian regime. This temple symbolized the corrupt institutional control of the worship of God, in league with the Roman overlords, a fact already made clear by Jesus' cleansing of the temple in 21:10–17. The verb *katalythēsetai* (v. 2) should be translated "will be overthrown" here, inasmuch as

Homiletical Perspective

With the opening words of chapter 24, "As Jesus came out of the temple and was going away," the setting for Matthew's story has made a sudden and dramatic shift. No longer in the temple, now outside of the city walls, we are on our way to another mountaintop. It is as if the change in setting signals the need for a change of perspective at this point in the story. We have been in and around Jerusalem since Jesus' triumphal entry in chapter 21, and there is a sense here that what Jesus has to say to his disciples requires a different vantage point, a different view. Jesus' next entry into Jerusalem will be far less celebratory. Since the disciples are almost too close to see the truth, a change of scenery becomes necessary.

It is only once Jesus and the disciples leave the city, that there can be some distance to talk truthfully about what is to come. The disciples, looking over their shoulders, casting their eyes back on the glory of the city and its temple, reflect the very nature of the human response when we start to imagine what lies ahead and when what lies ahead begins to invoke concern, uncertainty, and even fear. We look back, because looking forward is just too difficult, and we see only what we want to see.

There is something very touching in this moment, as if we catch a glimpse of the disciples longing for what could have been. Note that the actual feelings

Theological Perspective

is not just "one damn thing after another," with no purpose. When such prognostications help explain tragic events, such as the destruction of the holy place or anything once held sacred and meaningful, we are ready to listen. The alternative, the threat of purposelessness, is intolerable. There is, though, also a danger in "reading the signs" of history in search of a deeper or larger purpose.

As Stanley Hauerwas has suggested in his analysis of Matthew, both conservative and liberal Christians fall prey to the temptation to "read the signs" for their own particular purposes. Some take the language of war and famine literally, and posit that this or that particular contemporary event marks "the beginning of the end." Others, less literal, still seek to "determine the meaning and direction of history."[2] Both make the mistake that is suggested by the disciples' questions: we get fixated on wanting to know (or claiming to know) the specifics of the when and the what, and we miss the fact that Matthew's Jesus is offering instructions for a state of attentive readiness.

Apocalyptic discourse such as that found in Matthew 24–25 offers the promise of meaning in history, specifically that there is meaning and purpose to be found in tragic, devastating historical events. We are told that "nation will rise against nation, . . . and there will be famines and earthquakes" (v. 7). Matthew's community lived in a time of upheaval, of social and especially religious disarray, as do we. We welcome the implied consolation: although things are rough now, "this is but the beginning of the birth pangs" (v. 8). A new era will be born.

While grabbing on to the hope that these words offer, we must not be led into the temptation to justify the atrocities of our time in the name of some imagined and hoped-for future good. As the Jewish philosopher Emmanuel Levinas has warned, there is an important moral difference between finding meaning in our own suffering and justifying the suffering of others. For Levinas, suffering is a "given," it is "unassumable"; all that we can ultimately say about suffering is that it is useless, it is for nothing.[3]

The disciples ask about the end of the age: "when will this be, and what will be the sign of your coming?" (v. 3). Jesus does not answer these questions. Instead he warns, "Beware that no one leads you astray" (v. 4). He goes on to speak of "wars and rumors of wars . . . famines and earthquakes in

2. Stanley Hauerwas, *Matthew* (Grand Rapids: Brazos, 2006), 204.
3. Emmanuel Levinas, "Useless Suffering," trans. Richard Cohen, in *The Provocation of Levinas: Rethinking the Other*, ed. Robert Bernasconi and David Wood (London: Routledge, 2002), cited in *The Problem of Evil: A Reader*, ed. Mark Larrimore (Malden, MA: Blackwell, 2001), 371.

Pastoral Perspective

lost several times finding the gift shop. After finally locating it, she went in and bought one of those big Tweety Bird balloons, thinking that this would cheer up the very sick Tweety Bird fan whom she had come to visit. She got on the elevator with the Tweety Bird balloon bouncing off her head but then got off at the wrong place. So she got back on when the next elevator came and went back down to the desk to ask directions. She got back on the elevator, all the time with the balloon bobbing about. Finally, she found the room of the person that she had come to visit, and there was a sign that read, "Please check in at the Nurse's Station before entering." So she went to the desk. The woman sitting at the desk was on the phone, doing a very good job of studiously avoiding meeting Carol's eye. Finally she turned toward Carol and looked at her with a "what can I do for you, you irritant on a dog's back?" gaze. Carol said, "I'm here to see Jennifer Smith in Room 320, and the sign says to check here at the nurse's station." The woman said, "Hold on."

So Carol was standing there, holding her Tweety Bird balloon, and her back was hurting, but she was remaining calm. Then the woman said, "I can't help you. You have to check with her nurse Susan before you go in there," and then turned around in her swivel chair and looked off into space. Carol said, "Excuse me. Where might I find Susan?" With a look on her face as if she had just run over a basket of rotten eggs, the woman at the desk slowly pointed to the back of a nurse, just as a door marked "Staff Only" closed behind her. So Carol, aware that her back was still hurting and simultaneously thinking about her to-do list, which was lengthening with every tick of the clock, moved away from this delightful woman. Then suddenly a tiny unbidden thought poked its head up out of the irritation and anger that was swirling around in Carol's head. "I'm just going to stand and watch," Carol thought. "If I have to stand here a half an hour, I'm just going to stand here and watch."

So she did. For about fifteen minutes, Carol just stood and watched. She saw so many things that she would have missed otherwise. She saw Nurse Susan come and go, once to the phone with some intensity, her face heavy, her voice urgent. She saw an older man come out of a room in his blue striped hospital gown, holding it together in the back with one hand and pushing the IV cart with the other, saying, "I'm thirsty." From where Carol was standing, she could see five rooms, each of them with people who were alone and sick, and the thought came to her, "Pray

the destruction of the temple represents the over-throwing of a repressive human system in favor of God's reign.

Further, the destruction of the temple would have evoked memories of the exile in 587 BCE, when the Solomonic temple was destroyed by Nebuchadnezzar's forces. With its demise came the end of a particular stream of Zion theology that considered the temple God's eternal throne on earth. Although its demise was a tragedy of unparalleled dimensions, it paradoxically allowed for significant theological evolution in Yahwistic faith. Such concepts as Torah, book-based faith, vicarious suffering, and individual responsibility would not have been so prominent, had the temple remained intact. Jesus' pronouncement of the end of the temple in these verses would have evoked a similar theological disruption. It would have made space for a new understanding of atonement, independent of a single ornate building. The image of the tragic death of one sacred institution was itself pregnant with new possibility, of a new vision, of a new kingdom predicated on the Christ event.

As Jesus sits on the Mount of Olives, foretelling an end and making space for new beginnings, his disciples privately approach him in verse 3 asking the crucial question: "When will this be?" They ask for a sign (*sēmeion*) of the end of the age, and they add curious language about Jesus' "coming" (*parousia*). Though common to us, contemporary interpreters should note how unusual this would sound to the original audience, for the disciples to ask about the "coming" of the still-present Jesus.

The desire for the "sign of your coming" remains a persistent issue for Christians, as we continue to note appeals to all manner of issues—from climate change to prophesied doom dates to international tensions—as harbingers of the end of times and the return of Christ. This verse presumes that Jesus will at some time be gone, which Peter has denied (16:22), and the disciples do not really seem to understand. In fact, it is really only in this chapter after verse 22, as the "little apocalypse" unfolds, that the full connection between the Messiah and the *eschaton* seems to be evident in Matthew. It is interesting that Jesus' reference to the destruction of the temple, an event that Matthew's listeners would have known as a historical incident of the Judean exile, seems to be enough for them to imagine a shift in their conversation from the historical age to the apocalyptic age and the end of the world.

As he begins his response in verses 4–5, Jesus notes that there will be some who will seek to

of the disciples are not narrated. There are no exclamations of wonder or amazement about the temple, as in Mark, or any marveling about the temple's beauty, as in Luke. There is simply a drawing attention to its buildings: "his disciples came to point out to him the buildings of the temple" (v. 1).

This odd comment, however, reveals the heart of Matthew's christological claim. Jesus is God with us, Immanuel. If this is true, then the temple can no longer be the home of God. The emphasis here on the buildings reiterates this truth. The disciples do not point out the size of the temple or how it is adorned, but simply note its buildings. Buildings do not have permanence. They can topple over, fall down, be brought to rubble on the ground. This brief exchange about the temple foreshadows Jesus' promise at the end of Matthew's Gospel: "And remember, I am with you always, to the end of the age" (28:20). The presence of God cannot be confined to a building, but in the risen Christ will be with the disciples forever.

In many respects, Jesus' response to the temple comment from the disciples is meant to be the exact opposite of how it sounds. Whereas our initial reaction to Jesus' words might have been, "Well, that seems pretty hopeless," the disciples would have heard the reverberations of hope in the margins of Jesus' predictions. Chapter 24 of Matthew's Gospel is frequently called Matthew's "little apocalypse" or the "eschatological discourse." At the heart of apocalyptic literature is encouragement when all hope seems lost.

To some extent, this is Jesus at his pastoral best. That which looks like devastation and defeat will be God's victory. Out of the theological turmoil and confusion surrounding the destruction of the temple will be a new presence and power of God. Out of the suffering and death of their Messiah will be new life forever. God's new way of being in the world will turn a cross into resurrection and an empty tomb into eternal life.

Once again, the disciples find themselves alone with Jesus on a mountain. If the Sermon on the Mount was Jesus' inaugural address, announcing the coming of the kingdom of heaven, this mountaintop experience describes what happens when kingdoms collide. To be the salt of the earth and the light of the world does not come without cost in a world that rejects the love of God at every turn. New creation cannot be born into the world without the pains of labor. Putting these two mountaintop moments in conversation with each other can yield much for the interpretation and significance of Jesus' claims, as the

Matthew 24:1–8

Theological Perspective

various places" (vv. 6, 7), but his immediate response is an advisory warning. We must be vigilant and avoid being led astray, but we also are told to remain calm and not to be alarmed, "for this must take place, but the end is not yet. . . . All this is but the beginning of the birth pangs" (vv. 6, 8). We must live in a state of apocalyptic readiness, but note that this requires a rather paradoxical stance. On the one hand, we can be assured that the horrors of the day (both human-made and natural disasters) are what must take place; they are all part of the larger, cosmic battle and are unavoidable. Also (as if that is not enough!), on the other hand, we are reminded that the end is not yet. This is it, but not yet *it*. We must get ready and be prepared. Time, quite literally, is of the essence.

Perhaps, though, Jesus does answer their (and our) questions, through indirection, and we need to take seriously the implications of his answer. Perhaps we are easily led astray because of our anxiety and our need to know the signs; we look for signs, for answers, and find them, and are therefore easily misled. Like a Zen master, Jesus offers an answer that seems at first glance to be absurd; it seems a disjunction, it does not seem to follow from the question. However, ultimately it does function to reconnect the questioner to what is more fundamentally true. Despite the fact that chapter 24 goes on to give a fairly detailed account of the plot of the end times (then . . . and then . . . and then . . .), one that follows carefully the Hebrew prophets, the crucial warning here seems to be "do not be led astray." It is as if Jesus is offering the needed words of chastisement as well as a call to attention: "Focus, people!"

HANNAH SCHELL

Pastoral Perspective

for them. Pray for the old man with the IV. Pray for the nurses. Pray for all these people who are alone and sick. Pray for the irritating woman at the desk." So she just stood there, Tweety Bird balloon in her hand, and she prayed, not for anything in particular, just lifting them up into the light of God.

Carol says, "Now this would be a really great story if Nurse Susan had come and had seen me standing there; and seeing my face lit with compassion and a tender smile, she told me what a rough day it had been, and I told her that I understood, and Nurse Susan poured out her soul, and I prayed with her and handed her the Tweety Bird balloon as a benedictory gift. But that is not what happened. What happened was that Susan came out and asked, 'What do you want?' and I said, 'May I go into Room 320? The sign said to check at the nurse's station.' Susan said, 'That sign should have been taken down yesterday.' I said, 'Okay. Thank you.'"[2]

Carol said that this would be a good story if all the loose ends had been tied up in a nice, neat theological bow; but she did not really mean that. The story is so much better and truer the way it actually happened. What Carol discovered when she took the time simply to watch and to wait as a Christ follower, is that you get saved. You get saved from your irritation, and you get saved from your anxiety, and you discover—much to your surprise—that you are no longer alarmed.

ELIZABETH MCGREGOR SIMMONS

---

2. Carol Clark, unpublished sermon preached at Montreat West Youth Conference 2000, Fort Collins, CO.

deceive his followers regarding the moments of the end of times. The notion of many (*polloi*) coming in his name suggests that the attempts to deceive will be systematic and voluminous and that, worse, they will be largely successful, for "they will lead many astray" (v. 5). This concern for people being led astray by an abundance of upstart theologies is likely a common concern for those in the first generations of the Christian community, as "orthodox" Christian theology had yet to crystallize.

There were likely many assumptions about the Parousia of Jesus that were common among the people. The claim "I am the Messiah" is not one that Jesus explicitly makes at any point in this or any of the other Gospels, although others make that claim about him, and he may consent to a parallel claim about himself in Pilate's interrogation of him (27:11; cf. Mark 15:2; Luke 23:3; John 18:34–37). The presumptuousness of the personal claim of messianism by the pretentious should itself be enough to indicate that the claimant is false; for Jesus himself, while never denying that claim, is far more subtle in his acknowledgment of his messianic identity, perhaps not wanting such a role to be misunderstood.

"Wars and rumors of wars" are tragic events that often beset humankind (vv. 6–7). Such events are common to human existence but should not be interpreted as definitive signs of the end. These events are common to apocalyptic imagery, as are dualistic battles between cosmic forces, signs and omens, and the inbreaking of the heavenly realm into historical time that we will see subsequently in this vision, noting the disrupted state of affairs that accompanies the *eschaton*.

Here, however, we are told that these are not the signs that should alarm us. In some ways this passage is reminiscent of 1 Kings 19:11–13, where Elijah expects God's presence to be manifest in elements of traditional theophanies but finds God instead in the "sound of the soft whisper" (NRSV "sound of sheer silence"; RSV "a still small voice"; NIV "a gentle whisper"). God is nothing if not unpredictable, and God's arrival will itself be evidenced in unexpected ways. These battles and catastrophes are just the "birth pangs" of the end, not its manifestation (v. 8).

RODNEY S. SADLER JR.

first words of his ministry, and now here as some of his last.

What has happened in the meantime? What difference does it make that these mountain experiences frame Jesus' ministry and his private occasions with his disciples? That these mountaintop discourses bookend Jesus' time with his disciples suggests that a change in perspective is often necessary and even essential for a life of faith and discipleship. It is important to ask how a new view of the world shapes one's beliefs. The mountaintops in Matthew are not simply lovely locales, but reinforce the belief that a different outlook on the world is now vital because of the inbreaking of the kingdom of heaven. Things cannot look or be the same anymore. The presence of Jesus has turned the theological kaleidoscope so that whole new shapes and colors come into focus, about God, about Jesus and his ministry, about ourselves, and about the world.

The disciples want a sign, both for Jesus' coming and for the end of the age. We always want signs, because they give us direction, they point us on the way; they are comforting because they give us a kind of certainty about our future. However, there can be no sign for either occasion, because Matthew's portrait of Jesus collapses these two events together: the end of the age is present here and now because God has already come in Immanuel.

It is no accident that the closing words of the Gospel of Matthew—and therefore Jesus' last words to his disciples—are identical to this moment in the story. When Jesus says, "And remember, I am with you always, to the end of the age," we discover that *when* Jesus comes is not really the right question. Jesus is present and will be present always. There will be no time or interval without him being with us. This is the promise of Immanuel.

KAROLINE M. LEWIS

Matthew 24:9–28

⁹"Then they will hand you over to be tortured and will put you to death, and you will be hated by all nations because of my name. ¹⁰Then many will fall away, and they will betray one another and hate one another. ¹¹And many false prophets will arise and lead many astray. ¹²And because of the increase of lawlessness, the love of many will grow cold. ¹³But the one who endures to the end will be saved. ¹⁴And this good news of the kingdom will be proclaimed throughout the world, as a testimony to all the nations; and then the end will come.

¹⁵"So when you see the desolating sacrilege standing in the holy place, as was spoken of by the prophet Daniel (let the reader understand), ¹⁶then those in Judea must flee to the mountains; ¹⁷the one on the housetop must not go down to take what is in the house; ¹⁸the one in the field must not turn back to get a coat. ¹⁹Woe to those who are pregnant and to those who are nursing

Theological Perspective

Having warned the disciples not to be led astray in 24:3–8 (a message that continues in these verses), Jesus counsels patience and the necessity for endurance in the face of great suffering. A crucial line comes in verse 13: "The one who endures to the end will be saved" (cf. 10:22).

At one level, 24:9–28 is a continuation of Jesus' description of the details of what the "end of the age" will look like, and is part of the larger apocalyptic discourse of chapters 24–25. In these verses, where Matthew more loosely adapts Mark, he does not so much relay the plot of the end times; rather, he warns and advises about the coming time of great suffering, "such as has not been from the beginning of the world until now" and never will be again (v. 21). The suffering that is to come will be unique in its magnitude.

When the moment of crisis comes, it will be definitive and require urgent response. Making explicit reference to the book of Daniel, especially to "the abomination that desolates" (Dan. 9:27; 11:31; 12:11), Matthew draws an analogy to the "desolating sacrilege," the statue erected in the temple by Antiochus IV Epiphanes in 167 BCE. While Luke uses the phrase from Daniel to describe the destruction of Jerusalem in 70 CE, Matthew leaves the analogous

Pastoral Perspective

Barbara Brown Taylor remembers that one of her professors once told her that the second coming of Christ was an idea cooked up by some church father with only two fingers. "The truth, he said, is that Christ comes again, and again, and again—that God has placed no limit on coming to the world, but is always on the way to us here and now."[1]

In contrast to the nearsighted, two-fingered church father referred to by the professor, Matthew, in including this speech of Jesus in his Gospel, holds up ten fingers to past and present readers. Christ comes again, and again, and again, Matthew emphasizes. When he comes, believers are not to be surprised that their old lives are upended.

According to Jesus, one manifestation of his coming is internal division within the community of faith. During the first century, the division was marked by "many [who] fall away" and people who "betray one another and hate one another" and "many false prophets [who] arise and lead many astray" (vv. 10–11). In the twenty-first century, it might be a disagreement over theology or worship style, or the feeling that the church has gotten too

---

1. Barbara Brown Taylor, *The Seeds of Heaven: Sermons on the Gospel of Matthew* (Louisville, KY: Westminster John Knox Press, 2004), 113.

Feasting on the Gospels

infants in those days! ^{20}Pray that your flight may not be in winter or on a sabbath. ^{21}For at that time there will be great suffering, such as has not been from the beginning of the world until now, no, and never will be. ^{22}And if those days had not been cut short, no one would be saved; but for the sake of the elect those days will be cut short. ^{23}Then if anyone says to you, 'Look! Here is the Messiah!' or 'There he is!'—do not believe it. ^{24}For false messiahs and false prophets will appear and produce great signs and omens, to lead astray, if possible, even the elect. ^{25}Take note, I have told you beforehand. ^{26}So, if they say to you, 'Look! He is in the wilderness,' do not go out. If they say, 'Look! He is in the inner rooms,' do not believe it. ^{27}For as the lightning comes from the east and flashes as far as the west, so will be the coming of the Son of Man. ^{28}Wherever the corpse is, there the vultures will gather."

Exegetical Perspective

A brief overview of this complex section is in order before we examine specific details. There is a careful use of repeated words ("then," *tote*, in vv. 9, 10, 16; "many," *polloi*, in vv. 10–12) and themes (flight, false christs or prophets) that serves to emphasize the focal issues of this apocalyptic passage. As it begins in verse 9, the "then" statements suggest that the actions described follow those that preceded them in the prior pericope. Thus the tragic geopolitical and cosmological crises described above (vv. 6–7) mark the "birth pangs" of this apocalyptic period that is more fully evident here. The focus of verses 9–10 is on the negative impact of these times upon the faithful, who will suffer and die because of their fidelity (v. 9), and the internal divisions that will undermine the integrity of the community (v. 10). The recurrent use of the adjective "many" demonstrates the prevailing negativity of this period as "many" will "fall away" (v. 10), "many false prophets will arise" (v. 11), and many will have their "love . . . grow cold" (v. 12). Verse 13, about which more will be said below, becomes a focal verse in this overall passage, demonstrating Jesus' intent in describing the entire eschatological scenario. Finally, verse 14 offers the answer to the disciples' question back in verse 3 about the coming "end of the age." With this, the first section of this pericope concludes.

Homiletical Perspective

As if nation rising against nation, and kingdom against kingdom, and famines and earthquakes in various and sundry places were not enough, the continuation of Matthew's apocalyptic discourse brings on torture, hatred, suffering, and death. There seems to be no escape from the doomsday mood of this section of Matthew, but the truth of the matter is that Jesus is simply telling it like it is. If we view this section through the lens of a community whose temple, city, religious life, and construction of God have all been destroyed in one fell swoop by a foreign empire, it does little good not to state the obvious. This is a moment of truth for the disciples, their own personal "come to Jesus" talk. While we are far more comfortable with sugarcoating and placating our heartrending realities, Jesus does not allow for pretense and falsehood. In fact, when we ignore the truth, even in its difficulties, we can easily be led astray.

Jesus warns his disciples to be watchful for false Messiahs and false prophets who are capable of doing signs, much like what he can do. This is not unlike the description of the second beast in Revelation 13, who is also able to perform signs, to do "messiahlike" things. Therein lies the problem. That which is false, which is evil, which could lead us astray, can all too often have an appearance of

Matthew 24:9–28

Theological Perspective

historical event unspecified.[1] When the time comes, Matthew promises in verse 27, the signs will be unmistakably clear, like "lightning . . . from the east and flashes as far as the west." The challenge, Matthew's Jesus instructs, is to be ready and to be vigilant. Once more, we are warned not to be taken in by false messiahs and false prophets who "will produce great signs and omens" and potentially lead astray "even the elect" (v. 24). These passages teach how to endure the period between now and then. As Daniel likewise advised, "Happy are those who persevere" (Dan. 12:12).

In the previous verses Matthew has described political and even geological upheaval—nations fighting against nations, famines and earthquakes (24:7). Here, he turns his attention to the moral and spiritual confusion that will be a part of the unfolding turmoil. Jesus refers to "the increase of lawlessness [*anomia*]" and the effect that it can have on even the stalwart and the devout. The threat of disintegration will come not just from without but also from within the community: "many will fall away, and they will betray one another and hate one another. . . . The love of many will grow cold" (vv. 10, 12).

It would be easy to skim over these lines. However, as Daniel Harrington reminds us, predictions of communal discord (what Ezra called the "tumult of peoples") were an important aspect of Jewish apocalyptic writing.[2] Harrington suggests that these passages in Matthew 24 can be read as parallel to 2 Esdras 5:1–2, 9–10, which gives a slightly fuller account of the human toll that is taken with the increase of lawlessness. In this time, "the way of truth shall be hidden, and the land shall be barren of faith. Unrighteousness shall be increased . . . and all friends shall conquer one another; then shall reason hide itself, and wisdom shall withdraw into its chamber, and it shall be sought by many but shall not be found, and unrighteousness and unrestraint shall increase on earth." When the threat comes from outside the community, whether political or natural disaster, people can take refuge in their solidarity with each other. When the threat comes from within, when the community itself is in conflict, even the faithful are shaken, and they too will grow cold.

What is required is moral and spiritual endurance. Like a long-distance runner, the one who is able to endure to the end is the one who has trained

Pastoral Perspective

involved in politics, or a belief that the church is not involved enough in matters of social justice, that begins to fray the seams of congregational unity. The eyes of the members of the community become diverted from their previous steady focus upon the Christ; their ears close to the life-giving vibration of the good news, and, as Jesus so acutely presages, "the love of many will grow cold" (v. 12).

As this essay is being written, a congregation close to the writer is being riven by conflict. A news article noting the resignation of the lead pastor cites his leadership in accommodating traditional and contemporary preferences for worship without the kind of dissension created at other congregations about styles of worship. It refers to his continuing the congregation's legacy of social justice advocacy, including its embrace of a diverse membership. A lay leader in the congregation is quoted as saying, "I think most people who know and love him . . . think about the many times he has officiated at a funeral or been there for . . . a wedding. He's had an extraordinary emphasis on pastoral and hospital care. He's best known for that."

In a letter in which the pastor announced his departure to his congregation, he wrote: "This decision did not come to me easily. No doubt, most of you have heard that a vocal group of members is eager for my ouster. I hold no animosity toward them; they want the best for [the congregation], as do I. Others of you have urged me to 'stay and fight.' Our congregation has been torn apart in the past, and we have repaired it; but I am not confident that we could do so again. . . . It's really sad for me and not something I hoped or planned or wanted to do. But a vocal group of congregants made known their strong opposition to my . . . leadership. I decided my resignation was the only way to avoid a destructive and divisive situation in the congregation."

Jesus foretold destruction and division within the body of Christ. Matthew's first-century church experienced it, and the twenty-first-century church is identified far more often by fission than by fusion.

According to Jesus, destruction or division such as this is to be expected. Not only is it to be expected, but indeed this is a sign of Christ's coming again and again and again. In the face of the destruction and division that mark Christ's new age, believers are exhorted not to lose heart, but to view upheaval and disorientation as an opportunity to reorient themselves to the love of God that is manifest in Jesus and to endure to the end, for through their endurance "the good news of the kingdom will be proclaimed throughout the world."

---

1. My reading here depends heavily on Donald Senior, *Matthew* (Nashville: Abingdon Press, 1998), 269.
2. Daniel Harrington, *The Gospel of Matthew* (Collegeville, MN: Liturgical Press, 1991), 334.

Exegetical Perspective

As we approach verse 15, the focus of the passage has shifted to a discussion of the particulars of the end, including its chief marker (the arrival of the "devastating abomination" [my trans.], v. 15), the flight from Judea (vv. 16–20), the time of "great suffering" (vv. 21–22), the arrival of false christs and false prophets (*pseudochristoi* and *pseudoprophētai*, vv. 23–24), a brief intervening note about the sudden arrival of the "Son of Man" that answers the disciples' question about the Parousia of Christ from verse 3 (v. 27), and a final note about the inevitable success of the false prophets described in terms of "vultures" and carrion (v. 28). Thus, the disciples' original question is answered in two sections: verses 9–14 lead up to the end of the age, while verses 15–28 portray the end itself, immediately prior to the return of the Christ. The entire pericope frames this period with apocalyptic imagery.

As we examine the message of this passage, it becomes clear that being a Christian is not without its consequences. In verse 9 we see that the fidelity of Christians to their witness for Christ will lead them to be tortured and killed; they will become martyrs because of their witness to what God has done in Jesus. Being a Christian can get you killed; at least it could during the time of the early church. Perhaps more difficult than dying for Christ is living for Christ, even in the time of the early church. The alienation of those who live for Christ is the key concern in verse 9, for it suggests that affiliation of the follower with Christ alone is a cause for being hated by "all nations." Such universal disdain, however, is not to dissuade Christians from enduring the hardships they will encounter for the sake of his name. Though this passage is an apocalyptic text addressing a first-century community under the oppressive authority of the Roman Empire, the questions that it engenders are those faced by the Christian community in every subsequent generation.

The fears raised in verse 10 seem to be fears of the early community that people will recant their costly commitments to Christ and fall back into more comfortable patterns, leading to the decline of the nascent church. Worse, the fear is that the pressures from the larger world will cause rifts and infighting among those who are within the community and lead to its disintegration. Such fears seem to have been realized in the church at Corinth and in several of the seven Asian churches to whom John writes in his Apocalypse, among other places in the New Testament. Thus this fear is consistent with the concerns

Homiletical Perspective

what is good. Our perceptions of power and authority are tethered to our human expectations. This is perhaps one of the most difficult things about the incarnation.

When God becomes familiar, we then make God even more familiar, as if God's becoming human would then conform completely to our views of humanity. If God becomes human, it becomes all too easy to make God like us; to look for God in human ways and human forms; to hold God to our standards, thinking, hoping, praying, that we might finally "get" God. However, nothing that is coming down the pike for the disciples is going to help them understand God. In fact, it will be just the opposite for them and for Jesus.

Moving into the last chapters of this story, the disciples need a reality check, and so do we. The next few days for the lives of the disciples and for the life of Jesus are going to be nothing short of the kind of chaos experienced when the world as you knew it crashes down around you. Jesus' words to the disciples in this passage speak the truth about what we see, what we do not want to see, and call us to question in what we put our trust. They are important words for us to hear, acknowledge, and even speak in times when the lives we have constructed—and over which we think we have control—are crumbling all around us, falling into ruins and rubble like the buildings of the temple.

We might wonder if there can be anything hopeful to lift up, or if there are any words of encouragement in the midst of such catastrophe. While it may be necessary that Jesus states the obvious at this point, we desperately need something to shine some light into the bleak forecast that Jesus has presented. It is a little hard to find in this passage, but the claim that "this good news of the kingdom will be proclaimed throughout the world, as a testimony to all the nations; and then the end will come" witnesses to the abiding and ongoing proclamation of God's good news beyond what we can immediately see. The term "nations" will be used again in the last verses of Matthew's Gospel, typically known as the Great Commission.

The commissioning of Jesus' followers to go and make disciples of all nations, baptizing and teaching, assures them that the good news is possible beyond this moment and gives them a purpose beyond the pressing, despairing prophecies they have heard. There is a profound hope in such an invitation and partnership. It creates the possibility that you will survive and that you need to survive for the sake of

Matthew 24:9–28

Theological Perspective

well, keeps a steady pace, has deep resources from which to draw in order to keep going, and is not easily deterred or distracted. Spiritual endurance is not passive; it is neither resignation nor a "wait and see" attitude. The kind of endurance spoken of here is active; it requires hope and activity. Spiritual endurance in the face of human tumult is a grave and difficult thing. It requires believing in something beyond what is readily apparent. It requires a stoic patience that justice and righteousness will prevail but also continued commitment to practices that help ensure the prevailing of righteousness.

Kent Keith's "Paradoxical Commandments" exemplify these qualities of spiritual endurance: "People are illogical, unreasonable, and self-centered. Love them anyway. If you do good, people will accuse you of selfish ulterior motives. Do good anyway."[3] His commandments—often paraphrased and recast as a poem titled "Anyway"—are popular because they encourage an active faith in a hoped-for future in which truth and righteousness win out.

Concluding lines that were added as the commandments were turned into a poem counsel a kind of turning away from the world and other people, when they advise that "in the final analysis, it is between you and God; it was never between you and them anyway." All too often we embrace this message and invoke . . . the idea of "spiritual endurance" for the purposes of *self*-help Christianity. We imagine the world as an antagonistic environment where individuals must seek a competitive edge; but it is not about winning a race. When Matthew speaks of "the elect" in verses 22 and 24 (and again in v. 31), we must remember the communal nature of salvation. The elect are plural, and will be gathered. The ability to endure is not an individual achievement that is recognized with a prize. Endurance is active engagement with the world, alongside fellow men and women working together to mitigate the threats of lawlessness.

HANNAH SCHELL

Pastoral Perspective

During times of division and destruction, it is tempting to focus on what is being lost. Jesus, however, calls humanity back to the enduring love of God, which can never be lost or taken away. In one of William Sloane Coffin's sermons, he spoke of how years after the death of Gertrude Stein, her companion Alice B. Toklas gave tribute to Stein by saying, "It wasn't what Gertrude gave me, which was so much, it was what she never took away." Coffin then said, "I often think of God that way. What impresses me is not only what God gives, but what God never takes away. Put differently, it's a wonderful thing to be loved by someone who is never in competition with you, someone who wants only your well-being. God is that person."[2]

God's love is in you, Jesus says to every person and to the church; so endure to the end. People at school may grab your backpack and throw it on the ground and say things to you that make your heart hurt, but God's love is in you, and no one can take it away, so endure to the end. You may bump up against people in this world who wish you ill or you may lose your job or your marriage may fall apart or people you love may die and your whole world may seem to be a desolating sacrilege, but God's love is in you, and no one can take it away, so endure to the end. Your church may be full of gossip and lies, but God's love is in you, and no one can take it away, so endure to the end. The diagnosis may be grim and the hour of your death approaching, but God's love is in you, and no one can take it away, so endure to the end.

Endure to the end, Jesus says, because Christ is coming to you, to the church, and to the world, again and again and again!

ELIZABETH MCGREGOR SIMMONS

---

3. Kent Keith, *Anyway: The Paradoxical Commandments* (New York: Berkley Books, 2001). The poem "Anyway" is often attributed to Mother Teresa because a copy of it was found on the wall of a Calcutta orphanage where she worked.

2. William Sloane Coffin, *Living the Truth in a World of Illusions* (San Francisco: Harper & Row, 1985), 105.

known to have been prevalent in the larger Christian community during this time.

Verse 13 raises the focal concern for the entire pericope. Apocalyptic passages often provide a word of hope for those who are enduring or soon to be enduring great suffering and travail. The promise here is that the one who remains faithful and "endures" the difficulties that are to come will find salvation. This promise, like that in 1 Thessalonians 4:13–18 and in the scope of the Apocalypse of John, is meant to increase the faith of the community of believers by assuring them not only of the correctness of their way, but also of the certainty of their deliverance. Such words that remind us of God's providence can prove useful to contemporary communities enduring the travails that attend to life in the early twenty-first century as well. It is always helpful to be reminded that "the one who endures to the end will be saved."

The final moment that determines the advance of the end in this pericope is the universal proclamation of the "good news of the kingdom" (v. 14). God's justice is again revealed inasmuch as all nations (*pasin tois ethnesin*, v. 14) will be given the "good news of the kingdom." God's concern for the entirety of the world should not escape our notice. God is not a parochial deity concerned only for those of a single nationality, with a particular ideological perspective, or from similar backgrounds. It has always been part of God's plan to have a global orientation and to have the good news reach all, friends and enemies alike; at its root, the gospel that we proclaim is a message whose scope is universal.

RODNEY S. SADLER JR.

something beyond yourself. Of course, the question is, how does one get through what is to come, make it to the other side, or just plain survive?

The clue to this kind of endurance and fortitude is found in Jesus' words, "But the one who endures to the end will be saved" (v. 13). The verb translated as "endure" can also mean "continue, resist, stay behind, stand one's ground, hold out, survive." There is a sense that all of these meanings come into play when we think about what the disciples will face and when we are forced to look toward our own desolate predictions. In a literal sense, the word combines the verb "to remain" or "abide" with the preposition typically rendered as "under" or "below." An interpretation of "enduring to the end" could quite possibly communicate an impression of "staying, abiding, or remaining under." This compound word intimates that what is being experienced feels like a crushing weight.

In addition, the use of "to the end" in this passage and again in 28:20 implies that this end will not be reached alone. Jesus assures his disciples that he is in the midst of it all: "I am with you always." Jesus' promise of his future with them is brought back into the disciples' present reality. The good news in this particular call to endurance is that it is not simply one more coping mechanism or some sort of cheerful platitude to make us feel better. "The one who endures to the end" acknowledges that this reality is a profound burden, yet one that Jesus himself enters and knows.

This section of Matthew testifies to the theology of faith, a telling of the truth twice, so to speak: first about our brokenness, our sinfulness, our despair, and then about God's promises to us that allow us to look forward. While acknowledging the incredible challenges of the present, this passage continually looks forward, moving us not only into the postresurrection future of the end of the Gospel, but also beyond the pages of its story to speak into our own lives.

KAROLINE M. LEWIS

Matthew 24:29–41

²⁹"Immediately after the suffering of those days
the sun will be darkened,
   and the moon will not give its light;
the stars will fall from heaven,
   and the powers of heaven will be shaken.
³⁰Then the sign of the Son of Man will appear in heaven, and then all the tribes of the earth will mourn, and they will see 'the Son of Man coming on the clouds of heaven' with power and great glory. ³¹And he will send out his angels with a loud trumpet call, and they will gather his elect from the four winds, from one end of heaven to the other.

³²"From the fig tree learn its lesson: as soon as its branch becomes tender and puts forth its leaves, you know that summer is near. ³³So also, when you see

Theological Perspective

"Tell us, when will this be, and what will be the sign of your coming and of the end of the age?" In Matthew 24:29–41, Jesus gives only a partial answer to his disciples' question in verse 3. Although he tells them *what* the signs will be, he never tells them *when* he will return. Ironically, Jesus' incomplete answer offers a profound theological insight into his identity as Son of Man and as one who is both God and human.

One of the most beneficial ways to reflect theologically on this text is to focus on two elements: human anxiety about the future, and the human and divine natures of Jesus Christ. To begin, all people want to know what will happen to them, their families, and friends in the future. The first-century readers of Matthew's Gospel lived only one generation after Jesus. The Jerusalem temple had been destroyed, and Matthew's Jewish Christian audience was expecting Jesus' imminent return. They wanted guarantees about the future so they could better understand the political and religious instability of their time and put their hope in Jesus' return in glory. This text also testifies to the paradox of human existence. Although humans *should* be able to read the signs of the times, they most often do not. They fail to watch, they ignore the budding of the fig tree, and, like the people of Noah's time, they eat and

Pastoral Perspective

The imagery in these verses of Matthew is both poignant and provocative. Beginning with the "trumpet call" and the gathering of the "elect," this story invites a powerful sense of God's authority. At the same time, there is the clear reminder to be careful, as some are gathered up and others are left behind. The commitments of the writer of Matthew compel the hearers to be steadfast in the midst of what feels like an unfriendly or unsafe world around them.

This passage, in particular, reminds me how Scripture can sometimes evoke more fear than it does compassion. There are times when our feelings of insecurity or threats from others—those with whom we deeply disagree, or those who make us uncomfortable because they do not fit our normative way of seeing the world—move us to speak in ways that foster a fear-based religion. We need to exercise care in reading this passage today, because religion based on retribution or damnation does not compel people into the steadfast faith in which the writer of this passage trusts. Where we see only condemnation and violence, the early Christians likely also saw a reassuring acknowledgment of God's guiding hand through the chaos of history.

Fear, in and of itself, is not a negative emotion. The study of neuroscience and psychology suggests that fear is a basic emotion that arose first in

all these things, you know that he is near, at the very gates. ³⁴Truly I tell you, this generation will not pass away until all these things have taken place. ³⁵Heaven and earth will pass away, but my words will not pass away.

³⁶"But about that day and hour no one knows, neither the angels of heaven, nor the Son, but only the Father. ³⁷For as the days of Noah were, so will be the coming of the Son of Man. ³⁸For as in those days before the flood they were eating and drinking, marrying and giving in marriage, until the day Noah entered the ark, ³⁹and they knew nothing until the flood came and swept them all away, so too will be the coming of the Son of Man. ⁴⁰Then two will be in the field; one will be taken and one will be left. ⁴¹Two women will be grinding meal together; one will be taken and one will be left."

Exegetical Perspective

After Jesus' prediction of the destruction of the temple (24:2), his disciples ask him when these events will occur and what will be the sign of his coming and of the end of the age (24:3). Jesus' long, winding answer, describing times of upheaval and immense suffering, now finally addresses "the coming of the Son of Man." Modern readers usually construe the coming of the Son of Man in terms of the final judgment of individuals, with but two possible outcomes, salvation or judgment. Matthew's focus in these verses, however, is on the judgment of human empires, the comprehensive reach of the Son's authority, and the certainty of his coming.

In the prophetic tradition, the "day of the Lord" is frequently associated with astral portents like those that precede the Son of Man's coming (v. 29). They signal God's judgment of the nations and empires that oppose God's rule and enslave God's people (e.g., Isa. 13:10, Amos 5:20, Ezek. 32:7–8, Joel 2:2). Daniel 7:13–14, which depicts the end of human empires and the everlasting dominion of the Son of Man, provides the image of his "coming on the clouds of heaven" (24:30). More than the judgment of individual sinners and saints, the coming of the Son of Man means the end of idolatrous, violent, and oppressive human rule, whether of Egypt, Assyria, Rome, the Jerusalem authorities, or any other imperial power.

Homiletical Perspective

Sermon preparation is generally easier when we know what the text is all about. After all, if Scripture is going to speak to us here and now, it helps if we know what it was saying there and then. So here, with this passage from Matthew, we are at something of a disadvantage. Is Jesus speaking of things that were destined to happen soon, like the fall of Jerusalem, which amounted to the end of the world for Israel? Is he, rather, talking about the end of the world in a greater, cosmic sense? Scholars disagree, and we try to follow their arguments while we ponder falling stars, trumpet blasts, and fig trees. It is no wonder if we feel tempted to give up and to check out the other readings instead.

Sticking with this passage, however, it is best if we set it in its wider context. Earlier in the chapter the disciples have asked Jesus, "What will be the sign of your coming and of the end of the age?" (24:3). In other words, when are you going to reveal yourself in power and bring in the new order? Jesus had given them cause to think this was going to happen soon. The disciples had been pointing with awe and wonder at the great temple that dominated the city of Jerusalem, and Jesus had informed them that this was due for demolition, that it would soon be attacked and razed to the ground. The disciples assumed that this would be the catastrophe that would usher in God's

Matthew 24:29–41

Theological Perspective

drink when they should be watching for God's activity in human history.

This brings us to one of the pitfalls of this text—interpreting verses 29–41 as a way to calm human anxiety about the future. Too often people have relied on this passage when estimating the precise day of the coming or return (*parousia*) of Jesus Christ or when predicting what political and ecological events will accompany the last days. It is interesting that some scholars and preachers use eschatological passages like Matthew 24–25 to interpret current events such as natural disasters or to judge who will be left. After all, does not this text testify to human anxiety about the future, the limits of reason, and human inability to read the signs of the times? "But about that day and hour no one knows" (v. 36). There is a richer theological fruit to harvest from this passage, however. These verses have much to teach us about who Jesus Christ is as the Son of Man, and they offer wisdom about his divinity and humanity.

One of the most fascinating theological claims comes in verse 36, when Jesus refers to himself as the Son of Man and says that even *he* does not know the hour of his return. What does this say about who Jesus is as God with us? The expression "Son of Man" is the subject of numerous sermons, commentaries, scholarly books, and articles. At the risk of oversimplification, one can discern three significant streams of interpretation. First, several New Testament scholars, such as Barnabas Lindars, argue that the expression "Son of Man" was not used in the Jewish world of Jesus' time to refer to an apocalyptic messiah. Lindars suggests instead that "Son of Man" may have been Jesus' way of referring to himself as a member of a specific class of persons. In other words, Jesus was simply saying, "a man in my position."[1]

A second proposal suggests that Jesus never used the expression himself. Rather, the Gospel authors added the designation to associate Jesus with the Son of Man sayings found in the book of Daniel (7:13–14). Even Old Testament scholars, though, do not agree on the meaning of "Son of Man" in the book of Daniel. It may have indicated a human leader, prophet, or king who would represent the Jewish people before God, or it may have denoted an apocalyptic leader who would return to establish God's kingdom on earth.

A third and more modest interpretation argues that since Matthew's Gospel was written for a Jewish

Pastoral Perspective

our earliest encounters with danger. With a feeling of threat the amygdala—that part of our brain that moves into reaction-and-protection mode—steps up its pace. In the face of fear, we may withdraw or move into the characteristic fight-or-flight response, or we may be paralyzed and unable to access any sense of agency or ability to take action. We also know that some fear is actually designed to protect us, as it engages our more watchful responses. Learned responses to danger accumulate and are stored in our memory systems over time, so that they may be accessed when they are needed. While heightened fear can hijack our other capacities to think rationally and deliberately, it can also keep us mindful of the potential for danger. Our brain and our being respond in ways that are designed to protect us. In moments of fear, it is possible for our more deliberate and rational processes slowly to emerge as we recognize that not all experiences of fear are the same.[1]

It is important to remember that the kind of fear that some people live with constantly, or cumulative fear, can function negatively in our personal and spiritual lives. Such fear often makes people feel as if they are always living on the edge of danger. Those who survive the trauma of war, the abuse of childhood, the ongoing assault of violence, or the threat of annihilation know what it means to live in a constant state of heightened fear or impending doom. Such experiences can leave people feeling paralyzed and reactive. Often we refer to persons who are survivors of daily heightened levels of fear as those who bear the symptoms of posttraumatic stress. Once again, the brain and our emotions work together in ways that protect us, but that can also immobilize us or stand in the way of our efforts to live full and healthy lives.

What rests between the fear that functions to keep us safe and the fear that traumatizes us is a more generalized apprehension that is nurtured by the daily violence in the world around us. Those who live with uncertainty about their safety or with the vulnerability of marginalization—those who experience daily the very real threats of racism, heterosexism, classism, or other oppressions that keep many people feeling insecure on a daily basis—develop a wisdom that is important to their survival. By constantly scanning the horizon in an attempt to be aware of any emerging threat, people can develop

---

1. Barnabas Lindars, *Jesus, Son of Man: A Fresh Examination of the Son of Man Sayings in the Gospels in the Light of Recent Research* (Grand Rapids: Eerdmans, 1983), 23.

1. Louis Cozolino, *The Neuroscience of Human Relationships* (New York: W. W. Norton, 2006), 247.

Exegetical Perspective

The authority granted to the Son of Man reaches across the dimensions of cosmic geography, including the earthly (human) and divine realms, and the astral regions between. English translations obscure Matthew's precise nuances in the use of "heaven" and "heavens" (far more common in Matthew) by employing the singular "heaven" for both. In Matthew the singular form (used in vv. 29d and 30a, c) signifies the sky or air, that is, the upper portion of the earthly realm, in contrast to the plural "heavens" (vv. 29e and 31c), which designates the divine realm. The coming of the Son of Man is thus first evident in the darkening of sun, moon, and stars (v. 29b–d)—the bodies that govern day and night in the earthly realm (Gen. 1:16–18). His coming also shakes the powers of the "heavens," the divine realm itself (v. 29e). The "sign of the Son of Man" is visible in "the sky," and he comes on "the clouds of the sky with power and great glory" (v. 30). In verse 31 (cf. Mark 13:27) the Son's own angels gather the elect both from the "four winds" of the earth and from one end of "the heavens" (the divine realm) to the other. The Son of Man's authority, both to judge and to redeem, extends into every nook and cranny, every dimension of life.

The enigmatic sayings in verses 32–35 have generated endless speculation about the nature of the events—"all these things" (vv. 33, 34)—that precede the coming of the Son of Man, but their primary purpose is simply to affirm the certainty of his coming, especially in the face of the trials Jesus and his disciples after him will endure. In 24:8 "all these things" (false prophets, wars, famines, etc., vv. 3–7) signal not the end, but "the beginning of the birth pangs" (vv. 6, 7). "All these things" may also refer to the events that transpire in Jerusalem, culminating in Jesus' death and resurrection, when he is granted "all authority in heaven and on earth" (28:18). What is certain, however, is that the Son of Man is coming, just as certainly as summer follows the end of spring, signaled by the leafing of the fig tree (vv. 32–33).

The claim that "this generation will not pass away until all these things have taken place" (v. 34) has led many to assert that Jesus miscalculated the proximity of his own return, even though in verse 36 he affirms his ignorance of the time. Modern readers presume that "this generation" refers simply to Jesus' contemporaries, whether his disciples or others. Matthew, however, seems to use "this generation" more to designate a particular ancestry or lineage, such as the (evil) generation (of Cain, 23:31–36) that is preparing to kill Jesus. In Matthew, every occurrence

Homiletical Perspective

new creation, that out of the ruins of the temple God would raise up a whole new world.

It may be that the community to whom Matthew is writing some years after Jesus' death—and indeed after the destruction of the temple—is wondering when this new world is going to appear. People who thought that they would see this world out are dying. History seems to be dragging its feet. So Matthew is reminding them of Jesus' words, "About that day and hour no one knows, neither the angels of heaven, nor the Son, but only the Father" (v. 36). Here Jesus takes us back first to the days of Noah, when great storm clouds were gathering over the world and people were living life as usual, oblivious to the threat that was about to engulf them. He goes on to speak of two men in a field and two women grinding at a mill: suddenly two are gone and two are left. These are images of the hour of crisis that is to come.

What we might focus on here, however, quite apart from the end of the world, is Jesus' depiction of normal human life. Forget for now about the end of time. Forget about the return of Christ, whatever that might mean. What we have here is a picture of the world as it is, all too familiar to us.

The former U.S. secretary of defense, Donald Rumsfeld, was famous for his sometimes garbled rhetoric. Speaking about the intelligence surrounding the Iraq War, Rumsfeld famously said, "As we know, there are known knowns. There are things we know we know. We also know there are known unknowns. That is to say, we know there are some things we do not know. But there are also unknown unknowns, the ones we don't know we don't know."[1] This is what Jesus, albeit in less tangled language, is telling us. There are things in the world, says Jesus, that are known and that can be anticipated. Look at the fig tree. When its shoots appear, you know that summer is near. There is pattern and order and regularity in the world, the very basis of science and technology, and it means that we have a measure of control, without which life would not be viable.

There are also, however, "known unknowns." Life is ordered and reliable, but we know that it is also precarious and unpredictable. However much we may feel in control, we are always vulnerable. We know that we are always susceptible to the unexpected and the unplanned that suddenly throws our routine lives into turmoil and confusion. This is the hour of crisis, when the abyss opens beneath us; it comes in

1. http://www.defense.gov/transcripts/transcript.aspx?transcriptid=2636; accessed February 12, 2012.

Matthew 24:29–41

Theological Perspective

audience, the Gospel author may have used the designation "Son of Man" to point to the uniqueness of Jesus and portray him as the man who fulfilled many of the prophetic claims and eschatological hopes found in the Hebrew Bible and the hearts of the Jewish Christians.

This complex passage from Matthew contains yet another claim that has challenged biblical scholars and theologians. Verse 36 indicates that Jesus Christ does not know the precise time of the Parousia. If Jesus does not know, how can Christians confess him as fully divine and fully human? Does not divinity imply omniscience? Scholar Francis Gumerlock identifies several different ways that theologians have interpreted Jesus' supposed ignorance.[2] Augustine—one of the most important theologians of the early church—argued that Jesus was speaking figuratively. Jesus knew, but chose not to reveal the time of his return. Bishop Gregory of Tours suggested that the term "Son" actually refers to the people of God (not to Jesus Christ), meaning that the church does not know when the Parousia will occur. Other theologians—such as Athanasius of Alexandria—taught what became accepted as the orthodox interpretation, namely, that only the *human* nature of Jesus Christ was ignorant. Athanasius wrote, "He knows also the hour of the end of all things, as the Word, though as man He is ignorant of it, for ignorance is proper to man."[3] Ironically, this way of reading "But about that day and hour no one knows" emphasizes one of the central claims of the Christian faith: that Jesus Christ was a true human being, with creaturely limitations, as well as God with us. This text—which can be problematic because Jesus did not know everything—actually witnesses to the good news that God became fully human, and therefore humans need not be anxious about what is to come, because our future is in God.

MARY ELISE LOWE

Pastoral Perspective

courage and the capacity to persevere in the midst of daily fear. The strength of the gospel of hope, which counters genuine fear and does not allow for religious commitments to bear fruit through hate or violence, empowers people to move boldly into the world, not to escape from it.

Fear is a God-given emotion that functions both positively and negatively in our lives. There are specific times when fear is helpful, pushing us to react immediately to something around us: a parent sees a child running toward a road and instinctively runs toward the danger; a farmer sees one of the animals in trouble and reacts with a knowledge born out of experience and wisdom; a potential car accident in front of us compels us to swerve out of the way, lest we become entangled in the twisting of metal; an unemployed worker recognizes the family's need for food and shelter and strategizes about how best to move to action.

In the right moments, fear is an appropriate response to situations we encounter in our lives. Fear captures our attention, moves us to react in ways that protect us and those whom we love, and assists us in seeing new possibilities in the midst of turbulent times. Seeing this capacity for fear to motivate positive action allows us to see this text as more than simply inducing a fear-based belief.

Contemporary readers of this text may see it as more fearsome than hopeful. The writer of Matthew, however, is not invested in scaring people into belief, but in encouraging the listeners of the Gospel toward trust, living out of their redemptive experience of Jesus. It is written to Christians to help them interpret their experience of hostile opposition from their neighbors as part of the sufferings of the end times—the impending "day of the Lord." By placing their sufferings in the context of God's wider work, they are swept up in God's sovereignty. We are called to believe not out of fear but out of a genuine desire to listen for "the trumpet" and to live the abundant life. This eschatological discourse—like most apocalyptic literature—is designed to engender hope in God's mighty and mysterious works of salvation.

JORETTA L. MARSHALL

---

2. Francis X. Gumerlock, "Mark 13:32 and Christ's Supposed Ignorance: Four Patristic Solutions," *Trinity Journal* 28, no. 2 (2007): 205–13.
3. Athanasius of Alexandria, *Four Discourses against the Arians*, Discourse 3.43, quoted in Gumerlock, "Mark 13:32," 210.

Exegetical Perspective

of "this generation" and its variants designates Jesus' adversaries (11:16; 12:39–45; 16:4; 23:36) or the faithless, including his own disciples (17:17). "This generation" thus refers to all those—from Cain to Caiaphas to our own contemporaries—who resist God's will and ways. Verse 34 may thus be a reminder that this faithless and violent generation will remain until the coming of the Son of Man. Jesus' word, the promise of his coming, is more certain than the reality of heaven and earth itself (v. 35). In Isaiah 65:17 and Revelation 21:1, the passing of heaven and earth also marks the revelation of the glory of the new creation that follows God's judgment of the world's empires.

Throughout this discourse, Jesus answers his disciples' request for signs with both warnings of suffering and strong reassurances of his coming, but nothing that would help them know precisely where they are on a timeline. Only the Father knows the day and hour (v. 36). As time passes, disciples must resist returning to business as usual. The sayings in verses 37–41 all stress the sudden, surprising, and disruptive character of the Son of Man's coming. In the days of Noah, people conducted their lives as if all was well—eating, drinking, and marrying—right up to the moment when the floods swept them away (vv. 38–39). The images of disruption in verses 40–41 are the source of language associated with the "rapture," in which the elect are suddenly lifted from the earth, with loved ones and coworkers "left behind." In the other scenes in Matthew that depict such division, however, it is not the elect but the wicked who are taken first—for judgment (24:51; 13:40–42, 49–50). Being "taken" would likely have reminded Jesus' disciples of Roman military actions; it is better to be left behind. Jesus does not tell us when the Son of Man will come, only that his certain, sudden coming brings the end of human empires and the assertion of God's redeeming power into every dimension of reality.

STANLEY P. SAUNDERS

Homiletical Perspective

many guises, some more dramatic, some less dramatic. It may be the loss of a loved one. It may be an experience of failure or rejection. It may be a cancer diagnosis, a loss of a job, or a betrayal by someone we trusted. What happens, though, is that our familiar world is ruptured and thrown into disarray—as in the days of Noah. It is then that our lives are judged. It is then that our resilience is tried, that our foundations come under scrutiny. It is then that our faith is tested. While we do not know when such things may strike, we know that they are part of life.

Jesus here is reminding us, then, that life is more than "known knowns." We delude ourselves if we think that we are in control, for too much is precarious and uncertain. Forget Rumsfeld's third category of "unknown unknowns"—we can do nothing at all about them. We can, however, do something about the known unknowns. We can prepare for them, and we do this by living faithfully in the known knowns. It is in living out our faith conscientiously when life is stable and ordered that we prepare for the unexpected, for the time of trial.

It is in following Jesus faithfully through the familiar land of the known knowns that we are equipped to navigate the strange, frightening territory marked "known unknowns." Living that way also prepares us for the greatest "known unknown" of all, the last day, when we will be called to account for our lives and how we have lived them. That it will come is a known; when it will come is an unknown. So be prepared.

LANCE STONE

Matthew 24:42–51

42"Keep awake therefore, for you do not know on what day your Lord is coming. 43But understand this: if the owner of the house had known in what part of the night the thief was coming, he would have stayed awake and would not have let his house be broken into. 44Therefore you also must be ready, for the Son of Man is coming at an unexpected hour.

45"Who then is the faithful and wise slave, whom his master has put in charge of his household, to give the other slaves their allowance of food at the proper time? 46Blessed is that slave whom his master will find at work when he arrives. 47Truly I tell you, he will put that one in charge of all his possessions. 48But if that wicked slave says to himself, 'My master is delayed,' 49and he begins to beat his fellow slaves, and eats and drinks with drunkards, 50the master of that slave will come on a day when he does not expect him and at an hour that he does not know. 51He will cut him in pieces and put him with the hypocrites, where there will be weeping and gnashing of teeth."

Theological Perspective

This passage poses three difficult theological questions for contemporary preachers: How should Christians live in between the past event of the resurrection and the future return of the Son of Man? How can we interpret Matthew's claim that wicked servants will be cut off from God's love in Jesus Christ? How shall we read New Testament passages that condone, or at least do not challenge, slavery?

Many scholars claim that one of the central messages of Matthew 24 is that Christians should be watchful and work diligently while they wait for Jesus Christ to return. There is much less agreement among theologians, however, about the nature of the time in which we live and wait. These debates fall within the field of eschatology, the doctrine of last things, which investigates the resurrection of the dead, final judgment, heaven, hell, and eternal life. Eschatological passages such as Matthew 24:42–51 ask readers to reflect on the relationship between God's future kingdom and our present time. Has the kingdom already begun on earth? Is it a future event? Is God's kingdom, rather, present in an anticipatory way? How do we understand the time in which we watch, work, and wait?

Over the last hundred years, Western theologians and biblical scholars have disagreed about how to interpret eschatological statements in the New

Pastoral Perspective

In the city where I live there are two times during the year when churches become partners in a program called "Room in the Inn." These events coincide with the highest temperatures of heat and the lowest temperatures of cold, for these are times when it is physically most dangerous for people who survive on the streets. At these moments diverse church communities gather their resources in order to respond to the call of Matthew's Gospel to be faithful and diligent activists who are always alert to the needy, the poor, and the dispossessed. The members of these churches are working on the tasks that God calls them to, while they wait for the Master who is delayed.

In this particular text Matthew encourages the readers to remain steadfast and alert, drawing upon their resources in ways that are faithful and compassionate. We are not to squander our abilities, but to live out a radical discipleship in response to the needs of those around us. Biblical scholar Warren Carter suggests that part of the intent of Matthew's Gospel is to encourage the building of a community marked by an inclusion that sets it as distinct among other communities. Matthew's call to that community includes this unique call to "respond to God's love and mercy with practical mercy to the sick, homeless, hungry, naked, and imprisoned. . . .

Exegetical Perspective

The disciplines of "watchfulness" and "readiness" distinguish the followers of Jesus as they await the coming of the Son of Man. Watching patiently for signs of Jesus' appearance is one of the foundational disciplines of the church, a mark of its self-awareness as an eschatological people, living faithfully across time at the edge of history.

In the preceding section of the eschatological discourse (24:29–41), Jesus has affirmed the certainty that the Son of Man is coming, that his authority comprehends every dimension of reality, whether in heaven or the created realm, and that his coming will be sudden, surprising, and disruptive. Jesus now affirms repeatedly that the timing of his coming will be unknown and surprising. This does not pose a riddle for the disciples to solve, but affirms the conditions that will compel them to remain constantly awake and ready.

Jesus' insistence that the time of his coming is unknown and will remain so has not deterred his followers from endless quests to discover what "only the Father knows" (24:36). Keeping the time hidden prevents us from altering our behavior accordingly. Two reminders of what we do not and cannot know—"You do not know on what day your Lord is coming" (v. 42) and "the Son of Man is coming at an unexpected hour" (v. 44)—frame the vignette about the house owner and the thief (v. 43).

Homiletical Perspective

Absence. It "makes the heart grow fonder," but it can also sorely try us. When it is someone we love, when it is someone we are waiting for, when it has gone on far too long, it can leave us listless and impatient, and we just want it to be over with and to be replaced by presence.

Perhaps it is because absence can be so difficult that Jesus in this passage is beginning an extended discourse preparing his disciples for the fact that he is very soon going to go away and leave them. In the next chapter he will tell a story about ten maidens who are invited to a wedding, but the groom is delayed—he is absent. Then he will tell another story about a man who goes away and leaves his servants money to invest while he is gone. Here in our passage the story is similar, about a slave put in charge of a master's household while he is away.

Jesus seems pretty preoccupied with the fact that his disciples will soon experience his absence, and his great concern is how they will fill the time and whether they will be ready for his return. His urgent directive is that they should "keep awake," for they do not know when he will come. Jesus' immediate concern seems to have been the destruction of Jerusalem, which he could see on the horizon and which for him meant the coming of the Lord and the beginning of a new age. This would be the thief

Matthew 24:42–51

Theological Perspective

Testament. Some argue that verses about cataclysmic signs, the return of the Son of Man, and the final judgment refer to events that occurred during Jesus' lifetime. Others suggest that eschatological claims were never made by Jesus, but were inserted by the Gospel authors, and therefore Christians should not assume that Matthew's Jesus was speaking about his literal return.

Despite these debates, most scholars agree that eschatology is central to Christianity. Protestant theologians Jürgen Moltmann and Wolfhart Pannenberg claim that Christian eschatological theology is not about predicting when the Son of Man will return or who will be cut in pieces. Rather, it illustrates that all of temporal creation will be taken up into God's eternity. They also contend that God's coming reign is already present in an anticipatory way, because it comes to us from the future in which all things are reconciled to God. This means that all persons and all creation are already being drawn into God's coming future of reconciliation, judgment, and healing. Rather than being with God *after* the final judgment, our whole life is in God *now*. Moltmann writes, "Men and women will find again with God not only the final moment, but their whole history . . . as the reconciled, the rectified and healed and completed history of their whole lives."[1]

If our theological reflection is guided by this anticipatory eschatology, then Matthew 24:42–51 can be read as good news that we are already blessed in this time. The Trinitarian God is already present in every moment of our lives, and we are already living into that which we will be in God's eternity. Pannenberg even says that the identity of every human being and finite creature has its origin, present, and future in God: "God is the future of the finite from which it again receives its existence as a whole as that which has been, and at the same time accepts all other creaturely being along with itself."[2]

In light of this assertion, perhaps one could venture an alternate interpretation of Jesus' teaching about the absent master and the wise and wicked slaves. It is true that the master—the Son of Man—is physically absent, and that he will return. However, God is already present now through the Holy Spirit. So the servants, both wise and wicked, are not actually alone; the master is present in an anticipatory way. The servants are living toward—and in light

Pastoral Perspective

Among the marginal Christian community, Emmanuel is encountered."[1] The church is to be a leader among those who are called to tend to the household and to be watchful in our expectation and waiting. We are most aware of those causes that are dear to our hearts. This text reminds us that we need to stay alert for the surprising and multiple ways in which Immanuel is encountered. By listening to those with whom we are least familiar—and sometimes most uncomfortable—we are compelled by a gospel God who is bigger than we ever imagined.

In our complex world there are many situations to which faithful communities respond. Misdiagnosed or untreated mental illness incapacitates many individuals, working against a sense of wholeness in families and communities, and resulting in lost lives through suicide, imprisonment, homelessness, and constant experiences of fragmentation. The rate of unemployment in our country compels us to be aware of the increased vulnerability, not only of those who chronically live on the outermost socioeconomic margins, but also of middle-class families who are experiencing need in new ways.

Increased awareness of the connections within our global community encourages campaigns to support missions and extraordinary opportunities to work with humanitarian organizations across religious and national lines. Economic self-protection moves some to secure borders and identify those who belong and those who do not, while others develop missions in the desert to protect boundary crossers caught in the struggle to survive. Inaccessibility to adequate basic health care globally puts women and children in particular in constant danger. Devastation from disasters (caused both by natural elements and by humans who act out in violence) decimates communities and creates deep spiritual, physical, and emotional needs. The list is long and tiring, and we can easily grow weary of the ongoing invitation to engage our compassionate hearts in response to all of the world's pain.

Out of an awareness of the massive global needs that cannot easily be met, an accompanying weariness exists among those who strive to respond to the needy, the poor, and the marginalized. We discover that it is difficult to be alert when we are dead tired or when the tasks in front of us seem insurmountable. Many of us have the experience of wanting to stay awake for a conversation in the middle of the

---

1. Jürgen Moltmann, *The Coming of God: Christian Eschatology*, trans. Margaret Kohl (Minneapolis: Fortress Press, 1996), 71.
2. Wolfhart Pannenberg, *Systematic Theology*, trans. Geoffrey W. Bromiley (Grand Rapids: Eerdmans, 1998), 3:607.

1. Warren Carter, *Matthew: Storyteller, Interpreter, Evangelist*, rev. ed. (Ada, MI: Baker, 2004), 88.

Would it not be a good thing, we might ask, to know when the thief is coming? Then the householder could sleep until it is time to get up and thwart the intruder. Jesus, however, does not want disciples who are awake some of the time and asleep the rest. Preparation for the coming of the Son of Man requires perpetual vigilance, not calendars and alarm clocks. Thieves, in any case, do not call ahead. Constant readiness, not precise foreknowledge, is the important thing. The householder must be "awake" and "ready." The disciples will not know, cannot know, and should not know the time of the Lord's coming, but must be watchful and ready at all times. Watchfulness and readiness are thus matters of ongoing discipline, not occasional practices reserved for the last moment of the eleventh hour.

Jesus' teaching about the "faithful and wise slave" (vv. 45–51) continues to explore the theme of readiness for the Lord's unexpected coming. The two scenarios he presents focus not so much on the character of the two slaves, one good and one bad, as on the differing ways their sense of the master's absence, or delay, shapes their behavior. Both scenarios have the same starting point: the master, who will presumably be absent for a time, puts a slave in charge of the household, with particular responsibility to make certain that the other slaves are fed and cared for appropriately (v. 45). The first scenario (vv. 46–47) represents the ideal: the master returns to find the slave "working," that is, ready for his return, and rewards him with even greater responsibilities, the management of all his possessions.

In the alternative scenario, when the slave perceives that the master's return is delayed, he proceeds, in direct contrast to his mandate, both to abuse his fellow slaves and to share the household's resources with drunkards. The slave may imagine that he will have time to set things right again, or that the master will never return. In any case, he abandons the tasks assigned to him for the time when the master is absent. He acts as if he were a newly minted householder exploring with abandon the power that wealth and status bring.

The master does arrive, unexpectedly (v. 50a, recalling v. 44), at a day and hour the slave does not know (v. 50b, recalling v. 36). When he finds the slave acting irresponsibly, the master cuts him in pieces and puts him among the "hypocrites," "where there will be weeping and gnashing of teeth" (v. 51), a stock expression in Matthew for dire judgment.

These scenarios provide an analogy for what Jesus requires of his disciples as they await his return,

coming in the night to plunder and to steal and for which they must be ready. Christians have extended Jesus' reference to his return at the end of the time and for us too; therefore, the warning is clear: Be ready! Be prepared! Keep awake!

It is very hard, however, to live in a state of permanent alert. In the early twenty-first century, when we are growing accustomed to an ever-present terrorist threat, we are always being urged to be vigilant. In the United Kingdom there are levels of terrorist threat that range from "severe" to "high" to "elevated" to "guarded" to "low"; it is difficult to know how we should distinguish among these and act accordingly. Of course the longer time passes without an attack, the harder it is to stay alert. That is the problem with Jesus' return. In the early days of the church, it may have been easier to live on tiptoe, but it has been two thousand years now, and it is hard to keep up a state of continuous watchfulness. There are only so many times we can be warned to be on our best behavior today, just in case Jesus comes back.

So what might it mean for us to keep awake, as we are instructed here and elsewhere in the New Testament? Perhaps one way into this is to consider when we are most aware of Jesus' absence, where we feel it most painfully. After all, when we are separated from someone we love and for whom we yearn, their absence is constantly mediated to us. There are continual reminders: the space in the bed beside us, the empty chair, the silence at the table, the old pullover, the folded newspaper. These are the things that gnaw at our hearts and keep us awake at night. These are the things that make us restless.

So too with Jesus' absence. If we are watchful, we sense it everywhere, whether it is in the vicious spiral of war, the agony of the bereaved, the beggar on the street, the arrogant smirk of the dictator, or the pitiful eyes of the starving child. These are antisacraments, signifying a vacuum, a void. As Christians we are trained to recognize the presence of Christ in bread and wine in our central act of worship, and to discern Christ there is to learn to discern him everywhere in the world around. With that recognition goes an ever-heightened sense of the signs of his absence from the world. Here too we are wakeful, and restless.

Jesus calls us, however, to more than just a listlessness, an unease. As we read here about the master who puts his servant in charge of his household while he goes away, two words come to mind: "responsibility" and "accountability." If religion has

Matthew 24:42–51

Theological Perspective

of—their coming reconciliation with all creation in God's eternity.

Interpreting the return of the Son (Master) as present in an anticipatory way does not mean that readers can ignore this passage's claim that some will be cut off from God. According to the author of Matthew's Gospel, those who do not watch diligently for the master and fail to serve the household will be cut off and put with the hypocrites. Some readers may be tempted to count themselves among the watchful, faithful, and wise who will be blessed by the master. Recall, though, that Matthew 24 also teaches that humans are anxious about the future, misread signs, fail to wait and work diligently, get caught up in earthly distractions, and do not know the date of the master's return. Perhaps one way to interpret this tough text is to admit that all persons fail to achieve the wise faithfulness that is expected by the master.

Finally, contemporary theologians and preachers must not shy away from questioning Matthew's approval of slavery. In chapter 24, Jesus seems to accept it as a necessary social and economic institution. If Jesus did not challenge slavery, then on what grounds can Christians reject slavery, child labor, exploitation of workers, or human trafficking? In his widely read text *The Good Book*, former Harvard chaplain Peter Gomes challenges the Bible's acceptance of slavery. Gomes looks to the overarching biblical principles of compassion and new creation and reminds his readers to engage the Bible with a contemporary moral imagination guided by the Holy Spirit. This way of reading can help modern Christians set aside the Bible's acceptance of sexism and slavery. He writes, "The racial theories based on the tortured inheritance of the sons of Noah . . . have yielded to Saint Paul's notion of the new creation in Christ and the transformed, renewed mind."[3] Gomes's appeal to the new creation in Christ resonates with claims of Moltmann and Pannenberg that we live in light of God's coming creation. We watch and work hopefully in the present, trusting that God's reign has already begun, and we wait expectantly for the Son to return, when we will be called into the blessing of the Master.

MARY ELISE LOWE

Pastoral Perspective

night; the conversation is important to someone else, but we are so exhausted that we cannot fully listen or be present to the person's story. Similarly, when we feel alone in our response or feel overly responsible, our souls become numb. At these moments it is important to realize that God calls us as a community, not as individuals who are solely responsible for meeting all of the needs around us.

Among mental health and pastoral care professionals, there is a growing literature on the impact of "compassion fatigue," "secondary trauma," or "vicarious traumatization" in the lives of individuals, families, and communities.[2] When reaching out is met with constant need or ongoing chaos, those offering care can experience despair, trauma, and hopelessness themselves. Eventually people lose the ability to access their inner soul, full of resiliency and hope.

When our desire to care for one another—to follow the call of the gospel to love justice and to practice mercy—creates fatigue, weariness, and hopelessness, the best of our pastoral wisdom suggests that appropriate interventions include such things as taking some time out, working with a spiritual director or pastoral caregiver, reconnecting with friends and family in order to renew our vitality, and reminding ourselves that we are not able to meet all of the needs of the world by ourselves. These are sound reminders that care of self and soul is a requirement for those who are alert, and those who watch and wait.

Matthew encourages us to be ready, to be diligent, and to be aware of the needs of those around us. In other words, we are to be constant in our love and care, remaining alert for ways we can serve God by responding to the needs around us. Such diligence also requires that we be watchful on behalf of our own soul, lest it grow so weary by our endeavors that we actually miss the very presence of God.

JORETTA L. MARSHALL

---

2. Andrew J. Weaver, Laura T. Flannelly, and John D. Preston, *Counseling Survivors of Traumatic Events: A Handbook for Pastors and Other Helping Professionals* (Nashville: Abingdon Press, 2003), 173–79.

3. Peter Gomes, *The Good Book: Reading the Bible with Mind and Heart* (New York: William Morrow, 1996), 99.

Feasting on the Gospels

not an allegory of divine behavior. Jesus' return is certain, yet subject to neither temporal mapping nor any other human projection. The analogy is both "secular" (drawn from everyday life) and hyperbolic, particularly in the dramatic images of judgment that Jesus piles up. Neither God nor secular masters would cut a slave in pieces and also put him with the hypocrites.

The central point is that the "faithful and wise" slave/disciple maintains the vigilance appropriate to the expectation of the master's imminent return, regardless of delays or shifting temporal expectations. Like the owner of the house who does not know when the thief is coming, the disciple must be prepared—"working" on the appointed tasks, producing the fruit of God's kingdom—whenever the Son of Man returns. Jesus will continue to illustrate the need for readiness in the next story, where foolish bridesmaids not only fail to come prepared with adequate oil for the wedding feast, but fall asleep when the groom is delayed, rather than take advantage of the time to secure the oil they need (25:1–13).

Jesus does not here name explicitly the practices that constitute "readiness," but there are some hints. The slave is appointed the task of making sure the other slaves are appropriately fed. The faithful and wise slave is thus like the followers of Jesus who "produce the fruit of the kingdom in its time," that is, who practice hospitality, forgiveness, reconciliation, and care for those in need (3:8; 7:15–20; 12:33–35; 21:43).

In the second scenario, the slave's judgment includes being given a place among "the hypocrites," a term Matthew uses especially to designate the Jewish elites who use their time and resources to serve their own interests, rather than to share God's gifts with those who suffer or to work for the restoration of God's people (21:33–39; 23:13–36). Disciples "stay awake," "watching" both for the Lord's coming and their neighbor's need, for "the Son of Man comes in his glory" among the hungry, naked, sick, and imprisoned (25:31–46).

STANLEY P. SAUNDERS

ever provided an excuse for taking our eyes off this world and focusing them on the next, this passage alone ought to be a sufficient corrective. God entrusts us with responsibility for the world, and we are accountable to God for how we have lived in it and cared for it.

We are told here that the master commissions his servant with the task of giving the other servants their food, their proper share. What impact might that make on an unequal world, accustomed to malnutrition and starvation, if we really lived it? We are told that the servant is put in charge of the master's possessions; they own nothing, for everything is his. How might we steward the world's resources and regulate the financial markets, if we really believed that and acted upon it? When the master returns, we will be held accountable for these responsibilities delegated to us. What difference might that make to a world that has no sense of any accountability to anyone apart from ourselves, which seems to mean in practice that the powerful always end up with free license? This is wakefulness. This is how our restlessness is expressed, by living in the clear light of responsibility and accountability.

There is much more to be said about Christ's absence. There is of course the coming of the Holy Spirit, which means that we are not left abandoned. The wonder of the Spirit's presence does not overrule the awareness of Christ's absence; it heightens it, for God's Holy Spirit sensitizes us to every denial of Christ's rule, every antisacrament. May that same Spirit keep us ever awake to the sense of responsibility and accountability with which the Master entrusts us.

LANCE STONE

¹"Then the kingdom of heaven will be like this. Ten bridesmaids took their lamps and went to meet the bridegroom. ²Five of them were foolish, and five were wise. ³When the foolish took their lamps, they took no oil with them; ⁴but the wise took flasks of oil with their lamps. ⁵As the bridegroom was delayed, all of them became drowsy and slept. ⁶But at midnight there was a shout, 'Look! Here is the bridegroom! Come out to meet him.' ⁷Then all those bridesmaids got up and trimmed their lamps. ⁸The foolish said to the wise, 'Give us some of your oil, for our lamps are going out.' ⁹But the wise replied, 'No! there will not be enough for you and for us; you had better go to the dealers and buy some for yourselves.' ¹⁰And while they went to buy it, the bridegroom came, and those who were ready went with him into the wedding banquet; and the door was shut. ¹¹Later the other bridesmaids came also, saying, 'Lord, lord, open to us.' ¹²But he replied, 'Truly I tell you, I do not know you.' ¹³Keep awake therefore, for you know neither the day nor the hour."

Theological Perspective

"The groom has been delayed." The delay of the second coming of Christ and the reign of God (*basilea tou theou*) created a problem for Christian theology almost from the beginning. By the year 50 CE, just twenty years after Jesus' death, some of the apostle Paul's converts are already growing a little restless. Their loved ones are dying, and Christ has not returned. Paul explains to the Thessalonians that "the Lord will come like a thief in the night" (1 Thess. 5:2), and that they should therefore "keep awake and be sober" (1 Thess. 5:6). He assures them that "God will bring with him those who have died" (1 Thess. 4:14) and that "the dead in Christ" will rise from the dead to join with the living "to meet the Lord in the air; and so we will be with the Lord forever" (1 Thess. 4:16–17).

By the time 2 Peter was written, well into the second century CE, restlessness had turned to impatience and even scoffing: "Where is the promise of his coming? For ever since our ancestors died, all things continue as they were from the beginning of creation!" (2 Pet. 3:4). The apologist here begs for patience and stretches time: "With the Lord one day is like a thousand years, and a thousand years are like one day. The Lord is not slow about his promise, as some think of slowness, but is patient with you, not wanting any to perish, but all to come to repentance" (2 Pet. 3:8–9).

Pastoral Perspective

"What are you waiting for?!" That is usually a critique posing as a question, because we live in a society uncomfortable with waiting. We are encouraged to act, to get moving, much like the bridesmaids who could spare no time to fill their lamps. Jesus too seems to live in a manner that wastes no time, privileging the present moment. He tells Peter and Andrew to follow him and immediately they drop their nets (4:19–20). In the Sermon on the Mount he implores people not to worry about tomorrow (6:34). He heals the leper right when they meet: "I do choose. Be made clean" (8:3).

However, according to this parable Jesus also understands there is waiting to be done. Amid his many end-time predictions and declarations comes this timely parable about waiting. The bridesmaids who bring enough oil for the long haul are lauded, for we "know neither the day nor the hour" (v. 13). To refuse to wait would be foolish, for it denies the possibility of a future outside one's own design. To bring enough oil is to be wise, because the night might be longer or darker than expected. Still, the belief is that the morning will come. Waiting is an act of faith.

Modern life has traded oil lamps for electric, slowly burning wicks for technologies meant to speed up the pace of life, but much time is still spent

Exegetical Perspective

The Gospel of Matthew presents a lucid and compelling portrait of Jesus as the Jewish Messiah for third-generation Christians. Having shown Jesus to be descended from David and Abraham (1:1), and fulfilling all righteousness (3:15), Matthew addresses followers of Jesus with such issues as the way of the kingdom (5:2–16), the order of the church (18:15–20), and the Great Commission (28:18–20). Along with John, Matthew was the great teaching Gospel of the early church, and it continues to be a favorite for discerning Christian living in every generation.

Emerging from the Christian movement centered in Jerusalem, and finalized in a Jewish setting such as Antioch (around 90 CE), Matthew's presentation of the fivefold teachings of Jesus matches the fivefold law of Moses. Chapters 5–7 emphasize fulfilling the law by getting at its radical center; chapter 10 outlines Jesus' instructions to disciples as he sends them out on their traveling ministries; chapter 13 features parables of the kingdom regarding the reception and rejection of the gospel; chapter 18 calls for accountability and graciousness in managing community affairs; and chapters 24–25 call for followers of Jesus to be ready, faithful, and responsive as they await the return of the Son of Man.

As the first of three parables in Matthew 25, verses 1–13 present us with the parable of the Ten

Homiletical Perspective

If Jesus had been a college professor, this section of Matthew would have been his last lecture. In many ways the meaning of the parables in this chapter seems obvious: be like the wise bridesmaids and the wise investors and the faithful ones who feed the hungry and visit the sick. How can we hear these parables as open-ended stories that invite conversation, rather than static allegories with few surprises? The meaning of today's parable seems clear enough: the bridegroom is Jesus, the Human One, who has promised to return. Jesus has not returned, and Matthew's community is weary of waiting. Some are prepared, and whenever Jesus returns, they will be ready, and he will invite them into the banquet. Some are not prepared at all; when Jesus appears, they are off at the market. They will beg to get in, but Jesus will answer, "Truly I tell you, I do not know you" (v. 12).

Some things in this parable are odd. Take the ending, for example: "Keep awake therefore, for you know neither the day nor the hour" (v. 13). All ten of these women fell asleep and were not scolded! The warning to stay awake made sense in the previous chapter. People who were eating and drinking and getting married were surprised by the flood, and Noah went safely into the ark (24:38–39). "Keep awake therefore," said Jesus, "for you do not know on what day your

Matthew 25:1–13

Theological Perspective

Our story from Matthew's Gospel falls somewhere in between Paul's letter and 2 Peter and offers simple and fairly flat advice: "stay ready." The groom has been delayed so long that some have fallen asleep. In Matthew's story, all the maids who are waiting to accompany the groom start to doze. Then at midnight there is a shout that wakens them: "Look! Here is the bridegroom! Come out to meet him" (v. 6). Some have stocked up on oil and are found ready. Others have not and are therefore shut out.

One could preach a rather safe sermon or teach a safe class that sticks to Matthew's simple message to stay ready. So long as the sermon or Bible study traffics in evocative images and practical implications, this could even be done without leaving the impression that the preacher (or the teacher or the congregation) actually believes in a literal second coming of Christ. However, for the brave hearted, this text may give an opportunity to tackle head-on the problem of translating ancient eschatological texts into the language of a scientific age. Certainly the sales numbers for Tim LaHaye's *Left Behind* series[1] and the continued ability of doomsday prophets to grab headlines witness to the need of courageous mainline Christians to do so. The groom has been delayed for thousands of years now. So what do twenty-first-century Christians do with texts like this?

What is needed is an engagement with ancient eschatological texts as what theologian Paul Tillich called "broken symbols." Broken symbols are symbols that are recognized as symbols. Religious symbols refer to the ultimate or the transcendent. They use finite, worldly images to invoke something beyond. Religious symbols are stories, rituals, and practices that drive us beyond the symbol to ultimate meaning, to the sublime, to the abyss, to unfathomable depths, or to unreachable heights. The danger in dealing with symbols is that sometimes the symbol, rather than the reality to which the symbol points, becomes the object of worship or loyalty. It is good that a symbol is broken, then, so that the meaning of the symbol is no longer imprisoned in the symbol. The symbol points beyond itself to a reality that cannot be contained in the symbol. The power of the symbol lies in its ability to point beyond itself and thereby participate in that to which it points.[2]

The first step in engaging ancient eschatological texts as broken symbols may be to recognize their

Pastoral Perspective

waiting. Some waiting is inconsequential, but much is significant. People wait with bated breath for good news or bad, from doctors' diagnoses to business reports, from struggling family members to strangers across the globe facing unknown crises. At other times, the wait is for the unknown itself, uncertainty about what is next at work, at home, in relationships.

The parable reveals a tension between planning for the future and living in the present. On the one hand, Jesus' example urges his followers to act now, while, on the other hand, he speaks of the need to be prepared, to wait well. The proper response to this reality is to "keep awake." Wait urgently. Jesus' commitment to the present moment and his commandment to be prepared belong together. They define each other. The need for action in the world is informed by a preparedness that avoids hastiness. The need for urgency propels active waiting, steering it away from apathy and complacency. Clarity of purpose and direction is at the core of this dual calling. Rather than into an exhausting struggle to stay awake, the parable invites hearers into an *awakening*, a growing awareness of the world around them and God's coming into it.

To trust in this coming is no more difficult for people today than for those in the first century (both are "in Jesus' time"). There is a challenge to waiting both preparedly and expectantly, with the belief that something, and someone, is actually coming. Sensationalist doomsday prophets have long bellowed out end-times predictions in ways that tend more to incite paralyzing fear or mocking laughter than to inspire faithful living. In spite of the temptation to become cynical, one can discover something genuine and sacred about waiting for the fulfillment of God's promise. For its citizens, the coming kingdom of heaven requires, and creates, a new orientation to the world around them and a new way of being in it.

Waiting with expectation and preparation will not magically open up some padlocked doors to a walled-off palace, but it will foster in the believer openness to the coming kingdom of God. Waiting with true anticipation for the kingdom to come, in turn, brings into focus the traces of the kingdom that are already all around. Because, as Jesus earlier asserts, "the kingdom of heaven has come near" (10:7), the faithful find courage to live as if the kingdom has already arrived, loving radically and fearlessly. Moreover, as individuals and communities become attuned to the signs of the kingdom, they become increasingly able to participate in its coming by living according to its ways. The prophecy itself awakens in its hearing.

---

1. Tim LaHaye and Jerry B. Jenkins, *Left Behind: A Novel of the Earth's Last Days* (Wheaton, IL: Tyndale, 1995).
2. See Paul Tillich, *Dynamics of Faith* (1958; repr., New York: Perennial Classics, 2001), esp. chap. 3.

Bridesmaids, emphasizing the importance of being ready for the bridegroom, as the hour of his appearing remains unknown. In contrast to the five foolish bridesmaids, who allow the oil in their lamps to run low, the wise bridesmaids keep their lamps full, so to be prepared for the unannounced appearing of the bridegroom. In Galilean culture, upon the bridegroom's appearance, the bridesmaids would accompany the wedding party with lamps and torches from the bride's house to that of the groom, where the celebration would then begin. This parable follows Jesus' apocalyptic teachings in the previous chapter (24:3–8) on signs of the end of the age, which will include persecutions (24:9–14), the desolating sacrilege in the temple, and false messiahs (24:15–28), before the appearance (*parousia*, 24:3, 27, 37, 39) of the Son of Man (24:29–31). Therefore, believers should be watchful, taking lessons from the budding fig tree, as one keeps guard against a thief in the night (24:32–44). As a laborer seeks to be found productively at work when his master shows up, the faithful and wise servant seeks to be diligent—serving his master well whenever he should return (24:45–51).

In contrast to these fear-producing warnings, anticipating the celebration of a wedding is far more joyous in its motivating thrust (vv. 1–13). As the high privilege of the bridesmaids is to welcome the groom (some mss. add "and the bride," v. 1) and launch the celebration, they want to be ready for the groom's part of the wedding party, whenever it should arrive. Therefore, keeping their lamps filled and lit would have provided a joyous welcome and procession, whenever the unscheduled event should happen.

The foolish bridesmaids, however, have not prepared themselves for the wait. Perhaps they thought the bridegroom would come sooner, or perhaps they imagine being able to borrow oil from others. Their foolish lack of preparation, however, forces them to leave the scene to procure more oil, resulting in their missing out on the great joy of the wedding. As a result, the door is shut, and despite their excuses, the master of the feast declares he never knew them (vv. 11–12). The final point is made bluntly: "Keep awake therefore, for you know neither the day nor the hour" (v. 13).

As a collection parallel to the Sermon on the Mount (chaps. 5–7), the final cluster of Jesus' sayings in Matthew (we might add chap. 23 to chaps. 24–25) emphasizes embracing the way of the kingdom and living by its standards, so that believers may be found ready and worthy before the returning Lord. Therefore, Matthew adds specificity to Mark's

Lord is coming" (24:42). However, in this parable the problem is not falling asleep. The problem is running out of oil. This parable is about an oil crisis, and Jesus needs a different ending: "Therefore, I tell you, be prepared and bring plenty of oil."

Perhaps Matthew tacked the ending from another parable onto this story. Does it matter that they were women? The *Inclusive Language Bible*[1] calls them "attendants"—wonderfully inclusive but a stretch from the Greek word *parthenos*. That is the same word we heard in the first chapter of Matthew: "A virgin [*parthenos*] shall conceive and bear a son" (1:23). The word could mean simply a young woman; so some translations say "maidens" or "girls." The choice of "bridesmaids" (NRSV) moves further from the Greek, but fits the wedding. Today, people who hear "bridesmaids" may see ten women in matching gowns carrying lamps instead of flowers—and wondering where the bride is.

If Matthew brought two stories together—one about staying awake, the other about being prepared—maybe he put his own spin on the women in the story too. The women are labeled and divided from the start: five are "wise" and five are "foolish." Was Matthew concerned about the role of women in his own community? Were some women in the community doing or saying things that were foolish? We know there were divisions within the community, because Matthew in an earlier chapter (18:15–20) includes Jesus' detailed instructions for reconciliation. Was Matthew using this parable to warn the community about "foolish maidens" in their midst? Marie-Eloise Rosenblatt wonders who those foolish women might have been:

> Were they Gnostic teachers? Restless young women who sought new theological ideas in the market places? . . . Was the community divided because some were nervous and others deeply inspired by these prophetic women? Were the women themselves divided, and the male pastors "forced" to exercise "authority" by exiling some of the recalcitrants from the community?[2]

Even the wise women come off as harsh when their sisters ask for oil: "No! There will not be enough for you and for us; you had better go to the dealers and buy some for yourselves" (v. 9)—which would seem impossible at midnight, unless they

1. *The New Testament of the Inclusive Language Bible* (Notre Dame: Cross Cultural, 1994).
2. Marie-Eloise Rosenblatt, "Got into the Party after All," in Amy-Jill Levine, ed., *A Feminist Companion to Matthew* (Cleveland: Pilgrim Press, 2001), 193.

Matthew 25:1–13

Theological Perspective

inherent fantastic and mysterious tone. They are fantastic visions, featuring a breakdown of the predatory nature of the cycle of life: "the wolf and the lamb shall feed together, the lion shall eat straw like the ox" (Isa. 65:25). They are otherworldly dreams featuring dragons and seven-headed beasts (Rev. 12–13). They are earth-shattering imaginings in which "the sun will be darkened, and the moon will not give its light; the stars will fall from heaven, and the powers of heaven will be shaken" (Matt. 24:29). They are slightly less fantastic but perhaps even more mysterious parables, like our story of the delayed groom.

In every case these symbols do not merely refer to some future event. Instead, they strain to give voice to a hope that transcends the limitations of current circumstance and even language itself. These symbols are where the reality of human suffering meets the mystery of human hope. In fantastic and mysterious imagery, these symbols insist that sin and death are not the final words and that the darkness of the night need not necessarily lead to hopelessness and despair. The symbols envision a new day and a new creation. They open a way where there is no way.

Our parable from Matthew can transcend the flat advice to "be ready" for a literal second coming, if we engage it imaginatively. The story envisions a great feast that comes at the end of long waiting. The parable invites us to live our lives in celebratory anticipation, not sleepy apathy. It encourages us to stock up on lamp oil, despite the darkness of the night and the seemingly endless delay of the guest of honor. The parable dares us to be awake, vigilant, and, most importantly, hopeful.

DANIEL J. OTT

Pastoral Perspective

Such a faith becomes a well of resources from which to draw in the midst of life's deepest troubles. God's ushering in of the kingdom of heaven is a reminder that life is not lived in isolation. Just as the bridegroom of the parable has been away, presumably negotiating the wedding contract with the father, so too does Christ continue to intercede on behalf of God's children. Moreover, Christ provides assurance that acts of faithful waiting, which are either overlooked or downright opposed in the world, are not in vain, for they are recognized by the very Lord who comes. Finally, this kind of waiting serves as a daily reminder of how the story ultimately ends; God's promise to bring things to completion in the future provides strength to live in the present.

In the end, the mistake of the unwise bridesmaids is not that they fail to believe the bridegroom is returning. If they did not believe, they would not have gone to meet him in the first place. Neither is it that they fall asleep, for the wise and the foolish alike succumb to the human need for rest. Rather, the mistake of the foolish is to fail to invest in what will prepare them to see God's kingdom when in fact it does come. For them it was the oil that burns a lamp. For contemporary hearers, it may be hearts that burn with prayer, eyes that study God's word or recognize God's work in the world, ears that hear the crying of God's children, hands that reach out to those in need, feet that find those who have been lost, or simply a developed taste to know God's goodness. One thing is clear: what is required in this time of waiting is an awakening of all the senses to what God is doing and promises to do in the world.

What are you waiting for? Is it truly for the kingdom of God and the coming of the Lord? The question is an honest one, and its faithful answer will provide enough light to endure the longest night.

ROBERT M. MCCLELLAN

Exegetical Perspective

warnings against the scribes, adding seven woes against the scribes and Pharisees (23:1–36; cf. Mark 12:38–40), condemning outward religiosity despite inward corruption and doing violence and injustice to the righteous and the needy. Matthew 5–7 and 23–25 are well read together as being mutually instructive.

Matthew 24–25, then, builds upon the apocalyptic discourse of Jesus that Matthew finds in Mark 13, adding three emphases on watchfulness for the Lord's return: parallels with the flood of Noah, two men in the field, two women at the mill, and the householder's vigilance (24:37–44; cf. Luke 17:26–36; 12:39–40); the parable of the Good and Wicked Servants (24:45–51; cf. Luke 12:41–46); and the parable of the Ten Bridesmaids. These parables expand upon the exhortation of Jesus in Mark 13:33–37 to watch and be ready for the return of the master.

So what does it mean to be ready and prepared for the Son's return? Luke's Jesus puts it bluntly: "I tell you, he will quickly grant justice to them. And yet, when the Son of Man comes, will he find faith on earth?" (Luke 18:8). To be prepared for the returning master is to be found in living faithfully and full of faith. Faithful living involves embracing the countercultural standards of the Beatitudes as salt and light in the world (5:2–16), living by the heart of the law instead of its legalistic fringe (5:17–37), breaking the spiral of violence by loving enemies and showing mercy (5:38–48), and practicing inward devotion over and against outward piety (6:1–18). The way of faith is characterized by trusting in God's provision—anxious for nothing (6:25–34), supplanting judgmentalism with graciousness (7:1–6), and trusting the Father fully for the provision of one's needs (7:7–11).

Only in faithful living and with living faith can one be prepared for the unannounced return of the bridegroom. Neither false messianic hopes, nor hostile demands of a persecuting world, nor apocalyptic signs in the heavens (24:2–36) should distract from the believer's central focus: being prepared for the wedding feast, and being suitably dressed for that wondrous celebration (vv. 1–13; 22:1–14; cf. 1 Thess. 3:6–13).

PAUL N. ANDERSON

Homiletical Perspective

lived in New York City. Five of the women are rejected twice—once by their sisters and again by the bridegroom. Maybe Matthew thought this needed to happen within his community of believers.

If Matthew merged two different strands in telling this parable to his community, how would we tell this parable in our communities? We may wish the wise women had chosen sisterhood over lighting the way to the bridegroom's banquet, but we cannot make things up or say whatever we would like to say. We pay attention to our own communities and to the larger vision of Matthew's Gospel. Why should women be pitted against each other at the end of this Gospel? After all, Matthew began with a genealogy that includes women who should not have been there: Rahab, Tamar, Ruth, and the wife of Uriah—foreigners or sexually suspect or both! Their inclusion in the genealogy is downright foolish if Matthew wanted to establish Jesus' credibility.

Let us start over, then, without labeling the women before the story unfolds. "Ten young women took their lamps and went to meet the bridegroom. As they walked together they asked one another, 'Did you bring extra oil? You know it could be a long night!'" Can the church be a community where we help one another through the long days and nights of waiting? Can we ask one another, "What do you need to keep going?"

Friends of mine lost their son to cancer at a young age. They were overwhelmed with grief, and the light of faith seemed an ember ready to go out. "We went to church," they said, "but we couldn't sing." Nevertheless they kept going Sunday after Sunday. "We let others sing for us and we listened until we could sing again." Instead of labeling one another wise or foolish, can we enter this parable together, asking what oil we need to keep the light of faith burning? After all Jesus said, "You are the light of the world" in his first teaching session (5:14). What is the oil in this parable? Some have said the oil is love, others faith or tradition or church teaching. Jesus will fill in the metaphor at the end of this chapter. The oil has everything to do with caring for the least among us who are members of Jesus' family (25:40).

BARBARA K. LUNDBLAD

¹⁴"For it is as if a man, going on a journey, summoned his slaves and entrusted his property to them; ¹⁵to one he gave five talents, to another two, to another one, to each according to his ability. Then he went away. ¹⁶The one who had received the five talents went off at once and traded with them, and made five more talents. ¹⁷In the same way, the one who had the two talents made two more talents. ¹⁸But the one who had received the one talent went off and dug a hole in the ground and hid his master's money. ¹⁹After a long time the master of those slaves came and settled accounts with them. ²⁰Then the one who had received the five talents came forward, bringing five more talents, saying, 'Master, you handed over to me five talents; see, I have made five more talents.' ²¹His master said to him, 'Well done, good and trustworthy slave; you have been trustworthy in a few things, I will put you in charge of many things; enter into the joy of your master.' ²²And the one with the two talents also came forward, saying, 'Master, you handed over to me two talents; see, I have made

Theological Perspective

The parable of the Entrusted Money presents several possible theological pitfalls. The parable works as a simple injunction to stay ready and active while awaiting the second coming (Parousia), but the use of commerce as an allegory for faithfulness and the characterization of the returning master as a hard boss begin to threaten notions of divine justice and grace.

Lest the preceding story, about maids who merely stocked up on lamp oil and then slumbered until the groom's return, lead the reader to justify passive waiting, Matthew follows it with this story about the need for faithful activity. Two servants embark on business endeavors to increase the money entrusted to them by their parting master. The third servant plays it safe by engaging in the then common practice of burying the money entrusted to him. For this, he is dubbed a "wicked and lazy slave" (v. 26) and cast into "the outer darkness, where there will be weeping and gnashing of teeth" (v. 30). Contemporary readers may have some sympathy for the safe play; after all, there was no FDIC and certainly no government bailout for Jewish entrepreneurs living in the Roman Empire. Other writers then and since, though, condemn the passive slave just as harshly.

Matthew's message is reminiscent of John of Patmos's message to the church in Laodicea: "I know your works; you are neither cold nor hot. I wish

Pastoral Perspective

Life presents plenty of opportunities for fear. An uncertain future because of difficulty at home or in the workplace is frightful. Global threats send shock waves into everyday homes, although they are accompanied by the added feeling of helplessness. On scales large and small, the world is full of people who choose to use fear to get what they want, unconcerned for those they leave in their wake. Some scare people into hating others, by vilifying the unknown or misunderstood. Others scare people into a life of consumption and overindulgence, based on the lie that it will make for a fulfilling life or the misguided fear that there is not enough to go around. Still others scare people into burying their talents as a way of controlling them for selfish profit or gain.

Rather than serving as a source of steadying or fortifying faith, however, the church has often sadly been a contributor to the climate of fear and anxiety. By biblical calls to "fear the Lord" (e.g., Isa. 11:2–3; Prov. 1:7; 9:10) or by ceaseless talk of damnation, pastors have often tried to frighten people into coming to church; in doing so, they have frightened many more away. People have been taught to live in fear of punishment rather than in grateful praise.

On the surface, the passage commonly known as the parable of the Talents looks like part of the

two more talents.' [23]His master said to him, 'Well done, good and trustworthy slave; you have been trustworthy in a few things, I will put you in charge of many things; enter into the joy of your master.' [24]Then the one who had received the one talent also came forward, saying, 'Master, I knew that you were a harsh man, reaping where you did not sow, and gathering where you did not scatter seed; [25]so I was afraid, and I went and hid your talent in the ground. Here you have what is yours.' [26]But his master replied, 'You wicked and lazy slave! You knew, did you, that I reap where I did not sow, and gather where I did not scatter? [27]Then you ought to have invested my money with the bankers, and on my return I would have received what was my own with interest. [28]So take the talent from him, and give it to the one with the ten talents. [29]For to all those who have, more will be given, and they will have an abundance; but from those who have nothing, even what they have will be taken away. [30]As for this worthless slave, throw him into the outer darkness, where there will be weeping and gnashing of teeth.'"

Exegetical Perspective

The parable of the Talents in Matthew 25:14–30 provides continued instruction for believers living in the interim between first and second comings of the Son of Man (chaps. 24–25). As one of several parables Matthew adds to Mark's apocalyptic discourse (Mark 13), the second of three parables in Matthew 25 bears the closest parallels with Luke (Luke 19:11–27). It also coheres with the master-servant parables and references elsewhere in Matthew: pray to the lord of the harvest so send forth laborers, 9:37–38; a servant will suffer as did his master, 10:25; laborers need not uproot the tares, as such will be gathered and burned before the harvest, 13:24–30; the servant receiving mercy from the master should have shown mercy to his lesser debtors, 18:23–35; the vineyard owner pays the same daily wage to early and late-coming workers, 20:1–16; the wicked tenants refuse to pay their dues and even kill the vineyard owner's son, 21:33–42; the wise servant is faithful and just, versus one who is slothful and cruel, 24:45–51. Similarities and differences are intriguing.

In sum, Jesus here describes the master's entrusting three servants with different amounts of money (a talent, *talanton*, would have been worth six thousand days' wages, between fifteen and twenty years' earnings): five talents, two talents, and one talent—each according to his ability (*dynamis*, power).

Homiletical Perspective

Jesus' parable of the Talents has enjoyed—or been subjected to—a host of interpretations over the centuries. Because the setting is the last week of Jesus' life, we know he will soon go away and will entrust his followers with the gospel. Some will give all their energies to spread the good news. Others, out of fear or embarrassment, will keep the good news to themselves. In the rhythm of the church year, this parable often comes during Stewardship Month. We remind people that Jesus was talking about talents of many kinds—singing in the choir, volunteering in the food pantry, and teaching Sunday school. Do not bury your talents but use them to the glory of God (and do not forget to sign your pledge card). Some will hear this parable as strong affirmation of capitalism: those who work hard and invest wisely will be rewarded, and those who are lazy will lose what they have. This parable challenges us to think about who God is in our lives. Is God harsh and demanding or gracious and merciful?

Parables are complicated and many layered. Recent scholarship has brought new interpretations shaped by realities of the Roman Empire where Jesus lived and was crucified. New Testament scholar William Herzog is among those who urge us to ask different questions: "What if the parables of Jesus were neither theological nor moral stories, but political

Matthew 25:14–30

Theological Perspective

that you were either cold or hot. So, because you are lukewarm, and neither cold nor hot, I am about to spit you out of my mouth" (Rev. 3:15–16). In the fourteenth century, Dante goes a step further in his condemnation of those who live life with neither blame nor praise. These souls are imprisoned in hell's vestibule, where they are caught in a rushing, whirling wind chasing a banner that never "takes a stand."[1] "These wretches, who had never truly lived, went naked, and were stung and stung again by the hornets and the wasps that circled them and made their faces run with blood in streaks; their blood, mixed with their tears, dripped to their feet, and disgusting maggots collected in the pus" (*Inferno* 3:64–69).

The message is clear, if overstated in all three cases: to take the easy road, to be lukewarm, never to take a stand, really is not to live at all. The one who buries his treasure will never gain anything. The one who is neither hot nor cold really has no temperature at all. Only the one who does nothing with her life can avoid all blame or praise.

The problem with Matthew's parable, though, is not only the excessive harshness of the punishment given to the slave who buried his treasure, but the very nature of rewards and punishments given by the master to the servants. The active servants are commended with a line often repeated at funeral services: "Well done, thou good and faithful servant: enter thou into the joy of thy lord" (KJV). What did these servants in the story do to earn such praise? They feverishly went to work investing and utilizing the entrusted money to make gains for a greedy boss, so that they might get their just deserts.

Surely this is not the kind of activity we mean to connote as we repeat these words at graveside. Even if we parse the allegory and say that the entrusted money stands for time and talents or spiritual gifts, still the theology can easily go wrong. Faithful service is not rightly done in fear of a harsh boss, nor is it done in hopes of future reward. This sort of interpretation dangerously flirts with a kind of works righteousness. The faithful serve due to their awe, obedience, and gratitude. God gives benefits out of sheer grace, not in response to the harried work of greedy servants.

For this reason, we should hasten to say that the boss of this story and God cannot be the same person. The third servant describes the boss as "a harsh

Pastoral Perspective

problem, a tale of an angry God waiting to punish the faithless person. When a property owner leaves for a time and entrusts possessions to three servants, it is the servant who takes the safest approach who is punished. Never mind the fact that burying such riches in the ground was, at the time, a common method of protecting valuables from thieves.[1] Despite the fact that the return on investments, then as now, is not always either profitable or predictable, the master calls the two who risk their talents on the market "good and trustworthy," while the one who hides the treasure safely away to protect the master's wares is called "wicked and lazy."

A deeper look, however, reveals a truer and far richer meaning and a picture of a God more gracious than vengeful. The parable pivots not on risk and reward, but on mutual trust. The master has given the servants talents, "each according to his ability," trusting in their ability to make good use of them on the master's behalf. Similarly, the good servants trust in their master's goodness, both in the master's wisdom in apportioning talents, but also in their master's reaction to their good-faith efforts. The mistake of the wicked servant is not in failing to trust the market, but in failing to trust the master. His poor management strategy is to operate out of fear rather than gratitude and faith. He says to the master, "I knew that you were a harsh man" (v. 24), but that is his greatest miscalculation, for what is most evident is that the servant does not know the master. Otherwise, he would have surely recognized the master's true character in trusting him with talents.

The word "talents" is a fitting pun in English, even if it is not so in the original Greek. If, in the allegory, the master is God, then it follows that God entrusts people not only with material resources, but personal and social ones as well, talents in the modern English sense of the word. These too are not to be buried beneath a bushel, but rather employed for the service of the master and the kingdom, for the benefit of all. This story is about vocation far more than it is about investment.

What does it mean to live into the gifts God has provided? This was as critical a question for Jesus' followers as it is now. In Matthew, the people are facing the approaching reality that Jesus will leave them. The parable helps them see how they have been equipped for the time when "the master is away." Today, the lesson is just as germane; God has

---

1. Dante Aligheri, *The Divine Comedy: Volume 1: Inferno*, trans. Mark Musa (New York: Penguin, 2003), 90–91.

1. Daniel J. Harrington, *The Gospel of Matthew* (Collegeville, MN: Liturgical Press, 1991), 352.

While the servants entrusted with five talents and two talents double their master's investments, securing his praise and commendations, the steward entrusted with one talent buries it for fear of the master. At this, the master scolds him harshly—revealing indeed his fearsome character—giving his single talent to the man with ten. At least he could have invested it to garner interest. The last verses declare the point of the parable directly (vv. 29–30): "For to all those who have, more will be given, and they will have an abundance; but from those who have nothing, even what they have will be taken away. As for this worthless slave, throw him into the outer darkness, where there will be weeping and gnashing of teeth."

While this parable seems terribly unfair and devoid of the graciousness characterized by other Matthean parables, it adds the themes of responsibility and entrepreneurial initiative to what it means to be prepared for the Lord's imminent return. As a means of bolstering the appeals of Jesus, Matthew adds "weeping and gnashing of teeth" warnings a total of six times (8:12; 13:42, 50; 22:13; 24:51; 25:30; Luke adds the motif to the teaching on the narrow and the shut door (Luke 13:22–30; cf. Matt. 7:13–23; 8:11–12; 19:30). Such a device would have challenged the teachings of Pharisees during the Jamnia Period (70–90 CE) in their motivating adherence to the way of Moses as they understood it, employing the rhetoric of eternal consequences. It also would have emboldened believers regarding the Roman destruction of Jerusalem (67–70 CE), calling on them to remember eternal rewards as followers of Christ, over against competing political sirens of the times.

Some of Matthew's emphasis becomes clarified when this parable is compared and contrasted with the parable of the Pounds in Luke 19:11–27; both are expansions upon Mark 13:34. In Luke a nobleman going to a far country to receive a kingdom calls ten of his servants together, entrusting each with one pound (mina, worth three month's wages) with which to trade (versus a man's going on a journey and entrusting his servants with five, two, and one talents, Luke 19:12–13; Matt. 25:14–15). Upon his return two of his servants have produced tenfold and fivefold profits, whereupon the nobleman places them in charge of ten and five cities accordingly (versus those doubling the five and two talents, receiving the master's praise, Luke 19:14–19; Matt. 25:16–23). The fearful servant hides his pound in a napkin (versus burying a talent in a field, Luke 19:20–21; Matt. 25:24–25). The master condemns

and economic ones? What if the parables are exposing exploitation rather than revealing justification?"[1] For Herzog, Jesus' parables were meant to be discussion starters. What kind of discussion does this parable open up?

We need to resist the temptation to turn this parable into an allegory. The master of this estate is not God. He is what Jesus says he is—a wealthy landowner with substantial property, servants, and enough money to go on a long journey. Before he leaves, he distributes talents to three of his servants. Jesus is talking about exorbitant sums of money, because one talent was worth about twenty years' wages. Imagine a yearly salary of $30,000 in today's money. Even with that rather low salary, one talent would be worth $600,000. The servant who receives five talents is handling $3 million! It is not unlikely that slaves would be entrusted with such huge sums. These slaves must be overseers who have slaves under them. They collect payments from peasant farmers who are trying to work off debts to the landowner. When these farmers cannot pay, their master takes their land. Those who hear Jesus' parable would nod their heads in recognition. For them, this story is not an allegory.

Herzog says these servants are given "a first-century form of venture capital."[2] How can they turn a profit, not only for the owner, but also for themselves? They can exploit the slaves below them, especially those who are in debt to their master. Jesus' hearers have to contend with such overseers every day. In the parable the servants have plenty of time to double their master's investments and get something for themselves as well. After all, the master of the household is gone a long time.

"Well done!" says the master to the two servants who double his money. "I will put you in charge of many things. Enter into the joy of your master!" What about that third servant? He gets more attention than the first two servants combined. If he fears a reprimand, you would think he would flatter his master. Instead, he is audaciously honest: "I knew that you were a harsh man, reaping where you did not sow, and gathering where you did not scatter seed." That is exactly how a wealthy landowner operated in Jesus' day—he extracted land and produce from poor farmers without doing any of the work himself.

We can hear the sarcasm in the master's voice as he mimics the third servant: "You knew about me,

1. William R. Herzog II, *Parables as Subversive Speech: Jesus as Pedagogue of the Oppressed* (Louisville, KY: Westminster John Knox Press, 1994), 7.
2. Ibid., 159.

Theological Perspective

man, reaping where you did not sow, and gathering where you did not scatter seed" (v. 24). Notice that the servant may be understating things when he calls the boss "harsh." The implication is that the boss is not only harsh, but unethical and unjust. The boss makes no effort to deny it. In his rebuke of the "wicked" slave the boss exclaims, "You knew, did you, that I reap where I did not sow, and gather where I did not scatter? Then you ought to have invested my money" (vv. 26–27). Then the boss says the most damnable thing: "For to all those who have, more will be given, and they will have an abundance; but from those who have nothing, even what they have will be taken away" (v. 29).

It would be difficult at best to align such a statement with sayings such as "The last will be first and the first will be last" (20:16) or "Blessed are the poor in spirit, for theirs is the kingdom of heaven" (5:3) and "Blessed are the meek, for they will inherit the earth" (5:5). Matthew's boss seems at odds with the heart of Matthew's Gospel. This cannot be God. God is not a harsh God. God is not an unethical landlord who steals the crops that others have planted. God is not a ruthless master who takes from the poor and gives to the rich. God does not say, "To those who have, more will be given." God blesses the poor and rewards the meek.

This is a tricky parable indeed. The internal logic of the parable works to encourage active faithfulness, but the reader will have to avoid allegorical interpretations wherein the characters and action of the parable stand for interactions between God and God's servants. Perhaps, instead, the commerce metaphors and the character of the hard boss can be held in creative tension with the gospel message of God's mercy and grace and the humble and active service that is intended for those who know that grace.

DANIEL J. OTT

Pastoral Perspective

provided God's people with talents and gifts that will enable them not simply to endure, but to thrive and to flourish. This interpretation should resist the platitude that "God only gives us what we can handle," which places God in the role of the one who doles out tragedy. It instead should stand as a powerful reminder that God, as revealed through the master in the parable, is the one who gives great gifts. The question facing God's people is, how should one receive the gift, with faith or with fear?

The criterion with which God will make an accounting, then, is not the ability to attain a return on investment. Even metaphorical markets are volatile. It is in the ability to transform a fearful orientation into one of trust, to move from terror to faith. The world is full of those who would use fear to motivate and manipulate, but the church has an important response to a world ruled by fear: faith is more powerful, for faith originates from the true ruler of all.

The church is not the master, but is composed of the ones charged with carrying forward the master's story. The church and its leaders stand in this world as the ones who will give their lives to tell the master's story. The church inspires faith, trust in God, by reminding people of all the trust that God shows, from the giving of God's only Son to the gifts given to each of God's children. In doing so, the church empowers people to share what they have been given—indeed, even themselves—for the good of all. Master and servant become bonded, each to the other. What from the outset appeared to be a mere contractual arrangement becomes true relationship. The result, for those who can move from fear to faith, is a return on a heavenly investment with interest.

ROBERT M. MCCLELLAN

the man and gives his pound to the one who had ten (similar to giving the single talent to the man with ten, Luke 19:22–24; Matt. 25:27–28). Despite the cry of unfairness ("Lord, he has ten pounds!"), to those who have much, more is given, and from those who have little, even that shall be taken (versus the lack of an explicit mention of unfairness, although both traditions feature the rewarding of the productive, Luke 19:26; Matt. 25:29). The enemies of the nobleman are slain for not wanting him to rule over them (versus the casting of the worthless servant into outer darkness, where weeping and the gnashing of teeth will abound, Luke 19:14, 27; Matt. 25:30). Coming through clearly in both renderings is the call to responsible and productive ingenuity, even while awaiting the Lord's return. Both traditions also focus on the unfairness of the master's rewards (implicitly in Matthew; explicitly in Luke), but such informs the way of the wise versus that of the foolish.

The call to faithful and productive ingenuity would have rung true on several levels for Matthew's audience. First, as believers in Thessalonica become troubled over the delay of the Parousia (1 Thess. 4:1–18), Paul calls for them to hold on to their hope in Christ's return, but also not to give up their day jobs. If one does not work, neither shall he or she eat; believers must continue to be responsible on conventional levels, despite awaiting the imminent return of Christ (2 Thess. 2:1–17; 3:1–15).

A second level of meaning may simply have applied as a wisdom parable: the most productive will be most amply rewarded. Therefore, all persons are called to be proper stewards of that with which they are entrusted—in physical resources and otherwise—in furthering the work of the master.

A third level of meaning applies to the stewardship of the gospel. In all seasons and times, despite waiting for the Lord's return, believers are exhorted to further the good news in ways creative and effective. After all, only after the kingdom is "proclaimed throughout the world, as a testimony to all the nations" will the end finally come (24:14). If this parable is seen to continue the thrust of the previous one, perhaps keeping one's lamp filled and lit involves prospering the kingdom.

PAUL N. ANDERSON

did you? You think you're so smart! Well, you're fired!" His next words describe the reality of life for poor farmers: "from those who have nothing, even what they have will be taken away" (v. 29; cf. 13:12). For refusing to play along with the system, the third slave is thrown into the outer darkness with those who own no land, those who are on their way to extinction. Where is Jesus in this parable? Jesus is with the one who is thrown outside. That is where he dies—outside the city as darkness covers the whole land (27:45).

Is this the correct interpretation? We have the right to argue. If Jesus stands outside with the third slave, that is the place "where there will be weeping and gnashing of teeth" (25:30). We have seen this description before in Matthew. Who are the ones cast out? They are the heirs who refuse to receive Jesus (8:12) and the children of the evil one (13:42). The guest without a wedding garment is out there (22:13) and the slave who mistreats his fellow slaves when the master is delayed (24:51). Is Jesus outside with all of them or only with the slave in the parable of the Talents?

We would like to know for sure, but Jesus' parables are complex and many layered. They have a surplus of meaning. This parable may mean using our God-given talents to spread the gospel rather than burying it in the ground. This parable may call us to consider how we see God. If God is gracious and merciful, we can take the radical risks Jesus calls for in Matthew's Gospel: pray for our enemies, refuse vengeance, forgive extravagantly, and stop worrying about tomorrow.

Let us also be open to the possibility that this parable is about real-life farmers and landowners, about money and exploitation. Jesus talked about wealth and poverty more than anything else except forgiveness. Maybe, when we pray, "Your kingdom come. Your will be done, on earth as it is in heaven" (6:10), Jesus wants us to include economics.

BARBARA K. LUNDBLAD

Matthew 25:31–46

³¹"When the Son of Man comes in his glory, and all the angels with him, then he will sit on the throne of his glory. ³²All the nations will be gathered before him, and he will separate people one from another as a shepherd separates the sheep from the goats, ³³and he will put the sheep at his right hand and the goats at the left. ³⁴Then the king will say to those at his right hand, 'Come, you that are blessed by my Father, inherit the kingdom prepared for you from the foundation of the world; ³⁵for I was hungry and you gave me food, I was thirsty and you gave me something to drink, I was a stranger and you welcomed me, ³⁶I was naked and you gave me clothing, I was sick and you took care of me, I was in prison and you visited me.' ³⁷Then the righteous will answer him, 'Lord, when was it that we saw you hungry and gave you food, or thirsty and gave you something to drink? ³⁸And when was it that we saw you a stranger and

Theological Perspective

Everything turns on how you translate one little phrase: *panta ta ethnē* (v. 32). The phrase literally means "all the nations," but many times in Matthew both *ethnē* and *pante ta ethnē* clearly refer to the Gentiles, the non-Jews. If the phrase refers to Gentiles, then the term "least" mentioned later in the passage (vv. 40 and 45) most likely refers to Jesus' followers or missionaries, and the passage tells the story of Gentiles judged according to their hospitality to Jesus' "little ones" (cf. 10:40–42).

If, on the other hand, *panta ta ethnē* refers to "all the nations," including Israel and the Gentiles, then the passage takes a much more universal tone, and the "least" may simply refer to the hungry, the thirsty, the stranger, the naked, the sick, and the prisoner. In this case, the passage has to do with all people being judged according to their care for the poor and needy. This essay will treat both translations as viable and pursue the theological implications of each in turn.

"The Gentiles will be gathered." New Testament scholar Daniel J. Harrington points out that the interpretation of this passage as a judgment of Gentiles according to their reception of Jesus' followers is often rejected because it leaves the passage "with little relevance for contemporary ethics or

Pastoral Perspective

Visitors, or those considering visiting the church, often approach me with a trace of trepidation in their eyes. They want to know what we believe, not in general, but about heaven and hell. "Where are you on *damnation*?" a woman nervously asked after curiosity (or the Spirit) led her into the church one weekday afternoon. She had not set foot in a church for years. More important than my answer about God's sovereignty, about God's overwhelming grace, was the question the woman's query had provoked. Why are so many "recovering Christians" walking the earth, carrying with them painful scars inflicted by the churches of their youth?

The story of the sheep and the goats is of course a story about us, but it is not faithfully told when it is told in order to incite fear. Whether or not Jesus' image of the king casting those at his left into "eternal fire" (v. 41) is hyperbole, it is a frightful image, and simple fear does not move people into a life of vibrant discipleship. To make this image the center of the passage is a mistake. The lesson of the preceding parable is that operating out of fear is not the way to live in response to God's provision (25:14–30). Fear paralyzes, and if Jesus was about anything, it was motion, moving us into a different reality called the kingdom and the Spirit of God who moves constantly through the world.

welcomed you, or naked and gave you clothing? ³⁹And when was it that we saw you sick or in prison and visited you?' ⁴⁰And the king will answer them, 'Truly I tell you, just as you did it to one of the least of these who are members of my family, you did it to me.' ⁴¹Then he will say to those at his left hand, 'You that are accursed, depart from me into the eternal fire prepared for the devil and his angels; ⁴²for I was hungry and you gave me no food, I was thirsty and you gave me nothing to drink, ⁴³I was a stranger and you did not welcome me, naked and you did not give me clothing, sick and in prison and you did not visit me.' ⁴⁴Then they also will answer, 'Lord, when was it that we saw you hungry or thirsty or a stranger or naked or sick or in prison, and did not take care of you?' ⁴⁵Then he will answer them, 'Truly I tell you, just as you did not do it to one of the least of these, you did not do it to me.' ⁴⁶And these will go away into eternal punishment, but the righteous into eternal life."

Exegetical Perspective

The parable of the Sheep and the Goats is one of the most moving, yet most vexing among the teachings of Jesus. Found only in Matthew, this parable concludes its final collection of Jesus' sayings in ways striking and disturbing. Over and against earlier emphases about being prepared for the unannounced coming of Christ, here the Son of Man sits as the heavenly judge of the gathered nations, along with his angels, dividing humanity between the sheep and the goats. The sheep, at his honoring right hand, will receive a heavenly welcome; the goats, at his dishonoring left, will be led away into eternal punishment.

How will such distinctions be made? Will the righteous be rewarded for keeping the Law, attaining outward or inward purity, or being watchful for the coming Son of Man? None of these worthy values will do on the final day of judgment according to this parable; only putting the commandments of Christ into practice—loving God and loving neighbor (22:37–40)—will suffice.

On the final Day, the Son of Man shall say:

Come, you that are blessed by my Father, inherit the kingdom prepared for you from the foundation of the world; for I was hungry and you gave me food, I was thirsty and you gave me something

Homiletical Perspective

This last teaching in Matthew 25 does not begin as the parable of the Talents began: "For it is as if a man, going on a journey . . ." There is no "as if" clause here. Jesus seems to be saying this is how it will be when the Son of Man comes in glory. He says nothing about faith or doctrine, nothing about being born again or being a member of the church. Indeed, this is not a picture of *ecclēsia* but of *ethnē*—not the church but the nations. The righteous ones have not been raptured up at some earlier time but stand with everyone else before the throne of glory.

Jesus is filling in the metaphors of the parables in chapters 24 and 25. This is what it looks like to stay awake when the master comes at an unexpected time. This is what it means to bring extra oil for the long nights of waiting. The oil has become food and drink, clothing and hospitality. This is what it means to invest your talents while the master is away. Invest in those who have nothing to eat or drink, those who are naked and sick, those who are strangers or imprisoned—those who probably will not increase your stock portfolio. This is Jesus' last lecture in his fifth and final teaching block in Matthew. Surely he must have saved the most important for last.

While this last teaching puts flesh on Jesus' metaphors in his recent parables, it is equally true that he has already filled in this judgment scene with

Theological Perspective

homiletics."[1] What, though, could be more pertinent in our time than the question of the ethical treatment of the religious other?

Notice that even the righteous had no knowledge that they were caring for the Son of Man. When would these Gentiles have had any opportunity to do so? Nevertheless they "inherit the kingdom" (v. 34) as a reward for their ethical treatment of Jesus' little ones, who would have been to them religious and ethnic others. There is no mention here of their "toleration" of the missionaries' religious views or of any sort of conversion to the faith of the missionaries. The righteous simply cared for the strangers that came among them. They knew nothing of any potential reward or punishment. They merely did what was right. Likewise, the goats are judged harshly, not due to any lack of faith, but as a result of their moral failure.

The question naturally arises: If the Gentiles, who knew nothing about the Jews' deep tradition of caring for strangers and knew nothing about Jesus' message to love as God loves, are expected to know enough to feed somebody who is hungry, clothe somebody who is naked, and heal somebody who is sick, regardless of where they are from and what they believe, then how much more should good Jews and Christians care for all people, regardless of their race or faith? Interfaith dialogue is tricky business to be sure, but interfaith caring, at least according to the logic of this passage, should be basic.

"All the nations will be gathered." Interpreting *panta ta ethnē* as referring to all people forces theological questions about the role of works in justification. The works/grace debate dates back at least to Augustine's arguments with Pelagius, but more recently there seems to be some ecumenical agreement that the doctrine of justification by grace through faith in no way negates the necessity of good works. Grace is given freely without regard to merit, but obedience to the law of love is still demanded of the faithful.

The problem arises because the sheep and goats story envisions the Son of Man's issuing judgment only according to the works of the nations that are gathered, while the church's doctrine teaches that we are not judged according to our own works or our own merit; rather, we will be judged according to the work that Jesus did on our behalf and according only to his merit. In the end, the interpreter of this

1. Harrington suggests, "The right problem is: By what criterion can non-Jews and non-Christians enter God's kingdom?" (*The Gospel of Matthew* [Collegeville, MN: Liturgical Press, 1991], 360).

Pastoral Perspective

Fear is used, nonetheless, by those who would try to dominate the world. Leaders use it for political advantage. Businesses use it for private profit. Groups of all kinds use it to advance their agendas. When read with faith rather than fear, this passage actually moves the reader into a space of holy assurance that empowers action more fitting in the kingdom. When read with trust in the faithful God, the focus shifts from a prospect of damnation to the possibility of participation in the coming kingdom of heaven and eternal life.

Fear causes people to fixate on the many things they have not done or cannot do, obscuring their ability to see the innumerable essential things they can do. "I throw food away while others starve!" we say. "I turn my head when I pass a homeless man on the street!" "I have more clothing than my closets can hold while some go cold!" "I am afraid of hospitals so I stay away!" While self-reflection is critical to the life of faith, it is only when accompanied by grace and forgiveness that a better vantage point is found.

With discernment comes clarity about the simplicity of the tasks before us and the God-given ability faithfully to fulfill them. Food, water, clothing, hospitality, companionship: these are not only the most necessary elements for communal life; they are the most readily available gifts to give. The lesson of the sheep and the goats is good news, because it asks each to share precisely what each has. That is the true center of this passage. Whether it is food or water, a compassionate ear or an open heart, everyone has something to share. Parishioners of all tenures—longtime members and visitors alike—should feel enlivened by this passage, for it calls them to serve in ways firmly within their grasp. It is a reassuring lesson from a story so commonly portrayed as frightening.

There is another piece of good news in this passage. If the most frightened question I receive from parishioners is about belief in heaven and hell, the most frequent is about belief at all. "What if I am not sure what I believe?" they ask. Christians have long concentrated on right belief, good teaching, and a proper theological understanding of how God works in the world. Councils have been formed, creeds written, and wars fought to determine how we are to believe in God. To be sure, what we believe is important. How we think about God is inextricably related to how we live our lives and interact with the world around us. Doctrine can be extremely helpful for guiding our lives, and shaping our beliefs. However, belief can strangely be a stumbling block

to drink, I was a stranger and you welcomed me, I was naked and you gave me clothing, I was sick and you took care of me, I was in prison and you visited me. . . . Truly I tell you, just as you did it to one of the least of these who are members of my family, you did it to me. (Matt. 25:34–36, 40)

By the same token, failing to do such things to "the least" of brothers and sisters (*adelphoi*) is to fail to do so also to Christ. While some interpreters have seen "the least of these" siblings of Jesus as referring only to believers, limiting them to the Christian fold misses the point entirely. It includes all persons, regardless of their religious or social status, as God's children and siblings of the Son.

At work here is a multileveled approach to Christ-centered living. On the first level, Jesus' followers are to obey his dual commandments to love God and neighbor, thereby summing up the heart of the Law. Whereas Luke's Jesus connects unlikely Samaritans with one's "neighbor" when focusing on the commandment to love the other (Luke 10:25–37), Matthew's Jesus includes the hungry, the thirsty, the naked, and the imprisoned among the ones his followers are called to love.

On a second level, disciples are called to imitate the vision of Jesus, who dined with "sinners," thereby extending divine forgiveness even before they repented (9:9–13). Seeing others as God sees them embraces the neglected, inviting them into redemptive relationship and the fellowship of grace.

On a third level, Jesus' followers are to perceive "the other" as though he or she were Christ himself. As Fritz Eichenberg portrayed in his wood-block print *The Christ of the Breadlines*,[1] the serving of the needy should be approached as serving Christ himself. How can genuine followers of Jesus neglect the prisoner, the hungry, the thirsty, or the naked if they see in these the very image of Christ? Christ-centered living thus transforms disciples' actions, their sight, and their perspectives; and anticipating the Lord's return brings such a vision for living into sharper focus.

Perplexing problems with this parable, however, abound. First, if salvation is a factor of receiving grace through faith, does Jesus here declare salvation to be dependent on one's works? Such an inference is hard to avoid; the Johannine Jesus also declares the Son of Man to award resurrections to life and condemnation according to persons' merits (John

his words and actions earlier in this Gospel. The "righteous" ones do not simply show up at the end of time; they are living the kingdom life now. From the beginning of Matthew, Jesus has been passionate about righteousness. Joseph was a righteous man, called to go even beyond righteousness to take Mary as his wife (1:19–20). Jesus' passion for righteousness is abundantly clear in his first teaching session, the Sermon on the Mount. Not once but twice he blesses those who yearn after righteousness (5:6, 10). Jesus' passion for righteousness in this Gospel is far from passive. While we may confess that we can never do enough to make ourselves righteous, Jesus calls us to active righteousness in his first teaching session: Go and be reconciled with your brother or sister before you bring your gifts to the altar (5:24). Do not seek revenge (5:38–39). Love your enemies and pray for those who persecute you (5:44).

Jesus has already done what he calls his followers to do in this judgment scene. He has fed hungry people on the hillside (14:16–26; 15:33–16:4). He has welcomed tax collectors, sinners, and other strangers to his meals (9:10). We could go verse by verse through this Gospel and find one clue after another pointing to Jesus' vision of righteousness and kingdom living. His first teaching overlaps his last teaching. Judgment day intersects the present hour. We live in a double-exposed photograph in which the last day and the present day are part of the same picture. When and where will the reign of God come? Jesus told us in his first public words in Matthew: "Repent, for the kingdom of heaven has come near" (4:17). Judgment is happening all the time, and righteousness is happening all the time, and Jesus is with us all the time.

Jesus is clear about the timing of the last judgment: the gospel will first be proclaimed to all the nations, and no one knows when the end will come (24:14, 36). Though we do not know the time, we do know what Jesus expects us to do: feed people who are hungry, quench their thirst, welcome the stranger, clothe the naked, care for the sick, and visit those in prison. The righteous ones are shocked to be blessed, wondering when they have ever seen Jesus. "Truly I tell you," he says, "just as you did it to one of the least of these who are members of my family, you did it to me" (v. 40). Those who failed to do these things are equally astonished; if they had seen Jesus they would surely have given him something to eat.

Is this last teaching a parable? Is Jesus speaking metaphorically? Separating the sheep and goats is a metaphor; this is not a lesson in animal husbandry!

---

1. Fritz Eichenberg, "The Christ of the Breadlines," in *The Catholic Worker* (1953).

Matthew 25:31–46

Theological Perspective

passage may have to live with, or perhaps better live in, this tension.

Matthew's vision is an important reminder that what we do matters. God's grace and love are given freely, and there is nothing that we do to earn them, but that does not mean that we can forget to care for the least. After all, the least too are members of Christ's family. In fact, the story presses even further than that and insists that our care for the least is care for Christ himself. If we do not care for Christ, then how can we expect him to judge in our favor?

Notice again, though, that the people do not realize that it was Christ for whom they were caring or failing to care. When the judge condemns the goats and commends the sheep for their respective ethical activities, both respond, "When? When, Lord?" The implication is that the action was not done out of any expectation of reward or punishment. The righteous cared for those in need because they saw need, and the unrighteous simply failed to do the same.

Interpreted in this way, this passage has the potential to mitigate a kind of "mission-trip mentality" emerging in American Protestantism. There are two expressions of this mentality. The first has a tendency to romanticize poverty by locating Christ as mystically present among the poor. This has the potential to consecrate poverty rather than to recognize poverty as a curable evil. Mission work needs to be focused on ending poverty, not communing with Christ in the person of the impoverished.

The second expression of the "mission-trip mentality" is more therapeutic in nature. It is marked by the oft-heard phrase, "I gave so little and gained so much." Here the mission worker feels a sense of accomplishment and fulfillment as a result of his or her service or discovers a renewed thankfulness as a result of comparing his or her own plight to that of the poor person being served. Perhaps Matthew's fantastic scene of judgment can be used to shock us out of these kinds of self-serving mentalities and return us to ministering to the poor and suffering simply because they are poor and suffering.

DANIEL J. OTT

Pastoral Perspective

as well. Often people feel somehow less Christian because they have trouble with one of our tradition's positions or statements. They feel somehow left on the outside because they are not sure of their beliefs. As a result, they feel less suitable for the work of the church, less likely to engage in it, and thereby less likely to have the very experiences that will inspire the faith they feel they lack.

What this passage provides is relief from the pressure to have all of the answers before being able to act. Whereas people hesitate at the sight of doctrine, they are quite willing to jump into action when they see someone in need. Think of those who might be on the margins of the worshiping community who spring to life when it is time for the yearly mission trip. Consider the longtime attendee who refuses to join on the grounds of theology, but who leaps into action to organize meals for someone in need. This too is faith and, according to this passage, perhaps more blessed than someone who believes all the right things, but fails to put the faith into actual practice. Moreover, in the same way right belief can foster faithful action, right action can nurture belief. I carry around with me plenty of unsettled theological questions, but it is in moments of the kind of service Jesus describes that I feel God closest and my faith most unwavering.

In the end, the two are not opposed. Action and belief become so intertwined that the faithful move through life, not as those afraid of a vengeful king doling out eternal punishment, nor as those riddled with guilt about what they can or cannot profess about the sovereign God, but simply and wonderfully as those changed by the transformative Spirit and Word into those who feed, share drink, welcome in, and clothe. It is they who are truly ready to inherit the kingdom.

ROBERT M. MCCLELLAN

Exegetical Perspective

5:25–29). One could argue, of course, that the fruit of authentic faith is one's loving works, and that authentic believers—if they really see others as children of God—would of course respond lovingly.

This leads to a second problem: why do believers fail to see the face of Christ in the faces of the needy? Indeed, the most earnest of endeavors may also blind the most ardent of believers, unless they retain an awareness of the overall mission: extending God's love to those who need it most.

A third problem involves how not only to deal with poverty and hardship as symptoms of social ills, but how also to address their causes. In long-range terms, Christ's calling us to care for the hungry, the thirsty, the naked, and the imprisoned calls for believers also to address generational factors of poverty. Just as Jesus calls his followers to break spirals of violence by the transforming love of enemies, he calls them also to break cycles of poverty, beginning with glimpsing the face of Christ in the countenance of the other.

For members of Matthew's audience, called to hope for the Lord's return and also to be ready for its advent, the parable of the Sheep and the Goats poses a fitting climax to the final instructions of the Lord. Here Jesus reminds believers of what it means to be the salt of the earth and the light of the world (5:13–14). Just as one's light should not be hidden under a bushel, one's talent should not be buried in the ground. To have one's lamp filled and lit, to multiply the entrusted resources of the master, to be numbered among the sheep rather than the goats, finally involve continuing Jesus' work by extending his love to the forgotten corners of the world.

In the last verse of Matthew's final parable (v. 46), Jesus thus redefines righteousness for his followers in all ages. Righteousness abides neither in performing rites of purification nor in heeding legal mandates; it involves embracing the way of the kingdom, which imbues the world with divine love and extends healing grace to all. In that sense, it defines living faith as faithful living, and it invites believers to put into action the Prayer of the Lord: that God's kingdom would come and that his will would be done on earth as it is in heaven (6:10).

PAUL N. ANDERSON

Homiletical Perspective

However, Jesus does not give any indication that his pictures of righteousness are metaphors. Giving food to the hungry is not preaching a sermon, and visiting people in prison is not calling on people who are captive to the Internet. Jesus is talking about food that hungry people can eat. Jesus means visiting people who are in prison, even if we think we do not know any. While we may not know people in prison, there are congregations and communities where everyone knows someone in prison.

A pastor told me recently, "When people in our congregation talk about 'going upstate for the weekend,' they are not going to their weekend home. They are going to visit their father or brother or son in prison." Some are visiting their mother or sister or daughter. No matter where we live, we can visit someone in prison. After all, the United States imprisons more than two million people, more than any other country. Of all U.S. prisoners, about 67 percent are people of color, although people of color make up only about 30 percent of the population.[1] Visiting someone in prison may change the way we think about prisoners and the system that puts more young African American men in jail than in college.

"When will Jesus come again?" is the wrong question. Jesus is already here. We see him in those we may consider least among us. We see Jesus in the child going to bed hungry. We see Jesus in the stranger who is of a different ethnic group, someone who does not look like me. We will see Jesus in the prisoner if we ever go to visit. These sisters and brothers are not metaphors, and neither is Jesus.

BARBARA K. LUNDBLAD

1. Department of Justice statistic cited by Rachel Herzing, "What Is the Prison Industrial Complex?" http://www.publiceye.org/defendingjustice/over view/herzing_pic.html; accessed October 2, 2012.

Matthew 26:1–5

¹When Jesus had finished saying all these things, he said to his disciples, ²"You know that after two days the Passover is coming, and the Son of Man will be handed over to be crucified."

³Then the chief priests and the elders of the people gathered in the palace of the high priest, who was called Caiaphas, ⁴and they conspired to arrest Jesus by stealth and kill him. ⁵But they said, "Not during the festival, or there may be a riot among the people."

Theological Perspective

The providential and redemptive action of God is often embedded in the tormented and tangled actions of human beings. When Joseph suddenly reveals himself to his brothers, he insists that their "selling" him into Egypt is encompassed in God's larger intention of sending Joseph before his brothers "to preserve life" (Gen. 45:5). Again, at the time of Jacob's death, when Joseph's brothers fear that a righteous vengeance may be exacted for their earlier fratricidal deed, Joseph replies, "Even though you intended to do harm to me, God intended it for good, in order to preserve a numerous people, as he is doing today" (Gen. 50:20). For Joseph, devious human actions are no final impediment to the divine purpose to create, sustain, and redeem life.

So it should not be a great surprise that a similar conviction is operative in Matthew's introduction of Jesus' passion. Just as the most horrendous human actions come on stage seeking to thwart the will and purpose of God embodied in Jesus, Matthew takes pains to refocus his audience. He is clear that the tangled and tormented actions of humans in Jesus' passion are superintended by the merciful and redemptive action of God, embedded in and sovereign over all those human efforts. Matthew begins to make this point as Jesus restates his three earlier predictions of the suffering that is to come (16:21;

Pastoral Perspective

In the life of faith, those who follow Jesus understandably would like to be informed as to what is ahead, where the path will take them. The word "understandably" is in place because in all of life it is only natural to want to know what the future promises and what threats lie ahead. Heading into strange territory without a road map is foolish. Roads can lead through perilous twists and turns in the mountains, or across deserts where service stations may not be available for many miles. Heading into new territory also can mean promise. Children impatiently ask, "Are we there yet?" because "there" is where grandparents await them, with presents and adventures.

On the path of faith, followers have profound reasons for wanting to know what lies ahead, because their destinies—and they know it!—are tied to where Jesus will lead them. They have memorized words from the Twenty-third Psalm, where God has them rest in green pastures, beside still waters. They want to be in such places, under divine protection. So far, so good. Disciples lean forward to hear hints and whispers about such protections. In the Gospel stories—just as is the case with believers today—they are uncertain, puzzled, and sometimes frustrated, until they get clear words about the future. They keep listening because they have faith and hope, and

Exegetical Perspective

Matthew 26:1 concludes the last teaching discourse of Jesus, using a variation of the same words found at the end of each of the four previous discourses (7:28; 11:1; 13:53; 19:1). Unlike in the other occurrences, though, here Matthew inserts the word "all": "when Jesus had finished saying all these things." This means that verse 1 not only concludes the fifth discourse (24:1–25:46); it also completes Jesus' teachings.

Once the teachings of Jesus are concluded, Matthew moves immediately into the passion narrative. Matthew rewrites Mark's account so that it is Jesus who announces, "You know that after two days the Passover is coming, and the Son of Man will be handed over to be crucified" (v. 2), rather than the omniscient narrator. Matthew's Jesus is aware of what lies ahead, and he has spoken previously of his passion (16:21; 17:22–23; 20:17–19). In verse 2, Jesus addresses his disciples by reminding them of what they know: that the Passover will occur in two days and that the Son of Man will be crucified. In the earlier passion predictions, Jesus stated where the passion would occur but gave no indication of when. Here he is linking the event of Passover with his passion. Matthew eliminates Mark's reference to the Feast of Unleavened Bread (Mark 14:1), perhaps in order to focus more strongly on the exodus story itself. Jesus' death will be the new Passover.

Homiletical Perspective

We arrive at the point in the Gospel when instructions about exhibiting the kingdom of God end. Previously, on four different occasions, Matthew has concluded a series of teachings by noting, "When Jesus had finished saying these things" (7:28; 11:1; 13:53; 19:1). The ominous "all" in verse 1 indicates that Jesus' teaching is completed. The disciples must now turn from thinking about what they are supposed to do toward honoring what Jesus was ultimately sent to do. The preacher is well served by letting the text show us how Jesus and his obedience to God are the primary focus of this text. We simply watch from the sidelines as the passion events begin to unfold.

Indeed, we will soon smell the sweet perfume of anointing and taste bread broken by Jesus' own hands for us, but we do not have the capacity to follow in his footsteps any further. Jesus responds in unwavering obedience to the call of God that is his alone. The homiletical invitation of this brief introduction to Matthew's passion narrative is to proclaim what solely God in Jesus Christ does, apart from any faithful response we might muster.

The preacher can echo the thrust of this text by reminding the listening congregation what we already know about time. All time is in the hands of God and beyond our control. Jesus establishes the

Matthew 26:1–5

Theological Perspective

17:22–23; 20:18–19): "You know that after two days the Passover is coming, and the Son of Man will be handed over to be crucified" (v. 2).

The embedded and sovereign action of God in tangled human behavior begins to emerge as this reiteration of the passion is compared with those earlier statements. Notice first of all what is left out of this declaration of the passion. While those previous passion predictions mention not only the suffering that is coming, but also the resurrection after three days, this one stays resolutely focused on the passion. No quick and easy passing over the brutal reality of the human action of crucifixion is countenanced. If God is going to be discerned in this passion, it will not be because it is a "pretend" suffering promptly surpassed by a "real" resurrection. In anticipation of the subsequent creedal formulation of the church, Matthew is insisting that Jesus will be "crucified, dead, and buried." Tangled, tormenting human deeds will have undeniably anguished consequences for Jesus.

Notice also what is added to those earlier passion predictions. It is the specification that the "handing over" of Jesus to be crucified will be done at the Passover. Perhaps there is a deliberate ambiguity regarding who is "handing over" Jesus for crucifixion. Later the role of Judas becomes obvious (26:14–16). At the level of human agency, it seems clear that he will be the one "handing over" Jesus. Here, though, Jesus announces the whole chain of events in a manner that seems actually to set them in motion and make God the actor of greatest significance: "You know that after two days the Passover is coming, and the Son of Man will be handed over to be crucified" (v. 2).

Most importantly, the timing of the handing over is tied indissolubly to the Passover. This is Matthew's way of echoing the Joseph story, as Joseph addressed his brothers: "You intended to do harm to me, [but] God intended it for good, in order to preserve a numerous people" (Gen. 50:20). The Passover connection interprets Jesus' coming passion as more than the distorted and destructive human deed it surely was. It interprets it also as tangled human action encompassed by the wider and more pervasive redemptive purpose of God. Just as the sacrifice of the Passover commemorated the deliverance of the Hebrew people from Egyptian bondage, so Jesus' death during the Passover festival identifies it as God's new and greatest act of deliverance. Thus God's intention to attend to the well-being of all humanity is embedded in and sovereign over what Judas and others intend.

Pastoral Perspective

they want a foretaste of everything to which these point.

Whoever wants to draw a crowd in the life of faith is tempted to advertise the values and rewards their particular view of God's promises offer. They then find it alluring to coat with sugar their interpretations of what Jesus was always and only about: good things, good events, good thoughts. One leader in the church noted that the people commended to his care asked him always to be "pastoral," a form of leadership related to the work of the shepherd, which, in Latin, is *pastor*. He noted that, for them, "pastoral" meant "soft," always cushioned against demands that go with leadership. No, he had to say: like the original followers of Jesus, believers today have to be prepared for "hard" stuff, through which their Lord will lead them.

The words in Matthew 16 are certainly hard to hear, to absorb, to interpret, to test. Through the chapters of Matthew we read often about what discipleship means. The noted leader Dietrich Bonhoeffer, who gave his life in witness to and efforts against the Nazis, noted that when Jesus calls someone, he calls that person to die. Dying is not the end of the story for the faithful, but it is a painful, exacting, sometimes terrifying turn in the Christian's walk. Being informed that there are risks, perils, and exactions ahead does not remove them. However, assurance from the words of Jesus helps those who hear them to be prepared so they can draw strength that they will not be abandoned in the bad times, that Jesus, who had to endure temptations, questionings, and sufferings, will not abandon them. Believers today are right there with the disciples, and they want help.

In the chapters of Matthew we find that Jesus was very generous with the knowledge he was imparting. In fact, Matthew ends the story about them with a great etcetera, as in "When Jesus had finished saying all these things" (26:1; cf. 7:28; 19:1). It turns out that there is even more, a postscript that makes everything that has gone before it now more intense, more urgent. To be sure that the urgency is recognized, the Gospel writer puts the events ahead on a rather precise calendar: "You know," he reminds them of what now they really know: that in two days they will witness and be part of the appalling apparent end of Jesus' life—and of their hopes. "The Son of Man," which is what Jesus sometimes calls himself when he wants to reveal something about himself, "will be handed over to be crucified."

No doubt many of them had seen crucifixions by the Romans at Golgotha or Calvary, on a hill that

As he has done elsewhere, Matthew elaborates on the more succinct Markan narrative. In verse 3, the chief priests and elders of the people (elders are absent in Mark, who instead includes scribes) assemble in the palace of the high priest, whom Matthew names as Caiaphas. In Mark, the chief priests and scribes are looking for an opportunity to arrest and kill Jesus. Matthew strengthens their resolve. They are no longer simply leaving it to chance. The chief priests and elders "consult together" (NRSV "conspired," v. 4). The Greek word, *synebouleusanto*, is related to the terms used for political councils. A *symboulē* was the deliberation of the *boulē*, or council of citizens. The chief priests and elders of the people agree to arrest Jesus and to have him put to death, but they plan to do this after the upcoming festival, for fear of a riot. As the story unfolds, their plans are accelerated. Jesus will actually be arrested on the evening of Passover.

In the first century, Passover, the Festival of Pentecost, and the Feast of Booths were the three festivals that brought Jewish pilgrims to Jerusalem. Exodus 23:14–17 established the pilgrimage cycle, which originally followed the agricultural calendar. The seven-day springtime celebration of Unleavened Bread occurred during the barley harvest. The ingathering of wheat occurred in early summer. Finally, in late fall, olives, grapes, and other fruits were gathered. Later the pilgrim fests became associated with various moments in Israel's salvation history: the exodus, the giving of the Law, and the wanderings in the desert.

Passover and the Feast of the Unleavened Bread commemorated the original exodus experience, where each family was to slaughter and eat an unblemished lamb and sprinkle its blood on their doorpost. This spared the Hebrews from the plague of the firstborn (Exod. 12:1–13, 21–28). They were also to fix unleavened bread, since they were preparing in haste for the journey out of Egypt.

On the first day of Passover, the lambs would be sacrificed in the temple (Mark 14:12) and their blood sprinkled on the altar. The Synoptics and John disagree in their chronologies of the Last Supper and the crucifixion in relationship to the festival of Passover. Following Mark, Matthew is clear that the Last Supper occurs on Passover (26:17–19), and Jesus' death occurs the next day. John places Jesus' death during the time of the slaughter of the lambs (John 19:14).

The chief priests and elders of the people have reason to fear a riot, should they attempt to arrest Jesus, since political and religious tensions ran high

time frame of his arrest and crucifixion during the Passover, which recalls the formative mighty act of God's deliverance of ancient Israel. His announcement of the time of his betrayal stands in stark contrast to the fearful murmurings of religious leaders behind closed doors. They declare the arrest must not take place during Passover, when the city is filled with crowds, while there is safety in numbers, and a festival spirit might arouse religious yearnings for a new march toward freedom. Jesus' pronouncement of the time comes first, however, echoing previous passion predictions, but now with the specificity of a ticking clock counting down two days. He locates the moment of his arrest at Passover, as if to say that no earthly manipulations of the timing of things can overpower the deliverance that is about to take place at God's chosen hour.

Although the chief priests and elders may have a judicious strategy as they consider the right moment for Jesus' arrest, little do they know they are up against the power that parted the waters of the Red Sea to stand up like walls beside an evacuation route across a seabed of solid ground. They may be sequestered in the palatial home of the high priest Caiaphas to scheme against Jesus, and they may have the military acumen of Rome on their side, but they are no match for the God of the Passover, who was, and is, and forever will be in charge of the history of salvation.

Now that the teachings of Jesus are completed, we might imagine Jesus' disciples begin to fall away, no longer able to hang on to his every word. In contrast to the powers of Rome and Caiaphas, he may appear to them and to us as incredibly vulnerable. Indeed, as the narrative unfolds, he will say very little in comparison to all that he has said before, from the long Sermon on the Mount to his summary parables in the preceding chapter. Jesus' own clock-setting word, however, is spoken with a power unmatched by any other human tinkering with the rightness or wrongness of timing. Human betrayal, religious fearfulness, and the military power of the occupying Roman government may be orchestrating the details of how this pending execution will take place, but the timing is clearly out of human control. Some things God alone can appoint in due season.

The brevity of these five verses exemplifies the brusque reality of how the timing of any death is out of our control. The preacher might invite the listener to consider how Jesus' announcement of his upcoming death resonates with how we hear and absorb the sad news of the pending deaths of loved ones. The

Matthew 26:1–5

Theological Perspective

As others have observed, there is one more feature of these opening verses of Matthew's passion story that underscores his intention to declare God's redemptive activity at work in the midst of nefarious human scheming. The point unfolds in the deliberations of the religious leaders in caucus with Caiaphas, wherein they both conspire "to arrest Jesus by stealth and kill him" (v. 4) and decide it best be put off until after the Passover festival (v. 5). So there is tension between the intended action of the conspirators to avoid the Passover and the intentions of God to invoke the Passover. The subsequent fact of Jesus' arrest on Passover (26:47–50) is "a sign that God's will is prevailing through all human scheming and plotting. . . . The religious authorities believe that they are in charge of Jesus' fate, but it is God's will that governs the course of events. They will arrest Jesus, the savior of the world, the one who gives freedom and deliverance, on Passover, the day celebrating freedom and salvation."[1] Against their best laid conspiratorial plans, they arrest Jesus not when they think wisest but when, in the providence and mercy of God, his hour has come.

As in the suffering of Joseph, so in the suffering of Jesus: in all things God works a redemptive purpose that desires the well-being of all that God has made. Paul provides the appropriate New Testament echo: "For I am convinced that neither death, nor life, nor angels, nor rulers, nor things present, nor things to come, nor powers, nor height, nor depth, nor anything else in all creation, will be able to separate us from the love of God in Christ Jesus our Lord" (Rom. 8:38–39). Embedded in and sovereign over even the worst actions that humans may perpetrate has been and is the saving purpose of God. No theological conviction is more basic to what Matthew wants us to understand about the passion story that he begins to tell in these brief verses. No theological conviction is more basic to the Christian capacity to confront the ragged edges of life with an abiding trust in the goodness and graciousness of God.

D. CAMERON MURCHISON

Pastoral Perspective

had all the beauty of a garbage dump and evoked all the terror one could imagine. Jesus was not telling "soft" pastoral things, but he was telling the truth that would ultimately benefit them. People today who want to package happy-talk "prosperity" gospels include lessons on how to gain happiness and prosperity by being identified with Jesus as a strong agent of his destiny, an optimistic strong man. Yet he speaks in opposite terms. He will not be in command of his destiny. Others will, and they do not mean well. The Gospel does not say—although it could, since other Scriptures do—that Jesus would deliver himself over to be crucified. No, this time he is weak, even powerless, passive: he would "be handed over" by those who in that hour, during the Passover, had the power to seize him and deliver him for a trial that would lead to death.

Is that story and that way of telling the story something that we can call "gospel," good news? At the moment it sounds as if the people in power, the religious establishment, in a place of power, the palace of the high priest, have everything the way they want it. Yet Jesus' being "handed over" is the crucial part of the plot of his life, his relation to us. In that climactic moment he does not come on like a hero in a Greek drama, a muscular, bragging Olympian. If his act in the circumstances of that Passover can be a passage to victory, from death to life, then no circumstances that anyone now can dream up or act upon can interrupt the life-giving motion of God. This God brings strength out of weakness, life out of death, and passes them on to us, who are also powerless and therefore dependent on a God of love, whom Jesus calls Father.

MARTIN E. MARTY

---

1. Thomas G. Long, *Matthew* (Louisville, KY: Westminster John Knox Press, 1997), 291.

Exegetical Perspective

during Jerusalem's pilgrimage fests. Ordinarily the Roman prefect, Pontius Pilate, resided in Caesarea Maritima, but during festivals, when the city was flooded with pilgrims and potential rebels, he and his cohort relocated to the praetorium. Acts 5:36–37 describes two different rebels who attempted to overthrow the Romans: Theudas and Judas the Galilean. The first-century Jewish historian Josephus also mentions Theudas (*Ant.* 20.5.1) and Judas (*Ant.* 18.1.1), as well as a third insurrectionist known as the Egyptian (*Ant.* 20.8.6).

The setting for verses 1–5 may be the Mount of Olives, since it was here that Jesus began his fifth discourse (24:3). Matthew 26:6–16 will open in Bethany. The Mount of Olives is part of a ridge of hills that overlooks Jerusalem from the east. The ridge is two and a half miles long and has three summits. The highest summit, Mount Scopus, at the north end, is 2,690 feet above sea level. The Mount of Olives is the second summit, 2,660 feet in height. It is directly across from the city and the temple area. At the base of the Mount of Olives is the traditional site for the Garden of Gethsemane and the valley of Kidron. The village of Bethany is located on a ridge adjacent to the Mount of Olives to the southeast. In the first century, a Roman road crossed over the Mount of Olives, traveled through Bethphage and Bethany and continued a steep decline into Jericho. Along the route to Jericho, the Judean wilderness drops 3,900 feet over a distance of fifteen miles to the Dead Sea.

In this brief pericope, Matthew concludes his portrait of Jesus as a teacher like Moses. As the story continues, Jesus will move deliberately toward his passion and death. As verse 2 makes evident, Jesus is aware of what lies ahead, prior to the machinations of his enemies (vv. 3–5). In his life and teaching Jesus is presented as the new Moses (see esp. the Sermon on the Mount). In his crucifixion, burial, and resurrection, he will become the new Passover.

LAURIE BRINK, OP

Homiletical Perspective

dying are often ready to accept a terminal diagnosis and admit their human frailty long before those closest to them. We may accompany them through shared holiday feasts, just as the disciples prepare to celebrate Passover with Jesus. We may try to deny their repeated refrains of accepting their own deaths in the deepest crevices of our minds, just as the disciples seem to turn a deaf ear to Jesus' repeated passion predictions. We may engage in mathematical maneuvering of their numbered days, reaching longingly toward the outer limits of probable ranges in time, but that limit will all too soon appear unavoidable. We may work hard to try to get ahead of our grief, disbelieving that the days of those we love are waning, and find ourselves yearning desperately for more control over time. However, the timing of another's death always happens apart from our own schemes of denial, mental maneuvering, and longing to manipulate time.

Indeed, even deaths we pray to come sooner, to bring release from whatever ails the dying, occur when the timing is God's and not our own. At this turning point in the Gospel, by sheer obedience to the Author of creation and all its orders, Jesus shows us how to accept that moments of life and death are solely in the hand of God.

While the pending death of Jesus and God's control over his time may resonate with our own experiences of anticipated deaths, a faithful proclamation of this text should not simply force a comparison. While he faces an excruciatingly human death, Jesus' journey forward into this passion narrative is still his to bear alone. His is an obedience to God we cannot mimic. His is a sacrifice we cannot imagine. His is an act of love we can barely fathom. His is a new Passover moment of deliverance we can pass through, only because he himself has parted the way for us. Some things only God can do.

AGNES W. NORFLEET

⁶Now while Jesus was at Bethany in the house of Simon the leper, ⁷a woman came to him with an alabaster jar of very costly ointment, and she poured it on his head as he sat at the table. ⁸But when the disciples saw it, they were angry and said, "Why this waste? ⁹For this ointment could have been sold for a large sum, and the money given to the poor." ¹⁰But Jesus, aware of this, said to them, "Why do you trouble the woman? She has performed a good service for me. ¹¹For you always have the poor with you, but you will not always have me. ¹²By pouring this ointment on my body she has prepared me for burial. ¹³Truly I tell you, wherever this good news is proclaimed in the whole world, what she has done will be told in remembrance of her."

¹⁴Then one of the twelve, who was called Judas Iscariot, went to the chief priests ¹⁵and said, "What will you give me if I betray him to you?" They paid him thirty pieces of silver. ¹⁶And from that moment he began to look for an opportunity to betray him.

Theological Perspective

A sharper ethical dilemma can scarcely be posed than that raised by the woman with the alabaster jar of "very costly ointment." She chooses to honor Jesus by pouring it on his head as he sits at table. The disciples, who have been following Jesus and learning to live a life of being merciful (5:7), immediately recognize an ethical conflict. In anger they name the act for what they are sure it is: a waste. Such a valuable resource is convertible to cash, which, in turn, can be readily made available to those in desperate need, the poor.

Familiarity with this story can easily blind one to the ethical edge of the disciples' complaint. Knowing that they are about to be rebuked by Jesus tends to short-circuit one's attention to their concern. Surely their point is a commendable one. Lavish celebrations to honor one person—no matter how worthy of honor—divert resources that could otherwise be used to sustain many people. Inaugural celebrations for U.S. presidents every four years come to mind as a case in point. That such expenditures are done with "private" instead of "public" funds does not alter the fact that, in a world of finite resources and virtually limitless human needs, any lavish expenditure of resources for celebration reduces by precisely that much what can be applied to those boundless needs. There is something deeply biblical, even Christian,

Pastoral Perspective

When a good storyteller like the author of Matthew catches our attention, he has to do two things: let the story lead somewhere so that we get the point, and vary the telling enough to keep our attention without grimly pursuing that point. That varying can include some humor or some sidetracking, as in, "Oh, by the way," or "Oh, that reminds me," or "I can't resist introducing something extra here, something that will make all this more memorable," or "In order for you to know more about the lead character—in this case, Jesus—I have to bring you up to date on a side character." Here in Matthew 26 is one, identified only as "a woman." What believers make of this story, this recorded incident, this woman, not only does not distract from the figure of the main character; it enhances the narrative and adds color to the point.

Such apparent (but only apparent) distractions as this one inspire curiosity and lead to commentaries on the Gospels, meditations, sermons, and works of fiction. This character, in many ways not important enough to warrant the mention of her name, is given numerous names. Tradition sometimes names her Mary Magdalene, a favorite for those who need a name to enrich their own stories. It may have been she, since the Gospels provide just enough clues about her to warrant storytelling and respect, although John thinks she is Mary of Bethany (John

Exegetical Perspective

In Matthew 26:1–5, Jesus reminds his disciples of his coming passion at the same time the chief priests and elders are plotting against him. Matthew 26:6–16 contains a similar juxtaposition as it introduces two very different responses to the person of Jesus: the unnamed woman who lavishly anoints Jesus' head with oil, and one of his disciples, Judas, who seeks to betray him.

Having finished his final teaching discourse (26:1), Jesus now enters the home of Simon the leper in Bethany, where he encounters an unnamed woman with an alabaster flask of costly perfumed oil (vv. 6–13, Matthew's adaptation of Mark 14:3–9). Luke locates the anointing during Jesus' Galilean ministry (Luke 7:36–50). The Gospel of John places the anointing in the home of Lazarus at the hands of his sister, Mary (John 12:1–8). Scholars propose that the differences among the evangelists may result from two different sources. One story, the one in Matthew, Mark, and John, spoke of a woman who anointed Jesus' head, and the action was interpreted as prefiguring anointing for burial. In the other, reflected in Luke's version, the woman bathed his feet as a sign of hospitality and gratitude.

Without any back story, the unnamed woman anoints Jesus' head, while others look on with indignation. Matthew says explicitly that those grumbling

Homiletical Perspective

The church lives within the tension of this text. We gather in the company of Jesus and find ourselves variously pulled between beauty and a sense of duty, between praise and doing good works, between worshiping God and ministering among the poor, between expressions of faithful adoration and betrayal. From the moment Simon opens his front door to receive this dinner party, where Jesus himself will recline at the table, until Judas Iscariot sneaks out the back door to betray him, Matthew fills this scene of Jesus' anointing with all manner of contrasts and incongruities. A faithful proclamation of this reading will not let go of its tension.

The setting in Simon the leper's house is distinctive and nuanced with theological undertones. Whether Simon has been healed or not, his appellation "the leper" reminds us of the wide circle of acceptance Jesus drew around the outcasts. In a few short verses we have moved quickly from the interior of the high priest's grand palace, where the ugly scheme to arrest Jesus is launched, to the humble room of an unlikely host, where a thing of unbearable beauty occurs. The location of a meal in the home of a leper would surely surprise anyone in Matthew's congregation who would be fully aware of the social and religious boundaries around the ritually unclean.

Matthew 26:6–16

Theological Perspective

about the concern that the disciples raise. There is something righteous about their anger.

Thus it is important to note that Jesus' response to them does not call into question their core ethical vision. Although easily cited as a reason not to be overly exercised about the poor and their needs, Jesus' affirmation that "you always have the poor with you" points in the opposite direction. It is a confirmation of the disciples' concern, not a refutation of it. Indeed, Jesus is likely echoing Deuteronomy 15:11, which draws the same conclusion as the disciples from the continual presence of the poor: "Since there will never cease to be some in need on the earth, I therefore command you, 'Open your hand to the poor and needy neighbor in your land.'"

The disciples are not mistaken about the ethical obligation to the poor. What they miss is the fact that the woman's act has posed a genuine ethical dilemma, a question of two competing goods that cannot simultaneously be realized. The disciples only see what the woman's action lacks: immediate responsiveness to the needs of the poor. They do not see what it embodies, a deep recognition of how the reign of God is being realized in Jesus' death. The disciples are focused on other-regarding action with *the poor* as the other. The woman is focused on other-regarding action with *Jesus* as the other.

Jesus makes this evident when he interprets her action: "By pouring this ointment on my body she has prepared me for burial" (v. 12). Her action redirects attention from any number of valid ethical obligations to the source of all ethical obligations for Christians: the boundless mercy of God toward a needy world, manifest in Jesus' death and, subsequently, the compassionate, powerful presence of the risen Christ, sustaining the world in the power of the Holy Spirit. "All acts of Christian ministry grow out of this one profound act of Jesus' ministry."[1]

Thus, against the opinion of the disciples, the woman's act calls attention to that which summons and sustains concern for the poor. That is why Jesus says, "What she has done will be told in remembrance of her" (v. 13). Whereas the male disciples are ready to speak on behalf of the poor, it is this unnamed woman who recognizes that the one who ultimately speaks on behalf of the poor (and all of us) is the one who is being "handed over" for crucifixion.

If the ethical question of the poor and its proper grounding in what is taking place in Jesus is worked

1.Thomas G. Long, *Matthew* (Louisville, KY: Westminster John Knox Press, 1997), 294.

Pastoral Perspective

12:1–11). There is a saint's day named after Mary Magdalene, and around the world there are churches of St. Mary Magdalene, just as there are shelves full of works of fiction and meditations on her meaning for moderns. Yet this little story within the big one carries its own weight and meaning. In case we are tempted to pass over it too quickly, we read that Jesus stepped in with explanations and guidance that we can still use.

Oh, by the way: the Gospel writer captures Jesus using the incident involving the woman to criticize some people who should have known better than they did when they criticized her. Those who would criticize the criticizers at least should see the incident as they did. Here is their friend, their teacher, their Lord, who has just turned their minds to the horrible death that is just ahead. They know him as homeless, poor, dependent, frugal, self-sacrificing and then— *then!*—he lets this woman use not a clay pot but an alabaster jar, filled not with mere ointment but with *very costly* ointment, to anoint him. The oil will not heal him, not endow him with kingship, as such anointing could do in some circumstances. No, she just pours it on and inspires the question we might have asked: "Why this waste?" Jesus' evident silence during the pouring of the oil, which messes up his hair, cheeks, and shoulders as its surplus falls to the floor, has to be broken with explanation. This is a teaching moment, and they do not get the point.

In the course of his words, Jesus says something that many have used to justify their own lack of generosity or their grudging attitudes to the poor. "You always have the poor with you" is an observation—not a shrug, a call to be callous, or worse, a call to treat the poor routinely and with neglect. The point is in the other part of the line: "you will not always have me with you." This is a reminder of the obvious, something that will start at Passover, in two days. The point is also the obverse of what is here: it is a reminder that "you" *do* now have me with you. Pay attention to Jesus' presence; do not argue about secondary matters involving secondary characters like "a woman" or the money she spends on nard.

The next lines then make this secondary character primary. First comes an explanation of her action and importance: "By pouring this ointment on my body she has prepared me for burial" (v. 12). He is calling attention to a Jewish rite and to the importance of "presence" and the "body." Jesus is not a ghostly spiritual phenomenon but a real human with hair and feet and a body that needs anointing. Anointing occurred with a king, who was

Feasting on the Gospels

are disciples (v. 8). Mark's version makes note of the cost—more than three hundred denarii (Mark 14:5; one denarius was a daily wage). Matthew recognizes the extravagance but is satisfied with a simple adjective, "very costly" (v. 7). The oil could have been sold and the proceeds given to the poor, or so the disciples complain (v. 9). The Matthean Jesus possesses an inner knowledge. As he knew of his impending death before the plotting of the chief priests and elders (26:2–3), so he now knows the critical thoughts of his disciples (v. 10). Since the woman appears suddenly on the scene, the reader must puzzle out her relationship to Jesus. Has she previously been forgiven by Jesus, as in Luke 7:47? Has she witnessed a miraculous healing, as in John 12:1–3? Mark's version gives no answer, nor does Matthew's.

Jesus responds to his disciples' criticism by reminding them that the poor will always be with them, paraphrasing Deuteronomy 15:11. Jesus interprets the gestures of the woman as anointing him before his burial (vv. 10–13). Ordinarily the body of the deceased would be anointed with scented oils in the family home before the public burial. The woman is commended for figuratively preparing for Jesus' burial. In Mark's Gospel, Mary Magdalene, Mary, the mother of James, and Salome bring spices to Jesus' tomb in order to anoint the body (Mark 16:1). Matthew lets this Bethany anointing stand. After the Sabbath, Mary Magdalene and the other Mary go to the tomb only to view it (28:1).

Almost as an aside, verses 14–16 describe Judas's betrayal. He is identified as one of the Twelve (v. 14), a privileged member of Jesus' inner group. He aligns himself with the chief priests (vv. 3, 14) by asking the price for betraying Jesus to them. The answer is found only in Matthew: thirty pieces of silver, a paltry sum according to Zechariah 11:13, and the price of a slave who has been gored by an ox in Exodus 21:32. When Judas Iscariot attempts to return the blood money, the chief priests and elders use it to buy a burial ground for foreigners (27:7–10).

Bethany on the Mount of Olives serves as Jesus' home away from home on his visit to Jerusalem. During times of pilgrimage the city's population would increase to four times its normal size, forcing pilgrims to find housing in the villages surrounding the city. Following the pilgrim route from Jericho, the town of Bethany sits halfway up the southeastern slope of the Mount of Olives. The travelers ascended from nearly 800 feet below sea level to 2,500 feet above sea level in about fifteen miles.

The anointing itself occurs amid a number of ironies. The unnamed woman and her extravagant devotion, according to Jesus, will be remembered down the corridors of time and throughout the world, and yet we cannot recall her by name. The perfume she pours over Jesus' head is of incalculable price, but Judas's betrayal can be counted out in thirty silver coins. Judas can be bought with a measured price; Jesus' messianic anointing cannot be reduced to any known sum. The woman anoints Jesus' body for burial while he is alive, which Matthew's audience will understand foreshadows a burial so anxiously hurried there will be no time for proper ritual preparation.

The tension within this text that troubles readers most, perhaps, is the lavish devotion poured out in costly oil upon Jesus' head when the same resource could be sold to support the poor. Throughout the Gospel, Jesus has instructed the disciples and crowds in sermons, lessons, and parables about the economics of the kingdom of God. He has confronted the human lures of material wealth, inviting a different kind of investment from citizens of the kingdom. His response to the disciples' concern that the woman's action is wasteful can sound puzzling. But Jesus makes clear that this is an act of hugely symbolic proportions. His time among them is limited. He has announced his death and has set his face with obedient determination toward the cross in all its horror. The poor are always present to be served and supported by Jesus' followers; Jesus, however, will not always be present to them in person to be worshiped and adored.

The anointing is beautiful because the woman sees in Jesus' death a thing of significance that the disciples cannot yet see. She has engaged in an ancient practice, the bestowal of priestly holiness upon a royal head. Messiah means "anointed," and by her gracious outpouring of extravagant oil she recognizes him as king. While the disciples are seeking to honor the lessons Jesus has taught them about love of God and neighbor, they simply cannot yet comprehend the sacrificial nature of Jesus' life.

In contrast to the woman's extravagant anointing, Judas's betrayal is cheap. He leaves the dinner party, with sweet perfume filling the air, while the body of the one who called and equipped him for discipleship is dripping with significance. With no detail given the stark setting of betrayal, Judas trades in his friendship for a handful of coins. Quickly the text jumps from the warmth of dinner among friends and the fragrance of worshipful devotion to cold and

Matthew 26:6–16

Theological Perspective

out in interplay between the woman, the disciples, and Jesus (vv. 6–13), the theological question of God's embedded sovereignty, resident even in human scheming, is reintroduced in the interplay between Judas and the chief priests (vv. 14–16). The intricate interweaving of human deception aimed at preserving a religious status quo and divine determination aimed at promoting the well-being of all that God has made is expressed in the verb "hand over/betray." The translators have rightly employed the first use of the term, "hand over," in 26:2, when Jesus speaks from God's point of view about what is happening in his passion. Now in verses 15–16, when the point of view is that of Judas, the term used is "betray."

To be sure, what Judas is about involves handing Jesus over to the chief priests, but with the unmistakable nuance of betrayal. What God is about is handing over Jesus, but with the unmistakable nuance of Passover sacrifice that demonstrates God's sovereign persistence in a redemptive purpose. The sacrifice theme is deepened by the financial consideration offered to Judas by the chief priests. The thirty pieces of silver recall the passages in Zechariah 11:12–14, in which the shepherd is paid but a pittance for tending the flock, and in Exodus 21:32, where the same niggling amount is paid if an ox gores a slave (contrasted with a ransom imposed if the ox should kill a free person).

So Jesus is not only handed over, but also betrayed—as a disrespected shepherd or a (relatively) worthless slave. Thus the human handing over is described in a way that makes the betrayal obvious. Yet God's embedded sovereignty guides the whole way of Jesus' passion. Jesus accepts human betrayal in order that the good shepherd who "emptied himself, taking the form of a slave" might become "obedient to the point of death—even death on a cross" (Phil. 2:7–8).

D. CAMERON MURCHISON

Pastoral Perspective

empowered in ceremonies of oiling. The simplest, poorest commoner might also be lavished with oil as he or she was being readied to be commended to the Creator of that body. Believers who pay attention to the body of Jesus are stressing that he is not a ghost but a flesh-and-blood being. They are honoring divine creation and the wonder of the human. We could have left the story there, but Jesus does not.

He implicitly congratulates the women for her generosity, her risk, her insight. Then he goes on to make his praise explicit to anyone who hears or reads this story. Not very often does Jesus in the Gospels single out a person as if to put up a memorial plaque or a monument or a literary boost. Here he does: "Truly I tell you, wherever this good news is proclaimed in the whole world, what she has done will be told in remembrance of her" (v. 13). True. One example is occurring at this moment, centuries later, far away, as the story is told or read. One hopes it is being acted upon, with ointment or not, with visible or invisible means, in media available to the eyes or only to the heart.

Here is another "Oh, by the way," a moment in which the Gospel introduces a human contrast to the good "woman." He has the name Judas, the vivid figure who plays a role opposite to the woman's. There is danger that the drama of his villainy could obscure the beauty of what happens next in the wonderful account of the first Last Supper. Throughout, given its chance to reach the depth of our souls with its picture of self-giving love, Judas does not stand a chance. That, however, is another story.

MARTIN E. MARTY

Exegetical Perspective

Scholars debate the origin of the name "Bethany." Modern commentators have argued that the village derives its name from *beth* or "house" of Ananiah (Neh. 11:32). The name could also be read as *beth hini*, which means "house of figs." The fourth-century church father Jerome defined the meaning of Bethany as "house of affliction," reading the Hebrew as *beth 'ani*, which can be translated as either "house of the poor" or "house of affliction/poverty." Support for Jerome's reading is found in the sectarian writings of the Dead Sea Scrolls. The Temple Scroll, discovered among the cache of ancient texts in the caves above the Dead Sea, describes the location of poorhouses that were to be built 1,500 yards outside the city of Jerusalem.

Interestingly, no information is given about Simon the leper, who the reader would presume has been cured of his disease if he is hosting a banquet. Jesus and his disciples would need to remain ritually clean in order to enter the temple, especially during the festival. The fact that this Simon (cf. Mark 14:3) has a house in Bethany may indicate that this village was a location of one of these "houses of the poor" in which people with diseases could reside a safe distance from the Holy City. Despite his former infirmity, Simon owns a home in the village, suggesting a long-term residence. Archaeologists have excavated at least four large ritual baths on the southern limit of ancient Bethany. The presence of so many installations could be in response to the needs of pilgrims preparing for ascent to Jerusalem. However, they could also be necessary if the area welcomed the sick poor.

The discussion about the use or waste of the expensive ointment (vv. 8–9; Mark 14:5; John 12:4–6) has new relevance if the village was known for its care of the sick poor. The mixture was derived from the root of the nard plant, which grew in Nepal and was transported across the Arabian Peninsula along caravan routes. The precious scent was carried in an alabaster jar, a translucent stone found in Egypt.

LAURIE BRINK, OP

Homiletical Perspective

calculated divvying up of money and the stench of betrayal. The contrast is pointed and painful.

The preacher can invite the church to consider how it is stretched between these opposing contrasts. The life of faith involves both extravagant worship and obedient faithfulness to serve among the poor. In every community of faith there is some tension among church members about what is more worthy of the allocation of time and resources. When the sanctuary needs to be renovated, one strident leader will inevitably ask, why should the church spend that much money on a room used infrequently during the week? When the minister of music hires a small orchestra to accompany a special worship service, there are always folk who think the money used to bring in the violins, horns, and tympani is a waste. After all, an embarrassing number of children at the public school down the street are on the free meal plan and do not have enough food or adequate housing or money for school supplies. The extravagance of the worship ministry can be considered a wasted effort by well-meaning, mission-oriented followers of Jesus.

Likewise, churches that spend most of their resources and energies reaching outward among the needy in the community and the world can neglect the stewardship of praise and adoration that reminds us that God is God. Christian disciples are called to exhibit the kingdom of God to the world, but we cannot save it. Communities of faith that become so strident about good works can forget the significance of the sacrificial death of Jesus in all its unlikely beauty.

By highlighting the tension within the Scripture reading and the life of faithful service, the preacher invites the congregation to consider how we both anoint and betray Jesus, how we vacillate between understanding and not understanding, how we balance pure praise with concrete acts of service. While we may variously occupy the roles of both the unnamed woman and the named betrayer, what never changes is Jesus' prime position at the table and in the midst of our salvation.

AGNES W. NORFLEET

Matthew 26:17–30

¹⁷On the first day of Unleavened Bread the disciples came to Jesus, saying, "Where do you want us to make the preparations for you to eat the Passover?" ¹⁸He said, "Go into the city to a certain man, and say to him, 'The Teacher says, My time is near; I will keep the Passover at your house with my disciples.'" ¹⁹So the disciples did as Jesus had directed them, and they prepared the Passover meal.

²⁰When it was evening, he took his place with the twelve; ²¹and while they were eating, he said, "Truly I tell you, one of you will betray me." ²²And they became greatly distressed and began to say to him one after another, "Surely not I, Lord?" ²³He answered, "The one who has dipped his hand into the bowl with me will betray me. ²⁴The Son of Man goes as it is written of him, but woe

Theological Perspective

The conflict that gives rise to Jesus' passion story may be understood in more than one way. It can be understood in terms of religious and political struggle in which an emerging, alternative religious perspective contends with an established pattern of religious practice countenanced by the dominant political arrangement. In this framework of understanding, Jesus appears as an unorthodox teacher from Nazareth arriving in Jerusalem at the time of religious festival, making the religious establishment nervous enough to collaborate with political rulers in a determined effort to maintain the status quo. Such an understanding is sufficient to explain the suffering and violence to which the story leads. It is not sufficient, though, to explain the theological meaning of that suffering and violence, to account for what God is bringing about in these tumultuous events.

In these verses, Matthew creates a laserlike focus on just such theological understanding, on an account of what God is bringing about as Jesus is arrested, tried, tortured, and killed. The occasion of the Passover meal is central to this purpose. Although Jesus' disciples approach the occasion as an obedient act of Jewish observance for which they are concerned to make preparation, his instruction to them is telling, not because he directs them to a "certain man" in the city of Jerusalem, but because of

Pastoral Perspective

After a few opening lines that provide insight into how Jesus planned important events, the text moves on at once to involve us readers in one of these events, pointing to its practice and meaning. The event goes by many names: the Lord's Supper, the Last Supper, Holy Communion, the Eucharist, the Mass. Each has invited complex interpretations, follow-up ceremonies, libraries full of controversial books arguing the meanings, debates at councils of churches. This snippet from this Gospel allows readers, whether in independent prayer and study or in the company of gathered believers, to see what in it stands out in the context Matthew provides.

We cannot resist stopping along the way to notice a truly mysterious exchange between Jesus and Judas. It is hardly necessary to heap further scorn on Judas than Matthew's telling does. He plays the role of the evil one in all texts for this central weekend in history, as Christian believers regard it. His presence in the story is one of the sources of what today we would call anti-Semitism, just as it has inspired anti-Semitism through the centuries. Judas is the faithless one, the conniver, the ultimately greedy one, the beside-the-point character—if identifying Jesus is the point, since those who came after Jesus hardly needed him to be recognized, notorious as he had become. With a pastoral interest in the care of souls,

to that one by whom the Son of Man is betrayed! It would have been better for that one not to have been born." [25]Judas, who betrayed him, said, "Surely not I, Rabbi?" He replied, "You have said so."

[26]While they were eating, Jesus took a loaf of bread, and after blessing it he broke it, gave it to the disciples, and said, "Take, eat; this is my body." [27]Then he took a cup, and after giving thanks he gave it to them, saying, "Drink from it, all of you; [28]for this is my blood of the covenant, which is poured out for many for the forgiveness of sins. [29]I tell you, I will never again drink of this fruit of the vine until that day when I drink it new with you in my Father's kingdom."

[30]When they had sung the hymn, they went out to the Mount of Olives.

Exegetical Perspective

Matthew 26 opens with the chief priests and elders conspiring against Jesus. It concludes with Peter's denial. Within this chapter of betrayal is the brief but significant event of the Last Supper, played out in three scenes: the preparation of the Passover (vv. 17–19); the announcement of the betrayal of Judas (vv. 20–25); and, finally, the meal itself (vv. 26–29).

Matthew has adapted Mark 14:12–16, creating a greater sense of solemnity. Although Mark is seldom loquacious, Matthew pares down the preparation scene, removing some of Mark's details. For example, Matthew excludes Mark's explanation that the Passover lambs were sacrificed on the first day of the Feast of Unleavened Bread (Mark 14:12). In Matthew, Jesus announces that his time draws near and states where he will hold the Passover meal (v. 18). Mark presents an omniscient Jesus who knows beforehand the details of the location of the Last Supper (Mark 14:13–16). The Jesus in Matthew is commanding and the disciples obedient (v. 19).

The preparation complete, the scene now changes to the beginning of the Passover meal, at which Jesus and the Twelve are reclining. As they are eating, Jesus announces that one of them will betray him (v. 21). Mark specifies that the betrayer is "one who is eating with me" (Mark 14:18), emphasizing the violation of table fellowship, an allusion to Psalm

Homiletical Perspective

When the new sanctuary of Holy Trinity Greek Orthodox Church in downtown Columbia, South Carolina, was completed, the public was invited to tour the building and learn about Eastern Christian iconography. An elderly artist and his team from Greece had spent months on scaffolding, adorning the domed ceiling and surrounding walls with pictures of the creation story, the prophets, the Gospel writers, and the life of Christ. On the front wall behind the altar is a depiction of Jesus serving the Last Supper to his disciples. All of them are attentively facing Jesus as he breaks the bread, with hands extended toward him to receive it, except for Judas, who from the far end of the table is turned away as if to take his leave.

What I learned about iconography, which literally means "image writing," is that this artistic style of flat characters is meant to be three-dimensional. The viewer's relationship with the icon, through which a spiritual reality is revealed, creates the third dimension. Similarly, Matthew's account of the Last Supper reveals a profoundly theological dimension of this Passover meal with Jesus. The preacher needs simply to point to the images in such a way as to invite the listener to embody them.

The text begins with curiously flat characters. Jesus sends his disciples into the city "to a certain

Matthew 26:17–30

Theological Perspective

what he tells them to say to the man: "The Teacher says, My time is near; I will keep the Passover at your house with my disciples" (v. 18). Thus, even at the point of preparing for the meal, Jesus connects his impending fate ("My time is near") to the occasion ("I will keep the Passover at your house").

So an initial hint of the passion's theological meaning, a first suggestion of what God is up to in the impending suffering and violence, is offered. The Passover is decisively connected to the fate that is about to befall Jesus. Whatever the Passover has meant heretofore, the way is now open to understand it in relation to the gathering storm of religious and political torture and violence sweeping toward Jesus. Jesus in a few verses will explore it further, but for now he simply makes the connection—"My time is near; I will keep the Passover at your house with my disciples"—asserting that his passion has a Passover meaning.

Before the Passover meaning of the passion is brought more fully into focus, an intermediate scene probes afresh a theological theme that has been evident in each of the two preceding sections of this chapter. As he sits at the Passover meal with his disciples, Jesus confronts the "handing over/ betrayal" that Judas has already initiated, naming for the disciples the truth that one of them will betray him. Matthew's account of their reaction differentiates between the disciples who remonstrate against any possible treachery on their part, addressing Jesus as "Lord," and Judas, who protests his innocence while addressing him as "Rabbi." The nuance is important, because even a great teacher is susceptible to being controlled by a cunning disciple, to being "handed over" and "betrayed." On the other hand, the acknowledgment of Jesus as Lord implies the awareness that the power of handing over resides elsewhere. Jesus notices the difference, responding to Judas, "You have said so" (v. 25).

Ironically, Judas's very language "betrays" him. So thoroughly has he opted into the assumption that he can exercise a controlling influence over the unfolding events, discounting the possibility that the Maker of heaven and earth is weaving a redemptive tapestry through the tangled web of deceit and violence, that Judas unconsciously convicts himself. Thereby he serves as a reminder that how we name Jesus is a clue as to whether we see in him God's redemptive work on behalf of a needy world, or whether we reserve such a prerogative to ourselves. What is in a name? The difference is between recognizing that God is at work in the complexities of Jesus' fate,

Pastoral Perspective

we can let his story tell itself and then move on to the positive incident.

The meal, which is observed by almost all Christian believers, in Matthew's version—one of four in the New Testament, each with a different accent—turns on two words that have much pastoral meaning: "covenant" and "forgiveness." The story is framed by attention to timing and location: it is evening, and Jesus locates himself "with the twelve" (v. 20), whether sitting or reclining, at the head of the table, in the middle as in classic Christian art, or anywhere that he can be heard and seen. Then follows the ceremonial meal. "While they were eating . . ." is a clue to a revelation. Jesus usually reveals something at the table. He takes bread, blesses and breaks it, gives it, and speaks. Later he takes a cup, gives thanks, gives it to the others, and leaves a command. We stress this because the faithful followers in churches through ages and times try to replicate the gestures in order to help them extract and be true to what can be known.

That having been noticed, those with a pastoral focus will get the most interpretation from two words captured by the writer of Matthew. We will take them up in sequence, after having paid attention to the role of thanking. It would be inconceivable to follow Jesus without using each step to pray a prayer of thanks. "Take, eat. . . . Drink from [the cup], all of you" (vv. 26–27). Jesus calls the cup of wine "my blood of the covenant." The focus on covenant, almost an obsession, is constant in Christian memory, observance, and hope. Whoever has seen two people who trust each other saying some version of the slang phrase, "Put 'er there!" and seen the partner respond to the commitment just spoken with a gesture that "puts 'er there" in the form of a handshake has a vivid human picture of God's action in making and keeping a covenant.

God made a covenant with Abraham and his inheritance for the ages, and we are in the story. God made a covenant with Israel, renewed through prophets who had to call Israel to justice when it forgot and wandered. God renewed a covenant by bringing Israel out of captivity to its enemies. God through Jesus called the Twelve and calls all disciples since then, with words and gestures and even the voice of silence in prayer. This time the point of the covenant is brought to brilliant prominence with the other key pastoral word: this blood is "poured out for the *forgiveness* of sins." Forgiveness is necessary because the heirs of Abraham, Israel, and the disciples are forgetful and neglectful of the covenant.

41:10. Luke further highlights the act of betrayal by placing it immediately after the bread and wine (Luke 22:21–23). All three Synoptic accounts include Jesus' statement that the Son of Man goes as it is written of him, but woe to the one by whom the Son of Man is betrayed (Matt. 26:24//Mark 14:21//Luke 22:22). After this statement, Matthew inserts a brief dialogue between Jesus and Judas (v. 25), creating a parallel with verses 21b–23. The disciples respond, "Surely not I, Lord?" (v. 23). Judas substitutes the title "Rabbi" when he asks the same question (v. 25).

Judas is introduced as one of the Twelve in 10:4, where the reader is informed that he will betray Jesus, an act that Judas himself will regret in 27:4. The Greek word found in verse 25 is a participle of the verb *paradidōmi*, which has the basic meaning of "to give from one's own hand." Other connotations include to entrust, to commit, to hand over, to deliver. In a legal context, *paradidōmi* refers to handing one over to the authorities (5:25; 10:17, 19, 21; 20:19; 26:15). Jesus is not the only one who will experience betrayal; in 24:9, Jesus announces that the disciples will also be handed over to persecution.

The encounter between Jesus and Judas ends, and Judas will not be mentioned again until the actual act of betrayal in the Garden of Gethsemane (26:48–49). The Gospel of John states explicitly that after Jesus' announcement of impending betrayal, Judas departs (John 13:30). Matthew only suggests this, since Judas is not among the disciples with Jesus at the Garden of Gethsemane.

The final scene in verses 26–29 returns to the meal. As he did with the multiplication of the loaves (14:19; 15:36), Jesus takes bread, says the blessing, breaks the bread, and distributes it to his disciples. Jesus then takes the cup, gives thanks, and gives it to the disciples. It is the blood of the covenant, shed for the forgiveness of sins (v. 28). The blood of the covenant echoes Exodus 24:8, in which Moses sprinkles blood on the people as part of the ratification of the covenant. That Jesus' blood will be poured out for the forgiveness of sins calls to mind the actions of the Suffering Servant of Isaiah (Isa. 53:12).

Matthew follows Mark closely, but with some notable differences. Matthew includes an imperative to drink the cup (v. 27, absent in Mark), providing a more complete parallel with the words over the bread. Matthew includes that Jesus' blood will be shed for the forgiveness of sins (v. 28). The Matthew-Mark version of the words of institution said over the bread and wine differs from the two variants found in Luke 22:19–20 and 1 Corinthians 11:23–25.

man" to make preparations for Passover. The man is to be told that "the Teacher" has sent them to his house, where he will host them for the festival feast. Who is this man? How are the disciples supposed to recognize him? Are we to assume he will know who "the Teacher" is? Why is this one unknown and nameless person included at this high holy moment with Jesus and his inner circle? These questions, it appears, urge the preacher to invite the listener into a new dimension. Something is happening beyond our full knowledge and understanding. Obedience to Jesus' command is all that is required to find a seat at his table.

Then come foreboding words of pending betrayal. Again, there are hints of anonymity as the disciples begin to question which one could be disloyal. Custom bound participants at a common table to protect one another from any possible intrusion of harm, and yet here Jesus proclaims an enemy at hand. Judas gives himself away by his question, and Jesus' power to recognize him as the betrayer is clear. The questioning uncertainty of the rest of them also foreshadows their falling away.

If sin is a matter of turning your back on God, and evil is turning your back and walking away, then Judas already fulfilled his role as the evil one when he accepted his thirty pieces of silver from the chief priests. He turned from God and walked away. While evil may bear the name of Judas, the rest of the disciples allow sinfulness a seat at the table with their anxious preoccupation with their own culpability.

By merely pointing descriptively toward Jesus' companions, the preacher can open up this text and invite the listener to resonate with the humanity of the characters portrayed. Once we find ourselves seated at the table, confessing our own denial and acts of betrayal, then we might more fully welcome Jesus' gospel word. For even as the clock in this sad scene ticks toward the hour of crucifixion, its centerpiece is a word of astonishing good news.

In the hands of Jesus, the meal proclaims the salvific efficacy of his death ahead of time. The broken bread and the lifted cup are signs of a new covenant "poured out for many for the forgiveness of sins" (v. 28). God is ever in charge of the time, and God's purposes extend beyond our time. Judas may have sought the opportune time to betray Jesus, but Jesus alone can claim that the time of his death is near. Jesus alone can proclaim what his death will mean before it comes. The disciples' betrayal and inquisitive denials are met by God's forgiveness in God's

Matthew 26:17–30

Theological Perspective

and believing that only human religious, moral, and political wisdom governs.

The familiar eucharistic words of verses 26–30 turn attention back to the Passover meaning of Jesus' passion. Having earlier asserted the connection, Jesus now reimagines that connection. Whereas the unleavened bread of the Seder reminded the Jewish faithful of the haste with which Israel needed to be ready to leave Egypt, Jesus refers to the bread as his body, pointing forward to his impending death. Thus he makes the bold claim that just as God was redemptively active in Israel's escape from slavery in Egypt, so God is freshly and redemptively active in his tortuous path toward the cross and beyond. The original Passover event involved the sprinkling of lamb's blood on the doorposts of the Israelite dwellings, sparing their households from the death of the firstborn and freeing them from Pharaoh's captivity. Jesus refers in this Passover meal to his blood, which has a twofold connection, to the blood sprinkled on the doorposts to protect God's own and to the blood of the covenant (cf. Exod. 24) now signifying God's perpetual covenant of forgiveness.

In all this, Jesus affirms the Passover meaning of his death and destiny. No longer does Passover refer only to the covenant inaugurated by God at Sinai and manifested in the exodus out of Egypt. Now it refers to a new exodus and a new covenant that sets God's people free from the reign of sin and for the reign of God. This imaginative reinterpretation of the Passover is the clearest representation that Matthew can offer concerning how the ominous clouds surrounding Jesus in Jerusalem can be most truly understood. To understand them in terms of contested religious perspectives and associated political machinations only begins to scratch the surface. Matthew wants to offer an account that shows how in all these troubled events, God is the ultimate one at work, bringing about something new.

For those seeking courage enough to read on into this tortuous story, or to live on into life that may seem to furnish a similar measure of conflict and terror, Matthew provides it in these verses.

D. CAMERON MURCHISON

Pastoral Perspective

They turn their backs, as if to walk out into the darkness. However, their rejection of the covenant does not mean that God forgets, neglects, or rejects the covenant.

So it is that readers of this text or followers of practices commanded in it get the full benefits of the promise of forgiveness. Jesus ends the meal and the discourse with a decisive word: he would not be physically present as he was at this storied meal, but he would be present to "drink" the blood of the covenant with his followers in his "Father's kingdom." Christians, as we noticed, have argued and will argue about the meanings of the meal, but the covenant, God's agreement and promise, never is withdrawn. The realization of "forgiveness" and being right with God also empowers a new way of life.

After all the tumult shown in these stories of Jesus' last days with the disciples and in full knowledge of what grimness is ahead, we read of a very quiet scene: "When they had sung the hymn, they went out to the Mount of Olives" (v. 30). With the hymn they had commended themselves to the maker of the covenant and the forgiver they had come to know in the Creator, the one Jesus called "Father," and to the Jesus who did the calling and who still calls. Careful attention to the call and its results makes clear that all these stories are not just recollections of the past, or literary forms that demand and deserve study. They are central to the care and cure of all who respond to them. As always, and ever anew.

Gospel stories help believers meet the limits and problems, the puzzles and paradoxes of daily living, and impart hope for richer life in what Jesus here calls "my Father's kingdom."

MARTIN E. MARTY

Exegetical Perspective

The Gospel of John includes the Last Supper but does not narrate Jesus' words over the bread or wine. The versions agree that Jesus took bread, blessed/gave thanks, broke it, and said, "This is my body." However, 1 Corinthians and the Gospel of Luke add "which is given for you. Do this in remembrance of me" (Luke 22:19; 1 Cor. 11:24). The cup follows the meal in Luke and Paul's versions, but Jesus does not give thanks. The sayings found in Matthew and Mark make explicit the connection between Moses and Jesus by describing the cup as the blood of the covenant (Exod. 24:8; Matt. 26:28//Mark 14:24). In the variants of Luke and Paul, it is "the blood of the new covenant," perhaps an allusion to Jeremiah 31:31 (the eschatological new covenant). Scholars propose that Paul preserves the earliest tradition.

The meal is concluded with Jesus giving a final passion prediction. He will not drink the fruit of the vine until he can do so with his disciples in the kingdom of his father (v. 29). Jesus prophesies his death but also anticipates the eschatological banquet that awaits him. Earlier in the Gospel, Jesus spoke of the experience of the kingdom of heaven as a grand banquet (8:11; 22:1–14; 25:1–13). The meal concludes with a hymn, and then Jesus and the disciples go out to the Mount of Olives (v. 30).

Christians tend to focus on the Last Supper of Jesus within its eucharistic context, but within the setting of the historical Jesus, the meal is meant to resemble the traditional Passover Seder. Although Exodus 12:11 says that the meal should be eaten by those ready to depart, the Passover celebration among first-century Jews had adopted the Greco-Roman custom of reclining. Ordinarily the meal occurred in the household with the family gathered. Jesus eats his last Passover with his disciples, perhaps a symbolic reconstruction of his new family (12:46–50). The Passover lamb slaughtered on the previous day would now be eaten, although no mention of this is made in the Synoptic Gospels (although cf. John 19:14).

LAURIE BRINK, OP

Homiletical Perspective

good time. God's saving acts in human history bear significance that transcends our accounting and creates a new dimension of God's power and purposes for us.

Many a student of Scripture has long struggled with the fact that someone so close to Jesus as to be counted among the Twelve is the one to betray him. Yet we know from our own experiences that is always the nature of betrayal. Betrayal takes place in the context of the most intimate of relationships. Marriage vows are broken. Children deny the honor due their parents. Parents fail their children in countless ways. Siblings go for years without speaking, because of caustic words, poorly chosen in the heat of a stressful moment. Longtime friendships can break apart at the seams because of the tiniest slight or misunderstanding. Judas has to be a friend to be believable. As through an icon, we can look at these characters Matthew has painted and enter a dimension that invites our participation.

We also participate in this gospel moment by the regular gathering around the Lord's Supper. We recall Jesus' ceremonial actions by taking bread, blessing it, breaking it, and announcing its significance. We lift the cup proclaiming a new covenant made by God for the forgiveness of sin. In so doing, we model the life of faith. We gather, we invoke God's blessing, we are nurtured at the hand of Jesus, and we are sent to share.

The rich texture of this dramatic meal during the last hours of Jesus' life encourages us to take our part in the life of faith. Jesus finds room for us to gather in the company of fellow disciples and find ourselves at the crux of the worshiping life. Together we move from faithful obedience to questions, to confession, to acceptance of Jesus' forgiveness. Then, having been nurtured at Table, we are sent forth singing, to relate to God and one another through an altogether new covenant, a new dimension.

AGNES W. NORFLEET

Matthew 26:31–35

³¹Then Jesus said to them, "You will all become deserters because of me this night; for it is written,
   'I will strike the shepherd,
      and the sheep of the flock will be scattered.'
³²But after I am raised up, I will go ahead of you to Galilee." ³³Peter said to him, "Though all become deserters because of you, I will never desert you." ³⁴Jesus said to him, "Truly I tell you, this very night, before the cock crows, you will deny me three times." ³⁵Peter said to him, "Even though I must die with you, I will not deny you." And so said all the disciples.

Theological Perspective

This passage is a conversation about two predictions. Jesus predicts what Peter will do, and Peter in turn predicts differently. Logically, they cannot both be right. If Jesus is correct, all the disciples will fall away, denying and disowning their teacher in his most perilous hour. If Peter is correct, then at least one disciple—namely, Peter himself—will stay true to the end. Their point of disagreement concerns the likely actions of Peter. Peter, one of the parties to the debate, is also the subject of the debate.

Ordinarily we might expect that the most knowledgeable expert on Peter would be Peter himself. If we bracket for the moment any ideas about Jesus' supernatural foreknowledge, and consider this only as a debate between a disciple and teacher, does it not seem likely that Peter is in the best position to gauge his own loyalty? Indeed, even if Peter should find loyalty more difficult than he anticipates, surely making such a public pledge of fealty would hold him accountable, would it not? How could Peter be so deluded about his capabilities?

When read from within a late-modern context, this text tests the fragility and contingency of selfhood as it has come to be commonly conceived. Many contemporary people have a sense of themselves not just as agents or even subjects, but precisely as selves. Selfhood goes beyond a reflexive awareness

Pastoral Perspective

We are setting our faces resolutely toward the cross. As we do, we remember where we have been, what has transpired in the previous scene. In the preceding verses, Jesus predicts Judas's betrayal and pronounces woe upon him. In the next moment, he presides over what will come to be called the Last Supper. It is hard to imagine the emotional whiplash it must have caused for Jesus to accuse Judas of treachery, then serve him (and the others) the bread and cup.

Jesus drops another bombshell in this passage. He announces that all his followers—*yes, even you, Peter*—will desert him at the vital hour. After hanging around for twenty-plus chapters with these twelve bumblers and yahoos, the audience is unlikely to find this revelation particularly shocking. Frederick Buechner has famously described the disciples as folks who were "continually missing the point, jockeying for position and, when the chips were down, interested in nothing so much as saving their own skins."[1] Of course they are going to desert him.

Sadly, we too are bumblers and yahoos. The pastoral, prophetic truth is this: we desert when the chips are down. Actually, we desert long before that. When the Christian life becomes inconvenient,

1. Frederick Buechner, *Wishful Thinking: A Theological ABC* (San Francisco: HarperSanFrancisco, 1993), 73.

Exegetical Perspective

The bread has been broken, the cup has been drunk, the psalms have been sung. Now Jesus leads his disciples to the Mount of Olives as in prayer he prepares for the ordeal that lies ahead. With this unit Matthew's passion narrative begins, a narrative framed by Jesus' prayer in the garden to "My Father" (26:39) and on the cross to "My God" (27:46).

The Mount of Olives. The Mount of Olives in Scripture is a place rich with associations that provide important background to the scene before us. The Mount of Olives is where David weeps when he learns that his son Absalom has led a revolt against him and that his trusted counselor Ahithophel has deserted him (2 Sam. 15:30). It is where the Lord's "feet shall stand" on the great, apocalyptic "day of battle" (Zech. 14:3, 4), the day of judgment and refinement (Zech. 13:9). The Mount of Olives is a place of betrayal, desertion, and judgment, yet it is also a place of triumph where "the LORD will become king over all the earth" (Zech. 14:9).

"You will all become deserters . . ." (v. 31). The first words Jesus speaks sound an ominous tone: "You will all fall away" (RSV/NIV). Eugene Peterson paraphrases it, "You will all fall to pieces."[1] The Greek

1. Eugene Peterson, *The Message: New Testament* (Colorado Springs, CO: NavPress, 1993), 66.

Homiletical Perspective

Matthew depicts the highly stratified Roman society of the agrarian provinces. For this reason, his Gospel is, in many ways, politically charged in comparison with the other Gospels. Jesus repeatedly frames his message of the "kingdom of heaven" over against the kingdom of Rome. In Matthew, John the Baptist, prophet and predecessor of Jesus, is executed by the state by the authority of Herod Antipas, tetrarch of Galilee. Jesus, therefore, is the leader of a movement of sorts, a marginal religious movement certainly, but nonetheless a movement that is concerned to support values and principles associated with a very different "kingdom" than the Roman Empire.

In this context, Jesus predicts that when he is killed his followers will scatter, as the ancient Scriptures predict. In similar ways the assassinations of leaders such as Che Guevara in Bolivia, Chico Mendes in Brazil, and Martin Luther King Jr. in the United States had the effect of scattering followers. This story, however, is not only about the potential dissemination or disruption of a *movement*; it is also about the disruption of the *relationships* that sustain the movement. When Peter speaks about never "deserting" Jesus—more literally, never being "scandalized" by virtue of being connected to Jesus—he is saying in no uncertain terms that he does not want to go it alone. Broken relationships, desertion, and

Matthew 26:31–35   291

Matthew 26:31–35

Theological Perspective

of one's existence; it is a sense that one has a vast interior realm that, while it can be shared, is private and one's own. Feelings reside in the self, according to this late-modern consensus, but so do beliefs and personality and neuroses and morals. Moreover, my self is posited as somehow the *most real* me, even (or perhaps especially) when none of the onlookers—who peer in from the outside—perceive me differently. One can be "true to oneself," bringing one's actions and beliefs into authentic compliance with what lies within one's inner realm. One can also "betray oneself" by acting in ways that are inauthentic to who one really is (or so the thinking goes).

This thick notion of the self as a seat of authenticity is, in fact, a historical development, as surely as e-mail and plastic and jet engines are historical developments. Like e-mail and plastic and jet engines, this late-modern self—this "real me" that is believed to reside somewhere within, as distinct from the outside world—arose as a captivating idea that helped make sense of the world people lived in. However, it was not always so. Just as first-century Palestinian Jews certainly communicated with each other (but did not use e-mail); and just as they also traveled (but not with the benefit of jet engines); so too did they operate as self-aware actors in the world, without having such a hefty and fraught sense of private inner selfhood.

Likely writing in the eighties, Matthew presents the Jesus movement as a sect within Judaism, and is fond of having Peter represent every would-be follower. Called to utter perfection, yet actually including a mixture of faithfulness and unfaithfulness: this is Matthew's church. What happens if one accepts, very carefully, Matthew's invitation to see Peter as a representative for every would-be Jesus follower?

With the proviso that neither Matthew nor Peter nor Jesus would have operated with anything like a contemporary sense of selfhood, the passage offers an unexpected bit of wisdom to those of us with this very late-modern preoccupation. This text shines a light on this fact of human life: Our knowledge of ourselves is not perfect, even when it is sincere. This is a lesson with special resonance to those of us who use the idea of selfhood to make sense of our lives. However much time we have spent mapping the intricate and cavernous spaces of our private interior realms, we may yet be mistaken. We may discover that we are—like Matthew's church—a mixture of good and bad. We may further discover that our very selves are obscure to us, such that we cannot even predict where the good and bad lie.

Pastoral Perspective

embarrassing, or costly (forget life threatening), we retreat into our cozy environs, whatever they may be: denial, economic comfort, silence in the face of injustice. We wring our hands. We convince ourselves that we could not have made a difference anyway. We desert.

In the passion story, the lion's share of the pathos naturally centers around Jesus. We have been taught to feel the isolation, the blows, the thirst, the piercing of thorn and spear. However, it is the disciples who tell our story. We stand beside them, or more accurately, run at their heels at the first sign of danger. Perhaps preachers might spend some time faithfully speculating about the internal struggle of Jesus' friends. They protest when he calls them deserters—we would too—but what is their heart-of-hearts response? Do they find it impossible to believe that they will forsake him when he needs them most? Do they, rather, squirm under the truth of his words?

Preachers should avoid browbeating with this passage. Jesus does not pour forth judgment on the deserters here, and neither should we. In the prior section, Jesus announces Judas's betrayal and says, "It would have been better for that one not to have been born" (26:24). Here, in contrast, Jesus makes a simple declarative statement about what will happen. There is no condemnation. In fact, Jesus' friends are simply sheep without a shepherd, but the shepherd will return in time and "go ahead" of them to Galilee (v. 32).

It would be a stretch to say that Jesus is hoping that his friends, whom he loves and intends to die for, will run the other way, leaving him to die alone and friendless. He must, though, be expecting it. If we were able to stand in perfect solidarity with him—courageous and steadfast—we would not need the redemption that Jesus will embody on the cross. The disciples' desertion may be unsurprising, yet it still manages to be ironic: if there were no desertion, no brokenness, no sin, then the crucifixion would be unnecessary. Without the cravenness of the disciples, the death of Jesus loses its meaning.

It is interesting the way Jesus phrases his charge: "You will all become deserters because of me." They will not simply desert him; they will *become deserters.* The NRSV's use of "become" suggests an ontological shift when the disciples flee Jesus' side. Many of us, by contrast, are careful to separate a person's actions from his or her essence. We may not use the phrase, "Love the sinner, hate the sin," but we easily live out the cliché in the ways that we care for broken people. "You did a bad thing, but you are a good person," we say reassuringly.

is *skandalisthēsesthe,* "you will . . . be *scandalized*" because of me. Matthew has used the same word in 11:6, where Jesus promises, "blessed is anyone who takes no offense [is not *scandalized*] at me," and in the parable of the Sower (13:21), as Jesus warns, "when trouble or persecution arises on account of the word, that person immediately falls away [is *scandalized*]."

". . . all become deserters because of me" (v. 31). Jesus' arrest and the threat of the disciples' arrest with him may have been the occasion for their desertion, but on a deeper level their desertion is rooted in the scandal of Jesus' whole way of being Messiah, embracing—not escaping—suffering and death, as the passion account will soon make brutally clear!

Jesus quotes from Zechariah 13:7, but he changes the wording from, "Strike the shepherd . . ." to "*I will* strike the shepherd, and the sheep will be scattered," thus making God the active subject. Throughout the passion of the Good Shepherd, even the complete failure of the disciples has its place in the divine "script" of redemption as the triune God takes the full depths of human sin, suffering, and betrayal into God's own divine life to overcome them.

"After I am raised up, I will go ahead of you to Galilee" (v. 32). The disciples will be scandalized and scattered, but not abandoned. Their faithlessness will not have the final word. The resurrecting God will. A word of pure gospel!

Throughout the Old Testament the liberating Lord of the exodus continually makes a way out of no way. Now once again, and decisively so, God will make a way for the mission of the Messiah to go forward on the far side of death. Despite the faithlessness of the disciples and the seeming finality of a God-forsaken death on a cross, the mission begun in Galilee will begin again there as resurrection leads to renewed mission to "all nations" (28:19), led by the risen Christ.

"Though all become deserters . . . I will never desert you" (v. 33). Peter, impetuous as ever, is cocksure that he will not lose faith. He will not fall to pieces. He will stand firm as "the Rock" Jesus nicknamed him (16:18). Jesus knows better. With the most solemn of emphasis ("*Amēn!*"), Jesus declares that before dawn "the Rock" will have crumbled. "Truly I tell you, this very night, before the cock crows, you will deny me three times" (v. 34; cf. 26:75).

fragmentation are the things that the principalities and powers have always used to prop up unjust systems and to create spaces in which to consolidate power. When people connect, organize, communicate across differences, establish common causes, and pursue a common good; it makes things more difficult for those in power.

When Peter cries, "I will never desert you!" (v. 33), we are tempted as preachers to pounce on him and convict him of pride, hyperbole, and lack of self-knowledge. How can he be so pompous and self-assured? Peter's words are more constructively understood, however, when seen from a more generous perspective. When Peter cries, "I will never desert you" (v. 33) "even though I must die" (v. 35), he is not speaking out of egotistical bravado. He is speaking out of his devotion to Jesus. Jesus is at the very center of his life. He has left everything for Jesus. His commitment runs deep.

Even more significantly, he is announcing precisely what he has learned from Jesus, the greatest truth of the Jesus movement: *never desert those who are most vulnerable.* As far as we know, Peter may have wondered deep within his heart whether he could in fact make good on his declaration. He nonetheless repeats the central, defining truth of the Jesus movement, what he knows implicitly as his deepest conviction as a follower of Jesus: "I will never desert you—even if I must die." We would do well to follow his prompting and declare: "No matter who or what system tries to disconnect us, I will never desert Jesus. I will remain connected. I will make common cause, no matter what, with Jesus, the Human One, who connects me so deeply and permanently to God and to all other vulnerable persons."

Over the years, preachers have delighted in putting Peter in his place, knowing, as we do, that his courage fails him miserably. However, when we preach the Peter of *this* text, we can never lose respect for what he has to say, because, no matter how paradoxically, he is repeating what is at the core of the gospel: "I will never desert you." These words echo everything we know about Jesus' life and teachings. What Peter cannot accomplish, Jesus will accomplish. The Good Shepherd promises that he will never desert the flock. Struck down, he will be raised up and go ahead of us. The good news that we preach, therefore, is on Peter's lips: as Christians we are followers of an "I will never leave you" God. So we become an "I will never leave you" people. No matter how feebly we utter these words, and no

Matthew 26:31–35

Theological Perspective

This is at once frightening and reassuring. Frightening, because that allegiance we swear may turn out to be hypocrisy. We may not exactly know whether we are building altars to God or to ourselves. Meanwhile, there is Matthew, insisting on perfection that surpasses even the requirements of Torah. There is, though, a strange sort of reassurance here too.

First, if our very selves are always going to be somewhat obscure to us, then we need not feel compelled to spend every moment cataloging our inner intricacies and desires. No perfect answer is forthcoming, so any self-examination is necessarily provisional and incomplete, and thus best undertaken humbly. Nor is it strictly unproblematic to look to other followers in the sect. Recall, for example, the earlier parable of the Weeds in 13:24–30. There are weeds, warns Matthew, growing alongside the good plants, weeds that have been placed there deliberately by an enemy in order to sabotage the planter's efforts. As an ecclesial allegory, this parable hardly inspires blind and uncritical trust in one's coreligionists.

Where, then, is the reassurance? The reassurance comes from the fact that there is one whose assessment proves true: Jesus. Earlier in Matthew, Peter confessed Jesus as "the Christ, the son of the living God" (16:16). Jesus responded by pointing out that Peter's insight did not come from any sort of familiar human knowledge, such as the knowledge sought by the Pharisees who had just asked Jesus for a sign. Rather, this knowledge was revealed to Peter by Jesus' Father in heaven (16:17). Peter's overconfident pledge in chapter 26 contrasts perfectly with the confession in chapter 16. The theological claim is clear: God's people are known first and foremost by God. Knowledge that proceeds from any other starting point cannot yield the kind of holiness Matthew understands God to be calling for. Instead, Matthew suggests, such attempts are likely to produce blunders as cringe-worthy, self-serving, grandiose, deluded—and, tragically, altogether sincere—as Peter's premature promise of loyalty to Jesus.

SARAH MORICE-BRUBAKER

Pastoral Perspective

Certainly we are not called to brand people with a scarlet letter. Jesus' testimony suggests that being and doing are not so easily separated. Once we transgress, we are humbled to realize what we are capable of: "I never thought I was the kind of person who could have an affair." "I got swept up in the get-rich scheme; I never intended to break the law." The fruit cannot be uneaten. Yes, redemption is possible: a resurrected Christ will be reunited with his followers—even Peter, thrice-denier of Jesus. Still, the desertion and the denial cannot be excised from the story.

A prayer of Thomas Merton is famous and well loved: "The fact that I think I am following your will does not mean that I am actually doing so. But I believe that the desire to please you does in fact please you."[2] Many of us have found comfort in its simple trust and its blunt admission that we are often clueless about the right way to go. An intention is a powerful thing, argues Merton; it is the true north that helps us chart our course. We cannot know the mind of God. We can simply discern God's leading the best we can and set the intent to please God through as many of the countless transactions of our lives as possible.

The problem is, the disciples want to please God too. Peter's sputtering, echoed by the others, is clear enough. Surely their protests are not just an attempt to save face; these are the folks who stood up when Jesus said, "Follow." The bumblers may become rascals before the night is over, but there is little doubt that they want to do the right thing. It is just that they cannot. As Jesus will tell them in the garden in just a few verses, "the spirit indeed is willing, but the flesh is weak" (26:41). Intentions cannot save them; not even right action can do that. Only the power of Jesus' death and resurrection can save them . . . and us.

MARYANN MCKIBBEN DANA

---

2. Thomas Merton, *Thoughts in Solitude* (New York: Farrar, Straus & Giroux, 1958), 77.

Exegetical Perspective

With stony self-confidence, or mindless bravado, Peter responds, "Even if I must [the word *deē* connotes divine necessity] die with you, I will not deny you" (v. 35). Peter is sure that he will not deny his Lord, no matter what the cost may be. All the rest of the disciples say the same thing. It is the last word they will speak in the text until the evangelist says, "all the disciples deserted him and fled" (v. 56). So much for their courage and commitment!

With ruthless honesty Matthew exposes the failures and faithlessness of Jesus' most intimate disciples. Despite their best intentions the disciples continually find themselves scandalized by their Lord's vulnerable, nonviolent way of being Messiah. The same proves true across the centuries as in one way or another the followers of Jesus run out on him—repeatedly, consistently, tragically. Therein is the ongoing story of the church. Filled with the intoxication of our own self-confidence, we imagine that with a little more effort on our part, or by a little more liberal or conservative moralizing and better organization, we can make the church strong and faithful and even victorious, all evidence to the contrary.

One of the lessons here, writes Dale Bruner in his commentary on Matthew, is for disciples "never to say never." "On our own we are much weaker than we think,"[2] even—or most especially—when we think our dedication is strong. Who knows what we might have been guilty of, had we lived in Germany in 1939? Who knows what self-deception we are guilty of this moment? One thing is clear. Without the strong undergirding of prayer, disciples then and now have no hope of withstanding the trials of discipleship, as we shall see in the next scene.

In this brief but powerful passage disciples across the ages are warned not to put excessive faith in their own presumed faithfulness. Martin Luther was right: "Did we in our own strength confide, our striving would be losing; were not the right man on our side, the Man of God's own choosing."[3] It is the enduring faithfulness of the risen Christ, not our wavering faith in him, that "wins the battle."

ALLEN C. MCSWEEN JR.

Homiletical Perspective

matter how many times we fail, we, like Peter, keep speaking and living into these words, striving never to desert the most vulnerable in our midst.

Jesus promises that he will return and "go ahead" of the disciples, and in like manner he goes ahead of us. Over and over again, in spite of our desertions big and small, he restores us to right relationship, and continues to lead us into a world in which many are deserted daily, utterly abandoned by social, economic, or family systems. We can imagine him going ahead of us, touching someone in the oncologist's office, whispering, "I will never leave you," despite the fact that you cannot afford health care. We can see him standing in a welfare line, saying, "I will never leave you," to persons unable to make a living wage. We can find him feeding a hungry child living below the poverty line, or lifting the social and cultural veil for those who are invisible, because they dwell beyond the color line. Millions of people are deserted every day, and it is in this context that we hear Peter repeat words he knows he must strive to live out: "I will never desert you." We can imagine that, after the resurrection, Peter keeps uttering these words, gaining courage once again as he struggles with us to follow Jesus who goes ahead of him.

When preaching this text, it is important to remember the ultimate goal that Jesus leads us toward in Matthew's Gospel: the kingdom of heaven. In this kingdom, no one is deserted. All are fed. Peacemakers are blessed. In this kingdom there is a Good Shepherd, and no one is scattered. All are in communion with God and one another. No one is deserted. This is a much-needed vision in today's world—one worth proclaiming, like Peter, with as much courage as we can muster.

JOHN S. MCCLURE

---

2. F. Dale Bruner, *Matthew: A Commentary*, rev. ed., (Grand Rapids: Eerdmans, 2004), 2:642.
3. Martin Luther, "A Mighty Fortress Is Our God," 1529.

Matthew 26:36–46

³⁶Then Jesus went with them to a place called Gethsemane; and he said to his disciples, "Sit here while I go over there and pray." ³⁷He took with him Peter and the two sons of Zebedee, and began to be grieved and agitated. ³⁸Then he said to them, "I am deeply grieved, even to death; remain here, and stay awake with me." ³⁹And going a little farther, he threw himself on the ground and prayed, "My Father, if it is possible, let this cup pass from me; yet not what I want but what you want." ⁴⁰Then he came to the disciples and found them sleeping; and he said to Peter, "So, could you not stay awake with me one hour? ⁴¹Stay awake and pray that you may not come into the time of trial; the spirit indeed is willing, but the flesh is weak." ⁴²Again he went away for the second time and prayed, "My Father, if this cannot pass unless I drink it, your will be done." ⁴³Again he came and found them sleeping, for their eyes were heavy. ⁴⁴So leaving them again, he went away and prayed for the third time, saying the same words. ⁴⁵Then he came to the disciples and said to them, "Are you still sleeping and taking your rest? See, the hour is at hand, and the Son of Man is betrayed into the hands of sinners. ⁴⁶Get up, let us be going. See, my betrayer is at hand."

Theological Perspective

In his anguished prayer, Jesus evidently desires something that he suspects may not be the will of God, or at the very least he cannot be sure is the will of God. The "something" in question is no trifle: he wishes to be spared the suffering and death that Matthew's intended audience—and we, the contemporary readers—know is coming. In short order, though, he accepts death if death is the consequence of God's will. It is a haunting, stark passage that portrays Jesus as an exemplar of courage and humility. What else might it tell us about Jesus—or, more specifically, about how Christians form beliefs about Jesus?

In the second through the fifth centuries CE, as Christianity was cohering into a distinct and then dominant world religion, there were a number of theological squabbles about Jesus. Was Jesus the Son of God eternally? Did God, rather, only start having a Son when Mary became pregnant? Was Jesus a holy man who was rewarded in his lifetime by being adopted as God's Son? Was Jesus maybe not really a man at all, but a kind of apparition through which God acted in the world? Did Jesus have a divine nature (*physis*) and a human nature, even though everything else has only one nature? Did Jesus have, perhaps, a divine mind directing a human body? Did "Christ" designate some sort of unprecedented divine-human hybrid?

Pastoral Perspective

Fresh from the news that they will desert Jesus in his time of need, the disciples accompany Jesus to Gethsemane for his vigil of prayer and then desert him in his time of need. They do not flee the scene—that will come later—but while he prays in agony, prostrate under the olive tree, they are not even able to stay awake.

I remember well the experience of being in labor with my first child. I was doing my best to rest and catch my breath between waves of excruciating contractions. At one point, I opened my eyes to find my husband, chin in hand, eyes closed, dozing peacefully in a chair nearby. I was incensed. *How dare you sleep while I suffer!* I silently seethed. *The least you can do is stay conscious!* Had I had the presence of mind, I would have barked at him in the way of Jesus: "Pray that you may not come into the time of trial, buster!"

Jesus chastises them, and the story suggests that Jesus genuinely covets their companionship; after all, he is "grieved and agitated" here in the garden. More importantly, he cannot help teaching them too. His words to Peter have an instructional tone to them—not out of character for Matthew's Jesus, who frequently quotes Scripture and connects the dots for his listeners. Here the clustering of disciples—some close to the action, others further away—suggests

Exegetical Perspective

In the preceding passage Jesus has prophesied that his disciples "will all become deserters because of me this night" (26:31). Peter vehemently denies it. So do all the disciples. Now on that very night Jesus' words begin to be fulfilled as he leads his disciples to the place called Gethsemane.

Jesus commands his disciples: "Sit here while I go over there and pray" (v. 36). Does he want them to stand guard while he prays? Does he want to spare them from seeing too closely their Master's agony, as John Calvin has suggested?[1] The text does not say.

Matthew says that as Jesus goes aside to pray, he takes with him "Peter and the two sons of Zebedee" (v. 37). Mark gives their names, James and John. Matthew names only Peter, presumably to keep the focus on Peter as spokesman and representative of the disciples throughout the passion narrative.

This is not the first time Jesus has taken Peter, James, and John aside. Earlier he has taken them with him up the high mountain where he is transfigured in glory (17:1). There they fall on their faces, "filled with awe" (17:6 RSV). Now it is Jesus who falls on his face, filled with anguish. The same three disciples who have witnessed their

1. John Calvin, *New Testament Commentaries* (Edinburgh: The Saint Andrew Press, 1972), 3:147.

Homiletical Perspective

After elaborate preparations for dinner with Jesus in the upper room, and the stress created by Jesus' prediction that he will be betrayed and die, it is only natural that the disciples are sleepy. They have good reasons to be completely exhausted. It is unfair, therefore, for preachers to paint this sleepiness as a direct analogy to a sleepy, uninvolved, uncaring church. The disciples *care*, they simply cannot *stay awake*. They are human beings, flesh and blood, and their worn-out bodies and minds keep them from doing what they most desire.

This, it seems, is precisely the point of this story. Matthew parallels the weakness and vulnerability of the disciples with Jesus' experience of his own weakness and vulnerability. He experiences "grief," "agitation," desire for companionship, fear for his life, and a sense of abandonment by both his friends and, seemingly, by God. When Jesus confronts the disciples with their sleepiness and inattentiveness, therefore, he is only reminding them of what he is experiencing himself: a willing spirit, but weak flesh. As Jesus confronts betrayal, isolation, and death, he also has a "willing spirit," making him capable of uttering profound, spiritually charged words of submission to God's will: "not what I want but what you want" (v. 39). This does not mean that his "flesh" goes immediately along for the ride. The flesh

Matthew 26:36–46

Theological Perspective

The theological problem framing all of these controversies, at least within the worldview of the day, was how properly to imagine divinity and humanity when speaking about Jesus. If Jesus was in no sense divine, or was less divine than God, then (according to some theological commentators) Christians could legitimately be called idolaters for worshiping a creature. On the other hand, if Jesus was entirely divine and in no sense human (a divine apparition, say), then one would have to wonder whether God had really acted decisively to save humanity. If Jesus was some hybrid creature—a bit of humanity and a bit of divinity mixed together into some new thing—then Jesus is some third thing, a theological Frankenstein's monster. Yet one could not too starkly separate Christ's divinity and humanity, ascribing certain actions to the man Jesus and other actions to the eternal divine Son. Such an arrangement would fail to bring about salvation, it was thought, precisely because it failed to bridge humanity and divinity in any decisive way.

Eventually, those in a position to hammer out a dominant theological position did so. Ecumenical councils at Nicaea, Constantinople, Ephesus, and Chalcedon mandated what one could say, and could not say, about Jesus Christ. The emerging position was this: Christ is one in being with God the Father, uncreated, eternal, the divine Word, the second person of the Trinity. Jesus is this divine person incarnate. He possesses a divine nature and a human nature that are undivided, unchanged, unconfused, and without separation. Beyond that, the relationship between the two is a mystery. That position became the go-to test of orthodoxy for many Christian traditions, although not all. (The Oriental Orthodox churches and the Assyrian Church of the East, for example, are ancient non-Chalcedonian communions with congregations and members all over the world.)

Here is Matthew's Jesus, seemingly expressing uncertainty about God's will. One in being with the Father, indeed! For us late-modern readers, this passage likely seems far removed from the solidity and fixity of ecumenical councils and their formulas. Perhaps some of us find the anguished Jesus "more human," not in the classical sense of "human nature," but in the psychological sense of "having deep feelings." None of those inclinations is wrong, necessarily, but they ought to be held humbly and with care.

The architects of classical Christianity brought their culture's own preoccupations to their theological deliberations, as do we all. Contemporary readers

Pastoral Perspective

tutorial groups. The three who are nearest to Jesus in the garden have a front-row seat in the lecture hall; they can see up close what true steadfastness looks like in the face of a terrible ordeal. These three are also the ones who saw Jesus transfigured (17:1–7). They have seen the glory; Jesus needs them to see the anguish too. It is as if Jesus is saying, "*You say you would rather die than desert me? Here is what that looks like. You had better be ready, body and soul, and I am not sure you have it in you.*"

"Keep awake" means more than staving off sleep. Jesus' friends are urged to be alert, ready. Jesus is talking about eschatology here, not narcolepsy, and he has hit these themes before: "Keep awake therefore, for you do not know on what day your Lord is coming" (24:42). He voices a similar sentiment in the parable of the Bridesmaids just one chapter before (25:1–13). Jesus is asking his friends to be attentive. All the spiritual senses need to be engaged, lest they miss the signs of God's reign breaking into their world. "People are going back and forth across the doorsill / where the two worlds touch," writes the poet Rumi, in words that evoke those of Jesus. "The door is round and open. Don't go back to sleep."[1]

Unfortunately in this case, God's reign is breaking in amid an excruciating act of betrayal and violence. The kingdom of God is evident in more than just healings, stilling storms, and feeding crowds of people. It is easy to see and celebrate God at work in these kinds of events. The kingdom of God is not Never-Never Land. Sometimes we must squint into the gloom to see the grace. The despair can overwhelm us until we become drowsy, lethargic. We must fight off our torpor with every ounce of strength we have. This is what Jesus teaches us, and it is a lesson both timeless and timely. Preachers are all too aware of the novel ways we find to numb ourselves, whether through television, the Internet, consumerism, or drugs, both legal and illegal. The spirit may be willing, but the flesh is weak, and our eyes are heavy.

"*I asked you to do this one little thing, and you could not even pull that off,*" we can imagine Jesus saying. On the other hand, sitting vigil with the dying is not a little thing. When death is the only outcome, being present can mean everything; in the end, it is the only gift that matters. The gifts flow in both directions, in ways both beautiful and heartbreaking. I am haunted by the story of the Kenyan mother with AIDS whose last act was to teach her

---

1. Coleman Barks, *The Essential Rumi* (San Francisco: HarperOne, 2004), 36.

Master's preresurrection glory now witness his soul-wrenching struggle in the garden.

As Jesus prays, Matthew says he "began to be grieved and agitated" (v. 37 NRSV) or "sorrowful and troubled" (RSV). Mark uses even stronger verbs to describe the feelings that assault Jesus: "Horror and dismay came over him" (Mark 14:33 NEB). The letter to the Hebrews has this scene in mind when it says, "Jesus offered up prayers and supplications, with loud cries and tears, to the one who was able to save him from death" (Heb. 5:7).

Jesus says to the three disciples, "I am deeply grieved, even to death" (v. 38). In his complete humanity Jesus does not face death with Socratic calm or stoicism. He experiences a sudden assault of fear and trembling, bordering on terror. With unflinching honesty the Gospel writer portrays the savior of the world in the most unheroic manner.

All Jesus asks of his disciples is that they remain with him and stay awake. In Matthew, to "stay awake" implies being on watch for signs of the coming kingdom of the "Son of Man" (24:42). Now, in the hour of his need, the disciples fall asleep, "for their eyes were heavy" (v. 43), weighed down by their own fear and despair.

Going a short distance apart, Jesus throws himself on the ground and prays in the anguish of his spirit, "My Father, if it is possible, let this cup pass from me" (v. 39). Jesus has taught his disciples to address God in prayer as "our Father" (*pater hēmōn*, 6:9) but in his unique sonship Jesus alone addresses God as "*my* Father" (*pater mou*, v. 39).

Jesus begins by asking earnestly if it might be possible to achieve the world's salvation in any way that would not require his suffering and death. He prays fervently, "Let this cup pass from me." On its simplest level the cup is a metaphor for death. Earlier Jesus has asked the sons of Zebedee, "Are you able to drink the cup that I am about to drink?" (20:21–22). There the cup clearly refers to death, their deaths along with his. Here there is likely a deeper, more disturbing aspect to the image. The prophets of Israel had often used the metaphor of cup to symbolize the judgment and wrath of God (e.g., Isa. 51:17, 22; Jer. 25:15–28). It is the drinking of that cup, symbol of the awesome judgment of God on the full range of human sinfulness, that fills Jesus with such intense anguish.

Nevertheless, he submits fully and freely to the will of God, however inscrutable, however terrifying it may be: "not what I want but what you want" (v. 39). As Jesus has taught his disciples, so he now prays his own "Lord's prayer," "Thy will be done."

is "weak." It creates distress, fear, and the desire to negotiate his way out of his predicament if possible: "if it is possible let this cup pass from me" (v. 39). Flesh is, by nature, "sleepy," "unwilling," not completely up to the task.

From this perspective, Gethsemane is about a shared confrontation between willing spirits and weak flesh. It is about exhausted disciples sleeping while the great spiritual drama of salvation unfolds in their very midst. It is also about Jesus entering deeply into this all-too-human flesh/spirit conundrum, uttering in the same breath, "Let this cup pass from me" and "yet not what I want but what you want" (v. 39). What Jesus sees in the disciples' sleepy oblivion only mirrors his own struggles. In his nagging at them, we may overhear his own fussing at himself, as he goes back and forth between pleading with God and submitting to God.

On the journey to the crucifixion, a big piece of what is happening christologically is the identification of God, through Jesus Christ, with humanity at its very depths. Although this identification achieves its fullest expression at the crucifixion, it begins to intensify in Gethsemane, as we see Jesus taking upon himself the struggle that exists perpetually between the human spirit and human flesh. Preachers can take the opportunity at this point to remind listeners of this divine/human identification and of its importance. Without God's identification with our humanity fully in Jesus Christ, there can be no redemption of our humanity at the cross.

At Gethsemane God remains silent, not intervening to change the course of events, but entering into human weakness, struggling with the weight of human "flesh." When we observe this struggle closely, we discover that Jesus *understands*. Just as Jesus' resurrection body, when presented to doubting Thomas, will continue to bear the wounds that we have inflicted upon it (John 20:26–29), so Jesus also experiences the wounds of our indecisiveness, our arguing with God, our sleepiness, and, at times, our utter unawareness of the drama of salvation in our midst. Jesus understands all of these things from the inside out, bearing them, along with many other human weaknesses, in his own body to the cross.

As the writer to the Hebrews puts it, "we do not have a high priest who is unable to sympathize with our weaknesses, but we have one who in every respect has been tested as we are, yet without sin" (Heb. 4:15). In the words of the hymn "What a Friend We Have in Jesus," "Jesus knows our every

Matthew 26:36–46

Theological Perspective

who see here a relatable, sensitive Jesus might be surprised to learn that this very story was used as evidence in one of the classical dogmatic debates that strike us today as so stultifying. The monothelite controversy was a seventh-century argument about whether Christ had one will or two. Parties to the controversy gravitated to this text, for obvious reasons. Monothelites, who believed that Christ had two natures but only one will, interpreted this story to mean that Christ's singular will was different from God's. Dyothelites, on the other hand, believed that Christ had two natural wills, as a logical consequence of his having (as Chalcedon insisted) two natures. They cited this story as proof of their position, with some even arguing that Jesus said these words precisely in order to demonstrate that he had two wills.

"Why would someone use this passage only to score points in an abstract theological debate?" we might ask, and it is a fair and important question. However, it is worth remembering that past generations of Christians would balk at the thought of reading Scripture in the hopes of identifying a relatable Jesus with deep inner feelings. Are we wrong? Are they? The more salient point, in my opinion, is that there are two definitions of "human" at stake: one metaphysical and one psychological. Such should be expected. Everyone probes theological mysteries from his or her own perspective, and humanity has defined itself differently in different contexts. Sometimes the emphasis has been upon a quantity called "human nature." Sometimes the scientific definition of *Homo sapiens* has held explanatory sway. Sometimes people imagine a human person as a unique individual possessing inner feelings and emotional depths. Sometimes people make sense of the world by thinking of humans as rational animals. At various points in history, groups of people have been functionally denied full humanity, due (for example) to their race or gender or ability.

In fact, one often encounters a hodgepodge of the above definitions, and widespread confusion over whether and how they can be true at the same time. Careful and thoughtful theological reflection must address rival understandings of what it means to be human—not accepting one version uncritically, and not blithely accepting an incoherent blur of contradictory definitions. We owe our predecessors, and ourselves, that kind of charitable scrutiny.

SARAH MORICE-BRUBAKER

Pastoral Perspective

young daughter how to bury her. The dying can teach us, if we are awake enough to receive the lesson. Nowhere is that more evident than in the story of Jesus' passion.

Still, even without his friends bolstering him with spiritual support, Jesus appears to get what he needs from the time of prayer. Mark's rendition of this prayer has Jesus saying the same thing each time: "Abba, Father, for you all things are possible; remove this cup from me; yet, not what I want, but what you want" (Mark 14:36). Matthew's Jesus, by contrast, evolves in his prayer. He begins as Mark's Jesus does, but by the second time he prays, something has shifted: "My Father, if this cannot pass unless I drink it, your will be done" (v. 42). There is a subtle difference. In the first, Jesus petitions God, "Remove this cup from me." In the second, there is no imperative, no plaintive request. Jesus has come to a place of grim, steely acceptance. He does not relish what is to come, but he is ready, at least, to face it.

We see this readiness at the end of the passage, when he rouses his sleepy friends for the next scene in the drama: betrayal with a kiss, a brief flare of violence, and capture. Again Jesus' words contain eschatological overtones: "the hour is at hand." As the mob makes its way into the garden, he invites them twice to "see" what is happening. This is a key moment; their eyes cannot be heavy for it. *You will soon run away,* Jesus seems to say. *But for a little while longer, you must be a witness. Do not go back to sleep.*

MARYANN MCKIBBEN DANA

Exegetical Perspective

As he prays, the disciples sleep. All he has asked of them is to watch and pray with him. Finding them asleep, Jesus is dismayed. He rebukes Peter and charges him, "Stay awake and pray that you may not come into the time of trial [*peirasmon*]!" (v. 41). Again it is the same word used in the Lord's Prayer: "do not bring us to the time of trial" (6:13).

A second time Jesus goes apart and prays. Note the subtle shift in his petition. "My Father, if this *cannot pass* unless I drink it, your will be done" (v. 42). It is becoming clear to Jesus that faithfulness to the will of God will indeed involve drinking the cup of death and judgment to its dregs.

As the disciples still sleep, Jesus goes aside again and prays a third time. As Jesus had faced a threefold temptation by the devil in the wilderness, so now in the garden he faces a threefold inner struggle to submit fully to the will of God, even unto death.

Three times Jesus prays. Three times he finds the disciples asleep. Now with his resolve tempered in the furnace of agonized prayer, Jesus is prepared to face "the hour . . . at hand" as "the Son of Man is betrayed [*paradidotai*, "handed over"] into the hands of sinners" (26:45b). Earlier Jesus had prophesied that "all the tribes of the earth . . . will see 'the Son of Man coming on the clouds of heaven' with power and great glory" (24:30). For now Jesus urges the disciples to rise and go with him: "See, my betrayer [*paradidous*—my "hander-over"] is at hand [*ēngiken*, v. 46]." Ironically and significantly *ēngiken* is the same word used both by John the Baptizer and by Jesus in proclaiming that the kingdom of God "is at hand" (3:2; 4:17). As the passion narrative moves from the local darkness of Gethsemane to the earth-encompassing darkness of Golgotha, and from the passive sleep of the disciples to their active denial and betrayal, Matthew would have us know that the kingdom Jesus proclaims and embodies is indeed "at hand."

ALLEN C. MCSWEEN JR.

Homiletical Perspective

weakness."[1] This is indeed true, if by "knowing" we mean that Jesus *experiences* our every weakness. How else could these weaknesses ever find forgiveness and healing? In the end, this is good news that can be preached in spite of the apparent gloominess of this story.

Arguably the greatest idea promoted by the famous rhetorical theorist Kenneth Burke was his idea that genuine communication is not so much about "persuasion" as it is about "identification."[2] By identification he meant that all true communication is about mutual role taking or "getting into the shoes" of others to the point of sharing their experience in all of its depth and complexity. Only then can we experience what he calls "consubstantiality," or a sharing of life substance with one another. In this view, communication is not about persuading someone to enter a preconstructed world, but about inviting each other into a new, shared experience in which we are transformed by what each party brings to the table.

For Christians, this is at the heart of our Christology. Even as God in Christ took upon himself our "nature," we partake of his "nature" by eating and drinking the bread and wine of Communion. The result is a new redemptive reality, beyond what either party could fully anticipate prior to the transaction.

Gethsemane follows immediately upon the Last Supper, a supper at which the betrayer sits. Rightly so, for Gethsemane is focused on Jesus' increasing experience of the ways in which the flesh betrays us all. Jesus in this story is moving toward full consubstantiality with his disciples. He is communing more deeply with them in their sleepiness, betrayals, fears, agitations, and negotiations. By virtue of this, one day soon they will be able to be more fully with him, as they discover that God is not a distant, angry judge, but one who loves them to the point of sharing every aspect of their experience, even death.

JOHN S. MCCLURE

1. Joseph Scriven, ca. 1855, "What a Friend We Have in Jesus," in *Presbyterian Hymnal: Hymns, Psalms, and Spiritual Songs* (Louisville, KY: Westminster/John Knox Press, 1990), #403.

2. Kenneth Burke, *A Rhetoric of Motives* (Berkeley: University of California Press, 1969), 20–23.

Matthew 26:47–56

⁴⁷While he was still speaking, Judas, one of the twelve, arrived; with him was a large crowd with swords and clubs, from the chief priests and the elders of the people. ⁴⁸Now the betrayer had given them a sign, saying, "The one I will kiss is the man; arrest him." ⁴⁹At once he came up to Jesus and said, "Greetings, Rabbi!" and kissed him. ⁵⁰Jesus said to him, "Friend, do what you are here to do." Then they came and laid hands on Jesus and arrested him. ⁵¹Suddenly, one of those with Jesus put his hand on his sword, drew it, and struck the slave of the high priest, cutting off his ear. ⁵²Then Jesus said to him, "Put your sword back into its place; for all who take the sword will perish by the sword. ⁵³Do you think that I cannot appeal to my Father, and he will at once send me more than twelve legions of angels? ⁵⁴But how then would the scriptures be fulfilled, which say it must happen in this way?" ⁵⁵At that hour Jesus said to the crowds, "Have you come out with swords and clubs to arrest me as though I were a bandit? Day after day I sat in the temple teaching, and you did not arrest me. ⁵⁶But all this has taken place, so that the scriptures of the prophets may be fulfilled." Then all the disciples deserted him and fled.

Theological Perspective

"All who take the sword will perish by the sword" (v. 52) is a saying of Jesus that does not appear in the other Synoptic Gospels. Although the other Gospels include in the story of Jesus' arrest the disciple who brandishes his sword, only Matthew has Jesus speak these specific words of rebuke, with their apparent wider implications about violence. Nonetheless, the saying has become a folksy maxim about the danger of falling victim to one's own worst methods: "All who live by the sword will die by the sword." More substantially, it has received centuries' worth of theological scrutiny as Christians have considered the question: May a Christian take up arms against another, or must Christians be pacifists?

At first glance, the question itself may seem odd. Indeed, if framed as a simple descriptive question—Are there any Christians who have taken up arms?—the answer is an obvious yes. Not only are there Christians who have taken up arms to defend themselves or their homelands against aggressors, but there are Christians who have taken up arms specifically in the hopes of advancing Christianity (or their particular version thereof).

Looking deeper, though, we find that Christians have long considered the possibility that obedience to God requires some refusal to take up arms. During the first two centuries or so after Jesus' death,

Pastoral Perspective

Jesus' prayer in the garden immediately prior to this passage (26:36–46) evolves from "remove this cup from me" to "thy will be done." Consider that Jesus has moved through a stage of grief—from bargaining to acceptance—in short order. In today's passage, there is no agony, no hesitation. Judas and the crowds arrive while he is still speaking—but he is ready for them. He even helps to guide the action. He receives the betrayer's kiss from Judas, but also spurs him on: "Do what you are here to do" (v. 50). It is as if he is directing the action in the scene.

Not only is Jesus the director and the protagonist; he is also the interpreter and commentator, ready with explanations, scriptural citations, and advice. When violence erupts, he quells it, but then expounds on it theologically. He rebukes the disciples for resorting to violence, assuring them that if a battle were called for, Jesus would have battalions of angels to summon. Instead, he goes to his fate nonviolently, thus modeling a more excellent way. He proclaims to the disciples, and later to the crowd, that these things happening to him are part of a larger narrative that he not only understands, but also endorses: "All this has taken place, so that the scriptures of the prophets may be fulfilled" (v. 56).

He may utter these words mournfully, but not reluctantly. This self-assuredness is very typical of

Exegetical Perspective

Matthew, with his fondness for groupings of three, opens his passion narrative with three scenes. After Jesus' last meal with his disciples, he leads them to the Mount of Olives, where he prophesies their desertion and Peter's denial. Then, in the garden of Gethsemane, he struggles in agonizing prayer to know and follow the will of his Father. Now, in the third scene, Jesus is betrayed and arrested and the disciples flee.

The Betrayal of Judas and Arrest of Jesus. Matthew opens the betrayal scene in midsentence as it were: "While [Jesus] was still speaking, Judas, one of the twelve, arrived" (v. 47). All the Gospel writers identify Judas as "one of the twelve." Every time Judas is mentioned in the Synoptic Gospels, he is identified either directly or indirectly as one of the Twelve. The evangelists will not let followers of Jesus forget that betrayal is an inside job. Judas, the betrayer, is one of the chosen Twelve, one of those who know and presumably love Jesus best.

The Sign of the Kiss and the Arrest of Jesus. When "a large crowd with swords and clubs" arrives in Gethsemane, Judas identifies Jesus with a prearranged signal, a greeting and a kiss, presumably to ensure that the right man is seized by the arresting squad.

Homiletical Perspective

This story is a crisis point in the life of Jesus. Everything he stands for comes to a head at one time. Although he has offered himself in friendship to his disciples, he is betrayed by a kiss from Judas. Although he considers himself a Jewish teacher, his relationship to the Jewish chief priests and elders has drifted into irreconcilable antagonism. Although he has taught that peacemakers are blessed in the kingdom of heaven, he watches one of his followers cut off the ear of the slave of the high priest. Although he has been an easily accessible teacher in the temple, he finds himself suddenly treated as a terrorist and a fugitive. We can only imagine his sense of discouragement and futility. In many ways, this story finds Jesus utterly bereft. Both his ideas and his companionship seem to be of no real value to anyone. As if to add a final punctuation mark, the closing words of the narrative read: "then all the disciples deserted him and fled" (v. 56).

Although the story of the arrest of Jesus is one of the most frightful and seemingly negative stories in the New Testament, it is possible for preachers to invert each of the negative aspects in the story and gain a front-row seat in the kingdom of heaven. In other words, if we look at what is going wrong in this text, we can see with striking clarity what Jesus desires most for us in his kingdom. By looking at

Matthew 26:47–56

Theological Perspective

many—although not all—of his followers did indeed eschew military service, not least because serving in the imperial military would have entailed performing pagan rituals. Moreover, during the Jesus movement's early days, many of the movement's faithful would have been faithful Jews and considered as such by Rome, and thus excused from serving in the imperial army. The early Christian author Tertullian wrote approvingly about a Christian soldier of his acquaintance, "more steadfast than his brethren," who refused first the outward insignia of military membership and then gave up even the sword, "which was not necessary either for the protection of our Lord."[1] Two years after his conversion in the fourth century, Martin of Tours, who would later be canonized as a saint, determined that he could not continue to fight as a soldier while also being a Christian.

Centuries later, the Anabaptist movement emphasized simple and thorough obedience to the words of Jesus in all matters. They refused—and many of their spiritual heirs still refuse—to wage violence, swear oaths, or hold office. Other theological luminaries have responded to the question, "May a Christian wage violence?" with a more qualified, "Yes, under certain conditions." In constructing their arguments, these theologians have also contended with Jesus' words in Matthew's Gospel and, more broadly, with the persuasiveness of the Christian pacifist position. For example, Thomas Aquinas and, later, John Calvin both acknowledged the force of the argument that Jesus' rebuke removed the option of justified violence for Christians. "It would seem," wrote Thomas in the *Summa theologiae*, "that it is always sinful to wage war," for "those who wage war are threatened by Our Lord with punishment, according to Mt. 26:52."[2] Calvin agreed, pointing out that the disciple's defensive maneuver was really rather moderate, and reasoning that if Jesus rebuked even *that* gesture, then "Christ appears to tie up the hands of all."[3]

How, then, do Aquinas and Calvin craft a theological argument in qualified support of certain wars? They do so by drawing distinctions and carefully considering the conditions under which the war takes place. What authority has declared it? Has the

Pastoral Perspective

Matthew, who is meticulous in connecting the dots between the life and ministry of Jesus and the fulfillment of the Hebrew Scriptures. *"All of this took place to fulfill what had been spoken through the prophet,"* Matthew asserts again and again in the Gospel. From a narrative standpoint, the constant citing of Scripture can disrupt the flow and make events seem pro forma and canned. Too much exposition disturbs the pace of the movie: *"Is there anything about the Jew from Nazareth that astonishes his biographer?"* we may throw up our hands and ask. Theologically, of course, such citations are essential, as Matthew builds the case for Jesus to his audience. Jesus is not strictly an iconoclast; he is also the fulfillment of everything that has gone before him (see 5:17–20).

These Scripture quotations also function to heighten the gulf that exists between Jesus and us. Jesus' life was one that went "by the book." His teachings, healings, rejection, death, and resurrection are all written in the stars, or at least in the scrolls. Was there a grim comfort for Jesus in knowing that his life was not a random series of events, that his crucifixion was going to mean something? His gruesome death is not an act of random violence; it is required in order for the Scriptures to be fulfilled. The cross is the only way that the story can end—although, of course, it is not the end.

For us, on the other hand, it is not so simple. Do our lives have any inherent meaning and value? This is one of the existential questions of humanity. Some of us address this question with pious certainty, even when bad things happen to us: "God has a plan." "This is God's will." It gives our suffering meaning to imagine that it is taking place so that the Scriptures (or at least God's purposes) can be fulfilled. However, some tragedies cannot be so easily explained. Some events seem too unspeakably terrible, too random, to have a higher God-ordained purpose.

As people of faith, we affirm that positive things can come out of trials and tribulations, and that all things can work together for good—even horribly ugly things (Rom. 8:28). That is not the same as saying that God desires for them to happen or that our suffering is somehow written into the biblical narrative, as it is for Jesus. When people explain their own misery (or that of others) in such terms, I am left feeling half-awed and half-dismayed. I am awed at the steadfastness of their faith and witness; I am dismayed because only God really knows how the dots connect—indeed, whether they connect at all. We do not bridge the divide between God and us through

---

1. Tertullian, "The Chaplet, or De Corona," chap. 1, trans. S. Thelwall, in Alexander Robinson and James Roberts, eds., *Latin Christianity: Its Founder, Tertullian*, in *Ante-Nicene Fathers* (Buffalo: Christian Literature Publishing Co., 1887), 4:93.

2. Thomas Aquinas, *Summa theologiae*, 2-2, q. 40, a. 1.

3. John Calvin, *Commentary on a Harmony of the Evangelists, Matthew, Mark and Luke*, vol. 3, trans. William Pringle (Edinburgh: Calvin Translation Society, 1845). *Christian Classics Ethereal Library*, http://www.ccel.org/ccel/calvin/calcom33.ii.xxxii.html; accessed July 31, 2012.

The meaning of the greeting and the "Judas kiss" are much debated and cannot be settled exegetically. Interpreters must weigh a variety of options. The word with which Judas greets Jesus, *chaire,* was as common as our "hello" or "good morning." In itself it would not arouse suspicion, as perhaps was intended.

Judas proceeds to address Jesus as "rabbi." It could be a simple term of respect, "my teacher," but earlier in 23:7–8, Jesus has told his disciples that they are "not to be called rabbi" because he is the "one teacher," and at the Last Supper it is Judas alone who refers to Jesus as "rabbi" (26:25). In Matthew's Gospel only nondisciples address Jesus as "rabbi." Thus Judas's use of the term suggests that he is already outside the circle of the Twelve.

Even more ambiguous is the infamous "Judas kiss." Again, a kiss of greeting would not be suspicious. It was as common in that culture as a handshake in ours. The Greek word Matthew uses for "kissed" (*katephilēsin,* v. 49) is intensive, indicating that Judas kissed Jesus warmly or affectionately. Why? Was the kiss a blatant act of hypocrisy? Was it a means of holding on to Jesus until he could be seized by the mob? Was it a heinous expression of betrayal? Could it have been, as some have suggested, a sign of genuine remorse and affection, even in the act of handing Jesus over in accordance with the purposes of God? To the end Judas's discipleship remains as ambivalent and conflicted as our own.

Jesus' response deepens the ambivalence and the irony: "Friend, do what you are here to do" (v. 50). Twice before in Matthew Jesus has used "friend" (*hetairos*) in an ironic way that implies disapproval (20:13; 22:12). Could Jesus be exposing the insincerity of Judas's greeting with his own ironic response? Even more difficult to decipher is what Jesus says to Judas, literally, "for what you are here." The reader must supply the missing verb. The NRSV and most recent English translations treat Jesus' words as a command: "do what you are here to do." The RSV views it as a question: "Friend, why are you here?" Some interpreters understand it as a statement: "I know what you are here for." Eugene Peterson combines elements of all three: "Friend, why this charade?"[1]

Responses to the Arrest of Jesus. Again Matthew narrates three responses to the arrest of Jesus. The first is a response of violent retaliation. "One of those with Jesus" (v. 51) draws a sword and cuts off the

the "underside" of the text, we begin to see its "overside"—what God's final redemption of our all-too-human failings will look like.

First, if we look at Judas's betrayal through the kiss of friendship, we anticipate that the kingdom will be a place of genuine friendship. Jesus addresses Judas, his betrayer, as "friend," even in the moment of his betrayal (v. 50). As Christians, we anticipate that one day this scenario will be forever reversed: there will be no more betrayals of friendship. Those who have betrayed the trust of a friend will be forgiven and restored. Friendships will endure, and trust will reign supreme.

In many situations today, betrayal disrupts our ability to develop or sustain genuine friendships. Soldiers returning from Iraq and Afghanistan, for instance, testify that they suffer from a serious distrust of those around them. Having learned to suspect everyone as a potential betrayer—even young children—they find it difficult among family and friends at home to regain confidence in human relationships. In the same way, many who have experienced divorce, childhood sexual abuse, or a career sabotaged by a coworker yearn to regain their basic trust in human nature. Many today long for genuine, trustworthy friendships.

Second, the kingdom will be a place of authentic communion and renewal between Christians and Jews. The large crowd pushing their way into the Garden of Gethsemane brandishing swords and clubs and the disciple who was quick to pull out his sword and fight are merely instruments of the antagonism that had developed between the Jewish authorities and the followers of Jesus. If we imagine a redeemed future that will reverse this scenario, we can envision a situation where Jews and Christians overcome their fear of one another. In this realm, all those who seek earnestly after the truth of the God of Abraham will listen to one another with open hearts and minds and grow in understanding and wisdom. Although it is difficult to imagine what this new relationship will look like in the reign of heaven, many Christians and Jews today long for a different kind of relationship than the one found in this biblical story.

Third, and perhaps most important, this story anticipates the reign of nonviolence and lasting peace. If ever there existed a situation in which the disciples and the authorities could become involved in hand-to-hand combat, this certainly is it. When one of the disciples strikes out with a sword, however, Jesus makes his most emphatic statement in the New Testament against the idea that the best way

---

1. Eugene Peterson, *The Message* (Colorado Springs, CO: NavPress, 1993), 67.

Matthew 26:47–56

Theological Perspective

enemy done something that is an affront to justice? What are the intentions in waging war? Some who have heard the phrase "just war theory" believe mistakenly that, according to the theory, war is justified under nearly any condition.

Rather, Christian just-war theorists continue to place careful limits around the moral case for war. What of violence that falls short of the scope and scale of outright war, such as self-defense or capital punishment? Calvin, in the same commentary passage cited above, makes a distinction between one person's taking up arms against a robber and a government's acting in its proper capacity. The former, he says, is not strictly morally wrong. However, in order to avoid sinning, someone who takes up arms against a robber must not be excessively angry, must not hate or desire revenge. As Calvin points out, this almost never happens. Yet that, he says, is an altogether different matter than violence done in the name of the rule of law. Rule of law hinges on the state's being able to threaten lawbreakers with violence and make good on that threat. God, Calvin reasons, cannot will anarchy; indeed, to let murderers murder and thieves steal would insult a just God.

This theological debate has persisted for centuries, with strong arguments on both sides. Its existence hints at a perhaps more fundamental ambivalence. Are Christians to refuse violence, even if doing so seems to permit injustice? Are Christians, rather, to use the instruments of coercive power in the hope of making the world run properly? One's answer to that question has profound implications for one's definition of faithfulness. It is important to realize, however, that both pacifism and just war place restrictions on Christians. There is no tradition of Christian reflection that allows someone to overpower another, simply to get what he or she wants.

SARAH MORICE-BRUBAKER

Pastoral Perspective

the answers and explanations we find. Jesus bridges the divide through his life, death, and resurrection.

Oddly enough, Jesus' affirmation that the Scriptures will be fulfilled (v. 56) is his last word to his disciples. Here is his final lesson before they desert him and flee into the night. It feels anticlimactic that these should be the last words they hear from their teacher before his death. No last-minute "love one another"? No pithy one-liner about the kingdom of God? Surely Jesus could have come up with something better than this. A pastor friend reports sending his teenage daughter out the door on her very first date by yelling in desperation, "Remember your baptism!"

Maybe in a strange way these words can be a comfort. *"What is happening is not evidence of failure on your part,"* Jesus suggests. *"This is how it must be."* The disciples abandon him utterly. Peter will weep with shame before the night is over. We humans are adroit at making a mess of things. Nevertheless even our most excruciating failures will not ultimately stand in the way of what God is planning to do, has planned to do from the beginning of time. On reflection, Jesus' parting word—*"Let the Scriptures be fulfilled"*—is one of the more pastoral things he could leave them with.

It is going to get worse before it gets better. Jesus will be dragged before Caiaphas. Peter will lurk nearby but say he does not know Jesus. Pilate will interrogate Jesus further. A notorious prisoner will be exchanged for the sinless one. There will be a crown, a cross, darkness, a loud cry. There will be a tomb. Then, something else will happen, something astonishing, something so powerful that not even the disciples' profound failure can stand in its way.

MARYANN MCKIBBEN DANA

Exegetical Perspective

ear of the high priest's slave. Which one? John says it was Simon Peter who cut off the ear of Malchus (John 18:10), but Matthew leaves the perpetrator unnamed, to keep the reader's focus on the command that Jesus addresses, not to one, but to all: "Put your sword back into its place; for all who take the sword will perish by the sword" (v. 52). Earlier, in the Sermon on the Mount, Jesus has commanded his followers, "Do not resist an evildoer. But if anyone strikes you on the right cheek, turn the other also" (5:39). Throughout the passion narrative Jesus fully embodies the way of nonviolent love that he teaches his disciples.

Violent retaliation is both forbidden and unnecessary. It is forbidden because violence begets more violence and is antithetical to the way of self-giving love. It is unnecessary because, if it were the will of God to protect Jesus from harm and suffering, he could have unimaginable power at his disposal: "Do you think that I cannot appeal to my Father, and he will at once send me more than twelve legions of angels?" (v. 53). In his prayerful struggle in Gethsemane, Jesus has learned that in fulfillment of "the scriptures of the prophets" (v. 56) his passion must indeed unfold "in this way" (v. 54)—not with his escape, but with his death.

The second response narrated by Matthew is found in Jesus' words to the crowd: "Have you come out with swords and clubs to arrest me as though I were a bandit?" (v. 55). The word translated "bandit" (lēstēs) carries the connotation of an armed revolutionist. Jesus denies that he is a terrorist operating in secret to overthrow the Roman Empire. His whole ministry has been conducted nonviolently in public, teaching openly for all to hear.

Once again Jesus asserts that all that is happening is in accord with the divine script first narrated by the prophets and now being played out in his life and the lives of his disciples. As the scene comes to an end, the disciples offer their response. The disciples, who once had left everything to follow Jesus, now desert him and flee for their lives, just as he has prophesied.

ALLEN C. MCSWEEN JR.

Homiletical Perspective

to curtail violence is through more violence. Jesus asserts, "All who take the sword will perish by the sword" (v. 52). Jesus makes it clear that the power of God within his reign is not power over the world. The reign of heaven is not ruled by a militaristic God who sends "more than twelve legions of angels" (v. 53) to help believers out of their conflicts. Rather, it is ruled by the power of self-giving love, the power of the Suffering Servant.

Among the nations, and in our local communities today, many continue to believe that the best way to solve conflicts is through violence. Civil warfare plagues many countries, and refugees flood across borders in search of relief. Nations continue to discover ways to manufacture weapons of mass destruction. Military budgets everywhere are the last to be slashed. Violence is also a common way to solve problems in local communities. Neighborhood gangs protect street turf, weapons are carried in public places, and bullying is a serious issue in many schools.

At the same time, however, many people around the world long for a day when swords are beaten into plowshares and spears into pruning hooks (Isa. 2:4; Mic. 4:3). New Israeli-Palestinian peace movements have garnered many followers. The United Nations International Day of Peace has attracted a large number of participants, both secular and religious.[1] Nonviolent activism on behalf of peaceful policies and programs is increasing.

This little story of the arrest of Jesus, therefore, is of tremendous importance for the world today. It is a snapshot of three of the most significant evils that God will one day transform in the new creation: betrayal in relationships, interreligious conflict, and violence. Preachers, therefore, can identify these evils, and then stand this text on its head, and proclaim boldly what Jesus desires most for us: genuine friendship, interreligious communication and renewal, and nonviolence.

JOHN S. MCCLURE

---

1. http://internationaldayofpeace.org/; accessed April 15, 2012.

⁵⁷Those who had arrested Jesus took him to Caiaphas the high priest, in whose house the scribes and the elders had gathered. ⁵⁸But Peter was following him at a distance, as far as the courtyard of the high priest; and going inside, he sat with the guards in order to see how this would end. ⁵⁹Now the chief priests and the whole council were looking for false testimony against Jesus so that they might put him to death, ⁶⁰but they found none, though many false witnesses came forward. At last two came forward ⁶¹and said, "This fellow said, 'I am able to destroy the temple of God and to build it in three days.'" ⁶²The high priest stood up and said, "Have you no answer? What is it that they testify against you?" ⁶³But Jesus was silent. Then the high priest said to him, "I put you under oath before the living God, tell us if you are the Messiah, the Son of God." ⁶⁴Jesus said to him, "You have said so. But I tell you,

From now on you will see the Son of Man
    seated at the right hand of Power
    and coming on the clouds of heaven."

⁶⁵Then the high priest tore his clothes and said, "He has blasphemed! Why do we still need witnesses? You have now heard his blasphemy. ⁶⁶What is your verdict?" They answered, "He deserves death." ⁶⁷Then they spat in his face and struck him; and some slapped him, ⁶⁸saying, "Prophesy to us, you Messiah! Who is it that struck you?"

Theological Perspective

This passage, like others in Matthew's account of the passion, contains a challenge for the contemporary preacher, since at its heart is a conflict between Jesus and Jewish leaders of his time. Matthew's account of the trial before Caiaphas has been used to support Christian anti-Semitism for so long that anyone who preaches or teaches from this text needs to be careful to preach it in a way that does not foster anti-Semitism, but instead communicates the gospel message that is appropriate to Christians today. So as to avoid the Christian anti-Semitism that so easily gravitates to the trial before the Sanhedrin, we should be certain to speak to the difference between Matthew's first Jewish Christian readers and ourselves as Gentile Christians hearing Matthew's Gospel nineteen centuries later.

Matthew's Gospel is often called the most Jewish of the four Gospels, but we should bear in mind that there is a conflict in Matthew's time, decades after Jesus' life. Matthew is a Jewish Christian speaking to others of his persuasion who have accepted Jesus as the Messiah, the Christ. The high priest in the passage, Caiaphas, failed to accept Jesus as the Messiah, but other Jews did. Contemporary hearers of Matthew's Gospel need to be reminded that the conflict over Jesus' identity continued as an intra-Jewish conflict throughout the first century. Even in the story

Pastoral Perspective

The trials of Jesus are first about him. Whatever contemporary readers may think of their motives, the Roman and Jewish officials haul Jesus into their courts in order to determine, on their terms and from within their worldviews, the truth about what Jesus has said and done. They seek to know who he claims to be. They ponder how his actions and claims affect their responsibility to maintain civil order, their desire to preserve their own positions of influence, and, in the case of the Jewish leaders, their responsibility to protect their faith.

Historically, Jesus was on trial; now, his story tries those who read it. As Matthew describes the examination of Jesus by Caiaphas, readers find themselves examined. When the high priest presses Jesus to say who he is, readers' own identities are probed: Are they like the officials who try Jesus, anxious about perceived threats to God's honor and to the uneasy peace that exists between their minority community and the dominant Roman Empire? Are the readers, in other words, defensive on God's behalf and fearful on their own? Are they, like Peter, torn between loyalty to Jesus and uncertainty about what such loyalty might mean for their own safety? Are they—like that wavering disciple—following Jesus closely enough to see how his story will end (v. 58), but distantly enough to avoid jeopardy for themselves? Are the

Exegetical Perspective

The present passage is part of the passion narrative, for which Matthew seems to follow Mark very closely. It depicts the trial of Jesus at the house of Caiaphas right after his arrest at Gethsemane on the first evening of the Feast of the Unleavened Bread, which is another name for the Passover (26:17). Joseph Caiaphas was appointed as the high priest by the Roman prefect Valerius Gratus, in 18 CE. He succeeded his father-in-law Annas, who had been deposed by the Romans in 15 CE. Caiaphas held the office of the high priest during the prefecture of Gratus and his successor Pontius Pilate until 36 CE, when both Pilate and Caiaphas were removed from their respective offices by the Syrian governor Lucius Vitellius (Josephus, *Antiquities* 17.90). Caiaphas's exceptionally long tenure as the high priest indicates that he collaborated very well with the Roman colonial regime. On the other hand, even while Caiaphas was holding the office of high priest, Annas seems to have remained a powerful political force as a retired high priest, which may have contributed to the discrepancy in which Luke calls Annas the high priest, when in fact Caiaphas is the one (Acts 4:6; Luke 3:2).

Matthew presents this event as an interrogation by the chief priests and the entire Sanhedrin (v. 59), which here refers to the supreme council in Jerusalem headed by the high priest. Josephus uses the

Homiletical Perspective

Dr. Paul Scott Wilson has been heard to remind us that when we study a text we should listen for the trouble in the text. Examining this text with homiletical eyes requires that we hear that trouble in the text. Examining the text allows the contemporary echo of the text to speak simultaneously to our spirits. It would be a mistake to lift up the passages and highlight the ancient tradition without drawing the contemporary parallels inherent in the text.

Dr. Henry Mitchell, professor emeritus of homiletics at the Interdenominational Theological Center, has reminded us that the preacher should look for universal ideas when constructing a message. For example, the ideas of love, hope, suffering, and grace speak beyond the concerns of Matthew's own time and beyond any ancient esoteric concept.

Matthew beautifully sets up the passion narrative, building tension and juxtaposing this conclusion of the life of Jesus with the dramatic entrance of Christ into the Galilean community. According to Matthew 1–2 Jesus begins his life accompanied by religious objectives, political intrigue, and failed assassination attempts. Now in Matthew 26–27 the lens of Matthew turns to the final act of the life of Jesus, and we are confronted again with the conflicts he witnessed during the sunrise of his ministry.

Matthew 26:57–68

Theological Perspective

of Jesus' trial, this later conflict can be seen woven through the narrative.

What is important to Matthew is that Jesus is the Christ for believers and followers. This message is still available to us, but needs to be carefully distinguished from its original Palestinian setting, since it is too easy for contemporary Gentile Christians to blame the Jews of the first century in a way that renders contemporary Jews as Christ's victimizers and rejecters. It is worthwhile, therefore, to call attention to the fact that our situation is quite different religiously from that of Matthew's original Jewish Christians, and then to call today's hearers to see some of the features of the trial narrative as gospel that continues to speak across culture and time.

In the conflict, Jesus accepts the role of Messiah in a somewhat cryptic way. When asked to tell the council if he is the Messiah, the Son of God, Jesus says, "You have said so," making his accuser someone who has testified to his identity. He then goes on to claim the Son of Man tradition from Daniel for himself. From the point where he says, "From now on you will see the Son of Man seated at the right hand of Power and coming on the clouds of heaven" (v. 64), there can be no doubt that Jesus is claiming to be the Messiah. So here we have the two basic complaints about Jesus that would haunt the early church and slow Jesus' acceptance in the Palestinian Jewish community: that he said he would destroy the temple, and that he was the Messiah. Matthew presents these charges offered by perjured (or compelled) witnesses, but then Jesus affirms his messiahship in his own voice.

Matthew's purposes in the passage appear to be several in number. First, he has Peter witness all that goes on during the trial; he has Jesus stand up to unfair charges; and, most importantly, his Jesus truthfully reveals himself to be the Messiah. Then Matthew has the high priest Caiaphas misunderstand Jesus' answer as a blasphemous claim. Even in the midst of the high priest's rending his garments in anger, Matthew's Jesus reveals who he is and who we know him to be.

Christians today, therefore, need to hear the strong claim on Jesus' lips that he is the expected Jewish Messiah, the fully Jewish son of the covenant and the Son of God, the culmination of God's saving activity in Israel and for the nations. That Caiaphas (and perhaps the Sanhedrin) rejects Jesus as a blasphemer from their positions of religious power (which was itself under the scrutiny and boot of the Roman emperor) is for Matthew a tragic

Pastoral Perspective

readers somehow like Jesus, unwilling to allow their identities to be distorted by people who do not understand their experiences of God, experiences that have shaped the identity they now question?

This narrative has a way of revealing readers' own less-than-faithful reactions to Jesus. As it does so, they might be tempted to divert attention and deflect responsibility onto the Jewish officials who conduct the trial. To do so would be to repeat a tragic error that is often made and that sadly contributes to shameful anti-Judaism. To avoid such a simplistic and misguided reading of texts like this one, it is important to remember that the lived experience of the people involved in the arrest, trial, and crucifixion of Jesus is significantly different from the lived experience of the Gospel writers who have recorded their actions and the Christian interpreters who have reflected upon them.

Between Jesus' death and the writing of Matthew's Gospel, the city of Jerusalem fell, and in 70 CE the temple was destroyed. Those events precipitated a severe crisis in Jewish identity and drove a wedge between "Jews" and "Christians." With an urgency that had not existed before, both groups scrambled to establish substantially separate identities. Such radical separation did not exist when Jesus was tried and crucified. As Raymond E. Brown has reminded us, "*The religious dispute with Jesus was an inner Jewish dispute. . . .* It is true that in the passion narratives of Matthew and John, written after 70, 'the Jews' appear as an alien group over against Jesus; but on the level of history Jews were dealing with a fellow Jew."[1] The Jews were not "them" to the followers of Jesus at the time of his crucifixion.

For that reason, Christians who read about Jesus' trial at the hands of the high priest, Caiaphas, the scribes, and the elders (v. 57) should not assume that all of the Jews of Jesus' time had thoroughgoing contempt for him or sinister motivations for their examination of him. Even among the leaders of the Jews, there were people sympathetic to, or at least willing to forgo condemnation of, Jesus. One clear example is the Gospel of John's portrait of Nicodemus, "a Pharisee and leader of the Jews" (John 3:1–10; 7:50–51; 19:39). Despite Matthew's polemical claim that "the people *as a whole*" took responsibility for Jesus' death (27:25), the New Testament's portrait of Jewish responses to Jesus, a fellow Jew, is more nuanced than Matthew's stark version reveals.

1. Raymond E. Brown, *The Death of the Messiah: From Gethsemane to the Grave* (New York: Doubleday, 1994), 1:396.

term *synedrion* in multiple ways as a reference to the council in Jerusalem (*Ant.* 14.167–68), regional governing councils (*Ant.* 14.89–91), or various other groups of royal advisors and consultants (*J.W.* 1.537). Precise information about the makeup, function, and prerogatives of the Jerusalem Sanhedrin is not available. Even the question whether or not the Sanhedrin during the time of Jesus held the judicial authority to impose capital punishment for religious offenders cannot be determined with accuracy.

In the present passage, this episode would not have been an official Sanhedrin trial, since it was the very first evening of the Passover. It was most likely a preliminary investigation in preparation for the trial by Pilate, who certainly had the ultimate authority to impose capital punishment. At this scene the adversaries of Jesus are the scribes, the elders, and the chief priests (vv. 57, 59). The Pharisees, who were among the primary opponents of Jesus in the previous parts of the Gospel until chapter 23, recede into the background for the moment, only to reappear later in 27:62.

Matthew characterizes the motive of this interrogation as an attempt to obtain false testimony against Jesus to secure a death sentence (v. 59). The prefix *pseudo-* meaning "false" is added by Matthew to the Markan original, which simply says "testimony" (*martyria*, Mark 14:55). This casts the whole proceeding as fraudulent right from the beginning, and it reflects Matthew's consistent criticism of the Jewish religious leadership. Now Matthew is holding the highest-ranking Jewish leaders primarily responsible for eliciting the death sentence for Jesus from the Roman authority. This should not be taken as an anti-Jewish stance on the part of Matthew. Rather, it is a focused disapproval of the highest-ranking religious leaders who condone and support the Roman colonial power and manipulate the ordinary people to demand of Pilate the execution of Jesus (27:20).

In verse 60 Matthew mentions two witnesses coming forward to accuse Jesus. This seems to allude to Deuteronomy 17:6, which stipulates that at least two witnesses are required for a death sentence to be executed. Their testimony that Jesus said he could destroy the temple and build it in three days (v. 61) may or may not be false. At least within Matthew's story there is no such saying of Jesus. His prediction of the destruction of the temple in 24:2 does not say who will destroy it. Whether true or false, this testimony does not seem to constitute a serious enough offence for capital punishment. So the high priest changes his tactics and puts Jesus under oath, which

There are several possible options for a preacher preparing to preach on this text.

One can place a stake here looking from the vantage point of the opening and closing acts of the life of the Messiah and witness how conflict and trouble follow a man committed to transformation. Why does trouble follow love? Why does conflict seek to snuff out hope? A ministry committed to transformation is also a life connected to struggle. These are all great universal themes to examine as one is attempting to construct a message.

This would, of course, be a broad view, but there is plenty of rich homiletical material to mine from this narrative observation. The obvious point of examination, for many, will be the conflict of the religious leaders with Jesus. The teaching ministry and healing power of a nonviolent, rural, and revolutionary Jew has caused the urban religious elite to organize resistance to this nonviolent movement of love. The plot to kill Jesus is partially the elite's response to the democratization of religious teaching. Jesus represents a new paradigm of religious leadership—a model that seeks to reach out to a broad and diverse public. Parables, rural metaphors, outdoor seminary training, and practical field education are creating a disturbance across the theological landscape.

A person of authority, who does not have the blessing of the Roman government or the religious establishment, is drawing people to his teachings. The religious elite begin to panic as this new theological movement infects the Hebraic landscape. For the elite, the concern for power, status, authority, and favor overrule a passion for the poor and sensitivity to the Spirit of God. Violence becomes a solution to achieve political and theological submission.

One can turn to these ideas of conflict and political intrigue and look at them from an external or an internal gaze. Externally, the question can be raised: How is our world similar to the world of those first-century religious elites? Mahatma Gandhi spoke powerfully of the fact that British officials knew they were wrong when they opposed Indian independence, but political orthodoxy overruled moral authority. In our own time we see instance after instance where people in power—including church leaders—seek to evade justice in order to protect an institution. The human personality is wired in this manner, to have a proclivity toward comfort and orthodoxy, to protect ourselves even when the lives of others are at stake.

Much can be said from an external vantage point, building a critique of structures and religious

Matthew 26:57–68

Theological Perspective

misunderstanding but not—emphatically not—a rejection by the whole Jewish people of Jesus as the Christ.

We are not to read this passage in our time as triumphant victors. It would do us well to read the passage seeing ourselves as Caiaphas. How often have our apprehensions of what is going on been distorted by our religious, social, and economic presuppositions? When God is doing a new thing, how often might we, who believe we are doing God's work in observing God's ways, miss God's inbreaking in our lives? Tragic figures caught in tragic misunderstandings are the substance of many great narratives. The kings Agamemnon and Oedipus in classical drama, and Othello, Hamlet, Romeo and Juliet, and King Lear in Shakespearean drama are all examples of misunderstandings that create essential action and give the action that follows its tragic character. In a similar manner, Caiaphas fails to see the Messiah standing right before him, but unlike a classical or Shakespearean character, he is not a tragic hero, only someone who has failed to participate in God's larger drama.

So we see that the actions of the high priest and the council help propel Jesus toward Calvary, but Matthew intends readers of his Gospel to continue reading so as to see that God has the last word in Christ. This passage is powerful in its evocation of conflict between Jesus and the religious leaders of his own people, yet today's preacher or teacher needs to approach this passage mindful that Matthew's purpose in this passage is to lead to the good news that is found in the totality of Jesus' life, death, and resurrection. The trial does not stand by itself; rather, it leads to Christ's glory, even while it helps explain how it is that not all accepted God's Messiah when they beheld him.

JAMES HUDNUT-BEUMLER

Pastoral Perspective

Historically, the Roman authorities bear at least as much, if not more, responsibility for the crucifixion of Jesus. Theologically, *everyone* for whose forgiveness and liberation Jesus died is responsible for his death. Jesus lived and died and rose again for all; all share responsibility for his death; and all—Gentiles and Jews—are embraced in his love and grace.

Today the church's own leaders are the ones sifted by this account of Jesus' trial. How do the church's leaders resist God's saving but threatening newness made continually available through Jesus and cling, instead, to a lifeless but familiar status quo? How does their investment in prior understandings of God, self, and world blind and deafen them to the unsettling but transformative truth that, in Jesus, stands always before them? These are sobering questions, from which readers might wish to turn aside, but as Rowan Williams, the former archbishop of Canterbury, has written, "Matthew's narrative does not allow the believer—in particular the articulate and educated believer, the teacher, the expert—any fixed answer to the question of how I might know that I am still with Jesus rather than with Caiaphas."[2]

This text cautions all followers of Jesus that, if there is nothing in their understanding of him that stretches them or that requires them to surrender old patterns of thinking, feeling, and living for new ones, then their understanding of him is incomplete. The way of Jesus, as the New Testament presents it, is so challenging that it causes even his most loyal followers—like Peter—to stay safely in the shadows rather than risk themselves along with him. If Jesus asks only for what his followers are already eager to give, then they need to look more closely, walk more nearly, and listen more intently to discover Jesus more fully.

GUY SAYLES

2. Rowan Williams, *Christ on Trial: How the Gospel Unsettles Our Judgement* (Grand Rapids: Eerdmans, 2000), 36.

is also a Matthean redaction, to tell if he is the Messiah, the Son of God (v. 63).

For this crucial question, the Markan Jesus answers, "I am" (Mark 14:62), while Matthew changes it to "You said" (NRSV "You have said so," v. 64a). In contrast to the unambiguous affirmation in Mark's version, this Matthean version is elliptical in form and elusive in meaning. If it is an affirmative answer, it is a highly qualified one. Earlier, in 26:25, Jesus gives the exact same answer ("You said"; NRSV "You have said so") to Judas, and later, in 27:11, he gives a very similar answer ("You are saying"; NRSV "You say so") to Pilate. In all these cases, there is an irony of discrepancy between what is said and what is connoted. In the present passage, this evasive answer of Jesus alerts the reader to recognize the discrepancy between what Caiaphas means by Messiah and what Jesus means by the same.

Then Jesus adds an apocalyptic prophecy about the Son of Man seated at the right hand of God and coming on the clouds of heaven (v. 64b). The word "Messiah" is conspicuously missing in this statement of Jesus. The high priest condemns it as blasphemy. Leviticus 24:15–16 stipulates that anyone who blasphemes the name of the Lord should be put to death by stoning. In this statement Jesus does not say anything really blasphemous. He even has the scruple of using the word "power" (*dynamis*) as a euphemism for the name of God. Claiming messiahship for oneself would not necessarily constitute blasphemy either, so long as one has the potential to deliver what is expected of the Messiah, especially if messiahship is taken in a political sense, as is the case with Bar Kokhba. In that sense, the verdict of the high priest is without ground and therefore unjust.

On the other hand, his interrogation of Jesus has elicited an important basis for accusation in the Roman court. By managing to coerce Jesus to admit, even evasively, that he claims to be the Messiah, Caiaphas can now deliver him to Pilate as one of the political instigators who try to overthrow the Roman colonial government and restore the nation of Israel, which is exactly what he does the next morning.

EUGENE EUNG-CHUN PARK

orthodoxy. However, to stay with the external and not turn Matthew's beautiful narrative inward excludes an important aspect of the text.

The text builds the case that the people closest to Christ and the community Christ seeks to save also play their part in the movement toward his destruction. The distance of Peter—standing outside at the trial of Jesus—speaks clearly to the human proclivity to cowardice in relation to God. How often are we the enemies of God, planning the deaths of good things? Religious people can be dangerous. We live for doctrine, pronouncements, liturgy, but often fail to understand why we do what we do and for whom we do it. Matthew indicts us all. We at times are seduced by the religious elites, or we cowardly walk at a distance from Jesus, close enough to see Christ, but too far away to have a relationship or a conversation. We keep a safe distance, condemning ourselves with the illusion of safety. We are willing to follow him, but only so far. When danger looms, we all too easily retreat to our comfortable alliances with the powers that be, to the safety of the familiar.

Another more imaginative approach that the preacher might use is to preach on the courtroom saga within the text. The juxtaposition of powerful men orchestrating a legal drama to entrap and execute an innocent man is ripe with plenty of issues to engage homiletically.

An unequal legal system biased toward money and Roman ethnicity is presented in the text. In these verses we see an unjust legal system designed to protect and serve the wealthy. We see an unjust legal system where lives are ruined by false testimony, poor defense, and zealous prosecution. An unjust legal system is presented in the text, where the crucifixion of that time scarily foreshadows the executions and the uses of the death penalty in our own time. If one desires to approach a creative prophetic homiletical perspective, the minister could raise questions and re-create the sounds, images, and burdens of this ancient legal system. The intersection between ancient and contemporary issues boldly stares in the face of the minister as he or she grasps the text and desires to speak to the people of God.

By either of these strategies the preacher shows us how much both the violence and the promise of those ancient texts still speak to judge and bless our own times.

OTIS MOSS III

⁶⁹Now Peter was sitting outside in the courtyard. A servant-girl came to him and said, "You also were with Jesus the Galilean." ⁷⁰But he denied it before all of them, saying, "I do not know what you are talking about." ⁷¹When he went out to the porch, another servant-girl saw him, and she said to the bystanders, "This man was with Jesus of Nazareth." ⁷²Again he denied it with an oath, "I do not know the man." ⁷³After a little while the bystanders came up and said to Peter, "Certainly you are also one of them, for your accent betrays you." ⁷⁴Then he began to curse, and he swore an oath, "I do not know the man!" At that moment the cock crowed. ⁷⁵Then Peter remembered what Jesus had said: "Before the cock crows, you will deny me three times." And he went out and wept bitterly.

Theological Perspective

In this passage Peter, the eyewitness of the trial in 26:57–68, comes to his moment of denying Christ three times. Matthew's depiction of Peter's denial of Christ is a rich passage for theological reflection. Peter has, throughout Matthew's Gospel, been the most enthusiastic disciple in the good moments of Jesus' ministry. He was the first to recognize that Jesus is "the Messiah, the Son of the living God" (16:16). Jesus responded to Peter's faith by saying, "You are Peter, and on this rock I will build my church" (16:18). Peter expressed his willingness to die with Christ (26:35).

Matthew's first readers know, of course, that Peter became the leading apostle in the founding of the postresurrection church. So this passage comes as a dramatic illustration of how being a follower of Christ can be difficult in the face of violence. Peter has just followed Jesus to the house of Caiaphas and watched him accused, abused, and condemned to die. As much as Peter believes in Jesus, he now feels fear and does not know how he is going to survive his association with Jesus. He had said he was willing to follow Jesus to the death. Jesus then questioned not his sincerity, but rather his ability to stay the course. Jesus has even told him that before the cock crows he will deny him three times (26:31–35). Imagine then Peter's disappointment in

Pastoral Perspective

In the last week of Jesus' life, some of his closest followers find themselves trapped in webs of betrayal, denial, and defection. While their teacher and friend struggles and suffers, they become mired in discreditable greed, in fearful confusion, or in a desperate drive for self-preservation. The Gospel of Matthew particularly focuses on Judas's betrayal of Jesus (26:14–16, 47–50) and, in this text, Peter's denial of him: a denial about which Jesus has earlier warned his friend (26:31–35). In response to that warning, Peter has confidently said: "Even though I must die with you, I will not deny you" (26:35). Although he is determined never to do it, Peter denies Jesus. His denial underscores how the promises people make when threatening conditions are remote can get broken under the pressure of risk and danger, despite people's conscious intentions.

There is no reason to doubt the sincerity of Peter's promise. Doubtless he means what he says; but he does not take sufficient account of how, under pressure, people are capable of abandoning their best friends, forfeiting their most cherished principles, and sacrificing their truest identities on the altar of survival.

Preaching amid the urgent uncertainties and perplexing problems that the Second World War left in

Exegetical Perspective

There are two trial scenes of Jesus in Matthew's passion narrative: the interrogation of Jesus by the high priest Caiaphas (26:57–68) and the trial of Jesus by the Roman governor Pilate (27:11–25). Sandwiched between them are two reports about disciples of Jesus who fail him in their respective ways. One is the denial of Peter (26:69–75); the other is the suicide of Judas Iscariot (27:3–10). In these stories, both Peter and Judas commit betrayal and subsequently regret what they have done. Within the narrative world of the passion of Jesus in the Synoptic Gospels, there is no redemption or rehabilitation for either of them, though there is for Peter in John 21:15–19.

Earlier, in 26:31–35, as they were going from the Passover meal to the Mount of Olives, Jesus foretold the betrayal of all the twelve disciples. Peter spoke up in protest and swore that he would never desert him. Upon hearing this, Jesus predicted Peter's denial of him in specific terms: "This very night, before the cock crows, you will deny me three times" (26:34). Peter adamantly denied the possibility of his denial of Jesus. This verbal exchange makes Peter's eventual denial of Jesus all the more tragic and poignant. Indeed, when Jesus was arrested at Gethsemane as a result of the betrayal of Judas, all the disciples abandoned Jesus and fled (26:56). Once they had fled,

Homiletical Perspective

Our attention once again is drawn to the passion narrative. We witness the final days of Jesus, his journey to the cross, as he accepts his undeserved but necessary journey to Calvary. Now we fix our eyes, our theological gaze, on Peter the disciple (the Rock) denying Jesus.

When we look at Peter from a different angle, the power of this text can be revealed in a nontraditional manner. Peter signs up to follow Jesus early in his ministry and is elevated in the Synoptic Gospels as a very vocal disciple. Peter speaks up to protect Jesus and speaks up to declare the need to build a temple to commemorate the transfiguration moment. Peter speaks up again to communicate his desire to be empowered to walk upon water. Anna Carter Florence, homiletics professor at Columbia Theological Seminary, has sometimes framed Peter as the "insecure disciple," always speaking up to compensate for his insecurity. Peter reflects the personality of the parish. Peter lives in constant contradiction, yet he has a deep love for Christ. His failures are wonderfully public, and have the hint of insecurity.

What is fascinating about Peter is the residue of his class distinction. A deeply committed disciple, who is in partnership with men and women who are from different socioeconomic sectors of Palestine, Peter is called as a young man without means. Yet he

Matthew 26:69–75

Theological Perspective

himself when he denies his association with Jesus three times in the early morning hours, just as Jesus has predicted.

The three accusations Peter denies indicate the substance of his fear of association with a condemned man as a follower, in his proximity, and in his ethnicity. These were not surprisingly some of the very reasons early Christians failed to follow through in their commitments. Most significantly, for today's believers these same fears cause contemporary believers to deny their associations with Christ. Peter's first response to the servant girl who accuses him of being with Jesus the Galilean is to deny it before those in the courtyard with a hedging statement: "I do not know what you are talking about" (v. 70). When he moves from the courtyard to the porch, another servant girl tells the bystanders, "This man was with Jesus of Nazareth." Again he denies it, but this time with an oath, "I do not know the man" (v. 72). The move from the first denial to the second is one of increased intensity. Association with Jesus in this moment may lead Peter to a violent end, which he clearly fears. So in spite of his earlier avowed promise to follow Jesus wherever he goes, Peter is not prepared to go there right then. Finally a kind of additional evidence is offered, that Peter must be with Jesus, for his Galilean accent betrays him. He is not from Judea, but rather from Galilee. Why else would he be here, except for being a follower of Jesus of Nazareth? Once again Peter's response intensifies. He begins to curse and swears again, "I do not know the man!" (v. 74). Then the cock crows three times, and Peter realizes what he has done. Peter goes out and weeps bitter tears.

One has to ask, What is the purpose of taking one of the heroes of the first-century Christian faith to this nadir? Why does Matthew destroy Peter's credibility from earlier sections of his Gospel when he knows Peter will go on to preach courageously and even die himself on the cross later? One cannot know for certain why Matthew narrates the passion this way, but the effect can be seen immediately in the narrative itself. One of Jesus' closest friends has denied him, and the Jesus movement is at its lowest. Human beings will not save Jesus; only God will do that. We also see Peter's disappointment in himself in Matthew's telling of the story, a story that rings true for those of us who say we are committed to Christ and then disappoint ourselves.

Theologically, we can also see that the story of Peter's denials, when seen in a larger historical context, have an encouraging aspect. If one of such great

Pastoral Perspective

its wake, Harry Emerson Fosdick, then pastor of the Riverside Church in New York City, said:

> What we really are always comes out in the testing of an emergency. . . . And when an emergency comes there is so little time to get ready. One must be ready. Life is a series of ambushes. Trouble does not commonly evolve by slow gradations; it rather leaps upon us, and when that happens there is so little time to get ready—one must be ready.[1]

When Jesus is arrested by the temple guard and taken to Caiaphas's residence for a late-night trial (26:57), Peter is ambushed. Suddenly trouble leaps on him, and he makes his way to the high priest's house under the heavy weight of simultaneous loyalty to Jesus and dread for his own fate. He "followed Jesus at a distance" and "sat with the guards in order to see how this would end" (26:58). When it is over, Peter sees not simply the Jewish officials' verdict on Jesus, but also his own capacity for deception and denial. He fails the test of this emergency.

Just as Jesus has been tempted three times by Satan (4:1–11) and has, in Gethsemane, wrestled with God's will through three long seasons of prayer (26:36–46), Peter is now confronted three times with the choice of whether to honor his commitment to Jesus or to deny him. Three times, contrary to his promise to remain loyal to Jesus, Peter disavows any connection to him. After his last denial, "the cock crowed" and "Peter remembered what Jesus had said, 'Before the cock crows, you will deny me three times.'" In abject shame and grief, he "went out and wept bitterly" (vv. 74–75).

About Peter's weeping, theologian and ethicist Stanley Hauerwas writes: "Peter's bitter tears must always be the tears of the church, for the church, like Peter, finds itself in the position of having denied that we know Jesus."[2] The church denies Jesus when it opts for the safety of isolation from the world and its struggles, rather than for the risky adventure of engaging the world with justice and mercy; when its practices prop up the way things are, rather than point toward the way they could be in the transformational rule and reign of God; and when its presence polarizes, rather than reconciles people who are divided by differences and misunderstanding. Followers of Jesus deny him when self-absorption hinders self-giving, when fear strangles love, and

---

1. Harry Emerson Fosdick, *On Being Fit to Live With: Sermons on Post-War Christianity* (New York: Harper & Bros., 1946), 152, 158.
2. Stanley Hauerwas, *Matthew* (Grand Rapids: Brazos, 2007), 228.

they never returned to Jesus until after his resurrection—except for one, Peter.

In the immediately preceding passage of the trial of Jesus at Caiaphas's home, Peter reappears as following Jesus into the courtyard (26:58). Matthew's editorial remark says Peter's purpose for doing this is "to see how this would end," which is not found in Mark. Obviously, in Matthew's version, Peter thinks that it is all coming to an end, now that Jesus is arrested and is most likely going to be executed, in spite of his thrice-repeated prediction of his death and resurrection (16:21–23; 17:22–23; 20:17–19). This implicit criticism of Peter in Matthew's redaction is in accordance with the recurring characterization of the disciples as having "little faith" (*oligopistoi*, 6:30; 8:26; 14:31; 16:8; 17:20).

The present passage immediately follows the report that those who are present at the house of Caiaphas mock and deride Jesus after the consensus about the death penalty has been reached. Verse 69 locates Peter sitting "outside [*exō*] in the courtyard." This implies that the trial and the ensuing derision of Jesus take place inside the house of Caiaphas, while bystanders including Peter stay outdoors in the courtyard. A servant girl comes to Peter and says, "You were with Jesus the Galilean." A person-to-person statement, it is not even presented as an accusation, although it could have suggested guilt by association. However, Peter denies it "in front of all" (NRSV "before all of them," v. 70), which is Matthew's redactional addition to Mark. Then Peter goes out toward the gate. In the Markan version, it is at this point that the cock crows for the first time (Mark 14:68), but Matthew deletes that detail and makes the cock crow only after the third denial by Peter (v. 74).

As Peter goes out to the gate, another servant girl sees him and says to those who are present, "This man was with Jesus of Nazareth" (v. 71). The imperfect tense of the verb *eimi* here says that Peter, who used to have the privilege of being with Jesus, is no longer with him, which is sad enough, but Peter is now denying with an oath even his past association with Jesus (v. 72). The third denial is occasioned by the bystanders both in Mark and Matthew. In Matthew's version, they recognize Peter as a Galilean through his accent (v. 73). There is no evidence that Aramaic had a distinctive Galilean accent, but there are certainly local peculiarities in any language. This time Peter begins to invoke a curse (*katathematizein*) and to swear an oath (*omnyein*) to deny the charge (v. 74). According to Jewish tradition, the embedded

is placed in partnership with James and John, who are both children of privilege. The contradiction of Peter is the schism of the parish; often we serve people of great gifts and deep commitment, but they suffer from the spirit of insecurity.

The dichotomy of Peter is his deep love, insecurity, courage, cowardice, faith, and fear—all woven together in one soul. The tapestry of Peter is the cloth of humanity. Peter's contradictions are on display throughout this biblical narrative. The patriarch Abraham also has the residue of this contradiction. He sits upon the pedestal of sanitized quasi-sainthood, but the reality is different from the romantic story. However, when preached from the pulpit, the story about how Abraham was a liar and potential exploiter of his spouse oftentimes is edited out of his biography. David, another lauded character, brings shame to the throne publicly and is the catalyst for the destruction and continued dysfunction of his family.

The point is that Peter's contradictions should never be preached in isolation or as an anomaly, but in the broader context of human error and foolishness. Peter's consecration as a future ecclesiastical leader is never redacted from the biblical narrative or the church's history. Peter's denial of Christ is not reciprocated by Jesus, and the future achievements are not marred by his past cowardice. Here we witness the good news. The mourning of this moment and the tragic tone of the narrative never shut the door on the redemptive nature of God's love.

A message recalling Peter's life and demonstrating the struggle of a person living in poverty in Palestine under Roman colonial rule has the potential to connect universally with the majority of the world's population. Peter's life is echoed in places such as the Congo, Flint, Cleveland, Newark, Los Angeles, and many other cities and countries across the globe.

Much of the world knows a portion of Peter's context, the struggle of living with few resources yet with the potential within a person who recognizes God's call. The challenge of living among people of means can weary even a person of great spiritual promise. It can confuse the psyche and wear upon the spirit. The internal struggle of inadequacy and the tragic moment of shame and disappointment are ideas that speak universally.

The story of Peter does not end in the denial stage, though, just as the story of Christ refuses to fade to black and ask the audience to exit the theater at Calvary. Peter's low point is one chapter in a longer story.

Matthew 26:69–75 317

Matthew 26:69–75

Theological Perspective

faith as Peter will eventually demonstrate can have doubts and nevertheless become Christ's witness and his martyr, so too can Matthew's early readers, who are beset by people who doubt Christ and his ways.

As bad as Peter seems at this moment, he serves as an inspiration to believers with their own moments of doubt, denial, and desperation. For we know that Peter recovered and reoriented his life to preaching the one whom he has sadly denied. For early Christians facing persecution and separation from their communities, therefore, this negative moment could paradoxically serve as a positive encouragement to stand fast in the face of fear and not to deny Christ. It could also offer a second chance to believers who had fallen away from their earlier association with Christians.

Matthew's passage can also function in a hopeful way for contemporary Christians, as reassurance in the face of difficult moments in the life of faith. If the only people who can be Christians are people who have no doubts, no fears, then there is little hope, for all will fall short of the glory of God and of Christ, God's Son. Nevertheless, if we can turn to Peter as our brother in the faith, we can recognize our humanity in his fears for his life. Though he saw Jesus face to face and watched him preach and perform miracles, Peter was brought low by fear. We are also to remember that Peter made a comeback and that the church was founded on the faith of Peter and others, whose faith proved stronger than their fear about what others would say about them or do to their bodies. Today's Christians are to be encouraged to recognize themselves in Peter at the point where he denies Christ, but never to leave themselves or Peter on the porch in the moment of denial.

JAMES HUDNUT-BEUMLER

Pastoral Perspective

when despair silences hope. Bitter tears are the right response to such denials, especially if they prepare the heart for renewing grace.

Were it not for such grace, the report of Peter's weeping might be the last words about him in the New Testament. Because there is grace, though—because the crucified Jesus rose from the dead and offered mercy and forgiveness to all who betrayed, denied, and forsook him—bitter tears are not where Peter's story ends.

To the community for which Matthew wrote his Gospel, Peter was a leader held in great esteem. He bore significant authority and influence, which Matthew's church believed Jesus had granted to him (16:13–20). It is astonishing, then, that Matthew is so honest about Peter's weakness in a time of testing and his abject denials of Jesus. There is no hiding or pretending in this account; Matthew candidly admits that his church's most visible and trusted leader was widely known to have failed dramatically. There is good news in such honesty; it provides assurance that grace and mercy have remarkable power.

Our culture shines the spotlight on success; it celebrates victory and achievement. It also broadcasts the news of failure. It does not allow people to fail quietly; the reports go up on Facebook, creditors call, neighbors gossip, and colleagues whisper. It is a harsh and cruel place in which to fail. The harshness and cruelty are surprising, since everyone fails. Potential goes unrealized and dreams become nightmares. Commitments are shattered, and promises get broken. To fail is to lose, and part of what people lose is "face": failure robs people of respect in the eyes of others and esteem in their own.

Failure does not have to be the final verdict for any of Jesus' followers. Peter's story makes that truth compellingly clear. In Jesus, God forgives even the most shocking failure and restores those who fail to the dignity of usefulness and service.

GUY SAYLES

meaning of the curse would be, "May I be accursed by God if I am found to be lying in my statement that I do not know the man." Then immediately a cock crows, fulfilling the prediction of Jesus (26:34). Peter remembers it, so he goes out (*exō*) and weeps bitterly (v. 75).

This weeping of Peter indicates his remorse and even regret, but it does not lead him to repent, which would have meant turning around and going to Jesus to be with him. The series of three adverbial expressions of locality Matthew uses in this passage—that is, "in the courtyard" (v. 69), "into/toward the gate" (v. 71; NRSV "out to the porch"), and "out" (v. 75)—symbolically trace the change of location of Peter as a centrifugal movement away from Jesus. That is, even as he bitterly (*pikrōs*) regrets his denial of Jesus, Peter still continues to flee from the plight he fears he would be in, were he implicated with Jesus.

In the narrative world of Matthew, this is the very last scene in which Peter appears as an individual character. From this point on, Peter is conspicuously absent from the suffering and the crucifixion of Jesus. In the Markan version of the empty tomb story Peter's name is singled out as a primary beneficiary of the news of Jesus' resurrection in the message of the young man in a white robe (Mark 16:7), but Matthew deletes Peter's name in his revised edition (28:7). In the last scene of the reunion of Jesus with the eleven disciples on the mountain in Galilee (28:16–20), it is presumed that Peter is among them, since their number is eleven. However, his name is never mentioned. In fact, he may very well be one of those who doubt (*hoi de edistasan*) in 28:17. If the Gospel of Matthew had been the only available story of Jesus, Peter would have appeared as one of the tragic dramatis personae who spectacularly fall from top to bottom, never to recover.

EUGENE EUNG-CHUN PARK

Another fascinating approach to this text is to examine Peter's denial in context and from the viewpoint of a servant girl. What rich material to preach and teach sits behind this nameless woman who recognizes Peter as a man of faith following Jesus of Nazareth. Here again is a hidden homiletical gem. Here are some questions to raise for the person constructing a message around this nameless person: Why was she watching Peter? What caused her to speak out? What was her daily routine as a servant girl? Was this a simple statement? Was this an act of defiance or jealousy? Was this woman looking to talk more with Peter and learn more about his life? The answers are not clear, but the questions help us to think about the role of the servant girl and reconstruct the life of a young woman in ancient Palestine.

The preacher has the option to explore this very small crevice in the Scripture and help the wider community understand the ancient world and the connections with contemporary society, developing and understanding the role of a servant girl, both in her society and in this narrative. Why is the servant girl written into the narrative rather than an officer, a tax collector, an unknown individual who is male? Matthew's primary audience should be considered along with the narrative structure to examine this small corner of the text.

The preacher should be encouraged to turn the Scripture in several directions. Read it aloud with emphasis upon different words and syllables to gain a better understanding of how the Scripture might have been heard and how the oral story would have been passed on. What impact would this story have on a young girl hearing it? What is the feeling one would have hearing the story of a person of particular socioeconomic means, Peter, denying Jesus, and then another person, even lower on the socioeconomic ladder, pointing out the contradiction and cowardice of this looming biblical character?

This text is full of possibilities. With work, imagination, prayer, and strong exegesis, a creative message can be structured theologically to excavate the roots of the text and create a relevant message that will be palatable and understandable to the postmodern worshiper.

OTIS MOSS III

Matthew 27:1–10

¹When morning came, all the chief priests and the elders of the people conferred together against Jesus in order to bring about his death. ²They bound him, led him away, and handed him over to Pilate the governor.

³When Judas, his betrayer, saw that Jesus was condemned, he repented and brought back the thirty pieces of silver to the chief priests and the elders. ⁴He said, "I have sinned by betraying innocent blood." But they said, "What is that to us? See to it yourself." ⁵Throwing down the pieces of silver in the temple, he departed; and he went and hanged himself. ⁶But the chief priests, taking the pieces of silver, said, "It is not lawful to put them into the treasury, since they are blood money." ⁷After conferring together, they used them to buy the potter's field as a place to bury foreigners. ⁸For this reason that field has been called the Field of Blood to this day. ⁹Then was fulfilled what had been spoken through the prophet Jeremiah, "And they took the thirty pieces of silver, the price of the one on whom a price had been set, on whom some of the people of Israel had set a price, ¹⁰and they gave them for the potter's field, as the Lord commanded me."

Theological Perspective

The first story in this passage raises the question whether Judas was truly repentant of his betrayal of Jesus, and if so, whether he might find grace and forgiveness from God.

No figure of history has been more vilified than Judas. Often portrayed as the archdemonic figure, he has been consigned eternally to the depths of hell. Is this not an accurate extension of the biblical judgment on Judas? Does not Jesus pronounce woe on the one who will betray him and say that it would have been better if he had never been born (26:24)?

At the outset, we must acknowledge that there are two accounts of the death of Judas in the New Testament, and they differ in important ways. Distinctive of Matthew's narrative is that Judas "repented" (v. 3), returned the thirty pieces of silver he had received from his coconspirators, acknowledged that he had "sinned" by betraying innocent blood, and in complete despair hanged himself. By contrast, according to the account in Acts, the blood money is kept by Judas, there is no mention of his repentance, and his death is portrayed not as a suicide but as an involuntary explosion: he fell and burst open, "and all his bowels gushed out" (Acts 1:18). Since these two accounts obviously cannot be harmonized, it is only in relation to the story as told by Matthew that questions arise whether the repentance of Judas

Pastoral Perspective

Judas Iscariot ranks among the great villains of all time. He betrayed the Savior of the world with a friendly kiss. That despicable action set in motion a chain of events that resulted in the humiliation, rejection, torture, and death of Jesus.

Why did Judas betray Jesus? He may have had his material gain in mind. Perhaps he had trouble adjusting his expectations of how the Messiah should act to Jesus' way of handling things. It is also possible to imagine that somehow God needed Judas to play a necessary, if unpleasant, role in the drama of salvation by handing Jesus over to the religious and Roman authorities. Each of these possibilities calls for further reflection.

Let us suppose, first, that Judas acted freely and from selfish motives. Betraying Jesus to the religious authorities may have seemed like a good idea at the time. A cash payment sufficient to buy a piece of real estate in the Jerusalem area might have made a certain amount of sense to Judas, particularly if he was worried about finding a way to secure his future.

With respect to the second possible explanation for the behavior of Judas, one could well imagine that he had become disenchanted with Jesus' vision and way of doing things. In this scenario, Judas and Jesus have different visions for messianic behavior. Judas—like the rest of the apostles (see 24:3 and Acts

Feasting on the Gospels

Exegetical Perspective

As Matthew's story has arrived at Jesus' crucifixion, readers should keep the following sociohistorical realities in mind. First, the first-century Mediterranean world, including Israel, was under Roman rule, which shaped the politics, economics, and religion of the region. Second, these three components of life were inextricably intertwined in the Roman world. Roman propaganda declared that the gods had chosen Rome to bring peace and prosperity to the world. Caesar was either the son of a god or a god. Priests in the various provinces wielded political power, having received their positions by collaborating with Rome and becoming its "client rulers." Their political roles included overseeing the collection of taxes and tributes so that they also benefited from Roman economic policies. When they did their jobs well—that is, when they served Rome's interests in the region—Rome rewarded them with greater wealth and expanded authority. Third, the religious leaders in Jerusalem were thus politically connected, exercised political power, and had obtained positions that enriched them. They were allies of Rome and part of the privileged class in Israel. Matthew presents them as leaders devoted to their privilege, which drives their practice of their religion.

Consequently, this context demands that we not read the story of Jesus' fate as "Christianity versus

Homiletical Perspective

The death of Judas by his own hand forces us to consider an important theological consideration: Did the actions of Judas as they involved his betrayal of Jesus in the Garden of Gethsemane constitute "the unpardonable sin"? Were the actions of Judas so terrible, at least in his own eyes, that he came to believe that he could not go on living? This is no small or incidental question. We who preach the gospel of Jesus Christ may need to wonder aloud about the fact that there is a little of Judas in all of us. All of us have had days when we betrayed the Lord in word or deed. All of us have had days when our actions and our attitudes seemed to deny our claim of being intimately associated with Jesus. When we face such moments in our own lives, we live with the hope and the faith that God will forgive us of our sins and cleanse us from all unrighteousness (1 John 1:9). The question that is being raised here is whether the same possibility existed for Judas.

This passage yields many lessons that can be carried into the pulpit. There is the lesson of the economics of sin, or the notion that when we go off in pursuit of the trinkets and baubles of this world, walking away from God in the process, what we lose is always more than what we gain. Judas gained thirty pieces of silver, blood money that he did not live long enough to spend. What Judas lost was the

Matthew 27:1–10

Theological Perspective

was genuine and whether it might be met by God's forgiveness.

So did Judas truly repent, and can he be saved? Dante and Calvin, among many others, do not think so. Dante places Judas in the lowest ring of hell, where Satan chews on his head and claws at his back for all eternity. Calvin is sure that Judas was only "touched" with repentance, not manifesting "real conversion." His horror and despair at what he had done did not lead him back to God, but simply plunged him into darkest despair. He became "an example of a man banned from the grace of God," who handed him over to Satan "for torment without hope of relief."[1]

Karl Barth's reflections on the New Testament accounts of the end of Judas move in a different direction—not that he excuses Judas or downplays the seriousness of his sin. Sin for Barth is never anything less than despicable. Barth's point, however, is that the gospel proclaims God's grace as greater than our sin, however atrocious. Was the sin of Judas infinitely worse than the abandonment of Jesus by the disciples during his passion and crucifixion? Was it worse than the threefold denial of Jesus by Peter? Had they not also betrayed their Lord? Must we assume that forgiveness of sins is categorically ruled out in the case of Judas? Did Jesus not also die for him? In Christian theology's all-too-assured exclusion of Judas from the grace of God, might there lurk an effort to hide our own betrayals of Jesus and to immunize ourselves against the judgment of God, which we are content to see fall on Judas (and, tragically, on the people so closely associated with his name)?

The great question that haunts those who insist on sending Judas to hell is whether allowing the possibility of his redemption would irresistibly drive us toward a doctrine of universal salvation. If Judas may find forgiveness, why not also Hitler, Stalin, and all others who repudiate the grace of God and violate humanity? Reflection on the story of Judas thus confronts us with opposing alternatives. On the one hand, there is nothing in either of the New Testament accounts of the death of Judas that gives us permission to conclude that God accepted his repentance and forgave him. On the other hand, as Barth points out, particularly if we focus on the Matthean account, the question at least arises whether even an admittedly heinous sin is necessarily outside

Pastoral Perspective

1:6)—thought that the Messiah should act like King David of blessed biblical memory. In the Davidic version of messianic expectation, God would raise up a messiah in order to lead a military uprising against an occupying Gentile power and to reestablish a free Israelite nation. In marked contrast, Jesus' vision for the Messiah entailed a Suffering Servant (Isa. 52:13–53:12) whose nonviolent sacrifice would lead to the salvation of Jew and Gentile alike. In this conflict-of-messianic-expectations scenario, Judas may have betrayed Jesus to jump-start the process of violent revolt against the Romans. Maybe he succumbed to the bitterness that comes from disenchantment with a charismatic leader.

A third option for making sense of Judas's behavior presents the most disturbing scenario theologically. What if God had determined to use Judas as a necessary player in the unfolding drama of Jesus' passion and death? In order for the Suffering-Servant drama to play out, God needed someone to betray Jesus into the hands of the religious and civil authorities. In other words, betrayal was a dirty job, but God needed someone to do it.

No matter how we may think about it, upon closer inspection Judas seems more a tragic figure than a coldhearted villain. Making self-interested choices, clashing with a beloved authority figure, or playing an unwitting role in a larger drama all have the air of tragedy about them. In many ways, Judas was not so very different from the other apostles. Come to think of it, he may not be that much different from us and from the people we hold dear. Do we not sometimes make decisions on the basis of what will serve our personal interests? Do not our visions of the way things should be done conflict with authority figures or partners? Are we not sometimes swept up in larger dramas to play parts not necessarily of our own choosing?

The most tragic part of the story of Judas may lie in the fact that he gave up on hope. Once he had come to himself and realized the terrible implications of what he had done, Matthew tells us simply that "he repented" (v. 3). More than merely having feelings of remorse over his actions, Judas's anguished feelings led him to take steps to repair the damage he had done. He returned to his coconspirators and tried to give the betrayal money back. When the religious leaders refused to take the money back, he left it with them anyway. In the end, he chose not to profit from his shameful deeds. Although it was a case of "too little, too late," it cannot go unnoticed that Judas actually felt badly about

---

1. John Calvin, *A Harmony of the Gospels,* Calvin's New Testament Commentaries (Grand Rapids: Eerdmans, 1978), 3:175.

Judaism" or as anti-Semitic in any way. The conflict in Matthew's story is not between Jesus and "the Jews," but between a peasant Jew who announced that the apocalyptic promises of God were being fulfilled, and powerful Jews and Romans who understood his claims to threaten their privilege.

In the flow of Matthew's narrative, this text ties up loose ends in the portrayal of the betrayers in the story. Peter denied Jesus, then wept bitterly when he recognized his failure (26:69–75). Judas conspired with the religious leaders to "hand over" or "betray" (*paradidōmi*) Jesus to them (26:14–16) and had succeeded (26:47–56). What of his reaction to these events?

The result of Judas's action is related in verses 1–2. Jesus was "handed over" (*paradidōmi*) to the Romans, which guaranteed his death. Did he expect the religious leaders to remove Jesus quietly back to Galilee? Did he expect Jesus to perform a great miracle to stop his execution and dazzle Jerusalem? Did he think Jesus would call on his followers to fight for him? When we put speculations regarding Judas aside, we find that the text tells only of his remorse when he saw that Jesus was as good as dead because the Romans had him.

The "handing over" of Jesus to the Romans appears to be for Judas what the rooster crowing was for Peter, the moment when his betrayal "hit home." Like Peter, Judas appears in these verses as genuinely remorseful. He had done a horrible thing for money (the only motivation Matthew offers, 26:14–15) and was horrified by his act. He tried to return the money (v. 3). He confessed his sin in "betraying" (*paradidōmi*) Jesus and bore witness to Jesus' innocence in doing so (v. 4a). When the religious leaders would not hear his confession or accept his repentance (v. 4b), he hanged himself (v. 5). In the shame-honor culture of this world, his suicide can be read as a "falling on his sword" act, that is, a recognition that he had acted dishonorably and paid the price so as to restore some honor to his name.

Christians have vilified and demonized Judas for centuries. So perhaps we are surprised to note that he is the sympathetic figure in this story. The "villains" are the upstanding figures of the time, the religious leaders who wear phylacteries and prayer shawls, who are given the places of honor at banquets and important seats in the synagogues, who are greeted happily in the marketplace (23:3–7).

While readers today are likely not surprised at the villains, our centuries of demonizing the Jewishness of the "chief priests and the elders" may have dulled

ability to live with himself and his own conscience. What he lost was the right to be numbered among the ranks of the followers of Jesus, persons whose names have continued to echo through the millennia. We all know about hospitals, schools, towns, and our own children that are named after Peter, James, John, Matthew, and all the others—all, that is, except Judas. Nobody in their right mind would name anything of worth or value after Judas. I do not know anyone who has even named a pet after Judas. Judas Iscariot is a name that lives in infamy. He may have gained thirty pieces of silver, but what he lost is far more than he gained.

Another lesson that can be learned from the story of Judas is that the Bible is full of good people who had a few bad days. For most of his three years with Jesus, there was no mention of Judas's causing any problems. John 12:4–6 suggests that as the keeper of the money Judas might have been guilty of taking a little out for himself from time to time. Who among us can say that we have not had days when we bent a rule or ignored a policy or simply broke a covenant of trust in pursuit of some personal advantage? The actions of Judas look bad when viewed from a distance, but when they are viewed through the lens of our own lives, we discover there is not that much difference between Judas and us.

Like Moses and Abraham, like David and Solomon, like us and those who hear us preach on a regular basis, Judas was probably a good man who was prone to having an occasional bad day. The day described in this passage was an especially bad day. We should be cautious, however, about judging him too harshly or believing that his sin was beyond the reach of God's grace and forgiveness. If God cannot forgive the sin of Judas, then God may also choose not to forgive our sins. That might be what Jesus had in mind when he said, "Do not judge, so that you may not be judged" (7:1).

The final lesson we can learn from the life of Judas involves the life of Peter during the same period of time. What did Judas do that was so much worse than what Peter did? Indeed, what Judas did with his betrayal of Jesus occurred only once. What Peter did with his denial of Jesus occurred three times. In both instances, Jesus seemed to know the heart of the people involved. Jesus knew that Judas would betray him. Jesus knew that Peter would deny him. Why is it that Judas has seemed to us to be beyond redemption, while Peter rose to the top of the list of the followers of Jesus? Perhaps the answer is that Peter lived long enough to find out that his

Theological Perspective

Pastoral Perspective

the scope of God's forgiveness.[2] Faced with this interpretive dilemma, is it not best to leave the matter of final judgment on Judas and on all others in the hands of God alone, while also holding fast to the good news that "where sin increased, grace abounded all the more" (Rom. 5:20)?

Turning to the second part of our text, what theological yield is there to be found in the account of the chief priests' purchase of the potter's field with the paltry thirty pieces of silver that Judas returned? In the story in Acts, the chief priests have no part in the purchase of the field; instead, Judas is reported to have kept the blood money and used it to purchase the field for himself. Equally significant, the Acts account omits any mention of a positive purpose the field might eventually serve. It is simply described, in fulfillment of prophecy, as a place of desolation where no one should live (Acts 1:20).

By contrast, and in accord with his own emphasis on prophetic fulfillment throughout his Gospel, Matthew finds a special meaning in the chief priests' purchase of the potter's field—later known as the Field of Blood—to provide "a place to bury foreigners" (vv. 7–8). The inclusion of this story is surely more than a curious desire to explain the origin of a name. Matthew's is a missionary Gospel, concluding with the commission of the risen Jesus to proclaim the gospel to all the nations. Although the chief priests know nothing of the redemptive significance of Jesus' death, their purchase of the potter's field with the blood money paid to Judas will attend to the needs of "foreigners," a term likely including Gentiles.

Matthew's story of the potter's field suggests that in the smallest details of the passion and crucifixion of Jesus, God's work of redemption reaches out to all people. If this reading is correct, even Judas's blood money is used by God to offer a sign of inclusion of the Gentiles in the benefits of Christ's death and in the proclamation of God's coming kingdom to all the nations.

DANIEL L. MIGLIORE

what he had done and tried to do something about it. Far from a heartless, cold-blooded sociopath, Judas actually had a functioning moral conscience, even to the very end. His story is one of truncated repentance. Yet it goes deeper than that.

The deepest level of tragedy in this story lies in the fact that Judas looked only to human beings for forgiveness and restoration. Why did Judas stop with the religious leaders? Why did he not turn also to God, pouring out his repentant soul and asking for God's mercy by using the well-worn words of Psalm 51? Why did he come to believe that he was beyond any hope of redemption? Why did he give up on God?

The account of Judas in Matthew speaks powerfully and deeply about the importance of hope in God. For whatever reasons, Judas came to see himself as beyond help and beyond hope. This is the real tragedy of Judas. It is a tragedy that continues to play out all around us in the lives of people in society, in our workplaces, in our churches, in our families, and in our own lives. Even though he had screwed things up so horribly, and even when his sincere attempt to fix the mess came to nothing, he could still have thrown himself on God's mercy. If only he had not taken matters into his own hands yet again, if only he had waited longer, surely grace would have been given to him, just as it was given to the disciple who had denied Jesus three times.

The lesson we learn from the tragedy of Judas is that no one is ever beyond help and beyond hope—no matter how heinous the choices, no matter how terrible the consequences of those choices, and no matter how feeble our remorse and attempts to make things right. There is always hope in and through God. The gospel of Jesus Christ is ultimately a message of radical hope for undeserving sinners. To embody this message is the primary calling of the church and its members.

GORDON S. MIKOSKI

---

2. Karl Barth, *Church Dogmatics*, II/2 (Edinburgh: T. & T. Clark, 1957), 476.

Exegetical Perspective

us to the impact Matthew hoped to make with his account. The problem in this story is not the Jewishness of the chief priests and elders. The problem is their devotion to their privilege, power, and wealth. They are quite religious according to Matthew; note how they will not deposit the money Judas returned into the temple treasury, because "it is not lawful" to put "blood money" there (v. 6). However, as Matthew's story goes, their religion is a means to achieve and maintain their own plans and desires.

The chief priests and elders in this story were neither the first nor the last religious people to use their religion to serve their own ends. Neither is such behavior a problem for *Jewish* religious leaders only. Christians who think so know little about the dark shadows in our history. Matthew was shining a light on a *human* problem and its consequences. In difficult times, these religious leaders collaborated with the oppressors of their people to secure a good life for themselves. To maintain this security, they bribed, plotted, and schemed; they participated in lies and sanctioned violence; but they would not put "blood money" in the treasury, because that was "against the law." They did what was necessary to work with the Romans, as they continued to be terribly religious. However, the fruit of their practice betrays them (note 7:15–20): Judas hanged himself, and Jesus was "handed over" to the Romans.

The money Judas returned glitters on the temple floor, demanding our attention. What will we do for money? How hard are we willing to work to hide what we have done? Judas betrayed someone close to him. The religious leaders also betrayed Jesus for money: they bought a solution to a threat to their place, then hid their actions by laundering the money. Money and betrayal are joined in this story. What kind of challenge does this pose to us in our capitalist, consumer culture?

The irony, and even hope, in this story is that none of these betrayals prevents God from keeping the promise of renewal. When the religious leaders use the blood money to buy a "potter's field as a place to bury foreigners" (v. 7), they unwittingly fulfill prophecy, according to Matthew (vv. 8–10). Participants in evil can (and will) do their worst, *and* the promises God has made continue to be fulfilled.

MITZI MINOR

Homiletical Perspective

sin was not the unpardonable sin—a discovery that Judas might also have made if he had not hanged himself.

Something like this is intimated in Mark 16:7, when on the morning of the resurrection the angel tells Mary Magdalene, "Go, tell his disciples and Peter that he is going ahead of you to Galilee." The angel is talking to someone who knows all of the disciples personally. If the instruction were to go and tell the disciples, there is no doubt she would tell Peter as well. So why this special emphasis on "tell his disciples *and Peter*"? Can it be that a message is being sent especially to Peter that his actions a few days earlier did not and would not mark the break of his relationship with Jesus? Go tell Peter that he is still a part of the family. Go tell Peter that his actions have been forgiven. Go tell Peter that he still has a part to play in the days ahead. "Go, tell his disciples and Peter."

Is it possible that the angel might have expanded the message of resurrection morning to say, "Go tell his disciples, including Peter and Judas"? The greatest sin of Judas may not have been what he did to Jesus; it may have been what he did to himself—not his suicidal action, but his failure to believe what he had heard and seen for the preceding three years. Sins can be forgiven. Lost souls can be restored. If that is not true even for Judas, then can we be sure it is true for us?

MARVIN A. MCMICKLE

Matthew 27:11–26

¹¹Now Jesus stood before the governor; and the governor asked him, "Are you the King of the Jews?" Jesus said, "You say so." ¹²But when he was accused by the chief priests and elders, he did not answer. ¹³Then Pilate said to him, "Do you not hear how many accusations they make against you?" ¹⁴But he gave him no answer, not even to a single charge, so that the governor was greatly amazed.

¹⁵Now at the festival the governor was accustomed to release a prisoner for the crowd, anyone whom they wanted. ¹⁶At that time they had a notorious prisoner, called Jesus Barabbas. ¹⁷So after they had gathered, Pilate said to them, "Whom do you want me to release for you, Jesus Barabbas or Jesus who is called the Messiah?" ¹⁸For he realized that it was out of jealousy that they had handed him over. ¹⁹While he was sitting on the judgment seat, his wife sent word to him, "Have nothing to do with that innocent man, for today I have

Theological Perspective

Who is responsible for the condemnation and death of Jesus? This is the central theological question raised by this passage, and the appropriate answer is: All of us. While straightforward enough, this answer draws us inexorably into disturbing reflections on the nature of religion, state power, and mob mentality.

The Chief Priests and Elders. The first group Matthew holds responsible for the trial and execution of Jesus is "the chief priests and elders" (v. 12). When Jesus is brought before Pilate, it is the chief priests and elders who act as the prosecuting attorneys. As the official defenders of the faith and law of Israel, they are certain they know better than anyone else what the will of God is, and they will tolerate no challenge to their authority, least of all from this upstart teacher from backwater Galilee.

Matthew has previously shown how Jesus' teaching and healing aroused the hatred of the religious leaders and their determination to destroy him. In this passage, the evangelist continues his portrayal of the dark side of religion. No doubt religion can sometimes serve noble aims: it can give people a sense of purpose; it can inspire them to help others; it can give them hope. This, though, is far from the whole story. It is the chief priests and elders

Pastoral Perspective

In this dramatic scene, Jesus stands before the Roman governor Pontius Pilate. In the interactions portrayed in this part of the passion story, ironies abound. At first glance, we think we know what is going on in this story. Every element of this episode has a straightforward meaning that lies on the surface of things. The religious authorities bring a notorious troublemaker before the judgment seat of Rome. A brief interrogation yields little information, hardly enough evidence for punishment, let alone execution. The crowds demand something that makes little to no sense. The highest-ranking government official in the region, Pilate, weighs his options and vacillates between idealism and expediency. In the end, he caves in to public pressure and gives the people what they want. A knowing miscarriage of justice occurs, but such is the business of politics in the real world.

Just below the surface, we find an abundance of ironies and contradictions. While it seems that Jesus is on trial by the civil power, it is actually the civil power that is on trial before God. The powers of this world fail to see the plain truth, even when it stands before them in bodily form. Almighty Rome, represented and embodied in the person of Pilate, appears weak and uncertain before the incarnate Son of God. Jesus—the one who has no political power of any

suffered a great deal because of a dream about him." [20]Now the chief priests and the elders persuaded the crowds to ask for Barabbas and to have Jesus killed. [21]The governor again said to them, "Which of the two do you want me to release for you?" And they said, "Barabbas." [22]Pilate said to them, "Then what should I do with Jesus who is called the Messiah?" All of them said, "Let him be crucified!" [23]Then he asked, "Why, what evil has he done?" But they shouted all the more, "Let him be crucified!"

[24]So when Pilate saw that he could do nothing, but rather that a riot was beginning, he took some water and washed his hands before the crowd, saying, "I am innocent of this man's blood; see to it yourselves." [25]Then the people as a whole answered, "His blood be on us and on our children!" [26]So he released Barabbas for them; and after flogging Jesus, he handed him over to be crucified.

Exegetical Perspective

First-century Palestine is an occupied country. Pilate, as Roman governor of Judea, has formed alliances with the local ruling elites, the chief priests who are his "clients," to maintain Roman control of this restless province. They will work together to rid themselves of Jesus of Nazareth.

Matthew jumps immediately into an account of Jesus' trial, noting with minimal preamble Pilate's question, "Are you the King of the Jews?" (v. 11). "King of the Jews" had been Herod's title (see 2:2–3) when he was Rome's client king in Israel. Asking Jesus in this context if the title applies to him is to ask if he is leading a resistance movement against Rome. In response, Jesus neither confirms nor denies the implied charge. His "You say so" (v. 11) leaves Pilate to figure out the answer. Then he is silent (vv. 12–14).

Indeed, why *should* Jesus answer? This trial was never about justice, despite Roman boasts regarding its superior law. So why should he participate? Furthermore, how *can* he answer when, ironically, the true answer is both "yes and no"? In Matthew's Gospel Jesus is King of the Jews and is leading resistance to Roman rule, but not with swords, clubs, and violence (26:55), not to become like the emperor. So Pilate's response is amazement (v. 14), that is, he does not understand Jesus. Does he expect Jesus to

Homiletical Perspective

Over the years there have been many courtroom dramas that have left an indelible impression, not only on our minds, but on history itself. The Nuremberg trials of 1945–1946 were a courtroom drama where the surviving civilian and military leaders of the Nazi Party were brought to justice for their war crimes. The 1931 trial of nine young black men who came to be known as the Scottsboro boys, who were falsely accused of raping a white woman, was a courtroom drama where racial prejudice obscured any rational pursuit of justice. There was the 1925 Scopes trial in Tennessee, where a high school science teacher was prosecuted for teaching about the idea of evolution.

The nation was enraptured by the 1994 trial of Byron De La Beckwith, who was convicted, thirty years after the fact, of the murder of civil-rights leader Medgar Evers. On the other hand, there was the 1955 trial of two white men who were found innocent of the brutal murder of a fourteen-year-old black youth named Emmett Till, even though they had boasted about having killed him. That case, along with the 1896 U.S. Supreme Court ruling of *Plessy v. Ferguson*, reminds us how injustice can be inscribed into the law. However, the 1954 *Brown v. Board of Education* ruling reminds us of how courtroom dramas can right past wrongs. The 1973

Theological Perspective

Pastoral Perspective

who, in vigorous defense of their religion, play the leading role in bringing Jesus to trial and eventual crucifixion.

In Christian theology, the sinister potential of religion has been found primarily in Israel's rejection of Jesus as the Christ. This is, however, merely a protective maneuver. We are adept at sanitizing our own religious tradition and its history, even as we label all others diseased and dangerous. Every religious tradition, however, has a dark side, and when this dark side takes control, nothing is more destructive. One need not agree that "religion poisons everything"[1] to acknowledge the truth that religion can and often does harbor poison. It can hide hatred of others and the desire for revenge if wounded. Evil in its religious guise takes the form of our sole and absolute possession of the truth and even the determination to bring destruction on all who pose a real or imagined threat to our self-certainty.

Pilate. The second group depicted as responsible for the miscarriage of justice and the consequent execution of Jesus is the leaders of the state, represented in the person of Pilate. State power, like religion, can be a monster. It can be used to destroy or repress all opposition, including the murder of children, as Matthew tells us in the story of Herod's massacre of Jewish infants when he hears of the birth of a king of the Jews (2:16–18). Pilate can be brutal too, but here he is mostly a self-serving politician. His primary concern is to avoid a riot that would inevitably get him in trouble with his superiors in Rome.

In addition, Pilate suspects that Jesus is innocent of the charges against him, and the report of his wife about her disturbing dreams only makes him all the more nervous. So Pilate tries two ploys to get himself off the hook. One is to offer the crowd the choice of releasing Jesus or a notorious prisoner named Barabbas. When that does not work, he publicly washes his hands to proclaim his innocence and to signify he will have nothing further to do with the matter. A little hand washing, however, cannot wipe away the fact that he shares responsibility for the condemnation and death of Jesus.

As Matthew portrays him, Pilate is a representative of what Hannah Arendt calls the "banality of evil."[2] She uses this phrase to describe Rudolf Eichmann, the man who helped implement the

kind—demonstrates strength of character and integrity of purpose in the midst of high-stakes political maneuvering.

Further ironies abound. When Pilate should listen to his wife, he ignores her. When he should trust his instincts and ignore the political power play by the religious leaders, he caves in to their demands. Jesus, the Son of God the Father, is rejected in favor of Jesus Bar-Abbas (literally, "the son of the father"). The giver and redeemer of life is condemned to die, while the one who has presumably committed acts of violence goes free. The Roman ruler—the only one in Jerusalem who can do anything—"saw that he could do nothing" (v. 24). The Jewish crowds who despise Roman occupation beg for a favor from imperial Rome. In short, just under the surface of the details of this story, everything is ironically inverted.

The episode with Pilate serves as prelude to the much larger irony of the cross. Through the execution of Jesus as an enemy of Rome on a barren hill resembling a skull, God grants forgiveness of sin, reconciliation, and new life to the world. The sinless one dies that sinners might be reckoned as righteous. Through one man's death, new life becomes possible.

The pithy episode of Jesus before Pilate, with all of its ironies and contradictions, does more than provide necessary filler for the hours between the anguished prayer of Jesus in the Garden of Gethsemane and the heartbreaking prayer of Jesus on the cross. This scene discloses something that points to the heart of our daily lives in this world. Just below the surface of things, our lives are filled with irony. Things are rarely simply what they appear to be at first glance. The plain truth appears before us, and we take it for something insignificant. We, like Pilate, brush past the truth of God as a distraction from our more pressing concerns. Too often, we fail to listen to those who have our best interests in mind, and we pay attention to those who have ulterior motives. We allow ourselves to be persuaded to demand what we do not need and should not want.

Beyond laying bare the many ways in which we find our lives implicated and under judgment, this episode also discloses several ironies crucial to our faith and practice as Christians. We find here the King of kings and the Lord of lords engaging the violent and corrupt forces of empire in a way that says something profound about the reign of God. Jesus Christ reigns not with power, violence, threat, and coercion; he reigns with deep integrity, by means of uncalculated goodness, and with simple testimony

---

1. Christopher Hitchens, *God Is Not Great: How Religion Poisons Everything* (New York: Warner, 2007).

2. Hannah Arendt, *Eichmann in Jerusalem: A Report on the Banality of Evil* (New York: Penguin, 1976).

beg for his life? To deny the charge? To rant about Roman oppression?

At this point Matthew notes that Pilate has a "practice" of releasing a prisoner during Passover (v. 15). Scholars note that no historical evidence for such a practice exists, although Roman governors exercised discretion over prisoners and did release them at times. Still, since Passover celebrated Israel's liberation from Egypt, the festival would be a good time for Pilate to "liberate" a prisoner so as to manipulate the crowd by demonstrating Rome's "goodwill." Certainly, as the narrative unfolds, Pilate works at manipulation. So he offers the crowd a choice: shall I release Jesus or Barabbas? (v. 17). Barabbas, in Matthew's telling, is a "notorious prisoner" (v . 16), a description with broad meaning, including someone who engages in violent, terrorist-type activity (cf. Mark 15:7; John 18:40).

In Christian history, Pilate's choice has often been seen as Matthew's distancing Rome from Jesus' death or as a sign that Pilate knows Jesus is innocent, hopes the crowd will ask for Jesus and get him off the hook. Rome does not operate that way, however. The text says Pilate understands the envy of the religious leaders toward Jesus (v. 18), which means he also understands Jesus' popularity with the people and, thus, the threat he poses. Therefore, we should expect that Pilate's goals through all that transpires are to remove a potential threat, secure his own position, and support his clients/allies. No wonder, then, that he offers to liberate a Jewish prisoner for the Jewish people during Passover. He is working the crowd.

Suddenly inserted into the narrative is a message from Pilate's wife about her dream of Jesus' righteousness (v. 19). Christians have often read this occurrence as another indication that Pilate knows Jesus is innocent but is too weak to stop unfolding events. The text, however, says no such thing. In fact, it says nothing of Pilate's response to her. Instead, this insertion presents an extreme outsider—a woman, a Gentile, the wife of a Roman official—who bears witness to Jesus' righteousness. She has a dream, apparently from God (see Matt. 1:20–21; 2:12–13), which she is apparently willing to receive and consider. As a result she assesses the situation more wisely than the insiders in the story. She is the counterpart in the death story to the magi in the birth story—outsiders who, even as evil things are unfolding, grasp that God is at work and bear witness.

Despite his wife's message, Pilate offers the crowd Jesus or Barabbas, which readers can understand as a choice between two ways of responding to their

Supreme Court ruling known as *Roe v. Wade* and the 1995 made-for-television trial of O. J. Simpson all tell us that courtroom dramas have a way of capturing our imaginations and altering the course of history at the same time.

Matthew 27:11–26 is another pivotal courtroom drama. Begin with the fact that the defendant in this case, Jesus of Nazareth, is the only innocent person in the courtrooms in which he is made to stand trial. His ordeal begins with the Sanhedrin, the leaders of the Jewish religious and political establishment. It shifts quickly to Pontius Pilate, the Roman governor. Pilate, like so many political leaders of every generation, is guilty primarily of a lack of courage and conviction. The text makes abundantly clear that Pilate does not think Jesus is guilty of anything deserving death. Pilate's wife sends him a message urging him not to get involved in the case at all. Rather than taking her advice, or simply exercising the power he has as a Roman governor and reinforcing it by dispatching a few dozen Roman soldiers to disperse the mob, he washes his hands of the problem. In so doing he writes himself into one of the darkest chapters of history.

The people to whom Pilate turns for direction are guilty of flip-flopping, as the current political jargon describes people who take first one position and then another as they suddenly change their views. Many in the crowd that cries out for Jesus to be crucified may well be among those who just a few days earlier were shouting, "Hosanna," as Jesus made his way into the city of Jerusalem. This leads us to the chief priests and the elders, who are guilty of jury tampering when they persuade the crowd to ask Pilate to release from prison a man named Barabbas and to send Jesus to be crucified.

The most remarkable part of this courtroom drama is this person Barabbas, who becomes the beneficiary of the judicial proceedings. This "notorious prisoner" is very likely someone who was captured during an insurrection when the Jewish people attempted to free themselves from Roman rule. In fact, Mark 15:7 states clearly that Barabbas committed murder during the insurrection. He may have killed a Roman soldier. Despite his obvious guilt, the people are willing to clamor for his release and for the crucifixion of Jesus. Despite his assumption that Jesus is innocent, Pontius Pilate the Roman governor is willing to release a notorious prisoner like Barabbas. Preachers need to ponder how this can happen.

In the case of both the crowd and the governor, someone persuades them to do something that

Theological Perspective

Nazi policy resulting in the destruction of millions of Jews. Eichmann was no titanic figure of evil like Hitler. He more closely resembled a mediocre, undistinguished bureaucrat. At his trial he protested that he was simply doing his duty, making sure that he discharged efficiently the responsibilities of his office. He utterly lacked the moral convictions and courage that might have moved him to resist the murder and mayhem that was taking place around him. The banality of evil is manifest in Pilate no less than in Eichmann. He declares his innocence in the face of gross injustice; he wants to occupy the high moral ground above the petty jealousy of the chief priests and the dangerous frenzy of the crowd, all the while being up to his neck in complicity with them. In the end, Pilate releases Barabbas and hands Jesus over to be crucified (v. 26).

The Crowd. Finally, there is "the crowd" (v. 15). They too are culpable for what happens to Jesus. When given the choice of having either Jesus or Barabbas released, they choose Barabbas. They want Jesus crucified. It is useless to say that enlightened people like us would have acted differently because we are self-reliant individuals who think for ourselves and would have resisted becoming faceless members of a crowd. Matthew's narrative does not cater to this sort of self-deception. He knows all too well that an individual betrayer like Judas or an individual denier like Peter can help bring about the death of Jesus, no less than can a maddened mob.

In this passage, Matthew depicts the complexity and pervasiveness of evil that opposes the reign of God Jesus proclaimed and inaugurated. His narrative shows that evil appears in self-righteous religious guise; that it is at work in the use of state power to brutalize others or simply to wash one's hands when innocents are brutalized; that it finds expression in the frenzy of crowds, communities, and nations seeking to relieve their own failure, anger, guilt, and bitterness by projecting these on some scapegoat. For the howling crowd depicted in Matthew's Gospel, Jesus is a convenient scapegoat.

Meanwhile, in spite of all the poison and the pretense surrounding him, Jesus refuses to answer his accusers. In silence he remains obedient to the Father's will that he pour out his life "for many for the forgiveness of sins" (26:28).

DANIEL L. MIGLIORE

Pastoral Perspective

to the truth. Jesus does not resist religious and civil corruption with violence or with power plays. Instead, he resists such machinations of religion and politics with the power of nonviolent love. He does not pander to the powerful, nor does he angle for the approval of the crowds; he stays true to what he knows to be right, and he lives (and dies) by the courage of his convictions. He willingly stands alone in the face of both official condemnation and popular rejection.

The account of Jesus before Pilate suggests something of the importance for Christians of embracing the theme of irony. Perhaps irony alone can disclose to us the true character of our personal hypocrisies and the depths of corruption in church and state. If we take Paul the apostle seriously, only irony can help us to see the true meaning of God's action in the crucifixion and resurrection of Jesus (for a fuller account of this theme in relation to the gospel, see 1 Corinthians 1 and 2). Only irony can unmask our personal and corporate sin. Only irony can help us to see the beauty of divine love at work in the face of a disfigured "man of sorrows" (Isa. 53:3).

Tertullian, one of the greatest theological minds of the early church, once made the surprising claim that he believed the gospel precisely because it is absurd. Though he has often been branded as anti-intellectual, Tertullian actually grasped the same core dynamic of the gospel that we see operative in Matthew's account of Jesus' trial before Pilate. At first glance, the whole passion story appears as a comedy of errors or as a terrible tragedy. Upon deeper reflection, it helps us to enter into the mind-set of ironic reversal in which our sins are laid bare and the love of God is established once and for all.

GORDON S. MIKOSKI

world. The *way of Jesus* centers on God's mercy and justice, nonviolence and love for enemies, care for the "least of these," and trust in God's judgment. The *way of Barabbas* (and of Rome) chooses force and violence, so as to conquer enemies. Will the crowd choose to be part of the kingdom of heaven or of a kingdom like Rome?

The crowd cooperates with its leaders and chooses the way of violence (vv. 20–21), which is underscored by their demand that Pilate not only let Barabbas go but also crucify Jesus (vv. 22–23). The crowd, with the encouragement of the leadership, has become a bloodthirsty mob.

Pilate is quite willing to let Barabbas go. Rome operates as Barabbas does, by force and violence, but they are better at it. Indeed, as Matthew wrote his Gospel, Israel had actually chosen the way of Barabbas and engaged in violent revolt against Rome in 66 CE. Roman violence was indeed bigger and better. By the year 70, Jerusalem was in ruins and awash with blood.

When Pilate realizes he has gained all he can from the crowd, so that further effort is unnecessary, he washes his hands before them, declaring himself "innocent of this man's blood" (v. 24). His declaration of innocence has sometimes been read as the final indication that Matthew was trying to exonerate Rome for Jesus' death. Portraying Pilate as powerless before a subject people, however, would hardly endear Christianity to Rome. Instead, we can read Pilate as having achieved his goals. In the end, a Jewish mob calls for the murder of a fellow Jew and absolves Pilate of responsibility for a Jewish death. He destroys a threat, avoids a riot, placates his clients, and secures his own position. Shrewd politics on Pilate's part.

Christians have often used verse 25, where the crowd calls for Jesus' blood to be "on us and on our children," to justify their anti-Semitism, claiming that God's judgment fell on "the Jews" right here. However, this crowd is not "the Jews," nor is it a representative sample of "the Jews" in Matthew's story, many of whom have hung on Jesus' words. This crowd has become a bloodthirsty mob. Should we allow such a mob to define a whole group of people? Should we expect God to comply with the rants of a bloodthirsty mob? Really?

MITZI MINOR

neither might have done on their own. The people are persuaded by their leaders, and Pilate is persuaded by the people. Can anybody persuade us to do something different from what we believe to be true? Are we all so firm in our convictions that no person and no emotionally charged atmosphere can persuade us to behave differently from what our core convictions tell us to do? Perhaps a better question would be, do we even have any core convictions upon which we stand? Many people in the church may be susceptible to what Paul calls being "tossed to and fro and blown about by every wind of doctrine, by people's trickery, by their craftiness in deceitful scheming" (Eph. 4:14).

Consider this issue at an even deeper level of faith and faithfulness. Can anyone or anything cause us to choose Barabbas over Jesus? Matthew's story is less about the positive selection of a notorious criminal named Barabbas, and more about the rejection of Jesus and the claims being made about him. It may be that both then and now the claim that Jesus of Nazareth is the God-sent savior for all sinners who put their faith in him is more than can be believed or endured. It may be that the disciplined lifestyle taught by Jesus, marked by service and suffering and sacrifice, is something people do not want to embrace. It may be that political correctness trumps theological conviction, and so sociopolitical injustice endures because so many people lack the courage to stand against an unjust status quo.

We should not stand on the outside of this text and wonder about those people. We should stand inside this text and ask ourselves what we would have done differently. Is it possible that in a similar situation we too would have cried out, "Give us Barabbas"? False pride might incline us to say no, but when we look at ourselves more closely (and remember trials like the Scottsboro boys), we may end up appearing as guilty as those in this text whom we so easily condemn.

MARVIN A. MCMICKLE

Matthew 27:27–37

²⁷Then the soldiers of the governor took Jesus into the governor's headquarters, and they gathered the whole cohort around him. ²⁸They stripped him and put a scarlet robe on him, ²⁹and after twisting some thorns into a crown, they put it on his head. They put a reed in his right hand and knelt before him and mocked him, saying, "Hail, King of the Jews!" ³⁰They spat on him, and took the reed and struck him on the head. ³¹After mocking him, they stripped him of the robe and put his own clothes on him. Then they led him away to crucify him.

³²As they went out, they came upon a man from Cyrene named Simon; they compelled this man to carry his cross. ³³And when they came to a place called Golgotha (which means Place of a Skull), ³⁴they offered him wine to drink, mixed with gall; but when he tasted it, he would not drink it. ³⁵And when they had crucified him, they divided his clothes among themselves by casting lots; ³⁶then they sat down there and kept watch over him. ³⁷Over his head they put the charge against him, which read, "This is Jesus, the King of the Jews."

Theological Perspective

This is one of those passages of the Bible that requires a strong stomach to read. The mistreatment of Jesus by the soldiers of Pilate is appalling. It disturbs us at the deepest level of our being, for two reasons.

The first is that we are confronted here with the utter humiliation of a human being. Jesus is brutally tortured. Even before being nailed to the crossbar of torture called crucifixion, he is assaulted by an entire Roman battalion. After a flogging, he is stripped and draped with a scarlet robe, a crown of thorns is placed on his head, and a reed is put in his hand to represent a royal scepter. Then the soldiers bow before him, all the while laughing and mockingly calling him king of the Jews. They toy with him in this way for a period and then, bored with the game, they spit on him and take the reed from his hand and strike his head with it. Note that the subject of these actions is in the plural. The soldiers take turns battering Jesus with their blows.

A reading of Matthew's account alerts us to the fact that the secret agencies of modern states and their specially trained interrogators are not the inventors of torture. The Roman military had developed "enhanced" ways of dealing with political prisoners long before the use of water-boarding and other forms of modern brutality. To say that

Pastoral Perspective

In the last stop on the way to the cross, we come face to face with torture: cruel, inhumane, and degrading treatment of a political detainee. In the end, the passion story brings us face to face with the execution of an innocent man at the hands of empire. After the cruelly ironic encounters with Pontius Pilate, the religious authorities, and the crowd, Jesus is delivered into the hands of the Roman military. The soldiers torture Jesus and beat him mercilessly. After they use him as a punching bag for their sadistic play, the soldiers drag him outside to be executed in the most humiliating and excruciating manner possible.

According to a 2009 survey conducted by the Pew Forum on Religion and Public Life, 54 percent of those who attend church on a weekly basis support the use of torture and inhumane treatment against suspected terrorists.[1] Shockingly, the study found that the more likely Americans are to go to church on a weekly basis, the more likely they are to support the use of torture and mistreatment of detainees. Large numbers of American Christians also support state-sponsored execution of criminals. How can this

1. "The Religious Dimensions of the Torture Debate," The Pew Forum on Religion and Public Life, May 7, 2009, as found on http://www.pewforum.org/Politics-and-Elections/The-Religious-Dimensions-of-the-Torture-Debate.aspx; accessed January 30, 2012.

Exegetical Perspective

A major challenge for us is to read this story without attaching two thousand years of atonement theology to it. Since Matthew knew nothing of these debates, we need to set our atonement theories aside and allow Matthew to tell his story his way, if we hope to read it well.

We begin with Matthew's sociohistorical context and the first-century Roman occupation of Israel, giving particular attention to the propaganda of the glories of the *Pax Romana*. On buildings, monuments, and coins, via proclamations and festivals, Rome proclaimed its successes: "Look at the system of roads we have built! Look at the end of piracy on the seas! See how trade and commerce flourish, how wealth and prosperity expand! Look at our art and architecture! See the end to border wars, the advance of efficient government, our superior system of justice! What a time we live in, when the gods have chosen Rome to bring peace and prosperity to the world!" Through such propaganda Rome sought to convince the masses that a system created to benefit the few served the interests of all.

Those who experienced Roman rule as less than beneficial—those taxed into debt, those whose lands were taken so a ruler's wealth expanded, those whose crops were confiscated to feed the Roman army, those who encountered a government designed to

Homiletical Perspective

The crucifixion of Jesus was a demonstration of imperial power at its worst. One good way to study this passage is to start with verse 37 and work backward. Rome was showing what happens to anyone who dares call himself (or who is acclaimed by others to be) the king of the Jews. In any province controlled by Caesar and his legions, there was no room for any king they did not sanction or appoint. There was plenty of room for King Herod, because they knew he posed no threat whatsoever to Roman rule. This man from Nazareth, though, came across as being a bit more dangerous. As James Cone argues in his book *The Cross and the Lynching Tree*, Jesus was cruelly and unjustly put to death by the same set of fears and prejudices that have resulted in other innocent people's being lynched.[1]

It is an understatement to say that Jesus was simply killed. Even the word "crucifixion" does not carry the full weight of what Jesus endured at the hands of his tormentors. This passage takes us inside of what is commonly called "the passion" of Jesus. Many preachers talk about the cross of Christ as being central to the Christian faith. In their haste to get to the celebration of the resurrection, however, they do

1. James Cone, *The Cross and the Lynching Tree* (Maryknoll, NY: Orbis Books, 2011).

Theological Perspective

such treatment violates "universal human rights" as understood in late modernity is true as far as it goes, but it does not go far enough. Torture as it took place in the Roman praetorium after Pilate had washed his hands of the matter, or as it occurs in modern prisons with obscure names like Abu Ghraib, is a violation of the creation of every human being in the image of God. All human beings have a God-given dignity and worth that deserves respect and protection from degrading treatment, whatever the circumstances.

Our visceral response to this ugly behavior in the praetorium is immeasurably heightened by knowledge that the Roman soldiers lack but believing readers of Matthew's Gospel have: the person being tortured is the Son of God. To be sure, the theological tradition has tried to give us some protection from the intolerable realization that for our sake God incarnate is brutalized in a way that we would not countenance in the treatment of a wild animal, and is finally nailed to a cross. God is not capable of suffering, some theologians have assured us. God the almighty is omnipotent and inviolable. Jesus must therefore suffer only in his human nature. In his divine nature he is immune from all the messiness of torture, suffering, and death. However well-intentioned such claims may be, they serve only to soften the horror of the passion story. No, Jesus of Nazareth, the incarnate Son of God, is truly tortured and crucified. Matthew's account shatters our porcelain images of God. It tells the story of a "crucified God."[1]

When the Twin Towers in 2001 collapsed in a ball of fire and smoke, along with thousands inside them and the hundreds who were lost in the attempts at rescue, some believers lost their faith. How can any God permit an evil event like this? Matthew's passion story would seem to answer: It is not a matter of an all-powerful and aloof deity's permitting evil events. It is a matter of recognizing that the true God is profoundly present when God seems most absent, or as Bonhoeffer puts it, "Only the suffering God can help."[2] There is no gospel of the resurrection without the prior reality of the crucifixion. Only if God for our sake does in fact descend into the hell we create for others and suffer at the hands of others, only if God lets our inhumanity and brutality, our sin and guilt, burn themselves out in God incarnate, is there any hope for redemption and new life.

1. See Jürgen Moltmann, *The Crucified God* (London: SCM, 1974).
2. Dietrich Bonhoeffer, *Letters and Papers from Prison* (New York: Macmillan, 1972), 361.

Pastoral Perspective

be? How can Christians—whose Lord and Savior was himself a victim of torture and execution by an occupying military power—support practices that so blatantly contradict both Jesus' teachings and his profound example of love in the face of violence?

Doubtless, many American Christians turn a blind eye toward torture and abuse of detainees because they are motivated by a deep instinct for self-preservation. Some support torture or state-sponsored execution because of a desire for revenge. Untold numbers have been desensitized to the dehumanizing aspects of torture and violent mistreatment of detainees, as well as state-sponsored execution, through watching fictionalized accounts of torture and execution on television or in film. Tacit supporters of torture and state-sponsored execution tend to calculate that the severe mistreatment of a few bad apples might save the lives of thousands. Besides, the reasoning goes, none of those tortured or executed is likely to be an innocent like Jesus.

Lest we think that these matters pertain only to members of rogue groups of Muslim radicals, we should face the fact that torture and abuse of human beings go on within the bounds of our country. Our prisons are full of people who regularly experience mistreatment and abuse. Not only that: a disturbingly high number of our homes are also the sources of unspeakable violence. Spousal abuse and severe mistreatment of children in their homes are things that most people do not wish to discuss in polite company. Very few people want to talk about domestic violence and the torture of innocent children—whether in our slums or in our more respectable neighborhoods—at all.

Matthew's account of the torture and execution of Jesus does not allow us to hide from the ugly realities of torture and execution. Jesus Christ, the One who is "ground zero" for our faith, is a victim of both torture and state-sponsored execution. From a Christian point of view, support for torture and state-sponsored execution simply does not compute. Even though God worked to bring something good out of Jesus' torture and execution, we should not confuse God's ability to bring good out of evil in the case of Jesus with divine support for evil practices like torture and execution. Instead, followers of the man of love, who was savagely beaten and heartlessly executed by government personnel, should oppose all forms of torture and execution. Those who mourn the mistreatment of the Crucified should cry out "No!" and "Never again!" whenever the specter of torture and execution of prisoners rears its ugly head.

protect the interests of the ruling elite, those who experienced Roman violence—rarely got to tell their story. So Matthew gave his witness. Rome's brutal rule is on full display in verses 27–37. In these verses Matthew works like a whistleblower: "The empire may proclaim its glories, but I can show you what Roman rule is really like in the story of Jesus of Nazareth!"

Having been "handed over" (the Greek verb *paradidōmi* has been key in the story of Jesus' fate) for crucifixion (v. 26), Jesus is taken first into the praetorium for the dehumanizing practices characteristic of violent rule. How are soldiers capable of such horror as crucifying a fellow human being? They make him less than human—a thing, an object of scorn, a fool. People fret less over the suffering of an object than that of a human being. So the soldiers mock and spit on him, strip and beat him (vv. 28–30), with the result that they carry out their task with (apparently) clear consciences (note vv. 35–36).

The bitter irony is that, in the midst of the dehumanization, they make fun of Jesus as "King of the Jews" (v. 29). They intend to show the absurdity of this naked, beaten, condemned man's being any kind of king (Caesar in all his glory was king, not this fool!). Nevertheless Matthew insists that the soldiers are right, that Jesus *is* "the King of the Jews" (note 2:2; 25:31–34)—although not as the Romans conceive of a king. They do not understand a king committed to God's righteousness, who beats swords into plowshares and brings justice to the poor and vulnerable ones. So they mock Jesus, but as they do, they demonstrate the need for his kind of kingship.

The bitter ironies continue. As they lead Jesus out to crucify him, the soldiers force Simon of Cyrene to carry Jesus' cross (v. 32). This stranger's name is a haunting reminder that Jesus' friend, Simon Peter, is absent and unwilling to bear Jesus' cross. They arrive at Golgotha, and the soldiers set to their task. They offer Jesus wine (v. 34), which he refuses (we are not told why). Matthew gives no details of the act of crucifixion itself (v. 35a), for which we should probably be grateful. All we know about crucifixion says it is a gruesome way to die. Rome uses it to terrify into submission those who oppose its purposes. Matthew's audience likely needs no reminders of its horrors.

When the soldiers have crucified him, they divide his clothes among themselves (v. 35b) and sit down to watch (v. 36). Their dehumanization practices have worked. Although they have tortured a fellow human being, no pangs of conscience are evident.

not linger over the more graphic details of what Jesus experienced before he was even nailed to the cross.

We are given some idea of what awaited Jesus in 27:26, when we read that Pilate had him flogged and then gave him over to be crucified. There was something terrible that preceded being crucified. There was something awaiting Jesus that might have been worse than the crucifixion itself. The flogging would have ripped open his flesh and left him as little more than a mangled mass of blood and tears. That was followed by the pain and scarring of a crown of thorns pressed down upon his head. Then came the humiliation of being covered with the cloak of a Roman soldier and mockingly hailed as king of the Jews. Then they spat on him, beat him again and again, and then finally led him off to be crucified.

There is the fascinating appearance of a man from Cyrene named Simon, who was compelled to carry the cross of Jesus. This is more than a reminder that what Jesus had earlier endured at the hands of the Romans had left him too weak to drag his cross through the narrow streets of the ancient city of Jerusalem. It is also a tangible reminder of the African presence in the Bible, something that nearly all Hollywood movies on the life of Jesus have managed to ignore: Cyrene was a colony in present-day Libya. After all of that, Jesus was nailed to the cross and left to die. He was offered what amounted to a sedative or painkiller that might soothe him during his final hours, an offer he refused to accept. Then his executioners sat down at the foot of the cross and watched him die, while they gambled to see which of them would go home with his sole earthly possession, his cloak. This was what happened to the man whose crime was to be hailed king of the Jews.

What this Roman execution squad could never have imagined is that once again Rome was playing a leading role in God's plan of salvation. They could not have understood that in killing this man who had been accused of challenging Roman rule and authority they were, at that very moment, participating in the redemptive work of God. At the birth of Jesus, according to Matthew, Rome played a central, but unintended, role. Herod's treachery in chapter 2 precipitates the flight to Egypt that fulfills a prophecy from Hosea: "Out of Egypt I have called my son" (2:15).

The same thing was true in the events that surrounded the death of Jesus. Once again Rome played a central, although unintentional, role. In this instance, the death of Jesus was not only a brutal act perpetrated by a cruel political regime.

Matthew 27:27–37

Matthew 27:27–37

Theological Perspective

Our text continues with the story of Simon of Cyrene, who is compelled by the soldiers to carry the cross of Jesus when Jesus is unable to bear it any farther. Matthew tells us almost nothing about Simon except that he did not have a choice. He was "compelled" (v. 32). The Roman military does not take no for an answer. That is not the way of imperial power. If you can torture a condemned man, there is no reason why you cannot compel a bystander to do whatever you ask. Running through this entire reading is the stunning contrast of imperial power and the seeming powerlessness of the Christ and everyone associated with him. Jesus is exhausted from the ordeal, and Simon is helpless to do anything but comply with the command of the soldiers. However, the fact that his name (and the names of his sons, Alexander and Rufus, Mark 15:21) is remembered may indicate that he later became a Christian. If so, it would be a sign for believers that the powerless one whose cross Simon carried proved in Simon's own experience to exercise a power very different from and much greater than the soldiers' power to coerce and to crucify.

When the soldiers earlier called Jesus king of the Jews, it was mockery; when they inscribed the same title over his head on the cross, it was a warning. What the title really meant for them was that the crucified one was a powerless and laughable loser. Let no one mess with the supreme power of Rome. Let all beware: the real power of this world is the power of Caesar and his soldiers to command, cajole, and coerce, to give the crucified king gall instead of water, to cast lots for his clothes, and to sit calmly beneath the cross to "watch over him" and to make sure he stays there. Unless we recognize this apocalyptic conflict between the brutal power (but ultimate powerlessness) of empire and the radiant powerlessness (but ultimate victorious power) of the one hanging on the cross, we have not begun to understand the depths of Matthew's account of Jesus' torture and crucifixion.

DANIEL L. MIGLIORE

Pastoral Perspective

As a seminary student at Princeton Theological Seminary in the late 1980s, I vividly recall a sermon preached in chapel by William Sloane Coffin. He reflected on the crowds of people who stood around the cross, watching the whole terrible event unfold. He seized upon the verse from the Gospel of Luke that is parallel to Matthew's story: "And when all the crowds who had gathered there for this spectacle saw what had taken place, they returned home, beating their breasts" (Luke 23:48). The punch line of Coffin's sermon that hit me so powerfully was, "All it takes for evil to triumph in the world is for a lot of good people to go home beating their breasts." Some who do not actively oppose torture and violent abuse of prisoners would never see themselves as actively supporting violence and mistreatment of other human beings. Yet, by not actively opposing torture and abuse of detainees, they are contemporary versions of those who went home from the cross "beating their breasts" and saying how horrible it all is.

Pious American Protestants for over a century have asked themselves the question, "What would Jesus do?" when faced with a difficult decision. That is a very good question. I am certain that Jesus, a victim of both torture and state-sponsored execution, would support neither torture nor execution. Why do we, as Christian citizens of the most powerful nation on the earth, sit idly by and allow torture and execution of prisoners? Why do we who are followers of the preacher of the Sermon on the Mount tacitly support cruel, inhumane, and degrading treatment of other human beings, even of our enemies? Jesus commands us to love our enemies, not to torture or execute them.

Maybe our Christian faith goes only so far and so deep. Maybe we are followers of Jesus only on certain subjects or to a certain depth. Matthew's account of the passion narrative calls into question our willingness to follow Jesus into the torture chamber and to the cross. Come to think of it, not many of the original disciples of Jesus went with him to those places either.

GORDON S. MIKOSKI

Exegetical Perspective

Matthew portrays the Romans as utterly callous in this moment.

The callousness continues. On the cross above his head is the final reference to Jesus as "King of the Jews" (v. 37). The Romans intend further mockery of Jesus, but they are likely also mocking the Jews as a subject people, as in, "This naked, bloody fool is the best you can do?!" In addition, crucifixion is more than death for the victim. It is intended to terrorize and so to act as a deterrent. If others are thinking of resisting Roman rule, they should know that they can end up publicly shamed and crucified like Jesus of Nazareth.

Indeed, evil prevails by these kinds of deterrents, by horrifying resisters into submission. Rome wants subject peoples to fear reprisal, so that they will became collaborators at best or passive nonresisters at worst. When they do so, they help solidify Roman rule.

Matthew's story of Jesus of Nazareth presents one who will neither collaborate with nor passively accept the evil in his world. He actively resists Rome. He calls his people back to God's peace and justice, and practices what he preaches. As he does so, he challenges Rome's ordering of the world in favor of the few. When the ruling elite go after him, the religious leaders' collaboration with Rome and allegiance to their privilege are exposed. Jesus suffers the consequences of his allegiance to God's kingdom rather than Rome's. His willingness to bear this suffering, to take up the cross and trust in God's vindication, exposes the limits of the power of evildoers. Try as they might, they cannot stop him. He also exposes Rome's power as violent and destructive. There is nothing glorious about it. It is brutal and ugly, and Jesus refuses to succumb to it. In the words of theologian James Allison, Jesus "lived as if death were not" and showed his followers how to do the same.[1]

Matthew does not soften the reality of what evil ones will do to those who so live. The ruling elites could have executed Jesus simply and quietly, but they chose a public, gruesome death for him. What kind of courage and faith, then, did Jesus possess? Now, what of his followers?

MITZI MINOR

Homiletical Perspective

The crucifixion proved also to be a redemptive act performed by a gracious God. In this cruel setting on the cross, at the place of the skull, the words of John the Baptist from another Gospel came fully and finally into focus; Jesus was the Lamb of God who takes away the sin of the world (John 1:29). In this blood-soaked moment the words of Isaiah 53:4–6 that spoke of the work of the Suffering Servant took on new meaning:

> Surely he has borne our infirmities
>   and carried our diseases;
> . . . .
> He was wounded for our transgressions,
>   crushed for our iniquities;
> upon him was the punishment that made us whole,
>   and by his bruises we are healed.
> All we like sheep have gone astray,
>   we have all turned to our own way;
> and the LORD has laid on him
>   the iniquity of us all.

No doubt, as those Roman soldiers sat there and watched this death-penalty convict breathing out his last breath, they thought that would be the end of the story. They had undoubtedly presided over other crucifixions, and in every other instance the end of that life meant the end of the story. They left Calvary that day with a sense of "mission accomplished."

They could not have known what Peter came to understand and to declare to the world on the Day of Pentecost: "This man, handed over to you according to the definite plan and foreknowledge of God, you crucified and killed by the hands of those outside the law. But God raised him up, having freed him from death, because it was impossible for him to be held in its power" (Acts 2:23–24). Every preacher should join with Paul and preach Christ and him crucified (1 Cor. 2:2). This gruesome scene is the key to the gospel!

MARVIN A. MCMICKLE

---

1. James Allison, *Raising Abel* (New York: Crossroad, 2000), 66.

Matthew 27:38–44

³⁸Then two bandits were crucified with him, one on his right and one on his left. ³⁹Those who passed by derided him, shaking their heads ⁴⁰and saying, "You who would destroy the temple and build it in three days, save yourself! If you are the Son of God, come down from the cross." ⁴¹In the same way the chief priests also, along with the scribes and elders, were mocking him, saying, ⁴²"He saved others; he cannot save himself. He is the King of Israel; let him come down from the cross now, and we will believe in him. ⁴³He trusts in God; let God deliver him now, if he wants to; for he said, 'I am God's Son.'" ⁴⁴The bandits who were crucified with him also taunted him in the same way.

Theological Perspective

As is often observed by readers of Matthew's Gospel, his story of the crucifixion focuses much less on the act of Jesus' being crucified and much more on the actions and words of those looking on as it happened. In this particular part of that story, the focus is on the variety of people who taunt Jesus as he hangs on the cross. It was not enough that Jesus was condemned by more or less due judicial process and was hung on a cross to die. In his dying, he also was subjected, according to Matthew, to derisive taunts that scornfully underscored the unprotected vulnerability in which he stood.

What is of greatest theological interest is that the taunts have to do with Jesus' failure to make good on his purported claims of identity with God, either as God's Son or as God's Messiah. The fact that the taunts have echoes in Psalm 22 reinforces the point that misunderstanding of the shape of God's power and the ways of God's deliverance is long-standing. In this passage the point is made once and for all that the power of God is manifest not in Jesus' coming down from the cross, but in his enduring it.

The view of God's power that the passage rejects is a view shared across the sociological spectrum. There are passersby who were not intimately involved in the trial of Jesus, but perhaps had joined in the crowd's chorus of "Let him be crucified!"

Pastoral Perspective

It's loud around the cross
screaming taunts on Golgotha
press the case
of a miracle worker
now nailed up
bandits on either side
no sympathy
just commentary
on a God
who does not deliver.

Jesus is nailed to the cross and is surrounded. Bandits on either side and a crowd at his feet offer caustic commentary about Jesus' situation. He is the focal point of a public reaction to a spiritual leader who is condemned to die. Jesus' dying on the cross teaches us about the public and in turn political nature of the disturbance Jesus makes in the world. His ministry of love and healing has a ripple effect on the way the world is organized both economically and politically. Jesus is a threat to both systems. He teaches the world about the value of all people and upends the prevailing notion of the exclusion of any who do not match the world's current definition of "insider." For people who wonder if their faith in Jesus Christ has anything to do with their public life, this Scripture teaches us to consider the ways in which Jesus encourages us to move outside of the private nature

Exegetical Perspective

This scene follows directly on the heels of Jesus' crucifixion (27:35–37). After two bandits are crucified beside him, Jesus is mocked by three distinct groups of antagonists while he hangs on the cross. The author of Matthew has used Mark as a source throughout the arrest, trial, and crucifixion scenes, and that continues to be the case here (cf. Mark 15:27–32), although the author has made a few changes to the Markan text. Perhaps most significantly, the evangelist has added "Son of God" in two key places to reinforce Jesus' identity (vv. 40, 43). The entire scene is also permeated with irony, and with allusions to Psalm 22, a psalm in which a suffering, forsaken person is mocked by numerous opponents. In it, the psalmist is rescued by God in the end, and "all the families of the nations" worship God in response (Ps. 22:27). Thus, in Matthew's own unique spin on this text, the evangelist continues to present Jesus as the Son of God and the King of the Jews, the one who suffers the humiliation of crucifixion in obedience and in fulfillment of the Scriptures, in order to bring God's salvation to humanity.

Perhaps the most striking feature of this passage, which also functions to structure it, is the threefold mockery of Jesus (vv. 39–40, 41–43, 44). Three unique groups—the passersby, the Jewish authorities (which include the chief priests, scribes,

Homiletical Perspective

The cheering crowds are gone. Now he is alone, nailed to a cross, dying. The two thieves crucified with him summon cruel strength to mock him. Passersby deride him, as do the religious authorities who are watching, in scornful sarcasm: "He is the King . . . ; let him come down from the cross now, and we will believe in him" (v. 42).

The faithful come to church during Lent to hear a story they already know. It is such a powerful story that it needs retelling before it is interpreted. So the preacher should tell it again, amplify where appropriate, avoid exaggeration, and be careful about the propensity of this story to inspire anti-Semitism.

One way to hear the story is with Jesus not only as victim but as initiator of the action. From the moment he decides to go to Jerusalem, through his trial and torment, right up to his dying breath, he is in charge. He passes, with high intentionality, any number of opportunities to change the story's trajectory, quietly to return to a life of teaching and healing in the safety of rural Galilee. He is the innocent victim of a very human plot to preserve the privilege and authority of the powerful. However, he is much more than that. Jesus—not the religious officials, not the Roman governor, Pontius Pilate, not the soldiers—is in charge.

Rome reserved crucifixion for special cases: runaway slaves, insurrectionists, revolutionaries, any

Matthew 27:38–44

Theological Perspective

(27:22–23). They have a view of what it would take to undermine the passionate conviction to which the crowd had been led, that this deceiver claimed a status and role deserving to be destroyed. For that conviction to be overturned, it would take a demonstration that the claimed status was true. The only conceivable way for it to be shown true would be for Jesus to come down from the cross. The power of God is assumed to be power to resist the power of the death arranged by mortals.

The second group betraying an inability to grasp the nature of divine power at work in Jesus is the denizens of the religious establishment: the chief priests, scribes, and elders. These are clearly more than passersby to the crucifixion and all that led up to it. They are indeed its primary historical agents. Again reflecting the ancient taunts of Psalm 22, they suggest that one who is God's Son would surely be delivered by that same God. Whether by his own doing or by an act of God, his vindication would surely (and only) be manifest in his coming down from the cross.

Perhaps most puzzling in the array of those taunting Jesus in his dying are the words of the two thieves crucified with him. Representing the margins of society—outcasts in multiple senses of the term—here at their end they incorporate themselves into the dominant culture by joining in the taunts. In doing so, they reveal how pervasive the assumption about the character of divine power is. Though they are bandits who have flouted the conceptions and constructs of conventional society, this is one convention they cannot fight, flout, or otherwise transcend. They too want the divine power manifest in the only conceivable way, in Jesus' coming down from the cross.

Thus across the sociological spectrum Matthew reports a view of divine power that he clearly rejects. In portraying Jesus' endurance of these taunts, Matthew hammers home the theological point: divine power is found in the midst of human vulnerability, not in transcending it. The only hope for divine deliverance that any of the taunters harbor consists in deliverance from the fate of crucifixion. In this part of the story, Matthew makes the unflinching theological point that deliverance is in and through the suffering that Jesus endured on the cross—not in avoiding it.

Christian theology has struggled to encompass Matthew's witness to the power of divine deliverance in many ways, but nowhere more centrally than in its atonement theologizing. Ranging from stark

Pastoral Perspective

of our faith to consider the public implications of God's love and radical inclusion.

As Jesus hangs on the cross, subject to taunts about the ineptitude of God, we are alerted to the reality of outward challenges to faith and life. As an East Coast inner-city pastor for eighteen years, I learned from many faithful people about the ways destructive voices and even evil situations seek to destroy hope among children and adults alike. Toxic environments, chronic joblessness, generational poverty, and long-term violence can create a place where nurturing life becomes nearly impossible. What I learn from the people I serve now in another East Coast city is that these taunts at the cross are not manifest only in the outer world; they are also present in our inner world. We may have a whole medley of tapes in our own heads that seek to deride what is made of love and promise within each of us.

Our text invites us to look at our daily news and to find those places where such taunting and derision go on today. As we consider the media, notice the language that spiritual leaders, criminals, and public figures use to describe issues of inclusion and justice. Consider the cacophony around the world as different groups seek justice in the face of oppressive regimes. What taunts are used by the powers that hold control?

This text lends itself to a time of devotion in seeing that Jesus, who was once so full of life and hope and engaged in the world, is now suffering in a manner that is so utterly human that it can take our breath away. On the cross, Jesus becomes radically connected to the fate that we all share as humans: we will die someday. While we hear so much of what is going on around Jesus, what is Jesus contemplating in the silence of his own heart and mind? Perhaps Jesus is tempted as he hears what God could do but does not. Perhaps Jesus doubts the validity of his mission and ministry to love and bless the world. Perhaps he wants to jump off that cross and show the world what God can do. There are faithful people among us who have a sense that there is a spiritual battle going on around us. This battle is one between the forces that want God's mission to fail and the forces that want to manifest God in ever expanding ways. This text offers a vivid picture of that battle, one that still rages on around us.

While Jesus is surrounded by people as he hangs on the cross, where are his friends? Apparently they are at a distance. Has the relational net that Jesus has so lovingly crafted over his ministry been destroyed by this act of crucifixion? Acts of violence can be

Exegetical Perspective

and elders), and the bandits—mock Jesus in succession as he hangs on the cross. Matthew narrates this employing three distinct Greek verbs to describe the scope of the mockery: the antagonists "derided" him (*blasphēmeō*), they "mocked" him (*empaizō*), and finally "taunted" him (*oneidizō*). The author of the Gospel never describes the agony and suffering of Roman crucifixion that Jesus experiences, but he does report the humiliation and scorn heaped upon the condemned. As part of its very nature, Roman crucifixion was designed to be a shameful and public punishment and death. That Jesus is mocked by so many spectators is not surprising—it only adds to the humiliation of the crucifixion itself. Nevertheless, in spite of the mockery, the allusions to Psalm 22 cause readers to anticipate Jesus' deliverance and resurrection by God.

The passage begins as two bandits are crucified on either side of Jesus. Unlike Luke's Gospel, in which one of the two criminals repents and asks Jesus to "remember" him (Luke 23:39–43), here both bandits will later taunt Jesus in the story. Even among the criminals, Jesus receives no solace or support. It is unclear, however, exactly what type of condemned persons these two are. The Greek word *lēstēs* can suggest a bandit or robber, but can also signify a political insurrectionist. Curiously, in the arrest scene, Jesus says that he is being arrested as if he were a *lēstēs*, even though he clearly is not (26:55). It seems only appropriate that they execute him among bandits here.

There may be an allusion to Jesus' kingship in the detail that the bandits are crucified "one on his right and one on his left" (cf. 20:21, 23). If so, the irony that was evident in the inscription on the cross ("This is Jesus, the King of the Jews," 27:37) is also evident in this verse. Matthew has ironically depicted Jesus as the King of the Jews throughout the trial and crucifixion, and reinforces his identity as such here.

After all three condemned persons are crucified, those who pass by the site of the crucifixion "deride" Jesus, and the author uses the first of the three unique verbs to describe the way in which the various spectators mock Jesus in this scene. The Greek verb here is *blasphēmeō*. Literally, "they were blaspheming him" with their sarcasm and insults. Jesus himself was accused of blaspheming in his trial (26:65), and here the passersby blaspheme him in turn. They also "shake their heads," a direct allusion to those who mock the "forsaken one" in Psalm 22:7. These onlookers then ridicule Jesus for one of the charges leveled against him in the trial, that he

Homiletical Perspective

deemed a threat to the authority of Rome. Borg and Crossan call crucifixion "imperial terrorism," an act of "calculated social deterrence," the most cruel act in a cruel age, done as publicly as possible as a warning.[1] We seem to believe that it is acceptable to execute people, so long as we do not have to watch. The Romans did it as visibly as possible. Golgotha may have been the execution site for the capital city, with crosses permanently in sight. This, Rome said, is what happens to insurrectionists and troublemakers. To punctuate their contempt, the Romans put a sign over Jesus' head, "The King of the Jews"—a final insult to him who they had become convinced threatened their authority and also the people of Israel. Rome was saying, "This weak, helpless dying peasant hanging there on our cross is the only king you will ever see so long as we are in charge."

The preacher might explore the various ways the crucifixion has been understood. "Jesus died for our sins and the sins of the world," we have been taught in our liturgies and much of our hymnody. Classically articulated by Anselm, an eleventh-century theologian, this is one way to understand what happened when Jesus was crucified. God is just, Anselm said. Human beings are sinners, and an offence to the justice of God, which must be satisfied. God is also love, Anselm continued. So God provides a substitute victim to receive the punishment that we sinners deserve and God's justice demands. While there is truth here, some find less than satisfying the way God seems to be depicted as an angry judge who must be appeased. The Bible, and Jesus himself, talk about a God who is love and whose anger and justice are always tempered by love, a God who is like a parent dealing with wayward children, a God who is like a loving mother or father.

Borg and Crossan suggest that Jesus died, not so much *for* the sins of the world as *because of* the sins of the world. So his cross is, among other meanings, a symbol of holy love, not only a symbol of human sin and evil and compromise. It is supremely a symbol of God's love, come all the way down to us, to suffer as we do, to struggle and doubt and wonder where in the world God is in all of this, and, finally, to die our death.

Historian Garry Wills, in *What Jesus Meant*, puts it beautifully for us. The cross "is God's way of saying that no matter the horrors we face or the hells we descend to, he is coming with us." Then Wills

1. Marcus J. Borg and John Dominic Crossan, *The Last Week: A Day-by-Day Account of Jesus' Final Week in Jerusalem* (San Francisco: HarperCollins, 2006), 138–63.

Matthew 27:38–44

Theological Perspective

substitutionary accounts through moral exemplar patterns to *Christus Victor* themes, Christian theology of the atonement has struggled to comprehend Matthew's rejection of the assumption of the taunters.[1] What Matthew bears witness to by depicting Jesus simply hanging on the cross, as the onlookers beseech him to show God's deliverance by coming down, these traditions of theology have reflected in their varied ways.

Few theologians, and probably fewer ordinary believers, have been completely satisfied by these theological interpretations of Matthew's story. On the one hand, pure substitution seems to promise deliverance through a legal fiction, that is, one person is condemned in place of another, thus delivering the latter. On the other hand, moral exemplar approaches appear to engender deliverance only subjectively in those captivated by the exemplar. On yet another hand, *Christus Victor* requires deliverance to await the vindication coming in the resurrection. Still, whatever their shortcomings, all these efforts faithfully seek to echo Matthew's witness that Jesus did not come down from the cross—and therein the deliverance of God is manifest. They endeavor to utter a view that the characters in Matthew's story cannot fathom, that God's delivering power is present where general human opinion—across the full spectrum of any particular society—assumes it is absent: in the midst of Jesus' suffering.

This does not mean that all human suffering is redemptive in character. It means only that Jesus' suffering has this delivering, redemptive significance. Because Jesus' suffering on the cross does have such significance, it enables Christians to respond to whatever suffering may become their lot in the knowledge that the delivering power of God may be trusted.

D. CAMERON MURCHISON

Pastoral Perspective

isolating, as we may sometimes see today in the families we serve, or even in our own families. Perhaps we see this in victims of violence in our larger communities. Whether it is public violence like what Jesus experienced, or the more private form of violence that touches the people around us, violence has an isolating impact that does not dissolve or ever really go away. This text gives us a space that is safe enough to acknowledge that violence can be part of our experience and does not need to be hidden, particularly in our faith journey. Our relationship with Jesus includes what is messy about our lives.

This acknowledgment of Jesus' suffering on the cross gives people of faith the courage to face the sufferings of our world with the assurance that we do not do so alone. The Jesus of the cross, taunted and derided, is with us and among us wherever suffering happens. We have the freedom through Christ to bear witness to love even in situations that seem steeped in death and violence, knowing that somehow Jesus Christ is present, and in turn that love is forever stronger than death.

Further, because we have the witness that Jesus is present in suffering, we are invited and called to go forth into the world in mission, into those places where suffering exists. This can mean that we go into the clinics where people are receiving treatment for HIV/AIDS or into homeless shelters. We are called also to go into those public places in our world where suffering happens due to an economic or political system that forgets we are all God's children, even when others might be certain that God is unable or unwilling to act.

KAREN L. BRAU

---

1. See Gustaf Aulén, *Christus Victor: An Historical Study of the Three Main Types of the Idea of the Atonement* (London: SPCK, 1965).

would rebuild the temple in three days, as well as the claims that he is the "Son of God" (26:61, 63–64).

When the passersby have had their say, the Jewish authorities who are present also mock Jesus. Their insults also derive directly from Psalm 22:8. In the psalm the onlookers taunt the forsaken one with sarcastic pleas for God to "deliver" and to "save" him. The Jewish authorities in Matthew also speak sarcastically: they do not really think that Jesus is the "King of Israel" and they do not intend to believe in him, even if he does come down from the cross (v. 42). So they speak more truth than they know, and they too end up unwittingly testifying to Jesus' identity. Jesus has indeed saved others, and he truly is the King of Israel. Moreover, Jesus does trust God, and God will indeed deliver him.

Finally, in the last verse of this passage, the bandits that are crucified beside him taunt him as well, as if to add insult to injury. In spite of their own similar fate, the bandits' contempt for Jesus completes the sense in this scene that *everyone* present at the crucifixion is unsympathetic to, even hostile toward, Jesus as he hangs on the cross. The threefold mockery of this passage enacts and fulfills the words of Psalm 22:7: "All who see me mock at me."

In spite of the derision, the mocking, and the taunts heaped upon the crucified Jesus in this scene, God will save him in the end. Just as Psalm 22 anticipates the forsaken one's salvation by God, so too will readers of Matthew's Gospel find that Jesus' death by crucifixion is not the last word. God will raise him from the dead on the third day, just as Jesus himself predicted (16:21). Likewise, as Psalm 22 predicts that "all the families of the nations shall worship before him" (Ps. 22:27), God's salvation also anticipates the future mission to "make disciples of all the nations" (28:19).

ARTHUR M. WRIGHT JR.

illustrates the point with a personal story about his young son waking from a violent, frightening nightmare. When Wills asked what was troubling him, his son said that his parochial school teacher had told the children that they would end up in hell if they sinned. The boy asked his father, "Am I going to hell?" Wills, without any pretense of heroism, "instantly answered what any father would, 'All I can say is that if you're going there, I'm going with you.' If I felt that way about my son, God obviously loves him more than I do."[2]

The central affirmation of Christianity is that the almighty Creator of the universe is a God of love who lays aside almightiness to be with us and to be one of us. There is nothing quite like it in the history of human religion—a God who assumes humanness, human frailty, and vulnerability, a God who goes all the way to show God's love, all the way into the valley of the shadow to be with us.

Pastors know that people who suffer understand the cross better than most of us and hold to it tightly. If you are lying in a hospital bed with a serious illness and a not-very-promising prognosis, you do not need a theologian to explain the cross. You hold on to it. A political prisoner in a dark cell in a police state knows what the cross means. Whenever any of us faces a personal valley of the shadow, we stand gratefully beneath the cross of Jesus.

Music, finally, says it better than any of us: Mozart's *Requiem*, J. S. Bach's *St. Matthew Passion*, or Isaac Watts's hymn:

> Were the whole realm of nature mine,
> That were a present far too small:
> Love so amazing, so divine,
> Demands my soul, my life, my all.[3]

JOHN M. BUCHANAN

2. Garry Wills, *What Jesus Meant* (New York: Viking, 2006), 117–18.
3. Isaac Watts, "When I Survey the Wondrous Cross," *Hymns and Spiritual Songs* (1707).

⁴⁵From noon on, darkness came over the whole land until three in the afternoon. ⁴⁶And about three o'clock Jesus cried with a loud voice, "Eli, Eli, lema sabachthani?" that is, "My God, my God, why have you forsaken me?" ⁴⁷When some of the bystanders heard it, they said, "This man is calling for Elijah." ⁴⁸At once one of them ran and got a sponge, filled it with sour wine, put it on a stick, and gave it to him to drink. ⁴⁹But the others said, "Wait, let us see whether Elijah will come to save him." ⁵⁰Then Jesus cried again with a loud voice and breathed his last. ⁵¹At that moment the curtain of the temple was torn in two, from top to bottom. The earth shook, and the rocks were split. ⁵²The tombs also were opened, and many bodies of the saints who had fallen asleep were raised. ⁵³After his resurrection they came out of the tombs and entered the holy city and appeared to many. ⁵⁴Now when the centurion and those with him, who were keeping watch over Jesus, saw the earthquake and what took place, they were terrified and said, "Truly this man was God's Son!"

Theological Perspective

In these verses the theological focus shifts from that of the immediately preceding pericope. Whereas the theological focus has been on the inability of the onlookers to comprehend the power of God other than by Jesus' coming down from the cross, here the theological focus shifts to the manifest power of God in Jesus' suffering and death. It begins with his cry of dereliction, "My God, my God, why have you forsaken me?" (v. 46). At first glance this seems to affirm the taunting that has just taken place: God does not deliver; Jesus does not come down from the cross; his identity as God's Son goes unconfirmed; and he experiences abandonment by God.

However, the very cry is misunderstood by those inhabiting the scene. The mental filters with which they witness the whole episode require that they would mistake the "Eli, Eli . . ." as an appeal to Elijah, whom Jewish tradition regarded as a rescuing figure to appear as the messianic age was dawning. Still locked in their assumption that the only demonstration of the power of God would be in a forceful rescue of Jesus from the cross, they inevitably mishear the Hebrew word for God as an appeal to Elijah. Some appear even to be hopeful that Elijah's rescue is about to take place, and offer a sponge of sour wine as a pitiful contribution to reviving Jesus as Elijah approaches. Others take a more skeptical,

Pastoral Perspective

It's loud around the cross
desolation mounts
moans of abandonment echo
the earth groans and cracks
breaking open to crucified death
a preview of raising appears
skepticism transforms into
guarded conversion
a grief filled silence
settles in.

The public death of Jesus has a physicality to it that is palpable to those present and to us as readers and hearers. The public berating of Jesus recedes, and we hear from Jesus himself. His cry articulates his own despair, and after a second loud cry, he breathes his last breath. The public death of Jesus is observed by all who have gathered to mark his death, yet it is not humanity alone that is affected. The sky changes, the earth shakes, the temple curtain is ripped, and those who are dead break back into the world. There is a supernatural response to Jesus' death.

It seems that the political powers got their way on Golgotha. The threat they perceived in Jesus is gone. Nevertheless there are still guards in place, guards that show us how the political powers will not let up on this now-dead leader. It is in that supernatural response to Jesus' death that we learn again the impact

Exegetical Perspective

Jesus' moment of death in Matthew is accompanied by one of the most bizarre scenes in the Gospels. An important curtain in the Jerusalem temple is ripped in half, an earthquake shakes the ground, and dead saints are resurrected and enter the city. These eschatological events are presented by Matthew to show that something definitive happens at the moment of Jesus' death. It is a turning point in history, the beginning of something new that will be fully realized in Jesus' resurrection.

This passage divides cleanly into two parts. The first, verses 45–50, depicts Jesus' last moments of life, and the second, verses 51–54, depicts the eschatological events that happen as a result of Jesus' death, along with the response of some of the onlookers. Matthew is still using Mark as a source here but makes significant changes, including the major insertion of verses 51b–53 (cf. Mark 15:33–39).

The darkness that covers the land in verse 45 is the first of the eschatological signs that accompany Jesus' death. It is unclear what "land" (gē) Matthew intends that this darkness covers. Is it only Judea? All of Palestine? The entire Roman Empire, or even the entire world? The Greek word gē is generic enough to allow for any of these possibilities, although it is not difficult to imagine that Matthew has the whole world in mind with the cosmic scope of this scene. Because

Homiletical Perspective

New Testament scholarship observes that a significant portion of the Gospels is about the passion; that when Jesus enters Jerusalem on the first day of the week, Palm Sunday, the pace of the narrative slows dramatically, and the Gospel writers show a new interest in detail. When Mel Gibson's motion picture *The Passion of the Christ* was released several years ago, it set off a major debate about whether the cinema depiction was accurate historically. Biblical scholars opined that the film was more detailed, and certainly more physically violent, than the biblical texts warrant. Many Jewish and Christian advisors believed the film was anti-Semitic. Nevertheless the film was at least consistent with the artistic interest in—some would say, obsession with—the crucifixion of Jesus. Visit any art gallery and see how the death of Jesus has inspired some of the greatest art human beings have ever produced. Artists know that in the crucifixion there is either suffering and tragedy that almost everyone can identify with, or a final, ultimate truth about God and the human condition, or perhaps both.

New Testament scholars have observed that had Jesus returned to Galilee on that Monday of Holy Week, resumed his life of teaching and healing, grown old, and died a natural death, we would be left with a body of teaching and the example of a life

Theological Perspective

wait-and-see attitude, curiously standing by to see if in fact Elijah will appear.

Whether hopeful or skeptical, all these bystanders show the inability of the human easily to imagine the Divine. The mental straightjacket in which these bystanders abide illustrates the manner in which God's revelation is often missed. Able to conceive only one way for the manifestation of God's presence and power, they are oblivious to the fact that God's power is being enacted in the very place they consider it most absent. That is the theological point Matthew thunderously proclaims in the verses that tumble out after the crowd's ambiguous wait for Elijah.

As Jesus breathes his last—as he experiences not rescue by Elijah but death by crucifixion—all manner of strange things are enumerated in the narrative: the temple curtain is torn from top to bottom; an earthquake splits rocks and seems to shake the foundations; tombs are opened as many saints who have fallen asleep are raised. Exegetes have to work out for us the tension between verses 52 and 53, since the latter seems to qualify the former in an effort to make sure that the resurrection of Jesus is the first fruit of all resurrections. Matthew is less concerned with specific details than with a narrative showing that the power and presence of God is most dramatically operative at the point where human imagination assumes its absence: in the brutal death of an unrescued Jesus.

Christian theology, in consequence, has ever since been a theology of the cross. As such, it is a theology that has enabled the community assembled in Christ's name to find light in all kinds of darkness, not least the darkness of torture and death. While never welcoming—much less seeking—such untoward experiences, the community that lives in the light of Matthew's account of the crucifixion has turned out to be a resilient one. It is a community that has reason to believe that even when the worst circumstances take place, an eye should be turned toward the unexpected, surprising power of God working its way through them. The reason it has so to believe is nothing more and nothing less than the story of these verses. They narrate those accompaniments of Jesus' death that leave a stunned and terrified group of guards testifying in their amazement: "Truly this man was God's Son!"

Nowhere is the divine revelation at the center of these verses liturgically captured more simply and clearly than in the classic Anglican evening prayer: "Lighten our darkness, we beseech thee, O Lord; and by thy great mercy defend us from all perils

Pastoral Perspective

Jesus does have on the world, even in death. One of the guards, the centurion, has a conversion on the spot, acknowledging that Jesus was the Son of God. His conversion voices the accusation that got Jesus killed. So the uneasiness of who Jesus really is, even in his suffering and death, continues to have an impact on the physical world. This tension still resides with us today, and is further complicated as people of faith debate the way the vulnerability of the crucified Christ translates into our public life together.

When it comes to justice in our world, we see in this text a final solution promoted by the state. We see that Jesus, who did not argue on his own behalf before Pilate, is not only accused but put to death. This text can cause us to wonder about the many times the state gets the verdict wrong, and about how it is impossible to stop the wheels of "justice," once they are going. Although too often repeated before and since, the 2011 execution of Troy Davis in Georgia is a case in point. Many people organized against this, including the pope, but the state would not be stopped. Perhaps Jesus' public death needs to give us pause to reconsider what public deaths say about the health of our entire society.

Jesus' death and dying bring his humanity to the forefront, and this gives ordinary people a way to feel connected with him. His doubt and question, his anguish and distress are familiar to those of us who have been in those vulnerable places where life is sheer pain. Jesus allows us to acknowledge our own vulnerability as something that is part of a larger story of God at work. Whether it is in our family life or in our work, we can carry this humanity of Jesus with us.

Contemplating this section of Scripture, perhaps we hear ourselves crying out in despair to our God. At times it can be almost impossible to imagine that God hears our cry in any way. In fact it may seem that the only response we get is for our world to break apart. It is the earth-shaking portions of this text that remind us of the ways our own lives can be shaken deeply by death, whether the death of a single loved one or the catastrophic deaths of many in an act like 9/11. Yet look at this text again. Even in the earth's groaning, there is a preview that there is an awakening at the moment of Jesus' death, for our text tells us that the graves are opened and many dead saints come back to life. Perhaps this is part of the mystery of this text, that through Jesus Christ, death does not have the final victory.

In this all-encompassing scene at Golgotha, who is watching besides the guards? Jesus has a whole

Exegetical Perspective

Matthew has changed Mark's Greek so that it more closely conforms to the Exodus text, the evangelist may be attempting to draw a connection to Exodus 10:22, in which the darkness is an indication of God's judgment on Egypt and a sign of God's intervention to free the Israelites from captivity. Whatever the meaning of the darkness, it indicates that something significant is about to happen. Readers cannot help but hold their breath as the scene unfolds.

In verse 46, Jesus' cry from the cross in Hebrew and Aramaic (there is some disagreement among scholars about the language here) is a direct quotation from Psalm 22:1. Connections to Psalm 22 have been numerous throughout the crucifixion scene, and this quotation once again links Jesus to the suffering, forsaken narrator of that psalm. Matthew has changed Mark's *elōi, elōi* to *ēli, ēli* in verse 46 (cf. Mark 15:34), perhaps better to correspond to the text of Psalm 22. The change also functions to make sense of verse 47, in which the bystanders mistakenly think that "Eli" is short for "Elijah." In popular thought, the prophet Elijah provided help in times of distress.

Matthew also makes sense of the confusing text in Mark 15:36, where it is unclear why the same person gives Jesus wine and urges the others to "wait" to see if Elijah arrives. Verses 48–49 clarify that one of the onlookers gets a sponge soaked in cheap, sour wine to give to Jesus, while the others tell the first to wait. Presumably the first one hopes to extend the remaining moments of Jesus' life, while the others think that if Jesus' suffering increases, they will get to see Elijah appear and save him. There are a couple of significant connections here with the Jewish Scriptures. The offer of the cheap wine (*oxos*) alludes to Psalm 69:21b: "for my thirst they gave me vinegar to drink." Matthew has also changed "take him down" from Mark 15:36 to "save him" in verse 49 to better reflect the language of Psalm 22.

Elijah does not come to rescue Jesus, though, and Jesus cries out again. Matthew has modified Mark 15:37 in two significant ways here. First, Matthew has added that Jesus cries out "again," suggesting that he may have uttered the quotation from Psalm 22:1 a second time. Second, whereas Jesus "expires" or "breathes his last" in Mark (*exepneusen*), he "gives up his spirit" (*aphēken to pneuma*) in verse 50, suggesting that Jesus has composure and control as he dies. Because there is no possessive pronoun in the Greek text, it is also possible that Matthew is suggesting that Jesus "gives up" or "releases" the Holy Spirit into the world at the moment of his death.

Homiletical Perspective

lived compassionately, but we would not have the gospel. What is so very compelling about the narrative is its inclusion of Jesus' cry from the cross: "Eli, Eli, lema sabachthani?"—"My God, my God, why have you forsaken me?" (v. 46, from Ps. 22:1).

In one way or another everyone, sooner or later, asks that question: "Why have you forsaken me? Why has this happened to innocent people? Why me?" It is the human question; to be human is to ask it. There are many other psalms that raise the question: "How long, O LORD? Will you forget me forever? . . . How long must I bear pain in my soul?" (Ps. 13:1a, 2a). Some psalms complain about the simple injustice of innocent suffering while the unrighteous prosper: "Do you indeed decree what is right, you gods?" (Ps. 58:1a). "O God, you have rejected us, broken our defenses" (Ps. 60:1a). Job of course adds his voice: "How long will you torment me, and break me in pieces? . . . Are you not ashamed to wrong me? . . . I call aloud, but there is no justice" (Job 19:2, 3b, 7b).

The deep pain in those passages is as contemporary as today's newspaper. A stray drone attack kills twenty-five civilians in Afghanistan, many of them children; a tornado rips through a Midwestern American city destroying hundreds of homes, leaving many dead; a wonderful adolescent, outstanding student, a good swimmer, drowns in Lake Michigan, and his father speaks for every one of us: "They say everything happens for a reason. I wish I knew the reason this had to happen."

The preacher can count on the universality of the question, "why has this happened?" and the deep yearning for some way to live with innocent suffering, whenever and however it happens. There are suggested answers. After every natural disaster, hurricane, flood, earthquake, tsunami, someone announces that it was an act of God punishing human beings for some presumed infraction of God's justice. Most shudder to be told that the people of New Orleans suffered flooding because of their city's easy tolerance. Yet many wonder, if God is almighty and loving, powerful and compassionate, why does innocent suffering happen, ever? God is either not truly almighty or not truly loving. Perhaps God is not there at all. The philosophers have struggled with it from the beginning of time, and so do we, every one of us, when we witness or experience tragic suffering.

The preacher's first responsibility is to assure the congregation that no one knows enough to blame God for human suffering, that to assign God

Matthew 27:45–54

Theological Perspective

and dangers of this night; for the love of thy only Son, our Savior, Jesus Christ. Amen."[1] The prayer is resolute in its acknowledgment of darkness, which is not expected to be dispelled, but "lightened"; and of perils and dangers that are not avoided, but against which defense and deliverance are anticipated. The prayer grounds this anticipation in the very event of which Matthew's text speaks: "the love of thy only Son, our Savior, Jesus Christ."

Perhaps every great religious tradition has its particular way of coping with the presence of profound evil in the midst of human experience. There is no doubt that the Christian way of so coping is to be found in substantial measure in this witness from Matthew's Gospel. Evil is not explained by Matthew's witness. Neither is evil discounted, as something that only appears to be bad. Still less is evil escaped through some metaphysical sleight of hand. Rather, evil is endured—and then consumed by a more profound power of God to weave a new fabric of beauty and health and wholeness that evil seeks to destroy.

This theology of the cross that Matthew narrates echoes far and wide through the New Testament. It is classically apparent in Romans when Paul concludes the eighth chapter thus: "For I am convinced that neither death, nor life, nor angels, nor rulers, nor things present, nor things to come, nor powers, nor height, nor depth, nor anything else in all creation, will be able to separate us from the love of God in Christ Jesus our Lord" (Rom. 8:38–39). Because God in Christ endured the cross, the Christian community may live confidently, trusting the power of God that has been made perfect in this very specific weakness.

D. CAMERON MURCHISON

Pastoral Perspective

web of relationships across Jerusalem and the surrounding areas. Where are his friends and associates? Perhaps they are watching from afar. Maybe they have run off because it is too hard to remain with Jesus' suffering and death. There has been a vocal crowd around the cross, but they recede as Jesus dies and the earth responds with its own groaning. Yet again, the power of the crucifixion comes to us as we are drawn to look at the centurion and to hear his confession of who Jesus is. One of the gifts the centurion gives us is teaching that in situations where we hang in there through the suffering, we may be able to gain insight into the unusual ways God is made manifest in the world. This surprise can shake up the world as we know it.

The witness we have at Golgotha is that even at the place of death, God is present. The death of Jesus Christ evokes anguish, so much so that the earth shakes. Yet Jesus' death also calls forth the dead saints from their graves and the conversion of the centurion , a recognition that God is made real even—or especially—in the crucified man on the cross. As followers of Jesus Christ, we are set free by the cross to go into the places of death in our world with the confidence that God is present. We are freed to be at the bedside of a loved one dying, or to be in the inner city nurturing children who are being left behind. We are sent in mission to connect with what God is doing in the world, into places that are filled with turmoil and question, where the world groans and cracks, and even into the places where God seems silent. We can know we are not alone.

KAREN L. BRAU

---

1. *The Book of Common Prayer and Administration of the Sacraments and Other Rites and Ceremonies of the Church,* According to the Use of The Episcopal Church (New York: The Church Hymnal Corporation and The Seabury Press, 1979), 111.

Exegetical Perspective

The moment of Jesus' death in Matthew is exceedingly dramatic, continuing the eschatological signs that began with darkness covering the land in verse 45. Like Mark, Matthew reports that the curtain of the Jerusalem temple is torn in two. The detail that it is split "from top to bottom" (v. 51) hints at God's involvement and the curtain's utter ruin. This curtain is most likely the inner curtain of the temple that isolates the Holy of Holies, the innermost sanctum, from the rest of the temple. Multiple interpretations abound. The curtain's destruction could signify the departure of God's presence from the temple and foreshadow its destruction in 70 CE. It could also indicate that, because of Jesus' death, God's presence is now available to Gentiles, including the Gentile centurion and his companions who make a confession of faith following these events (v. 54).

In addition to the curtain's splitting in two, Matthew adds to the Markan source an earthquake, the splitting of rocks, and the opening of tombs (vv. 51–53). In the Hebrew Bible, earthquakes often indicate God's revelation in the last judgment (Isa. 5:25; 24:18). The power of the earthquake splits rocks, and the entrances of tombs are miraculously opened, possibly because the stones covering their entrances also split.

The resurrection of the dead saints prefigures Jesus' own resurrection as well as the general resurrection at the end of time. Note the unusual sequence of events, however. The dead saints are resurrected at the moment of his death, but they do not emerge from their tombs until Jesus himself has been raised. Thus, at least in one sense, Matthew can still claim that Jesus' resurrection is the first.

Jesus' death is tragic in Matthew, yet it also represents a decisive and triumphal moment in history. Through it, God acts in history to enact God's plans. The events that accompany Jesus' death are so powerful that the Roman centurion and his companions are terrified and respond with a confession of faith in Jesus: "Truly this man was God's Son!" (v. 54).

ARTHUR M. WRIGHT JR.

Homiletical Perspective

responsibility for suffering flies in the face of what we believe about God and what Jesus Christ reveals about God: that God cares deeply, that God is love, and that God acts in human history in ways that are meek and vulnerable, as in the birth of a child in Bethlehem and in the death of a beloved Son on a cross. Rather than visiting suffering on innocent people, God suffers with and weeps with all who suffer.

Matthew's depiction of God's own Son—unjustly accused, tried and convicted, humiliated, tortured, and executed, ridiculed by witnesses, abandoned by friends—is either an eloquent example of the meaninglessness of suffering and the utter absence of God, or it is something very different: namely, the presence of God in that suffering, God experiencing the human suffering that comes to all of us. That is the gospel, the good news.

Jesus called God "Father." Parents understand the limits of love. Parents understand that you cannot fully protect your child from suffering, that never to allow a child out of your sight is finally to deny a child's own freedom and self-determination. To parent is to love and grant freedom and then to be present with love and compassion when suffering results. To watch a child suffer because of freedom extended is exquisitely painful. Faith knows that God experienced such pain when Jesus died, and that God is present with us, experiencing our pain and grief with us.

Jesus was remembering a psalm he memorized as a child: "My God, my God, why have you forsaken me?" (Ps. 22:1). It is a powerful lament about suffering that pivots, halfway through, into an equally powerful affirmation of God's redeeming presence with Jesus, and with us:

> For he did not despise or abhor
>   the affliction of the afflicted;
> he did not hide his face from me,
>   but heard when I cried to him.
>   (Ps. 22:24)

JOHN M. BUCHANAN

⁵⁵Many women were also there, looking on from a distance; they had followed Jesus from Galilee and had provided for him. ⁵⁶Among them were Mary Magdalene, and Mary the mother of James and Joseph, and the mother of the sons of Zebedee.

⁵⁷When it was evening, there came a rich man from Arimathea, named Joseph, who was also a disciple of Jesus. ⁵⁸He went to Pilate and asked for the body of Jesus; then Pilate ordered it to be given to him. ⁵⁹So Joseph took the body and wrapped it in a clean linen cloth ⁶⁰and laid it in his own new tomb, which he had hewn in the rock. He then rolled a great stone to the door of the tomb and went away. ⁶¹Mary Magdalene and the other Mary were there, sitting opposite the tomb.

⁶² The next day, that is, after the day of Preparation, the chief priests and the Pharisees gathered before Pilate ⁶³and said, "Sir, we remember what that impostor said while he was still alive, 'After three days I will rise again.' ⁶⁴Therefore command the tomb to be made secure until the third day; otherwise his disciples may go and steal him away, and tell the people, 'He has been raised from the dead,' and the last deception would be worse than the first." ⁶⁵Pilate said to them, "You have a guard of soldiers; go, make it as secure as you can." ⁶⁶So they went with the guard and made the tomb secure by sealing the stone.

Theological Perspective

A certain quietness seems to pervade the scene in the aftermath of the taunting, torture, and crucifixion of Jesus. The raucous jeers at the one hanging on the cross, and even more the cataclysmic events recounted as accompanying Jesus' death, give way to women silently gazing from a distance as Joseph of Arimathea undertakes to provide a quiet, simple burial for Jesus. Matthew has by now made his decisive theological point that the power and presence of God were manifest as Jesus endured rather than escaped the cross. Here he prepares the way for the corollary theological claim that is coming, that death cannot encompass and contain God incarnate.

Matthew makes the move in this theological direction by following the subdued depiction of the burial with the anxious conversation of the religious leaders with Pilate on the following day. They approached Pilate with their concern about making the tomb secure, in order that the disciples might be thwarted in any body-snatching efforts designed to fuel rumors about a resurrection. Apparently they were not at ease with the fact that Jesus had not come down from the cross. They were now fretting about whether he might come out from the tomb. From Matthew's point of view, well they might!

Whatever one might make of contemporary theological debates concerning whether it is necessary

Pastoral Perspective

It is silent
at the mouth of the tomb
heaviness wraps
witnesses of death
with the certainty
of a tragic ending
the promised rising
an uneasy dream
sealed up in a tomb
women wait anyhow
there's nothing left to lose.

It seems as though the politicians have triumphed. Another troublemaker is dead, and the body of Jesus becomes a commodity handed over for a private burial. Still the state gets stirred up by warnings that a dead body may not stop the story of Jesus. A stop is what the leaders want. Extra guards and a sealed tomb make security complete. If Jesus and his teaching are in part about a change in the way the world is organized politically and economically, of course leaders will exercise caution as the story ends. They want to control Jesus' message of hope, making sure that the ending is clear from cross to sealed tomb.

We see messages controlled in our day too. Even though we use the word "hope" around political and economic systems, we have limited it to mean certain things. For our economy, there is "hope" that

Exegetical Perspective

This passage is composed of three distinct units. The narrator first reports an additional group of eyewitnesses at the cross, then describes the burial of Jesus, and concludes by relating a uniquely Matthean story in which the Jewish authorities enlist Roman support to secure Jesus' tomb. It is hard to draw clear boundaries here. The first two verses (vv. 55–56) can be read with the preceding passage, but also fit appropriately here, because of the connection with the women between these verses and verse 61. The burial scene functions as a bridge between Jesus' death and resurrection. The third scene operates in tandem with what follows in 28:11–15, to offer an apologetic in response to allegations contemporaneous with Matthew's own community in the late first century.

The Women at the Tomb (vv. 55–56). Matthew, like Mark, waits to describe the presence of women at the cross until after narrating Jesus' death (Mark 15:40–41). Although it comes as an aside from the narrator, it is not insignificant. Only female disciples are mentioned here, and their role is not a passive one. All of Jesus' male followers have fled at this point, withdrawing when Jesus is arrested (26:56). Peter attempts to follow Jesus after the arrest, but he too has departed after denying Jesus three times (26:75). Only the women who have supported

Homiletical Perspective

Religion that has the strongest popular appeal these days focuses on the positive, the potential, the possible. The scene represented in this text is not a positive one in any sense of the word. The cross, although transformed regularly into an elegant gold pendant, was ugly, not beautiful. Dying on it was terrible. Added to the excruciating pain of slowly suffocating was the scorn heaped on the victim by passersby, and the abandonment in terror by all his friends. It is no wonder that some contemporary churches are built without a visible cross in sight. There is enough pain and suffering in the world and enough stress in our lives. Who needs a symbol of cruelty, torture, and death?

Anne Lamott confessed (and many of us totally understand), "I don't have the right personality for Good Friday, for the crucifixion. I'd like to skip ahead to the resurrection. In fact, I'd like to skip ahead to the resurrection vision of one of the kids in our Sunday School who drew a picture of the Easter Bunny outside the open tomb: everlasting life and a basket full of chocolates. Now you're talking."[1]

It is the preacher's task today to "proclaim Christ crucified . . . the power of God and the wisdom of God" (1 Cor. 1:23–24), to help the congregation

1. Anne Lamott, *Plan B: Further Thoughts on Faith* (New York: Riverhead, 2005), 160.

Theological Perspective

for the tomb to have been empty to affirm belief in the resurrection, there can be little doubt where Matthew puts his theological foot down. He seems to relish the plight of the religious leaders in their conversation with Pilate. Even more, he revels in Pilate's enigmatic response that acknowledges that the religious leaders have all the ordinary means of securing the tomb at their disposal—"a guard of soldiers"—but also seems to level a challenge at them: "go, make it as secure *as you can*" (v. 65, emphasis added). In response, these leaders not only stationed the soldiers at the tomb, but took the additional measure of sealing the stone. Matthew's telling of this story accepts the challenge of letting these actors do all they can to assure that the tomb will not turn out to be empty.

There is a great reversal at this stage of the story, compared to the taunts that dared Jesus to come down from the cross. In that first stage of the story, few expected Jesus to come down from the cross (though some probably wondered if he would). However, at this stage the religious leaders are clearly worried that the one who had not come down from the cross might at least appear to have come out from the tomb. To their way of thinking, the only resurrection that could happen would consist of a body gone missing because of grave robbing. So it is important to Matthew that there be an account of their extra efforts to thwart any attempt to carry out such grave robbing. Matthew clearly wants these leaders to make the tomb as secure as they can. Only so will the interpretation of the empty tomb as the result of grave robbing be undermined.

Thus Matthew, in the same chapter in which he enshrines a theology of the cross as central to theological reflection, also prepares the way for a theology of glory, for a resurrection theology as its vindicating complement. While Matthew has shown his readers that the powerful presence of God was evident in the weakness of torture and death of Jesus, he also is going to show that God does not leave his faithful ones in the grip of evil. The same power of the state that sent Jesus to his death was now being employed in the securing of his tomb. Whereas God was ready for the incarnate one to endure the power of the state in Jesus' dying, God's readiness to allow state power to keep Jesus in the tomb was another matter altogether.

Cumulatively, the theological points of this chapter in Matthew are that human powers can indeed bring death and destruction, but not death and destruction that crowd out the powerful presence

Pastoral Perspective

upward mobility can be the motivator for people to hang in with a system that is characterized more by immobility than mobility. For our political system, "hope" masks the way large corporate interests outweigh the participation of regular citizens in the democratic process. "Hope" has little to do with God's love and promise.

What about Jesus being a public figure who embodies God's justice? We can open the news any day and see reports of the deaths of people who put their lives on the line for justice. They too may be major public figures like Jesus, or they may be ones who have quietly worked for the good of all sisters and brothers in Christ. Think of people throughout the world who are killed just because they are Christian. Think of people who are killed just because they love someone whom the society they live in says is off limits. It can seem, as with Jesus, that God's justice is killed off and put out of sight. There are many things that we bury away so as not to agitate for the change they demand.

There is a deep sadness at the foot of the cross that moves over to the tomb. In the text we hear about the women who have traveled with Jesus during his ministry, and how they have been observing the goings-on at Golgotha from a distance. The women and a rich man named Joseph of Arimathea move the dead Jesus to prepare him for burial. Loved ones care for the dead Jesus.

Grieving the death of a loved one is a common experience we share as people of faith. Sometimes the relationships are public, and we can grieve openly with a community. Sometimes the relationships are more hidden, and we feel isolated in our grieving. One of the consequences of serving in the inner city as a pastor for many years has been to learn about grieving that comes from ongoing neighborhood violence. There are long-term consequences for large numbers of people who live in a place that has the feeling of a war zone in the streets. Honoring the reality and heaviness of grief, beyond what we do around funerals, is a conversation we have to have in church.

The devotional quality of this text can be about a slow walk through the end of life that leads to our sitting with death. It can give us the courage to be present with death and its harsh reality. In the text it seems that a small portion of the web of relationships that Jesus has had in his ministry reappears in the ones gathered around him in their grieving and in their tending to Jesus' ending. They take on a variety of roles, just as we do when we deal with

him since his ministry in Galilee remain to witness his death and burial. Their persistence allows two of them to be the first to discover and then to announce his resurrection.

Mary Magdalene has not been mentioned in Matthew before now, but she and "the other Mary" witness Jesus' death here, see his burial at the tomb (27:61), and eventually will discover the tomb empty (28:1–7). The early Christian tradition surrounding Mary Magdalene is so strong that all four Gospels attest to her involvement. The identity of "Mary, the mother of James and Joseph" is uncertain, but it is possible that she is the mother of Jesus. Matthew does list James and Joseph as two of Jesus' brothers earlier in the Gospel (13:55). If Matthew intends to indicate that it is Jesus' mother at the cross, this is certainly an unusual way to do so.

The third woman named by Matthew, "the mother of the sons of Zebedee," has replaced Mark's "Salome" (Mark 15:40) and has already played a significant part in the Matthean narrative, requesting earlier in the story that Jesus choose her sons, James and John, to sit at his right and his left in his kingdom (20:20–23). The description of her as "the mother of the sons of Zebedee" may serve to further highlight the absence of Jesus' male disciples in this scene. All of these women serve an important role as witnesses to his death, burial, and resurrection.

The Burial of Jesus (vv. 57–61). All four Gospels attest that a man from Arimathea named Joseph collects Jesus' body from the cross and buries it after his death. Matthew adds to the Markan source by clarifying that Joseph is "rich," which Matthew may assume from the fact that he owns a tomb nearby, and his identification as affluent is consistent with the idea that Matthew's own community may have included many wealthy members. Matthew also says that Joseph is a "disciple" of Jesus, rather than a "respected member of the council" (Mark 15:43), to avoid linking him to the group that condemned Jesus to death (26:59–66).

It is the evening before the Sabbath begins when Joseph approaches the Roman governor to ask him for the body. Matthew omits Mark's exchange between Pilate and the centurion, in which the Roman governor wonders whether Jesus has already died (Mark 15:44–45), and Pilate hands over the body without delay. Joseph wraps it in a clean linen cloth and places it in his own new tomb. Matthew adds to Mark's text the details that the linen is "clean" and the tomb is "new" (vv. 59–60; cf. Mark 15:46).

understand the monstrous injustice, the crime, the shame of it all, and that Jesus was the victim of the kind of moral compromise made every day of our lives by vested self-interest. It is also imperative to remind the people that our most precious conviction is that the death of Jesus is more than an illustration of human sinfulness. It is supremely and finally a symbol of God's holy love for all of us.

In the meantime there are three fascinating details. First, there were women present. Each of the Gospel writers tells it slightly differently, but they agree that women were present, "many women" who had followed him from Galilee, among them Mary Magdalene and several other Marys. John remembers Mary, his mother, present as he died. I have always been struck by the fact that the men all flee and the women remain with him—perhaps at a distance, but they do not flee. They are not afraid to be identified with him. Perhaps the consequences of identification as his disciple were more severe for men. We do not know that. All we know is that the men flee and the women remain.

In Matthew's account, Mary Magdalene and Mary, mother of James and Joseph, are among many women who not only watch from afar, but minister to him, a tender detail. Did they speak comfort? Did they actually approach and touch him, pat him, wipe his brow? The two of them watch as Joseph of Arimathea takes the lifeless body down from the cross, and they are still watching as Joseph buries Jesus in his own tomb. These women are absolutely fearless. They will return, alone, to the tomb in the early morning, before dawn.

The second detail is that of Joseph of Arimathea, described as a rich man and a disciple of Jesus, who musters his courage and asks Pilate for the body of Jesus. Pilate orders his soldiers to give it to him, and Joseph, wealthy enough to own a garden with a private tomb, places the body of Jesus in it. Given what has transpired in the previous twenty-four hours— the arrest and trial, the frenzied crowd that had turned utterly on Jesus, the obvious political conclusion that Jesus was somehow a threat to Roman authority—it required considerable bravery for anyone to be identified with Jesus. Joseph's act was not only extraordinarily kind, but also courageous.

The third and most provocative detail is the Saturday visit by a delegation of old men calling on the Roman governor in his palace. It is a quiet Saturday, the Jewish Sabbath. The streets are empty. Yesterday's crowd is gone. The victim is dead, buried. Here they are again, the same old men who were so persistent

Matthew 27:55–66

Theological Perspective

of God. Moreover, human power cannot stymie the power of God to create life where death alone was thought to reign, to sponsor hope where human powers sponsor hopelessness, or to declare a new day of light where human powers herald only darkness. Such is the significance of sending soldiers to guard and seal the tomb, allowing human power to do everything in its reach to make sure the tomb stays occupied. The same deadly human power that took Jesus to the cross is deployed once again.

As readers of Matthew's Gospel, we have to wait for the concluding chapter to tell us the outcome of this final effort by the forces of evil. At this moment in the story Matthew is toying with those forces of evil, hinting more than broadly that they are at the precipice of their comeuppance. For no matter how excruciating the principalities and powers of this world may be, whatever mayhem and destruction they may bring, Matthew invites us to put them to this final test. He invites us to array the most force-ful forms of these powers available to us against the determination of God to empty the tomb of the one who did not come down from the cross.

The theological irony in all of this is that while the forces that human beings command can bring death, they can go no further. They have no lever-age when it comes to what happens next. Even when they try to ensure that no one would be able to mount either a plausible or a deceptive story of something happening next, the power of the God who intends that something will happen next leaves them desperately wanting.

If we would know the outcome of this head-to-head combat, Matthew invites us to read on into chapter 28!

D. CAMERON MURCHISON

Pastoral Perspective

the death of a loved one—some provide the funeral space, some prepare the body, others come and sit. The women in the text can also give us the gift to consider that there is something after death. They have heard Jesus' teaching that he will rise, and they seem to have a sense that Jesus' promise that the cross is not the end of the story could be true. How-ever, they want to see for themselves.

This text calls us to witness to the reality of death and to honor it. So much of our lives moves quickly, and we are accustomed to instant gratification; but grieving takes time. The rituals of the church are valuable in helping us to move with grief and to begin to process it. Traumatic deaths take a further measure of compassion and care for those who grieve. The church has a role in providing a space for immediate grieving and for healing the long-term consequences of traumatic death.

Because of our witness to Jesus' death on the cross, people of faith are set free in mission to go into the places of death in our world with the role of caring for the dead—whether that is in hospice, in our inner cities, or in areas where natural disas-ters have caused death. Some of the grandmothers I worked with in East Baltimore taught me that the struggles in the inner city can make it seem like every day is Good Friday. However, like the women sitting and waiting opposite the tomb, these grand-mothers also taught me to trust that there is some-thing more God will do, even in the face of death. These wise women teach us never to lose hope in a God whose Son has died for us all and who will make a way out of no way, over and over bringing new life that just might surprise us. They remind us, it is always darkest before the dawn.

KAREN L. BRAU

The linen cloth (*sindōn*) may be translated as "shroud" and has been connected in church tradition to the Shroud of Turin. There is, of course, nothing in the text itself to substantiate the connections. Speculation concerning the shroud is merely the result of developing traditions throughout church history. After taking care to place the body in the tomb, Joseph rolls a large stone in front of the door to seal it and to prevent the possibility that grave robbers will enter the tomb. He then departs, his act of devotion and piety complete.

Matthew, following Mark, reports that two of the women, Mary Magdalene and the other Mary, witness Jesus' burial. They know which tomb he is buried in, so there is no chance that they will go to the wrong tomb on the first day of the week to anoint his body.

Securing the Tomb (vv. 62–66). The scene that follows the burial is unique to Matthew and functions along with 28:11–15 as an apologetic against allegations circulating in the latter part of the first century. It is not hard to imagine that in Matthew's day some opponents of the Christian movement would claim that Jesus was not raised from the dead but, rather, that his body was stolen by his disciples from the tomb after his death. As a response, Matthew has inserted this story into his Markan source, along with 28:11–15, to counter the allegations by implying that it would not have been possible for the disciples to steal the body.

There is, of course, irony in this scene. The Jewish authorities think the disciples will attempt to retrieve the body, but the disciples will continue to remain passive in the story until the women inform them of Jesus' resurrection (28:16). In spite of the best efforts of the Jewish authorities, Pilate, and a contingent of Roman soldiers to make the tomb as "secure" as they possibly can, Jesus truly will be raised from the dead on the third day.

ARTHUR M. WRIGHT JR.

in their insistence that Jesus of Nazareth was not only committing the sin of blasphemy, but was also a political threat to Roman rule. I doubt that Pilate is pleased to see them.

We know these men. In fact, the more I think about them, the more human they seem. The chief priests and Pharisees were doing everything they could think of to preserve the autonomy of their temple, their religion, their nation. It was their compelling goal, their vocation, to keep the temple, and all it meant to the nation, open for business. So, from Caiaphas on down, they were prepared to make the compromises and do the deals that would serve their goal. We should not be too hard on them. For his part, Pilate, too, simply wanted to survive, to protect his position in the Roman bureaucracy, to keep the peace long enough to earn a positive review and promotion.

The old men want to secure the tomb. Pilate's response is theologically provocative, "You have a guard. Go, make it as secure as you can" (v. 65). The old men say they are afraid that Jesus' friends will steal the body, announce a resurrection, and their political and social positions will be more precarious than ever. Perhaps they are actually afraid that what he predicted will happen, that he will walk out of the tomb and nothing, nothing, will ever be the same again.[2]

It is helpful to read verses 55–66 as the prologue to the Easter pericope. The watchful women, the courageous undertaker, and the fearful protectors of the status quo set the stage for what is to come. As the sun rises on the morning of the first day of the week, Mary Magdalene and the other Mary return to the tomb and are the first witnesses to the dawn of a new reality, a new world, from crucifixion to resurrection, from death to life, from weeping to laughter and great joy.

JOHN M. BUCHANAN

2. See Frederick Buechner, *The Magnificent Defeat* (New York: Seabury Press, 1966), 74–81.

Matthew 28:1–10

¹After the Sabbath, as the first day of the week was dawning, Mary Magdalene and the other Mary went to see the tomb. ²And suddenly there was a great earthquake; for an angel of the Lord, descending from heaven, came and rolled back the stone and sat on it. ³His appearance was like lightning, and his clothing white as snow. ⁴For fear of him the guards shook and became like dead men. ⁵But the angel said to the women, "Do not be afraid; I know that you are looking for Jesus who was crucified. ⁶He is not here; for he has been raised, as he said. Come, see the place where he lay. ⁷Then go quickly and tell his disciples, 'He has been raised from the dead, and indeed he is going ahead of you to Galilee; there you will see him.' This is my message for you." ⁸So they left the tomb quickly with fear and great joy, and ran to tell his disciples. ⁹Suddenly Jesus met them and said, "Greetings!" And they came to him, took hold of his feet, and worshiped him. ¹⁰Then Jesus said to them, "Do not be afraid; go and tell my brothers to go to Galilee; there they will see me."

Theological Perspective

Matthew's account of Jesus' resurrection is literally earthshaking. More than any of the other Gospel accounts of what happened "as the first day of the week was dawning" (v. 1), this passage portrays the resurrection as an apocalyptic event with immediate public consequences. There is no missing the point that what happened when Jesus was raised from the dead shocked witnesses and affected the world itself. Three theological issues arise in reading this passage: What does it mean to claim that *Christ is risen*? What is the nature of his *risen body*? Is *fear* an appropriate response to this event?

First, what does "resurrection" mean? Jesus' being "raised from the dead" is not itself a visible, public event. All we see is the empty tomb and/or the risen Christ (in this passage, both). There are no witnesses to tell us what did or did not happen to Jesus' body. This is the mystery, the gap, the silence, in the center of Christian faith. What the Gospel writers seem keen to convey, however, is that something monumental happened that altered the world order, overturning expectations about the relationship of death and life and the coming of God's reign.

Some twentieth-century theologians (such as Rudolf Bultmann[1]) focus on resurrection as an event

Pastoral Perspective

When local church leaders besought Martin Luther King Jr. to ease up in his agitation for civil rights, King responded in a sermon in Montgomery that is often called "Our God Is Marching On." In that sermon King mocked the desire of white moderates for a return to a more comfortable, placid world. He vowed defiantly, "No, we will not allow Alabama to return to normalcy."[1] A world in which racial segregation made sense has ended. King eschewed normalcy, not as a savvy political strategy but, rather, because of his Christian faith: after God raised Jesus Christ from the dead, forget "normal."

It is the first day of the Jewish work week. After a violent weekend, the disciples of Jesus are hankering for a return to normality as a new day dawns. Alas, nothing is normal. Three women go out to the tomb to pay their last respects to poor, dead Jesus. Women? Where were the men? Who begins an important story with marginalized women? There is a "great earthquake." This earthquake serves as a metaphor for the unfolding story of people who are having their world rocked. An angel descends from heaven and perches impudently on the stone that is supposed to keep the body of Jesus safely sealed. Is this the same intrusive angel who began the Gospel

---

1. Rudolf Bultmann, *Theology of the New Testament*, trans. Kendrick Grobel (New York: Scribner, 1951–55).

1. "How Long, Not Long," March 25, 1965, http://www.mlkonline.net/ourgod.html; accessed on February 25, 2012.

Exegetical Perspective

Matthew's story of Jesus does not end with sealing a tomb and posting a guard (27:66). The witness of faithful women disciples, who were with Jesus at the cross (27:55–56), also continues. Two of them—"Mary Magdalene and the other Mary"—observe his lifeless body being placed in a tomb with a heavy stone rolled in front (27:57–61). These same two are the first witnesses of an emptied tomb and resurrected Jesus.

An Emptied Tomb (vv. 1–7). Matthew follows Mark 16:1–8 with some changes. A third woman in Mark's account, Salome, has dropped out. The two Marys are not there to bring spices or anoint the body (cf. Mark 16:1) but, rather, "to see the tomb." They grieve as Jesus is executed and his body laid in a tomb. They want to continue their mourning after Sabbath. The dawn of a new day and a new week, signaling the dawn of a new age, represents the best timing for grieving to continue (v. 1; Mark 16:2; Luke 24:1).

In Mark, the women wonder how they will be able to anoint the body if no one is there to move the stone (Mark 16:3). The women in Matthew have no expectations, since they have seen the tomb sealed shut two nights before. Yet they want to be near. Matthew describes why they see an emptied tomb,

Homiletical Perspective

One of the biggest decisions a preacher makes is whether to downplay the differences among the four Gospel accounts of Jesus' life, death, and resurrection, in order to present a united front to listeners, or whether to call attention to those same differences, in order to honor each evangelist's distinctive witness. This essay favors the second approach, both because the dissimilarities among the Gospels open such interesting homiletical doors, and because going through them offers listeners the opportunity to decide what is more important: establishing Christian facts or risking Christian faith.

Matthew's singular witness to Jesus' resurrection from the dead includes at least three details that may prove interesting to preachers in search of fresh handholds on the text.

1. Only Matthew Allows the Reader to Watch the Opening of Jesus' Grave. In the other Gospels, the stone has already been rolled away from the door of the tomb by the time the women arrive. In Matthew's account, Mary Magdalene and "the other Mary" arrive just in time for an earthquake. If they had been carrying spices for anointing Jesus' body, then there might have been some breakage, but according to Matthew they come empty-handed for the sole purpose of viewing Jesus' grave.

Matthew 28:1–10

Theological Perspective

in the life of the disciples, a mysterious transformation that led to faith in the crucified Jesus as the most profound sign of God's presence in the world. Although there is power in this interpretation, Matthew's Gospel offers a different lens. An earthquake. An angel descending in the sight of the women and the guards, rolling away the stone. Guards so terrified that they "became like dead men." This is no personal event in the lives of the disciples. It is a mystery that testifies to the inbreaking of God's reign in the world.

Second, although there is no account of what happened to Jesus' body in the tomb, the encounter of the women with the risen Jesus does raise the question: what kind of body is this? They meet him on the road, apparently have no trouble recognizing him (in contrast to accounts in Luke 24 and John 20–21), and take hold of his feet. All of this suggests a body that is recognizably similar to the one that was crucified and laid in the tomb three days earlier.

Recent decades have seen new interest in the nature of Jesus' risen body. The New Testament accounts have conflicting testimony, some more tangible (as here, the affirmation that the women "took hold of his feet") and others depicting the risen body as more radically different from the body of Jesus during his lifetime (e.g., Paul's encounter with the risen Christ in Acts 9). What is at stake in this debate? Two things: the relationship between the Jesus who lived and the Jesus who was raised, and the status of our bodies now in relation to our hope for God's future. It matters that Jesus' risen body is recognizably the same Jesus who taught and healed and fed the hungry, who walked the roads of Galilee with these women in the preceding years. This confirms that the historical, embodied life of Jesus matters to God, and that God draws *this* Jesus (not some other Jesus) out of death into new life. It also matters because it confirms that God cares about our bodies, and about the bodies of the world's victims, so that our hope lies not in some disembodied spirit realm, but in the redemption of our very bodies from death.

Finally, the repeated references to the *fear* of both guards and women (vv. 4, 5, 8, 10) raise the question about whether fear is the appropriate response to resurrection. Does fear indicate a disordered relationship to God, or the proper recognition of God's glory? Old Testament passages such as Psalm 34:11 portray the fear of the Lord as appropriate awe before God. Yet angels and other messengers of God (as in this passage) regularly tell their listeners, "Fear

Pastoral Perspective

by disturbing the sleep of Joseph (1:20)? Who knows? Lightning before dawn, snow in the Middle East (v. 3), a huge stone rolled away, and Caesar's finest shaking in their boots—we are not simply on the edge of dawn, we stand upon the precipice of a strange and wonderful, although confusing and badly shaken, new world.

"Come, see," the inviting angel beckons the women (v. 6b). Throughout Matthew's Gospel, we are being trained by the evangelist to see, to look at what the world fails to notice. That is not a bad definition of the purpose of any reflection on this text: come, peer into the darkness, see the wonder that God has worked among us. The earth has shifted on its axis, a badly damaged creation is being restored, and God is at last having God's way with our sin and death—but not without shake, rattle, and roll.

The angel preaches a three-point sermon for the women: Do not be afraid. You just missed Jesus, who is already on his way to Galilee. Go tell the men (cowards huddled together for safety back in Jerusalem) that the story between us and God is not ending; it is beginning.

The pastor is charged with telling this story to a congregation full of people who are fearful of disruption and therefore shield their eyes from the blinding truth of resurrection. Can it be that there is a victorious power loose in the world that is more powerful than Caesar, sin, and death? People who have been trained to think of religion as the cement of social stability, cultural conformity, and order may have difficulty believing in Easter. Can it be that God is on the move, peripatetic, and headed for the boondocks where we live? People who think that they have gotten up, gotten dressed, and gotten themselves to church in order to come close to God are thus surprised that the risen Christ is on his way to Galilee. Women bearing disruptive news, determined to give their testimony to the resurrection to hesitant and disbelieving disciples, are models for Christian preachers of every age.

Be honest. Lots of our sermons have as their goal the pacification of the discombobulation induced by a living God. Are you distressed by the vicissitudes of life? Come to church and we'll fix that. Have you had your world rocked by factors beyond your control? This sermon will give you a sense of inner peace. Disturbed by something you heard Jesus say? I can explain to you how he really did not say what you thought you heard him say. Thus, when confronted by the testimony of the women, the disciples (at least as told in Luke 24:11) attempt to defend

after all: "There was a great earthquake" (*seismos*, v. 2a). This natural upheaval occurs because "an angel of the Lord [*angelos kyriou*], descending from heaven, came and rolled back the stone" (v. 2b). Matthew often describes heavenly portents accompanying divine action. At the crucifixion, when Jesus "breathed his last" (27:50), Matthew reports: "At that moment the curtain of the temple was torn in two. . . . The earth shook, and the rocks were split. The tombs were also opened, and many bodies of the saints who had fallen asleep were raised" (27:51–52). Thus at crucifixion, resurrection unfolds. Here it occurs for Jesus with his "rock" removed by divine action in the person of an angel (cf. angelic interventions in Matthew's birth narratives, 1:20–21; 2:13). The angel sits on that rock to further denote God's power (v. 2c). The actions of the angel typify apocalyptic expectation, in which miracles accompany divine activity in the final days. The physical appearance of the angel adds to this eschatological motif. He looks like "lightning" with a garment "white as snow" (v. 3). The "young man" with a simple "white robe" in Mark 16:5 has become a divine messenger in Matthew, one who miraculously moves a heavy tombstone, sits on it in triumph, and frightens heavily armed Roman soldiers, almost to death. Note Matthew's irony: the angel will soon report that Jesus is no longer among the dead, while the guards watching his tomb "for fear [*phobos*] of him . . . shook and became like dead men" (v. 4).

To allay similar fears, the angel reassures the women: "Do not be afraid [*mē phobeisthe*]" (v. 5a). He acknowledges their desire to mourn the crucified Jesus, but has astounding news: Jesus no longer inhabits the tomb, "for he has been raised [*ēgerthē*]" (v. 7a). The passive voice indicates that God raised Jesus from the dead. Moreover, Jesus himself predicted this ("as he said," v. 6b; cf. 16:21; 17:22–23; 20:18–19). In each of these predictions, Matthew uses the passive form of "raised," indicating divine action, which involves elevation to new life rather than resuscitation of an old life.

The apocalyptic tone of the Gospel resurrection accounts, including this one in Matthew—and the fact that no two accounts are the same, and that they do not describe the actual resurrection, but rather focus on the impact of the empty tomb, the divine agency of the resurrection, and the witness of the women and others who experience the resurrection—preserves the mystery, power, and hopefulness of these accounts, rather than mere chronological facts. The angel, rather than describe what happened

Does the arrival of these witnesses trigger the earthquake, or would it have happened anyway? Matthew does not say, although he does say what causes it: an angel straight out of the book of Daniel arrives to roll back the stone, then sits down upon it. The angel looks like lightning, Matthew says. His clothing is as white as snow fallen straight from the sky.

This is quite a change from Mark's "young man" dressed in a white robe, sitting sedately *inside* the tomb when the women arrive (Mark 16:5). It also differs from Luke's account, in which the women encounter "two men in dazzling clothes" inside the tomb (Luke 24:4). While the men's clothing signals something different about them, they are still men— and the opening of the tomb remains a mystery.

Only Matthew lets the reader know how the rock that blocked the entrance to the tomb came to be moved. A grave robber did not do it. A Messiah-sympathizing soldier did not do it. A band of guerilla disciples certainly did not do it. An angel of the Lord did it, rearranging the landscape the same way God rearranged it with two earthquakes three days apart: one on the day of Jesus' death and another on the day of his resurrection. Only Matthew mentions these earthquakes. A physical resurrection apparently requires earthly resurgence as well.

If this is an interesting handhold, then the preacher is left with some equally interesting questions: Why are these details so important to Matthew? How do they fit with the rest of his Gospel? What is gained by knowing how the tomb was opened? What is lost?

2. Only Matthew Mentions Roman Guards at the Tomb.

While it is necessary to back up a few verses to discover who posted the guards and why, Matthew clearly considers them essential to his story. From the Roman point of view, the guards are there to keep Jesus' disciples from stealing his body in the middle of the night and proclaiming his resurrection falsely. They are there to prevent fraud.

From Matthew's point of view, they are there to prove that no such fraud occurred (although there will be some controversy about this later). Since only Matthew mentions the guards, it is possible that he added them to his story so that his congregation would have something to say to their critics decades later (when the story about Jesus' disciples stealing his body was still in circulation). Since Matthew's description of the angel rings with echoes of Daniel, it is equally possible that Matthew still has Daniel in mind: "A stone was brought and laid on the mouth

Matthew 28:1–10

Theological Perspective

not," suggesting that God should not be the cause of terror.

John Calvin points out two kinds of "terror" in this passage: that of the guards, who "became like dead men" and are not restored, and the terror of the women, which is twice met by reassurance. "Certainly," Calvin goes on, "it is proper that the majesty of God should strike both terror and fear indiscriminately into the godly, as well as the reprobate, that all flesh may be silent before his face. But when the Lord has humbled and subdued his elect, he immediately mitigates their dread, that they may not sink under its oppressive influence." He goes on to say that the women meeting Jesus on the road should not have been afraid, because "*fear, mingled with joy,* shows that they had not yet fully relied on the testimony of the angel."[2] Calvin implies that ongoing fear of God is evidence of a disordered relationship to God, a sign of absence of true faith. Although we might question Calvin's judgment on the women for their lingering fear (after all, they are meeting a man who was supposed to be dead!), his words of assurance are striking. Those who have heard the testimony to the gospel have no need for fear.

Jesus' resurrection declares that there is hope beyond death, and that all the death-dealing powers of the world do not have the final say-so over our lives. As William Placher put it, the resurrection "offers hope for the world's victims and challenges the lordship of all the forces in the world that can kill us. To the powers and principalities that threaten us, even with death, we can reply that Jesus survived the worst they can do, and so can we."[3]

MARTHA MOORE-KEISH

Pastoral Perspective

themselves by crying out in unison, "The women are nuts."

Another pastoral challenge for the church is that many people gather in our churches under the misapprehension that church is mostly about them. Church is where I come to get pumped up to do my bit to fix the world, to be given strength for my daily living, to see where I have taken the wrong path and how I can get on the right path, to discover what I'm searching for.

The story before us is not about us. It is a narrative of a God who is not simply love, but love for us, love in action, taking on our battles with sin and death, doing for us that which we could not do for ourselves. Petty, humanistic moralizing wilts in the face of omnivorous death. Can it be that there is a force loose in the world stronger than death, more powerful than Caesar's legions or our betrayal and infidelity? Here is a story that defies our tendency to reduce preaching either to pastoral care, as if our greatest need were for comfort and pacification, or to ethics, as if beneficent human action could change the world. This story rises above the merely ethical (What am I to do?) and pushes us into the threateningly theological (What is God doing?). No exclusively human, anthropological help is sufficient for us and our deepest need. Therefore the most interesting character in this drama is not us, or even the women who bravely testify. The most interesting actor is a God who raises the dead and makes a way when we thought there was no way. This is the new "normal."

Dare we come to church in the darkness and peer with the women into so great and inexplicable a wonder? The women leave the tomb with "fear and great joy" (v. 8). Any Sunday we contend with this story we leave church with a mix of emotion: joy at God's great vindication of crucified Jesus and fear at the earthshaking implications of God's great disruptive shaking of the world by resurrection. Come, see!

WILLIAM H. WILLIMON

---

2. John Calvin, *Commentary on a Harmony of the Evangelists: Matthew, Mark, and Luke*, trans. William Pringle (originally printed for the Calvin Translation Society, Edinburgh, Scotland; repr., Grand Rapids: Baker Books, 2003), 3:344.
3. William Placher, *Jesus the Savior: The Meaning of Jesus Christ for Christian Faith* (Louisville, KY: Westminster John Knox Press, 2001), 160.

to Jesus' body or where he is at the present moment, directs the women to "see the place where he lay."

More importantly, the angel urges the women to "go quickly and tell his disciples" (v. 7a). The male disciples, of course, had fled from the crucifixion scene. The women must testify that Jesus "has been raised from the dead" (v. 7b). Like Mark, but unlike Luke and John, the angel also directs the women to tell the disciples that Jesus will meet them in Galilee, their home turf, not in Jerusalem, the site of his death. Good news will come back home, where the movement had its start, not where its existence was threatened. There in Galilee they will see Jesus, and they will "rebuild, recall and renew."[1]

A Resurrected Jesus (vv. 8–10). Mark ends with the women fleeing the empty tomb in fear, with no indication that they will tell others (Mark 16:8). In Matthew, the two Marys do as the angel instructs. They "run" quickly to find the disciples and tell them the good news. Thus they become the first postresurrection "evangelists." They are not without fear about what they have just witnessed, but they also have "great joy" (v. 8). On their way to share the news they have another astounding encounter: "Jesus met them" (v. 9a). He does so with the simple, "Greetings! [*chairete*]." Their reaction fits the momentous occasion more than Jesus' standard salutation: They approach him, grab his feet and "worship" (*prosekynēsan*, v. 9b, also translated "pay homage").

Matthew narrates various similar instances in which persons kneel before Jesus to worship him (8:2; 9:18; 14:33; 15:25; 17:14; 20:20), but none more memorable than the magi who went to pay homage (also *prosekynēsan*) to the baby Jesus in 2:11. Thus, in birth and resurrection, "Jesus is worshipped in Matthew."[2] Jesus reiterates the words of the angel, allaying their fears and instructing that the disciples go see him in Galilee. Jesus calls his disciples "brothers" here, signaling forgiveness for their abandonment (v. 10). With this direct commissioning from Jesus, the women in Matthew (cf. John 20:11–18) become "prime witnesses and apostles" of the resurrected Lord.[3]

EFRAIN AGOSTO

of the den, and the king sealed it with his own signet and with the signet of his lords, so that nothing might be changed concerning Daniel" (Dan. 6:17).

If this is an interesting handhold, then note who faints when the apocalyptic angel comes to roll the stone away: the guards, not the women. Because the women imagine the world differently from how the soldiers imagine it, they are not destabilized by such angelic interruptions. Whether or not they have seen this sort of thing before, they have acquired the spiritual muscle to trust it. While one doubts that they had smelling salts to offer the unconscious armed men, one wishes they had.

3. Only Matthew Testifies That the Women Were the First to See, Touch, and Worship the Risen Christ. The longer ending of Mark says that Jesus appeared first to Mary Magdalene, but no one believed it (Mark 16:9–11). Luke says that the women received instructions from the two men in dazzling clothes, but no one believed them either (Luke 24:6–11). In John's Gospel, a tearful Mary Magdalene is the first to see and speak with Jesus. She tries to touch him, but he does not want to be touched. Although she is alone with him and thus has no other witnesses to support her testimony, the disciples apparently believe what she tells them (John 20:16–18).

With a single verse, Matthew adds a whole new scene to the story: "Suddenly Jesus met them and said, 'Greetings!' And they came to him, took hold of his feet, and worshiped him" (v. 9). The women want to touch him, and he allows himself to be touched. They are moved to worship him, and he allows them to do so. Since the disciples go to Galilee just as Jesus instructed, one presumes that they believed what the women told them.

If this is an interesting handhold, then wonder out loud how a church so dependent on the primary ministry and witness of women ever came to debate their gifts for congregational leadership. More importantly, in any sermon on the resurrection, note how all such debates (and the hierarchies on which they are based) vanish like snow on a warm stone in the light of Jesus' appearing.

BARBARA BROWN TAYLOR

---

1. J. Andrew Overman, *Church and Community in Crisis: The Gospel according to Matthew* (Valley Forge, PA: Trinity Press Int., 1996), 399.
2. Ibid.
3. Barbara Reid, *The Gospel according to Matthew* (Collegeville, MN: Liturgical Press, 2005), 144.

Matthew 28:11–15

[11]While they were going, some of the guard went into the city and told the chief priests everything that had happened. [12]After the priests had assembled with the elders, they devised a plan to give a large sum of money to the soldiers, [13]telling them, "You must say, 'His disciples came by night and stole him away while we were asleep.' [14]If this comes to the governor's ears, we will satisfy him and keep you out of trouble." [15]So they took the money and did as they were directed. And this story is still told among the Jews to this day.

Theological Perspective

This story, which is unique to Matthew's resurrection narrative, reveals the struggle of early Christians to define themselves in relation to the non-Christian Jewish community of first-century Palestine. It thus raises interesting and troubling questions for contemporary Christians about Christian-Jewish relations. Its focus on a "large sum of money" also invites reflection on how money is related to faith. Finally, the shocked and fearful reaction of the priests and the soldiers to the news of Jesus' resurrection returns us to the question of how and whether Jesus' resurrection challenges religious and political authorities, in his time and in ours.

John Chrysostom, in a sermon on this passage in the fourth century, focuses particularly on the *power of the money* given to the soldiers, lamenting

> Oh, covetousness! All things are become money; for this cause all things are turned upside down. If anyone declares another happy, he mentions this; should he pronounce him wretched, hence is derived the description of wretchedness. And all reckonings are made on this account, how such an one gets rich, how such an one gets poor. Should it be military service, should it be marriage, should it be a trade, should it be what you will that any man takes in hand, he does not apply to what is

Pastoral Perspective

It is hard to believe that there was a time when you had to pay people to disbelieve in the resurrection. Nowadays, disbelief in resurrection is the official position of nearly everyone. Ninety percent of all Americans believe in an amorphous, presumed beneficent entity called "God" who rarely intrudes into our affairs. Yet only those who risk gathering in your church this Sunday believe that "God" names the One who defiantly raised the crucified Jesus from the dead.

We have created for ourselves, in Pope John Paul II's words, a "culture of death."[1] When threatened by birth, we abort. When disrupted by stirrings of new life elsewhere, we bomb into submission. If invaded by the transcendent, we relegate religion to the margins, something tucked safely within. The modern world was invented, in great part, to give us more control. Through human progress, we need not cower in the face of pain, sickness, and death, or even bad weather. We have the whole world in our hands.

Alas, such thinking invariably produces some form of crucifixion. Modernity thrives upon the discovery of continuity and pattern in order to give

1. John Paul II, *Evangelium Vitae* (The Vatican: Libreria Editrice Vaticana:1995.03.25), 12. http://www.vatican.va/holy_father/john_paul_ii/encyclicals/documents/hf_jp-ii_enc_25031995_evangelium-vitae_en.html; accessed January 19, 2012.

Feasting on the Gospels

Exegetical Perspective

This text begins with the affirmation that the women at the tomb, who are instructed by both an angel and the resurrected Jesus, are indeed going to tell the disciples about the good news they have heard and seen: Jesus lives! (vv. 5–10). However, the Roman guards of the tomb are also witnesses of these strange proceedings, and they too have a story to tell, although from their perspective it is not a happy one. So "they went into the city and told the chief priests everything that had happened" (v. 11). Matthew has previously told his readers that the religious leaders in Jerusalem were already suspicious about resurrection predictions that Jesus himself had promulgated. Thus they secured from Pilate, the Roman governor of Judea and Jesus' official executioner (although Matthew tries to play down his role, 27:24), "a guard of soldiers" and a secure, sealed stone for the tomb where Jesus' body had been laid (27:62–66).

Now their worst fears have come to fruition—an empty tomb—and so they conspire to secure the cooperation of the guards by way of a bribe. From Matthew's perspective, this story, still being told in Matthew's day, pits the deception of the guards' testimony and their leaders against the integrity of the women and the disciples they would tell. Moreover, the real point of the pericope, which is unique to Matthew and "a narrative fiction," largely his

Homiletical Perspective

Matthew's story about the bribing of the guards never shows up in the lectionary, which means that published interpretations of it are scarce. This is excellent news for preachers, teachers, and students of the text, since it means that we cannot hitch a ride to an already established meaning. If meaning is what we want, then we will have to arrive at it on our own two feet.

The story that sets this one up (27:62–66) *does* show up in the lectionary—every year, on the Saturday before Easter—as part of a longer narrative about Jesus' burial. In that passage Matthew tells us that although the guards are Romans, posting them at Jesus' tomb is not Pilate's idea. They are the brainchildren of the chief priests and the Pharisees, who ask Pilate to help them prevent Jesus' disciples from leading the people any further astray.

Pilate grants their wish. The guardians of the faith get their military guard. As an added precaution, they put a seal on the stone in front of Jesus' tomb before posting the soldiers in front of it. Amateur sleuths cannot fail to appreciate this fine detail. If you want to know whether anyone has visited a crime scene during the night, just glue a single hair across the doorway.

Fast forward to the story at hand to discover that the technique has failed in every way. Not only has

Theological Perspective

proposed, until he see these riches are coming in rapidly upon him.[1]

Contemporary Christians may protest that it is not the money itself that is the problem, but the fear and the deception of the priests who seek to cover up news of the resurrection. Yet Chrysostom helpfully reminds us to pay attention to financial transactions in the narrative and ask: How is money used by those in positions of power to serve their own interests? What do our own financial transactions reveal about our commitments, about our faith? Money may not itself be evil, but it is a powerful motivator for action, and a powerful indicator of where we place our trust.

Whether or not "the love of money is the root of all evil" (1 Tim. 6:10), the center of the narrative presents the chief priests inventing and spreading the story that the disciples had stolen Jesus' body. As Matthew says, "this story is still told among the Jews to this day" (v. 15). This offers a glimpse of the lines being drawn between Christians in Matthew's community and their Jewish neighbors. In those early days, those who claimed Jesus as Messiah were beginning to define themselves over against the Jews who did not recognize Jesus as Messiah, although the boundaries were still porous.

As Christianity gained power in subsequent centuries, narratives like this became more problematic. Although Matthew (as compared to John) does not often target "the Jews" as the enemies of Christ's followers, his portrayal of the scheming priests for centuries fed Christian anti-Semitism. For too long, narratives like this nourished Christian images of Jews as greedy, driven by love of money (e.g., see Shylock in Shakespeare's *Merchant of Venice*). Such poison has no place in current proclamation of the gospel. Preachers will do well to avoid portraying the priests as "those *others*" who have betrayed "*our* savior."

Rather than targeting "the Jews" as those who tried to cover up the resurrection, we might recognize in the story just how frightening the news of Jesus' resurrection was for the religious authorities in the first century. Christian preachers in days past have ridiculed the flimsy story told here, pointing out how difficult it would be to believe it. John Wesley, for instance, scoffs, "*Say, his disciples came by night, and stole him while we slept*—Is it possible, that

Pastoral Perspective

us control, or at least the illusion of control. What is more predictable than taxes and death?

The death-dealing empire rules through threat of death. Killing is illegal—except for the state. Matthew tells us that, even after resurrection, the religious authorities, lap dogs for powerful politicians, are still doing business under the old assumption: Caesar rules. They hope that through a few bribes they can stop all this resurrection-induced commotion and negotiate a return to business as usual.

In a way, the world continues to attempt to protect itself from God by paying off those who assert resurrection. Modernity renders Matthew's stories of the world postresurrection as unbelievable. In our world, everyone must be a scientist to succeed. Earlier, wondrous works of healing and release from the demonic were thought to be typical of Jesus. Now we relegate his works to the margins as "miracles" and exclude them from the realm of possibility. An interventionist God violates our sense of normal and natural, our presumptions of self-control.

In modernity, religion is fine, as long as it is kept tucked away, confined to the realm of the private and the personal. Church can be helpful to the preservation of peace within the community, as long as the church does nothing to threaten the real sovereign—the all-powerful democratic state.

All of this makes perfect sense to us, seems quite normal and natural, because the government controls and subsidizes most of our ways of making sense. We have been indoctrinated to believe that there is no greater power present on earth than the legions of the empire. Our collective machinery of death makes perfect sense, seems to be "the way things are"—*unless the Easter testimony of the women is true.* If they are telling the truth, and the guards are lying, then we must go back and rethink everything we once thought was fixed and certain.

The guards become preachers! Money is offered them publicly to preach something other than what they have actually witnessed. (Is Matthew making a connection between faithless preaching and clerical covetousness? Ouch.) They have seen an event, albeit a strange, difficult-to-explain event. Still, something has happened. In violation of what they have seen, they will lie to the authorities and act as if nothing has happened.

Whenever confronted by this text in preaching or teaching, the church does not have to work up enthusiasm for some personal, inner, heightened spiritual experience. We must simply have the courage joyfully to testify to what we have seen. Christ

---

1. John Chrysostom, Homily XC, in *Homilies on the Gospel of St. Matthew*, in *Nicene and Post-Nicene Fathers* (Peabody, MA: Hendrickson Publishers, 1999), 10:532.

creation,[1] lies in its final verse (28:15). The soldiers accepted the bribe and "did as they were directed" (*edidachthēsan*, "they were taught," v. 15a), just as the women followed the instructions of both the angel and Jesus (vv. 8, 10). Yet for Matthew and his readers, the women had the correct teaching about the resurrection; the soldiers did not. Thus Matthew ends with this update on the impact of the conspiracy between the official leaders and their envoys, the soldiers: "And this story is told among the Jews to this day" (v. 15).

First, "they devised a plan" (*symboulion te labontes*, v. 12), which can also be translated "they took counsel," as the "chief priests," "elders," and "Pharisees" had done earlier in Matthew's narrative to entrap Jesus (12:14; 22:15; 27:1). Matthew depicts Jewish religious leaders of all types, whether Pharisees, Sadducees, scribes, or the chief priests and temple elders, as vehemently opposed to and consistently conspiring against the ministry of Jesus.

Second, this plan included a bribe, to give the soldiers a large sum of money (*argyria*, "pieces of silver," v. 12), as they gave to Judas to turn over Jesus to them (26:14–16; 27:3). However, here it is a "large sum" (*hikana*), while for Judas it was only "thirty pieces." As Eugene Boring notes, "It costs more to suppress the resurrection message than to engineer the crucifixion."[2] Third, the soldiers must tell the story that the disciples of Jesus came by night and stole his body while the soldiers slept (v. 13). Thus the very action the leaders were trying to avoid by having Pilate post a Roman guard has come to fruition, but only through the failure of the guards to do their job!

Thus the story to be told, as Matthew presents it, is full of holes. How did they know the body was stolen if they were asleep? Moreover, these were highly trained, professional Roman soldiers. Would they not have some soldiers on guard, rotating through while others slept? If so, the former would be heavily armed, so how could the disciples overcome them? All kinds of questions abound with the "story" (v. 15b), called a *logos* ("message") by Matthew to contrast it with the message to be brought to the disciples by the women witnesses of the empty tomb and the resurrected Jesus. According to Matthew, the soldiers, who are ultimately beholden to Pilate, but assigned to the chief priests

a violent earthquake destroyed the seal; an angel of the Lord has descended from heaven, rolled back the stone, and sat on it. This has frightened the guards so badly that they have become "like dead men," unable to interrupt the angel's instructions to the women who have come to look at the tomb.

When the soldiers revive, some of them go into the city to tell the chief priests what has happened. They do not all go, according to Matthew. Only some of them go. What do the rest of them do? Matthew does not say.

When the chief priests and the elders have digested the guards' report, they devise a plot involving a large sum of money—not to shut the guards up, but to get them to change their story. Since the new story requires the guards to confess that they fell asleep on the job (close enough to the truth, since they really did pass out from fear), it also involves ruining their reputations. The guards do not seem to care. The respectable people offering them the money apparently have Pilate in their pocket, or at least they think they do. They promise to keep the soldiers out of trouble with the governor.

"So they took the money and did as they were directed," Matthew says of the soldiers, providing another surefire plotting device (v. 15a). If you want to know who is ultimately responsible for the crime, just follow the money.

This story is over, though, as far as "the Jews" are concerned. Matthew's use of that phrase (which he never uses elsewhere in his Gospel except in four references to "the King of the Jews") lets the reader know that something fishy is going on here. Matthew is not only telling a positive story about Jesus' resurrection; he is also telling a negative story about "the Jews," who by all accounts were his chief detractors when he sat down to write his Gospel forty years after Jesus' death.

This is interesting behavior from the same evangelist who recorded Jesus' teaching about loving your enemies and praying for those who persecute you (5:44). Teachers and preachers alert to the anti-Jewishness in the text will go out of their way to hold Matthew responsible for his own enemy thinking instead of allowing him to pin it all on "the Jews." Two thousand years later, in churches populated and run by Gentiles, it is too easy to forget that "the Jews" included Jesus and all of his disciples, including Matthew.

Even preachers whose hermeneutic prevents them from "deconstructing" Matthew can still find a loophole in this story. What about the guards who

1. Ulrich Luz, *Matthew 21–28: A Commentary*, trans. James E. Crouch (Minneapolis: Fortress Press, 2005), 609.
2. M. Eugene Boring, "The Gospel of Matthew," in *New Interpreter's Bible* (Nashville: Abingdon Press, 1995), 8:501.

Theological Perspective

any man of sense should digest this poor, shallow inconsistency? If ye were awake, why did you let the disciples steal him? If asleep, how do you know they did?"[2] Though the story be flimsy, the action of the priests reveals how threatened they felt by Jesus' resurrection. If the one crucified under the sign "King of the Jews" has been raised by the power of God, then what has happened to their power?

The claim of resurrection would have signaled the coming of God's reign into the world. Some, at least, of the religious authorities believed that God would one day bring in a new reign of justice and righteousness, and that those who had kept God's laws would then be raised to new life. The unrighteous would either be raised to eternal torment, or they would not be raised at all. In 2 Maccabees, for instance, we hear the words of a man who refuses to cooperate with the authorities' command to abandon some of the Jewish laws and adopt Greek practices:

> You accursed wretch, you dismiss us from this present life, but the King of the universe will raise us up to an everlasting renewal of life, because we have died for his laws. . . . One cannot but choose to die at the hands of mortals and to cherish the hope God gives of being raised again by him. But for you there will be no resurrection to life! (2 Macc. 7:9, 14)

With these words ringing in their ears, the priests in the first century had good reason to fear if the news got out that Jesus' body was missing. People might think that this was the first person to be raised from the dead, which meant that God's new reign had really begun. There might be riots. Their own authority would be undermined. It would be tough to keep control.

Worse: what if it were true?

MARTHA MOORE-KEISH

Pastoral Perspective

is risen! We cannot explain that, need not attempt laboriously to argue that. We must simply stand and deliver that which we have seen, tell the truth of our collective surprise that, although the death-dealing world has done its worst in torturing Jesus to death, God refused to be defeated by death and defiantly vindicated Jesus' way as God's way by raising him from the dead.

We do not claim that the Easter message is popular, that it is easily squared with the messages that predominate in our culture, or that it will be useful to people in getting whatever it is for which they strive. We simply say that this is the truth about God. We cannot say for sure, at this point, all of the implications of the event we have witnessed— whether it will make life worth living, whether it will bring us fear or joy. All we know at this point is that something has happened, an event that is not self-made and not derived through human action. Of this we are witnesses.

Who is a Christian? This passage from Matthew invites us to define a Christian as someone with the guts simply to witness to what has happened, to stand up, all evidence to the contrary, and tell the truth: Surprise! God raised the crucified Jesus from the dead.

The church ought to testify to the truth that we have witnessed and not be dissuaded by money. Whether or not the world receives this Easter truth with joy and belief, this is our story, and by the grace of God we are sticking with it.

This is the beginning of the Christian faith: Something has happened. God has made God's move. The world has rendered its verdict on Jesus: crucify him. Now, in raising the crucified Jesus from the dead, God renders a verdict. We now know whose side God is on. We have witnessed a revealing, defiant act of God that tells us a great deal about God. We will spend the rest of the church's year, your next fifty or so sermons, trying to figure out what Easter means. God has defeated death, the church has truthfully testified to that which it has seen and heard.

Now what?

WILLIAM H. WILLIMON

2. John Wesley, Commentary on Matthew 28:13, in *Explanatory Notes upon the New Testament* (Naperville, IL: A. R. Allenson, 1958), 137–38.

for this occasion, must tell the story concocted by the religious leaders, if they are to survive Pilate's ire, should he find out (v. 14).

Matthew's depiction of polemics between Jesus and religious leaders is more intensified than in the other Gospels (with the possible exception of John's Gospel). This can be traced to the opposition that Matthew's community, at the time he wrote his Gospel, faces from fellow Jews who do not accept the former's claims about the messianic status of Jesus of Nazareth. None of these encounters is more disastrous in terms of the history of Jewish Christian relations and anti-Semitism than the statement by Matthew in the mouths of the crowd accusing Jesus before Pilate: "His blood be on us and on our children!" (27:24–26). For Matthew, this was a matter of an internecine battle between "synagogues," between the gatherings of Jewish believers in Jesus (also known as the *ekklēsia*, including increasingly Gentile cohorts) and synagogues of the descendants of the Pharisees and religious officials who seem to give Jesus such a hard time throughout the narrative in Matthew.

Of course, Matthew's Jesus gives them a hard time right back, calling them "hypocrites" and "blind guides" in the famous discourse against scribes and Pharisees in 23:1–39. Here in 28:15, these opponents are lumped together as *Ioudaioi*, which in John's Gospel refers to Judeans, that is, the leaders of the Jewish community who collude with Rome in Jerusalem, the capitol of Judea. In Matthew, it refers to the Jewish opponents of Matthew's community, who, because of their lack of belief in Jesus as the resurrected Lord, are like those original leaders who conspired to spread a "false interpretation of [Jesus'] resurrection."[3] These *Ioudaioi* continue to spread false rumors in the time of Matthew and his community about the nature of Jesus' resurrection. However, Matthew and his community continue to hope that Jews as well as Gentiles will accept the authentic witnesses to the empty tomb.

EFRAIN AGOSTO

did *not* go tell the authorities what had happened at the tomb? Whom were *they* telling about what happened?

According to Matthew, the very first people to proclaim Jesus the Son of God after his death were a centurion and those who were with him (27:54). As often as one may have imagined these soldiers standing at the foot of the cross, a close reading of 27:50–54 leaves open the possibility that they were among those guarding Jesus' tomb the following day.

The time frame in those five verses collapses as Matthew splices together things that happened on both sides of the two earthquakes that he reports (one at Jesus' death and the other on the morning the women found his tomb empty). Strictly speaking, the soldiers' confession comes *after* Jesus' resurrection (27:53), while he and those who were with him were "keeping watch over Jesus": When they "saw the earthquake and what took place, they were terrified and said, 'Truly, this man was God's Son!'" (v. 54).

Which earthquake was that, exactly?

Whether the proclamation was made at the cross or at the tomb, it is a reminder that Roman soldiers were among the first to see God at work in Jesus' death. Even the soldiers who did not see God at work still saw what they saw. A witness is a witness, and there is no way to predict what people will do with the visions they receive. Did not the apostle Paul start out as an enemy named Saul?

Centuries earlier, an ancestor of Jesus' named Joseph said something that could serve as a postscript to Matthew's story of the bribed guards: "Even though you intended to do harm to me, God intended it for good, in order to preserve a numerous people, as he is doing today" (Gen. 50:20).

BARBARA BROWN TAYLOR

---

3. Barbara E. Reid, *The Gospel according to Matthew* (Collegeville, MN: Liturgical Press, 2005), 146.

Matthew 28:16–20

¹⁶Now the eleven disciples went to Galilee, to the mountain to which Jesus had directed them. ¹⁷When they saw him, they worshiped him; but some doubted. ¹⁸And Jesus came and said to them, "All authority in heaven and on earth has been given to me. ¹⁹Go therefore and make disciples of all nations, baptizing them in the name of the Father and of the Son and of the Holy Spirit, ²⁰and teaching them to obey everything that I have commanded you. And remember, I am with you always, to the end of the age."

Theological Perspective

In these concluding verses of Matthew, eleven disciples go to Galilee, to an unspecified mountain "to which Jesus [has] directed them," where they see and worship the risen Jesus. He offers them final words, sending them to "all nations" to baptize and teach, and assuring them of his presence "to the end of the age." Although brief, this passage is rich with theological puzzles for the attentive preacher.

Doubt? "When they saw him, they worshiped him," says Matthew, and then, almost as an afterthought, he adds, "but some doubted" (v. 17b). From the very beginning, among those closest to Jesus, there was doubt. In this otherwise transcendent, triumphant narrative, there are some who do not really grasp or trust what is going on. Nevertheless these doubters are still sent out, and even to these doubters Jesus says, "I am with you always" (v. 20b). Doubt is not presented here as an obstacle to discipleship, but as an element of discipleship, from the very beginning.

Authority? Jesus' words, "all authority in heaven and on earth has been given to me" (v. 18), raise the tricky issue of power and authority. We know too well the dangers of power in this world, how too much authority in the hands of one person leads to corruption and cruelty. We know how Christians in

Pastoral Perspective

Since Moses, everybody knows that if we want to worship God, we must naturally go high up a mountain in order to get closer to the Divine. Now, upon an unnamed mountain in Galilee the disciples have the risen Christ come close to them. Throughout Matthew, the stress has been on faithful obedience. Now, after the resurrection, we see a closing vignette of faithful worship. We are offered a grand opportunity to reflect upon the peculiar nature of worship in the name of Jesus.

"Reveal yourself to us," we had prayed. "Show us glory!" we cried down through the ages. Now that God has shown up as a crucified Jew who lived briefly, died violently, and rose unexpectedly, a God whom we did not expect, the question is: Are you able to worship this God? Jesus was crucified because he failed to meet our expectations for and definitions of God. Now that God has raised the crucified Jesus, will we risk conversation with this loving, demanding, boundary-breaking God?

"But some doubted" (v. 17). What comforting words to the church! That is not a bad description of any congregation: some worship, full of faith, and some hold back due to doubt. Even with Christ standing bodily before them, his identity is not self-evident. He stands before them as a mysterious, not fully comprehensible presence, not as a knock-down argument.

Exegetical Perspective

This scene opens with "eleven disciples," not "twelve" (cf. 10:1–4), on a mountaintop in Galilee. The narrative assumes that the women who received instructions to direct an inner circle to Galilee to see Jesus have done so (28:1–10). There are only eleven because of the betrayal and subsequent death of Judas (26:14–16; 27:3–10). No particular mountain is named. Rather, Matthew echoes previous encounters with Jesus on mountains.

On a mountain, Jesus rejected a temptation to receive authority over all kingdoms in exchange for worshiping Satan (4:8–11). Now, with all authority ascribed to him by God (v. 18), the disciples worship him (v. 17). From a mountain Jesus taught disciples ethical expectations in God's kingdom (5:1–7:27). Now he instructs the disciples to "teach" many nations (v. 20). On a mountain, three disciples experienced a precursor to a resurrected Jesus (the "transfiguration," 17:1–8). The last words they heard from Jesus before they scattered and he was crucified came from the Mount of Olives: "You will all become deserters because of me this night. . . . But after I am raised up, I will go ahead of you to Galilee" (26:30–32). Now here they are, just as he predicted, on another mountain, in Galilee, with their abandonment forgiven, about to receive a final commission.

Homiletical Perspective

The last five verses of Matthew's Gospel have become known so well as "the Great Commission" that preachers who wish to give them a new hearing will begin with their own ears. Where there is no surprise for the preacher, there is no surprise for the listener. Here then are several provocations to traditional readings of the conclusion to Matthew's Gospel, offered to interpreters willing to leave the established path to the accepted meaning of the text.

What Is So Great about This Commission? Jesus never calls it great. He reserves that adjective for the commandment to love God with your whole heart, soul, and mind (22:37). "This is the greatest and first commandment," he says, adding a second one that "is like it" about loving your neighbor as yourself. On these two instructions, he says, hang all the law and the prophets.

While there is good reason to wonder about the difference between a commission and a commandment, there is also reason to wonder why this particular commissioning of Jesus' disciples has assumed the proportion of greatness in his followers' minds.

If the key word is "Go," then he also commissioned the disciples to go, be reconciled to their brothers or sisters before leaving their gifts at the altar (5:24); to go the second mile (5:41); to go into

Theological Perspective

authority have abused power in the name of Christ, from the medieval crusades to the church's complicity in South African apartheid. What then are we to make of Jesus' claim to absolute authority?

To begin with, in this statement Jesus identifies his own power with the one whom he called "Father," the author of creation and therefore its Lord. The risen Jesus is so joined with the Father that he too is Lord of all creation. The authority they share, though, is not a dominating lordship, not the kind of authority demonstrated by the Roman state when it crucified Jesus. In going to the cross, Jesus refused to exercise such coercive authority. Instead, here on the mountain he offers an alternative vision of power: an authority that seeks "all nations," calling all people to a new way of living.

It may sound coercive when he tells his disciples to teach the nations "to obey everything that I have commanded you" (v. 20)—until we remember what it was that he commanded them: Be reconciled to one another. Love your enemies. Do not retaliate against evil. Pray, fast, and give alms, but not in a way that draws attention to yourself. Deny yourself. Above all, love God and love your neighbor. This is the kind of authority that Jesus claims.

Notice: by saying that all authority has been given to him, Jesus subtly removes any human claim to absolute authority. Given *to me*, he says, not directly *to you*. This passage challenges our notion of authority in two ways: first, because Jesus' authority is the authority of *self-giving, forgiving* love, and second, because any authority we have is derivative, dependent on the one to whom all authority on heaven and earth has truly been given.

Baptism. Jesus commands his disciples to baptize "in the name of the Father and of the Son and of the Holy Spirit" (v. 19b). This text provides the baptismal formula now regarded ecumenically as one of the marks of a valid baptism. Of course, there were various baptismal formulas among early Christian communities, and only later did this triune name become the standard language for Christian baptism. Even so, baptizing in the name of Father, Son, and Spirit offers a significant summary of the faith, joining the baptized with Jesus in his own baptism, in which he is claimed by the Father and anointed by the Spirit. Despite the lines that divide Catholic, Protestant, and Orthodox Christians from one another, this baptismal language unites us, signaling a core of common faith in the triune God. This unity is worth celebrating.

Pastoral Perspective

The good news is that the risen Christ is undeterred by the doubts of his first followers. In this mountaintop congregation of intermingled believers and doubters, Christ comes, blesses, and commissions them. We can be thankful that Christ does not wait until we are full of faith, cleansed of all doubt, before he comes to us and utilizes us in his great move upon the world.

Galilee is where Jesus' ministry began (4:12). Having been called out of Galilee, his disciples are now reassembled there for one final teaching and sending forth. All times of Christian worship tend to be times when, even as we worship him, he teaches us, then sends us forth on his mission. He meets his disciples where they are, but he will not leave them where they are.

In our churches each Sunday there is a similar rhythm of gathering, then being sent forth, only to be regathered next Sunday. Jesus invites, "Come to me," and then he commands, "Go!" No worship of Christ, no matter how grand and glorious, is complete without this rhythm of gathering and sending. Worship and mission are inseparable. The church that is engaged in tough, demanding mission will need the refreshment and rest of worship. The church's worship is validated by the way we are engaged not only in worshiping Christ in church but in serving with Christ in the world. Here is the test of the fidelity of our Sunday worship.

While the disciples are told to teach the gospel, it is rather odd that Matthew (a Gospel that contains much teaching) does not include any instruction on the content of this gospel. Gentiles are to be made into disciples, baptized into a new, expansive family, not converted into a new philosophy.

In this, the most "Jewish" of the Gospels, it is rather amazing that the resurrected Christ tells his disciples to go, not only to Judea, but into the whole world and to enlist even Gentiles as disciples. Just as the resurrected Christ has a body that is not confined by the usual limitations of time and space, so the church is not confined to Judea. Now the church is free to show up anywhere. Just as on a mountain Moses was told what Israel needed to do to take the promised land, now the disciples on the mountain are told what to do to retake the world.

They think they are going out to a mountain in Galilee to search for God—only to have God come to them. There on the mountain Jesus promises to be present to his followers, not just on mountains but everywhere and throughout all ages. In a way, your church, gathered this Sunday in a place far away

Exegetical Perspective

The encounter between Jesus and the disciples starts simply: Upon "seeing him" (*idontes auton*), they "worshiped" (*prosekynēsan*, v. 17), as the women did at 28:9. In 14:33, the disciples "worshiped" Jesus after he walked on water. However, there was also some doubt. Peter attempted to walk on water, but faltered. Upon rescuing him, Jesus said, "You of little faith, why did you doubt?" Similarly in verse 17, the disciples "worshiped him; but some doubted" (*hoi de edistasan*). The *hoi* can be translated "they" or "some," and can mean that *all* the disciples both worshiped and doubted (or "hesitated"), or that some worshiped while *others* doubted, as in the story of "doubting Thomas" (John 20:24–28). For Matthew, disciples will always be "caught between adoration and doubt."[1]

Finally, Jesus speaks, approaching his disciples for the first time since they abandoned him a few days prior. His first words carry power: "All authority [*exousia*] in heaven and on earth has been given to me" (v. 18). In Matthew, Jesus teaches with authority (7:29). He has authority to forgive (9:6–8). His opponents question whether his authority is from heaven (21:23–27). Jesus authorizes his disciples to heal and exorcise (10:1). Here, Matthew confirms this authority and its all-encompassing nature in a postresurrection world. The angel came down from heaven with God's authority to release the crucified Jesus from his burial tomb (28:2, 5–6), and now that authority from heaven is to be fully exercised on earth. Moreover, on the basis of Jesus' authority, the disciples will now "go therefore and make disciples [*mathēteuō*] of all nations" (v. 19).

Discipleship has been a major theme in Matthew's Gospel. Matthew refers to "disciples" more than seventy times. Even the name "Matthew" is derived from the Greek term for disciple. Now these disciples, and all the disciples in Matthew's community that hear about this final exhortation from the risen Jesus, are charged with "making" more disciples. Matthew points out three aspects of disciple making. First, they will initiate them into the community through water baptism. John baptized Jesus to begin his ministry. Members of this new community should identify with the resurrected Jesus in a similar way. Moreover, just as God spoke at the baptism of Jesus about this being his "beloved Son," and God's Spirit made a visible appearance through a dove (3:13–17), so should new followers of Jesus be identified with this divine "family"—"Father, Son, and Holy Spirit"—in their baptism. This may have

1. John P. Meier, *Matthew* (Wilmington, DE: Michael Glazier, 1980, 1986), 369.

Homiletical Perspective

their rooms, shut their doors, and pray to their Father who is in secret (6:6); and to go sell their possessions and give the money to the poor (19:21).

He even commissioned them to go nowhere among the Gentiles, limiting their proclamation of the good news to the lost sheep of the house of Israel (10:6; cf. 15:24). "Cure the sick," he instructed them on that occasion, "raise the dead, cleanse the lepers, cast out demons." He also told them to do it all for free, taking no money with them, no luggage, no change of clothes, not even a staff to lean on (10:5–10).

What makes that first commission different from the last one, so that his followers remember the last one as the "great" one? Is it because Jesus has come back from the dead, with power to revise what he said before? Is it because he has lifted the restrictions on what they may take with them, freeing them from the dirty work of caring for the sick, in order to concentrate on the nobler work of evangelizing the nations? What benefits does the last commission grant to Jesus' disciples that might lead them to elevate it above all the others?

If Some of the Disciples Doubted, Why Were They Worshiping Jesus? Matthew's math is deliberate. Only eleven disciples returned to Galilee, he says, letting readers deduce who is missing. Of those who are left, Peter is the identified doubter in this Gospel, not Thomas (whose name appears only once, in Matthew's list of the disciples at 10:3). After Peter's poor performance at walking on water, Jesus diagnosed his problem out loud: "You of little faith, why did you doubt?" (14:31).

While some readers may point to doubting Peter's proclamation at 16:16 as proof of his cure ("You are the Messiah, the Son of the living God"), others may be relieved to suppose that faith and doubt are not mutually exclusive. Even here, on the mountain where Jesus appears to his disciples after his death, some of them doubt. Doubt what? Matthew does not say, although the Greek word he uses points straight to Peter.

Matthew uses it only twice—here and at 14:31—not as an adjective ("faithless") but as a verb that means "to hesitate" or "to sit on the fence" (literally, "to stand in two places"). Some in this small crowd are holding back. No one witnessed the actual resurrection, not even the women. Some are hesitant to step out on the water with no proof the surface will hold. Yet they are worshiping anyway, accepting the risk of devoting themselves to something that still

Matthew 28:16–20

Theological Perspective

However, the gendered language of this formula can also be problematic, if it feeds an image of God as male. As feminist theologians have reminded us since the 1970s, when we use only masculine language for God (such as "Father"), we bolster unjust patriarchal systems, and we worship an idol rather than the true God. Classical Trinitarian language needs to be treated with care. One contemporary study of this issue offers wise guidance:

> The language of Father, Son, and Holy Spirit, rooted in scripture and creed, remains an indispensable anchor for our efforts to speak faithfully of God. When secured, an anchor provides both necessary stability and adequate freedom of movement. If our lifeline to the anchor is frayed or severed, the historic faith of the one holy catholic and apostolic church risks being set adrift. With this anchor in place, however, we are liberated to interpret, amplify, and expand upon the ways of speaking of the triune God familiar to most church members.[1]

With You? Jesus' promise "I am with you always" is a profoundly odd statement. Jesus is not "with us" in any obvious way. What is meant by his ongoing presence, with the disciples then, and with us now? Unlike Luke, Matthew does not have an ascension narrative to distinguish the nature of Jesus' risen presence with the disciples from his presence in the rest of history. "I am with you always" seems to speak equally to all of us who are living before "the end of the age." With us how? Some theologians emphasize Jesus' presence "with us" as a deep personal knowledge of Jesus cultivated by prayer and contemplation. Others interpret the "with us" as the presence of Christ by the power of the Spirit in the gathered community, particularly in and through the proclamation of the Word and the celebration of the sacraments. The paradox of the "with us," in any case, is that Jesus is simply not available to us in any ordinary way. His promise thus signals a different order of presence, one that cannot be controlled or grasped, but can only be received and trusted.

MARTHA MOORE-KEISH

Pastoral Perspective

from that mountain in Galilee, gathering folk in so many ways different from those first disciples, is confirmation of Jesus' promise. What a comfort to know that our relationship to God is not predicated upon our earnest searching for the Divine; God comes out to where we are, meeting us there, as we are.

Note that we do not speak of resurrected Christ "sightings." These post-Easter epiphanies are known as Christ's *appearances*. His revelation to us is his *self*-revelation. His presence among us is at his loving initiative, not at our demand. Here is hope for those of us who think of religion as essentially something that we do, the Christian life as a way that we must act or think or feel. Our faith, our spiritual life, is, thank God, God's self-assigned task.

Two similarly stunning truths are set before the church whenever this text is contemplated: (1) The crucified Jesus has been raised from the dead. (2) The first thing the risen Christ does is to return to us, blessing even those who betrayed and forsook him (his disciples, us) with his presence. The God whom we worship is not only a God of love but One who in his resurrection and in his appearances and return to us is shown to be God's love for us.

I know someone who has tried to believe but, as yet, just cannot. I have told her to relax; in due season Jesus will come to her, not as her intellectual achievement, but rather as his loving gift. A young man in my church has committed a terrible wrong and now feels terribly alone and hopeless. I have advised him to take heart; Jesus not only sallied forth from the tomb on Easter (which might have been miracle enough). The risen Christ, in the days after Easter, miraculously returned to us. If he would come back to his best friends who were also his worst betrayers, then he can show up for anybody.

Jesus' most comforting words are "I am with you always."

WILLIAM H. WILLIMON

---

1. *The Trinity: God's Love Overflowing* (Louisville, KY: Office of Theology and Worship, Presbyterian Church (U.S.A.), 2006), lines 330–335.

Feasting on the Gospels

Exegetical Perspective

been an early baptismal formula practiced by some Christian communities, including Matthew's, while others baptized "in the name of Jesus" (cf. Acts 2:38; 10:48). However, more important for Matthew is this connection to the baptism of Jesus and the presence of the divine "family." No fully developed Trinitarian doctrine is in mind.

The second aspect of making disciples according to Matthew is teaching the new disciples to "obey" (RSV "observe") everything Jesus has commanded the first disciples (v. 20a). Matthew 26:1 reads, "Jesus had finished saying all these things." The story then shifts to the passion narratives. Until then, Matthew has included abundant teaching materials: the Sermon on the Mount (chaps. 5–7), the nature of discipleship (chap. 10), the type of Messiah that Jesus represents (16:13–28), discourses about church discipline (chap. 18), and so forth. These are not easy demands. Jesus argues that the interpretation of Mosaic Law by his opponents sometimes requires less than it should. Instead, he offers the formula, "You have heard that it was said . . . ; but I say . . . ," thus exacting much higher standards (5:17–48).

Finally, the commandment to go, make disciples, baptize, and teach must be for "all nations" (*panta ta ethnē*). Does Matthew advocate the end of mission among Jews and a turn toward only "Gentile nations"? Such interpretation connects to conflicts Matthew has with Jewish leaders throughout his narrative: many rejected Jesus and had a hand in his execution, so the mission must turn elsewhere—the *ethnē*—understood as non-Jewish nations, the "Gentiles." Earlier Jesus had instructed his disciples: "Go nowhere among the Gentiles, and enter no town of the Samaritans, but go rather to the lost sheep of the house of Israel" (10:5–6; cf. 15:24). Does his postresurrection commission abrogate the earlier one? More likely, the "all" in "all nations" includes rather than excludes Israel. Matthew's Jewish believers in Jesus will not stop making disciples, baptizing and teaching all peoples, Jew and Gentile, despite opposition from portions of both communities. Jesus' parting instructions are all encompassing.

However, Jesus does not really depart. There is no ascension here, as in Luke's writing (Acts 1:9–11). Rather, Jesus promises to be with his followers *all the time* until the end of history. Thus, Matthew ends his Gospel with a promise of eschatological presence among faithful disciple makers. With "all authority" these disciples will reach "all nations" with "all" the teachings of Jesus for "all time."

EFRAIN AGOSTO

Homiletical Perspective

makes their knees wobble. Is this hypocrisy or faith? Does the existence of doubt in the worship of Jesus mean that something is wrong, or does it mean that something is right—when people with no idea how deep the water really is step out on it anyway, trusting that even their doubt cannot separate them from the love of God?

What Does It Mean to Make Disciples? A cartoon in the *New Yorker* shows a man sitting alone on a bench seat, wearing a T-shirt that says, "ASK ME ABOUT MY RELIGION." The caption reads, "Another way to keep an empty seat beside you on the train." Depending on whom you talk to, it seems possible that nothing has cost Jesus more new disciples than the tactics of those most intent on recruiting them.

Does making disciples mean convincing people that the path they are on is doomed? Does it mean adding value to the gospel by attaching material incentives to it? Does it mean baptizing people straightaway and taking their questions later?

According to Matthew's Jesus, making disciples means two things: (1) baptizing them in the name of the triune God and (2) teaching them to obey everything that Jesus has commanded. In Matthew's Gospel, number two promises to take a lot more of the disciples' time than number one. It also promises to involve a lot more than talking. "Not everyone who says to me, 'Lord, Lord,' will enter the kingdom of heaven," Jesus said in an old sermon on another mountain, "but only the one who does the will of my Father in heaven" (7:21). If that teaching still applies, then the best way for the disciples to expand their numbers is to show the nations what doing the will of God looks like—not to talk about it but to do it—so that even those who still have their doubts are willing to enter the water.

There is no ascension in Matthew's Gospel. Jesus' last recorded words to his eleven disciples concern his enduring presence with them. "To the end of the age," he says, as if he were speaking over their heads to all of us who are here today because they did what Jesus commanded.

BARBARA BROWN TAYLOR

Contributors

Efrain Agosto, Professor of New Testament Studies, New York Theological Seminary, New York, New York

Paul N. Anderson, Professor of Biblical and Quaker Studies, George Fox University, Newberg, Oregon

Ellen Blue, Associate Professor of the History of Christianity and United Methodist Studies, Phillips Theological Seminary, Tulsa, Oklahoma

Frederick Borsch, Adjunct Professor of New Testament and Anglican Studies, Lutheran Theological Seminary at Philadelphia, Philadelphia, Pennsylvania

Stephen Boyd, Professor of Religion, Wake Forest University, Winston-Salem, North Carolina

Karen L. Brau, Pastor, Luther Place Memorial Church, Washington, D.C.

Linda McKinnish Bridges, Associate Dean of Admissions, Wake Forest University, Winston-Salem, North Carolina

Laurie Brink, OP, Associate Professor of New Testament Studies, Catholic Theological Union, Chicago, Illinois

Michael Joseph Brown, Director of the Malcolm X Institute; Associate Dean and Professor of New Testament, Wabash College, Crawfordsville, Indiana

Sally A. Brown, Associate Professor of Preaching and Worship, Princeton Theological Seminary, Princeton, New Jersey

Teresa Fry Brown, Professor of Homiletics and Director, Black Church Studies, Candler School of Theology, Emory University, Atlanta, Georgia

John M. Buchanan, Editor/Publisher, *The Christian Century*; Pastor Emeritus, Fourth Presbyterian Church, Chicago, Illinois

Andrew Foster Connors, Pastor, Brown Memorial Park Avenue Presbyterian Church, Baltimore, Maryland

Kate Foster Connors, Director, The Center, Presbytery of Baltimore, Baltimore, Maryland

R. Alan Culpepper, Dean and Professor of New Testament, McAfee School of Theology, Atlanta, Georgia

MaryAnn McKibben Dana, Pastor, Idlywood Presbyterian Church, Springfield, Virginia

Keith Errickson, Professor of Religion, North Carolina Wesleyan College, Rocky Mount, North Carolina

Richard A. Floyd, Pastor, Presbyterian Church (U.S.A.), Atlanta, Georgia

Liz Barrington Forney, Pastor, Spiritual Director, Charlottesville, Virginia

Lewis F. Galloway, Pastor, Second Presbyterian Church, Indianapolis, Indiana

Roger J. Gench, Pastor, New York Avenue Presbyterian Church, Washington, D.C.

W. Scott Haldeman, Associate Professor of Worship, Chicago Theological Seminary, Chicago, Illinois

Gary Neal Hansen, Associate Professor of Church History, University of Dubuque Theological Seminary, Dubuque, Iowa

J. William Harkins III, Senior Lecturer of Pastoral Theology and Care, Columbia Theological Seminary, Decatur, Georgia

Joseph S. Harvard III, retired Pastor, First Presbyterian Church, Durham, North Carolina

Susan K. Hedahl†, Professor of the Proclamation of the Word, Lutheran Theological Seminary at Gettysburg, Gettysburg, Pennsylvania

Olive Elaine Hinnant, Minister, United Church of Christ, Aurora, Colorado

E. Glenn Hinson, Senior Professor of Church History and Spirituality, Baptist Seminary of Kentucky, Georgetown, Kentucky

John F. Hoffmeyer, Professor of Theology, Lutheran Theological Seminary at Philadelphia, Philadelphia, Pennsylvania

R. Ward Holder, Professor, Theology Department, St. Anselm College, Manchester, New Hampshire

Dock Hollingsworth, Assistant Professor of Leadership and Supervised Ministry and Assistant Dean, McAfee School of Theology, Atlanta, Georgia

James C. Howell, Senior Pastor, Myers Park United Methodist Church, Charlotte, North Carolina

James Hudnut-Beumler, Anne Potter Wilson Professor of American Religious History, Vanderbilt Divinity School, Nashville, Tennessee

Edith M. Humphrey, Professor of New Testament, Pittsburgh Theological Seminary, Pittsburgh, Pennsylvania

George R. Hunsberger, Professor of Missiology, Western Theological Seminary, Holland, Michigan

Ada María Isasi-Díaz[†], Professor of Christian Ethics and Theology, Drew University School of Theology, Madison, New Jersey

Cynthia A. Jarvis, Minister, The Presbyterian Church of Chestnut Hill, Philadelphia, Pennsylvania

Nathan Jennings, Associate Professor of Liturgics and Anglican Studies, Seminary of the Southwest, Austin, Texas

Joseph R. Jeter, Emeritus Professor of Homiletics, Brite Divinity School at Texas Christian University, Fort Worth, Texas

Pablo A. Jiménez, Pastor, Iglesia Cristiana (Discípulos de Cristo) en Espinosa, Dorado, Puerto Rico

Skip Johnson, Senior Lecturer of Pastoral Theology and Care, Columbia Theological Seminary, Decatur, Georgia

Susan B. W. Johnson, Senior Minister, Hyde Park Union Church, Chicago, Illinois

Eunjoo Mary Kim, Professor of Homiletics, Director of the Doctor of Ministry Program, Iliff School of Theology, Denver, Colorado

Jin S. Kim, Senior Pastor, Church of All Nations, Minneapolis, Minnesota

Douglas T. King, Senior Associate Pastor, Brick Presbyterian Church, New York, New York

Michael D. Kirby, Pastor, Good Shepherd Presbyterian Church, Chicago, Illinois

Cynthia Briggs Kittredge, Professor of New Testament, Academic Dean, Seminary of the Southwest, Austin, Texas

Lisa Washington Lamb, Affiliate Faculty in Homiletics, Fuller Theological Seminary, Pasadena, California

Emmanuel Y. Lartey, Professor of Pastoral Theology, Care and Counseling, Candler School of Theology, Emory University, Atlanta, Georgia

David Lewicki, Co-Pastor, North Decatur Presbyterian Church, Decatur, Georgia

Jacqueline J. Lewis, Pastor, Middle Collegiate Church, New York, New York

Karoline M. Lewis, Associate Professor of Biblical Preaching and Chair, Leadership Division, Luther Seminary, St. Paul, Minnesota

Michael L. Lindvall, Pastor, Brick Presbyterian Church, New York, New York

David J. Lose, Chair in Biblical Preaching, Luther Seminary, St. Paul, Minnesota

Gregory Anderson Love, Associate Professor of Systematic Theology, San Francisco Theological Seminary, San Anselmo, California

Mary Elise Lowe, Associate Professor of Religion, Augsburg College, Minneapolis, Minnesota

Barbara K. Lundblad, Professor of Preaching, Union Theological Seminary, New York, New York

Joretta L. Marshall, Executive Vice President and Dean, Professor of Pastoral Theology and Pastoral Care and Counseling, Brite Divinity School at Texas Christian University, Fort Worth, Texas

Martin E. Marty, Professor Emeritus of the History of Modern Christianity, University of Chicago Divinity School, Chicago, Illinois

Robert M. McClellan, Pastor, Westminster Presbyterian Church, Tiburon, California

John S. McClure, Professor of Preaching and Worship, Vanderbilt Divinity School, Nashville, Tennessee

Marvin A. McMickle, President, Professor of Homiletics, Colgate Rochester Crozer Divinity School, Rochester, New York

Allen C. McSween Jr., Pastor Emeritus, Fourth Presbyterian Church, Greenville, South Carolina

Daniel L. Migliore, Professor Emeritus of Systematic Theology, Princeton Theological Seminary, Princeton, New Jersey

Gordon S. Mikoski, Associate Professor of Christian Education, Princeton Theological Seminary, Princeton, New Jersey

Mitzi Minor, Professor of New Testament, Memphis Theological Seminary, Memphis, Tennessee

Martha Moore-Keish, Associate Professor of Theology, Columbia Theological Seminary, Decatur, Georgia

Sarah Morice-Brubaker, Assistant Professor of Theology, Phillips Theological Seminary, Tulsa, Oklahoma

Otis Moss III, Pastor, Trinity United Church of Christ, Chicago, Illinois

D. Cameron Murchison, Professor Emeritus, Columbia Theological Seminary, Decatur, Georgia

Agnes W. Norfleet, Pastor, Bryn Mawr Presbyterian Church, Bryn Mawr, Pennsylvania

Daniel J. Ott, Assistant Professor, Department of Philosophy and Religious Studies, Monmouth College, Monmouth, Illinois

Eugene Eung-Chun Park, Professor of New Testament, San Francisco Theological Seminary, San Anselmo, California

Paul T. Roberts Sr., President and Dean, Johnson C. Smith Theological School at the Interdenominational Theological Center, Atlanta, Georgia

Rodney S. Sadler Jr., Associate Professor of Bible, Union Presbyterian Seminary, Charlotte, North Carolina

Stanley P. Saunders, Associate Professor of New Testament, Columbia Theological Seminary, Decatur, Georgia

Guy Sayles, Pastor, First Baptist Church, Asheville, North Carolina

Hannah Schell, Associate Professor, Department of Philosophy and Religious Studies, Monmouth College, Monmouth, Illinois

Mary H. Schertz, Professor of New Testament; Director, Institute of Mennonite Studies, Anabaptist Mennonite Bible Seminary, Elkhart, Indiana

Mary Hinkle Shore, Professor of New Testament, Luther Seminary, St. Paul, Minnesota

Elizabeth McGregor Simmons, Pastor, Davidson College Presbyterian Church, Davidson, North Carolina

Lance Stone, Pastor, Emmanuel United Reformed Church, Cambridge, United Kingdom

Barbara Brown Taylor, Butman Professor of Religion, Piedmont College, Demorest, Georgia

William H. Willimon, Professor of the Practice of Christian Ministry, Duke Divinity School, Durham, North Carolina

Patrick J. Willson, Interim Pastor, First Presbyterian Church, Albuquerque, New Mexico

Arthur M. Wright Jr., Affiliate Professor of New Testament, Baptist Theological Seminary at Richmond, Virginia

John Yieh, Professor of New Testament, Virginia Theological Seminary, Alexandria, Virginia

Author Index

Gary Neal Hansen — Matthew 19:13–15 TP; 19:16–30 TP

J. William Harkins — Matthew 16:24–28 TP; 17:1–13 TP; 17:14–21 TP

Joseph S. Harvard III — Matthew 16:24–28 HP; 17:1–13 HP; 17:14–21 HP

Susan K. Hedahl — Matthew 17:22–23 HP; 17:24–27 HP; 18:1–11 HP

Olive Elaine Hinnant — Matthew 19:13–15 PP; 19:16–30 PP

E. Glenn Hinson — Matthew 17:22–23 EP; 17:24–27 EP; 18:1–11 EP

John F. Hoffmeyer — Matthew 21:14–17 TP; 21:18–22 TP; 21:23–27 TP

R. Ward Holder — Matthew 17:22–23 TP; 17:24–27 TP; 18:1–11 TP

Dock Hollingsworth — Matthew 18:12–22 PP; 18:23–35 PP; 19:1–12 PP

James C. Howell — Matthew 18:12–22 EP; 18:23–35 EP; 19:1–12 EP

James Hudnut-Beumler — Matthew 26:57–68 TP; 26:69–75 TP

Edith M. Humphrey — Matthew 16:24–28 EP; 17:1–13 EP; 17:14–21 EP

George R. Hunsberger — Matthew 20:1–16 TP; 20:17–28 TP

Ada María Isasi-Díaz — Matthew 18:12–22 TP; 18:23–35 TP; 19:1–12 TP

Cynthia A. Jarvis — Matthew 21:28–32 TP; 21:33–46 TP; 22:1–14 TP

Nathan Jennings — Matthew 18:12–22 HP; 18:23–35 HP; 19:1–12 HP

Joseph R. Jeter — Matthew 19:13–15 HP; 19:16–30 HP

Pablo A. Jiménez — Matthew 20:1–16 EP; 20:17–28 EP

Skip Johnson — Matthew 20:1–16 PP; 20:17–28 PP

Susan B. W. Johnson — Matthew 16:24–28 PP; 17:1–13 PP; 17:14–21 PP

Eunjoo Mary Kim — Matthew 20:29–34 HP; 21:1–11 HP; 21:12–13 HP

Jin S. Kim — Matthew 22:41–46 PP; 23:1–12 PP; 23:13–33 PP

Douglas T. King — Matthew 22:15–22 EP; 22:23–33 EP; 22:34–40 EP

Michael D. Kirby — Matthew 20:29–34 PP; 21:1–11 PP; 21:12–13 PP

Cynthia Briggs Kittredge — Matthew 21:28–32 EP; 21:33–46 EP; 22:1–14 EP

Lisa Washington Lamb — Matthew 21:14–17 HP; 21:18–22 HP; 21:23–27 HP

Emmanuel Y. Lartey — Matthew 21:14–17 PP; 21:18–22 PP; 21:23–27 PP

David Lewicki — Matthew 21:28–32 PP; 21:33–46 PP; 22:1–14 PP

Jacqueline J. Lewis — Matthew 22:41–46 HP; 23:1–12 HP; 23:13–33 HP

Karoline M. Lewis — Matthew 23:34–39 HP; 24:1–8 HP; 24:9–28 HP

Michael L. Lindvall — Matthew 15:1–11 TP; 15:12–20 TP; 15:21–28 TP

David J. Lose — Matthew 22:15–22 HP; 22:23–33 HP; 22:34–40 HP

Gregory Anderson Love — Matthew 22:41–46 TP; 23:1–12 TP; 23:13–33 TP